Gallery of Best Resumes

A Collection of Quality Resumes by Professional Resume Writers

Fifth Edition

David F. Noble, Ph.D.

JIST Works
America's Career Publisher

Gallery of Best Resumes, Fifth Edition
A Collection of Quality Resumes by Professional Resume Writers
© 2012 by David F. Noble

Published by JIST Works, an imprint of JIST Publishing
7321 Shadeland Station, Suite 200
Indianapolis, IN 46256-3923
Phone: 800-648-JIST   Fax: 877-454-7839   E-mail: info@jist.com

Visit our website at **www.jist.com** for information on JIST, free job search tips, tables of contents, sample pages, and ordering instructions for our many products!

Quantity discounts are available for JIST books. Please call our Sales Department at 800-648-5478 for a free catalog and more information.

Development Editor: Heather Stith
Cover Designer: Alan Evans
Page Layout: Aleata Halbig
Proofreader: Jeanne Clark
Indexer: Ginny Noble

Printed in the United States of America
16 15 14 13 12 11   9 8 7 6 5 4 3 2 1

Library of Congress Cataloging-in-Publication Data

Noble, David F. (David Franklin), 1935-
   Gallery of best resumes : a collection of quality resumes by professional resume writers /
by David F. Noble. -- 5th ed.
     p. cm.
  Includes index.
  ISBN 978-1-59357-858-9 (alk. paper)
  1. Résumés (Employment) I. Title.
  HF5383.N62 2012
  650.14'2--dc23
                    2011026266

ISBN 978-1-59357-858-9

Contents

Introduction

Gallery of Best Resumes, Fifth Edition, is a collection of quality resumes from professional resume writers, each with individual views about resumes and resume writing. Unlike many resume books whose selections look the same, this book, like the first four editions, contains resumes that look different because they are representations of *real* resumes prepared by different professionals for actual job searchers throughout the country. (The writers have fictionalized certain information in the resumes to protect each client's privacy.) Even when several resumes from the same writer appear in the book, most of these resumes are different because the writer has customized each resume according to the background information and career goals of the client for whom the resume was prepared.

Instead of assuming that one resume style fits all, the writers featured in this Gallery believe that a client's past experiences and next job target should determine the resume's type, design, and content. The use of *Best* in this book's title reflects this approach to resume making. The resumes are not "best" because they are ideal types for you to imitate, but because the resume writers interacted with their clients to fashion resumes that were best for each client's situation.

This book features resumes from writers who share several important qualities: good listening skills, a sense of what details are appropriate for a particular resume, and flexibility in selecting and arranging the resume's sections. By "hearing between" a client's statements, the perceptive resume writer can detect what kind of job the client really wants. The writer then chooses the information that best represents the client for the job being sought. Finally, the writer decides how to best arrange the information for that job, often from the most important to the least important. With the help of this book—both in its advice and especially in the many examples of resumes that were successful for clients—you can create this kind of resume yourself.

Almost all the writers of the resumes in this Gallery are members of Career Directors International (CDI), Career Management Alliance (CMA, formerly Career Masters Institute), the National Résumé Writers' Association (NRWA), or the Professional Association of Résumé Writers & Career Coaches (PARW/CC). Many of the writers belong to more than one of these organizations. Each organization has programs for earned certification. For example, writers who have Certified Professional Résumé Writer (CPRW) certification received this designation from the PARW/CC after they studied specific course materials and demonstrated proficiency in an examination. Those who have National Certified Résumé Writer (NCRW) certification received this designation from NRWA after a different course of study and a different examination. For contact information for CDI, CMA, NRWA, and PARW/CC, see their listings at the end of the List of Contributors.

How This Book Is Organized

This book has three parts. Part 1, "Best Resume Tips," presents resume writing strategies, design and layout tips, and resume writing style tips for making resumes visually impressive. Many of these strategies and tips were suggested by the resume writers who contributed resumes. Often a reference is given to one or more Gallery resumes that illustrate the strategy or tip.

Part 2 is the Gallery itself, containing 182 resumes from 89 professional resume writers (if you include those who submitted only a cover letter) throughout the United States, Australia, and Canada. The resumes are presented in 18 occupational categories. Within each category, the resumes are generally arranged from the simple to the complex. Some of the resumes are one page, but most of them are two pages. A few are more than two pages.

The caption for each resume in the Gallery identifies which kind of resume it is. Resume writers commonly distinguish between chronological resumes and functional (or skills) resumes. A *chronological resume* is a photo—a snapshot history of what you did and when you did it, starting with your most recent accomplishments. A *functional resume* is a painting—an interpretive sketch of what you can do for a future employer. A third kind of resume, known as a *combination resume* (or a *hybrid resume*), is a mix of recalled history and self-assessment. Besides including "the facts," a combination resume contains self-interpretation and therefore is more like dramatic history than news coverage. A chronological resume and a functional resume are not always that different. Often, all that is needed for a functional resume to qualify as a combination resume is the inclusion of some dates, such as those for positions held. Almost all the resumes in this edition are combination resumes.

Part 3, "Best Cover Letter Tips," discusses some myths about cover letters and gives you tips on polishing cover letters. Much of the advice offered here also applies to writing resumes. Included in this part is an exhibit of 20 cover letters.

The List of Contributors is arranged alphabetically by country, state or province, and city. Although most of these resume writers work with local clients, many of them work nationally or internationally with clients by phone or e-mail.

You can use the Occupation Index to look up resumes by the current or most recent job title. This index, however, should not replace careful examination of all the resumes. Many resumes for some other occupation may have features that you can adapt to your own occupation. Limiting your search to the Occupation Index may cause you to miss some valuable examples. You can use the Features Index to find resumes that contain representative resume sections that may be important to you and your resume needs.

Who This Book Is For

Anyone who wants ideas for creating or improving a resume can benefit from this book. It is especially useful for active job seekers—those who understand the difference between active and passive job searching. A *passive* job seeker waits until jobs are advertised and then sends copies of the same resume, along with a standard cover letter, in response to a number of help-wanted ads or Internet postings. An *active* job seeker modifies his or her resume for a specific job target *after* he or she has talked in person or by phone or e-mail to a prospective interviewer *before* a job is announced. To schedule such an interview is to penetrate the "hidden job market." Active job seekers can find in the Gallery's focused resumes a wealth of strategies for targeting a resume for a particular interview. The section "How to Use the Gallery" at the beginning of Part 2 shows how to do this.

Besides the active job seeker, any unemployed person who wants to create a more competitive resume or update an old one should find this book helpful. It shows the kinds of resumes that professional resume writers are writing, and it showcases resumes for job seekers with particular needs.

What This Book Can Do for You

The Gallery offers a wide range of resumes with features you can use to create and improve your own resumes. Notice the plural of "resumes." An important premise of an active job search is that you have not just one "perfect" resume for all potential employers, but different versions of your resume for different interviews. The Gallery, therefore, is not a showroom where you say, "I'll take that one," alter it with your information, and then send out 200 copies of your version. It is a valuable resource for design ideas, expressions, and organizational patterns that can help make your resume a "best resume" for each new interview.

A good strategy is to create a basic resume in Microsoft Word or another word processing program that you can easily change and print out as needed to respond to specific job opportunities. If you don't have access to a computer, many public libraries offer computer and printer access. Quick-print shops and office supply stores also can print your resume on high-quality paper from electronic files. You will need to keep a few paper copies of your resume on hand to give to potential employers when you meet them in person or when application instructions require that you mail or fax your resume.

At some point in your job search, however, you will most likely have to submit your resume electronically. If you can send your resume as an e-mail attachment, you probably won't have to change it much. Most employers use Microsoft Word, so they will be able to view files created in that word processing program. If your resume has lots of graphics or unusual fonts, or you are using something other than Microsoft Word, or you use a Mac and the employer uses a PC, for example, consider converting your resume to a PDF file. PDF files preserve formatting and can be read with just about any computer system. You will need Adobe Acrobat or another conversion program (newer versions of Word have this capability) to create a PDF file.

You also should have a plain-text version of your resume prepared. A plain-text resume is a resume with all of the special formatting removed, such as bold, italic, bullets, lines, and tables. You use this type of resume when

- You submit a resume in the body of an e-mail message instead of as an attachment.

- You need resume text that you can easily copy and paste into an online resume or application form.

To create a plain-text resume, open your resume file in your word processing program, choose the Save As option, and select the Plain Text format. You will have to make some adjustments to the document to make it readable, such as shortening lines of text, adding more blank lines to separate sections, and using asterisks and other keyboard characters to replace lines and bullets. Refer to "Best Resume Design and Layout Tips" in Part 1 for more ideas.

When you apply online for positions, be sure you follow the submission guidelines posted by the employer. If they are not clearly explained, phone or e-mail the company to inquire. You don't want to be disqualified for a job that suits you well, because you did not follow the steps for successful submission.

If you are inexperienced with formatting word processing documents, most professional resume writers can make your resume look like those in the Gallery and help you convert it into the different formats you need. See the List of Contributors for the names, address-es, phone numbers, e-mail addresses, and websites (if any) of the professional writers whose works are featured in this book.

Besides providing you with a treasury of quality resumes with features you can use in your own resumes, this book can help transform your thinking about resumes. There is no one best way to create a resume. This book helps you learn how to shape a resume that is *best for you* as you try to get an interview with a particular person for a specific job.

You might have been told that resumes should be only one page long; however, this is not necessarily true. The examples of multiple-page resumes in the Gallery help you see how to distribute information effectively across two or more pages. If you believe that the way to update a resume is to add your latest work experiences to your last resume, this book shows you how to rearrange your resume so that you can highlight the most important information about your experience and skills.

After you have studied "Best Resume Tips" in Part 1, examined the professionally writ-ten resumes in Part 2, and reviewed "Tips for Polishing Cover Letters" and the cover let-ters in Part 3, you should be able to create your own resumes and cover letters worthy of inclusion in any gallery of best resumes.

Acknowledgments

To all those who helped make possible this fifth edition, I would like to offer my apprecia-tion. Again, I am most indebted to all the professional resume writers who sent me many examples of their work for inclusion in this book and other books. These writers took the time—often on short notice—to supply fictionalized resumes and any other requested information.

Special thanks go to my wife, Ginny Noble, for performing with proficiency and good sense many different tasks, such as updating, editing, and polishing all files, including her two indexes.

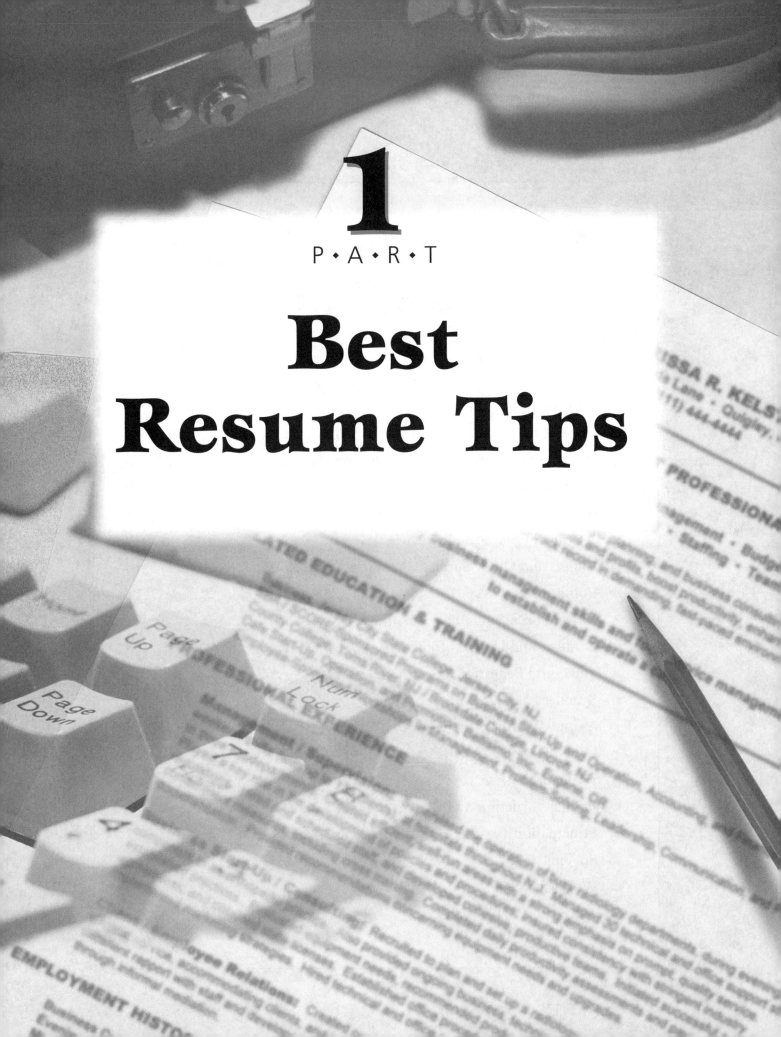

Best Resume Tips

P·A·R·T 1

Best Resume Tips at a Glance

Best Resume Tips

In a passive job search, you rely on your resume to do most of the work for you. An eye-catching resume that stands out from all the others may be your best shot at getting noticed by a prospective employer. If your resume is only average and looks like most of the others in the pile, chances are you won't be noticed and called for an interview. If you want to be singled out because of your resume, it should be somewhere between spectacular and award-winning.

In an active job search, however, your resume complements your efforts at being known to a prospective employer before that person receives it. For this reason, you can rely less on your resume to get someone's attention. Nevertheless, your resume plays an important role in an active job search, which may include the following activities:

- Talking to relatives, friends, and other acquaintances about helping you meet people who can hire you before a job is available

- Researching employers, using Internet and library resources to identify organizations that could use a person with your skills

- Creating phone scripts to speak with people who are most likely to hire someone with your background and skills

- Walking into businesses to talk directly to people who are most likely to hire someone like you

- Using a schedule to keep track of your appointments and callbacks

- Working at least 25 hours a week to search for a job

When you are this active in searching for a job, the quality of your resume confirms the quality of your efforts to get to know the person who might hire you, as well as your worth to the company whose workforce you want to join. An eye-catching resume makes it easier for you to sell yourself directly to a prospective employer. If your resume is mediocre or conspicuously flawed, it will work against you and may undo all your good efforts in searching for a job.

The following sections offer ideas for making your resume impressive. Many of the ideas are for making your resume pleasing to the eye, but a number of the ideas are strategies to use for special cases. Other ideas are for eliminating common writing mistakes and stylistic weaknesses. A number of these ideas came from the professional resume writers who submitted resumes for this book. Resumes that illustrate these ideas are referenced by their numbers.

Best Resume Writing Tips

All resumes contain the same basic types of information, such as a work history and list of skills. But the way in which this information is presented is the difference between a bad resume and a best resume.

Contact Information

Make sure your phone number, e-mail address, and other contact information are clear and easy to find on your resume. Keep these tips in mind:

- **Instead of spelling out the name of the state in your address at the top of your resume, consider using the state's postal abbreviation.** The reason is simple: it's an address. Anyone wanting to contact you by mail will probably refer to your name and address on the resume. If they appear there as they should on an envelope, the person can simply copy the information you supply. If you spell out the name of your state in full, the person will have to "translate" the name of the state to its postal abbreviation. Not everyone knows all the postal abbreviations, and some abbreviations are easily confused. For example, those for Alabama (AL), Alaska (AK), American Samoa (AS), Arizona (AZ), and Arkansas (AR) are easy to mix up. You can prevent confusion and delay simply by using the correct postal abbreviation.

  If you decide to use postal abbreviations in addresses, make certain that you do not add a period after the abbreviations, even before ZIP codes. This also applies to postal abbreviations in the addresses of references if you provide them.

  Do not, however, use the state postal abbreviation when you are indicating only the city and state (not the mailing address) of a school you attended or a business where you worked. In these cases, it makes sense to write out the name of the state.

- **When listing your phone numbers, adopt a sensible form and use it consistently.** Do this in your resume and in all the documents you use in your job search. Some forms of phone numbers make more sense than others. Compare the following:

123-4567	As area code regions continue to shrink, this form is becoming less acceptable.
(222) 123-4567	This form is best for a resume circulated in areas with different area codes.
222-123-4567	This form suggests that the area code should be dialed in all cases. But that isn't necessary for prospective employers whose area code is 222.
222/123-4567	This form is illogical and should be avoided. The slash can mean an alternate option, as in ON/ OFF. In a phone number, this meaning of a slash makes little sense.
1 (222) 123-4567	This form is long, and the digit 1 is unnecessary. Almost everyone will know that 1 should be used before the area code to dial a long-distance number from a landline, and most cell phones don't need it.
222.123.4567	This form, resembling Internet addresses, is becoming more popular, particularly with people in computer and design fields.

Note: For resumes directed to prospective employers outside the United States, be sure to include the correct international prefixes in all phone numbers so that you (and your references, if they are listed) can be reached easily by phone.

Professional Profiles and Skills Summaries

The information that immediately follows your name and contact information near the top of the first page is important. If this section fails to grab the reader's attention, he or she may discard your resume without reading further. Try these tips to create a great first impression:

- **Include a Profile section that is focused, interesting, and unique.** A Profile section can be your first opportunity to sell yourself. For examples of effective Profile sections, see Resumes 5, 19, 23, 55, 72, 83, 86, 110, 112, 134, and many others.

- **When your skills and abilities are varied, group them according to categories for easier comprehension.** See, for example, Resumes 28, 32, 54, 69, 70, 85, 88, 106, 111, 113, 114, 143, 162, and 169.

- **Consider including a Highlights section to draw attention to special accomplishments or achievements.** See, for example, Resumes 22, 31, 78, 111, and 135.

- **Summarize your qualifications and work experiences to avoid having to repeat yourself in the job descriptions.** See, for example, Resumes 4, 16, 46, 98, and 137.

- **Create a prominent Expertise section that draws together skills and abilities you have gained in previous work experience.** See, for example, Resumes 8, 28, 30, 45, 57, 58, 60, 83, 125, 160, 166, and 170.

- **Incorporate testimonials in your resume.** These can be quotes from performance reviews or comments from clients, for instance. Devoting a whole column to the positive opinions of "external authorities" helps make a resume convincing as well as impressive. See, for example, Resumes 36, 38, 43, 56, and 73.

Work Experience

When you write about your work experience in your resumes, consider these tips:

- **State achievements or accomplishments, not just duties or responsibilities.** The reader often already knows the duties and responsibilities for a given position. Achievements, however, can be interesting. The reader probably considers life too short to be bored by lists of duties and responsibilities in a stack of resumes. See, for example, Resumes 2, 12, 60, and 77.

- **If you feel you must indicate duties, call attention to special or unusual duties you performed.** For example, if you are an accountant, don't say that you prepared accounting reports and analyzed income statements and balance sheets. That's like being a dentist and saying, "I filled cavities and made crowns." What did you do that distinguished you from other accountants? To be noticed, you need to stand out from the crowd in ways that display your individuality, work style, and initiative. See, for example, Resumes 8 and 11.

- **Instead of just listing your achievements, present them as challenges or problems solved, indicating what you did when something went wrong or needed fixing.** See, for example, Resumes 18, 90, 135, and 159.

Best Resume Design and Layout Tips

Whether your resume is presented on paper or on-screen, it is important that it be inviting and easy-to-read. Otherwise, it might not be read at all!

Alignment

Misalignment can ruin the appearance of a well-written resume. Avoid this problem by following these tips:

- **Use vertical alignment in tabbed or indented text.** Try to set tabs or indents that control this text throughout a resume instead of having a mix of tab stops in different sections.

- **Try left- or right-aligning dates.** This technique is especially useful in chronological resumes and combination resumes. For an example of left-aligned dates, see Resume 32. For right-aligned dates, look at Resumes 7 and 125.

- **Resist the temptation to use full justification for text** (in which each line goes all the way to the right margin). The price you pay for a straight right margin is uneven word spacing. Words may appear too close together on some lines and too spread out on others. Although the resume might look more uniform, you lose readability.

Bullets and Special Characters

Special characters enhance the look of your resume, and using them correctly demonstrates your attention to detail. (Note that your word processing program may be set up to make some of these changes for you by default.) These tips will help you use bullets and other special characters effectively:

- **Use curly quotation marks (" and ") instead of straight ones (" and ") for a polished look.**

- **Use an em dash (—) instead of two hyphens (--) or a hyphen with a space on either side (-).**

- **To separate dates, use an en dash (a dash the width of the letter *n*) instead of a hyphen, as in 2010–2011.** If you use "to" instead of an en dash in a range of numbers, be sure to use "to" consistently in all ranges in your resume.

- **To call attention to an item in a list, use a bullet (•) or a box (❑) instead of a hyphen (-).** Browse through the Gallery and notice how bullets are used effectively as attention-getters.

- **Try using bullets of a different style, such as diamond bullets (◆), rather than the usual round or square bullets.** For diamond bullets, see Resumes 52, 58, 69, 104, 125, and 141. For other kinds of bullets, see Resumes 37, 46, 54, 84, 144, and 148.

- **Make a bullet a little smaller than the lowercase letters that appear after it.** Disregard any ascenders or descenders on the letters. Compare the following bullet sizes:

  • Too small   ● Too large   ● Better   • Just right

- **Brevity is not always the best strategy with bullets.** When you use bullets, make certain that the bulleted items go beyond the superficial and contain information that employers want to know. Many short bulleted statements that say nothing special can affect the reader negatively. For examples of substantial bulleted items, see Resumes 75 and 119.

- **Repeat a distinctive bullet type or other graphic element to unify a longer resume.** See, for example, Resume 55.

Fonts

Anyone with a word processing program and an Internet connection has access to a vast array of fonts for resume use. The tips in the section will help you make smart font decisions and avoid common pitfalls:

- **Consider using unconventional type in headings to make your resume stand out.** See, for example, Resume 14.

- **Beware of becoming "font happy" and turning your resume into a font circus.** Frequent font changes can **distract** the reader, AND SO CAN GAUDY DISPLAY TYPE such as this. Also, if you are e-mailing or submitting your resume online, uncommon fonts may not display correctly if the people receiving your resume don't have that font installed on their machines.

- **Try to make your resume more visually interesting by offering stronger contrasts between light and dark type.** Some fonts are light; others are dark. Notice the following lines:

  A quick brown fox jumps over the lazy dog.

  A quick brown fox jumps over the lazy dog.

  Most typefaces fall somewhere between these two. With the variables of height, width, thickness, serifs, angles, curves, spacing, and boldfacing, you can see that type offers an infinite range of values from light to dark. See, for example, Resumes 17 and 18.

- **If your resume will be printed, use a serif font for greater readability.** *Serif* fonts have little lines extending from the tops, bottoms, and ends of the characters. These fonts tend to be easier to read than *sans serif* (without serif) fonts, especially in low-light conditions. Compare the following font examples:

Serif	Sans Serif
Century Schoolbook	Gill Sans
Courier	Futura
Times New Roman	Helvetica

  Words such as *skill* and *abilities,* which have several thin letters, are more readable in a serif font than in a sans serif font.

- **If your resume will be read on-screen, consider using a sans serif font, which is the standard for on-screen text.** Sans serif fonts sometimes are used for section headings or your name at the top of the resume.

- **Avoid using monospaced fonts, such as Courier.** A font is *monospaced* if each character takes up the same amount of space. For example, in a monospaced font, the letter *i* is as wide as the letter *m*. Therefore, in Courier type, iiiii is as wide as mmmmm. Monospaced fonts take up a lot of space, so you can't pack as much information on a page with Courier type as you can with a proportionally spaced type such as Times New Roman.

- **Think twice about underlining words in your resume.** Underlining defeats the purpose of serifs at the bottom of characters by blending with the serifs. In trying to emphasize words, you lose some visual clarity. This is especially true if you use underlining with uppercase letters in centered or side headings.

- **When you want to call attention to a word or phrase, use bold or italic.** Boldfacing can make different job experiences or achievements more evident.

See, for example, Resumes 1, 6, and many others. You might consider using italic for duties, strengths, achievements, or company descriptions. For examples, see Resumes 50, 92, and 149. Be sure not to use italic too much, however, because italic characters are less readable than normal characters.

■ **Think twice about using all uppercase letters in your resume.** A common misconception is that uppercase letters are easier to read than lowercase letters. Actually, the ascenders and descenders of lowercase letters make them more distinguishable from each other and therefore more recognizable than uppercase letters. As a test, look at a string of uppercase letters and throw them gradually out of focus by squinting. Uppercase letters become a blur sooner than lowercase letters. If you like the look of uppercase letters in headings, consider using "small caps" instead.

To create a heading with "small caps" (a Font option in Word), first create a heading with upper- and lowercase letters. Then select the heading and assign Small caps to it by selecting that font option. Original uppercase letters will be taller than original lowercase letters, which now appear as small capital letters.

Note: In plain-text resumes (see the Introduction, "What This Book Can Do for You"), all uppercase letters are a good substitute for bold, italic, and other forbidden special fonts in headings and subheadings.

Lines, Boxes, and Other Graphics

You can use lines, boxes, and other graphics to enhance your resume in many ways:

■ **Use a horizontal line to separate your name (or your name and address) from the rest of the resume.** If you browse through the Gallery, you can see many resumes that use horizontal lines this way. See, for example, Resumes 16, 26, 32, and 151.

■ **Use horizontal lines to separate the different sections of the resume.** See, for example, Resumes 5, 11, 60, and 130. See also Resumes 13 and 17, whose lines are interrupted by the section headings.

■ **To call attention to a resume section or certain information, use horizontal lines to enclose it.** See, for example, Resumes 53, 141, and 177. See also Resumes 84 and 128, in which one or more sections are enclosed in a box. Resumes 33, 40, 46, 127, and 129 use shaded boxes or headings to make a page visually more interesting.

■ **Change the thickness of part of a horizontal line to call attention to a section heading above or below the line.** See, for example, Resumes 10, 98, and 141.

■ **Use a vertical line (or lines) to spice up your resume.** See, for example, Resumes 14, 39, 149, and 169.

■ **If you decide to use pictures or other graphics, try to make them match the resume's theme.** See, for example, Resumes 33 and 44.

■ **Visually coordinate the resume and the cover letter with the same font treatment or graphic to catch the reader's attention.** See, for example, Resume 14 and Cover Letter 16 and Resume 47 and Cover Letter 4.

Number and Length of Pages

No rule about the number of pages makes sense in all cases. The determining factors are your qualifications and experiences, the job's requirements, and the interviewer's interests and pet peeves. However, these general guidelines are helpful to follow:

- **Use as many pages as you need to portray your qualifications adequately to a specific interviewer for a particular job.** Try to limit your resume to one page, but set the upper limit at four pages. If you know that an interviewer refuses to look at a resume longer than a page, that says it all: You need to deliver a one-page resume if you want to get past the first gate. Sample one-page resumes include Resumes 59 and 64. For examples of two-page resumes, see Resumes 8, 56, and 75. For three-page resumes, look at Resumes 43, 58, 90, and 103. Resume 106 is an example of a four-page resume.

- **Make each page a full page.** More important than the number of pages is whether each page is a full page. A partial page suggests deficiency, as if the reason for it is just that information on page one has spilled over onto page two. Then it becomes evident that you don't have enough information to fill two pages. In that situation, try to compress all your information onto the first page. If you have a resume that is almost two pages, make it two full pages. Achieving this look may require that you adjust the character and line spacing settings in your word processing software.

Paper and Printing

If you will be printing your resume instead of sending it electronically, keep the following tips in mind:

- **If you use quality watermarked paper for your resume, be sure to use the right side of the paper.** To know which side is the right side, hold a blank sheet of paper up to a light source. If you can see a watermark and read it, the right side of the paper is facing you. This is the surface for printing. If the watermark is unreadable or if any characters look backward, you are looking at the "underside" of the paper—the side that should be left blank if you use only one side of the sheet.

- **Make certain that characters, lines, and images contrast well with the paper.** Your resume's printed quality depends on the device used to print it. If you use an inkjet or laser printer, check that the characters are sharp and clean, without smudges or traces of extra toner.

Spacing

A sheet of paper with no words on it is impossible to read. Likewise, a sheet of paper with words all over it is impossible to read. These tips will help you make your spacing just right:

- **Have a comfortable mix of white space and words.** If your resume has too many words and not enough white space, it looks cluttered and unfriendly. If it has too much white space and too few words, it looks skimpy and unimportant.

- **Make certain that adequate white space exists between the main sections.** For examples that display good use of white space, see Resumes 16, 22, 34, 44, 70, 124, and many others.

- **Make the margins uniform in width and preferably no less than an inch.** If the margins are less than an inch, the page begins to have a "too much to read" look. An enemy of margins is the one-page rule. If you try to fit more than one page of information on a page, the first temptation is to shrink the margins to make room for the extra material. It is better to shrink the material by paring it than to reduce the size of the margins. Decreasing the type's point size is another way to save the margins. Try reducing the size in your resume to 10 points. Then see how your information looks with the font(s) you are using. Different fonts produce different results. In your effort to save the margins, be certain that you don't make the type too small to be readable.

- **Be consistent in your use of line spacing.** How you handle line spacing can tell the reader how attentive you are to details and how consistent you are in your use of them. If, near the beginning of your resume, you insert two line spaces (two hard returns in a word processing program) between two main sections, be sure to put two line spaces between all the main sections in your resume.

- **Be consistent in your use of horizontal spacing.** If you usually put two spaces after a period at the end of a sentence, make certain that you use two spaces consistently. The same is true for colons. If you put two spaces after colons, do so consistently.

  Note that an em dash—a dash the width of the letter *m*—does not require spaces before and after it. Similarly, an en dash—a dash the width of the letter *n*—should not have a space before or after it. (An en dash is commonly used between a range of numbers, as in 2008–2012.)

  No space should go between the P and O of P.O. Box. Only one space is needed between a state's postal abbreviation and the ZIP code. You should insert a space between the first and second initials of a person's name, as in I. M. Jobseeker (not I.M. Jobseeker). These conventions have become widely adopted in English and business communications. If, however, you use other conventions, be sure to be consistent. In resumes, as in grammar, consistency is more important than conformity.

Best Resume Writing Style Tips

The following sections provide tips concerning style issues that commonly crop up in resumes. For more detailed information, consult a business writing style guide.

Capitalization

Resumes usually contain many of the following:

- Names of people, companies, organizations, government agencies, awards, and prizes

- Titles of job positions and publications

- References to academic fields (such as chemistry, English, and mathematics)

- Geographic regions (such as the Midwest, the East, the state of California, and Oregon State)

Because of such words, resumes are minefields for the misuse of uppercase letters. These tips address the most common pitfalls:

- **When you don't know whether a word should have an initial capital letter, don't guess.** Consult a dictionary, a handbook on style, or some other authoritative source, such as an official website of the organization or product in question. Often a reference librarian can provide the information you need. If so, you are only a phone call away from an accurate answer.

- **Check that you have used capital letters correctly in computer and technology terms.** If you want to show in a Computer or Technology Experience section that you have used certain hardware, software, or media, you may give the opposite impression if you don't use uppercase letters correctly. Note the correct use of capitals in the following names:

Adobe InDesign	LinkedIn	PowerPoint
AutoCAD	NetWare	QuickBooks
iPad	Microsoft Office	UNIX
JavaScript	Photoshop	Windows

  The reason that many computer product names have an internal uppercase letter is for the sake of a trademark. A word with unusual spelling or capitalization is more easily trademarked. When you use the correct forms of these words, you are honoring trademarks and registered trademarks and showing that you are in the know.

- **Use all uppercase letters for most acronyms.** An *acronym* is a pronounceable word or set of letters usually formed from the initial letters of the words in a compound term or sometimes from multiple letters in those words. Note the following examples:

CAD	Computer-Aided Design
OSHA	Occupational Safety and Health Administration

  Some acronyms, such as *radar* (*r*adio *d*etecting *a*nd *r*anging) and *scuba* (*s*elf-contained *u*nderwater *b*reathing *a*pparatus), have become so common that they are no longer all uppercase.

- **Use all uppercase letters without periods for common abbreviations that are pronounced as letters.** Using common abbreviations such as the following can save valuable space:

CEO	Chief Executive Officer
HR	Human Resources

Note: If you think that the person reading your resume might not recognize a certain abbreviation, spell it out the first time you use it in your resume. Also, you should never use abbreviations that represent informal, common phrases, such as FYI, in your resume or cover letter.

- **In headings, follow headline style with upper- and lowercase letters.** That is, capitalize the first word, the last word, and each main word in the heading, but not articles (*a, an,* and *the*), conjunctions (*and, but, or, nor, for, yet,* and *so*), and short prepositions (for example, *at, by, in,* and *on*) within the heading. Capitalize prepositions of five or more letters, such as *about*.

Hyphenation

Hyphenation is the root of many resume errors. These tips will help you deal with hyphenation issues:

- **Be aware that compounds present special problems for hyphenation.** Writers' handbooks and books on style do not always agree on how compounds (combinations of words) should be hyphenated. Many compounds are evolving from *open* compounds (two different words) to *hyphenated* compounds (two words joined by a hyphen) to *closed* compounds (one word). In different dictionaries, you can find the words *copy-editor, copy editor,* and *copyeditor.* No wonder the issue is confusing! Most style books do agree, however, that when some compounds that appear as an adjective before a noun, the compound should be hyphenated. When the same compound appears after a noun, hyphenation is unnecessary. Compare the following two sentences:

    I scheduled well-attended conferences.

    The conferences I scheduled were well attended.

- **Hyphenate so-called *permanent* hyphenated compounds.** Usually, you can find these by looking them up in the dictionary. You can spot them easily because they have a long hyphen (–) for visibility in the dictionary. Hyphenate these words (with a standard hyphen) wherever they appear, before or after a noun. Here are some examples:

all-important	self-employed
day-to-day	step-by-step
full-blown	time-consuming

- **Use the correct form for certain verbs and nouns combined with prepositions.** You may need to consult a dictionary for correct spelling and hyphenation. Compare the following examples:

start up	verb
start-up	noun
start-up	adjective
startup	noun, computer and Internet industry
startup	adjective, computer and Internet industry

- **Avoid hyphenating words with such prefixes as *co-, micro-, mid-, mini-, multi-, non-, pre-, re-,* and *sub-.*** Many people think that words with these prefixes should have a hyphen after the prefix, but most of these words should not. The following words are spelled correctly:

coauthor	midway	nondisclosure
cofounder	minicomputer	nonfunctional
coworker	multicultural	prearrange
microfiber	multilevel	reenter
midpoint	prequalify	subdirectory

Note: If you look in the dictionary for a word with a prefix and you can't find the word, look for just the prefix. You might find a small-print listing of a number of words that begin with that prefix.

For detailed information about hyphenation, see a recent edition of *The Chicago Manual of Style* (the 16th edition is the latest). You should be able to find a copy at your local library.

Parallel Structure and Consistency

Consistency is key to a polished resume:

- **Check that words or phrases in lists are parallel.** For example, notice the bulleted items in the Transitional Skills section of Resume 72. All the verbs are in the past tense. Notice also the bulleted list in the Executive Profile section of Resume 166. Here all the entries are nouns.

- **Make sure that you use numbers consistently.** Numbers are often used inconsistently with text. Should you present a number as a numeral or spell it out as a word? A useful approach is to spell out numbers one through nine but present numbers 10 and above as numerals. Different approaches are taught in different schools, colleges, and universities. Use the approach you have learned, but be consistent.

Punctuation

These tips address common punctuation pitfalls in resumes:

- **Use (or don't use) the serial comma consistently.** How should you punctuate a series of three or more items? If, for example, you say in your resume that you increased sales by 100 percent, opened two new territories, and trained four new salespersons, the comma before *and* is called the *serial comma*. It is commonly omitted in newspapers, magazine articles, advertisements, and business documents. However, it is often used for precision in technical documents or for stylistic reasons in academic text, particularly in the humanities.

- **Use semicolons correctly.** Semicolons are useful because they help distinguish visually the items in a series when the items themselves contain commas. Suppose that you have the following entry in your resume:

  > Increased sales by 100 percent, opened two new territories, which were in the Midwest, trained four new salespersons, who were from Georgia, and increased sales by 250 percent.

  The extra commas (before *which* and *who*) throw the main items of the series out of focus. By separating the main items with semicolons, you can bring them back into focus:

  > Increased sales by 100 percent; opened two new territories, which were in the Midwest; trained four new salespersons, who were from Georgia; and increased sales by 250 percent.

  Use this kind of high-rise punctuation even if just one item in the series has an internal comma.

- **Avoid using colons after headings.** A colon indicates that something is to follow. A heading indicates that something is to follow. A colon after a heading is therefore redundant.

■ **Use dashes correctly.** One of the purposes of a dash (an em dash) is to introduce a comment or afterthought about the preceding information. A colon *anticipates* something to follow, but a dash *looks back* to something already said. Two dashes are sometimes used before and after a related but nonessential remark—such as this—within a sentence. In this case, the dashes are like parentheses, but more formal.

■ **Use apostrophes correctly.** They indicate possession (Tom's, Betty's), the omission of letters in contractions (can't, don't), and some plurals (x's and o's), but they can be tricky with words ending in s, possessive plurals, and plural forms of capital letters and numbers. For review or guidance, consult a style guide or a section on style in the dictionary.

■ **Know the difference between *its* and *it's*.** The form *its'* does not exist in English, so you need to know only how *it's* differs from *its*. The possessive form *its* is like *his* and *her* and has no apostrophe. The form *it's* is a contraction of *it is*. The trap is to think that *it's* is a possessive form.

Spelling

A resume with just one misspelling is unimpressive and may undermine all the hours you spent putting it together. Worse than that, one misspelling may be what the reader is looking for to screen you out, particularly if you are applying for a position that requires accuracy with words. The cost of that error can be immense if you figure the salary, benefits, and bonuses you *don't* get because of the error but would have gotten without it. Keep the following tips in mind:

■ **Remember that your computer's spelling checker can detect a misspelled word but cannot detect when you have used the wrong word** (*to* for *too,* for example).

■ **Be wary of letting someone else check your resume.** If the other person is not a good speller, you may not get any real help. The best authority is a good dictionary.

■ **For words that have more than one correct spelling, use the preferred form.** This form is the one that appears first in the dictionary. For example, if you see the entry **trav•el•ing** *or* **trav•el•ling,** the first form (with one l) is the preferred spelling. If you make it a practice to use the preferred spelling, you will build consistency in your resumes and cover letters.

■ **Avoid British spellings.** These slip into American usage through books and online articles published in Great Britain. Note the following words:

British Spelling	American Spelling
acknowledgement	acknowledgment
centre	center
judgement	judgment
towards	toward

Word Choice

Make the correct word choices to ensure that your resume is clear:

- **Use the right words.** The issue here is correct usage, which often means choosing the right word or phrase from a group of two or more possibilities. The following words and phrases are often used incorrectly:

alternate (adj.)	Refers to an option used every other time. OFF is the alternate option to ON in an ON/OFF switch.
alternative	Refers to an option that can be used at any time. If cake and pie are alternative desserts for dinner, you can have cake three days in a row if you like. The common mistake is to use *alternate* when the correct word is *alternative*.
center around	A common illogical expression. Draw a circle and then try to draw its center around it. You can't. Use *center in* or *center on* as a logical alternative to *center around*.

  For information about the correct usage of words, consult a usage dictionary or the usage section of a writer's handbook, such as Strunk and White's *Elements of Style*.

- **Avoid using shortcut words, such as abbreviations like *thru* or foreign words like *via*.** Spell out *through* and use *by* for *via*.

- **Avoid using the archaic word *upon*.** The common statement "References available upon request" needs to be simplified, updated, or even deleted in resume writing. The word *upon* is one of the finest words of the 13th century, but it's a stuffy word in the 21st century. Usually, *on* will do in place of *upon*. Other possibilities are "References available by request" and "References available." However, because most readers of resumes know that applicants can usually provide several references, this statement is unnecessary. A resume reader who is seriously interested in you will ask about references.

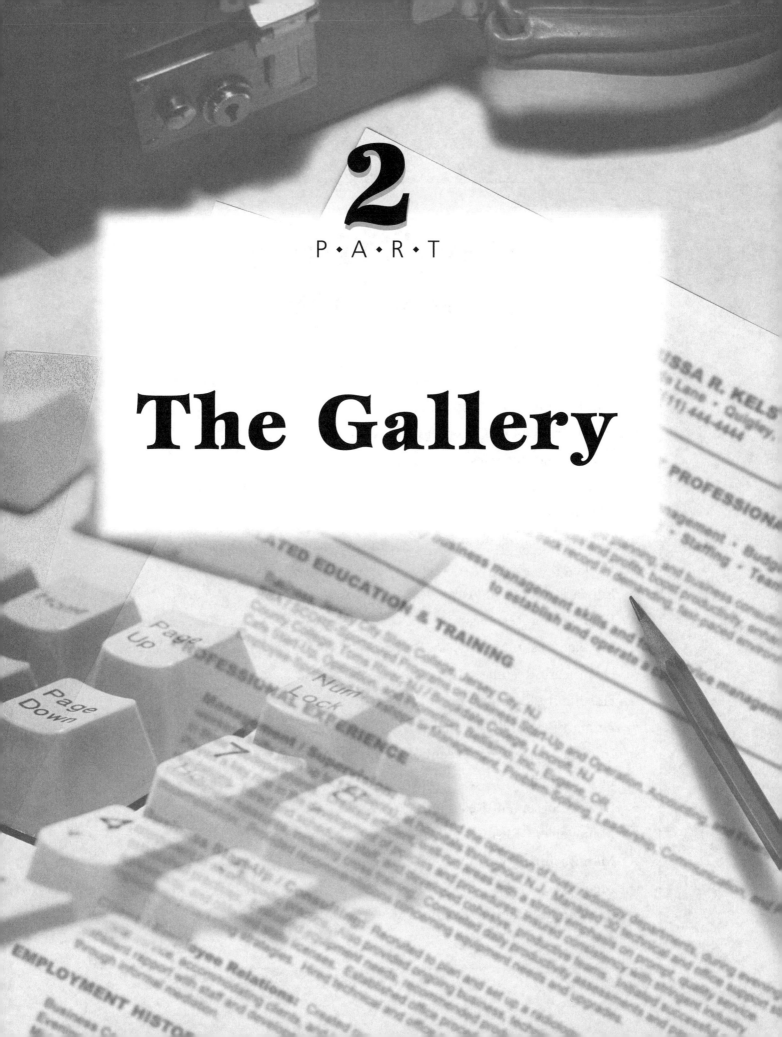

2
P·A·R·T

The Gallery

The Gallery at a Glance

How to Use the Gallery

You can learn much from the Gallery just by browsing through it. To make the best use of this resource, however, read the following suggestions before you begin.

Look at the resumes in the category containing your field, related fields, or your target occupation. Notice what kinds of resumes other people have used to find similar jobs. Always remember, though, that your resume should not be "canned." It should not look just like someone else's resume, but should reflect your own background, unique experiences, and goals.

Use the Gallery primarily as an "idea book." Even if you don't find a resume for your specific occupation or job, be sure to look at all the resumes for ideas you can borrow or adapt. You may be able to modify some of the sections or statements with information that applies to your own situation or job target.

Study the ways in which professional resume writers have formatted the applicants' names, addresses, and phone numbers. In most instances, this information appears at the top of the resume's first page. Look at type styles, size of type, and use of boldface. See whether the personal information is centered, spread across a line, or located next to a margin. Look for the use of horizontal lines to separate this information from the rest of the resume; to separate the address, phone number, and e-mail address from the person's name; or to enclose information for easier visibility.

Look at each resume to see what section appears first after the personal information. Then compare those same sections across the Gallery. For example, look at just the resumes that have a Profile or Summary of Qualifications as the first section. Compare the length, clarity, and use of words in these sections. Do they contain complete sentences or bulleted lists? Are some better than others in your opinion? Do you see one or more profiles or summaries that share similarities with your skills and experience? After you have compared these sections, try summarizing *in your own words* your professional history and/or skills.

Repeat this "horizontal comparison" for each section across the Gallery. Compare all the Education sections, all the Experience sections, and so on. As you make these comparisons, continue to note differences in length, the kinds of words and phrases used, and the content's effectiveness. Jot down any ideas that might be useful for you. Then put together similar sections for your own resume.

As you compare sections across the Gallery, pay special attention to the Profile, Summary, Areas of Expertise, Career Highlights, Qualifications, and Experience sections. (Most resumes don't have all of these sections.) Notice how skills and accomplishments are worked into these sections. Skills and accomplishments are *variables* you can select to put a certain "spin" on your resume as you pitch it to a particular interviewer or job. Your observations here should be especially valuable for your own resume versions.

After you have examined the resumes "horizontally" (section by section), compare them "vertically" (design by design). To do this, you need to determine which resumes have the same sections in the same order, and then compare just those resumes. For example, look for resumes that have personal information at the top, a Profile, an Experience section, and an Education section. (Notice that the section heads may differ slightly. Instead of the word *Experience,* you might find *Employment* or *Career Highlights.*) When you examine the resumes in this way, you are looking at their *structural design,* which means the order in which the various sections appear. The same order can appear in resumes of different fields or jobs, so it is important to explore the whole Gallery and not limit your investigation to resumes in your field or related fields.

Developing a sense of resume structure is extremely important because it lets you emphasize the most important information about yourself. A resume is a little like a newspaper article—read quickly and usually discarded before the reader finishes. That is why newspaper articles often have less-important information toward the end. For the same reason, the most important, attention-getting information about you should be at or near the top of your resume. What follows should appear in order of descending significance.

If you know that the reader will be more interested in your education than your work experience, put your Education section before your Experience section. If you know that the reader will be interested in your skills regardless of your education and work experience, put your Skills section at or near the beginning of your resume. In this way, you can help ensure that anyone who reads only *part* of your resume will read the "best" about you. Your hope is that this information will encourage the reader to read on to the end of the resume and, above all, take an interest in you.

Compare the resumes according to visual design features, such as the use of horizontal and vertical lines, borders, boxes, bullets, white space, graphics, and inverse type (white characters on a dark background), if any. Notice which resumes have more visual impact at first glance and which ones make no initial impression. Do some of the resumes seem more inviting to read than others? Which ones are less appealing because they have too much information, or too little? Which ones seem to have the right balance of information and white space?

After comparing the visual design features, choose the design ideas that might improve your resume. You will want to be selective and not try to work every design possibility into your resume. As with writing, "less is more" in resume creation, especially when you integrate design features with content.

Accounting

Resumes at a Glance

JAMES PARKER

222 Corner Lane Road • Bay Shore, New York 22222 • (555) 777-0000 • jraccountant@financialweb.net

---

Full-time accounting student with related experience seeking a part-time position in the capacity of

JUNIOR ACCOUNTANT

- Currently enrolled in a four-year accounting program; excel academically while working part-time.
- Well-rounded experience working in retail sales environments across foodservice and clothing industries.
- Analytical problem solver with a strong figure aptitude and ability to quickly grasp complex concepts.
- Disciplined with a strong character developed from extensive athletics and community involvement.
- Personable with innate relationship-building qualities; communicate effectively in English and Spanish.

EDUCATION

Bachelor of Science, Accounting, expected May 2014
LONG ISLAND UNIVERSITY, C.W. POST, Brentwood, New York
Honors: Phi Eta Sigma, Freshman Honor Society   **Current GPA:** 3.9

Coursework: External Reporting, Tax and Business Strategies, Managerial Accounting, Corporate Finance, Principles of Accounting, Microeconomics, Macroeconomics, Calculus, Business Law, Marketing, and Statistics

WORK EXPERIENCE

➤ **Supermarket City, Riverhead, New York**   **11/10–present**

Accounting Clerk, Internal Audit Department, Corporate Headquarters
- Perform general accounting functions focused on high-risk audits of daily inventory for 47 stores, weekly disbursements of short-term payable accounts, and mandatory reporting activities for management review.
- Research, identify, and investigate over/under charges through review and analysis of vendors' aging reports for all store sites; verify, reconcile, and approve payment for entry into network accounting system.
- Interface between major snack food and beverage vendors and Supermarket City's Accounts Payable/Receivable departments concerning invoice discrepancy issues and account billing cycles that include vendor discounts.
- Assisted Personnel during tax season to trace high-risk fraudulent employee activities for all store locations.
- Interviewed all levels of personnel to investigate incidents of false Social Security identifications and W-2 forms to cases of embezzlement, with a focus on bookkeepers, cashiers, and field auditors.

Produce Clerk, Produce Department
- Assisted in broad areas of customer service, sales, marketing, staff training, quality assurance, inventory control, delivery verification, stocking, vendor relations, catering services, and product merchandising.
- Selected to train four part-time clerks at another store location on daily produce department procedures.

➤ **Sales Representative, Garment Department, Discount Suits Corp., Riverhead, New York**   **12/09–11/10**
- Assisted in storewide functions, including sales counter and cashiering activities, part-time employee training, inventory control, stocking, merchandise display, purchasing, loss prevention, and problem resolution.

COMMUNITY INVOLVEMENT & AFFILIATIONS

Active Member, Accounting Society, Long Island University, C.W. Post
Cofounder and Chairman, Bay Shore Alumni Student Association

COMPUTER SKILLS

Windows 7; Microsoft Word, Excel, and Access; electronic tax research; Internet research; install, configure, and troubleshoot various hardware and software components

Combination. *Ann Baehr, East Islip, New York*

A full-time accounting student wanted to become a part-time junior accountant. A strong summary of skills and good academic credentials appear before beginning work experience.

JOHN T. SAMPLE

16 Melrose Ave., Anywhere NY 55555 ▪ Cell: 555.555.5555 ▪ getintouch@xxxx.com

SENIOR ACCOUNTANT / FINANCIAL ANALYST

Expert in: GAAP ~ Budgeting & Forecasting ~ Financial Statements ~ SOX

Dynamic bilingual professional who has earned fast-track promotions for proven ability to successfully direct all daily facets of organizational financial efforts. Extensive international experience in leading global branches and developing critical policies and procedures that consistently reduce company costs and dramatically improve productivity. Outstanding analytic, oral and written interpersonal skills in communicating effectively with all levels of the organization and producing clear, concise reports that provide key insight to Senior Management, allowing for sound business decisions. Skilled in negotiating partnerships and alliances, with extensive knowledge in multiple areas of technology and proven ability to implement technology-based solutions to combat key business issues.

CORE COMPETENCIES

Financial & Operations Management ~ Budget Planning & Development ~ Process Improvement ~ Change Management
Policy & Procedure Development ~ Organization & Communication ~ Accounting ~ Negotiations ~ Audits
Implementing Technology-Based Solutions ~ Risk Management ~ Financial Reporting ~ Forecasting
International Business Relations ~ SOX Compliance ~ Organizational Cost Savings

PROFESSIONAL EXPERIENCE

CITIGROUP, Tampa, FL   2009–Present
Senior Accountant / Financial Analyst

Played critical organizational role by supervising the administration, accounting, payroll, cash and banking, billing, risk management, insurance, negotiations, contracts, financial reporting (US GAAP and local Colombian statutory), tax reporting, budgeting and forecasting of all operations of foreign branch. Established organization's initial templates and procedures for reconciliations from local books to US GAAP, meeting corporate requirements. Also instituted company's initial policies and procedures for financial reporting, implemented structure and templates for month-end close and provided monthly financial data to Senior Management to ensure proper control and segregation of duties.

- Investigated and guaranteed international branch compliance with operational and financial controls, including SOX, internal and external audits and local requirements.
- Saved organization more than $2M via reduced branch importation transactions and an additional $1M in local taxes by providing local governmental authorities with corrected information.
- Reduced branch and corporate close process by 50% through revision of reporting priorities.

TEC DEVELOPMENT COMPANY, Sarasota, FL   2006–2009
Senior Accountant / Financial Analyst

Earned fast-track promotions by coordinating the consolidation of data for financial reporting (IFRS) for 40 global locations, while managing an annual operating budget of $500M. Directed staff trainings in examining work processes and utilizing new systems, saving organization more than $50K on fees. Designed and implemented innovative consolidation software, proving substantial savings and improving financial reporting efficiency with French parent company.

- Implemented Web-based payroll system, producing $4K monthly savings, improving tax reporting and eliminating manual payroll process.
- Developed and instituted financial reporting schedule consolidation, reducing preparation time from 12 days to 8.
- Implemented consistent single ERP system across all global sites, centralizing accounting information submission.

Continued

2

Combination. *Edward McGoldrick, Clearwater, Florida*

The opening paragraph serves as a profile, and the Core Competencies list contains many key-words useful in any online version of this resume. A pair of horizontal lines encloses each main

CONSOLIDATED GRAPHICS, New York, NY   2003–2006
Consolidations Accountant

Worked closely with Treasurer, overseeing all cash management activities, including investment portfolio, credit and risk management. Prepared financial instrument status reports for Senior Management, working with the legal department, finance and accounting teams to ensure all organizational financial goals were met. Produced internal and external financial reporting and assisted with budgets and SEC reporting, including preparing 10-K and 10-Q forms.

- Greatly impacted organization's bottom line by deleting receivable write-offs by $100K through developing credit policies, instituting aggressive collection strategies and establishing constructive dialogues with delinquent accounts, minimizing risk from marginal customers.
- Played integral role in negotiation of $1.3M loan and $500K working capital line, allowing organization to purchase assets with minimal principle cash contributions.
- Automated control cash disbursement process, increasing cash flow and reducing bank fees and related costs.
- Hand-selected to manage and then close Libya branch. Performed due diligence for company providing standard procedures on how to enter, open and establish branches in North Africa and most of the Middle East.

CW FIELDS, Anywhere, NY   2001–2003
Senior Analyst

Responsible for preparing and analyzing budget versus actual with variance explanations. Created, implemented and maintained various reporting tools to streamline processes in both Microsoft Excel and Access for entire portfolio. Abstracted all types of leases into the system, including purchase options, early termination fees, renewal options, tenant improvements, right of first refusal, right of way and various other components.

- Hired originally as Analyst and was promoted to Senior Analyst within a few months, managing a team of three people and 1,200 leases.
- Streamlined the budget process for the core and wireless portfolios, resulting in a decrease in completion time from three weeks to three days.
- Learned and implemented Sarbanes-Oxley rules as a third-party provider.
- Developed three significant consulting positions to the Army Corps of Engineers, equaling over $750K in annual revenue representing a 6.25% increase in overall company revenue over 2000.

EDUCATION

MBA in Finance, University of St. Thomas, Houston, TX

MBA in MIS, University of St. Thomas, Houston, TX

Bachelor's degree in Finance, Southern Illinois University, Carbondale, IL

CPA Examination, Currently pursuing and eligible by the Texas State Board of Public Accountancy
Possess more than 150 credit hours required by Board, including all accounting hours.

Fluent: English and Spanish.
Speak: Portuguese and French.

TECHNICAL SKILLS

Software:	Visual Basic, AS400, Timberline, Oracle 9 and 11i, PeopleSoft, Peachtree, Great Plains, SQL, Hyperion Essbase.
Applications:	Microsoft Office: Advanced Excel, Access, Word, PowerPoint

section heading, making the overall design easy to grasp at a glance. For each workplace, a paragraph indicates responsibilities and is followed by bulleted achievements. Many professional resume writers use this format.

DEBORAH HORTENSEN

555 Multnomah Street • Portland, OR 55555 • debhortensen@example.com • (555) 555-5555

CORPORATE ACCOUNTANT • SENIOR FINANCIAL ANALYST • REGULATORY EXPERT

Expert in implementing proper audit controls and scalable monitoring tools to ensure compliance

Accomplished, self-directed and critical-thinking lead financial analyst and accounting specialist combining a widespread comprehension of auditing cycles with analytical reasoning, research and requirements gathering skills. Readily implement and enforce pragmatic policy changes in accordance with FERC compliance guidelines. Gain credibility for getting the job done quickly and accurately, delivering quality and customer-satisfaction-driven results and products. Adept at developing and maintaining positive client and stakeholder relationships at all organizational levels. Provide experience from the ground up; equipped to integrate long-term financial strategies to foster exceptional cost savings and sustained business growth. *IT snapshot:* MS Office, OGE Corporate Reports, OGE CIS, QuickBooks and SAS. Demonstrated competencies in:

Internal and External Auditing • Financial Reporting • Budget Forecasting • Process Improvements
FERC Regulatory Compliance & Oversight • Analytical Problem Solving • Project Management
Presentation Skills & Communicating Project Plans • Staff Training • Relationship Management

CAREER HIGHLIGHTS

OREGON GENERAL ELECTRIC (OGE)—Portland, OR   1991–Present

Oregon's largest electric utility, OGE has 120 years of experience in generation and transmission of power from a diverse mix of resources, including hydropower, coal, natural gas and most recently wind and solar.

FINANCIAL ANALYST III, CORPORATE ACCOUNTING, RETAIL REVENUE   2009–Present

Appointed to front-line team leadership position during transition from General Ledger (GL) Operations, assigned to direct accounting functions for the Retail Revenue Division. Accountable for dedicated client support, provision of uncollectible customer A/R, reporting and support activities surrounding regulatory deferrals, high-level balance sheet and income statement analysis, auditor requirements gathering, forecasting and analysis for other revenues and taxes, analysis and SEC compliance disclosure as well as preparation and assessment of revenue-related journal entries. Serve in key function to evaluate payments and voucher information for low-income assistance, energy efficiency and public purpose charges.

Key Achievements:
- Reduced time to perform daily Customer Information System balancing by half.
- Took on additional accountability for activities including PCAM and ISFSI journal entries, serving in new position as Lead Analyst for regulatory deferrals.
- Trained and mentored all new analysts assigned to GL Operations.
- Chosen to review Oregon Public Utility Commission (OPUC) pages and organize publication of *OGE Quarterly* newsletter, containing mission-critical information used by various internal departments.
- Continue to support OGE Foundation: prepared journal entries, commitment sheets, ad hoc reports and financial statements; compiled Board materials and tax documents for its tax department.
- Streamlined several monthly processes and documentation systems, updated accounting software and implemented archival systems for documents for OGE Foundation.

FINANCIAL ANALYST II, CORPORATE ACCOUNTING, GENERAL LEDGER (GL) OPERATIONS   2008

Full ownership of GL Operations spanning preparation and monitoring of production scheduling activities, coordination of journal entries and commitment sheets, setup of user profiles and security access, report maintenance, updating cash reconciliation files, balance sheet reconciliation and analysis of income statement variances.

Key Achievements:
- Collaborated with IT team to create and benchmark a company-wide Datamart user template to simplify tool functionality for all users.
- Optimized efficiency by consolidating balance sheet reconciliation files and incorporating Datamart pivot tables into files for ledger summarization and quick update capabilities.

continued

3

Combination. *Sandra Ingemansen, Matteson, Illinois*

Section headings appear in shaded boxes, helping the reader to comprehend quickly the resume's shape. A two-line, italic description of the chief workplace is a front door into information about

debhortensen@example.com   **Deborah Hortensen • page 2**   **(555) 555-5555**

- Improved historically ineffectual reporting structure and eliminated unnecessary documentation by revamping VRW financial statements.
- Expanded role to oversee accounting responsibilities for the OGE Foundation, a nonprofit corporate foundation providing educational opportunities and access to the arts.

FINANCIAL ANALYST II, RATES & REGULATORY AFFAIRS, PRICING & OFFER DEVELOPMENT   2001–2006

- Promoted to ensure seamless preparation of rate case scheduling for rate increases and tariffs, with heavy involvement in the preparation of OGE tariffs through thorough pricing analysis.
- Point person to calculate bill comparisons for all commercial and industrial customers.
- Increased personal range of responsibility by gathering publishing rates information from various utilities on OGE intranet site and disseminated up-to-date information to various work groups.
- Known for providing 100% accuracy on daily power prices spreadsheets, crucial for Key Customer Managers.

OREGON GENERAL ELECTRIC–Portland, OR   1998–2001
FINANCIAL ANALYST I

Wholesale Origination
- Scope of accountability included all aspects of contract processing, gap identification and escalation.
- Consistently requested by Sales Originators to conduct research and analysis on potential customers and industries based on track record of providing the highest-potential leads.
- Performed crucial forecasting data analysis for Business Development Group and analysis of sales leads from various trade shows.
- Created and maintained status updates on 53 accounts for senior management.

Market Research and Intelligence
- Undertook market research and analysis, maintained company database, supported business development efforts and provided project support for all departments.

ENRICH BROADBAND SERVICES (PURCHASED BY OREGON GENERAL ELECTRIC IN 1997)–Portland, OR   1991–1998
FINANCIAL ANALYST I

Asset Accounting
- Spearheaded Fleet Tracking System Project by writing and distributing corporate-wide Accounting Practices and Procedure manual to decrease time spent on invoice returns and departmental queries.
- Provided instrumental administrative support to 10-member staff, balanced company payroll, aided in payroll tax preparation and processed Exempt and Non-Exempt payroll for over 2,100 employees.

Load Research
- Took on 2 stretch assignments: participated in strategic planning, forecasting and analysis functions on an Automated Meter Reading Project; coauthored Oregon Public Utility Commission report on Time-of-Use Project.
- Supported General Manager with key administrative functions, preparing monthly and quarterly internal financial reports for budget, billing and forecasting.

CREDENTIALS

BS in Business Administration, concentration in Accounting, *Eastern Oregon University (2007)*
Magna cum Laude, Recipient of "Outstanding Business Student Award for Academic Excellence"

AS, General Studies, *Clackamas Community College (2005)*

Professional Training: Risk Management, Introduction to Corporate Accounting and Applied Financial Accounting, IP Networks, various accounting/financial software applications

the applicant's work there. The "Key Achievements" subheadings call attention to what most prospective employers want to see in a resume: not just duties and responsibilities, but also especially the applicant's noteworthy accomplishments for a company.

DANIEL BROWN, CPA

SUMMARY OF QUALIFICATIONS

Performance-driven CPA with more than 20 years of accounting experience and a proven record of success in providing tax and financial services to corporate clients. Prominent accountant who is highly successful in attracting new business, building client trust, and retaining client accounts long-term. Knowledgeable and credible professional with a talent for explaining complex information in terms others can understand. Respected manager with strong mentoring and training skills. Technology-minded leader recognized for launch of numerous initiatives to automate operations and improve efficiency.

CAREER HIGHLIGHTS

Performance Excellence

- Accumulated wealth of tax accounting experience, building reputation as trusted and knowledgeable resource relied on for expertise not only by clients, but by other accountants as well.

- Established solid record in attracting new business, consistently bringing in from $80,000 to $100,000 in sales annually through word-of-mouth referrals.

- Earned confidence and respect of clients, successfully retaining many accounts long-term, including 2 that date to the 1980s. Maintain strong network of clients through knowledgeable support and commitment to service.

- As member of PASCPA's Professional Ethics Committee, gained broadened appreciation of ethics issues. Leveraged participation to enhance firm's ethics standards and ensure alignment with best industry practices.

- Set up first managed care group, setting up templates for maintaining books and records for group.

Technology Initiatives

- Played key role in bringing new technologies to the workplace: Among successes, researched and tested software alternatives, recommending and implementing applications that integrated tax prep and write-up to streamline back-office operations and facilitate data retrieval.

- Instituted and maintained company-wide data backups to protect and preserve key data.

- Installed all software updates and provided application training to 22 staff members during period of rapid growth. (Gold & Associates)

- Computerized accounting and tax preparation, automating manual process to improve efficiency. (Young & Sons Accounting)

- Selected and implemented company's first computer network, introducing new, leading-edge technology that streamlined operations. (Young & Sons Accounting)

continued

4

Combination. *Carol A. Altomare, Three Bridges, New Jersey*

A shaded box draws attention to the applicant's areas of expertise. Notice again the technique of using a pair of horizontal lines to enclose each section heading, enabling the eye to see each

PROFESSIONAL EXPERIENCE

J. PETERMAN ASSOCIATES, Philadelphia, PA   1998 to present

Senior Accountant/Manager

Manage up to 4 accountants, providing general accounting oversight while handling client caseload for firm that provides accounting services to small business clients.

GOLD & ASSOCIATES, Philadelphia, PA   1990 to 1998

Public Accountant

Managed staff of 5 in small public accounting office. Implemented software updates and delivered training.

YOUNG & SONS ACCOUNTING, Yardley, PA   1980 to 1990

Senior Accountant

Hired as junior accountant, progressed to senior-level position in small accounting office.

EDUCATION & PROFESSIONAL CREDENTIALS

PENN STATE UNIVERSITY, State College, PA
Bachelor of Arts in Accounting/Bachelor of Science in Economics, 1980

Certified Public Accountant since 1990

Member, AICPA, 1990 to present
Member, PASCPA, 1990 to present
    Professional Ethics Committee (2006 to present)
    State Taxation Committee (2003 to present)

TECHNOLOGY SKILLS

Microsoft Office (Word, Excel, PowerPoint), QuickBooks, Ultra Tax, Lacerte.
Internet and e-mail applications.

LEADERSHIP & SERVICE

Board of Directors, Germantown Hospital, 2001 to present
Manager, Yardley Little League, 2003 to present
Den Leader, Cub Scouts, 2000 to present
Manager, Yardley Recreational Softball, 2000 to 2005

Pro bono accounting work for Germantown Hospital, Yardley Little League, and Yardley Booster Club.

555 BROAD STREET ◆ PHILADELPHIA, PA 55555
(555) 555-5555 HOME ◆ (555) 555-5555 CELL ◆ danbrown@xxxx.com

section quickly and thus grasp the resume's overall design. Career highlights fill most of the first page, helping the reader see the most important information about the applicant. The first page is your main chance to stand out. Putting your best information there can be crucial.

PAUL KEENAN, CPA, CMA

Credentialed financial professional with expertise in GAAP and managerial accounting, excellent financial analysis skills, and a proven record in implementing effective cost-saving initiatives

PROFILE

Dynamic, results-oriented accountant with nearly 10 years of experience that include 5 years as a controller in a manufacturing environment. Top-notch CMA with demonstrated expertise in cost accounting, financial analysis, and financial reporting. Hands-on leader with open management style who is effective at creating a team environment. Accomplished negotiator with excellent relationship-building skills. Strong track record in implementing initiatives that improve financial operations. Respected financial advisor schooled in the use of EVA™ (Economic Value Added) metric system to guide corporate decision-making. Driven by challenge and the opportunity for development; thrive in diverse, fast-paced settings.

PROFESSIONAL EXPERIENCE

AFFILIATES OF AMERICA, New York, New York   Jan 2007 to present
Assistant Joint Venture Group Controller

Brought on to integrate financial operations of four affiliated companies with revenues totaling more than $800 million. Instrumental in building financial infrastructures and standardizing accounting procedures across all companies. Work closely with individual companies to prepare budgets and compile monthly and quarterly P&L forecasts. Coordinate monthly and yearly financial closing procedures.

- Served key role in the introduction, installation, and integration of new financial reporting system across four joint-venture companies. Successfully migrated existing data into new system while bringing books into compliance with general accounting standards.

- Instituted procedures that standardized operational reporting, simplifying calculations such as ROI and allowing more accurate comparison between groups.

- Identified best practices among units and incorporated them throughout affiliated companies.

- Successfully lowered monthly closing time from 10 days to 3 days across all four companies through effective introduction and coordination of improved financial closing procedures.

- Instituted use of FAS Asset Accounting software to manage all property, plant, and equipment (PPE) with aggregate value in excess of $72 million.

- Created policies for the management and disposal of all capital assets to ensure assets are accounted for and charged to appropriate cost centers. Established new tracking system to simplify asset accounting.

- Effectively negotiated property and casualty insurance renewals with brokers, leveraging prior experience in the insurance industry to obtain the most favorable rates.

- Reported financial results based on the EVA™ metric system, calculating and presenting findings on a monthly and annual basis to provide financial data to enhance corporate decision-making.

- Working closely with Big 4 audit firm, prepared supporting documentation, flux analysis for sales and inventory, fixed assets, and accounts receivable and payable for both quarterly and year-end audits.

- Routinely develop clear, cohesive financial reports that identify opportunities for cost savings throughout joint-venture companies.

PAGE 1

5 SIDNEY ROAD   •   BRIARCLIFF, NEW YORK 10001   •   (333) 333-3333
pkeenan5@aol.com

5

Combination. *Carol A. Altomare, Three Bridges, New Jersey*

This resume displays two characteristics of executive resumes: smaller type and longer lines. These help pack more information on two pages and still provide adequate white space. Placing contact

JOHNSON GROUP OF NEW ENGLAND, Greenwich, Connecticut   Nov 2006 to Jan 2007
Assistant Vice President

Acting as broker, worked closely with underwriters to negotiate acceptable financial terms for casualty insurance programs targeted towards Fortune 100 client companies.

- Negotiated programs for major clients, providing expert financial analysis related to loss-sensitive programs.
- Won major contracts through persistence and determined negotiating.

ACE INSURANCE CORPORATION, New York, New York   Jan 2003 to Nov 2006
Account Executive—Actuarial Services

Serviced Commercial Property & Casualty accounts in the National Account Department. Assessed underwriting data, prepared insurance specifications, negotiated premium, and made presentations to clients.

- Served as key member of team that serviced insurance portfolio worth $1 million.
- Developed financial models for loss-sensitive/cash-flow insurance programs.
- Designed computer training program for employees.

EDUCATION

YORK UNIVERSITY, New York, New York
Bachelor of Science in Accounting with concentration in Economics, May 2002

Post Graduation Education:
International Finance, Securities Analysis, Risk Management and Insurance, CPCU-7 Legal Environment, C/C++ Programming

CERTIFICATIONS & PROFESSIONAL AFFILIATIONS

Certified Management Accountant (CMA), 2012
Certified Public Accountant, New York, 2004

Member, The Institute of Management Accountants, 2010 to present

COMMUNITY ACTIVITIES

Member of the Board of Trustees & Volunteer Treasurer, Gentry Steering Committee, Yonkers, New York
- Manage books for this not-for-profit housing organization.
- Installed QuickBooks to automate accounting.

information in a footer on both pages makes room for important Profile information at the top of page one just below the person's name. The individual got a call for an interview from every company he contacted.

James M. Olson

9803 Clinton Avenue • Houston, TX 77068
(281) 000-0000 • name@msn.com

ACCOUNTANT

Detail-focused, highly ethical accounting professional with a BBA in Accounting and work experience demonstrating consistent achievement of organizational and fiscal objectives and goals. Able to pinpoint discrepancies and errors to prevent continuing and potentially unnecessary cost expenditures. Willing to accept responsibilities beyond immediate job duties and take on special projects at management request. Proficient in Excel, Access, other MS programs, J.D. Edwards, and proprietary software. *Knowledge and skill areas include*

- Audits & Financial Statements
- Accounts Receivable/Payable
- Financial Reconciliations
- General Ledger Accounting
- Record/Systems Automation
- Financial Research Projects
- Strategic & Financial Analysis
- Audit Review Procedures
- Teamwork & Communication

Education

TEXAS UNIVERSITY, Houston, TX
Bachelor of Business Administration (BBA) in Accounting, 2009

Accounting G.P.A.: 3.5 / Member, Beta Alpha Psi—for Honors Accounting, Finance, and IT students

Relevant Experience

Accountant, CITY OF NAME, Anywhere, TX   2010–Present

Fully responsible for several core accounting functions within municipality of 200,000 residents, including preparing financial statements and monthly reports/reconciliations, analyzing expense reports, integrating technology to facilitate accounting tasks, and completing special research projects as needed. Assigned significant role in managing finances, organizing large bodies of financial data, and preparing all financial statements for 2010 and 2011 audits. *Selected Accomplishments:*

- **Records Analysis & Error Identification**—Researched, identified, and helped resolve several large discrepancies in receivables and payables, all favorable to City of Name:
  - *$100,000 in A/R account for City of Name's power purchases;*
  - *$20,000 underpayment for A/R in General Fund Account;*
  - *$10,000 excess in A/P for Internal Service funds.*
- **Policy Development**—Played key role in development of new travel policy, with projected elimination of problems previously stalling productivity of accounting and internal audit functions.
- **Financial Analysis**—Compiled analysis of franchise fees subsequently used by Assistant City Manager in evaluating potential effects of pending legislation.
- **Audit Review Compliance**—Prepared cash flow and financial statements for external auditors on 13 Internal Service and 10 Special Revenue funds, with zero notes from auditors on review documents.
- **Teamwork & Collaboration**—Coordinated project with legal division that revived dormant accounts and ensured proper disposition. Worked with Chief Accountant to construct new reporting model.
- **Technology Improvement**—Changed automatic accounting instruction table in J.D. Edwards system, leading to correction of multiple unnecessary entries and subsequent cost/time savings.

Collection Agent, CITYBANK, Irving, TX   2006–2007

Trained new employees on account software; prepared detailed financial/customer reports for management.

Manager, TANNING SALON, Irving, TX   2005–2006

Managed A/P, A/R, payroll, and other financial functions in addition to general management activities.

6

Combination. *Daniel J. Dorotik Jr., Lubbock, Texas*

Notice how the three-dimensional horizontal lines work together as the top and bottom of a frame to enclose, and therefore direct attention to, the Accountant information. In the Relevant Experience section, shadowed square bullets, boldfacing, and italic call attention to selected accomplishments.

Advertising/Events Planning

Resumes at a Glance

THOMAS DORAN 555-123-4567

. . . .

EDUCATION

BA in Advertising, Minor in Marketing, ACADEMIA UNIVERSITY, Camary, Texas   *Fall 2013*
17 hours Spanish

FOREIGN EXCHANGE PROGRAMS

THE CENTER FOR BILINGUAL MULTICULTURAL STUDIES, Citalynda, Zapata, Mexico   *Spring 2012*
Studied Spanish six hours a day, five days a week. Lived with Mexican family and other foreign students, and
traveled throughout Mexico learning of foreign culture and economics.

- **Volunteered for Niños de la Calle.**

HUSTER HASS SCHOOL, Don Hogg, Holland   *Fall 2011*
Studied international marketing and management and organizational management for six months. Also studied Dutch
law. Lived in dorm environment, and traveled throughout Europe learning of foreign culture. Helped organize school
functions and give new-student orientations.

RELEVANT PROJECTS

ADVERTISING COALITION 2012 NATIONAL STUDENT COMPETITION
Selected out of 21 members to serve on creative team of three members. Created a four-year integrated marketing
communications plan book for auto dealership and manufacturer of products for the transportation industry.
Researched and analyzed industry; wrote creative brief; designed Web page and magazine ads; and targeted
portfolio to financial opinion leaders, stock- and shareholders, employees, and customers.

- **Won second place at nationals.**

CAMPAIGN BOOK FOR STATE LOTTERY COMMISSION
One of a group of five compiling proposals for awareness campaign for state lottery. Group is creating 13
advertisements to be presented to lottery commissioner.

WORK EXPERIENCE

Wait Staff, HOME COOKIN' CORNER, Bullnose and Camary, Texas   *2011–Present*
Provided standard wait-staff services and balanced out cash and tips each day. Transferred from full-time summer
job in Bullnose to part-time position in Camary.

- **Requested by regular customers.**

Director, WeeCare After-School Program, WEECARE, Camary, Texas   *2009–2011*
Oversaw five staff members who coordinated activities for 80 children ages 5–12. Handled discipline issues with both
staff and participants and dealt with collection issues. Facilitated complete program organization and facility
readiness.

- **Asked to return to director's position after study abroad.**

Full-Time Daycare Counselor, WEECARE, Bullnose, Texas   *Summer 2009*
Organized arts and crafts and play activities for children and created projects. Interfaced with parents and handled
issues. Acted as mentor to children.

ACTIVITIES

- Member, State Advertising Federation   *2012*
- Member and Social Chair, Kuptta Kai Fraternity   *2009–Present*
- Volunteer, Challenged Veterans Store   *2008*
- Volunteer, Heart Saving Association   *2007*

. . . . .

5555 55th Street ▪ Camary, Texas 55555 ▪ tdoran@yahoo.com

Combination. *Edith A. Rische, Lubbock, Texas*

This student had relevant experience both abroad and in academic competitions. His goal was
foreign advertising, so foreign language and exchange programs are highlighted. See Cover
Letter 1.

Christopher Rollins

138 Redwood Drive • Burlington Township, NJ 08016 • 609.555.5555 • CsRollins@earthlink.net

MARKETING DIRECTOR / ADVERTISING DIRECTOR
Expertise in Competitively Positioning Brands, Products and Services

Creative professional with a proven track record of successful projects from initial concept through completion. High-energy, results-oriented leader recognized for innovative tactics and strategies. Talent for building cohesive teams with strong problem-solving skills, able to manage time-sensitive projects with multimillion-dollar budgets.

Combine passion for marketing with commitment to contributing to an organization's bottom line. Consistently successful in conceptualizing, developing and orchestrating internal and external marketing initiatives to support national and international sales organizations. Excellent communications and interpersonal skills.

Areas of Expertise:

- Strategic Brand Planning
- Comprehensive Advertising Campaigns
- Direct Response Programs
- New Market & Customer Development
- Business Analysis
- Project Management

- E-Media
- Brand Building Goals
- Business Marketing and Promotions
- Cooperative Marketing
- Evaluate Market Trends
- Market Research Analysis

Professional Experience

HARRIS & SMITH COMMUNICATIONS, Cranbury, NJ (2008–Present)
A full-service, strategically driven agency with $29 million in revenues and diverse capabilities in advertising, all forms of media promotions, and public relations.

Account Supervisor

Lead the team responsible for Account Planning and day-to-day operations and management of key agency accounts. Responsible for setting budgets and forecasts, developing estimates and managing estimated vs. actual costs for all applicable clients. Hands-on involvement in each phase of client business, from campaign strategy through execution and program analysis.
- Conceptualized, designed and implemented programs ranging from brand salience to direct-response programs.
- Restructured underperforming accounts into profitable and successful client relationships.
- Created, planned and implemented programs ranging from strategic brand planning to direct-response campaigns for national and international brands including **Chase, Nordica Skis, Fedders, Bank of America, Prince Sporting Goods, Yardville National Bank, SQN Banking Systems,** and **New Jersey Economic Development Authority.**
- Successfully planned, directed and launched the initial U.S. **ING DIRECT** campaign.

Continued

8

Combination. *Beverley and Mitchell I. Baskin, Marlboro, New Jersey*

A page border on both pages ties together the two pages visually. After a profile, a pair of lines enclosing Areas of Expertise directs attention to them. To recognize the value of boldfacing, look

Professional Experience *(Continued)*

PMG VENTURES, Narbeth, PA (2003–2008)
A $25 million, 50-person international sports and entertainment marketing and management agency.

Director of Marketing (2006–2008)

Directed the design, creation and strategic planning for marketing campaigns for the Men's Worldwide Senior Tennis Circuit (WSTC), DiamondBack Racing, Limited Express Next Model Search and the Dave Schultz Wrestling Foundation. Developed integrated marketing programs with partners of the WSTC to maximize their sponsorship and achieve objectives. Some major accounts handled as sponsors were **Citi, Unilever, PricewaterhouseCoopers, Cadillac,** and **U.S. News.** Supervised and approved advertising media contracts for print, radio, TV and out of home. Successfully grew the company to 4 times its size in 5 years.

- Increased profits over a two-year period with budget reductions of 10%.
- Expanded WSTC sponsorships to record levels through innovative marketing concepts.
- Honored with the firm's "Man-of-the-Year" award for leading by example and for excellent performance.
- Trained and directed a staff of 10 regional marketing managers.
- Managed $1.1 million marketing budget for all U.S. events on the WSTC.

Creative Services Manager (2003–2006)

Initiated, planned and managed the implementation of the Creative Services department. Hired freelance graphic designers and illustrators and developed them into a cohesive team during the firm's rapid growth period. Assumed full responsibility for all printed advertising and promotional materials, including magazine, newspaper, out-of-home advertising, pop displays, sales brochures, direct mail, posters, capability brochures, corporate identification and proposals.

- Led negotiations with service bureaus and other vendors on all contracts.
- Charged with full P&L responsibility for the department's budget.

BARNES MARKETING & COMMUNICATIONS, Media, PA (2002–2003)

Graphic Artist

Given creative control of the design and layout of numerous brochures, corporate newsletters, direct-marketing pieces and magazine and newspaper ads. Responsible for corporate identity on all media. Managed each project from concept through completion.

Education

ASHLAND UNIVERSITY, Ashland, OH
BS, Visual Communications, with honors, 2002
BS, Business Administration, with honors, 2001

Honors and Activities

Current participant with AmeriCare, helping to rebuild homes in the Northeast
Outstanding Achievement Award; Association of Graphic Communications, New York, NY
Honors Award for Outstanding Leadership, Ashland University

just for it and let your eyes travel through the two pages. What you see first is what the applicant and writer want you to see: key information that is relevant to the target position and that convinces the reader that this particular applicant is someone to interview.

Frank Terman

555 Harvard Avenue ▪ Bridgetown, CT 55555 ▪ (555) 555-5555 ▪ frankterman@xxxx.net

Director/Vice President Advertising

Characterized by senior leadership as an *"exceptionally well-rounded innovative executive with attention to detail balanced by a broader integrated marketing vision, and by analytical skills blended with a creative flair."*

Strategist, cross-functional team leader and consensus builder with expertise in all marketing functions including advertising, market research, product positioning/launches, brand management and collateral development.

✓ **Project Management:** History of exceeding expectations in delivering projects on time and on budget.
✓ **Brand Advertising:** Create campaigns that position organizations globally and increase revenues.
✓ **Market Research:** Focus on developing actionable research plans that support sales processes and drive change.
✓ **Technology:** Well versed in technology as a business tool, including managing marketing Internet and intranet sites.

Successful in creating marketing solutions that **deliver double-digit revenues** and in building relationships that facilitate business goal achievement. Highlights:

✓ **Drove revenues from $30 million to $115 million** over 7 years by developing global advertising packaging strategy for 15 media products to target global sales channels.
✓ **Initiated brand perception survey that supported Internet business growth from zero to $11 million** in 15 months. **Launched a new financial services industry product with projected sales of $10 million annually.**

Professional Experience & Achievements

JOHNSON FINANCIAL SERVICES ▪ New York, NY ▪ 1999 to Present
Leading provider of financial services products for the retail advisory and institutional markets.

Director of Advertising and Market Research   **2004 to Present**

Overview: Tapped to lead the development and execution of internal and external actionable market research plans for product development, product management, sales and senior management, while also spearheading all advertising including product management, brand management, lead generation/tracking and product sales promotions. Manage advertising agency relationships, media schedule, trade press and $11.7 million budget. Oversee customer database services for direct marketing, focus groups and research, as well as Web site/intranet upgrading/maintenance.

Results:

● **Launched new product with national print ad campaign and research-based events that generated 3,000 leads and approximately 70 sales calls with clients' senior management teams, including company's 2nd largest client.**

 — Codeveloped 3 white papers on capturing affluent investors and building client loyalty.
 — Created newsletter that helped differentiate company from competitors.
 — Launched a series of transformational customer satisfaction and competitive surveys that led to new products.
 — Coauthored publication with the CEO, published in a Wall Street magazine.

● **Provided research and analysis uncovering key strategic issues that led to 4 new product launches and helped retain $160 million in revenue.**

 — Launched companion Web site, which now has 40,000 unique users in financial services.
 — Added sales specialists to support specific channels.
 — Initiated new ad campaign that was instrumental in creating statistically significant gains in research measures including end-user loyalty and satisfaction.
 — Results led Division to build a new product for the institutional side of the financial marketplace.
 — Redesigned all print and electronic sales and training collateral to be more customer-focused and hired PR agency to promote company as an innovative provider.
 — Doubled trade show participation to promote new image industry-wide.
 — Refocused training efforts and added 4 trainers to develop an online program to help end users build their businesses using company's content.

Page 1 of 2

Combination. *Louise Garver, Broad Brook, Connecticut*

Shaded boxes draw attention to the "Title" and main section headings. Boldfacing makes visible important information throughout the resume: a key quotation, areas of expertise, important

Frank Terman, frankterman@xxxx.net – Page 2 of 2

Director of Marketing / Director of Advertising and Sales Promotion   **2000 to 2004**

Overview: Overhauled and led the marketing efforts of all products as company transitioned the sales team from "order taker" to "solutions seller." Repositioned several products and launched new campaigns and brand advertising campaign that included print, television and radio. Completely revamped sales collateral and Web site to reflect current product offerings. Assisted sales staff in developing more effective sales presentations. Expanded a J. D. Power study about relationships between affluent investors and their financial advisors to include rankings of financial services firms and their perception by the affluent marketplace. Led development of multimedia presentations for direct email campaigns and the Web service for subscribers.

Results:
- Improved advertising ROI 40% by hiring new advertising agency and bringing projects in-house, which yielded more effective results—on a "shoestring" budget.
- Generated $1 million in revenue by increasing subscriber base for high-end product 10% over 6 months.
- Realized $250,000 in additional revenues by developing first co-op advertising program with vendors.
- Built company's first marketing database, which now houses 250,000+ end-user names and is instrumental in communicating new features and product introductions.
- Presented qualitative research data that led company to develop role-based products and retain revenues in core markets.
- Attained high-level meetings with clients' senior management teams to discuss research results, which led to revenue retention at major accounts.

Process Redesign Team   **1999**

Handpicked for a special assignment by the President of the International Division as the only person from Sales and Marketing on a team of 6 to improve the computing environment. Efforts led to rebuilding the company intranet with access to all offices around the world and workflow automation.

FINANCIAL SERVICES INTERNATIONAL • New York, NY • 1992 to 1999
Director of Marketing and Operations | Director of International Marketing Services   **1995 to 1999**

Consistently delivered double-digit revenue goals. Directed staff of 4 and operations of 15 sales and marketing offices globally with $127 million revenue and expense budget, while developing and implementing marketing strategies for global products. Led several product launches aimed at the advertising community including cable news stations in Europe and Asia.

- Achieved $6 million in new business with 63% margins within one year of launching a new publication to the U.S. advertising community.
- Developed and implemented value-added research program for an international advertiser that resulted in a $4 million global branding campaign.

Senior International Marketing Manager (1992 to 1995) | Marketing Manager (1992)

Supported sales staff's efforts to sell advertising in U.S., European, and Asian journals. Managed marketing budget and team of 3.

- Implemented first sales collateral to promote the publications as a global brand to the advertising community. Developed research program to provide value-added research for key advertisers.

Education

MBA; University of Michigan, Ann Arbor, MI

BS, Mass Communication; Emerson College, Boston, MA
- Graduated *Summa cum Laude;* Class Valedictorian

accomplishments, positions, overviews, noteworthy results, and dates of employment. Three kinds of "bullets" (check marks, round bullets, and em dashes [—]) direct attention to key points. Horizontal lines underscore the applicant's various positions.

Evelyn Waters, C.M.P.

1234 Main Street ▪ Silver Spring, Maryland 20901
240.555.5555 ▪ ewaters@emailaddress.com

Corporate Events Planner

~ *Domestic & International Expertise* ~

Sophisticated Certified Meeting Professional (CMP) and orchestrator of worldwide programs, promotions, trade shows, galas, and conferences. Savvy strategist and discerning consultant to multiple business units in evaluating and supporting event purpose through expert–level logistics planning, budgeting, service contracting, marketing communications, and sponsorship fulfillment. Talented cross–functional team leader accustomed to senior–level roles requiring a high degree of diplomacy and the confidence necessary to resolve crises through judicious decision making.

Key Strengths

☑ Strategic Show Assessment & Deliverables	☑ Global Travel & Lodging
☑ Multimillion–Dollar Budgeting & Allocation	☑ Speaking Talent & Extramural Events
☑ Vendor Sourcing & Contract Negotiations	☑ Facility Equipment & Technology
☑ Site Selection & Contract Negotiations	☑ Online Registration & Management
☑ Floor Plan Management & Exhibit Space	☑ Postwrap Research & Follow–Up
☑ Public Relations, Marketing & Collaterals	☑ Strong Communicator & Presenter

Career and Achievements

CONFIDENTIAL CORPORATION, INC. — Reston, VA ▪ 2007 to Present

Senior Director of Corporate Events

Lead domestic and international events and trade show operations from initial conception, strategy, and goal setting through planning, execution, and postshow follow–up. Partner with regional marketing and sales teams in assessing business directives, pinpointing a message, establishing a budget, and orchestrating semiannual and yearly events with more than 2,500 global attendees. Travel abroad to select facilities, negotiate service contracts, secure equipment and accommodations, and retain multitrade vendors. Oversee the creative development process for marketing communications, collaterals, menus, and programs. Liaise with speaker's bureaus in retaining top talent and coordinate extracurricular activities for attendees. Monitor budget line items to ensure a positive Return–on–Investment (ROI).

- Spearheaded an enterprise–wide sales event in Munich, Germany, with 2,800+ attendees at every matrix level; received formal, written commendation from President for a "job well done."
- Increased competitive positioning after organizing a national trade show with more than 5,000 attendees from competitive, horizontal, and vertical markets.
- Cut expenses 25% after developing an in–house creative team to eliminate external sources.
- Selected by executive team members to participate in rebranding and messaging campaigns for product and service lines; leveraged global market expertise to deliver constructive feedback.

. . . continued . . .

10

Combination. *Susan Barens, Cleveland, Ohio*

A pair of ornate horizontal lines (whose ornateness is less visible as all black in this printed version) encloses the applicant's chief role as Corporate Events Planner. Checked boxes are a

<u>MCI WORLDCOM</u> — Ashburn, VA · 2000 to 2005

Corporate Events Manager and Program Manager

Oversaw the research, evaluation, planning, and execution of corporate events, trade shows, seminars, conferences, charity events, and sponsored forums. Collaborated with external vendors and public relations firms in generating messages. Accountable for the entire project life cycle from conception, planning, site selection, and budgeting through milestone–setting, logistics management, lodging, and postevent follow–up. Sourced and obtained guest speakers, products, displays, demos, and product giveaways.

- Created and implemented quarterly marketing campaigns supporting strategic vision of multiple-business-unit events in order to meet corporate growth and profitability deliverables.
- Increased product- and service-line ROI by negotiating lower advertising and logistical rates and securing numerous guest speakers pro bono.

<u>SPRINT WORLDWIDE</u> — Reston, VA · 1999 to 2000

Communications Coordinator

Supported the corporate communications team by planning and executing project work, independent assignments, administrative functions, and budgeting activities. Conceptualized, developed, and executed internal and external marketing communications events and media relations programs. Held full accountability for project logistics, vendor contracts, public relations strategies, and sponsorship fulfillment.

- Provided interactive marketing support via Internet research and HTML support involving testing and content proofreading.
- Orchestrated national trade shows and corporate–sponsored events; created all collateral materials and displays while coordinating show logistics and attendee accommodations.

Previous career history discussed during a personal interview:

<u>America Online</u> — Vienna & Ashburn, VA · 1996 to 1999

Marketing Project and Program Coordinator

Formal Education and Credentials

VIRGINIA TECH — Blacksburg, VA

B.A. in Communication Studies

Professional Affiliations

Meeting Planners International (MPI)

Professional Convention Management Association (PCMA)

National Association of Women Business Owners (NAWBO)

different kind of bullet to point to key strengths. Center-aligned information throughout the resume helps to direct the eye down each page. Notice the use of boldfacing to highlight headings, positions, and other key information.

CHRISTINE CAMEO

5 Charleston Place • Fairfield, NJ 00000
chriscameo@email.com • 555-555-5555 (H) • 555-444-3333 (C)

PUBLIC RELATIONS / EVENT PLANNING

Special Projects & Events • **Media Relations & Communications** • **Advertising**

Accomplished and experienced Public Relations and Event Planning specialist. Journalist, Reporter, and Columnist for **award-winning publications,** as well as Speechwriter for Public Officials. Played central role in the **planning and execution of major ceremonial events and community projects,** in tandem with multilevel government, civic, and private organizations. Manage multiple projects simultaneously, adhering to strict deadlines in high-pressure settings.

- Journalism / Reporting
- Speechwriting
- Print & Broadcast Media

- Press Releases & Promotions
- Multimedia Advertising
- Web Site Development

- Event Management
- Budgeting & Expenditures
- Ad Copy / Photography

— **Planner / Coordinator of Key Events and Community Development Projects** —
— **Media Spokesperson to Major News Channels and Publications** —
— **Columnist for Award-Winning Newspaper** —
— **Political Speechwriter** —

PROFESSIONAL EXPERIENCE

MANOR NEWSPAPER GROUP — Middlesex County, NJ   2007–Present
Leading newspaper group with coverage extending across Middlesex County, including The East Brunswick Press, The South Brunswick Press *(Eastern and Western editions), and* The Press of Milltown and Edison.

Advertising Account Executive & Columnist

Manage advertising accounts for 4 weekly newspapers. Design print advertisements, including ad copy, photography, and layout. Meet with clients to develop marketing and advertising campaigns. Prospect for new business.

- Create ad copy for approximately 40 accounts within **4 award-winning newspapers**.
- Write a weekly column, **"Milltown Landing,"** for *The Press of Milltown & Edison* newspaper.

FAIRFIELD TOWN HALL — Fairfield, NJ   1997–2007
Chief administrative building for the town of Fairfield, New Jersey.

Assistant Director / Spokesperson — Department of Public Information
Community Service Aide — Constituent Services

Progressed to Assistant Director / Spokesperson, serving as liaison between town departments and the media. Wrote press releases, public service announcements, media advisories, and other material for media publication. Organized press conferences and media events. Prepared speeches. Maintained Town Web site.

- Pitched timely and relevant stories to major news organizations including **NBC, CBS, ABC, News12 New Jersey,** and *The New Jersey Record.*

...continued...

Combination. *Karen Bartell, Massapequa Park, New York*

This applicant was working as an Advertising Account Executive for a news group and wanted to return to public relations with a focus on event planning. The resume writer stressed the

- **Wrote speeches for elected officials, as well as articles** for town's award-winning "Economic Expansion" newsletter.
- Played key role in the organization and staging of the **grand opening ceremony of the Fairfield Mall Southwest Concourse,** incorporating one year's planning and coordination with all levels of government, private groups, and civic organizations.
- Instrumental in the year-long rigorous planning, coordination, and development of a Fairfield Town Hall **monument erected to honor the victims of September 11, 2001.**
- **Represented Town Supervisor and elected officials** at public meetings and functions.
- **Served on town's Web Site Development taskforce,** coordinating with department heads, civic leaders, and business representatives to design and launch a more comprehensive and user-friendly site.

THE BERGEN COUNTY NEWS / EAST RUTHERFORD BULLETIN — East Rutherford, NJ   1995–1997
Award-winning Bergen County newspaper in circulation for more than 120 years.
Reporter / Photographer
Collected, analyzed, reported, and wrote about breaking and feature news within the town of East Rutherford. Developed story ideas and took photographs to accompany news articles.

- Interviewed and wrote award-winning news article concerning a local public official.

EDUCATION AND CREDENTIALS

Bachelor of Arts in English — Concentration in Journalism
Montclair State University — Montclair, NJ

Professional Development
Journalism Research • Writing for Mass Media • Applied Journalism
Mass Communication in Modern Society • Public Relations and Advertising
Writing for Broadcasting and Film • Crisis Communication
Reporting and Writing for Online Media • Public Affairs Reporting

Professional Associations
Society of Professional Journalists (SPJ)
Public Relations Society of America (PRSA)
International Women's Media Foundation (IWMF)

Technical Proficiencies
Microsoft Word / Outlook; WordPerfect; Brainworks

applicant's role as a columnist (by mentioning the column) and downplayed her work in sales. Boldfacing of the opening heading, subheadings, achievements mentioned under the keyword list, and degree in the Education and Credentials section supports the applicant's targeted goal.

JOAN FISHER

55 Barnes Avenue ◆ Bronx, NY 55555 ◆ (555) 555-5555 ◆ joanfisher@xxxx.com

MANAGER — PLANNING & EXECUTION
MARKETING & PROMOTIONAL EVENTS

Meticulous "go-to" resource…
…with reputation for getting the job done.

Results-driven project manager with a history of success in planning and executing trade shows, meetings, and special events for well-known companies. Meticulous program coordinator who is adept in managing timelines and budgets, negotiating with vendors, and working collaboratively with others to achieve shared goals. Disciplined self-starter; a recognized "go-to" resource who can be relied on to get the job done no matter what the challenge. Solution-oriented team player with strong record in streamlining processes to improve efficiency and effectiveness.

Core Competencies

◆ Program Planning	◆ Needs Assessment	◆ Negotiation
◆ Event Management	◆ Client Support	◆ Vendor Relations
◆ Project Execution	◆ Relationship Management	◆ Problem Resolution

PROFESSIONAL EXPERIENCE

PFIZER, Brooklyn, NY   Jan 2006 to present
Associate Manager, Brand Promotion (1/10 to present)
Senior Planning Manager (5/08 to 1/10)
Convention and Meeting Planner (1/06 to 5/08)
Rapidly advancing to current role, provide meeting support to 3 brand teams and entire 1,000-member sales force, serving as liaison for promotional speaker programs coordinated through third-party vendors.

Planning Management Successes

- Taking on newly created role even before formal promotion, expanded group's influence by promoting services to and gaining acceptance from other brand teams, capitalizing on economies of scale to provide cost-effective promotional solutions to new clients.

- With added business, coordinated 4,300 speaker programs in 2009 (attracting more than 43,000 attendees total), a 30% increase over preceding year's results. Designed and implemented streamlined processes and procedures that supported increase without need to hire additional resources.

- Established stellar record in mediating issues and resolving problems, earning rave reviews from clients. Testament to success, achieved 98% satisfaction rating across all brands in 2009.

- Recognized for expertise, spoke at 6th Annual Pharmaceutical Meeting Planners Forum.

Meeting Planning & Support

- In meeting planner role, successfully coordinated participation at 38 conventions, managing design and staffing of booths from 100 to 1,600 square feet. Served as liaison between internal brand teams and third-party vendors, building record of success in meeting established goals.

- Developed and delivered preshow training to maximize return on investment. Coordinated literature orders and recommended ideas for premiums and giveaways to enhance company image and promote brand.

- Conceived and assembled survival kits for participating sales reps, adding small touches to keep them happy and productive while on duty in convention hall.

- Provided on-site support during convention, addressing arising issues while serving in reception role to meet prospects and draw them in to booth.

- Earned accolades for "Winning Culture" attitude.

(continued)

12

Combination. *Carol A. Altomare, Three Bridges, New Jersey*

The resume writer wanted to call attention to this applicant's many accomplishments. Just a long list of achievements can appear out of focus and imposing. The writer avoided this pitfall

Joan Fisher   joanfisher@xxxx.com   Page 2

Operational Improvements

- Launched computerized planning tool that simplified coordination of meetings and provided more accurate communication of needs to vendor. Trained sales force in its use and monitored compliance.

- Introduced streamlined process for reporting, developing, and delivering all activity reports (weekly, monthly, and ad hoc) to brand teams within established time frames.

- Collaborated with vendor to implement new communication tool for sales force, a Web-based announcement system that more effectively disseminated meeting information to field personnel.

- Created and executed online survey that streamlined data collection and evaluation, eliminating 3-week process to provide real-time gauge of success.

WESTCHESTER SYMPHONY ORCHESTRA, Valhalla, NY   Jun 2005 to Jan 2006
Special Events Coordinator (Part-time)
Working under direction of Special Events Director, assisted with organizing, planning, and marketing special events and fund-raisers.

- Provided on-site support at events, assisting as needed to ensure success while monitoring service levels delivered by vendors to gauge alignment with goals and targets.

NEW YORK BOTTLING COMPANY, Flushing, NY   Jan 1998 to Oct 2004
Senior Marketing Events Specialist
Provided strategic support to internal teams that increased participation in events and generated new business.

- Tapped to take over speaker's program from outside PR firm, initiated aggressive campaign that increased speaking opportunities by 62% while saving $600,000 in vendor fees annually.
- Managing 31 shows per year, effectively coordinated activities of internal groups to ensure all results were delivered within established time frames.

COMBINE SPORTS, Bronx, NY   Dec 1995 to Dec 1997
Trade Show/Events Coordinator
Coordinated development and setup of exhibit booths and related collateral for major industry events around the world. Also coordinated travel logistics for company participants.

- Designed event management tool, a first-ever compilation of shows attended and feedback collected, used to measure value and return of events and guide future participation.

SOUNDVIEW SEMICONDUCTORS, Larchmont, NY   Jun 1992 to Dec 1995
Budget Coordinator/Trade Show Assistant
Lead Tracking/Trade Show Assistant
Assisted with logistics for major international and domestic trade shows.

- Organized database of leads to facilitate customer contact and generate sales.

EDUCATION & PROFESSIONAL DEVELOPMENT

B.A. in English, Pace University, Pleasantville, NY

<u>Courses</u>
Strictly Business: The Dale Carnegie Immersion Seminar, 7/08
How to Communicate with Diplomacy, Tact, and Credibility, 7/06

TECHNOLOGY SKILLS

MS Office, FrontPage, Outlook; Raiser's Edge; Adobe Dreamweaver; Sage ACT!; database and Web navigation programs.

by grouping key achievements under three centered and underlined headings under the current workplace. Grouping, or clustering, related items under separate headings is a useful strategy to follow in any resume that has a long list, which may seem difficult to read as a whole.

SAMUEL E. THOMAS

5555 Pershing Avenue NW
Massilon, Ohio 55005

www.sethomas.com
sethomas@xxxx.net

Studio: 550-555-0050
Mobile: 550-555-5005

EVENT DESIGNER ~ FLORAL DISPLAY EXPERT
Logistics — Artistic Vision — Visual Displays — Styling

Respected, highly organized, and creative innovator with a passion for event planning with emphasis on functional, artistic design ... Excel in coordinating one-of-a-kind occasions customized to clients' personal styles and tailored to individual budgets and guest lists ... Thrive in challenging, multiproject, and deadline-driven situations ... Attend to myriad details without losing sight of big picture ... Travel extensively in search of new ideas and items ... Established worldwide network of major designers and vendor contacts for flowers, accessories, props, and furniture ... Charming and vivacious personality ... Exemplary interpersonal as well as oral and written communication skills ... Readily establish rapport with individuals at all professional levels and from diverse backgrounds ... Branded as Taste Master and Stylist talented in spotting, forecasting, and setting trends ... Bilingual (Hungarian and English).

EVENT PLANNING

▶ Oversee planning for functions with 12 to 1,200 attendees. Look at venue through eyes of client, truly listen to client to determine personality style and preferences, and make client's vision a reality. Evoke a "Wow!" impression from each guest entering the event site.

▶ Earned listing on preferred vendor list for all major hotels in Cleveland as well as country clubs based on reputation for reliability, respectfulness, practicality, willingness to assist on-site staff, and consistency in orchestrating successful and beautiful functions. Coordinate all facets of events with hotel management, bakers, musicians, photographers, caterers, and lighting and tent technicians.

▶ Dialog with clients to determine theme and develop a plan to incorporate that theme within a budgeted dollar range. Orchestrate event staff ranging from 10 to 50 members, including hotel management, bakers, musicians, photographers, caterers, lighting techs, and tent workers, to ensure details are appropriate to the function, anticipated audience, and established theme.

▶ **Examples of event themes:** Envision and deliver extraordinary designs exclusive to each client ... 50 unique affairs at the Ritz-Carlton ... Hot and spicy Moroccan ... Sleek, all-white contemporary ... Opulent, jewel-toned Russian ... Whimsically depicted summer evening ... Bold and dramatic Asian theme with red with black contrasts ... Traditional American fashion with a fresh-from-the-prairie feel ... Flemish still life emphasizing chiaroscuro light with deep colors and pelts of feathers.

CUSTOM FLORAL DESIGN

▶ Design live, cut, dried, and artificial flower and foliage arrangements that meet specific client requests for floral occasions. Incorporate design techniques to create uniquely personalized floral presentations from simple to extravagant; use specialty flowers and foliage as appropriate. Expert in procedure and processing of all floral and foliage material. Technically proficient with a vast knowledge of all styles of flower arranging. Personally maintain 3-acre garden; possess expert knowledge of annual, perennial, and woodland flowers and plants.

▶ Gain inspiration from clients, colors, textures, travel experiences, beauty of natural forms, and architecture. Intrigued by using flowers and candles to create a magical tablescape. Able to transform a carnation into a grand 7-foot statement of color and texture or highlight a single orchid in flickering candlelight.

▶ **Examples of styles:** Consistent, original, and unique approaches combine floral materials and accessories ... Create visual excitement by juxtaposing organic against opulent ... Rustic birch mixed with silver mercury glass and lavender anemones ... Embellish with colored glass with black lacquer and velvet textured roses ... Liquid gold with tufts of live moss, featuring yellow-centered, oversized whole Catelya orchids ... Sparkling crystal against wood grain surfaces with ethereal pink and lavender blossoms ... Amber shaded mirror with textured leather enhanced by woodland lady slipper orchids.

Continued on next page

13

Combination. *Jane Roqueplot, West Middlesex, Pennsylvania*

A challenge for a resume writer is to make each resume appear different from any other resume. Distinctive features in this resume are the use of ellipses (...) in the opening profile and elsewhere,

SAMUEL E. THOMAS, 550-555-5005 — *Page 2*

PROFESSIONAL HISTORY

Samuel E. Thomas Custom Floral & Design — Massilon, Ohio (www.sethomas.com)   1994–Present
Creative Floral and Event Design Studio — Cleveland, Ohio
PRESIDENT / OWNER

▶ Plan and manage event budgets up to $1 million. Supervise up to 15 employees with up to 50 staff for major installations. Direct all facets of functions, averaging 40 weddings; 20 parties; 150 retail orders; 15 home holiday décor installations; and multiple functions for 20 corporate, hospital, and university accounts annually. Some long-distance events require servicing by private plane.

▶ Coordinate unique parties, including Cleveland Air Show, NASA Anniversary, and Wright Brothers 100th Year of Flight.

▶ Organize events for celebrities, politicians, and sports figures, including Martha Stewart, Oprah Winfrey, Gloria Vanderbilt, Colin Powell, LeBron James, Travis Hafner, Johnny Peralta, and Don Shula.

▶ Create and implement four seasonal installations annually in two retail locations that include holiday theme trees and accessories. Introduce each season a new theme that tells a story and incorporates paint colors, lighting, props, and accessories. Handpick gift items, tabletop furnishings, etc., in showrooms in Chicago, Dallas, New York, and Atlanta.

▶ Presented floral design demonstrations for audiences of 30 to 200 and served as floral design judge for several organizations. Featured on radio and television, discussing topics such as wedding and special-event budgets, flowers, seasonal floral designs, holiday decorations, and entertaining.

Postcollegiate travels in Central Europe with Budapest, Hungary, as home base.   1991–1993
Taught English and business etiquette.

Donald Blanks Florist — Cincinnati, Ohio   1986–1987
FLORAL ASSISTANT
Prepared arrangements and installations for high-end wedding and party functions. Assisted with party designs. Created unique floral concepts for University of Cincinnati President's functions.

AWARDS / RECOGNITIONS

Best Wedding Florist in Cleveland, *Knot Magazine,* 2009
Philanthropy Award and Gala honored guest, Cleveland Hungarian Development Panel, 2009
Artistic Judge, St. Patrick's Day Parade, 2007–2009
"Master Tastemaker," *SoHo Magazine* cover feature, 2008
Best Parties of the Year, chosen by *The Cleveland Plain Dealer,* 2001–2008
Floral Design Judge, Cleveland Botanical Garden, 2007–2008
Best Floral Designer, *Cleveland Business Connects Magazine,* 2008

MEMBERSHIPS

Rockefeller Cultural Gardens | Cleveland Botanical Garden | Cleveland Museum of Art
Cleveland Hungarian Cultural Society

PUBLICATIONS

The News Herald | Currents Newspaper | SoHo Magazine | The Cleveland Plain Dealer | Cleveland Magazine

EDUCATION

Fine Arts/Communication Arts coursework, UNIVERSITY OF CINCINNATI — Cincinnati, Ohio

horizontal lines extending from the section side headings to the right margin, right-pointing triangular bullets, and centered awards/recognitions. Notice also the balanced format of the contact information at the top of the first page.

AMY VESTAL

Target:

Events Planner

Profile:

Creative, detail-oriented person with planning, implementation, troubleshooting, and follow-up experience needed to orchestrate successful events. Proficient craftswoman with talent for providing finishing details that make nice presentations. Flower arranging, invitation and announcement designs, and color coordination make accessories festive, elegant, or just plain fun.

5555 55th Street
Flower, Texas 79000

avestal@aol.com

(555) 555-1234

14

Promotions and Value-Added Projects . . . .

Increased sales by promoting Country Favorites gift shop through teaching design and craft classes. Organized teas and brunches as well as acquired guest speakers on subjects such as quilting, gardening, and cooking. Planned showers from beginning to end for customers, to include invitations, decorations, food, etc.

Remodeled two-story residence to house gift shop.

Created sales brochures, advertising, crafty displays, and backdrops for unique photography studio that produced finished cut-out, stand-up photos mounted on wood.

Conceptualized and implemented plan to convert expensive laser cut-out process to a more cost-effective local operation with laser-like results.

Business Development and Revenue Growth . . . .

Restructured failing photo business, taking it from operating in the red to a profit-producing enterprise in only one year. Concentrated effort on marketing, networking, advertising, and recreating props and backdrops. Lowered overhead by researching less-expensive ways to cut out photos.

Utilized previous experience in retail sales and buying to conceive and launch gift-shop business. Used creative marketing ideas to attract customers.

Developed business savvy to keep expenses down while increasing profits. Areas of expertise include strategic planning, business proposals, budget projection and management, employee development, accounting, marketing, building a strong client base, and networking.

Additional Skills . . . .

- Able to relate at any level with people of varied beliefs and backgrounds
- Talent for building rapport and trust with clients
- Efficient and professional time management
- Use instructional communication style to relate information
- Friendly, personable, and approachable
- Focus on customer needs to ensure satisfaction
- Open to new ideas and enjoy brainstorming
- Solve problems effectively and make informed decisions

Employment History . . . .

Cosmetic Technician, Permanent Makeup, Flower, Texas	2010–2012
Substitute Teacher, Flower ISD, Flower, Texas	2008–2010
Sales Representative, ChemMate, Centerville, Texas	2007
Administrative Assistant, Northbrook Life Insurance, Ty, Texas	2006–2007
Owner, Stand-up Photography Studio, Centerville, Texas	1997–2006
Clothing Representative, Eastmart Wholesale, Ty, Texas	1997–1999
Jewelry Department Manager, Sammy's Dept. Store, Ty, Texas	1993–1994
Owner, Country Favorites, Poppy, Texas	1992–1995
Manager/Buyer/Designer, Elite Decorating, River Creek, Texas	1992
Manager, Golden Touch, River Creek, Texas	1988–1991

Education . . . .

Bachelor of Arts in Interior Design—Texas Vocational University   1997

Combination. *Edith A. Rische, Lubbock, Texas*

To de-emphasize many job changes, the writer presents the work history as just one-liners. Design elements of this unconventional resume reflect the applicant's creativity. See Cover Letter 16.

Communications

Resumes at a Glance

ARLENE STONE
AStone@email.com

500 West End Street #55

New York, NY 55555

Residence (212) 555-5555

Mobile (917) 555-5555

MARKETING POSITION—FASHION PUBLISHING INDUSTRY

Recent graduate with proven ability to produce results in a fast-paced environment with critical deadlines. Outgoing and articulate communicator who gets along well with public and coworkers at all levels. Works well independently as well as collaboratively in a team environment. Learns quickly and enjoys challenges. Computer skills include Microsoft Word, Excel, PowerPoint and Access. Experience includes

Writing • Research & Analysis • Media Kits • Presentations • Problem Solving & Troubleshooting

---

EDUCATION

UNIVERSITY OF CALIFORNIA, Los Angeles, CA; May 2010
Bachelor of Arts in Communications; Minor in Marketing

PROFESSIONAL EXPERIENCE

STAR PUBLICATIONS—*MENS MONTHLY* MAGAZINE, New York, NY • 2010 to Present
Marketing Assistant
Relocated to New York after being accepted for position out of highly competitive applicant group from across U.S. Provide direct assistance to Advertising Director of prestigious men's magazine, gaining valuable hands-on experience. Day-to-day responsibilities vary and include the following:

- Prepare business proposals…Track competitive information…Run edit credits for various categories.
- Send out media kits to new clients, assemble presentations and manage contact card file. Collaborate with promotion department to organize databases for special events.
- Handle heavy phones, interacting directly with clients. Compose correspondence and memos, sort and distribute mail and manage complimentary subscription list.
- Track monthly expenses and coordinate travel arrangements.
- Organize weekly sales staff meetings and set up conference calls for outside offices.

MEDIA PRODUCTIONS, Hollywood, CA • Summer 2009
Production Assistant
Assisted in coordinating makeup and wardrobe for commercial and infomercial productions.

- Collaborated on identifying wardrobe theme; coordinated wardrobe selections with set decoration.

TOP SPORTS PUBLICATIONS / *FEELING GOOD* MAGAZINE, Woodland Hills, CA • Summers 2006 to 2009
Assistant / Intern
Worked closely with Editor-in-Chief, Fashion Editor, Beauty Editor, Senior Editor and Associate Editor of teen publication. Prioritized and coordinated multiple assignments, including transcriptions, research and follow-up. Contributed story ideas that resulted in publication, including the following:

- Assisted Fashion Editor at photo shoots. Contacted leading manufacturers to obtain sample merchandise; organized clothing for shoots; assisted with overall styling.
- Directly assisted in transforming and writing "Makeover" feature of magazine. Selected subjects; coordinated training with fitness instructors; arranged photo shoot; contributed to editorial staff meetings.
- Contributed ideas for retail accessories feature. Wrote captions, explaining new seasonal fashion trends.

15

Combination. *Vivian VanLier, Los Angeles, California*

Because the person's degree was only a year old and she graduated from a top-ranking university, education appears before professional experience. Bold italic emphasizes industry-related skills.

EILEEN ANDREWS

Accomplished teacher, trainer and administrator with extensive leadership experience and a flair for public relations and communications

SUMMARY OF QUALIFICATIONS

- Wealth of experience, including 13 years in highly visible and demanding leadership roles.
- Skilled grant writer with strong understanding of fund-raising strategies.
- Critical thinker. Able to develop compelling arguments.
- Outstanding interpersonal skills. Easily build productive, enduring relationships.
- Recognized as effective spokesperson for departmental programs and interests.
- Skilled in creatively promoting new products and programs.
- Energetic and organized. Able to effectively handle the demands of multiple projects.
- Committed to ideals of excellence.

PERTINENT SKILLS AND ACCOMPLISHMENTS

Grant Writing/Communications

- Working as a freelance grant writer, wrote effective grant proposals for organizations such as the Girl Scouts, Special Olympics, and the Los Alamos Chamber of Commerce.
- In leadership roles for local school board, wrote grant proposals to gain funding for key programs.
- Actively promoted all ancillary educational programs in the community. Represented township in the community-at-large.
- Developed the role of Director of Education, serving as liaison between the board of education and the local community.

Policy Development and Administration

- Established standards and goals and set up new policies and procedures to support them, bringing new credibility to the school system.
- Worked as liaison in helping individual groups set up consistent policies and procedures.
- As a member of the Board of Regents of financially troubled school, developed policy to ensure financial stability and initiated capital campaign.

Management

- Supervised activities of 350 employees and 500 volunteers in providing for the education of 1,600 children.
- Oversaw education budget in excess of $5 million. Hired and trained key employees.
- Stepped in as interim principal of troubled school and orchestrated its turnaround.
- Partnered with principal of struggling school and successfully facilitated the achievement of full-term accreditation.
- Effectively coached and mentored teachers and principals, helping them to hone their skills and motivating them to reach goals.
- Provided oversight function for district school.

PAGE 1

52 YORK ROAD • READING, NJ 11111
HOME (222) 222-2222 • FAX (333) 333-3333 • E-MAIL andrews@aol.com

16

Combination. *Carol A. Altomare, Three Bridges, New Jersey*

The individual wanted to get out of education and was looking for anything that her background might qualify her for. The writer put together many versions of the person's resume. This

Teaching and Mentoring

- Earned certificate in elementary education.
- Prepared training materials and delivered courses for students in all stages of life—children, college students, and adult learners.
- Initiated mentoring program for principals and entry-level teachers.
- Developed training and certification program for volunteer instructors.

Assessment

- Chaired 12 different visiting committees commissioned to evaluate schools and develop plans for improvement. Acted as resource to facilitate change.
- Assessed suitability of training materials for a given audience and program goal.
- Managed performance assessment of teachers and principals.

EMPLOYMENT HISTORY

Independent Contractor   2008 to present
Grant Writer

Los Alamos Board of Education, Los Alamos, NV   1989 to 2008
Director of Education, 2005 to 2008
Responsible for coordinating the activities and personnel of various groups and articulating the educational goals of the Board.

- Served as liaison between schools and state and federal government, and between the Board and the community.
- Developed policy handbooks.

Superintendent of Schools, 2001 to 2005
Responsible for hiring, supervising, and evaluating principals and maintaining school standards across schools in the local district.

- Chaired committees to assess schools and recommend plans for improvements.

Principal, Los Alamos School, 1995 to 2001

- Provided direction and leadership while handling day-to-day management issues.

Classroom Teacher, 1989 to 1995

- Taught 2nd and 7th grade, as well as 5th- to 8th-grade English.

EDUCATION

Master of Education in Educational Administration, University of California, 1995
Bachelor of Science in Elementary Education, University of California, 1989

particular version was very successful in getting the applicant interviews as a grant writer/development officer. She even got an offer sight unseen from a local community college; on the basis of her resume, it was assumed that she could write.

Elizabeth M. Singh

| 1775 Grover Street | Home: 410-837-5555 |
| Baltimore, MD 21201 | lizsingh@verizon.net |

PUBLIC RELATIONS / PUBLIC INFORMATION OFFICER

- **Award-winning public health information officer with bachelor's degree in journalism.** Track record of creating, editing and coordinating health information projects, website content, press releases and press events both independently and as a team member for more than 20 years.

- **Web content manager.** Gained reputation as expert web content writer and editor after successfully collaborating in state department website overhaul, as well as launch or rewrite of more than 25 sub-websites since 2012. Relied on by Webmaster to screen, organize and write wide breadth of content.

- **Experienced communicator and public spokesperson.** Adept at clarifying and communicating complex topics in easy-to-understand written content and charts. Senior spokesperson for large state government department, with widespread media, intra-agency and community relationships.

- **Consistently dedicated, meeting short deadlines while managing multiple projects.** Work well under pressure, formulating and/or editing written copy for high-level state government policy-makers. Serve as communications liaison between State Commissioner, outside agencies and government officials, management and staff, community organizations, MD consumers and media representatives.

AREAS OF EXCELLENCE

■ Web Content Writing & Editing	■ Writing & Editing	■ Public Health Education
■ Copyediting & Proofreading	■ Press Releases	■ Risk Communications
■ Media & Community Relations	■ Press Events	■ Project Management

PROFESSIONAL EXPERIENCE

MARYLAND DEPT. OF HEALTH AND SENIOR SERVICES (MDDHSS), Baltimore, MD   1992–present
Oversees public health and older-adult services statewide, including regulatory oversight of health-care institutions. $5.4 billion agency with 3,200 employees.

Public Information Officer / Senior Spokesperson & Web Content Manager
Cover diverse topics, including public health and environmental services, senior services, health-care policy and research, minority and multicultural health and health-related aspects of terrorism. Subject matter expert for community cancer concerns, disease outbreaks, anthrax/bioterrorism and West Nile virus.

- **Web Project Management.** Coled team that revamped DHSS website, in collaboration with Abernathy Consultants, to increase usability for consumers and showcase information, resources and links. Created online survey to query website visitors on usage patterns, information requested and needs.

- **Web Content and Web Policy Development.** Key contributor (organizing, writing, reviewing and editing) to primary and secondary multiple-page subsections of DHSS main website (at least 25 since 2009). Researched and developed new DHSS policy on web links.

  High-visibility projects included HealthLink, Bureau of Vital Statistics, Health-in-Schools, Community Health Centers, Education Campaign on Medicare Part D Drug Coverage, Patient Safety, Medical Milestones and Cultural Competency.

- **Press Releases and Events.** Prepare press releases, briefings, confidential memos and speeches, consulting with top policy-makers, scientists, physicians and Governor's Office. Organize press events that garner national, regional and statewide coverage. Publicize wide-ranging public health issues, including anti-tobacco initiatives and first major expansion of statewide Newborn Screening Program.

  Major press events for 2010: Hospital Performance Report, PAAD/Senior Gold Campaign, Minority Health Month, Cardiac Surgery Report, Discount Drug Program Expansion, Bariatric Report, HMO Report Card and Zonolite Health Consultations.

Page 1 of 2

17

Combination. *Susan Guarneri, Three Lakes, Wisconsin*

This longtime state employee needed to "justify" keeping her job with an incoming administration and wanted to move from a typical public relations role to the designated Web Content

Elizabeth M. Singh | Home: 410-837-5555 | lizsingh@verizon.net | **Page 2 of 2**

DHSS continued

- **Risk Communications.** Anticipate emerging media issues and advise Commissioner and key staff on response strategy. Collaborate with senior staff to prepare accurate responses, consistent with agency policy, to heavy volume of requests from state, national and international new organizations.

- **Health Information Project Management.** Given sole responsibility for high-visibility information projects, such as cardiac surgery report card, managed care report card and web-based report on hospital fines. Collaborate with reporters on long-term, multipart stories requiring special data runs and document requests. Associate editor and coauthor of department accomplishments report.

MARYLAND DEPARTMENT OF EDUCATION, Baltimore, MD   1989–1992
Public Information Officer

- Spearheaded communications (press releases, press conferences/events) for Basic Skills Testing Program. Developed communications handbook adopted by school districts statewide. Authored op-ed articles and executive-level speeches, including annual budget testimony by Commissioner to Legislature.

NEWS REPORTER   1979–1989
Staff writer, reporter and broadcast writer covering education, health, courts and government affairs. Wrote for Gannett News Service, *USA Today, The Press* (Washington, DC), *The News Enquirer* (Norfolk, VA), *The Associated Press* (Cleveland, OH) and others. Received local news reporting awards.

─────────────── **EDUCATION & TRAINING** ───────────────

Bachelor of Arts, Journalism, University of Maryland, College Park, MD
Graduated Phi Beta Kappa with 3.88 GPA
Internship, Washington Bureau, Knight Newspapers (bureau served *The Free Press, The New York Inquirer, Chicago Herald* and others)

Ongoing Professional Development
Terrorism Incident Reporting Structure, FEMA, Washington, DC—2011

TOBE 2010 (Top Officials Bioterrorism Exercise)—2010
MDDHSS partnered with United Kingdom, Canada, Connecticut and the U.S. federal government in largest bioterrorism exercise to date.

Maryland's Strategic National Stockpile Exercise—2009
Intra-agency simulation exercise regarding deployment of medications and medical equipment from the nation's stockpile to locations in Maryland.

Risk Communications, Center for Risk Management, Washington, DC—2008

Computer Skills: Windows 7, MS Office 2007 (Word, Excel, PowerPoint), Lotus Notes, Internet research

─────────── **PROFESSIONAL ASSOCIATIONS & AWARDS** ───────────

Federal Web Content Managers Forum—Member; National Public Health Education Coalition—Member

- ☑ Team Award: 2010 Gold Award for Excellence in Public Health Communications
  National Public Health Education Coalition. Outsourced Information Campaigns for "Maryland's Rapid HIV-Testing Campaign." Key contributor to Rapid HIV-testing web pages.

- ☑ Team Award: 2010 Bronze Award for Excellence in Public Health Communications
  National Public Health Education Coalition. In-house, Thinking on Your Feet: Real-time Risk Communications for "Smallpox—First Case in the U.S. in 15 Years."

Manager. The writer relegated to the second page the individual's typical PR duties and previous journalism experience and put on the first page the applicant's Web management and Web content accomplishments. Boldfacing makes key phrases stand out.

KRISTINE RULE

Senior Communications Executive
CRACKING THE CODE OF NEW MEDIA PR

- Giving Small Ad Agencies a Voice
- Making Global Organizations Relevant
- Driving Revenue by Shaping Opinions

Pioneer in advertising communications with repeated success achieving corporate goals through media relations, strategic alliances, social media, and search engine marketing/optimization (SEM/SEO). Expert at designing sophisticated, tightly targeted programs that capture attention and maximize ROI.

Top performer in every role. Combine PR skills with extensive media and industry network to achieve unprecedented results. Valued member of senior management team. Confidential CEO advisor and advocate.

PROFESSIONAL EXPERIENCE AND ACHIEVEMENTS

Epsilon Data—New York, NY   2007–Present

SENIOR VICE PRESIDENT, CORPORATE COMMUNICATIONS

Create/enhance agency's online presence. Raise visibility of individual locations and their leadership. Partner with NYC CEO to enhance reputation of Manhattan office.

Challenge: Present large global enterprise—with traditional ad agency roots dating back to the 1800s—as agile and creative, using social media and SEM to herald a new era in advertising.

- **Maximized traffic to corporate Web site.** Directed SEO analysis, introducing keywords and meta tags. Implemented Twitter and RSS feeds. Devised student outreach initiative to attract blog readers.
- **Showcased creative work online,** establishing strategic alliances with prominent marketing blogs.
- **Set Epsilon Data apart from competition,** marketing unbundled media group as key point of difference.
- **Introduced first multimedia digital bios,** incorporating portfolios, press coverage, and client results.
- **Promoted the most-watched YouTube video game content ever.**

Kristine Rule Communications, LLC—New York, NY   2006–2007

PRESIDENT and CEO

Partnered with agency clients, using deep industry and media knowledge to build high-impact communications plans. Advised principals on hot agency trends and use of press to attract search consultants and clients.

Challenge: Create distinctive brands and industry presence for small- to mid-sized agencies.

- **Secured unprecedented press coverage for little-known agency brands.**
- **Named "recommended associate" for A-Team Advisors,** consultancy of former 4A's execs.
- **Established KRC as new media PR leader,** attracting prominent clients including Lowe NY, Cheil Communications, Brushfire, and Amazon Advertising.

Draftcb—New York, NY   2003–2005

SENIOR VICE PRESIDENT, WORLDWIDE DIRECTOR OF COMMUNICATIONS

Pitched and secured stories featuring agency work, people, and innovations. Directed local and global distribution of corporate message.

Challenge: Rebuild Lowe NY's media presence, convincing reporters to "take a new look at Lowe" following a merger and worldwide management shake-up.

- **Transformed abrupt CEO departure into positive press by publicizing replacement.** Pitched and placed stories about new CEO in *USA Today* and *Womensbiz.* Boosted her industry presence, creating networking opportunities with Advertising Women of New York.
- **Won coverage of turnaround plan in *New York Times, Financial Times, Ad Age,* and *Ad Week.***
- **Secured Cannes Film Festival juror seat for Chief Creative Officer** (only 2 U.S. seats).

5555 Nottingham Drive, Montebello, NY 55555 ■ H: 555-555-4444 ■ C: 555-555-1234 ■ kmrule@xxxx.com

18

Combination. *Kim Mohiuddin, San Diego, California*

Large, square bullets catch the eye immediately and direct attention to key achievements, which are boldfaced to highlight their importance. If you "follow the bold" through the resume, you can

KRISTINE RULE   page 2 of 2

PROFESSIONAL EXPERIENCE AND ACHIEVEMENTS, continued

Young & Rubicam—New York, NY   2001–2003

SENIOR PARTNER, DIRECTOR OF COMMUNICATIONS

Positioned agency as go-to resource for creative talent. Executive responsibility for internal and external news distribution.

> Challenge: Drive successful transition from global network to national agency.

- **Defined corporate identity through 2 major M&A brand transitions.**
- **Boosted firm's creative profile,** achieving major coverage of awards including #3 ranking at Cannes.
- **Promoted Young & Rubicam's "creative boutique" culture by garnering publicity for CCO and CEO.**
  - Positioned Chief Creative Officer as leader of creative turnaround under CEO's mandate.
  - Built CEO's reputation as advocate for cutting-edge creative work. His later appointment as CEO of newly combined agency was largely due to this public perception.

Bozell—New York, NY   1999–2001

VICE PRESIDENT, CORPORATE COMMUNICATIONS

Developed 2-year plan for revitalizing firm's image, leading all communications, including announcements of new campaigns, new business wins and losses, and management changes.

> Challenge: Raise perceived value of firm in preparation for IPO.

- **Engineered multiple awards for firm,** including *AdWeek*'s Eastern Agency of the Year, Global Agency Network, and President's Award.
- **Pitched and won honors for President Lauren Scott** such as *Fortune*'s "Top 50 Women in Business," Ad Women of New York's "Advertising Woman of the Year," and *Ad Age*'s "25 Women to Watch."
- **Agency landed $200M Citibank account,** the then-largest consolidated account.
- **IPO raised $1B+, selling 16M shares.**

BBDO—New York, NY   1996–1999

VICE PRESIDENT, CORPORATE COMMUNICATIONS

Provided strategic and tactical communications plans for BBDO and major clients including Doritos, Pepsi, Pizza Hut, M&M's, Snickers, and HBO.

- **Inspired reporters to dub Super Bowl "BBDO Bowl" by publicizing quantity and quality of ads.**
- **Secured interviews for executives on *Today Show*, CNBC's *Power Lunch*, and CNN's *Biz Buzz*.**
- **Garnered coverage on *60 Minutes*, *Entertainment Tonight*, and *Dateline NBC*.**
- **Turned BBDO's TV research into major news item,** earning annual coverage in *TV Guide*, *USA Today*, *Wall Street Journal*, *Ebony*, and *Jet*.

PROFESSIONAL PROFILE

BFA—Adelphi University, Garden City, NY

Advertising Women of New York (AWNY):
Board Member and Winner of the Crystal Prism Award and President's Award

5555 Nottingham Drive, Montebello, NY 55555 ■ H: 555-555-4444 ■ C: 555-555-1234 ■ kmrule@xxxx.com

estimate at a glance the potential worth of this applicant to an employer. Current and former positions are all high-level executive positions, and these are cast in all-capital letters to make them stand out.

LINDA LAWRENCE

8777 BELLE COURT ◆ IRVINE, CA 55555 ◆ (555) 555-5555 ◆ E-mail: lindalawrence@xxxx.com

CAREER PROFILE

**Marketing Communications ◆ Advertising ◆ Public Relations ◆ New Product Marketing
Trade Show & Event Management ◆ Crisis Communications ◆ Business Development**

Innovative strategist of marketing, advertising and public relations plans that enhanced competitive market positioning, contributed to significant sales growth and won favorable media and customer recognition. Strategic planning, leadership and relationship-building strengths combine with successful project management, crisis management, image development, contract negotiations and public-speaking experience to deliver results.

PROFESSIONAL EXPERIENCE

MARKETING COMMUNICATIONS & PR MANAGEMENT, Irvine, CA ◆ 2000 to Present

Plan, design and manage execution of strategic sales, marketing and public relations consulting programs for corporate clients in diverse industries. Projects include promotions, advertising campaigns, product launches, special events, trade show coordination and collateral materials development.

Signature Achievements

- Played instrumental role in winning $1 million contract with the largest U.S. trade show producer.
  - Spearheaded planning and production of 13 trade shows for a global pharmaceutical company, launching its major new product line in U.S., Mexican, European and South American markets.
  - Created joint venture relationships with exhibit vendors globally, overcoming numerous logistical issues and language barriers to meet challenging deadlines for all 13 events.
- Designed new exhibit booth used at industry events nationwide for a $100 million food supplier.
  - Drove trade show revenues by $3 million over prior year.
- Enhanced local store marketing efforts for local restaurant chain through development of collateral and promotional materials that supported new product line introduction.
  - Results boosted customer traffic and led to 6% increase in incremental sales.

SOUTHLAND CORPORATION, Dallas, TX ◆ 1990 to 2000
New Product Marketing and Communications Manager ◆ 1996 to 2000

Tapped by management in recognition of outstanding performance results to join the New Product Marketing and Communications team. Led design and implementation of creative marketing and advertising plans for new product concepts, promotions, market testing and rollout for company's 9,000+ domestic stores. Authored departmental sales and marketing plans that contributed to company's strategic plan; evaluated new products and strategized product mix/positioning.

Directed 5 nationally recognized agencies to develop and execute nationwide marketing plans, communications, advertising materials and public relations strategies. Managed $1+ million budget for development of several new product concepts. Partnered with all internal departments, sourced new vendors and coordinated with agencies on presentations to store owners/operators to facilitate product testing and determine advertising dollar allocations.

continued...

19

Combination. *Louise Garver, Broad Brook, Connecticut*

The original resume was a "laundry list" of short projects, making the applicant look like a job hopper. The writer listed the applicant's consulting experience as one "organization" (her own)

LINDA LAWRENCE

Page 2 ◆ (555) 555-5555

SOUTHLAND CORPORATION *continued…*

Signature Achievements

- ◆ Revamped new product testing methodology and procedures and instituted Product Modeling System, which reevaluated products during 4 key stages of development. Results led to streamlined operations and saved company $10 million annually.

- ◆ Successfully launched 2 major product lines that drove sales 10% systemwide. Led development of marketing/public relations strategies, point-of-purchase materials, advertising and sales execution.

- ◆ Achieved $3 million in annual savings while significantly boosting visibility 30% through company-wide rollout of new menu boards, indoor/outdoor signage, billboard advertising and all point-of-purchase and collateral advertising materials.

- ◆ Helped heighten company visibility, opportunity for tie-in branded promotions and increased corporate revenue through development of nontraditional stores in retail outlets, universities, hospitals, athletic stadiums and convention sites across the nation.

Environmental Relations Manager ◆ 1990 to 1996

Selected by Senior Vice President to manage newly created Environmental Relations organization, assuming leadership role in creating marketing, crisis management and public relations strategies to combat company's major image problems during period of declining sales/market share. Key contributor on team that innovated $100 million green initiative, a recognized PR coup that operates as a stand-alone $1 billion program.

Signature Achievements

- ◆ Designed and executed marketing/public relations strategies that turned around public perception toward company in less than 2 years.
  - — Company achieved recognition as one of the nation's leading corporate citizens in the environmental area and winner of numerous awards from environmental organizations.

- ◆ Forged strategic alliances with key environmental groups and created grassroots lobbying campaigns, gaining substantial legislative support.

- ◆ Delivered well-received presentations at various educational and community organizations that strengthened company's image.

- ◆ Managed launch of 450 in-store recycling programs, including development of point-of-purchase brochures, advertising materials and training programs, in 5 key states nationwide.
  - — Led opening of recycling center in the Western U.S.

EDUCATION/ASSOCIATIONS

Master of Business Administration, Concentration in Marketing
UNIVERSITY OF CALIFORNIA, Irvine, CA

Bachelor of Arts in Marketing
NORTHWESTERN UNIVERSITY, Boston, MA

Member of
Public Relations Society of America | International Association of Business Communicators
California Advertising Federation

and bulleted the best examples of her work. With this revised resume, she went from no interviews for eight months to calls for interviews with every resume she sent out, and she landed a position quickly.

Scott Gronlund

000.000.0000 | s.gronlund@xxxx.com | Asheville, NC

Editor | Publications Manager | Senior Writer

Career Summary

√ **Award-winning editor** with more than eight years of professional journalism experience.
√ **Passionate about publication planning and editing,** transforming stories into optimal form while maintaining writer's voice.
√ **Creative and detail-oriented** writer holding bachelor's in journalism with honors and distinction.
√ Skilled at prioritizing and **coordinating multiple projects in fast-paced, deadline-driven environments.**

Proven Competencies

- Writing and Editing
- Project Management
- Staff Management
- Associated Press (AP) Style
- Layout and Design
- Print Production
- Website Editing and Publishing
- Creative Design
- Multimedia Production
- Copyediting
- News Writing

"Scott is doing an outstanding job. He has amazing attention to detail and is incredibly dedicated, conscientious, and productive. Scott has great planning ability and is excellent at multitasking. He is creative and always striving to make *People's Advocate News* better. He is an enormous pleasure to work with." — Supervisor and Director of Communications, People's Advocate

Professional Achievements

People's Advocate, Asheville, NC   2004–present
A nonprofit, nonpartisan national consumer advocacy organization.

Publications Editor (2006–present)

Editor, writer, and production manager of *People's Advocate News,* a bimonthly publication for People's Advocate members; copy editor for *Good Medicine* newsletter.

Key Points

- Earned Apex Awards for publication excellence, 2009, 2010.
- Improved layout and design of *People's Advocate News.*
- Added features to *People's Advocate News,* creating more engaging stories and formats.
- Met tight deadlines with minimal assistance.

Key Contributions

- Launched and directed redesign of *People's Advocate News,* creating greater organization and reader-friendly format, earning Apex Awards every year since.
- Introduced in-depth, magazine-style articles, staff spotlight, crossword puzzles, and other features receiving positive reader feedback and increasing reader donations.
- Conceptualized and created People's Advocate's annual report to distribute to potential donors.
- Completed annual congressional scorecard with minimal staff assistance and working after office hours to meet publication deadlines.

Assignments

- Edited articles providing constructive feedback about focus and style, simplifying complex consumer policy through interesting stories.
- Collaborated with staff and department directors to produce additional print publications.
- Posted and updated website text, using content management system.
- Negotiated and managed printing contract, ensuring publication deadlines were met.

Page 1 of 2

20

Combination. *Laurie Mortenson, Julian, North Carolina*

A gray-filled banner for the applicant's chief roles of editor, manager, and writer makes them stand out. The text box containing a testimonial captures attention almost immediately and "wins

Scott Gronlund

000.000.0000 | s.gronlund@xxxx.com | Asheville, NC

Professional Achievements (continued)

People's Advocate, Asheville, NC (continued)   2004–present
A nonprofit, nonpartisan national consumer advocacy organization.
    Public Outreach Coordinator (2004–2006)
      Part of the People's Advocate's group lobbying Congress about automobile safety issues.

News Reporter   1999–2003

Federal Journal, Asheville, NC (2001–2003)
Weekly news source for federal government information.
Reporter covering homeland security and government management issues.

The Asheville Star, Asheville, NC (1999–2001)
Daily newspaper serving the Winchester community.
Copy editor and staff writer covering homeland security, city government affairs, and state and national politics.

    Key Points and Contributions
    ◆ Quoted in *Legislature Research Service Report* and *Developing Issues in Homeland Security* publications.
    ◆ Created ambitious series covering city council elections with candidate interviews and snapshot profiles.
    ◆ Designed daily and business pages.

Editor-in-Chief

The Tar Heel, Chapel Hill, NC   1996–1999
Award-winning, daily student-run newspaper with circulation of 20,000, serving the University of North Carolina community.
Began as reporter; promoted to editor positions culminating in editor-in-chief (1998–1999).

    Key Points and Contributions
    ◆ Awarded Society of Professional Journalist Award for article about campus riot.
    ◆ Reorganized staff and created motivation program to overturn newspaper's downward spiral after large staff turnover, including three editors-in-chief in previous year.
    ◆ Expanded newspaper's arts section and introduced comprehensive weather feature, receiving positive reader feedback.

Education and Training

Journalism Intern, American Government Association, Washington, DC   2003–2004
Awarded and completed internship focused on teaching journalists about the American political process.

Bachelor of Arts in Journalism, English minor   1996–1999
University of North Carolina at Chapel Hill
   Phi Beta Kappa graduate with 3.74 GPA

    Awards: Society of Professional Journalists Award, 1999

               Gold Standard Award, 1999

               Schlinger Honors College Scholar

    Internships: *The Atlanta Courant,* Atlanta, GA, and *The Observer,* Carboro, NC

    Affiliations: Omicron Delta Kappa (leadership honor society)

                  Golden Key International Honour Society

Computer and Technical Skills

Microsoft Word; Adobe InDesign, Photoshop, Illustrator and Acrobat; HTML; Mac and PC operating systems.

over" the reader to the side of the applicant, which is what a well-crafted resume can do for you. A Career Summary and a three-column list of Proven Competencies reinforce the impression given by the testimonial. The battle for attention is won by the first half of the first page.

Monique Carson

New York, New York ▪ 555-555-5555 ▪ monique@email.com

EDITORIAL DIRECTOR

PR ▪ IMAGE MANAGEMENT ▪ BRANDING

Communications / PR Expertise: 10+ years managing communications in both public and private organizations; offer deep experience in managing all aspects of publications, corporate communications, marketing collateral, and social outreach. Talented leading teams of both direct and indirect reports; concentrate on building content and editorial programs that reflect the expertise and capabilities of staff while maintaining vision of organization.

Resource Management: Work closely with vendors and internal management to control expenditures, allocate resources appropriately, and bring in talented individuals within budget; history of creating streamlined processes that enhance productivity and reduce costs.

Community Activism: Deeply involved with several animal welfare organizations, working both as an animal care volunteer and pro bono director of PR, marketing, affiliate sales, and communications.

Computer Skills: Dual-platform proficiency in MS Office Suite; page layout using Quark, InDesign, and Photoshop, plus CMS, WordPress, and Dreamweaver.

NONPROFIT & VOLUNTEER PR EXPERIENCE

Leverage passion and talent to lend PR expertise to groups focused on personal health, education, animal welfare, and history. Build community, appeal to donors, and educate audience through engaging newsletters, annual reports, press releases, and marketing collateral. Recent work samples: <u>Newsletter</u>, <u>Website</u>, and <u>Blog</u>.

TopDog Lovers: 2009–Present ▪ Yoga House: Present ▪ Pound Puppies: 2009

Cat Candy: 2007 ▪ The Motivated Ones: 2006 ▪ Franklin Tupper Museum: 2006

CORPORATE COMMUNICATIONS & MARKETING EXPERIENCE

Editorial Director, OPTIMUM HEALTH SYSTEM: 2002–Present

Promoted through ranks to lead all aspects of large-scale communications vehicles for this suburban healthcare provider with 15 hospitals. Hired in 2002 as publication coordinator; quickly advanced to publications editor and managing editor positions. <u>Publications and work samples here.</u>

➢ **Initiatives:** Guide 7 diverse publications sent out up to 4x annually from content brainstorming through final printing; proposed in-depth newsletter focused on women's healthcare needs; ensure consistent brand messaging across every publication and story, through targeted content and photos/illustrations.

➢ **Management:** Reduced outsourcing costs with simple, effective reallocation of freelancers; streamlined internal processes by implementing clear editorial procedures with strict deadlines.

➢ **Leadership:** Lead group of 5+ staff and freelancers—including speechwriters, photographers, show producers, and PR reps—in creating content, layouts, pagination, and overall publication/brand management.

Freelance / Contract Writer: 1991–1995 & 2000–2002

Wrote, designed, laid out, and edited annual reports, manuals, marketing collateral, specialty articles, poster presentations, websites, catalogs, and newsletters for numerous special-interest and industry-specific publications.

➢ **Clients:** *A Life's Choice, Alternate Strategies, Boarders' Travel Times, Cart Now, Detergent Association of America, Expand!, Feng Shui Today, Halpern Hospital, LxWxH Magazine, Measure&Weigh, Offenders' Defense, Pool and Landscape Digest, Roundabout Music Hall, TamperProof.*

➢ **Writing Style:** Recognized for ability to dive deeply into complex subjects with clarity, including obscure issues requiring extensive research and numerous expert interviews.

Page 1 of 2

21

Combination. *Kimberly Schneiderman, New York, New York*

The applicant wanted to work as a director for a nonprofit company, so the writer listed on page one nonprofit and volunteer experience ahead of corporate experience and presented at the end

Monique Carson

555-555-5555 ▪ monique@email.com

Copywriter, JUST US BOOK CLUBS: 1997–2000

Created sell copy, blurbs, and headlines for this member-driven book catalog with 40+ pages of feature interviews, book reviews, and product blurbs. Teamed with creative staff and marketing department to execute print and direct mail advertising. Several work samples available for review.

➤ **Personality Interviews:** Interviewed author Jessica Johanson, among others, in preparation for full-issue spreads and book reviews for Just Us book catalog.

➤ **Marketing & Outreach:** Wrote direct mail collateral for prospective and renewing members; wrote/edited catalog copy and "buck" slips, handled compliance notifications, and worked closely with designers on look of materials.

➤ **CMS:** Captured and maintained corporate database history of advertising and marketing materials.

Publications Coordinator, NEW JERSEY PRESBYTERIAN HOSPITAL: 1995–1997

Brought in to handle wide range of PR and marketing initiatives designed to educate audience, reach out to community, and establish facility as a resource for residents. Directed all aspects of communications, including writing, trafficking, and creating materials.

➤ **Communications:** Managed press releases, advertorials, and marketing collateral from initial concept through final delivery; wrote executive speeches for fund-raisers, community meetings, and holiday events.

➤ **Newsletters:** Wrote, designed, and edited monthly newsletters focused on needs of hospital's local community and internal staff.

Early experience includes journalism and editing positions for trade magazines including
Direct Reach, Development, Rhythm & Bass Retailer, and Over the Top.

EDUCATION, AWARDS & VOLUNTEER AFFILIATIONS

Master of Arts (M.A.), Communications: *BUCHMAN INSTITUTE OF TECHNOLOGY*
Graduated with Highest Honors. Awarded merit scholarship five years.

Bachelor of Arts (B.A.), English: *ST. MARK'S UNIVERSITY*
Graduated with Honors.

Certificate in Public Relations Strategy & Execution: *CARSON UNIVERSITY*
Won award for Best PR Campaign (2009) for work with online PR service created by Council of Communications.

❧ INDUSTRY WRITING & PR AWARDS ❧

Platinum Hermes Creative Award, *Healthy Outlook* newsletter, 2010 ▪ Red Healthcare Advertising Award, *Child Centered*

newsletter, 2010 ▪ BIT, Extreme Excellence in Communication Arts, 2009 ▪ Health & Wellness Advertising Award, *Child Centered*

newsletter, 2007 ▪ Health & Wellness Advertising Award, *Healthy Outlook* newsletter, 2006 ▪ JUT Award, Optimum Health System

annual report, 2006 ▪ TUMI Award, *The Doctor* journal, 2004 ▪ JUT Award, Optimum Health System annual report, 2004 ▪

Semifinalist, Westerman Writers Film Project, 2002 ▪ Hit It Award, Just Us Book Clubs print ad, 1998

❧ Volunteer Work ❧

New York Animal Lovers League ▪ Hudson Paws Animal Welfare Coalition
Cat Candy of Queens ▪ Animal Life & Health Organization

Comprehensive portfolio available for review.

of page two an impressive array of awards and volunteer work. Gray-filled text boxes call immediate attention to the contact information at the top of both pages and to the centered section headings throughout the resume.

CAROL A. YOUNG

3 TABBY DRIVE • FLEMINGTON, NJ 08822
OFFICE (908) 237-5555 • CAY@WORLDRENOWNEDRESUMES.COM

Credentialed résumé writer with a demonstrated commitment to providing superior products and top-notch service

SUMMARY OF QUALIFICATIONS

Independent, self-motivated, and conscientious professional with strong customer focus. Excellent writing skills with extensive experience developing marketing materials, customer communications, and job search documents. Able to draw on diverse experience to understand client needs and develop effective, targeted résumés.

PROFESSIONAL HIGHLIGHTS

- Opened résumé business, coordinating all aspects of start-up including creating and producing all business communications materials: brochures, business cards, flyers, and the company's Web site.
- Established proven record of accomplishment in writing winning résumés and other job search documents.
- With background that spans the fields of research, development, manufacturing, marketing, technical service, administrative customer service, career development, training, and project management, successfully work with technical, administrative, and executive professionals at all levels.
- Competently draw out key information from clients to effectively market skills and abilities.
- Astute and analytical; always operate with the understanding that knowing and adapting to the audience is the key to effective communication.
- Recognized for leadership and commitment to quality improvement. Strong track record of providing outstanding customer satisfaction.

CERTIFICATION

Certified Professional Résumé Writer, Professional Association of Résumé Writers, 2009

EMPLOYMENT HISTORY

WORLD-RENOWNED RÉSUMÉS, *Owner,* 2008 to Present
RESUME.COM, *Elite Writer,* 2008 to Present
LIBERTY LIFE, *Implementation Consultant,* Voluntary Benefits Group, 2007 to 2008
KAPLAN, *Prep Course Instructor and Tutor,* 2007 to 2009
YORK OIL CORPORATION, *Senior Research Engineer,* Fuels Marketing Support, 2003 to 2007
SPECIALTY CHEMICALS, INC., *Staff Engineer,* Petroleum Catalyst Group, 1998 to 2003

EDUCATION

STATE UNIVERSITY, Master of Education (Counseling Psychology), 2004
CITY COLLEGE, Bachelor of Science (Chemical Engineering), 1998

22

Combination. *Carol A. Altomare, Three Bridges, New Jersey*

This resume writer's resume is included in this Gallery to give an example of at least one professional resume writer's background. Note her degrees in science and psychology.

Customer Service

Resumes at a Glance

❧ DONNA BERENGER ❧

CUSTOMER SERVICE SPECIALIST

*Highly regarded professional with top-notch interpersonal skills and a
proven record in sales and service*

❧ PROFILE ❧

- Customer-driven professional with a wealth of experience in sales and service.
- Skilled relationship-builder who is able to establish easy rapport with customers, building trust and respect. Highly service-oriented individual who is responsive to need and thorough in follow-through.
- Organized, effective multitasker with excellent coordination skills and a keen attention to detail.
- Respected team player known for dependability and commitment to achieving goals.
- Effective communicator who is always polished and professional, yet warm and engaging.

❧ EXPERIENCE ❧

<u>MADISON BMW</u>, Madison, CT   2005 to present
Service Consultant
Meet and greet customers, collecting information on repair and maintenance orders. Develop estimates for service. Follow up with customers on progress.

- Upgraded customer service standards, modeling behaviors to create pleasant, customer-first environment that conveys confidence and professionalism while promoting customer loyalty and trust.
- Achieved customer satisfaction ratings of nearly 99%, standout scores in corporation that prides itself on service excellence.
- Earned reputation for going the extra mile to improve the customer service experience. Consistently gain appreciation of customers for proactively offering beneficial input and advice.
- Successfully sold additional work and add-on services, leveraging relationship-building skills to grow sales.

<u>MADISON SERVICE CENTER</u>, Madison, CT   2000 to 2005
Service Writer
Handled invoicing and billing function, while serving as contact for customer inquiries and requests.

- Brought in on temporary, part-time basis to handle data-entry project, hired in full-time capacity as service writer based on knowledge and dedication to service.
- Overhauled billing system, eliminating redundancies and computerizing tasks to improve efficiency and minimize errors. Reorganized and streamlined accounts receivable function as well.
- Capably addressed customer inquiries, providing prompt response to all issues and concerns.

❧ EDUCATION ❧

<u>GATEWAY COMMUNITY COLLEGE</u>, New Haven, CT
Associate degree in Business, May 2000

---

55 ELM ROAD ◆ **MADISON, CT 55555**
(555) 555-5555 HOME ◆ **(555) 555-4444 CELL** ◆ **dberenger@xxxx.com**

23

Combination. *Carol A. Altomare, Three Bridges, New Jersey*

This resume highlights high customer satisfaction ratings and model performance. Ornate "bullets" enclose the applicant's name and the three section headings.

Taylor Mays

5555 Avenue
Detroit, MI 55555
Telephone: (555) 444-4444 Email: email.name@xxxx.com

Sales Ability * Analytical * Service Oriented * Proactive * Efficient

Team Player * Microsoft Office * Problem Solver

Professional Summary

Successful customer service professional with demonstrated experience in building positive rapport with team members, clients and leadership to support an organization's success. Well equipped to perform within diverse work environments, adapt to new procedures, contribute to the bottom line, and provide unmatched customer service.

Professional Work Experience

MIA Products   Detroit, MI
October 2005–Present

Product Service Specialist
Provide client service support for product managers on all aspects of product design and client feedback. Diligently sustain new and established business relationships.

- Deliver innovative suggestions to senior product management team, which has resulted in retention of 12 executive client partnerships.

- Support product life cycle promotions through effective partnerships with internal staff by research, analysis and delivery of customer feedback data to support client marketing decisions.

- Successfully track and monitor daily data submissions of product XYZ to ensure quality results are delivered.

- Respond to client inquiries to provide updates on product sales and resolution of any inquiries, concerns or general service requests.

Dollar Service Investors   Detroit, MI
February 1999–September 2005

Lead Quality Service Representative
Lead Quality Service Team to consistently meet the business objectives of each client in a timely and quality-focused manner.

- Awarded top **Quality Service Leader** recognition for 6 consecutive quarters in 2003–2004 for the North region.

- Trained 4 Quality Service Representatives on proper protocol to successfully deliver quality data to client customers in a call center environment.

- Implemented call inquiry process flow to decrease multiple responses for each customer, which resulted in a 10% decrease of return calls for the same inquiry.

- Responded to 60+ customer inquiries daily in high-volume call center through effective time management, strong problem solving and analytical ability.

Education

Detroit University
Detroit, MI
Associate degree in Business Management
December 2003

24

Combination. *Teauna Upshaw, Smyrna, Tennessee*

Three thin-thick-thin compound horizontal lines are the distinctive feature of this one-page resume, making it stand out. Experience exceeds education in importance.

MARY CARTRIGHT

123 Fortune Street
Philadelphia, PA 19119

mary_cartright@xxxx.com

Home: 555.555.5555
Cell: 555.444.4444

CUSTOMER SERVICE MANAGER

Dynamic, hardworking supervisor with demonstrated ability to motivate staff and build a solid team environment. Broad-based experience encompasses project management, process improvement and analysis for a Fortune 100 company. Demonstrated skill in assessing problem areas and recommending solutions, resulting in increased productivity and profitability while reducing expenses. Proven track record for meeting or exceeding customer satisfaction scores for more than seven consecutive years.

Core Competencies

- Consumer Trends Analysis
- Operations Management
- Quality Assurance
- Policy/Procedure Development

- Productivity Improvement
- Needs Analysis
- Risk Management
- Up-selling, Cross-selling, Value-added Sales

- Team Building
- Performance Management
- Account Management
- Microsoft Office (Word, PowerPoint, Excel)

PROFESSIONAL EXPERIENCE

VERIZON COMMUNICATIONS, Philadelphia, PA   2000–2012
93 billion-dollar telecommunications company

Process Improvement and Operations Manager (2005–2012)
Served as primary point of contact for high-priority residential customers, developing and implementing action plans to increase customer satisfaction. Fostered culture of continuous improvement, ensuring production needs and quality standards were met. Conducted 50+ remote observations of sales and service representatives' effectiveness. Interfaced regularly with director-level managers, field managers, and service representatives.

- Lowered percentage of repeat callers and improved performance in *Right the First Time* arena, increasing adherence to recapitulation guidelines 15% and customer satisfaction 10%.
- Positively impacted thousands of customers by initiating new call-out scripts and procedures for technicians; coordinated with management to increase server space to incorporate new system.
- Composed newsletter distributed to 100 senior executives and managers on trends and customer satisfaction.

Account Manager (2002–2005)
Directly assisted 550 medium-sized businesses with all telecommunication needs. Met frequently with clients to assess needs and recommend solutions, offering 24/7 availability when needed. Trained 75 sales personnel, using advanced coaching methods.

- Exceeded sales objective 251% in 2003; recipient of Winners Circle Award.
- Recognized as top 1% sales performer during entire tenure.

Sales/Service Representative (2000–2002)
Responded to sales inquiries, closed sales and finalized paperwork, receiving high client-satisfaction scores. Gained new business through handling all customer associations in a positive, professional manner. Selected to supervise office in the absence of manager. Instructed new representatives on sales and protocol procedures.

- Chosen to attend Quality Service Skills training; subsequently trained office of 100+ staff.
- Recognized as Top Sales Performer and Diamond Club Award Winner.

CRISIS COUNSELING CENTER, Philadelphia, PA   1998–2000
Nonprofit human services agency with annual budget of $20M
Assistant Program Manager
Oversaw residential program's daily functions. Administered billing for Housing and Urban Development program. Directed performance of six counselors and monitored consumer development plans.

- Received *Components Award* for exceeding management expectations.

EDUCATION

Bachelor of Arts in Psychology, PENN STATE UNIVERSITY, State College, PA, 1998

25

Combination. *Ginger Korljan, Phoenix, Arizona*

The inclusion of keywords in the Core Competencies section and bulleted accomplishments led to the selection of this resume over others. The applicant got a job quickly after submitting her resume via Indeed.

ROSIE SMITH

5000 Larkspur Lane #555   555-050-0000
Colorado Springs, CO 50005   rsmith@email.com

Talented Customer Service Representative with proven results in active listening, assessing needs, understanding issues, analyzing options and providing timely, helpful solutions. Able to effectively manage time and understand problem sensitivity while responding quickly. Knowledgeable in business operations and efforts that increase revenues. Adept at sales techniques, including persuasion and promotions. Strong interpersonal and communication skills. Talented in cultivating and maintaining long-term relationships.

PROFESSIONAL QUALIFICATIONS

CUSTOMER AGENT   **2006–2008**
AIRLINES INSURANCE AGENCY—San Diego, CA
Managed daily communications with prospects and customers by email, telephone calls and in-person. Assisted with coverage questions, quotes and insurance purchases. Coordinated documentation transactions including policies, notifications and payments.

- Successfully assisted customers with General Liability, Commercial Auto, Excess, Course of Construction, Professional & Tool insurance policies for California Contractors that averaged $3,500 annually by coordinating policy needs, gathering appropriate documentation, answering questions and collecting payments.
- Promoted from Customer Service Representative to Customer Agent through active listening to customer needs, being available to clients and providing timely solutions. Results included an average of 10 new monthly business accounts with a 95% renewal retention rate.
- Achieved personal and team goals by cultivating and maintaining relationships with clients and providing timely responses.
- Effectively communicated with prospects and clients regarding complex insurance policies in order to provide clarity and understanding, using effective oral and written communication skills.

CUSTOMER SERVICE REPRESENTATIVE   **2002–2006**
HAPPY INSURANCE AGENCY—Sacramento, CA
Responsible for assisting three sales agents with daily needs including customer contact, answering questions, gathering documentation and developing draft policies. Coordinated certificates and endorsements in order to enhance business.

- Coordinated sales activities for three liability agents, including answering questions, writing policies, assisting clients, accepting payments, invoicing, issuing certificates, processing insurance quotes and reinstating policies. Used time and priority management skills with multitasking.
- Provided outstanding service to prospects and clients regarding needs, questions and policies by researching answers and documenting information.
- Assisted with company communications and team knowledge by creating certificates and ordering endorsements from the insurance carrier in order to provide clients with necessary paperwork.
- Ensured that appropriate changes were made to policies in order to resolve customer issues or to address specific needs by clearly communicating with the customer and sales agent.
- Successfully conferred with customers multiple times in order to provide information about policies, to take orders or to obtain details regarding an issue using sensitivity and business knowledge.
- Resolved customer grievances by investigating reports, researching and collaborating with peers.

26

Chronological. *Ruth Pankratz, Fort Collins, Colorado*

This applicant was a full-time mom ready to return to work but worried about the gap in her professional work experience. The writer emphasized accomplishments of the applicant's previous

ROSIE SMITH

555-050-0000
rsmith@email.com

CUSTOMER SERVICE REPRESENTATIVE   **2000–2002**
EVERYDAY INSURANCE AGENCY—Los Angeles, CA
Coordinated office activities including answering phones, assisting visitors, typing and helping staff
members. Managed office flow of communications and supplies.

- Responded to 15 incoming phone lines representing various departments, listened to caller needs and
  directed the call to the appropriate location.
- Coordinated applications, including gathering information from agents; input details on applications
  and appropriate documents; and conferred with clients using attention to details and computer skills.
- Assisted with business growth by keeping company owner informed regarding lost business
  opportunities, such as unanswered prospect requests, resulting in a customer service adjustment.

MEDIA COORDINATOR   **1999–2000**
CHICO COMMUNITY COLLEGE—Chico, CA
Provided assistance to student employees and staff regarding issue resolutions, online learning labs, TV
class broadcasts, computer assistance, testing and study activities.

- Supervised four student employees and managed daily tasks using effective resource allocation skills.
- Coordinated computer testing and instruction activities for the site by maintaining equipment and
  resolving technical issues.
- Managed site operations and maintained efficiencies by fulfilling supply needs, placing work orders
  and assisting students and instructors.

MILITARY EXPERIENCE

UNITED STATES AIR FORCE   **2008–Present**
Military Spouse and Mother

UNITED STATES AIR FORCE   **1994–1998**
Signal Production Operator

EDUCATION & CERTIFICATIONS

- FRONT RANGE COMMUNITY COLLEGE—Westminster, CO
  Associate degree in Business Administration
- Certified Insurance Specialist
- Certified Customer Service Representative—Happy Insurance Agency

experience and downplayed frequent family military moves. She sent this resume to 21 potential employers,
received three calls for interviews, and got two job offers. This strong resume shows that people with full-time
family gaps can be accepted back into the workforce.

DORA M. VAUGHN

ENTRY-LEVEL PROFESSIONAL | FOCUSED ON PEOPLE

Enthusiastic, friendly, and motivated professional bringing to the workforce a **deep sense of responsibility and dedication** from focused experience as a stay-at-home mother and volunteer.

Broad-based distinct competencies in customer care, transaction completion, end-of-shift settlement, and documentation, with particular strength and previous experience in bank environments.

Excellent at resolving conflicts and problems by leveraging skills in **communication and critical thinking** to create win-win solutions.

Strong team player who works well under confident, participative leaders and in collaboration with colleagues to attain a shared goal.

VALUE OFFERED

Customer Service	Communication	Observant Listening	Adaptability	Independent Judgment
Numerical Ability	Attention to Detail	Honesty & Integrity	Fast Learner	Banking Knowledge

PROFESSIONAL EXPERIENCE

Restaurant Hostess, GOLDEN APPLE INN, Wayne, OH — 1989 to 1991

Provided courteous guest service to restaurant patrons. Ensured smooth flow of daily breakfast operations, with accountability for opening restaurant, preparing cash register, brewing breakfast beverages, stocking serving areas, and performing duties as required. Monitored guests' satisfaction and directed employees to cater to their needs. Conducted inventory of all food and service items.

- Valued by boss for reliability, and praised for ability to lead employees and restaurant without supervision.

Bank Teller, WESTERN NATIONAL BANK, Hartstown, PA — 1988 to 1989

Accurately and efficiently processed and recorded routine transactions for bank customers. Services included opening new accounts, cashing checks, accepting deposits and withdrawals, processing loan payments and money transfers, and promoting and advising on bank's products and services. Responsible for identifying customers; resolving issues and problems with customers' accounts; and balancing currency, cash, and checks in cash drawer.

- Recognized for background in marketing and asked to create promotional billboards with catchy slogans.

Additional Employment Considerations
Census Taker, SANDSBURG AREA SCHOOL DISTRICT, Sandsburg, PA — Summer 2010
Playground Instructor, SANDSBURG AREA SCHOOL DISTRICT, Sandsburg, PA — Summer 1982, 1983, 1984

COMMUNITY SERVICE | VOLUNTEERISM

Homeroom Mom, SANDSBURG SCHOOL DISTRICT, Sandsburg, PA
PTO (Parent Teacher Organization), SANDSBURG SCHOOL DISTRICT, Sandsburg, PA
Girl Scout Leader, GIRL SCOUTS OF AMERICA, Sandsburg, PA
Treasurer, SANDSBURG CROSS COUNTRY TEAM, Sandsburg, PA

EDUCATION

Bachelor of Arts in Business Administration, WESTMINSTER COLLEGE, New Wilmington, PA

5555 Hillsdale Rd. • Sandsburg, PA 50550 • (H) 555.505.0055 • (C) 555.505.0005 • dmv55@xxxx.com

27

Combination. *Jane Roqueplot, West Middlesex, Pennsylvania*

The graphic wheel of positive skills and results is the dominant eye-catching feature that makes this resume distinctive. "Value Offered" is a distinctive heading for skills and areas of expertise.

Design/Architecture

Resumes at a Glance

Alexander Parker

89 Toronto Drive • Mendham, NJ 07945 • 973.648.9604 • aparker@monmouth.com

GRAPHIC DESIGNER / DIGITAL PHOTO RETOUCHER / WEB DESIGNER

Creative professional with a proven track record of successful projects from initial concept through completion. High-energy, results-oriented leader recognized for innovative tactics and strategies. Reputation among peers for finding the most efficient way to facilitate a project or process without sacrificing quality. Possess strong problem-solving skills and an ability to manage time-sensitive projects.

Combine passion for aesthetics with commitment to contributing to an organization's bottom line. Excellent communications and interpersonal skills. Talent for writing and designing technical manuals and training programs. Comfortable working in Mac or Windows environments.

Areas of Expertise:

- Digital Graphic Design
- Brochure Design
- Web Design
- Project Management
- Multimedia Production
- Customer & Vendor Relations
- E-commerce
- Digital Photography

Software Proficiencies:

- Adobe Photoshop CS
- QuarkXPress
- CorelDRAW
- Novell NetWare
- Adobe Illustrator CS
- Apple Final Cut Pro
- Adobe GoLive CS
- Windows 7, XP; OSX

Professional Accomplishments

HANIFI DEVICES, INC., Fair Lawn, NJ (1977–2012)
The eighth-largest manufacturer of electronic pressure and vibration sensors for industrial and defense applications, with facilities in the U.S., UK, France, Germany, and Italy.

Supervisor
- Assigned creative control of the design and layout of numerous single-page and multipage publications and corporate identity packages.
- Created eye-catching logos, product brochures, flyers, mailers, trade magazine ads, and other promotional media.
- Photographed products, company employees, customers, and models for use in advertising and promotional materials.
- Balanced imagination with solid technical skills to create web pages using digital software to optimize all visual images to enhance the effectiveness of the company's website.
- Designed all training manuals and managed the training programs for new employees.
- Managed each project from start to finish, on time and within budget.
- Started with Hanifi as its third employee. Consistently given increasing responsibilities as process improvement suggestions increased efficiency and generated higher profits.
- **Presented with the company's first Process Improvement Award.**
- Streamlined product assembly operation into an efficient production-line process with fewer defects and a more attractive appearance.

Member of the Professional Photographers of America

28

Combination. *Beverley and Mitchell I. Baskin, Marlboro, New Jersey*

After a profile, two side headings—Areas of Expertise and Software Proficiencies—introduce other qualifications. Note that work experience is titled Professional Accomplishments.

Gregory Draper

http://www.creativehotlist.com/gdraper

5555 Cherry Dr., Unit 55A | Boston, MA 55555 | 555.555.5555 | gdraper@xxxx.com

GRAPHIC DESIGNER | ART DIRECTOR

Agency | Design Studio | In-House

Branding Concepts | Logo Design | Illustration | Layout | Story Boards | Production & Printing
Catalogues | Brochures | Packaging | Coupons | Apparel | Posters | Photo Shoots | Commercials
Web Sites | Landing Pages | Banners | Pop-Ups | Facebook | Twitter | E-newsletters

PROFESSIONAL EXPERIENCE

Art Director / Graphic Designer   Feb. 2008 to present
MASSACHUSETTS'S MOTOCROSS, Chelsea, MA

Lead, create and oversee the production and implementation of all in-house advertising and
marketing initiatives while acting as a one-man design shop.

- Developed, distributed and analyzed current client surveys; analysis used to expand desired
  product offerings, increase competitive advantage and improve business differentiation.
- Designed and managed magazine, print and pro bono advertising campaigns, outdoor
  boards, merchandising displays, retail and trade show signage banners, brand identity logos,
  coupons, posters, T-shirt and sticker graphics, e-newsletters, Web banners, pop-ups, social
  networking exposure, point-of-purchase (POP) brochures, postcards and signs, etc.
- Collaborated with sales manager to create a profitable ongoing sales program and campaign;
  conceived and implemented initiative that has maintained success for over a year and a half.
- Designed and regularly update the company's e-commerce Web site.

Designer / Production Artist   June 2007 to Aug. 2007 & Dec. 2007
AQUAMAUREEN CREATIVE, Boston, MA

Carefully managed time and priorities while contributing design and production experience to
various client projects through contract work at this small creative firm.

- Made advances in projects for City Market, IHOP, Cinnabon, the Children's Hospital
  Boston, Sundown Industries, the World's Best Cat Litter and the Clover Foundation.
- Developed campaign published in *Boston Magazine,* created a tri-fold invitation, designed
  raffle tickets and custom sponsorship lighted displays for a nonprofit fund-raising event.
- Retouched images and designed vinyl and metal signs, menu boards, posters, coupons, etc.

Associate Art Director   Aug. 2002 to Aug. 2003
ADVENTURES DESIGN & MARKETING, Seattle, WA

Worked closely with agency copywriters in developing original concepts, headlines and taglines
and assisted the creative directors in conceptualizing and managing numerous client projects.

- Actively contributed during creative team meetings; involved in all project stages, from
  concept to layout to delivering client presentations to production.
- Collaborated with the senior designers to exceed the expectations of a new client, Group
  Health Cooperative; developed a headline/concept and rolled out a multimedia ad campaign
  that offered the client the branding differentiation that it sought.
- Located photographer and led photo shoot for a Group Health Cooperative ad campaign.
- Worked on magazine and ad campaign, product info sheet, poster design and commercial
  development for Wells Fargo.

29

Combination. *Melanie Lenci, Denver, Colorado*

This resume was originally a three-page resume that the writer compressed to two pages. Things
left out: language specific to the applicant's latest position, most school-based information and

Gregory Draper gdraper@xxxx.com

AdVentures Design & Marketing **(continued)**

- Earned additional work from the University of Seattle's Athletic Department after impressing staffers with an original headline for their 2003 football marketing campaign.
- Executed numerous layouts, print advertisements, POP materials and corporate identity logo designs for clients, including Value Saver Pharmacies, Virginia Mason Hospital, the Cattlemen's Association, Seattle Yellow Pages, Campbell's Soup and Elite Lighting.

FREELANCE EXPERIENCE

Independent Designer / Art Director Jan. 2010 to present
Strictly Creative, Boston, MA
Work directly with clients to assess and answer their unique advertising objectives.

- Create magazine ad campaigns, POP brochures, brand identity logos, posters, promotional displays, etc., and oversee production as needed.
- Designed cardboard cutout to be displayed at all Boston Regal theaters this fall and winter.
- Work with a broad range of clients, including EchoStar, Goodyear, ThumperTalk, IFMA Freestyle, Mass Nutrition and *Welcome to the Neighborhood* magazine.

Industrial Line Drawing Illustrator / Graphic Designer Mar. 2004 to Apr. 2008
Angie Green & Saunders Crane Corp., Seattle, WA
Hired by Angie Green independently after working under her direction at Saunders.

- Performed line drawing and user manual illustration work at Saunders in 2004.
- Designed graphics, retouched photos and periodically updated the design, layout and content of fashion design student's Web site, as needed, for four years.

INDEPENDENT PROJECT SAMPLES

Book Jacket Designer Aug. 2008
Margery, *Book of Poetry,* Charlottesville, VA

POP Production Designer Feb. 2007
Shine Advertising, *Catalogue Design & Layout for firm's client, MINI,* Boston, MA

Logo & CD Cover Designer Dec. 2006
The Winter, *Alternative Band,* Danbury, CT

Menu Designer Summer 2006
Water View Fresh Fish Company, *Restaurant,* Danbury, CT

Industrial Line Drawing Illustrator Summer 2002
Valley Creative Group, *Creative Studio,* Seattle, WA

Pumpkin Carving Pattern Designer Fall 2001
Zombie Pumpkins, *Retailer,* Boston, MA

TECHNOLOGY

Adobe Creative Suite: Acrobat | Illustrator | InDesign | Photoshop | After Effects | Flash Dreamweaver | Premiere Pro

Microsoft Office: Word | Excel | PowerPoint

Other: Mac OSX | PC | QuarkXPress | iMovie | Final Cut | HTML

EDUCATION

BFA, Graphic Design ▪ International Academy of Design & Technology ▪ Seattle, WA ▪ 2002

experience, and any graphics that would draw attention from the individual's work experience. With this resume the applicant became confident in his job search and had a successful interview a few weeks later.

JASON S. CLARKE

5555 75th Street · Indianapolis, Indiana 00000 · (H) 555.555.5555 · jasonsclarke@email.com

INTERIOR DESIGNER / SALES SPECIALIST

LEED Accredited Professional • Registered Interior Designer (Indiana & Illinois) • NCIDQ Certified

Innovative, customer-oriented interior designer with impressive network of industry contacts, poised to excel in consultative sales role. Skilled in creating tailored sales presentations and demonstrations to drive achievement of revenue goals. Experienced in interviewing clients to uncover needs and develop customized concepts and pricing. Adept at partnering with clients throughout sales cycle to identify issues and recommend cost-effective solutions. Expertise in creating interior spaces that reflect clients' personalities and lifestyles.

~ Areas of Expertise ~

- Interior Design Project Management
- Proposal and Estimate Preparation
- Space Planning / AutoCAD Drafting
- Relationship Building
- Customer Retention / Satisfaction

- Sales Presentations / Demonstrations
- New Business Development
- Customer Service / Client Relations
- Home Consultations / Measurements
- Contract Negotiations

EXPERIENCE HIGHLIGHTS

ABC TOP ARCHITECTS, Indianapolis, Indiana
Interior Designer, 2007–2009
Served as sole interior designer for regional architectural firm primarily serving the Indianapolis metropolitan area. Led variety of small- to medium-sized projects ranging from 1.5K to 85K sq. ft., including build-outs and renovations for commercial and medical offices, retail buildings, and religious spaces. Developed project budgets, schedules, illustrations, full construction documents, and custom millwork designs. Produced schematic layouts and conceptual planning to include furnishings and equipment.

- Created sales presentations and proposal documents to support sales cycle.
- Enhanced client retention by maintaining high level of quality.
- Managed price negotiations with contractors to minimize costs.
- Improved library by updating materials and identifying and removing outdated resources.

SPACE + DESIGN, Indianapolis, Indiana
Interior Designer, 2004–2006
Created visually exciting and functional atmospheres for architectural and design firm specializing in corporate, legal, government, and healthcare industries. Led meetings with clients, contractors, and vendors. Selected furnishings, color palettes, and finishes. Participated in redesign of 75K sq. ft. hospital center, 43K sq. ft. office on 2 floors, and 20K sq. ft. office within Federal Reserve Bank Building in Chicago.

Continued...

30

Combination. *Michelle P. Swanson, Edwardsville, Illinois*

The applicant wanted to leverage his background in interior design to move into a sales role within the design industry. Gray shading makes the opening banner and centered section

555.555.5555   **JASON S. CLARKE** – *Page 2*   jasonsclarke@email.com

- Prepared sales presentations for use by leading architects, which involved outlining estimated timelines and creating detailed schematic drawings.
- Provided brochures of recommended products for client review.
- Consulted with clients from early design conception through project completion, ensuring compliance to specifications and full client satisfaction.

DESIGN ASSOCIATES, Indianapolis, Indiana
Project Manager / Designer, 2000–2003
Represented clients of architectural and interior design firm throughout project life cycle of renovations ranging in scope from 4K to 67K sq. ft. Implemented internal branding, established palette, and created concept space accountancy solutions. Produced construction documents and reviewed product / shop drawings. Partnered with sales teams to close deals; updated customer databases.

- Selected furnishings, established palette, and specified architectural finishes.
- Served as lead designer for historical renovation of Wilson Hall banquet and conference facilities. Balanced elegance of historic 19th century hall with modern technology.
- Led design and installation for international law offices, and designed technical office and foyer for investment bank and brokerage firm.

THE DESIGN GROUP, INC., Indianapolis, Indiana
Assistant to Architect, 1999–2000
Provided comprehensive design, documentation, and administrative support to architect with firm focusing on commercial tenant development and large retail design. Produced full tenant redevelopment programs, space plans, full construction documents, fixture specifications, and schedules. Designed handicapped accessibility and ADA building code renovation improvements.

- Supported development and execution of diverse projects, ranging from tenant improvement for 25K sq. ft space to full architectural plans for 32-floor high-rise office building.
- Administered project budgets ranging from $10K to $300K.

**   ***   **

Additional experience as **Theatrical Lighting & Scenic Designer** *with Broadway National Tours, Steppenwolf Theatre Company, Boston Ballet, American Repertory Theatre, and Scenic Studio.*

EDUCATION & CREDENTIALS

Bachelor of Fine Arts in Lighting & Scenic Design, *Magna cum Laude*
INDIANA UNIVERSITY, Bloomington, Indiana

Certifications & Licenses
LEED AP • Registered Interior Designer: Indiana and Illinois • NCIDQ Certified

Affiliations
U.S. Green Building Council (USGBC), Indianapolis Chapter, 2008–Present
International Interior Design Association (IIDA), 2005–Present

headings eye-catching. Square bullets point to notable achievements for all of his designated work experiences. For each of these, the writer provided a paragraph of duties followed by a list of bulleted achievements, a format popular among professional resume writers.

ALEX GRANT

55 Pleasant Run Road ◆ Briarcliff Manor, NY 55555
555-555-5555 Home ◆ 555-555-5555 Cell ◆ grant55@xxxx.com

ARCHITECT/PROJECT MANAGER
Commercial Design and Construction
Needs Assessment ◆ Plan Design ◆ Survey/Site Documentation ◆ Project Oversight

Delivering design solutions that offer the best of efficiency, functionality, and style.

Accomplished architect with a wealth of experience in managing commercial design and construction projects, developing and delivering creative, energy-efficient design solutions to meet a broad range of business needs and corporate styles. Respected project resource committed to Green Design and Lean Project Management principles.

Core Expertise

✓ Developing creative designs to meet a range of tastes and budgets, leveraging creativity and resourcefulness to identify low-cost solutions while making the most of available resources.

✓ Leading design and construction projects, meticulously developing plans and managing all details to consistently deliver results on time and within budget constraints.

✓ Overseeing site construction, leveraging ground-up industry experience to build collaborative work environment while effectively motivating teams of contractors to achieve shared goals.

✓ Incorporating green building practices into designs, striving to achieve best blend of efficiency and functionality.

SELECT CAREER HIGHLIGHTS

◆ **Established stellar record of accomplishment in commercial design and construction, successfully taking on a broad range of projects in various roles (designer, project manager, construction manager, etc.).**

✓ Developed and delivered commercial design solutions large and small, from a 2000 sq. ft. hospital project to a 240,000 sq. ft. warehouse conversion. Maintained standards for on-time delivery with minimal disruption.

✓ Managed projects both locally and internationally, overseeing design work for prestigious New York offices as well as distant overseas locations (Indonesia and Iraq).

✓ Handled design projects for range of clients—banks, pharmaceutical companies, a telecommunications giant, financial firms, national retailers, hospitals, and colleges, among others—designing customized solutions to meet a broad range of styles and needs.

✓ Developed expertise in all aspects of commercial design and construction projects, offering comprehensive service packages to provide turnkey operations to clients.

◆ **Cultivated signature architectural/design style that resonates with discriminating/value-conscious corporate clients:**

✓ Advocating Green Design practices, established reputation for creating designs that combine functionality and efficiency in attractive, cost-effective package.

✓ Won accolades for ability to develop creative designs that reflect local styles. For example, adapted basic bank design to maintain light, airy feel, but incorporate more utilitarian elements required in urban neighborhood. Similarly, included design touches to reflect roots of Flatiron District in local design project.

✓ Developed expertise in creating expensive looks from inexpensive materials, leveraging creativity and resourcefulness to offer sophisticated designs to meet a broad range of budgets.

◆ **Built strong following among clients, consistently earning rave reviews for creative ideas and flawless execution. Among achievements:**

✓ Developed and implemented creative design for bank that featured curved flow; lights that created an open, airy feel; and top-line construction materials in customer areas to reflect company image and philosophy. Earned Reach Higher award for performance excellence associated with well-received design.

31

Combination. *Carol A. Altomare, Three Bridges, New Jersey*

The original resume was a dry, lengthy list of project details. The writer turned it into this compelling document that clearly communicates the applicant's expertise and brand. A Select Career

- **Built strong following among clients, consistently earning rave reviews for creative ideas and flawless execution. Among achievements: (Continued)**
  - ✓ Designed modular dormitory system that accounted for required systems and shaftways so well that five 3-story buildings were successfully erected and made operational in just 10 days.
  - ✓ Developed cutting-edge raised floor office area for telecommunications giant, implementing design to facilitate future moves. As part of project, worked with leading furniture manufacturer to design $4 million in new furniture. Functional and attractive office space was featured in company sales brochure.
  - ✓ Created themed façade for resort complex, integrating 3 different looks for 3 different entrances for 3 different but related businesses. Successfully implemented design, earning rave reviews from client.
  - ✓ Designed sophisticated disaster recovery and data center that maintained controlled environment by placing air-conditioning units under floor. Identified simple solution to reduce cooling costs, recommending a change in roof color from black to white.
  - ✓ Designed showroom in SoHo, introducing innovative lighting solution that combined upward-facing fluorescent lights with downward-pointing incandescent fixtures to create a warm, welcoming environment.
- **Introduced initiatives and strategies to improve organizational effectiveness:**
  - ✓ Advocated use of new technology to improve business operations. Recommended use in promotional materials (client presentations) to help close sales. Used new design tools to improve accuracy of designs, identifying systems conflicts before they happen.
  - ✓ Leveraged ground-up construction industry expertise to identify and rectify construction issues before they became problems. For example, noticing welding issue with modular dormitories, worked collaboratively with contractors to help them recognize problems and initiate corrective action that saved project timelines.
  - ✓ As member of Green Team at Gould, launched and maintained first-ever recycling program for employees.

PROFESSIONAL EXPERIENCE

Construction Services Manager, PRESTIGE SOLUTIONS, 2008 to present
Architectural Project Manager, GOULD CORPORATION, 2006 to 2008
Project Designer, PFIZER, 2002 to 2006
Project Designer, YARROW ARCHITECTS, 2000 to 2002
Senior Project Manager, NORTH STAR BANK, 1999 to 2000
Engineering Coordinator, P.C. ASSOCIATES, 1997 to 1999
Project Manager, GOLDMAN ARCHITECTS, 1993 to 1997
Project Designer/Manager, CHOICE ASSOCIATES, 1990 to 1992

EDUCATION & CERTIFICATIONS

Bachelor's degree in Architecture, Pennsylvania State University, University Park, PA

Working toward LEED Certification through the U.S. Green Building Council.
Certified by the American Institute of Building.

TECHNOLOGY SKILLS

General:	Access, PowerPoint, Excel, Word
Design:	AutoCAD, Revit
Project Management:	MS Project, Prolog, SureTrak

Highlights section, placed where a Work Experience section usually appears, indicates a range of what the applicant can do. The Professional Experience section on page two amounts to a work history with just positions, names, and dates.

LINDA A. BUILDER
Licensed Architect

1227 Oak Avenue	Home: 331-271-9952
Lantern, Texas 77391	Cell: 331-271-9953

ARCHITECT / PROJECT MANAGER with experience in the planning, design, and construction of diverse project renovations (major and minor) and architecture projects such as institutional, recreational, and health care facilities. Extensive background in **urbanism** and all infrastructure, directing all project phases from design through completion of construction, coordinating the efforts of contractors; architectural, engineering, and landscaping consultants; and government agencies. Excellent technical qualifications complement an **innate sense of creativity** in the design of aesthetically attractive, architecturally strong, and utilitarian space. Highly organized and proficient in AutoCAD. Meticulous perfectionist who works well under pressure.

AREAS OF PROFICIENCY

Experienced in all phases of design from program definition through working drawing. Expertise in
- Construction estimating, cost analysis, feasibility studies, and project budgeting
- Negotiation and contract administration
- Inspection and supervision of construction

▶ Solid design and construction experience in commercial projects, including landscaping, office buildings, schools, churches, hotels, and restaurants.

▶ Established a **regional reputation** for excellence and developed a loyal following. Highly successful for project profitability and investor ROI.

▶ Strong **management skills,** including personnel and project scheduling, employee and subcontractor supervision, budgeting and finance, problem solving, client relations, and quality control.

▶ Seasoned **sales and marketing skills.** Demonstrated ability to gain trust and confidence of prospects. Personable and highly ethical.

▶ Proven **communications ability** that is straightforward, honest, and articulate, yet tactful and diplomatic. Sincere sensitivity to unique needs and aspirations of all segments of a community. Active listening and consultation skills with talent for respecting and responding to divergent opinions and interests. Strengths in blending idealism with political reality and devising new methods to improve procedural and system efficiency.

▶ Computer literate: Microsoft PowerPoint, Adobe InDesign, CorelDRAW, Harvard Graphics.

▶ Fully bilingual: Spanish and English.

CAREER HIGHLIGHTS

ARCHITECT
Planin Consultores, S.A., Caracas, Venezuela

2012	Designed, drafted, and supervised the building project for the new Emergency area for Adults and Pediatrics at the Hospital Clinico de Caracas.
2011	Remodeled living quarters on the second floor of the Caracas Hospital (4 models).

Page 1 of 3

Combination. *Myriam-Rose Kohn, Valencia, California*

Contact information is presented in a balanced format and is separated from the rest of the resume by a double line. The first paragraph is a profile of the applicant. Boldfacing enhances

LINDA A. BUILDER

2010   Designed individual family units for private owner.
              Participated in all project phases from initial client contact and presentation through
              conceptual design; production of contract documents; interface with engineers and
              outside planning consultants; and development of interiors, finishes, and specifications.

2009   Key member of design team responsible for the renovation of the Adult Emergency area
              at the Public (County) Hospital in Caracas (Hospital Universitario de Caracas). While
              work was in progress, intervened and adjusted the specifications to improve production.

ARCHITECT
G.P. Arquitectura, S.A., Valencia, Venezuela

2008   Assigned as architect in charge for the Main Control Room project at the Energia
              Eléctrica (Electrical Energy) of Venezuela (**ENELVEN / CAUJARITO**), approximately
              1000 mt2.

2006   Designed and drafted the remodeling of the main offices at the Investment Bank of
              Welles Orvitz. Served as director of field operations. Reviewed project specifications,
              researched previous designs, and prepared designs for customer presentation and
              approval. Maintained in-house library of design materials and references.

ARCHITECT
Faculty of Architecture, University of Apure, Cabimas, Venezuela

2002–2005   Supervising Architect on several relocation projects, among which were the communities
              of *El Hornito* (252 acres, $300 million budget, 325 houses from 7 different models,
              church, elementary school, community center, clinic, and fishing processing center) and
              Villa Hermosa.

              Reviewed development proposals for adherence to county zoning and other ordinances,
              and aesthetically based design guidelines. Dealt with
              -   Zoning administration   -   Community development
              -   Site plan review and approval   -   Stormwater drainage
              -   Subdivision regulation   -   Surface hydrology
              -   Wastewater distribution   -   Parking lot design
              -   Design ordinance administration   -   Environmental impact
              -   Economic development   -   Public relations
              -   Historic preservation   -   Urban redevelopment
              -   Environmental impact and planning   -   Administrative management
              -   Policy analysis

              Directed and facilitated the design and construction of new development projects
              and improvements to transportation facilities, streets, sidewalks, and utility systems.
              Coordinated/supervised an interdisciplinary team of professional consultants and
              construction inspectors to meet individual project time and cost objectives. Analyzed
              impediments to project goals; quickly identified and implemented solutions.

              Prepared graphic files for inspection and critical path schedules; analyzed construction
              schedules from contractors. Monitored project construction daily and represented the
              interests of client at progress meetings. Prepared design revisions when required by
              unknown field conditions. Analyzed requirements of plans and specifications to deny or
              justify claims by contractors for extra work. Facilitated public involvement in planning
              decisions by communicating merits of project(s), which in turn promoted community good
              will and continued support. Explained or modified construction activity to respond to
              public concern. Assisted with final project designs and construction drawings.

information of interest to the prospective employer. Boldfacing also highlights certain skills in the Areas of
Proficiency section. The value of the applicant's bilingualism becomes evident in the Career Highlights section.
Here and in the Education section, the reader may infer that Spanish is her native language and English her

LANDSCAPE ARCHITECT
Faculty of Architecture / Agronomy, University of Apure, Cabimas, Venezuela

2003   Collaborated with horticulturist Carmen Avila (partner in El Guacamayo Company) on the
            design and development of the exterior landscaping at *La Cabana Hotel* (Aruba, Antilles).
            Ensured *El Guacamayo Garden* was executed in accordance with client specifications.

PATENTS AND PUBLICATIONS

Faculty of Architecture
Research Institute I.F.A., University of Apure, Cabimas, Venezuela

In collaboration with Carlos Fidere, Dean, School of Architecture:
-   Authored and published ***Informe Final,*** Relocation Project of the community of *El Hornito*.
    Presented material in Barcelona, Spain (2006).
-   Authored, designed, and published ***Memoria Descriptiva,*** Relocation Project of the community of
    El Hornito, which became permanent reference in the library at the Faculty of Architecture.

EDUCATION

Diploma, **Architect,** University of Apure, Cabimas, Venezuela.

Completed highest level of English courses at Santa Fe University, Santa Fe, NM
Introductory computer and English courses, University of Apure, Cabimas, Venezuela
Courses in Excel for Windows, Beginning and Advanced AutoCAD.

second language. As you read the Career Highlights section, you learn quickly that an architect's activities are essentially achievements because of the creative nature of those activities. The variety of projects and the section on Patents and Publications are impressive.

Education/Training

Resumes at a Glance

SAMANTHA McLAUGHLIN

Prekindergarten Teacher

454 Swordfish Drive • Brentwood, NY 55555 • (555) 555-0000 • no1teacher@planet.edu

"Did you hear the good news? Samantha McLaughlin wants to teach on Long Island!"

CERTIFICATION	New York State Permanent Certification in Elementary Education, K–6 New York City Permanent Certification in Early Childhood Education, Pre-K–6
EDUCATION	**Master of Science, Elementary Education** LONG ISLAND UNIVERSITY AT C.W. POST, Brentwood, NY **Bachelor of Arts, Elementary Education** ENGLEWOOD COLLEGE, Englewood, NY

TEACHING EXPERIENCE

2005–present

Prekindergarten
2007–present
First Grade
2006–2007
Kindergarten
2005–2006

TEACHER
John Kennedy Elementary School, P.S. 18, Jamaica, NY

- Manage a structured, stimulating classroom with responsibility in all areas of teaching, assessment, behavior modification, and coordination of academic and social activities.
- Create a fun, warm, and exciting atmosphere where children play and learn while strengthening skills in areas of fine/gross motor development, math, reading, and writing readiness, and acclimate to daily routines and the school environment.
- Plan, develop, and institute educational activities that promote quality teaching in accordance with New York State teaching standards and Bloom's Taxonomy.

Thematic Units/Differentiated Lessons

Jungle Habitat, Farm Animals, Growth of a Seed, Shapes & Colors, Dental Hygiene, Martin Luther King, Self-Expression, The Four Seasons, and Ocean Life

Employ an integrated approach towards teaching, utilizing the following methods:

Charts/Diagrams	*Learning Centers*	*Poetry/Reading*	*Compare/Contrast*
Writing/Big Books	*Cooperative Learning*	*Story Mapping*	*Five Senses*
Sentence Strips	*Group Discussions*	*Brainstorming*	*Bulletin Boards*
Sight Vocabulary	*Games/Puzzles*	*Role Playing*	*Cooking Projects*

- Proactively communicate with parents to acknowledge superior work and areas of concern through discussion, newsletters, progress reports, telephone calls, and home visits; encourage parent involvement/volunteer assistance throughout the school year.
- Collaborate weekly with musicians to provide children with basic music appreciation through exposure to a diverse range of musical instruments and lyrics.
- Successfully use enrichment activities and behavior-modification techniques as a motivator for completing projects, following rules, and maintaining classroom conduct.
- Encourage group participation, and develop students' character exercising a strong respect for self, others, the community, and diversity.
- Recognized as the only teacher to attend PTA meetings in three years, attend Parent-Teacher Conferences, and coordinate Meet the Teacher Night and monthly field trips.

2001–2005	**PREKINDERGARTEN TEACHER** St. Agnes Head Start, Bay Shore, NY
2000–2001	**PREKINDERGARTEN TEACHER** Lutheran Elementary School, Massapequa, NY
1987–2000	**PREKINDERGARTEN TEACHER** Hauppauge Freedom Day Care Center, Hauppauge, NY

33

Combination. *Ann Baehr, East Islip, New York*

The writer made a fun resume for a teacher who was changing districts. She displayed a catchy statement at the top and used a custom logo for the name. Note the strong teaching experience.

Sheilah J. Curtis

email@email.net

21 Grove Place
Ridge Township, MA 00000

Home: (555) 555-5555
Cell: (555) 555-4444

Lesson Planning / Student Evaluation / MCAS Preparation / Program Development & Implementation

EDUCATION / CERTIFICATION

Michigan State College, Township, MI
Bachelor of Science, Education, 2011
Majors: Elementary Education / Natural Science & Mathematics
Elementary Teaching Certification Grades 1–6

Alpha Phi Chapter of Alpha Upsilon Alpha, the honor society of the International Reading Association

Tri Beta Life Sciences Honor Society

Who's Who Among Students in American Colleges and Universities, 2011

QUALIFICATIONS

- Plan and develop daily lessons for up to 24 students in multicultural classrooms.
- Interact with mainstream special education students.
- Develop and implement learning units to integrate unique learning models.
- Championed innovative program-development project *"Words on Vacation,"* a communication skills–based strategy utilized to prepare students for MCAS testing.
- Expand learning styles, IEPs, and educational plans through design and development of hands-on, inquiry-based techniques.
- Establish and demonstrate interdisciplinary thematic units on subjects including biodiversity, biographies, and rocks and minerals.
- Actively participate in parent conferences, student evaluations, core meetings, and grade and departmental team meetings.

TEACHER ASSISTANT/STUDENT TEACHING EXPERIENCE

Potter Road Elementary School, Framingham, MA   2/12–Present
Grade 4 Classroom

Longfellow School, Cambridge, MA   9/11–12/11
Grade 6 Classroom

Johnson Elementary School, Natick, MA   5/10–12/10
Grade 1 Classroom

Hemenway Elementary School, Framingham, MA   12/06–4/10
Grade 4 Classroom

PROFESSIONAL MEMBERSHIPS

International Reading Association
Massachusetts Marine Educators Association
Massachusetts Reading Association

34

Combination. *Rosemarie Ginsberg, Franklin, Massachusetts*

The resume writer put an Education/Certification section, list of honors, and a bulleted Qualifications list at the top of this resume in order to highlight the strengths of this recent college graduate. Her student teaching experience was put lower on the page.

Elizabeth Swanson

3461 N. Drake Ave. #324
Chicago, IL 60624

773-555-2166
eswanson4@ymail.com

Respected **Early Childhood Educator** with proven leadership skills both in and out of the classroom. Committed to creating a positive atmosphere that influences students' attitudes toward future learning and provides a solid foundation to help them reach their potential. Adept at cultivating parental involvement in the classroom. Possess early childhood training.

Professional Experience

IMMACULATE CONCEPTION CATHOLIC SCHOOL • Chicago, Illinois • 1994–2012
Prekindergarten Teacher

◆ Taught all-day prekindergarten program to approximately 24 students from diverse ethnic and socioeconomic backgrounds; created environment to effectively meet students' cognitive, social, emotional and physical needs.

◆ Developed and implemented early childhood curriculum; adapted instructional delivery to accommodate students' individual learning styles and functioning levels. Ensured complete preparation for promotion to kindergarten.

◆ Supervised teacher aides; solicited and coordinated parent volunteers in the classroom.

Extracurricular Activities (current and past)

◆ Service Learning Liaison with Chicago Public Schools
◆ Faculty Representative to Immaculate Conception School Board (1996–2003)
◆ Public Relations Committee
◆ Primary Department Chairperson
◆ Cochair of PTA

◆ Principal Search Committee (2000)
◆ Boys & Girls Night Out (originated program)
◆ Yearbook Committee
◆ Cheerleading Coach (7th–8th grade)
◆ Staff Social Director
◆ Garden Club Facilitator
◆ Art Teacher for Summertime Days

Related Experience

CHICAGO PUBLIC SCHOOLS • Chicago, Illinois • 1987–1994
Playtime Regional Director (1989–1994)

• Interviewed, selected, trained, managed and evaluated 32 leaders for summer Playtime programs.
• Contributed to program planning and organization; planned and conducted workshops.
• Interviewed and placed 250–300 program workers each summer.

Adult Education Instructor (1988–1989)

• Taught basic education to mentally and emotionally impaired adults.

Playtime Leader and **Assistant Leader** (1987–1988)

Education

ILLINOIS STATE UNIVERSITY
Bachelor of Science (1994)

• Child Development major/Chemistry minor

LOYOLA UNIVERSITY
Liberal Arts course work (1987–1989)

Continuing Education

XAVIER UNIVERSITY
Performance Learning Systems (1999)

• 10 graduate hours

CHICAGO STATE UNIVERSITY
Early Childhood Planned Program (1995–1998)

• 20 graduate hours

Certification

◆ Illinois Elementary Teaching Certificate
  • Early childhood–qualified

Affiliation

◆ National Association for the Education of Young Children

35

Combination. *Janet L. Beckstrom, Flint, Michigan*

Because of a personality conflict with new school management, this teacher had to seek other work. The resume writer emphasized with diamond bullets the teacher's vast experience and potential. See Cover Letter 9.

Judy Cassidy

123 Main Street, Anytown, USA 19000-0000
(555) 555-5555 ■ JudyC@kmail.net

PROFILE

ELEMENTARY EDUCATOR with more than 20 years of experience fostering academic learning and enhancing critical-thinking abilities. Incorporate effective cooperative learning techniques and unique classroom management style to establish creative and stimulating classroom environment. Dedicated, resourceful teacher skilled in building rapport and respect with students and student teachers.

Honored with **New Teacher Mentor Award** for Outstanding Service (2012)

"Miss Cassidy is an exceptional teacher. She is respectful to and of her students, and that respect is reciprocated. Using a variety of materials and techniques, Miss Cassidy challenges her students to excel. Her classroom is a warm, nurturing atmosphere where children are called to be their best selves."   A.F., School Administrator

EDUCATION AND CERTIFICATIONS

Instructional II—Permanent Certification, State of Pennsylvania (2010)

Master of Arts—**ANY UNIVERSITY** (2002)

B.S., Elementary Education—**ANY STATE COLLEGE** (1996)

SELECTED CAREER HIGHLIGHTS

- Successful in developing and executing **Everyday Math Program** at John Smith Elementary School (2007). Implementation of program resulted in overall math grades improvement by 180 points in 2010 *(versus previous-year scores)* along with instituting greater math awareness and mathematical thinking among all students. Participated in ongoing staff development and district training sessions to ensure utilization of hands-on, cooperative learning approach along with reinforcement and assessment techniques.

- Selected to serve as **Middle States Team Evaluator** for Brooklyn Diocese School System (2006). Collaborated with four colleagues in accreditation process comprised of interviewing teachers, meeting with committee, writing evaluation report, and creating recommended action plan. Conducted comprehensive academic assessment in similar capacity as **Catholic Elementary School Evaluator** for Diocese of Camden (2003).

- Directed and facilitated **Multidisciplinary Learning Project** at John Smith Elementary School to meet promotional requirements for students graduating to fifth grade (2007–2010). Through intensive interaction, students developed research, writing, and computer skills to accomplish long-term school project *(with City Year members)* and effectively strengthen individual student knowledge, pride, and enthusiasm with 90% passing rate.

PROFESSIONAL TEACHING EXPERIENCE

Metropolitan Public School District, John Smith Elementary School   2007–Present

ELEMENTARY TEACHER—Fourth Grade

Plan, implement, and evaluate various curriculum areas. Encourage cooperative learning and peer interaction, and increase achievement levels among disadvantaged and challenged students. Appointed by principal as Grade Chairman and Mentor (2008–2011).

continued

36

Combination. *Darlene Dassy, Reading, Pennsylvania*

This teacher had been a nun serving the Catholic community for more than 20 years. Nuns are moved around a lot, and she didn't want her resume to give the false impression that she was

PROFESSIONAL TEACHING EXPERIENCE (continued)

Sacred Heart School   2003–2006

ELEMENTARY TEACHER—Third Grade

Instructed students in subject areas of reading, integrated language arts, religion, and social studies. Coordinated and implemented language arts program for first- to fourth-grade students.

State Area Parochial School System   1997–2003

   ELEMENTARY TEACHER—Third and Fourth Grade

   - Saint Joseph Regional School
   - Blessed Sacrament School
   - Our Lady of Perpetual Help

Metropolitan Parochial School System   1986–1996

   ELEMENTARY TEACHER—First and Second Grade

   - Immaculate Heart of Mary School
   - Our Lady of the Holy Souls School
   - Saint Timothy School

TEACHING TESTIMONIALS

"Judith has, from the outset, displayed a level of professional competence and a striving for professional development which has benefited her students, our staff, and the entire school community in concrete ways. She introduced and implemented a variety of innovative classroom management strategies, such as Workshop Way and Integrated Language Arts, having been the first to pilot such a program in our school. She has challenged and motivated students to achievement and activities which have not only developed each child's personal gifts and talents, but also developed cooperative learning strategies to foster collaboration and interaction among her students."

                                                                                G.S., Principal

"Judy's professionalism, enthusiasm, and talent as a teacher are evident on a daily basis. Judy employs a thematic approach, and the varied learning experiences the children have to showcase their talents are not just one-time activities but related to all curriculum areas. Judy is comfortable with and flexible in following many different styles of administration and has been recommended to assume leadership roles many times during her career."   F.B., School Administrator

PROFESSIONAL DEVELOPMENT COURSES

Attended and participated in various courses from 2006–2012, including

   - The Middle Years Literacy Framework
   - Middle Years Balanced Literacy
   - Academy of Reading Program
   - Bringing Curriculum to Life
   - Accelerated Reading Program
   - Professional Education for Central-East AAO
   - Rigby Guided Reading & Literature Circles
   - Improving Decision-Making/Values Clarification
   - Improving Ability to Communicate Mathematically
   - Everyday Math Program & PowerPoint for Educators

a "job hopper." The writer therefore focused on the teacher's accomplishments, credentials, and testimonials so as not to draw attention to dates of employment. The administrators' testimonials near both the beginning and the end are tributes to the quality of her teaching.

Allie L. Rees

alrees@yahoo.com
Home Address: 30 Summit Trail ▼ Sparta, New York 12345 ▼ 555.123.4567
School Address: 26 East State Street ▼ The Plains, Ohio 45780 ▼ 740.797.0000

" ... Wow! Very attractive and engaging materials ... love to see students 'beg' to learn using her created materials for the Learning Center ... confident and positive; her students' self-esteem was enhanced by this ... exhibited an excellent knowledge base and understanding of the nature and needs of students with special needs ... she will be an asset in any educational environment."

~ Excerpts from Student Teaching Evaluations

OBJECTIVE

Special Education Teacher

Enthusiastic and creative educator offering a solid educational background, including B.S. in Education with a major in Special Education. Successful student-teaching experience and observations as evidenced by excellent evaluations from supervising teachers and university professors. Skilled in meeting the needs of special-education students—experienced in working with IAT, MFE, and IEP planning and implementation. Additional experience in testing and assessment.

EDUCATION & HONORS

OHIO UNIVERSITY, Athens, Ohio (June 2012)
Bachelor of Science in Education ▼ Major in Special Education, Mild Moderate
Education GPA: 3.52/4.0 ▼ Overall GPA: 3.24/4.0 ▼ Successfully passed PRAXIS exam
Kappa Delta Pi Education Fraternity ▼ Dean's List ▼ POWER (Nationally Certified Peer Health Educator)

Computer Skills
Computer proficient—experienced in use of various forms of assistive technology, PowerPoint, Microsoft Office 7/XP, Internet and e-mail functions

RELATED EXPERIENCE

Student Teacher—MORRISON ELEMENTARY SCHOOL, Athens, Ohio (January–March 2012)
- ▼ Developed and implemented lesson plans in K–4 Resource Room in conjunction with supervising teachers.
- ▼ Established attainable educational goals for students, which promoted personal and educational growth.
- ▼ Participated in IAT, MFE, and IEP planning sessions with parents, teachers, and administrators.
- ▼ Tailored educational curriculum to IEPs for children with a variety of disabilities.
- ▼ Gained experience utilizing the Stevenson program for presenting phonic patterns and testing.
- ▼ Created an entire learning center based on IEP goals—used Pokemon theme to significantly increase children's interest and participation.

Field Experience—MORRISON ELEMENTARY, Athens, Ohio (Spring 2011)
Field Experience—THE PLAINS ELEMENTARY, The Plains, Ohio (Fall 2010)
- ▼ Gained valuable experience observing a variety of teaching techniques and implementing daily lesson plans in diverse settings (K–6 classrooms).
- ▼ Served as a classroom aide and assisted with tutoring and assessing/teaching groups of 1–14 students with mild to moderate disabilities.
- ▼ Participated in data collection for the Positive Behavior Supports program implemented at Luke Middle School in Luke Valley, Ohio.

Child Care Counselor—WILLOWGLEN ACADEMY, Newton, New Jersey (Academic Breaks 2008–2010)
- ▼ Counseled children with severe behavior disorders.
- ▼ Gained experience working with autistic children while serving as a teacher's aide and working in group homes.

COMMUNITY INVOLVEMENT

- ▼ Tri-County Mental Health and Counseling—Volunteered with patients and planned recreational activities.
- ▼ Good Works—Volunteered at this temporary homeless shelter.

37

Combination. *Melissa L. Kasler, Athens, Ohio*

A challenge with education resumes for college graduates with the same credentials and experience is to separate an applicant from the competition. Quotations from evaluations can do just that.

Lara Carson

Home: 555.555.5555 • Mobile: 555.555.4444

555 South Hill Road • Los Angeles, CA 55555
E-mail: laracarson@hotmail.com

Professional Endorsements:

"Lara has been teaching Spanish to my children for the past year and is an exceptional teacher. She has boundless energy and patience, and the children respond to her with incredible enthusiasm. They are extremely motivated to learn Spanish because that is Lara's language, and they love anything having to do with her."

Private Client

***

"Lara has the ability to teach both the complex and simple aspects of Spanish quickly and efficiently. She understands how to use conversation about everyday subjects to get across vocabulary and grammar. Her empathy and sense of humor coupled with professional bearing make her an exemplary teacher."

Colleague

***

"Lara kept us wanting to learn more and looking forward to the next class. I am excited to take another class."

Student

***

"Lara is enthusiastic about teaching and energizes her class. She is fantastic and gave me great skills to continue on with."

Student

TEACHING PROFESSIONAL — SPANISH LANGUAGE

Creative, enthusiastic and dedicated native-speaking instructor who skillfully uses play, art, music and other tools to engage students in the language-learning experience.

- Excellent lesson-planning, organizational and presentation strengths.
- Skilled in teaching a range of students, from children to adult learners.
- Able to tailor instruction to individual learning needs and assist students in reaching their learning goals.

EXPERIENCE

INTERNATIONAL LANGUAGE INSTITUTE, Los Angeles, CA
Private language school that offers World Language, ESOL (English for Speakers of Other Languages) and ESOL Teacher Certificate programs. Accredited by the Council for Continuing Education and Training.

Spanish Instructor (2011 to present)

- ▶ Provide language instruction to nonnative speakers, including business professionals and other adult learners at a language-based institute.

- ▶ Use multiple teaching techniques, focusing on speaking, pronunciation and listening in a learner-centered and participatory environment.

- ▶ Effective at teaching students of different skill levels and creating a positive, engaging learning experience.

Private Spanish Instructor, Los Angeles, CA (2010 to present)

- ▶ Develop instructional materials and teach Spanish to private students of varying abilities.

MEMORIAL HOSPITAL, Los Angeles, CA
Medical Records — Office Volunteer (2009 to 2011)

PRIOR TEACHING EXPERIENCE

UNIVERSITY OF MEXICO CITY, Mexico City, Mexico
Instructor (1999 to 2009)

- ▶ Developed curriculum and taught courses in the cytology program at a major health institute.

EDUCATION

B.S. in Cytology (U.S. equivalent), 1999
National Institute of Medicine, Mexico City, Mexico

Additional: Completed intensive teaching training at the International Language Institute.

38

Combination. *Louise Garver, Broad Brook, Connecticut*

This part-time Los Angeles teacher wanted a full-time position in Florida. The resume writer included glowing quotations, and the teacher received a job offer from every school she applied to. See Cover Letter 2.

CERTIFICATIONS:	**Alexandra Stack**		
Elementary N–6 Special Ed. K–12	931 Columbia Street ❧ Poughkeepsie, NY 00000	astack22@dmail.net	(555) 555-5555

Objective

Secondary Special Education Teaching Position
Society benefits when all individuals are able to achieve their maximum learning potential.

Spirited, optimistic, and reflective individual with an outstanding attitude and a strong motivation to develop a caring learning community where students with exceptionalities can more fully participate. Offer positive interaction skills and the creativity necessary to accommodate unique needs. Respect a broad range of instructional methodologies and prepared to take collaborative approaches to teaching.

→ Capable of making sound educational judgments (formed by theory, research, and best practices).

→ Eager to promote understanding/respect for individual differences and unique learning needs.

→ Skilled at gaining the trust and respect of youth and conveying confidence in their abilities.

→ Possess a sound understanding of developmental issues and exposed to a wide range of disabilities.

Education

Union College, Troy, NY	**May 2011**
B.A. in Psychology / Special Education / Elementary Education	GPA 3.49

Herkimer Community College, Herkimer, NY	**January 2007**
A.A. in Liberal Arts and Science—Humanities and Social Sciences	

Student Teaching

Connor Stevens High School (Westchester CSD)	1/11 to 3/11

Reading I & Reading II (Special Education)
Formulated intensive reading lessons, incorporating multiple modalities and engaging *all* students—inviting them to listen, share, explore, and reflect. Utilized Orton Gillingham methods and devised creative approaches to integrating literacy and technology. Established well-organized classroom routines, set appropriate academic expectations, and provided positive experiences to build self-esteem.

Titusville Elementary School (Mohawk CSD)	4/11 to 5/11

Sixth Grade (Inclusion Class)
Structured a positive and supportive environment that maximized student participation and success. Commended on effectiveness in teaching both small and large groups. Created integrated math and science lessons and made appropriate adaptations to address individual learning styles.

Freedom Plains Elementary School (Hyde Park)	9/10 to 12/10

Preschool (3 & 4 year olds)
Developed age-appropriate centers that incorporated proactive social-skill activities. Developed lessons that focused on reading and math readiness and incorporated enrichment activities. Utilized many hands-on activities, manipulatives, and discovery learning to develop large motor skills.

Additional Areas of Experience

- Devising developmentally appropriate lessons
- Cross-disciplinary coordinated service delivery
- Lexia Learning Systems/phonics-based programs
- Structuring a positive, encouraging environment
- Establishing clear expectations and class routines
- Adapting instruction based on ability levels

Volunteer Experience

Titusville School, *Cafeteria Aide / Playground Monitor*	2008 to 2009
Mohawk Elementary School, *Parent Helper, Kindergarten*	2007 to 2008
Pine Plains School, *Lunchroom Aide / Playground Monitor*	2002 to 2003

39

Combination. *Kristin M. Coleman, Poughkeepsie, New York*

This resume may look difficult to create, but it can be done as a three-column table in which the first column has the headings, the second is narrow for space, and the third is wide for the information.

TRAVIS KENSETH

9803 Clinton Avenue ▪ Lubbock, TX 00000 ▪ (000) 000-0000 ▪ name@ntws.net

FOCUS & OVERVIEW	**Career Target: Secondary Education Instructor & Coach** ▪ *Profile*—Enthusiastic, dependable teaching candidate with solid knowledge base/skills in instruction and coaching-related functions that include instructional strategies, scouting, student relations, special populations, and professional ethics. ▪ *Evaluations*—Earned recognition from university professors and supervisors in employment positions for consistently meeting and exceeding expectations. ▪ *General Traits*—Effective communicator and multi-tasker; adapt readily to changing circumstances. Value diversity within school groups; favor student-centered teaching. ▪ *Specific Skills*—Proficient in MS Office suite ▪ First-Aid Certification—Responding to Emergencies ▪ Strong knowledge in and advocate of functionalism theory in sports.
EDUCATION	**Teacher Certification Program** ▪ NORTHLAND COLLEGE, Northland, TX ❑ Expected completion in 5/12 for secondary education certification program. ❑ Engaged in combination of lectures, class assignments, and formal observations. **BS in Kinesiology, 2009** ▪ UNIVERSITY OF TEXAS, Austin, TX *Key Courses & Projects:* ❑ **Administrative Theory/Practice in Athletic and Sport Regulatory Organizations**—Analyzed process for securing professional position within sports industry; examined ethical, legal, philosophical, and professional development issues. ❑ **Facilities, Equipment, and Budget for Athletics**—Created and presented plan to class for construction of sports facility, including blueprints, materials, and cost analysis. Utilized software, Internet research, and phone calls to local businesses. ❑ **Movement for Special Populations**—Worked one-on-one with disabled student in locomotor and object control activities, followed by creation of adapted physical education lesson plan. Gained insight into mainstreaming of special ed. students. ❑ **Coaching Football**—Sent on assignment to scout TCU-UTEP football game. Applied extensive prior study of scouting techniques and proper formats to follow in charting plays, analyzing individual performances, and summarizing findings. *Additional Upper-Level Courses:* Sociology of Sports ▪ Coaching Football ▪ Motor Behavior ▪ Psychology of Sports Physiological Bases of Exercise & Sports ▪ Coaching Individual Sports **AA & AS Degrees, 2006/2005** ▪ WEATHERFORD COLLEGE, Weatherford, TX
WORK EXPERIENCE	**Customer Service Associate** ▪ HOME DEPOT, Austin, TX (2006–Present) ❑ Recognized frequently by customers for providing solutions to meet individual needs, leading to repeat/referral business and requests for personal service. **Courier** ▪ TEXAS BANK, Austin, TX (2004–2006) ❑ Managed multiple tasks effectively in deadline-driven environment. Delivered inter-office mail, transferred daily deposits, and prepared supplies for all branches. **Customer Service Representative** ▪ RENTER'S CHOICE, Austin, TX (2003–2004) ❑ Maintained excellent record of resolving problems and handling stressful situations that involved collection activities and challenging customers.

40

Combination. *Daniel J. Dorotik Jr., Lubbock, Texas*

The applicant's work experience was unrelated to his career target, so the writer emphasized skills and school-related project work. Shading helps distinguish headings from the information.

Meets Federal Highly Qualified Teaching Standards   *Available for relocation*

CARLTON MARNER
214 Central Street • Montgomery, Alabama 36100 • cm200@sss.com • ☏ 334.555.5555

WHAT I CAN OFFER YOUR SCHOOL AS A **HISTORY TEACHER** _____

- The **character** to establish and maintain classroom discipline.

- The **academic background** to make my subject come alive for your students.

- The **tact** to establish strong "partnerships" with peers, parents, administrators, and students.

EDUCATION AND RELEVANT INSERVICE DEVELOPMENT _____

- **Masters of Education in History Education,** Corona State University, Montgomery, Alabama, Aug 09

  Earned this degree while working 40 hours a week by day and carrying a full academic load at night. GPA: 3.75.

- **B.S., History,** Mark State University—Montgomery, Montgomery, Alabama, Aug 07. *GPA 3.95+,* **Dean's List.** *One of very few college students to be inducted into two national honor societies for* **academic achievement.**

- More than 32 hours of the following **inservice training** over the last two years alone:

DAT Inservice	Special Education Issues	Bullying Issues
Writing Assessment	Gifted Characteristics	Co-operative Discipline
School Safety	Yes, We Can Get Along	SAT 10
Special Education Team Development	SAT Testing and Interpreting Scores	Integrating Technology in the Classroom
7th Grade Writing Assessment	Effective Classroom Management	ESL
Teacher Mentorship Program		

- "Guidance Counseling," U.S. Army, five weeks, 85. *Selected by senior decision makers for this course. One of very few to have experience requirements waived.*

RECENT WORK HISTORY WITH EXAMPLES OF PROBLEMS SOLVED _____

- **School Teacher,** Tether Middle School, Montgomery, Alabama, Aug 09–Present

  Tether has an average total enrollment of 760, of which I teach five classes averaging 30 students per class, including mainstreamed special education students. AY is nine months.

  Turned around, gently but firmly, a disruptive special education student whose behavior had thwarted other teachers for months. Parents had become so frustrated that they sued—and won—to keep him enrolled. *Outcomes:* He **met every class's academic standards and passed**—a great confidence builder for him.

More indicators of performance your school can use ☞

41

Combination. *Don Orlando, Montgomery, Alabama*

This writer successfully presents a fresh approach in resumes. Information other than the candidate's name is at the top of the first page. A phone symbol signals the phone number. "What I

Carlton Marner	**History Teacher**	334.555.5555

Took on a challenge others shied away from: teaching a failing student whose parents had pulled him from school. Volunteered to work closely with school counselors to cover the entire curriculum at his home, after normal hours. *Outcomes:* **He's now learning at his grade level.**

Stepped in smoothly when an influx of Korean students, with nearly no proficiency in English, were mainlined throughout the school. With my wife's volunteer help, soon gave the newcomers confidence to learn to their potential. *Outcomes:* **Every Korean student getting straight "A's"** — after only one year with us.

Joined with one other faculty member to take on the additional duty of guiding the Student Council. Took the lead to reestablish close ties with community leaders. *Outcomes:* **Students raised nearly $5K for needy children over the last two years.**

- Full-time student. Completed **B.S., History** and **Masters in Education**, 05–09

- *More than 20 years of experience in positions of increasing responsibility as a non-commissioned officer in the U.S. Army, serving in these capacities from 81 to 05:*

  Overhauled an education program I inherited that wasn't giving our team members the skills they needed to reach high school students. **Did the needs analysis** and then **built the right curriculum.** *Outcomes:* In three months, our group turned in its **best performance ever.** All done without spending an extra dime.

  Reached out to faculty and administrators in local minority schools. Found a way to **equip their guidance counselors** with a **comprehensive assessment instrument** and the training they needed to use it well. Sponsored career days. *Outcomes:* **Demand** for our participation **grew steadily.**

LICENSURE _____

- Certified 6th- through 12th-grade history teacher, State of Alabama, expires 14.

COMPUTER LITERACY _____

- **Expert** in proprietary program that **matches people to jobs** and **assesses student values and aptitudes.**

- Fully proficient in Microsoft PowerPoint, Excel, and Word and Internet search methods.

SKILLS USEFUL TO A DIVERSE STUDENT BODY _____

- Working knowledge of Korean language and culture.

Can Offer…" introduces the first main section. Comments in italic appear throughout the resume. Solutions to problems narrated in prose paragraphs are indicated as "Outcomes," with key information enhanced with boldfacing—a novel way to present achievements.

BRYSON CARSON

265 Charlotte Street
Cookville, NC 00000

(555) 000-7893 *home*
(555) 111-7893 *cell*
bcarson@hometown.net

HISTORY TEACHER
North Carolina License, Social Studies 9–12

PROFILE	Proactive, uncompromising focus on improving reading, writing, and critical-thinking skills. Use flexibility, resourcefulness, and organizational and interpersonal skills to assist that learning through a positive, encouraging environment.

Strengths

"A page of history is worth a volume of logic."—Oliver Wendell Holmes

- Capable teacher thoroughly grounded in U.S., Middle East, World, and European history.
- Rapport-builder with parents, able to gain their involvement, trust, and respect in creating a participative environment.
- Adept, available, and adaptable classroom manager—combine discipline plan with effective procedures and varied lessons to attract the inattentive and enforce student accountability.
- Student motivator—can use cooperative learning, jigsaw, and other student-directed, process learning techniques to foster a team spirit and build teamwork and goal-setting skills.
- Develop useful daily lesson plans and instructional resources.
- Friendly, interactive, dependable.
- Some fluency in Spanish (can read Spanish newspaper).

EDUCATION

B.A., History, Magna cum Laude, December 2011
North Carolina University, Polk, NC

Coursework

- U.S. History, Medieval Europe, Politics of the Middle East, Political Science, Chinese History (Revolutionary China), Afro-American History, Human Rights & International Politics, Humanities. Dean's List every eligible semester.

Student Teaching

"I teach skill in asking questions through my skill in asking the right questions...."

- Hall High School, spring and fall 2011—11th-grade college-prep classes in U.S. history. Selected to teach AP U.S. history class due to knowledge of material.
  - Contributions included judging senior projects, proctoring end-of-course tests, and sponsoring the fledgling Debate Club.
  - Because my co-op was on the school improvement team, was able to observe planning and goal-setting functions in the effort to meet constantly changing requirements.
  - Participated positively in parent-teacher conferences.

Honors & Affiliations

Cited by department faculty for original, critical thinking....

- Selected for Phi Alpha Theta History National Honor Society (high GPA and faculty recommendation).
- Selected by History Department faculty for the Mike Bolson History Scholarship as a promising student in the field of history, despite being on an education track.
- Participant, NCU History Association.
- Alpha Phi Omega National Service Fraternity—Chapter President; as Vice President of Service, initiated projects involving boys' and girls' clubs; fund-raising for pediatric brain tumors; highway beautification; food bank.

42

Combination. *Dayna Feist, Asheville, North Carolina*

The applicant was a man in his 50s whose previous careers were in the Navy, fishing, and manufacturing. When his manufacturing job moved to Mexico, he returned to college for a degree

bcarson@hometown.net · (555) 111-7893 *cell* · (555) 000-7893 *home*   **BRYSON CARSON**

Prior Education	**Diploma, Welding** (one-year program), 1988 WNC Technical Community College Coursework in Anthropology, Biology, Spanish, 1981 University of Massachusetts—Boston

---

PRIOR EXPERIENCE

BOILER OPERATOR: Culverton Textiles, Foster, NC—1989–2006
Operated steam and electric generating utility for largest textile mill of its kind in the world, on 10 acres, with its own waste-treatment and water-filtration system; a self-contained mini-city, it generated much of its own power. Member of 2-man team: managed electrical control room, maintenance, welding, machinery repair, pipefitting.

ENGINEER: 100-foot Bluestocking fishing boat, Gloucester, MA—1979–1988

MACHINIST MATE: United States Navy—1975–1979
Trained Navy personnel (including firemen and 3rd class petty officers) to work with tools and operate equipment.

COMMUNITY REINVESTMENT

- Coached Roller Hockey for boys' and girls' clubs, ages 13–18, in league competition.
- Tutor, Afterschool Club, Salvation Army.
- Big Brothers/Big Sisters, 1988–1991. Mentored 7-year-old boy (gardening, movies, sports, homework) until he moved to another state.
- Member of church Inquiry Committee—answer questions to assist one in deciding whether to join the church; prepare lesson plans and curriculum for those interested in doing so.

under a special teachers' program to teach history. His goal was a highly competitive position at the school where he student-taught. The resume writer sought to show how this individual will bring "an interesting mixture of authority, geniality, and intelligence to the classroom."

Barbara Joanne Blake B.A., B.Ed.

2222 Augusta View S.W., Pinehurst, Alberta A1A 1A1
Phone: (444) 222-8888
bblake@ontario.net.ca

Visual Arts Teacher
Intermediate & Senior

> *"Mrs. Blake is one of the most outstanding teachers I have met in my 22 years of teaching."*

Creative and dedicated Visual Arts teacher committed to creating meaningful and stimulating art programs to improve students' ability, creativity, appreciation, perception, awareness, concentration, confidence, and motivation. Exhaustive teaching experience in a wide range of visual media. Skilled in designing arts programs to complement core courses. Able to inspire children to stretch themselves and their work. Extensive leadership experience in school, volunteer, and community activities.

Teachable media include basic and advanced programs in

- Clay
- Free Form
- Group of Seven / Inuit Art
- Paint / Pencil
- Mixed Media
- Van Gogh
- Wire Sculpture
- Photography
- War / Militaria

> *"She demonstrates an enthusiasm for the subject matter which is infectious."*

EDUCATION & PROFESSIONAL DEVELOPMENT

Visual Arts—Part 3, Specialist	OISE, University of Augusta
Integrated Arts	Ontario Arts Education Institute
Meaningful Activities to Generate Interesting Classrooms	O.P.S.T.F.
English as a Second Language—Part 1	Pinehurst University
Canadian Art History	University of Ontario
B.Ed.—Visual Arts 2 / School Librarianship	University of Ontario
B.A.—Fine Arts	University of Manitoba

TEACHING EXPERIENCE

Developed and implemented dynamic lessons designed to teach a rich variety of artistic techniques, appeal to multiple intelligences, and enrich student learning. Established dynamic learning environments that highlight student work and stimulate creative expression. Introduced and led Intermediate art clubs ("Creatots") that allowed students to create art projects for school and charitable initiatives (posters, play backdrops, etc.).

> *"Barbara's creative mind, knowledge, and teaching ability combine to produce student work that is totally reflective of the keen interest, desire, knowledge, and skill level she has developed in her students."*

Placements include the following:

Bayridge Hill Elementary School, Berry Hill, Ontario **Visual Arts Teacher**—Grades 6, 7, & 8	2003–2011
Holy Trinity Catholic School, Berry Hill, Ontario **Visual Arts Teacher**—Grades 9 to O.A.C.	Oct.–Nov. 2003
Bayridge Secondary School, Berry Hill, Ontario **Visual Arts Teacher**—Grades 9 to O.A.C.	2002–2003
Augusta Region Board of Education—Area Central **Occasional Teacher**	1999–2002
St. Avenue Secondary High School, Sarnia, Ontario **Visual Arts Teacher / Teacher-Librarian**—Grades 9, 10, & 11	1985–1989

Continues

43

Combination. *Ross Macpherson, Whitby, Ontario, Canada*

Quotations in the left column of each page acquaint the reader with this teacher's abilities, enthusiasm, creativity, artistic skills, concern for students, effectiveness, helpfulness as a team

Barbara Joanne Blake   (444) 222-8888   Page 2

...

"Barbara uses her incredible ability as an artist and art teacher to affect every aspect of school life."

...

"[Barbara] has demonstrated extraordinary qualities of respect, dedication, and commitment to her students, to fellow human beings, and to her community."

...

"The work displayed consistently by her students is to be marvelled at!"

...

CURRICULUM DEVELOPMENT

Art Action Team: Augusta Region District School Board (ARDSB)—Selected to participate in the planning and facilitation of art workshops for teachers across the board.

Van Gogh: A Guidebook for Looking at Art, Grades 1–8—Worked with ARDSB Art Consultant to develop an integrated curriculum kit on Vincent Van Gogh, including history, books, materials, prints, and activities.

Teach Art 3: A Visual Arts Curriculum Guide—Invited by Heather Hearst to participate in focus group contributing to the development of a Grade 3 Art curriculum.

Outcome-Based Learning Study Team—Served as Art Representative on school committee developing an outcome-based learning curriculum.

ARTS ADVOCACY

- Developed and directed *Arts Alive: Series 2003 Performing Arts Program for Junior Kindergarten–Grade 8.*
- Coordinated *Careers in Art* After-School Speakers Series.
- Coordinated *Portraits of Our Past Art Show* in partnership with the Town of Berry Hill Heritage Centre.
- Coordinated Annual *Celebrate the Arts Night.*
- Presenter: Outdoor Education Weekend (Topic: Natural Dyes).

SCHOOL & BOARD COMMITTEE INVOLVEMENT

- 10th Anniversary Committee (school mural)—Bayridge Hill Elementary School.
- Member of ARTSLINK Action Team Committee (ARDSB Millennium Project)— Secured Federal funding for program and coordinated school art shows boardwide.
- Committee Representative—ARDSB *Together We're Better* Conference.
- Intermediate Division Career Day Committee.
- School Fundraising Committee.
- Arts Representative—Bayridge Hill Elementary School.
- Staff Representative—Bayridge Hill Community School Advisory Council.
- Anti-Bullying Conference—Staff Support.

EXTRACURRICULAR INVOLVEMENT

- Coordinated the Alternate Winter Sport Activity Program.
- Decorated display cases and bulletin boards to showcase student artwork and holiday themes.
- Annual Graduation Exercises Committee Coordinator (decorations).
- Coordinated art displays for Education Week .
- Volunteer Teacher (after hours)—Inuit presentations, watercolours, clay.

PUBLISHED ARTICLES

"CIA: 'Careers in Art' Program" – **Teachers Resource** (Curriculum & Instructional Services), ARDSB, Fall 2008.

Continues

player, global altruism, and positive influence on others. Such testimonials support all the factual data in the resume and help portray this teacher as the one to consider seriously for a job opening. This teacher's contributions "were so impressive that three pages were easily justified." If the writer had kept the resume to

• • •

"[Barbara] is a fabulous team player and always looks for ways to help her colleagues. She has the biggest heart of anyone (save my immediate family) that I know."

• • •

"Under her leadership and direction, staff, students, and parents have increased their knowledge of the plight of those less fortunate in other parts of the world."

• • •

"Barbara is a talented, dependable, knowledgeable, reliable, caring individual who continues to have a positive effect on those with whom she works and lives."

• • •

CHARITABLE / VOLUNTEER CONTRIBUTIONS (ACADEMIC)

Washington Hospital Burn Center Project—Spearheaded a student relief project supporting victims of the September 11 Pentagon attack. Student contribution published in *Center Profiles*, the Washington Hospital magazine.

Canadian Feed the Children: Sierra Leone, Africa Project—Coordinated school-wide initiative that provided 100+ knapsacks full of school supplies to children in Sierra Leone.

Project Love—Created and led program that provided school supplies to schools in Ghana and Senegal.

Operation Shoebox: Covenant House—Conceived and led a successful school-wide initiative that supplied 300+ shoeboxes of personal items to street children.

Help the Afghan Children—Coordinated program to sell snacks during lunch period ("Loonie Tuesdays"). All proceeds quadrupled by CIDA and donated to World Vision.

Warm Hands Warm Hearts—Initiated school program to collect winter clothing for Salvation Army.

CHARITABLE / VOLUNTEER CONTRIBUTIONS (NON-ACADEMIC)

Royal Canadian Air Cadets: 234 Banshee Squadron—Clothing Coordinator, Parent Volunteer, and member of 30th Anniversary Committee.

Deer Creek Alliance Church, Deer Creek, Ontario—Special Events Committee Member, Sunday School Teacher, and Coordinator of Grade 6 Sunday School Puppetry Program.

Augusta Region Skating Academy Winter Club—Member of Board of Directors responsible for all publicity and communications.

Canadian Figure Skating Association, Central Augusta Section—Developed and produced the programme booklet for the Sundial Sectional Championship (2003).

The Christian Alliance Church of Canada—Created all conference stage decorations for the 10th Biannual National Assembly.

Bayridge Hill Elementary School—Past President of parent-teacher liaison group (Partners in Education).

PERSONAL ACTIVITIES

Enjoy learning new crafts (calligraphy, stained glass, fabric arts, quilting), walking, and biking.

two pages, the employer would not get to read about the teacher's charitable/volunteer work—information that is as diverse as it is impressive.

Jeremy Cloud

Current Address: 125 West Gibbs Street • Shade, Ohio 45701
Permanent Address: 231 Louise Avenue • Racine, Ohio 45771
jcloud@bluesky.net •740.696.0000

High School Science Teacher

"Jeremy will make a great teacher ... builds great rapport with the students ... makes learning fun!"
– Sally Ball, Biology Teacher, Nelsonville-York High School

PROFILE

Enthusiastic educator with an avid interest in all areas of science. Offering a solid educational background including degree in Secondary Life Science as well as certifications in Project Wild and Project Learning Tree. Computer proficient. Seeking a high school teaching position with an interest in coaching track/cross country and/or advising extracurricular clubs.

EDUCATION & HONORS

OHIO UNIVERSITY, Athens, Ohio (June 2012)
Bachelor's Degree in Secondary Life Science
Major GPA: 3.24 • Dean's List

Relevant Courses
Microbiology ... Physics ... Chemistry ... Biology ... Plant Physiology ... Evolution

Certifications
Certified in Project Wild
- Interdisciplinary conservation and environment education program exploring wildlife; supported by natural resource agencies

Certified in Project Learning Tree
- Interdisciplinary environmental education program for educators working with students in Pre-K through Grade 12 focusing on the total environment; land, air and water

RELEVANT EXPERIENCE

Student Teacher — NELSONVILLE-YORK HIGH SCHOOL, Buchtel, Ohio (April 2011–present)
- Develop and implement lesson plans for anatomy, physiology and biology classes

Tutor — PHILLIPS CENTER, Ohio University, Athens, Ohio (September–November 2010)
- Effectively tutored student athletes in math, chemistry and geology resulting in improved test scores

ADDITIONAL WORK EXPERIENCE

Student Worker — BROMLEY DINING HALL, Ohio University, Athens, Ohio (June 2010–March 2011)
- Utilized strong work ethic and excellent interpersonal communication skills while rotating through various areas of dining hall

Cashier/Baker — BRITISH PETROLEUM (BP), Bellevue, Ohio (Academic Breaks, October 2008–January 2010)
- Performed a variety of duties with strong focus on providing superior customer service

Lifeguard — CEDAR POINT AMUSEMENT PARK, Sandusky, Ohio (June–September 2008)
- Ensured safety of guests; responded successfully to a spinal injury emergency

44

Combination. *Melissa L. Kasler, Athens, Ohio*

This person was a new graduate with a teaching degree. The cloud graphic was relevant to his last name and goal of science teaching. The graphic got many good comments, and he received a quick job offer.

CHRIS CHAVEZ

55-555 Main Street • Honolulu, HI 00000
Home: (808) 555-5555 • Office: (808) 555-5551, Ext. 555
Cellular: (808) 555-5552 • E-mail: chavezc@coconut.org

AREAS OF EXPERTISE

Human Behavior

Adolescent Education

Peer Education/
Counseling

Peer Counselor
Training

Service Learning

Program
Development

Curriculum Planning

Classroom
Management

Procedures Planning

Parent/Student/
Teacher Liaison

Research

Workshops/
Seminars

*Relocating 6/2012
to San Francisco, CA*

PROFESSIONAL EDUCATOR
Making a Difference in the Lives of School Children

Dedicated educator seeking position as **Psychology Teacher.** 10+ years of related experience includes positions as high school counselor and teacher, substitute and volunteer teacher, and private tutor. Particularly adept at curriculum planning and program development. Task oriented. Solid organization and time-management skills.

M.S. in Educational Psychology • B.A. in Psychology

CAREER TRACK

Junior High Counselor/   4/2008–Present
Peer Education Teacher
Pacific Rim Institute—Honolulu, HI
Accredited K–12 private institution for girls. Total enrollment 2,500.

Assist 375 students with transition to high school. Provide personal and social counseling in areas of academic progress, career awareness, peer conflict, and other adolescent challenges. Train peer counselors.

• Developed peer education and counseling program from scratch within 1 year. Teach entire curriculum. Foster sense of community awareness by incorporating service-learning program with Young Students Club of Honolulu. Program currently has active student peer counselors.
• Revised faculty grade-check procedures, including comprehensive follow-up system. Resulted in improved communication among faculty, students, and parents.
• Rewrote counseling procedures to conform to national standards of ASCA, ACA, and APA.

Substitute Teacher   2007/2008 school year
Island Substitute Services—Honolulu, HI

Functioned as "on-call" substitute. Reported to various private schools on island of Oahu. Assignments varied from 1 day to 3 weeks. Class sizes of 20 to 30.

• Consistently followed teachers' curriculum requests. Accepted all assignments offered. Earned reputation for reliability.
• Acquired valuable teaching experience through assignments in various school settings.

Career Track Continued on Page 2 ⇨

45

Combination. *Peter Hill, Honolulu, Hawaii*

The applicant, a counselor, was relocating to another part of the country and was seeking a position as a psychology teacher. The writer directs immediate attention to the individual's

CHRIS CHAVEZ
Page 2 of 2

EDUCATION

M.S. Degree, Educational Psychology
3/2011

Accredited Distance Learning Program of Chicago University— Chicago, IL
❋ *GPA 3.9/4.0*

B.A. Degree, Psychology
2000

Chicago University— Chicago, IL
❋ *GPA 4.0/4.0*

COMPUTER SKILLS

Internet, Outlook, Outlook Express, Eudora, Word, Publisher, PowerPoint

Tutor   2005/2006 school year
Tutors-R-Us—Honolulu, HI

Worked one-on-one with home-schooled or struggling students (1st through 9th grades). Kept student records. Wrote progress reports for in-house and parent use.

- Developed strong time-management skills. Required to cover large amounts of material in limited time.
- Obtained functional one-to-one communication skills through contact with children of various ages.

Volunteer Teacher   2000–2004
California Unified School District—Vista, CA

Taught basic Spanish to 2nd- and 5th-graders. Wrote weekly newsletter for 2nd-grade class and organized all activities. Also volunteered as ESL instructor until full-time teacher was hired. Class sizes of up to 27.

❋ *Previous experience as flight attendant with major airline.*

PROFESSIONAL DEVELOPMENT

Career Assistance Training	2010
State Counselor Association Conference	2009
Peaceful Intervention	2009
Psychobiology of Mental Control	2008
Statewide Conference on Conflict Management	2008
Counselor Education, Hawaii University	2005
National Student Assistance Program	2004

CERTIFICATIONS

Hawaiian Private School Professional Academic Certificate	2008
Hawaii Department of Health Substance Abuse Prevention Partner	2008
Student Assistance Training Certification	2007

AFFILIATIONS

American Psychological Association
American School Counselor Association
Hawaii School Counselor Association
American Counseling Association

formal education in psychology. The modified page border (not a full page length) is attractive on both pages and unifies them visually. Shading in the left column on each page directs attention to Areas of Expertise on page one and to the Education and Computer Skills sections on page two.

Felicia Bowman

Corporate Trainer

Summary of Qualifications

1 Master's degree in Adult Education/Training with hands-on delivery and development

2 Experience in training and program development for major corporation

3 Delivered dozens of workshops for team building, technical training and other workplace topics

4 Conducted analysis of work teams and job & task components and presented findings

5 Excellent computer skills, including development of online training and tools

6 Member: ASTD (national and local), SHRM, and ISPI

555 Wilshire Road
Tampa, Florida 33624
(813) 555-0248
fbowman@hotmail.com

Educational History and Degrees

University of South Florida
Adult Education–Training–Human Resource Development, M.A.
Tampa, Florida, 2006

University of South Florida
Psychology, B.A.
Tampa, Florida, 2003

Key Strengths

Creativity—Ability to create unique solutions, analogies and illustrations for complex problems

Patience—Ability to work with all departments with all levels of employees

Knowledge—Ability to use extensive insights in Adult Learners' understanding and information processing

Structured—Ability to plan and prepare programs and workshops in a long-term, time-based critical path schedule in order to meet targeted launch dates

Communication—Ability to express complex ideas and important points in a way that is understandable and simple for the majority of Adult Learners

Professional Experience

Training and Documentation Specialist, Lockheed Martin
Lakeland, Florida, 2007–Current

Team member of highly creative Training Group for corporate offices and 3 major business sectors of this $27 billion company.

✓ Completed 12 major job and task analysis projects to document technical work processes.

✓ Designed 4 training programs, each in multiple forms of media, including the Internet, CD-ROM, PowerPoint and NetMeeting.

✓ Used interactive team development processes to assess the functionality of teams in the Shared Services division.

✓ Delivered 3 specialized training modules for highly technical computer systems.

✓ Facilitate team-building exercises, communication enhancement workshops and ongoing meeting facilitation.

✓ Offer constructive and strategic input on organizational structural changes.

✓ Participate in business development projects and strategic planning.

Continued on Page 2

46

Combination. *Gail Frank, Tampa, Florida*

This corporate trainer was looking for a nontraditional format for a traditionally worded resume. She wanted to stand out from the pack when applying for jobs through the local ASTD

Program Assistant, Counseling Center for Human Development, University of South Florida
Tampa, Florida, 2004–2007

Created policies, procedures and training for clients of USF's Counseling Center. Also provided administrative and computer troubleshooting support.

✓ Produced detailed publications and handbooks, including the Counseling Center's Handbook, internship materials and brochures.

✓ Designed and produced promotional materials and presentations for professional workshops to clients and university administration.

✓ Trained staff on Internet usage and software programs such as Microsoft Word, Excel, PowerPoint and Outlook.

✓ Resolved client issues and provided customer service. Took incoming calls and provided referrals to other resources.

✓ Provided computer support for staff in the areas of software support and system troubleshooting.

✓ Conducted administrative support for the campus-wide Employee Assistance Program.

Program Assistant, University of South Florida, Veteran Services
Tampa, Florida, 2002–2003

Performed administrative and financial services in USF office that serviced veterans in their search for continuing education and employment.

✓ Reported directly to the Veteran Services Program Coordinator and ran the office when she was not present.

✓ Supervised 3 employees and ensured that reports and forms were properly filled out.

✓ Provided training in office procedures and policies.

✓ Handled all travel and budgeting administration.

✓ Solicited assistance from other campus offices in providing opportunities for work placement openings.

✓ Counseled veterans on their education and work options, and helped them define goals.

✓ Coordinated VA Work-Study Program for USF.

Courses Completed During Master's Program

Adult Education in the United States	Program Management
The Adult Learner	Foundations of Research
Methods of Teaching Adults	Consulting Skills
Instructional Design	Group Processes
Trainers in Business and Industry	Personnel Policy

Sample Presentations & Projects Completed During Master's Program

Experiential Learning in Adults

Presentation Skills Workshop

Future Trends in Adult Learning

Book Review: The Adult Learner, A Neglected Species

Andragogy Versus Pedagogy: Adults Are Different Than Kids

Professional Associations

Member of top local and national training organizations

National Chapter of American Society for Training and Development (ASTD)

Suncoast Chapter of American Society for Training and Development (ASTD)

Society for Human Resource Management (SHRM)

International Society for Performance Improvement (ISPI)

2 . . . .

chapter (American Society for Training and Development). The writer chose a newsletter format and added the graphic of a trainer to convey the applicant's creativity and playfulness and to offset somewhat dry "trainer-speak." Master's degree coursework and presentations provide keywords.

555 ● 555 ● 5555

B. Rae French
1003 Ironton Avenue ● Skyview, Texas 79000
brfrench@nts.net

CORPORATE TRAINER

SUMMARY OF QUALIFICATIONS

- BS in Interdisciplinary Studies with emphasis in Mathematics and Communications
- Eight years of teaching experience with measurable accomplishments
- Nine years of concurrent experience as sales representative for cosmetics line and portrait studio
- Director for live and video dramas; play actor
- Proven speaking, public relations, communication, and interpersonal skills

TEACHING EXPERIENCE

Math Teacher and *Cheerleading Sponsor,* MAC JUNIOR HIGH SCHOOL, Skyview, Texas   **2005–2010**
As teacher, trained individual students to increase their mathematical, logical, and reasoning skills. Ensured classroom safety, abiding by all safety requirements. As cheerleading sponsor (2007–2010), scheduled and organized special events such as pep rallies, fund-raisers, and tryouts. Motivated parents, staff, and cheerleaders to increase school allegiance. Authored directives.

Key Achievements:

- Advanced from teaching seventh-grade math to eighth-grade and freshman algebra.
- Instrumental in improving student assessment passing rate: 2006—86.2%; 2007—95.1%; 2008—97.6%.
- Teaching techniques resulted in 100% of seventh-grade class passing TAAS Test (2009).
- Collaborated with other volunteer teachers to implement Saxon Math Program that produced amazing results.
- Invested large amounts of time working with cheerleaders; getting to know them, organizing tryouts, attending camp, and coordinating activities.
- Completely restructured cheerleading program: Organized paperwork, published schedules, involved other programs, established rules and guidelines, and utilized open communication with parents and administration.

Math Teacher, PROJECT INTERCEPT (ALTERNATIVE SCHOOL), Skyview, Texas   **2003–2005**
Organized and prepared curriculum to accommodate 7–12 grade levels. Taught as many as four subjects to students in class size of 8–10. Collaborated with other teachers in areas of discipline and student achievement. Utilized consistency and awareness to manage classroom.

Key Achievements:

- Gained recognizable progress with several difficult students through an accepting attitude and creative teaching techniques.
- Esteemed for motivating students, retaining their attention, and cultivating a zest for learning.

Continued ─────

47

Combination. *Edith A. Rische, Lubbock, Texas*

This teacher wants to become a corporate trainer, so the writer highlights transitional skills, such as writing directives, public speaking, and mentoring, which are relevant to a corporate

B. Rae French ● *Page 2*   brfrench@nts.net

OTHER EMPLOYMENT

Portrait Consultant, PAUL'S PHOTOGRAPHY, Church Division, Skyview, Texas   **2011–2012**

Traveled multistate territory selling computer-generated portrait packages to church members. Created and presented attractive packages with best overall poses, motivating customers to make a purchase with warmth and sincerity.

Key Achievements:

- Ranked in top 10 portrait consultants among 30 district representatives in first three weeks of employment.
- Trained for only four days rather than two weeks due to quick learning capacity.
- Outsold trainer in first two days as sales consultant.

Sales Consultant, PRECIOUS COSMETICS, Lubbock, Texas   *CONCURRENT*   **2003–Present**

Market product and conduct facials to sell cosmetic products. Recruit sales consultants. Attend regular training sessions and yearly conventions.

EDUCATION

Bachelor of Science in Interdisciplinary Studies, RELIGIOUS UNIVERSITY, Skyview, Texas   **2003**

- **Major:** Secondary Education in Mathematics and Communications
- Teacher certified by the Texas Education Association

AWARDS AND ACTIVITIES

- Active participant in improving TAAS scores instrumental in Mac Junior High's Texas Education Association rating as "Recognized" campus 2006, 2007, and 2008; and as "Exemplary" campus 2009
- Mentor in Leadership Training for Christ Program, 2006–2010
- Student Teacher of the Year, 2003
- Dean's List and National Dean's List, 2002–2003
- Participant in community and children's theater programs

SPECIAL SKILLS

- Working with PCs and Macs and Microsoft Office software
- Presenting material with a variety of audiovisual and electronics equipment
- Playing piano and guitar, singing, and acting

environment. The writer also presents achievements such as successful teaching and program development to strengthen the candidate's hiring potential as a trainer. An unusual page border makes the resume distinctive. The use of bold and underlining helps achievements stand out. See Cover Letter 4.

Natasha Carer

1111 6ᵗʰ St.—Local City, CA 90000—(111) 111-1111—ncarer@abc.com

Nonprofit Education and Outreach Professional

Through education and employment/volunteer experience, have developed and demonstrated strong professional abilities in public/mental health and counseling services. Assignments have included peer, student, and rape victim counseling and related programs. Knowledgeable regarding theories and approaches in working with adult and child personalities. Key strength is developing and implementing relevant service programs that meet client needs through quality care and attention to detail.

Skill Areas:

- Written/oral communications
- Basic medical protocols
- Ease of interactions with children and adults of varied age, ethnic, economic, social, political, and educational group levels

- Needs analysis and problem resolution
- Resource acquisition/management
- Program representation
- Staff orientation/supervision

Employment History:

2003–2011   ***Educational & Community Resource Volunteer***—Peace Corps Non-USA
Trained to improve primary school education programs and adult programs designed to improve economic and educational statuses of people of varied ethnic and national identities.
   Key Contributions:
   - Surveyed needs and developed resources and services that involved cross-cultural adaptation.
   - Developed work plans and strategies for primary and secondary school projects.
   - Facilitated Peace Corps Non-USA governmental and nongovernmental working partnerships.
   - Aided in developing a permanent library site and secured book donations through Non-USA and Rotary Clubs.
   - Helped provide career guidance and HIV/AIDS information programs.
   - Consulted with primary schools implementing Non-USA's New Educational Act.

2001–2002   ***In-Home Outreach Counselor***—Non-USA Intervention Program Team
2000–2001   ***Peer Advisor***—Educational Equity Program, CSU, Some City, CA
2000–2001   ***Child Care Worker***—Children's Denominational Homes of USA, Some City, CA
1998–1999   ***Psych Aide/Assistant Peer Group Counselor***—Good Care Clinic for Schizphrenics
1998–1999   ***Teacher's Aide***—Campus Child Development Center, Small City College

Education/Training:

2010   M.P.A., California State University, Some City
2001   B.A., Psychology, California State University, Some City
        Internship: Hotline Peer Counselor/Peer Counselor

Personal: Able to travel and/or relocate.

48

Combination. *Nita Busby, Orange, California*

An Employment History section makes it possible to telescope limited work experiences before activity in the Peace Corps and to call attention to significant work experiences in that organization.

Engineering

Resumes at a Glance

GEORGE CRANDALL, EIT

0000 Smith Avenue
Houston, TX 79000

Home: (000) 000-0000
name@lycos.com

Career Profile

ENVIRONMENTAL ENGINEER-IN-TRAINING

- Focused, analytical professional with strong engineering educational background complemented by work experience involving field research and evaluation projects.
- Able to balance creative thinking with logical design ideas; enjoy opportunities to develop solutions that address challenging environmental problems.
- Work effectively in both self-managed and team-based projects; maintain high ethical and quality standards, professional demeanor, and cooperative attitude.
- Use hands-on, detail-oriented approach in completing projects and assignments.

Knowledge & Skill Areas:

Field Research • Report Writing • Experimental Design & Methods • Project Planning Quality Assurance Standards • Research & Development • Environmental Hazards Systems Analysis • Regulatory & Safety Compliance • Engineering Documentation Environmental Sample Analysis • Risk Assessment • Client/Customer Communications

Education

Master of Environmental Engineering, 2010 / GPA: 3.75
Bachelor of Environmental Engineering, 2008 / GPA: 3.30
University, Houston, TX

Selected Upper-Level Coursework:

- Design of Air Pollution Systems
- Solid & Hazardous Waste Treatment
- Environmental Impact Analysis
- Environmental Systems Design

- Design of Wastewater Treatment Plants
- Groundwater Contaminant Transport
- Geoethnical Practices for Waste Disposal
- Environmental Law & Policies

Project Highlights:

- **"Best Bench Scale Demonstration Award"**—Worked with group of 6 students to plan, develop, and present winning bench scale model (addressing water quality issues) at 2 Design Competitions, 2007 & 2008, at the Waste Energy Research Consortium.
- **"Design of Wastewater Treatment Plants"**—Played key role in design project for treatment plant based on quality assurance and regulatory compliance factors. Delivered well-received presentation to Master-level class upon completion.
- **"Environmental Impact Statement"**—Developed proposal-oriented report detailing most effective, environmentally sound strategies for controlling brush within region.

Work Experience

Research Associate, 2010–Present
Research Assistant & Laboratory Technician, 2006–2009
Research Assistant, Summer 2009 (Texas National Environmental & Engineering Lab)
University, Houston, TX (2006–Present)

Conduct research, sample collection and analysis, experimental design, and explosives evaluations using high-performance liquid chromatography, and perform other related activities in positions involving field studies and frequent travel to various counties within East Texas region. Report directly to Laboratory Manager; additionally responsible for daily maintenance of weather stations.

- **Bioremediation of Explosives in Vadose Zone**—Conduct explosives contamination studies and evaluations for government agency Pantex to recommend strategies for remediation projects with highest potential for success.
- **Overall Work Performance**—Put forth consistent effort in meeting and exceeding job requirements; worked overtime hours and maintained full-time class schedule throughout employment. Recognized for intelligent, thorough work habits.

Activities

Society of Environmental Professionals—Member, 3 years; Secretary, 1 year
Civil Engineering Honor Society—Chi Epsilon

49

Combination. *Daniel J. Dorotik Jr., Lubbock, Texas*

Including information about school-related projects is a way to offset a recent graduate's relative lack of work experience. See, for example, the Project Highlights in the Education section.

ANDREW S. MILLER

345 Maryland Lane • Eatontown, NJ 07724 • (732) 780-2673 • asm423@hotmail.com

TEST ENGINEER / TECHNICAL SUPPORT / PROJECT SUPERVISOR

Industrial ~ Government ~ Military

Results-driven and well-organized *Technical Professional* **who combines hands-on experience with a solid educational background in applied physics and engineering.** Strong skills in planning, implementing, upgrading, and maintaining high-tech semiconductor equipment. Reputation for solving problems with creativity and out-of-the-box solutions.

Extensive knowledge of applications, integration, hardware, and quality testing. Excellent team building, communication, and interpersonal skills. Provide outstanding customer service in high-pressure situations to advance the public's health, safety, security, and welfare.

Competencies Include

• Project Management	• Problem Solving	• Performance Optimization
• Testing & Evaluation	• Statistical Analysis	• Training
• New Hardware Startup	• Secret Security Clearance	• Computer Systems Expertise
• Customer Support	• Troubleshooting	• Mechanical Repair

Professional Achievements

Testing, Evaluation, Data Reduction, and Analysis

- Testing and evaluation of high-tech security-related explosive- and weapons-detection equipment, aircraft load impact on concrete runway structures, and anti-tank guided missile countermeasures.
- Generated project plans, test plans, and procedures applying multidisciplinary approaches.
- Performed literature search and consulted with area experts to assess technology and determine best approach.
- Developed methods unique to analysis being performed in coordination with organization and outside vendors.
- Data collection, reduction, statistical analysis; interpreting results to determine integrity, validity, significance, and formulated conclusions.
- Provided recommendations based on final test data analysis and actual results.
- Identified new methods or approaches based on technology assessments and results interpretations.
- Prepared project final reports and classified reports.

Project Supervision, Management, and Task Leadership

- Managed and supervised day-to-day test conduct and coordinated test activities.
- Prepared test/program assessment reports.
- Developed work breakdown structures and tracked project activities.
- Coordinated production activities and requirements.
- Trained and lectured students on advanced characterization of materials at the graduate level.
- Trained students in laboratory techniques and safety practices and policy.

Research, Development, and Design in Scientific Laboratory Environment

- Engineering design and fabrication of highly complex scientific laboratory hardware and equipment.
- Developed an innovative scheme for scanning and digital processing transmission of electron microscopy images of superlatice interfaces.
- Simulation studies of solar wind erosion contributions to atmospheric constituents.
- Supervised and maintained high-energy particle beam/materials interactions, modification, and analysis laboratory.
- Experience with ultra-high vacuum and cryogenic technologies, mass spectroscopy, and nondestructive organic and inorganic materials analysis and detection techniques such as Rutherford backscattering spectrometry, particle-induced X-ray and gamma ray emission, forward recoil detection, and secondary ion mass spectrometry.

Computer Proficiency

- Computer programming in Visual Basic, Pascal, BASIC, and FORTRAN. Familiar with UNIX and C code and algorithms. PC repair and upgrading. PCI-controlled data acquisition and instrumentation. ISDN connectivity setup.
- Proficient with software packages such as Microsoft Office suite (Word, Project, PowerPoint, Excel), Visual Basic macro development, WordPerfect, EMACS, AutoCAD, Visio, Pinnacle Video, and Photoshop.
- Introductory use and understanding of LabVIEW and Matlab capabilities.
- Computer hardware and instrumentation for high-speed data collection.

Page One

Combination. *Beverley and Mitchell I. Baskin, Marlboro, New Jersey*

The Professional Achievements section displays the value of clustering a long list of achievements into groups with separate subheadings. Without the subheadings, the task of comprehending the

Page Two   asm423@hotmail.com   ANDREW S. MILLER

Employment History

Self-Employed   2006 to present
   Technical and legal research and writing, training, and general services.

JHGC Sensor Technology Specialists, Fort Monmouth Army Labs   2/2006 to 9/2006
   Senior Engineer/Scientist
   U.S. Army CECOM RDEC Intelligence and Information
   Warfare Directorate Seeker Effects Laboratory

TRF, Inc. & Orion Scientific Corp., FAA William J. Hughes Technical Center   6/2001 to 6/2005
   Senior Engineer/Test Engineer/Systems Engineer
   Aviation Security and Airport Technology Research and Development Divisions

Contractor   1/1994 to 5/2001
   Traxx Technologies, Crier Metals, Ocean Specialty Gasses, NJIT

Princeton University, Princeton, NJ   9/1991 to 9/1993
   Chief Engineer
   Accelerator Research and Development Lab

Bell Laboratories, Holmdel, NJ   5/1985 to 9/1991
   Senior Technical Associate
   Radiation Physics Research Department, Interactions, Modification, and Central Diagnostics/Analysis Lab

Education

Pennsylvania State University
Graduate Research Assistant, Applied Physics/Metallurgy
   Research Assistant in field ion microscopy study of hydrogen embrittlement of Fe-Ti alloys. Teaching assistant in electronics/electromagnetic theory/laboratory techniques.

Pennsylvania State University
BS Physics
   Advanced studies in nuclear magnetic resonance techniques.

AT&T Bell Laboratories	Computer science, UNIX, C, MicroProcessor Primer, and hazardous chemicals safety training
Stevens Institute of Technology	AT&T–sponsored postgraduate studies Solid-state technologies, electrical engineering
Rutgers University	Postgraduate studies in various fields: Physics, electrical engineering materials science, ceramic science, and computer science
Brookdale County College	Preradiology program studies
Continuing Education	Legal research and writing Computer programming, PC repair, and upgrade certification training Tool-and-die machining Instrumentation, LabVIEW

Publications
   Author or contributing author of 20 technical papers; frequently lecture on advanced characterization of materials.

Awards
   Orion Scientific, Letter of Commendation and Award, July 2004
   FAA, Letter of Acknowledgment/Appreciation, March 2004
   Toastmasters, Best Table Topics Speech, 2002
   Princeton University, Letter of Commendation, 1993

many achievements would be immense. With each group of achievements under a subheading, the reader can fathom a shorter list and focus on a group of particular interest. Clustering is a useful strategy to use in any resume section with a long list.

BARRY H. SCHMIDT

1817 Orleans Drive   barrys@anyisp.com   Home: 555-555-5555
Elk Grove Village, Illinois 60007   Mobile: 000-000-0000

MANUFACTURING EXECUTIVE
Mechanical Engineering...Production...Plant Management

Seasoned professional with comprehensive experience and visible achievements in diverse manufacturing arenas, including machined parts, fabricated parts, plastic parts, die casting, mechanical power transmission, and powder metallurgy. Proven track record for implementing strategies that enhance productivity and profitability. Experienced in supervising engineers and technicians, as well as drafting and shop floor personnel. Recognized as an industry expert and published author on mechanical power transmission products. Academic credentials: MBA; BS in Physics.

Tradition of Performance Excellence in

- **Profit & Loss Responsibility**
- **Job Shop Operations**
- **Vendor Cost-Benefit Analysis**
- **Statistical Process Control**
- **Engineering Design Calculations**
- **Machining and Welding Operations**
- **Production Management**

- **Daily Plant Operations**
- **Staff Development**
- **Quality Assurance**
- **Creative Problem-Solving**
- **Job Costing and Routing**
- **Union Management Experience**
- **Continuous Process Improvement**

- **Computer literate** in MRP programs (MAPICS, Visual Manufacturing, ACCPAC, UA Corporate Accounting, PRO-MAN), AutoCAD, CADKEY, Windows XP/7 and MS Office applications.
- **Affiliations:** ASME, IEEE Magnetic Society, Charter Member—Chicago Chapter of Vibration Institute

PROFESSIONAL EXPERIENCE

REX-TEC CORPORATION   2009 to Present
Privately held, $2 million master distributor and manufacturer of mechanical power transmission products. 20+ years in business.
Manufacturing/Engineering Manager

Hired to develop new magnetic coupling product line, to offset 40% downturn in the machine tool industry (previous primary market for company); this included standardization of design, sourcing of components, and development of in-house manufacturing processes. Challenged with expanding sales of new product line from $100,000 to $1 million. Empowered with full accountability for manufacturing and assembly, design, application engineering, purchasing/vendor qualification, quality assurance, job costing, margin calculations, new materials evaluation, and staff development. Advise President in all aspects of new business development, market expansion, capital expenditures, and operating budgets. *Key Accomplishments:*

- **Transformed company from warehouse distributor to manufacturer, saving $10,000 per year in out-plant costs, offering 24-hour delivery, and generating additional sales of $20,000 annually.**
- **Successfully developed new magnetic coupling product line, projected to generate a 56% profit margin.** This new product line is designed for small-quantity customers and large OEMs. Usually, this product is customized by individual OEMs for internal use or built by magnet manufacturers not offering a complete power transmission solution.
- **Increased profit margins by another 10–15% after securing new vendors via E-sourcing.**
- **Achieved revenue increase in new product line from zero to $100,000 in the first year; projected to increase tenfold by FY12.**
- **Initiated and developed Quality Assurance procedures and manual and established a quality level for product manufacture, according to MIL-I-45208.**

PAGE 1 OF 2

51

Combination. *Joellyn Wittenstein Schwerdlin, Worcester, Massachusetts*

This manufacturing executive had long-term experience in large organizations and drew on it to help his most recent employer, a considerably smaller company, expand its traditional product

BARRY H. SCHMIDT

CONTAINERS, INC.   1998 to 2009

Privately held $4 million manufacturer of steel industrial refuse containers and cart-dumpers; 25 years in business; customers included City of Chicago Department of Streets & Sanitation, BFI, and Waste Management.

Plant Manager

Managed daily manufacturing operations and P&L of a 3-shift, heavy-gauge sheet metal and fabrication union shop. Supervised 7 direct reports (3 foremen, buyer, and engineering support staff) and 35 indirect employees (welders and assemblers). Responsibilities included purchasing materials and supplies, staffing, delivery, shop floor scheduling, vendor evaluation and selection, capital budgeting and implementation, and reorganizing shop floor for maximum productivity. ***Key Accomplishments:***

- **Significantly reversed $100,000 operating loss to $750,000 profit in 9 months** by raising prices to reflect costs plus fixed margins, and preparing/adhering to monthly production schedules, which further decreased costs by eliminating production shutdowns for special product runs.

- **Reduced welding manufacturing costs by $500 per day through re-engineering of the labor force,** assigning lower-salaried material handlers to stock work cells and move semifinished products to painting holding area, instead of highly paid welders, and adding a 3rd shift of painting operations to improve work flow.

- **Proactively negotiated payments with new vendors at a 15% cost savings on steel ($250,000) and established a new vendor for hydraulic cylinders at a savings of $50,000 per year at regular terms and no prepayment,** after obtaining a large, multiyear contract and a prepayment, preventing company from closing. Previously, the company had been paying bills on 120 days and many vendors had ceased business relationships or required advance payment on a year's worth of inventory.

POWER-TRANS, INC.   1984 to 1998

100-year-old privately held $30 million global manufacturer of mechanical power transmission products. Primary customers include Caterpillar, Gardner-Denver, GE, FMC, John Deere, WW Grainger, and McMaster-Carr.

Director of Research & Development

Progressed from R & D Engineer to Senior Application Engineer, Quality Control Manager, Engineering Manager, and Director of Research and Development. Contributed to company's growth from $6 million to $30 million during tenure. Managed design, application, manufacturing engineering, and quality assurance departments, which included supervision of 13 direct reports. ***Key Accomplishments:***

- Created Quality Control Department and accompanying Quality Control manual, establishing the MIL-I-45208 Inspection System. Reduced scrap and return rate from $400,000 to $100,000 against $20 million in sales.

- Developed a super-strong, wear-resistant U-joint, using this design to secure multiyear, multimillion-dollar parts contracts for the M-1 tank, F-16 fighter, Harrier aircraft, and Bradley fighting vehicle.

- Won the coveted "Bachner Award" after developing plastic universal joints and flexible couplings.

- Reduced costs of sintered products, saving 40,000 pounds of material (4% reduction) per year, lowering shipping costs by $30,000/annually, improving tooling life, and increasing throughput.

- Developed new products, including material development, tooling, vendors, and manufacturing processes.

- Presented lecture series on power transmission couplings; also presented technical papers at industry conferences and authored magazine articles addressing flexible couplings, vibration, and universal joints.

EDUCATION & TRAINING

- MBA, Olivet Nazarene University, Kankakee, Illinois (4.0 GPA)   2010
- MAPICS for the Engineer, GMD   1996
- Effective Engineering Management, NYU School of Continuing Education   1989
- Advanced Plastics Product Design Engineering   1987
- BS, Physics, Illinois Institute of Technology, Chicago, Illinois   1983

1817 Orleans Drive • Elk Grove Village, Illinois 60007 • 555-555-5555 • 000-000-0000 • barrys@anyisp.com

line. In the Professional Experience section, a brief company profile in italic under each company name helps the reader assess the applicant's career history. The heading Key Accomplishments in bold italic and the use of bullets make the individual's achievements in each workplace stand out.

Thomas P. Redmond, PE

256 Musket River Road • Washington, NJ 07882 • 908.555.5555 • TRedmond999@comcast.net

ENGINEERING / PROJECT MANAGEMENT
Maintenance Management ~ Project Engineering ~ Metals Industry

Results-driven and well-organized *Engineering Professional* able to combine a unique blend of formal technical education with a solid, hands-on background in the metals industry.

Extensive knowledge of manufacturing environments. Versatile team player with an ability to incorporate new concepts and interact with all levels of professionals. Expertise in industrial construction: foundations, structural steel, plumbing, and electrical. Work closely with management, consultants, vendors, and tradespeople.

Competencies Include

- ◆ Project Management
- ◆ Maintenance Management
- ◆ Equipment Selection and Installation
- ◆ Vendor Negotiations

- ◆ Troubleshooting
- ◆ Planning and Development
- ◆ Process Optimization
- ◆ Cost Reduction Strategies

Professional Achievements

As an Independent Consultant, and as a Maintenance Manager and Mechanical Engineer for Northeast Cast Iron Pipe Company, I developed expertise in the following areas:

Project Management—Provided design, project planning, and implementation for a variety of large projects that had a major impact on improving operations, efficiency, and profits.

- Specified, selected, and managed the installation of a 150,000cfm pulse jet dust collector utilizing a 600hp blower, with more than 2,000 bags and 150-ft.-tall discharge stack. The project resulted in a drastic improvement in the air quality of the manufacturing area.
- Managed the design and implementation of a cooling tower for the cupola, for maintaining cool shell temperature. The 2,000-ton-capacity system included 150hp pumps running at 2,000gpm with extensive piping, all completed by in-house personnel.
- Renovated a 150-ft.-long annealing furnace with new burners, gas trains, blowers, ductwork, refractory, structural work, and control room, to significantly increase production and efficiency.
- Directed the installation of seven air compressors, totaling more than 800hp, in three climate-controlled rooms, to provide reliable shop air pressure.
- Consulted with a spray specialist on paint machine improvements in order to decrease paint use and improve the appearance of the product. Developed and managed the conversion process, which included a new spray system, all new controls, paint storage tanks, hydraulic unit, pipe conveying system, and overspray removal.

Industrial Maintenance—Managed a maintenance team of more than 50 employees covering three shifts of operation. Personnel included a superintendent, nine foremen, millwrights, electricians, machinists, carpenters, and mechanics.

- Maintained the entire foundry consisting of scrap-loading cranes, 60 tons/hr charging system, cupola system, pollution-control equipment, wastewater treatment plant, cooling towers, hot-metal cranes, core department, six casting machines, annealing furnace, quality control, pressure-testing equipment, cement-lining station, seal-coating station, pipe lifts, air compressors, machine shop, buildings and grounds, and mobile equipment.

Continued

52

Combination. *Beverley and Mitchell I. Baskin, Marlboro, New Jersey*

If it were not for the Employment section on the second page, this resume would be altogether a functional resume. A profile, areas of competence, and achievements in a Professional

Professional Achievements *(Continued)*

Environmental Compliance—Performed/supported storm-water testing and permitting, yearly stack testing, hazardous waste removal, solid waste storage, dust collector performance evaluations, monitoring well testing, wastewater treatment operations and testing, materials recycling program, and continuous emissions monitoring.

Operations—Supported operations in various capacities, including start-up, troubleshooting, environmental compliance, production upgrades, quality-control testing, maintenance, and new equipment commissioning.

Engineering Procurement—Procured items including pumps, bearings, gears, couplings, valves, pipe fittings, structural steel, fasteners, motors, cranes, gearboxes, hydraulic units, blowers, tooling, machined and fabricated parts, obsolete part substitutions, and pneumatic and hydraulic components.

Civil Engineering Design—Completed extensive design of reinforced concrete foundations, walls and slabs, structural steel building design and detailing, underground water supply and drain piping design, grading and paving throughout plant, and transit layout work.

Machine Design—Designed an assortment of machinery and machinery parts. Well-versed in fabrication and machining techniques and rebuilding of machinery (pumps, cylinders, gearboxes, cranes, lathes, etc.).

HVAC—Performed HVAC calculations, primarily blower and ductwork sizing. Designed, specified, and installed systems to provide furnace waste heat for pipe drying, fresh-air supply for control rooms, gas heaters for freeze protection, and infrared tube heaters for curing rooms.

Quality Control—Supported the plant's efforts in the ISO 9002 certification process. Experienced in product physical testing methods including Charpy impact, tensile, hardness, metallurgy, dimensional gauging, weighing, and pressure testing.

Piping—Designed and installed numerous piping systems for water, air, oxygen, nitrogen, natural gas, oil hydraulics, wastewater and sludge, powder conveying, fuel oil, and paint. Utilized several types of piping (carbon steel, stainless steel, cast iron, hydraulic tubing, copper, and plastic).

Materials Handling—Specified, operated, and maintained overhead cranes, forklifts, conveyor belts, pneumatic conveying systems, screw conveyors, bucket elevators, scissors lifts, conveyor chains, and pipe transfer cars.

Employment

- Independent Construction Consultant working on various construction projects   5/08–present
- Maintenance Manager, Northeast Cast Iron Pipe Co.   6/07–4/08
- Mechanical Engineer, Northeast Cast Iron Pipe Co.   4/98–6/07

Education/Professional

- New Jersey Professional Engineering License, 2010
- B.S., Mechanical Engineering—New Jersey Institute of Technology, 1997
- Computer skills include Internet proficiency, AutoCAD, and Microsoft Word and Excel.
- Bilingual—English and Spanish

Achievements section take up almost all of the resume. Boldfacing and underlining help the reader see the many areas of expertise indicated at length on pages one and two.

SEAN L. STEEPER

17 Woodcliff Road
Westboro, MA 01581

Home: 333-333-3333
slsteeper@hotmail.com

INDUSTRIAL ENGINEER
New Product Design • *Manufacturing Process Redesign* • *Project Management*

EDUCATION

University of Massachusetts ~ Amherst, MA
B.S. Industrial Engineering ~ Graduated with Honors ~ May 2011

RELEVANT COURSEWORK

Engineering Design • Systems Engineering • Computer Integrated Manufacturing • Production Systems
Production Engineering • Operations Research • Oral and Visual Communications
Industrial Psychology • Ergonomics • Quality Management

ACADEMIC PROJECTS

- Researched and recommended alternative methods for coating coronary stents for a leading manufacturer of cardiovascular products. Designed and manufactured prototype for spray-coating each stent, as opposed to the current practice of dipping them, which resulted in a 25% reduction in defects.
- Designed a facility and assembly-line layout to optimize production for an electronics products company.
- Generated a comprehensive Safety and Development Plan for a medical devices company.
- Created an ergonomically efficient material-handling trolley.

ENGINEERING EXPERIENCE

ABC Cardiovascular, Amherst, MA   5/10–10/10
Industrial Engineer, Co-Op

- Designed, developed, and implemented a unique device for facilitating the movement of coronary stent and catheter products from one workstation to another, resulting in a 20% decrease in scrapped product.
- Revised and simplified the Standard Operating Procedure for a label-printing machine that included detailed, easy-to-follow troubleshooting procedures and digital photographs.
- Analyzed production reports associated with a crimping machine and successfully identified one product that was consistently more prone to defects than others. Recommended machine adjustments to alleviate defects.
- Optimized floor space by rearranging and redesigning four production cells within a tightly constricted space.
- Member of a team that prepared for a critical FDA audit. Ensured machines were fully validated and safety guards were properly and securely in place.

ADDITIONAL EXPERIENCE

Albright Roofing and Painting, Framingham, MA   9/11–Present
Construction Laborer—Contribute to roofing and home painting projects.

Dunmore Plastering, Southboro, MA   Summers 09 and 11
Plasters Foreman—Organized and monitored building materials and inventory levels.

Independently Employed, Amherst, MA   1/07–5/09
Agricultural Contractor—Performed agricultural contract work for farmers.

53

Combination. *Jeanne Knight, Tyngsboro, Massachusetts*

As the writer of this resume notes, "The focus on Education, Relevant Coursework, Academic Projects, and Engineering Experience nicely positions this new graduate for a full-time position as an industrial engineer."

Finance

Resumes at a Glance

Helene Hirsch

46 Brook Hollow Road
Selden, New York 11700

(631) 382-2425
hirsch@online.com

Qualifications

➢ **Fifteen years** of progressive experience handling multiple lines of insurance claims.
➢ Experience in handling Property, Commercial Auto Liability, Bodily Injury, and General Liability lines.
➢ Knowledge of applicable insurance contracts (commercial P&C), laws, and DOI regulations.
➢ Interfaced effectively with policy holders, claimants, physicians, medical providers, attorneys, and repair shops.

Work History & Summary of Key Skills

Claims Department Manager/Supervisor (15 years), ProCar Insurance, Garden City, New York
Initially hired as a Claims Representative Trainee and was quickly promoted to Senior Claims Representative and ultimately was selected as Claims Department Manager/Supervisor. **Prevented losses, contained costs,** and exercised initiative and independent judgment.

Effective Negotiation Abilities	Negotiated property-damage and personal-injury claims on both first- and third-party claims. Authority to **negotiate up to $500,000** per claim.
	Evaluated settlement strategies and alternatives. Determined settlement value and analyzed the potential costs, benefits, and risk of litigation.
	Attended mediation conferences and claim committee meetings to **achieve fair and equitable settlements.**
Keen Investigative Skills	Investigated commercial auto-property damage claims. Acquired information and maintained accurate records regarding accidents from policy holders and claimants.
	Conducted investigations of accidents, screened vehicles, researched missing information on claim forms, and processed claims from cradle to grave.
	Arranged independent medical exams, reviewed reports, and followed up on inconsistencies and/or coverage issues.
Strong Leadership Qualities	Managed a staff of 6 claims representatives, 2 claims processors, and 2 appraisers.
	Assigned incoming claims and **monitored process** to ensure accurate and timely handling of all claims. Held biweekly claim committee meetings to evaluate and delegate authority to settle third-party claims.
	Interviewed and trained staff in technical software, company procedures, and claims regulations/statutes.

Education

Bachelor of Arts, Finance, State University of New York at Stony Brook, Stony Brook, New York

54

Functional. *Linda Matias, Long Island, New York*

This insurance professional had been out of work for many years, so the writer did not include dates in the resume. She did mention the applicant's 15-year work history but embedded the information in the text.

EDWARD POTTER

752 Dexter Street #17
Santa Clara, CA 95050   edwardp@pacbell.net   408-333-2222 (home)
408-333-8000 (cell)

MANAGEMENT PROFILE

Business Intelligence management professional with a track record of significantly enhancing company operations. Define requirements aligned with strategic plans developed by senior management. Initiate partner relationships with IT staff to deliver critical decision-making information.

Key Strengths & Expertise

➢ Corporate strategic and tactical planning
➢ Project management to reduce risk
➢ Continuous process improvement
➢ Cross-functional team leadership
➢ Relational and OLAP database modeling

➢ Revenue-driven information management
➢ Focus on cost-effective problem solving
➢ Effective change agent and communicator
➢ Delivery of automated, accessible customer solutions
➢ Hands-on experience with Essbase, VBA, and Excel

PROFESSIONAL EXPERIENCE

Capsule Magic, Inc. / CapsuleMagic.com, Inc., Arcadia, CA / Santa Clara, CA   Jan. 2010–Feb. 2012

Director, Online Development and Corporate Planning (Capsule Magic, Inc.)
➢ Requested by senior management to remain with the newly combined company during the transition period to execute a comprehensive knowledge transfer, which included communicating the relationships among Web traffic, site transactions, direct and indirect revenues, and the expenses required to drive revenues.
➢ Designed and built multiple Essbase models, including a dealer-profitability model that provided margin visibility and analytical capability to Marketing, Sales, and Finance at the supplier and customer levels across several consumer and fulfillment brands.
➢ Interacted with IT and business managers to achieve data definitions suited to their needs and to create the necessary data sets.

Director, Online Development and Corporate Planning (CapsuleMagic.com)
➢ Managed the Finance and Business Intelligence team, which included a Financial Systems Manager, a Business Analyst, and a Web Site Analyst.
➢ Formed a cross-functional metrics team that worked with senior management to define operational reporting requirements and centralize tactical decision-making. Enabled transformation of a pro forma financial loss of approximately $1.0 million per month into a break-even situation by re-architecting the forecasting process for greater visibility and access to product-line managers.
➢ Delivered support to Marketing and Product Management for measuring and analyzing the success of new Web site features / products and online marketing campaigns.
➢ Directed the development of tools to optimize partner / affiliate relationships from the standpoint of both cost and performance.
➢ Initiated a company-wide report inventory that identified over 500 existing reports. Communicated with business managers and IT staff to select critical reports for retention and thereby reduce the resource commitment needed to support the reporting function.
➢ Contributed significantly to preparing the company for sale to Capsule Magic. Key actions included
  ▪ Modeled performance of major portal relationships to support the CFO and CEO in successful contract renegotiations.
  ▪ Prepared due diligence materials, including driver-based models, to assist synergy modeling and analysis of historical expenses and revenues.
  ▪ Designed and built an Essbase model to enable senior management to analyze and restructure the combined company prior to closing the sale.

Continued

55

Combination. *Georgia Adamson, Campbell, California*

This situation was complex: the applicant wanted to move to a higher management position, but the company he was leaving had been sold, and he had been asked to stay awhile to facilitate the

EDWARD POTTER edwardp@pacbell.net **PAGE 2**

Manager, Business Intelligence (CapsuleMagic.com)
➢ Interacted with the senior management team to clarify business objectives and develop corporate restructuring scenarios. Created and implemented strategies to transition the company from a dealer-referral model to one focused on the larger information-services market.
➢ Planned, directed, and implemented significant Essbase-related actions, including the following:
  ▪ With an outside consultant, developed a Hyperion Essbase model to provide actionable financial and transaction information, as well as accurate forecasting ability.
  ▪ Managed a consultant and a staff programmer, who developed front-end templates for entering data in and generating reports from Essbase.
➢ Developed the information architecture required for the IT staff to provide high-quality data for financial and Web site performance analysis.
➢ Teamed with the Director of Online Development to design a Web-traffic and transaction-analysis model that provided decision support for partner deal analysis and negotiation.
➢ Recruited by the company to investigate and resolve a number of problems. Key actions included partnering with the Controller to improve operating efficiency as well as board and SEC reporting.
➢ Promoted to Director of Online Development and Corporate Planning.

Petroni Winery, Tracy, CA Feb. 2007–Jan. 2010

Associate Financial Systems Analyst, Corporate
➢ Streamlined consolidation of domestic and corporate financials by re-engineering the International Finance reporting system. Prepared consolidated monthly reports and performed monthly closings.
➢ Contributed to successful migration of International Finance to an Essbase system. Researched and identified opportunities to streamline and automate data flow in a mixed NT and UNIX environment.
➢ Created aids for management reporting and profitability analysis by developing Essbase front-ends using Excel and VBA. Trained key analysts in the front-end development process.

Associate Financial Analyst, International
➢ Analyzed and revamped the group's forecasting for potential problems, which involved dealing with information from subsidiary operations in 78 countries.
➢ Developed automation tools and leveraged corporate data systems (Data Warehouse / Data Marts) to eliminate manual data entry, reduce errors, and shorten the financial closing cycle.

Business Analyst
➢ Provided critical support to the cross-functional team that redesigned the company's domestic distribution network. Reduced the network design time of analysts and reduced annual costs more than $1.0 million by developing a database-driven, distribution-network-modeling application. Started with a pilot program in Louisiana, followed by nationwide rollout.
➢ Reduced tax overpayments and potential penalty exposure by designing and building a system to reconcile tax payments made by third-party warehouse operators. Trained Compliance staff in usage.

EDUCATION, PROFESSIONAL DEVELOPMENT, AND AFFILIATIONS

➢ **M.B.A. in Finance**—one year completed, California State University—Hayward, Hayward, CA, 2008
➢ **B.A. in Political Science,** California State University—Hayward, Hayward, CA, 2005
➢ **A.A. in Political Science,** Mission College, Santa Clara, CA, 2003
➢ **Essbase Bootcamp,** FP&A Train, San Mateo, CA, June 2007: OLAP technology and Essbase application development
➢ **Visual Basic Programming,** Certificate of Merit, Tracy, CA, September 2008
➢ **Institute of Management Accountants (IMA),** member since 2008

transition to the new entity. A number of his recommendations could not be shown as achievements because they had not yet been implemented. The writer decided to mention senior management's request that he stay on and to refer to some of his suggestions that were implemented.

MICHAEL FISHER, MBA, CPA

717-222-8988
fisher@email.com
2283 Atlantic Avenue, York, PA 17404

SENIOR MANAGEMENT EXECUTIVE

Finance ... Change Management ... Procurement ... Purchasing

Visionary strategist with a demonstrated ability to deliver corporate objectives. Solid 13-year career creating market advantage; reducing and controlling expenses; and fostering a culture of teamwork, shared mission, and dedication to customer satisfaction. **Key strengths:**

"You quickly jumped in with both feet and made an immediate contribution to our team. Specifically, your analysis and projections of our financials and operational metrics within our group have been right on track."

John Jones
General Manager

Michael *"improved his revenue standing as the manager from the #6 position to the #2 position in about 60 days."*

Loren Hughes
Director
Consumer Ops

Leadership ... Pioneered a service program to improve customer service ratings that exceeded quarterly targets and captured the #1 position among 7 teams. The program was adopted by corporate and rolled out in 21 offices.

Cost Reductions ... Collaborated with intradepartmental managers and senior executives to implement a cost-reduction plan company-wide. Negotiated a telecommunications contract that generated $1.8 million in savings annually.

Change Management ... Drove the organization ranking from #6 out of 7 to #2 in sales performance within 60 days by introducing an empowering, team-based management style.

Vendor Sourcing ... Consolidated temporary services sourcing from 50 providers to one national contract, generating $200,000 in annual expense savings.

Team Building ... Championed employee development, recognition, and open communication that positioned the call center as #1 in product retention within a 9-state region in 5 months.

New Product Launch ... Introduced incentives and measurement tools that positioned the territory as #1 in telephone sales within a 5-territory region.

Participative Management ... Partnered with the Communications Workers of America (CWA) union to create a performance-based work environment, establishing best-in-class benchmarks for management practices.

Training & Development ... Key member of a 6-person team tasked with developing sales effectiveness training and implementing a certification process. Drove 15% annual sales increases post-implementation, garnering the VP/GM "Shining Star" Award.

PROFESSIONAL EXPERIENCE

BANK OF AMERICA, York, Pennsylvania

Director of Expense Management & Procurement — 2010 to 2012
Recruited to take over leadership of a department with a history of ineffective leadership, lack of performance, escalating expenses, and excessively high budgets. Manage a 15-person staff and $100 million expense budget; report directly to the Controller.

- Reduced expenses by $2.5 million through detailed reports and analysis of travel, telecom, express mail, copier leases, office supplies, document management, and cell phone policies.
- Partnered with the Human Resource Director to negotiate a 10% contract reduction on a national temporary services contract, yielding an annual expense savings of $200,000.
- Pioneered the department's first-ever incentive performance plans.

Continued

56

Combination. *Cindy Kraft, Valrico, Florida*

Most of the applicant's background was within the telecommunications industry. When that industry faltered with the economy, he was ready to transition to a new industry. "He submitted

MICHAEL FISHER   Page 2   717-222-8988

VERIZON, Tampa, Florida

Hired as a Senior Internal Auditor, launching a successful 10-year career holding increasingly responsible management positions with this Fortune 100 communications services company. Recruited for a special assignment as Finance Manager with P&L responsibility for a $200 million expense budget.

Manager of Sales/Service/Retention, Consumer Services — 2009 to 2010
Selected to drive sales and ensure customer service and retention. Managed 12 direct reports and 100 union-represented employees.

- Personally selected by senior management from among 1,000 candidates to participate in the Gateway Leadership Program.
- Completely turned around sales performance, taking the team from #7 to #2 in 60 days. Maintained the second-position slot for the balance of 2009.
- Initiated the customer service and satisfaction program that took ratings from #3 to #1 in 60 days.
- Built team unity and empowered employees to achieve corporate goals, establishing the team as #1 in product retention and beating the company's regional retention rate by 8%.

Manager of Sales Excellence, Consumer Services — 2008 to 2009
Personally chosen for leadership, product knowledge, vision, and financial expertise for this newly created position.

- Developed the Sales Effectiveness Training program that standardized training, strengthened the overall regional sales organization, and led to annual revenue increases of 15%.

Finance & Call Center Manager, Consumer Services — 2005 to 2008
Promoted to finance manager and within 12 months assumed additional responsibilities directing a 13-person team in the special-needs call center.

- Resolved a $20 million shortfall in sales goals to finish #1 in booked revenues by benchmarking internal performance, reallocating revenue goals between sales and service departments, and employing performance metrics for sales representatives.

Financial Analyst, Consumer Services Finance — 2004 to 2005
Conducted post-promotion marketing reviews for profitability; recommended marketing and operations funding prioritizations; reviewed income statement categories to evaluate financial trade-offs; and analyzed activity-based costing system results.

PRIOR RELEVANT EXPERIENCE

Financial & Compliance Auditor, FLORIDA AUDIT DEPT., Tallahassee, Florida — 1998–2000
Staff Accountant, Audit Staff, ERNST AND YOUNG, Nashville, TN — 1997–1998

EDUCATION

Master of Business Administration, University of Florida, Gainesville, Florida — 2009
Bachelor of Science in Accounting, Purdue University, West Lafayette, Indiana — 1997

CERTIFICATIONS

Certified Public Accountant (CPA) • Certified Internal Auditor (CIA)
Certified Information Systems Auditor (CISA)

this resume and had three offers on the table simultaneously...two with banks and one with a restaurant." The shaded box with testimonials is an attention-getter, buttressed by the list of key strengths of the same height and close to it. Bold italic makes these key strengths stand out.

Peter M. Dube, CPA, CMA, CFM

9391 Birch Avenue
Caldwell, NJ 07006

Home: 975-618-5555
Mobile: 975-930-5555
petedube@verizon.net

CORPORATE FINANCE EXECUTIVE
CFO / Controller / Audit Director—High-Growth & Multinational Corporations

- **Versatile finance professional with 23-year track record** of top-notch corporate finance and Sarbanes-Oxley Section 404 Project Management expertise. Achieved billions of dollars in financial gains through cost reductions, strategic business development and efficient business redesign.

- **Experienced cross-cultural communicator, international liaison and customer relationship manager.** Well-honed presentation and negotiation skills (English and German). Recognized consultative business partner to clients, integrating technical, financial, project management, human resources, transaction structuring and sales and marketing know-how to achieve business objectives.

AREAS OF EXPERTISE

- Sarbanes-Oxley Section 404
- Financial Planning & Analysis
- Strategic Business Development
- Client Relationship Management

- Internal Audit Assurance
- Finance & Cost Controls
- Risk Management
- Audit Compliance

- Executive Negotiations
- Acquisition Due Diligence
- Team Building & Motivation
- Budgeting & Forecasting

PROFESSIONAL EXPERIENCE

COMPUTER CONTROLS, INC. (CCI), New York, NY (corporate headquarters)   2010–present
Global provider of internal audit assurance services for 300 publicly traded Fortune 500 companies with international subsidiaries. 800 consultants worldwide. Annual revenues of $50 million.

Senior Manager, Mid-Atlantic Region, New York, NY (Jan. 2011–present)
Promoted to full-time position overseeing SOX 404 engagements for 250 small-to-mid-size Fortune 500 companies, with primary focus on risk management and compliance advisory services.

- **SOX 404 Project Management.** Develop and direct project planning and supervise SOX engagements, ensuring client retention by assuring high quality and meeting all project deliverables on time.

Manager (Consultant Contractor), SOX 404 Project Engagements (Sept. 2010–Dec. 2010)
Project 1—American Graphics, Inc., New York, NY (corporate headquarters)
- **Internal Audit Control.** Evaluated internal control structure (SOX 404) for publicly traded company with 3,500 employees and annual revenues of $116 million. Revised and updated Narratives and Risk Control Matrix for Revenue Cycle (Revenue Recognition, Accounts Receivable, Collections and Bad Debt).

Project 2—U.S. Computers (premier software company), New York, NY (corporate headquarters)
- **Project Leadership.** Headed up SOX 404 testing in Germany. Served as test lead, project manager and primary local interface with client. Completed testing one week ahead of schedule, despite 2-week delay in preparation by client. Motivated team to work weekends without monetary incentives or swap-outs.

- **SOX Testing.** Reviewed test scripts, selected and validated samples and performed Phase 1 testing for 9 cycles (327 Key Control Activities). Field work, including first level of review, completed within 4 weeks.

SARBANES-OXLEY, SECTION 404 CONSULTING—Internal Controls   2009–2010
- **European subsidiary of PharmaInternational, Inc.,** Munich, Germany (Oct. 2009, Jan. 2010)
  Verified narratives of accounting processes and tested controls for design suitability and effectiveness.
- **Edison Computers, Inc.,** Edison, NJ (March 2009). Wrote test procedures for internal controls.

KELLERMAN AG (multinational conglomerate), Berlin, GERMANY   1987–2008
Controller, Enterprise Division—Sales RSA, Kellerman AG, Germany (2007–2008)
Appointed to turn around ailing Regional Unit of South Africa (RSA) with $50 million in business volume.

- **Turnaround Financial Analysis.** Instrumental in identifying root cause of dysfunctional income reporting system. Recommended financial systems improvements centered on eliminating inadequate accounting systems and procedures and replacing them with state-of-the-art accounting systems.

Continued

57

Combination. *Susan Guarneri, Three Lakes, Wisconsin*

This person studied for his CPA during two years of consulting and passed with high scores on his first attempt. In Education & Certifications, a single bullet highlights these scores. The writer

Peter M. Dube, CPA, CMA, CFM | petedube@verizon.net | **Page 2**

CFO Network Division—Kellerman Communications Ltd., UK (2003–2007)
Tasked with establishing Network as major contender in UK. Business volume $95 million; 8 direct reports.

- **Strategic Business Development.** Propelled Network to top-3 supplier status in highly competitive market. Captured business from Euro-Telecommunications (ET), top-10 carrier worldwide. Negotiated multimillion-dollar contracts and created profitable business relationships in expanding market.

- **Cost Management and Revenue Generation.** Managed resource adjustments during economic downturn. While competition struggled, won $15 million systems contract from ET by creating atmosphere of trust and dependability. Result: $50 million annual sales (Network now viewed as strategic ET supplier).

- **Debt Collection.** Spearheaded collection of $15 million in doubtful receivables from financially troubled customers. Negotiated settlements and created payment schedules satisfying all stakeholders.

BA Dept. Head—Sales International Network, Kellerman AG, Germany (Jan.–June 2003)
Short-term assignment to gain knowledge of ET in preparation for CFO assignment in new Network Division.

- **Financial Operations.** Managed 4 BA Executives in delivering sales budgets and forecasting for $220 million in business volume. Generated monthly variance analyses and oversaw risk management.

- **Contract and Pricing Leadership.** Created terms and conditions (T&Cs) for $500 million in long-term RFPs and sales contracts. Researched and prepared international competitive pricing for bids and offers.

Program Controller—Kellerman AG, Germany (1999–2002)
Appointed to oversee restructuring program for $6 billion Telecom Networking Division (predecessor of Communications Networking Division). Reported directly to Group President and CEO.

- **Financial Control.** Devised and launched financial control system to capture restructuring program results. Implemented control tools to measure program-induced cost savings of $300 million.

- **Revenue Oversight.** Closely monitored impact of sales stimulation projects. Group sales increased to $8.5 billion during program restructuring period.

- **Cost Reductions.** Saved $2 million in consulting fees by initiating rigorous consultant bidding procedure, as well as crafting tight consultancy agreement (adopted by all German subsidiaries).

Audit Director / Manager—Kellerman Corporation, New York, NY (1994–1999)

- **Audit Performance.** Appointed to senior-level audit team as Audit Team Leader (10 Audit staff). Resolved major fraud incidence involving senior sales managers at second-largest U.S. operation.

- **Cost Savings.** Initiated cost-savings proposals of between $20 million and $50 million for each audit project. Achieved average adoption rate exceeding 80% for audit proposals to company boards.

- **Acquisition Due Diligence.** Participated on Due Diligence Team in proposed $500 million acquisition. Team identified $100 million tax risk exposure, which led to abandonment of acquisition initiative.

BA Executive—Domestic Network Sales, Kellerman AG, Germany (1987–1994)

- **Business Development.** Fast-tracked to Team Leader, supervising 4 BA Executives and 1 Team Assistant. Oversaw $150 million in business volume with partnering agreement T&Cs up to $50 million. Key role in introduction of interworking technology to German Network, with initial order of $1 million.

─────────────────── **EDUCATION & CERTIFICATIONS** ───────────────────

Bachelor & Master of Economics, Diplom Volkswirt, Berlin University, Berlin, Germany
Certified Public Accountant (CPA), University of Chicago Graduate School of Management—2010
  ☑ Passed on first attempt. Audit & Attestation—perfect score (99%), Overall Average Score (93%)
Certified Management Accountant (CMA), Institute of Management Accountants (IMA) since 1995
Certified in Financial Management (CFM), Institute of Management Accountants (IMA) since 2005
Technology Summary: Windows XP/7, MS Office XP/7 (Word, Excel, PowerPoint), MS Outlook
Prof. Associations: Illinois CPA Society, American Institute of Certified Public Accountants (AICPA), IMA

used the summary and shaded Areas of Expertise to play up the applicant's career direction in Sarbanes-Oxley (SOX) Project Management (an evolving field in finance), as well as his cross-cultural expertise. Professional Experience displays the person's SOX projects and achievements.

JEFFREY L. JACKSON

333 Lullaby Road—Cradlerock, MN 33333
999-555-6666—jljack@msn.com

CHIEF FINANCIAL OFFICER

Strategic Growth Management, Start-ups, Turnarounds
Equity and Debt Financing, IPO Process, M&A Experience and Restructure Operations

Senior executive with broad hands-on financial management and analysis background. P&L responsibility for national and international companies with multisite divisions and gross revenues of more than $200 million. Skilled in integration of acquisitions. Identify and exploit opportunities to maximize ROI and create significant shareholder/VC value. Proven team builder who delivers effective CEO support and serves as a catalyst creating new business opportunities, establishing strategic partnerships and overcoming regulatory barriers. Broad administrative and operations management experience. Public company experience. CPA. Strengths:

- Turned around company, reversing $9 million loss in one year by restructuring manufacturing and marketing operations. Completed international LBO with Merrill Lynch and Citicorp.

- Closed $2 million source code sales contracts and negotiated software and system integration contracts of up to $5 million.

- Spearheaded decision to exit business venture to focus on core business. Acquired major competitor, solidifying market share.

AREAS OF EXPERTISE

Financial Planning and Analysis	Cash and Asset Management	SEC Compliance and Reporting
General Accounting and Reporting	Human Resources	Sales and Marketing Strategies
Manufacturing Cost Systems	Equity and Debt Financing	Credit and Risk Management
Tax Planning	Investor and Analyst Relations	Forecasting and Due Diligence

PROFESSIONAL EXPERIENCE

ABCD, INC., Cradlerock, MN, XXXX–XXXX
Publicly traded conglomerate providing enterprise software and Internet technology, hosting and e-commerce solutions internationally with $800 million in revenues.

Chief Financial Officer, Treasurer and Executive Vice President, ABCD, INC., XXXX–XXXX
Publicly traded company specializing in digital content management and e-commerce advertising software and services.

Recruited to lead reorganization, gain financial control and provide stability during CEO departure. Served as #2 in command with COO responsibilities. Led strategic decision to exit nonperforming Internet advertising business to concentrate on core company enterprise software. Full P&L accountability. 8 direct and 42 indirect reports globally.

- Negotiated termination of $55 million of pre-reorganization real estate and equipment leases, bandwidth and service contract commitments at a working capital cost 70% below investment banker's estimates. Preserved $20+ million of working capital for company operations.

- Negotiated additional $25 million intercompany working capital financing and positioned company for favorable intercompany ownership change.

- Created analytical models and reports to convey key issues. Developed strategies to quickly maximize cash flow and improve business processes. Provided product cost analysis, operational flow charting, short- and long-term cash flow forecasting, financial modeling and budget variance analyses. Managed IT/MIS, investor and analyst relations, SEC compliance and reporting; directed capital expenditure process.

58

Combination. *Sally McIntosh, St. Louis, Missouri*

When an individual has had a long career, held high positions within large companies, and accomplished much, a resume of three or more pages is warranted, as shown in this example. Lines enclose profile information and help separate visually the companies where the individual

JEFFREY L. JACKSON

Chief Financial Officer, XYZ, Inc., XXXX
Privately held, $60-million, joint-venture (with Sun, Novell, and Compaq) start-up developing Internet operating network and infrastructure software.

Formulated and achieved projected business plan. Reported to Chairman of the Board. P&L responsibility.

◆   Positioned company for merger with corporate engineering infrastructure company.

Chief Financial Officer, EFGH, INC., XXXX–XXXX
Privately held core start-up in roll-up and build-out plan providing technology and infrastructure solutions to the e-commerce industry.

Concurrently held COO responsibilities. Led financial dealings, potential public offering (pre-IPO and IPO roadshows) and investment analyses. Dropped IPO initiative prior to S-1 completion due to adverse market conditions. Participated in due diligence process of assessing potential investments. Focused on global customer base. P&L oversight. 2 direct and 8 indirect reports.

◆   Responsible for due diligence and supervised negotiations in acquiring premier systems integrator with 375 employees. Supervised integration of project management and technical proficiencies.

◆   Grew workforce from zero to 450 through acquisitions and organic growth.

RSTUV, INC., Chicago, IL XXXX–XXXX
VC core company in a roll-up plan within the high-end access control, CCTV, telecommunications and security software industry. Provides engineering design, installation and maintenance.

Chief Executive Officer, XXXX–XXXX
Chief Financial Officer, XXXX–XXXX

Brought in to turn around company and to evaluate the validity of the original roll-up plan. Built systems and procedures for operations and financial reporting required due to operating problems since XXXX acquisition. Worked directly with principals of the VC investment fund. Oversaw real estate and facilities management. Established best practices in cash management, contract cost accounting, financial analysis, forecasting, budgeting and reporting. Full P&L responsibility.

◆   Positioned company for sale to maximize return to investor group.

◆   Grew sales 10% by realigning marketing approach to target middle market.

◆   Won $5 million installation contract for new terminal at Kennedy Airport.

MNOP, INC., Springfield, IL, XXXX–XXXX
Represented aftermarket products to automobile dealerships for resale to customers, including surface protection products and warranties, accessories, credit and insurance products. Company entered into joint ownership agreement with retail group operating in Canada.

Internal Business Consultant

Marketed products to larger automotive dealerships. Restructured marketing concept, product offerings and go-to-market strategy for potential franchise launch. Redesigned "point-of-sale" presentation system, materials and dealership sales training program.

◆   Improved gross margins 30% by renegotiating representation agreements and by acquiring highly competitive product line.

◆   Established contract sales employee program to place trained aftermarket personnel in dealerships.

has held top executive positions. Diamond bullets point to stellar achievements quantified with high dollar amounts and significant percentages. Line spacing between bulleted items ensures adequate white space,

JEFFREY L. JACKSON   jljack@msn.com

UVWX, INC., Springfield, IL, XXXX–XXXX
Privately held international manufacturer of children's clothing sold in 1,100+ specialty and department stores in the U.S., Canada and Japan. Company sold to international women's clothing company, XXXX.

Chief Operating Officer

Recruited to develop management systems in entrepreneurial company and to position company for IPO or sale/merger. Oversaw operations including sales, manufacturing, garment dye operations and administrative areas.

- ◆ Grew sales 10% and gross margins 8% in first year by developing retail concept and implementing multiple store operations.

- ◆ Saved 10% by bringing fabric management and cutting operation in-house.

LMNO, INC., Jacksonville, IL, XXXX–XXXX
Privately held manufacturer and importer of stainless steel and silverplated flatware and hollowware, and china and glassware. Also manufactured safety-critical precision forgings/assemblies for the foreign auto industry.

President and Chief Operating Officer, XXXX–XXXX
Executive Vice President, XXXX–XXXX
Member of Board of Directors, XXXX–XXXX

Completed $20 million leveraged buy-out of World Tableware International in XXXX from Insilco Corporation in association with Merrill Lynch Interfunding, Citicorp, U.S. and Citicorp, N.A., Taiwan, ROC. Obtained financial commitment prior to IPO roadshow offering process to obtain equity. Identified business drivers and key issues threatening survival of company turnaround. Increased product quality and manufacturing efficiency of Taiwan plant, improving competitive position, improving margins and increasing inventory turn. Acquired major competitor, solidifying market share.

- ◆ Defended and won United Trade Commission petition by Oneida to raise import duties.

- ◆ Secured $16 million domestic and international refinancing to provide working capital for operations growth and strategic acquisitions.

- ◆ Grew sales 10% and improved gross margins 8% in first year by redefining product lines by market segment and simplifying pricing strategy.

Other positions held: 123, INC., **Chief Financial Officer/VC Sponsored Internal Consultant,** Springfield, IL, XXXX; 456, INC., packaged consumer goods, **Vice President Administration and CFO,** XXXX–XXXX; IJKL Corporation, diversified international Fortune 500 company in electronics, computers, communications, consumer goods, auto, publishing and housing industries, XXXX–XXXX; NOPQ Company, **VP Administration and Treasurer, Director of Internal Audit, Audit Manager,** XXXX–XXXX.

EDUCATION AND PROFESSIONAL AFFILIATIONS

BS in Business Administration and Accounting, American International College, Chicago, IL, XXXX

Certified Public Accountant, Minnesota

preventing the resume from looking cramped in spite of all its information. Boldfacing makes the job positions stand out.

LAWRENCE WEEKS

555 Broadway Ave. · San Francisco, CA 55555 · 555.555.5555 · lawrenceweeks@example.com

TOP EQUITY DERIVATIVES TRADER

Resourceful, tech-savvy and performance-focused trader. Recognized as a valued advisor to executive management for in-depth knowledge of finance, statistics, risk metrics and derivative valuation models. Logical and analytical approach to research and analysis with expertise in trading multiple strategies and pricing options across a broad range of sectors, time frames and situations. Equipped to quickly recognize and implement new requirements and prioritize multiple concurrent projects in high-stress, deadline-oriented environments. Develop and maintain positive client and stakeholder relationships at all organizational levels. Immediately able to leverage industry networks, superior presentation skills and business acumen into a mid-level management role. Specialized talents in the following areas:

Portfolio Management / Financial Analysis / Problem Solving / Trading Compliance / Option Pricing
Risk Management / P&L / Team Training / Market Research / Customer Relationship Management

Technology Snapshot: MS Office, Internet research, Bloomberg, Derivix, Egar, AT Financial, Microhedge and Aqtor.

CAREER HISTORY

EQUITY DERIVATIVES TRADER (options), Bay Hall Capital Management—Danville, CA   2008–2010

Secured position as stakeholder point person on the portfolio management team, tasked with trading correlation and dispersion in all sectors; functioned as sector trader for equity and index options in financial, energy, pharmaceuticals, industrial and consumer sectors. Personally developed and improved proprietary models for all event pricing.

- Full authority for specific event and relationship pricing, involving relative pricing of options as well as the volatility of specific events.
- Successfully traded near-term and long-term volatility, non-normal distributions (both vertically and forward volume), takeovers and special occurrences.
- Actively served as Risk Manager, a key player on the Risk Committee.
- Integral in cultivating market research for the group, continually conducting market and economic research to stay current on market trends and events.

EQUITY DERIVATIVES TRADER (options), PTS Trading—Chicago, IL   2007–2008

Instrumental in strategizing a competitive edge as top trader, leveraging deep-rooted technical analysis skills into buying and selling of equity options. Set strategic direction of trading models to align with market conditions while researching and analyzing trade data.

- Proficiently leveraged various strategies to facilitate successful executions; located and provided recommendations on high potential options, including those outside personally managed sectors.
- Ensured strict compliance with company risk management protocol with comprehensive assessment of financial data.

FUTURES TRADER, Bay Hall Capital Management—San Francisco, CA   2002–2007

Enlisted as independently contracted day trader, trading short-term futures while managing a personally developed portfolio.

- Integrated trading disciplines and comprehensive market insight into notable profitability.
- Conducted thorough technical analysis by the use of Candlestick Patterns, Elliot Wave, Fibonacci and Market Profiling.

LEAD MARKET MAKER, SJT Trading—San Francisco, CA   1997–2002

Delivered value as a lead market maker on the Pacific Coast Options Exchange with full accountability to maintain markets and ensure customer liquidity. Facilitated weekly Options Theory classes, training/mentoring clerks and junior traders.

- Continuously maintained option quotes, updating implied volatilities across skew and term structure; disseminated quotes and traded on those markets.
- Ensured constant updates on the volatility of all options for a diversified portfolio of 30 stocks.
- Provided market depth to large customers and ensured continuous maintenance of an orderly marketplace.
- Co-opted to listing committee for the exchange, tasked with locating appropriate stocks on which to list options.

EDUCATION

BS, ACCOUNTING AND INTERNATIONAL STUDIES, *Indiana University*—Bloomington, IN

59

Combination. *Sandra Ingemansen, Matteson, Illinois*

This lead market maker on the Pacific Coast Options Exchange had been laid off and was seeking a similar role. The resume shows his knowledge of trading in a variety of sectors.

MICHAEL R. BROWN, CPA

5555 Winding Creek Drive • Ann Arbor, MI 55555
Home: 555-555-5555 • Cell: 555-555-5555 • mrbrown@xxxx.net

CHIEF FINANCIAL OFFICER

Versatile and resourceful **Senior Finance Executive** offering extensive experience in financial leadership, business planning, operations, and management reporting in diverse industries including manufacturing, healthcare, Internet services, professional consulting, and public accounting. Combine hands-on project management skills, well-developed analytical ability, and in-depth technical accounting knowledge. Possess unique ability to grasp the big picture, focus on the important details, and prioritize multiple projects. Self-directed leader who can build and motivate high-performance teams and cultivate effective working relationships with key stakeholders. Recognized as a trusted advisor and business partner. Committed to adding value and exceeding expectations through creative idea generation, collaborative problem solving, intuitive business judgment, and disciplined decision making.

AREAS OF EXPERTISE

- Strategic Planning
- Mergers & Acquisitions
- Joint Ventures
- P&L Management
- Financial Reporting
- Financial Analysis

- Budgeting & Forecasting
- Debt & Equity Offerings
- Cash Management
- Restructuring
- SEC Filings
- Internal Controls

- Cost Reduction
- Process Improvement
- High-Level Negotiations
- Change Management
- Business Development
- Coaching & Training

PROFESSIONAL EXPERIENCE

Recruiters National, Inc., Ann Arbor, MI • 2009–Present
Start-up national recruitment agency providing recruiting outsourcing services on a contingent fee basis.

Chief Financial Officer
Assist the CEO/Founder with fund-raising efforts, including developing financial projections, investor presentations, and business plans. Establish all financial and accounting policies and procedures; prepare and maintain accounting records; and manage relationships with critical vendors, bankers, attorneys, and CPAs.

Key Accomplishments
- Raised initial proceeds from investors to transition company from start-up phase and begin initial operations.
- Collaborated directly with outside legal counsel to update and refine franchise documents and offered advice and counsel to CEO/Founder on executing franchise agreements.
- Negotiated directly with potential franchisees and ultimately executed the company's first agreement.

Proserv International, Detroit, MI • 2005–2008
An international professional services firm and wholly owned subsidiary of PeoplePower, Inc., that provides risk advisory, tax, and finance and accounting consulting services.

Regional Finance Director
Delivered client services, planned engagements, and managed service delivery teams; met with management and boards of directors to address issues, communicate status, and present deliverables.

Promoted to Regional Director while continuing role as Michigan Practice Director. Worked directly with regional Finance Operations Directors to develop consistencies in service delivery, practice management, hiring, training, and professional development. Reviewed new client opportunities and developed marketing strategies to win new work.

Collaborated with the managing director to develop the Michigan Practice marketing plan, identify potential clients, and meet with target companies. Sold interim accounting services, account reconciliation services, financial process improvement, first-year SOX implementation and recurring testing of internal controls, and SEC services, including registration statement preparation and writing and reviewing periodic SEC reports (Form 10K / 10Q). Built service team by recruiting experienced business professionals and consultants. Created and provided training programs and regularly met with team to review performance and develop goals and personal improvement plans.

Page 1

60

Chronological. *Christopher J. Bilotta, Blue Bell, Pennsylvania*

The original resume had an objective statement instead of an opening summary, lacked a section on competencies, and overused bullets where job descriptions and accomplishments were mixed

MICHAEL R. BROWN, CPA   **Page 2**
Home: 555-555-5555 • Cell: 555-555-5555 • mrbrown@xxxx.net

Key Accomplishments

- Grew practice from three clients and eight client service employees to an average of 20–25 clients each year and more than 20 direct reports.
- Consistently ranked in the top 20% of the firm's directors in key performance metrics, including revenue per director, revenue per billable hour, and practice profitability.
- Drove client satisfaction scores for office and practice to be among the firm's highest.
- Successfully led project for a manufacturing client to bring three years of past-due SEC filings current, which eventually resulted in winning a major SOX engagement with the same client.
- Developed for an international financial services client processes related to foreign currency transactions, leading to numerous additional projects throughout the client's finance and accounting organization, which generated annual revenues of $1.2 to $2 million over several years.

Financial Consultant, Detroit, MI • 2003–2005
Provided various financial consulting services to clients, including writing business plans, developing short-term and long-term financial forecasts, general accounting, and finance services.

HealthCare Containment Corporation, Detroit, MI • 1994–2003
Publicly traded provider of cost-containment services to healthcare payers and providers doing $30 million in revenue with approximately 180 employees.

Chief Financial Officer
Directed all company financial, accounting, and tax functions by leading a 12-person staff. Managed relationships with shareholders, investors, lenders, and outside accountants. Supported the CEO and COO by developing and implementing strategic business plans and short-term and long-term financial forecasts. Created, implemented, and continually refined accounting department functions after completion of divestiture program in June 2001, and prepared and filed all required SEC reports. Led efforts to develop and refine internal accounting controls and implement procedures to comply with Sarbanes-Oxley.

Key Accomplishments

- Negotiated a loan extension with current lenders and developed vendor payment plans with key suppliers that allowed the company to avoid filing for bankruptcy and ultimately saved approximately $1 million.
- Improved EBITDA during five of six quarters by comprehensively reviewing all significant customer contracts, establishing a vendor review program for best available pricing, and adding spending accountability.
- Heightened company morale during difficult times by effectively negotiating with healthcare provider to offer a more comprehensive package with better coverage and additional benefits at no significant cost to the company or its employees.
- Developed revenue forecasting and cash collection models that helped senior management proactively manage the business and identify potential issues, improving credibility with bankers and board members.
- Implemented cash management systems and controls that reduced accounts payable from over $4 million to $2 million while increasing available cash from $200,000 to over $2.7 million on flat revenues.
- Played key role in negotiating and restructuring bank debt from $70 million to $40 million in April 2002.
- Increased cash from $22 million in 2001 to $29 million in 2002 with a run rate of $31 million in 2003.

Prior Experience: Held progressive leadership roles including *Chief Financial Officer* and *Director of Finance* in private and public manufacturing companies. Directed all corporate finance, treasury, and accounting functions. Also served as a *Senior Audit Manager* for a large regional public accounting firm.

EDUCATION
Bachelor of Science in Accounting, Michigan State University, East Lansing, MI

PROFESSIONAL AFFILIATIONS
Michigan Institute of Certified Public Accountants
American Institute of Certified Public Accountants
Institute of Management Accountants
Financial Executives International

together. This new version provides a summarizing profile, a focused Areas of Expertise section, and bulleted achievements listed under each "Key Accomplishments" subheading. Centered section headings direct a reader's vision down through the two pages.

Edward M. Goodchild

555 Green Hill Road • North Reading, MA 01864
(555) 555-5555 • (555) 000-0000 (mobile) • emgood@sbcglobal.com

Executive Profile

- Accomplished **Senior Finance Management Professional** and **School Business Manager** with 085 Certification and broad financial management and operations expertise—from overseeing finance, human resources, and capital budgets to effectively managing operations and facilitating complex negotiations, managing in both union and nonunion environments.

- Proactive senior-level manager with keen business acumen and strong strategic-planning and project-management skills. Track record of leveraging exceptional value from business relationships through expert negotiation and communication skills.

- PC skills include Phoenix, Solomon, JD Edwards, DTR/TMM, Maxcim, and Microsoft Office suite.

- Dynamic leader and dedicated team player
- Diversified business-operations experience
- Analytical and problem-solving expertise

- Solid business builder; track record of consistently improving performance
- Extensive finance and management skills

Experience & Accomplishments

READING BOARD OF EDUCATION • Reading, MA   2009–Present
Business Manager
Directly support Superintendent of Schools and manage finance and administration of $37 million public school district with 2,800 students across seven elementary schools, two middle schools, and one high school. Additionally, directly manage finance and administration, transportation, human resources, and cafeteria business matters for the entire district.

- Completed ED01 and budget presentation and approval for fiscal year 2010–2011.
- Saved $434,000 in health costs for fiscal year 2011–2012.
- Worked with IRS to complete audit of Reading Public Schools for the year 2008 (prior to tenure) and successfully reduced fine by 83%.
- Provide monthly reporting to the Reading Board of Education.
- Serve as contributing member of the Contract Negotiation Team.
- Created and handled competitive bid process for both transportation and food service contracts; generated savings of more than $95,000.
- Oversee grant management of $2.2 million.

TECH SYSTEMS, INC. • Wakefield, MA   2006–2009
Chief Financial Officer
A $35 million service company and Hewlett-Packard reseller supporting high-profile organizations (companies, universities, hospitals, etc.) throughout New England, New York, and New Jersey. Recruited to spearhead 50% growth opportunity for company targeting major expansion.

- Managed finance organization, customer service, and asset management (10 direct reports); managed Human Resources function for 7 months.
- Decreased Accounts Receivable DSO from 52 to 40 days. Reduced billing cycle from 8 to 4 days.

Continued

61

Combination. *Jan Melnik, Durham, Connecticut*

This individual wanted to transition from a private-sector, corporate-finance background to a public-sector, management opportunity and give back to the community. He was interested in

Experience & Accomplishments (continued)

GERO ENGINEERING DESIGN, INC. • Tewksbury, MA   2003–2006
Chief Financial Officer

A $20 million manufacturer of industrial products with 3 locations (Maine, New Hampshire, and Massachusetts). Recruited to address turnaround opportunity requiring broad management skills for treasury, operations, and accounting as well as sales costing and quoting abilities.

- Hired 3 new direct reports and fully reengineered finance department; implemented finance controls and closing procedures.
- Increased inventory accuracy from 90% to 99%.
- Initiated and requoted 2 production jobs, presented to customers, and increased profit margin by 7%.
- Implemented new manufacturing software package to provide company-wide integration; result: improved profitability and provided better management tools.

AERO-ONE TECHNOLOGIES CORP. • Cambridge, MA   1999–2003
Chief Financial Officer / Sales Manager

A privately held, high-technology contract manufacturing company serving a global niche market, in both commercial and governmental (aerospace) sectors; annual revenues of $16 million. Oversaw finance, human resources, and sales for company cited as one of "Massachusetts Fast 50 for 2002."

- As CFO, hired to turn around poorly capitalized startup venture; successfully restructured finances, renegotiated debt, and sourced funding partners to secure company operations and energize for future growth. Successfully negotiated lines of credit and restructured state loans.
- Managed sales department, comprising 3 salespeople, 1 sales representative, and 4 inside sales reps; played pivotal role in increasing revenue from $9 million to $16 million.
- Established cash flow plans and capitalization to sustain annual growth rates of 25%–35%.
- Standardized hiring process and implemented regular system of salary reviews and evaluations; administered corporate health and 401(k) plans; key familiarity with state and federal requirements.

DYNAMIC SERVICE SYSTEM, INC. • Boston, MA   1996–1999

One of the nation's largest commercial-building service and support companies with global divisions producing annual revenues totaling more than $750 million.

General Manager, New England (1998–1999)
Assigned to turn around faltering business unit; within 9 months, implemented successful operations and sales plan that preserved annual revenues of $30–$35 million.

Controller, Mall Services Division (1997–1998) • **Division Finance Manager, Massachusetts** (1996–1997)

Education

RENSSELAER POLYTECHNIC INSTITUTE • Troy, NY
- **Master of Business Administration—MBA** (2003)

UNIVERSITY OF MASSACHUSETTS • Lowell, MA
- **Bachelor of Science, Accounting** (1996)

---

applying his management expertise to a large public school system. The writer showed the applicant's achievements in each position while indicating skills (negotiation experience, public school administrator's certification, and so on) that would best transfer to academia.

FRANK JAKOVAC

609 Candlewood Lane
Pittsburgh, PA 15212
412.302.1218
fjakovac@msn.com

* SENIOR EXECUTIVE PROFILE *
Providing Financial & Operating Leadership to
High-Growth Ventures, Start-Ups & Turnarounds

Top-performing, **solutions-driven** executive with 25+ years of experience leading organizations through start-up, change, revitalization, turnaround, and accelerated growth. Personally credited with driving significant gains in revenues and bottom-line profits through strategic financial leadership. **Decisive** and **results-oriented** with **outstanding negotiation** and **crisis management** skills. An engaging, **professional communicator** with the ability to put others at ease, quickly building relationships based on mutual trust and benefit. Combine cross-functional expertise and experience in different arenas.

Business Development, Leadership, and Management

- Built entrepreneurial venture from start-up to $300M in four years; built another privately held venture from start-up to $100M in assets in five years.
- Develop and nurture proactive working relationships with chief executive officers, Fortune 500 corporations, bankers, investors, business partners, and other personnel critical to corporate growth, expansion, and profitability.
- Design and implement organizational infrastructures and business plans that maximize performance, quality, efficiency, and bottom-line profits.
- Key executive in successful turnaround and merger of a public company into restructured business opportunity.

Network Technology

- Astute strategic understanding of leading-edge technologies to leverage resources and to optimize productivity.
- Designed, implemented, and maintained large Local Area Networks (LANs) for major corporations—equipment included that of IBM, Amdahl, Hitachi, Memorex, and Compaq.

PROFESSIONAL EXPERIENCE

* President/CEO/Director *

A-FIRST SPORTSWEAR & GOLF CORPORATION   2009–PRESENT
A wholly owned subsidiary that designed, manufactured, and marketed distinctive premium and moderately priced sportswear. A-First sold its products primarily through golf pro shops and resorts, corporate sales accounts, and better specialty stores.

Challenge: To lead a financially unstable organization through aggressive dissolution, turnaround, and business process reengineering initiatives for corporate restructuring.

Key Accomplishments:

- Executive management responsibility for total restructuring and realignment of strategic planning, operations, marketing, finance, regulatory affairs, administration, technology, and P&L.
- Realigned budget process and developed/implemented strategic plans to achieve organizational goals.
- Completed successful merger with United Companies Corporation. Credited with leading AFSG through the revitalization process into business decisions that left the corporation able to pursue business opportunities.

Continued

62

Combination. *Sharon Pierce-Williams, Findlay, Ohio*

An attractive font (Imprint MT Shadow) for the name is the first sign that this is a distinctive resume. Next, the two-tone horizontal lines divide the text with flair. A pair of opening and

FRANK JAKOVAC

609 Candlewood Lane
Pittsburgh, PA 15212
412.302.1218
fjakovac@msn.com
Page 2

PROFESSIONAL EXPERIENCE (continued)

* President & Co-Founder *

AVID VENTURES, INC., Pittsburgh, PA   2006–2009
- Worked with other venture capitalists to develop and manage projects ranging from information technology to land development.

* Chairman, CEO, & Founder *

Challenge: To launch entrepreneurial ventures from start-up in an intensely competitive market while creating strong infrastructures supporting continued growth.

GATEWAY MANAGEMENT SERVICES & GATEWAY ARCHIVES, INC.   2000–2006
Largest independent disaster recovery provider in the country. Also provided information management and IT consulting services. Merged with Business Records Management to form BRM/Gateway.

GATEWAY CAPITAL FUNDING, INC.   1998–2005
Specialized in large-scale, mixed-use land development projects in the Southeast with major focus in North and South Carolina.

GATEWAY GROUP, INC., *parent corporation of*   1995–2003
Gateway Financial Corp., Inc.
Gateway Network Services, Inc.
GFC specialized in the leasing arena, concentrating on the large-scale mainframe market. The equipment included that of IBM, Amdahl, Hitachi, Memorex, and Compaq. GNS provided on-site maintenance and data processing services to corporations with a minimum of 200 computer terminals and PCs. The major focus was on utility markets.

Key Accomplishments:

- **Entrepreneur of the Year Nominations** by *The Pittsburgh Business Times/INC. Magazine—* 1997, 1998, and 2000.
- Built new privately held Gateway Archives from concept to $3M in annual revenues—an off-site business information retrieval and retention service that provided 21st-century solutions to old storage requirements.
- Gateway Capital funded $100M in assets from leasing operations. Launched 1,000-acre development of "King's Grant," the largest retail land development project in the history of the Carolinas. In 2007, the Concord Mills regional mall opened on King's Grant.
- *Who's Who in America, Who's Who in Business and Industry, Who's Who of Emerging Leaders in America.*

* President *

MEMOREX FINANCE CO. *A wholly owned "captive finance" organization of Memorex Corp.*   1983–1994
MEMOREX CORP. *Started as sales trainee within Memorex Corp. and became President of Memorex Finance Co.*

Key Accomplishments:

- **Leasing Manager of the Year**—1989, 1990, 1991, and 1992
- Key player in building Memorex Finance Co. from start-up to $300M in annual revenues in four years.
- Selected as one of three to start the first captive financial organization for a peripheral manufacturer—a prototype that IBM Credit Corp. currently uses.
- Branch Manager of the Year, 1987
- Senior Salesman of the Year, 1985

EDUCATION & AFFILIATIONS

Bachelor of Science, Edinboro University of Pennsylvania
Executive Extended Master Program in Business Administration, University of Pittsburgh
Board of Trustees, Alumni Board of Directors, Edinboro University of Pennsylvania

closing asterisks (not a common feature in resumes) flags several centered headings of particular importance. Explanations in italic promote understanding.

WALTER D. SAKS

98 Ben Franklin Drive
P.O. Box 219
Cherry Hill, New Jersey 07896   wdsaks@aol.com

Home: (609) 888-1111
Cell: (609) 888-5555
Home Fax: (609) 888-7777

REAL ESTATE DEVELOPMENT MANAGER / ENTERPRISE MANAGER

Results-driven management executive with an in-depth understanding of real estate development and construction. Exceptional ability to comprehend multifaceted problems and frame effective solutions, achieving multiple goals. Proficient in financial analysis, strategic development and implementation, staff management, and preparation of financial reports and statements. Outstanding communication and interpersonal skills, with expertise in developing and maintaining strong and productive working relationships with clients and staff at all levels.

- Land Purchase Contracts
- Strong Real Estate Knowledge
- Requisite Feasibility (Due Diligence)
- Construction Contracting & Negotiation

- Leasing Criteria
- Lease Negotiations
- Purchasing Scope Definition
- End-User Space Use Requirements

REAL ESTATE EXPERIENCE

DAIKCONS, INC. — New Jersey, NJ

General Partner

President/CEO of partnership developing commercial real estate projects in metro New Jersey area. Managed and directed construction of partnership ventures; negotiated sales and leases; performed evaluations and due diligence studies; negotiated loan draw schedules and terms; prepared loan packages and projections; developed marketing/sales material; directed architects, engineers, and staff.

- Recognized within the local real estate community as a credible professional with a track record of closing early sales/leases and meeting client delivery requirements. Interest saved due to early sales resulted in increased profits for venture partners and permitted acceleration of project phasing.
- Established strategic business relationships with brokers and agents for early access to potential development sites, expanding new and existing business opportunities.
- Championed project management of Corrs Professional Village ($12.2 million), Kinney Office Park ($19.5 million), Syman Office Park ($24 million), and Bowen Office Park ($18 million).
- Successfully prepared loan packages and projections for efficient line of credit construction loans, maximizing use of relatively small loan values.
- Led and negotiated strategic business alliances with commercial real estate developers to further expand market reach.
- Astutely controlled and established budgets for hard and soft costs, cash-flow projections, project phasing, and sales projections.
- Successfully performed evaluations and due diligence studies on sites, including evaluations for office parks, commercial warehousing projects, shopping centers, and commercial condominium projects.

CONSTRUCTION EXPERIENCE

SAKS CONSTRUCTION, INC. — New Jersey, NJ

President/CEO

President/CEO for general contracting company managing construction projects for federal government agencies and departments, state governments, large corporations, and individuals.

63

Combination. *Jennifer Rushton, Sydney, New South Wales, Australia*

This individual wanted to return to the real estate/construction industry after having worked a little while for a nonprofit organization. The writer highlighted his real estate and construction

WALTER D. SAKS

Experience Continued

- Successfully created financially viable company within 6 months by securing industry relationships, enhancing profile and market awareness.
- Led project management of 15–20 construction projects each year, with scope of projects ranging from commercial renovations to major new construction projects.
- Successfully bid for and performed contract construction work for local government agencies and the federal government through its various contracting arms, including General Services Administration, Navy, Army Corps of Engineers, Air Force, and NASA.
- Encouraged team communication by holding regular staff meetings, maintaining and facilitating communication about projects, avoiding potential problems, and contributing to a successful, results-driven organization.
- Pioneered innovative technological improvements through the design and installation of a detailed cost accounting system. Cost reports, which were taking several weeks to produce by hand, were available for weekly labor production analysis.

MARBLE PRODUCTS, INC. — Cherry Hill, NJ

Manager/Partner

- Full autonomy for profitability of operations, including margins, mark-ups, contracting, billing, collections, and negotiation of all disputes.
- Evaluated competitive market trends and implemented product positioning strategies to ensure long-term, sustainable growth. Re-engineered light structural steel designs of architects and structural engineers, conforming to applicable codes, to gain price edge over competing iron/steel companies.

ADDITIONAL EXPERIENCE

NEW JERSEY COUNTY AIRPORT ASSOCIATION (NJCAA) — New Jersey, NJ

Treasurer

Currently serving as Treasurer for NJCAA, a volunteer nonprofit organization. Former roles included President and Vice President.

- Instrumental in doubling active membership during tenure as President, through increased association activity and relationships with FAA and county government.
- Initiated and developed programs and safety presentations for local airport pilot community; liaised with county government and officials on behalf of local airport and general aviation community.

CAREER CHRONOLOGY

Treasurer — New Jersey County Airport Association	2006–Present
General Partner — Daikcons, Inc.	1989–2006
President/CEO — Saks Construction, Inc.	1973–1989
Manager/Partner — Marble Products, Inc.	1969–1973
U.S. Navy	1963–1969

EDUCATION

UNIVERSITY OF NEW JERSEY — New Jersey, NJ
Bachelor of Civil Engineering

PROFESSIONAL TRAINING

Management & Managerial Development • Construction Scheduling & CPM Implementation
Managerial Accounting • Purchasing Agent Practices & Principles
Contract Negotiations & Principles

experience by listing it first. Bullets in the Experience sections point to achievements. A Career Chronology on the second page let potential employers know that the applicant was currently working and had no resume gaps. See Cover Letter 3.

John H. Dinsmore

555 N. County Line Road #555 ▶ Chicago, IL 55555   555.555.5555 ▶ johndinsmore@example.com

SENIOR FINANCIAL ANALYST / HEALTHCARE ACCOUNTING SPECIALIST

Driven, business-savvy and technically inclined financial professional and auditing expert with notable success in executing a broad range of cost-saving, process-change initiatives for effective internal control and efficiency. Proven aptitude in financial reporting, compliance, general ledger automation and application of lean principles to streamline financial operations. Relationship builder and team leader with the ability to liaise from grass roots to senior administration. Quickly gain credibility by disseminating highly complex technical and financial information in non-technical terms. Analytical thinker and problem solver, able to adapt to any circumstance in ever-changing, patient-oriented healthcare environments. Technical snapshot: Word, Excel, PowerPoint, Kronos, SunPort QMF, Visionware. Specialist skills in:

**Finance & Accounting / Market Forecasting & Budgeting / Cost Model Development / Statistical Analysis
Federal & State Tax Returns / International Tax Laws / Financial Compliance & Reporting / Process Changes
Project Management / Analytical Problem Solving / Training / Requirements Documentation & Reporting Audits**

EDUCATION & CERTIFICATIONS

Six Sixma Green Belt Certified (2010) *SixSigmaSchool*—Chicago, IL
Bachelor of Science, Business Administration in Finance (2007) *Anderson University*—Ann Arbor, MI

ABC HEALTH GROUP—Chicago, IL
2007–Present

Excelled in financial analytics and accountancy roles with the largest not-for-profit Christian healthcare provider in the nation. Positions include:

FINANCIAL ANALYST   2009–Present
Appointed to position of increased responsibility, serving as point person for clinical managers. Enlisted by senior executives to produce daily productivity reports for 6 hospitals across the region as well as quarterly hours analysis. Coordinate with various department heads to develop budgets. Organize and perform tailored audits for HR and finance departments. Tasked with month-end analysis and accruals for contract staff. Provide payroll department with "paid days off" figures.

- Presently **collaborating with CFO, Director of Central Supply and several department directors to integrate lean operating principles into supply chain operations** for one of the group hospitals. Leveraged Six Sigma Green Belt certification into securing the assignment.
- Integrated a new benefits audit process, **conducting 5 audits a year to reclaim ~$800K in costs.**
- **Selected by CFO to execute an overtime audit** for each facility, subsequently **saving $400K each year** in employee overtime costs.
- **Fostered $129K+ in annualized savings** by performing an on-call employee audit, analyzing more than 4,000 personnel on the system.
- Increased personal scope of responsibility by taking full ownership of budget preparation for a critical access facility in Midwest region, including forecasting, complex spreadsheet preparation and financial analysis.

CASH ACCOUNTANT   2008–2009
Promoted to manage accounts and general ledger activities for revenue accounts, bank transactions and billing. Assisted with financial closing functions through preparation of journal entries, account reconciliations and performance of financial analysis; accountable to resolve issues with unclaimed property and process all returned checks for the Midwest region.

- Supported financial services department by generating daily lockbox activity reports.
- Expanded role to include processing and filing of Sales and Use tax for all 6 hospitals.
- Placed in charge of setting up new credit card locations and maintenance of existing machines for the entire region.

STAFF ACCOUNTANT   2007–2008
Total accountability for month-end close process and accruals for regional medical professional fees, utilities and rental properties. Collaboratively performed monthly financial analysis and reconciliations for balance sheet accounts; responsible for daily, monthly and quarterly journal entries, creating cash entries as well as identifying any balancing discrepancies. Took on accountability to reconcile patient clearing activity for one of the regional hospitals and to compile daily hourly earnings reports for all group hospitals across the Midwest.

64

Combination. *Sandra Ingemansen, Matteson, Illinois*

The applicant was seeking a senior-level, financial-analyst role in healthcare/hospital environments. The resume highlights his recent Six Sigma Green Belt qualification.

WAYNE J. MENENDEZ

20 North Street $ Port Jefferson, NY 11777 $ (631) 555-1111 $ WayneJMenendez@xxxx.com

JUNIOR TRADER | JUNIOR FINANCIAL ANALYST | PORTFOLIO JUNIOR ASSISTANT

Recent graduate who is passionate about investments and possesses a willingness to learn and develop, as demonstrated by three years of successful personal trading.

PERSONAL SNAPSHOT

Highly motivated, determined, analytical, intelligent and responsible. Bilingual with interest in international travel. Possess strong interpersonal and intercultural skills and would be an asset interfacing with Latin American clients.

Future goals: *Pursue M.B.A. in Finance. Manage portfolio of investments. Analyze stocks and implement recommendations for employer.*

Skills: Microsoft Word, Excel and PowerPoint.
Languages: Native Spanish, basic conversational French.

EDUCATION

Adelphi University, School of Business, Garden City, NY
Bachelor of Business Administration, Management, December 2008
Cum Laude, **G.P.A.—3.53**

SPECIAL PROJECTS:

Advanced Management Financial Analysis—Integral part of research project management team relating to financial crisis and involvement of government, AIG, Bear Stearns and JP Morgan. Advanced detailing of returns and analysis of options activities as well as BETA/ALPHA stock analysis. Achieved A- for efforts in this quantitative finance course.

Options/Futures/Swaps—Conducted individual report on five stock options indicating fictitious purchasing of derivatives and analysis of profit/loss.

Investment Management Portfolio—Managed $500,000+ in school funds to invest in individual stocks as agreed by class. Introduced fundamental and technical analysis of Johnson and Johnson and Quest Diagnostics.

Restaurant Management—Participated in class project of operating on-site restaurant as head treasurer in charge of modeling and forecasting sales. Tracked sales, managed expenses and achieved 80% ROI.

Applicable Coursework

➤ Advanced Financial Analysis
➤ Options, Futures and Swaps
➤ Micro/Macroeconomics
➤ Negotiations
➤ Investment Portfolio Management
➤ Organizational Behavior
➤ Managerial Accounting
➤ International Marketing

PAYING FOR EDUCATION

STAPLES, Commack, NY   **2005–Present**
Assistant Supervisor   2006–Present
Entry-Level Salesperson   2005–2006

Key Accomplishments
➤ Used strong interpersonal skills to effectively communicate company goals, expectations and progress through performance worksheets.
➤ Trained sales associates to ensure comprehension of products and business model.
➤ Achieved highest-level sales representative with supervisory tasks and responsibilities.
➤ Ranked as second-highest department sales associate; dedicated to showcasing superior products and services offered.

65

Combination. *Michelle Riklan, Morganville, New Jersey*

This applicant was enthusiastic about earning money for his future employer and for himself, conveyed by dollar signs in the contact information. He got an entry-level position quickly.

PHYLLIS FREDERICKS

555 First Street ◆ Phillipsburg, NJ 00000 ◆ (555) 555-5555 ◆ phyllis@xxxx.com

---

FINANCIAL ANALYST
*Strategic Financial Planning—Cash Flow Analysis—Regulatory Compliance
Auditing—Financial Reporting—Expense Control—Process Improvement*

Tenacious, detail-oriented Financial Analyst with **10 years of experience providing stellar financial support and analysis to Fortune 500 companies**. Exceptional talent for analyzing and identifying ways to **reduce company costs**. Out-of-the-box thinker who consistently devises strategies to **improve operational processes and procedures**. Exceptional technical skills including proficiency with MS Office applications, Oracle, SAP, Basel II, QuickBooks, and Peachtree.

PROFESSIONAL BACKGROUND

Ameriprise Financial, New York, NY
FINANCIAL ANALYST, 1/2005–Present

- Provide detailed financial analysis, which entails analyzing financials and general ledgers, reviewing profit and loss, monitoring expense variances, supervising accountants in bank and balance sheet reconciliations, and preparing year-end audits with external auditors.
- Prepare FINRA Focus filings and consolidate/audit financial statements for broker and dealer subsidiaries with a net capital of $500M.

Initiatives & Accomplishments:
- ✓ Identified and corrected $5M in booking errors through comprehensive research and analysis.
- ✓ Developed accounting procedures to facilitate internal controls and SOX compliance.
- ✓ Reduced cost on Blackberry usage by 30% through implementing effective work streams.
- ✓ Analyzed and monitored records of private equity investment with $850M in assets by working with Internal Counsel and Portfolio Manager on IPO valuation.

Morgan Stanley, New York, NY
ACCOUNTANT, 6/2001–1/2005

- Performed a myriad of accounting functions including fund accounting, fund performance report preparation, financial statement auditing, operating expense processing, and month-end closings.
- Managed relationships with investors by maintaining investor lists, calculating and executing investor capital calls and distributions, answering investor inquiries, and addressing concerns.

Initiatives & Accomplishments:
- ✓ Managed numerous domestic and offshore employee private equity funds, including NAV valuation, FASB 157 reporting, and analysis.
- ✓ Saved department $30K annually by negotiating printing contract with external vendor.
- ✓ Streamlined financial statement preparation by linking financial statements between MS Word and Excel, resulting in improved efficiency and 50% increase in turnaround time to auditors.
- ✓ Exacted challenge of executing monthly consolidation of and corporate reporting for each fund to ensure compliance with FASB 46.

A.G. Edwards & Sons, Bethlehem, PA
PORTFOLIO MANAGEMENT ASSISTANT, 9/2000–6/2001

- Maintained regular communication with clients, financial consultants, and brokerage houses, and worked daily with fixed income and equity trading rooms.
- Assisted with currency conversions, preparation of client reports, and trade execution.

EDUCATIONAL BACKGROUND

LEHIGH UNIVERSITY, Bethlehem, PA
Bachelor of Science in Accounting & Economics, *GPA: 3.81*

66

Combination. *Colleen Georges, Piscataway, New Jersey*

A shaded text box and boldfacing draw attention to must-see information at the top of the page. Adding "Initiatives" to the Accomplishments side headings is a strong twist to a common heading.

Healthcare

Resumes at a Glance

EVA RAMIREZ

7704 Greenland Place • Powell, Ohio 43065
Home: 614-237-9671 • Cellular: 614-294-4544
Email: eva@sevilla.com

COSMETIC SUPPLY TERRITORY MANAGEMENT • COSMETIC ARTISTRY

Cosmetology Techniques/Methods • Mask Applications • Facial Spa Equipment • Maneuvers • Manipulations

Customer-oriented cosmetology professional with valuable blend of business ownership and management experience combined with noticeable talent in esthetic skin care leading to customers' enhanced appearance and well-being. Utilize history as licensed **Cosmetologist, Manager and Instructor** to propel all facets of client care, organizational management and strategic planning agendas. Extremely well organized, dedicated and resourceful, with ability to guide operations and associates to **technique improvements, maximized productivity and bottom-line increase.**

AREAS OF STRENGTH

- Relationship Building • Customer Service •
- Time Management • Creative/Strategic Selling •
- Follow-Up • Merchandising/Promotion •
- Relationship Management •
- Product Introduction • Inventory Management •
- Expense Control • Vendor Negotiations •
- Client Needs Analysis •

EDUCATION

TIFFIN ACADEMY OF COSMETOLOGY ... Tiffin, Ohio
• Cosmetology • Manager • Instructor •
Licenses

TIFFIN ACADEMY OF HAIR DESIGN ... Tiffin, Ohio
Graduate in Hair Design

SEMINARS & SPECIALIZED TRAINING

Continuing Education Units
(to meet requirements of 8 credits annually)

Certificate of Achievement for Advanced Basic
Esthetics and Spa Therapies, August 2009

Several seminars held by various cosmetic
associations

ADDITIONAL BACKGROUND

The Hair Place ... Dublin, Ohio
Manager of Licensed Cosmetologists
(1998–2001)

Beverly Hills Salons ... Worthington, Ohio
Licensed Cosmetologist
(1995–1998)

PROFESSIONAL CAREER

PRINCESS SALONS ... Powell, Ohio (2001 to Present)
Full-service and independent customized hair, nails and tanning boutique positioned in strip mall (suburban locale) setting; operations staffed by 5 employees, contractors and technicians.

Owner/General Manager
Administer entire scope of operations while simultaneously contributing as cosmetologist in one station of four-station salon. As single owner of small business, administer profits and losses, undertake all facets of decision making, strategically guide salon operations and productivity, and assume complete responsibility for revenue performance.

Management responsibilities include cosmetic/accessories sales, customer service and client management, accounting and finance, associate development/management, regulation compliance, business/operations legal requisites, retail merchandising and advertising, inventory procurement and control, vendor relationships, contract negotiations, booth rental contracts and leases to licensed cosmetologists and nail technicians.

→ **Successfully conceived and launched full scale of operations** and guided business to strong reputation for quality output of product and services; consistently met challenges of market conditions and business atmosphere to persevere throughout years of ownership.

→ **Maintain operating costs at lowest possible point by reducing inventory and labor hours during seasonal periods.** Also negotiate with vendors to secure better pricing for goods and services.

→ **Facilitated revenue increase by bringing in cosmetic line to enhance product offering to clients.**

→ **Recognized opportunity to supplement revenue** and spearheaded remodel of existing tanning space to provide for salon.

→ **Expanded market visibility by becoming member of Powell Chamber of Commerce.**

→ **Modify policies and procedures to ensure employee compliance with changing licensing regulations.**

→ **Work in concert with American Cancer Society to provide styling services to cancer patients** with aim of improving appearance, outlook, confidence and self-esteem.

67

Combination. *Jeremy Worthington, Columbus, Ohio*

This cosmetologist owned her own shop and, as an artist with creativity, wanted to promote and develop her business. To that end, the writer designed this resume to be attention-grabbing by using Microsoft Word's Table feature.

LAURA S. CORD, RN, BSN, CPC-H

5555 Hampton Drive ~ New Berlin, WI 55555 ~ 555-555-5555 ~ cord@xxxx.com

PROFILE

"Laura demonstrates exceptional professional knowledge with regard to making coverage decisions in appeals and Medicare claims." —**Debra W., Claims Supervisor, Health Government Services, LLC**

LICENSE / CERTIFICATION

CAREER EXPERIENCE

MEDICAL CASE / RECORDS REVIEW

Claims Review & Analysis ~ Fraud Investigation ~ Consulting / Training

- More than **12 years of comprehensive case review experience** specializing in personal injury, Medicare, and managed care.
- Accumulatively **saved $77M+** by uncovering unsubstantiated claims and fraud for insurance companies, attorneys, and Medicare / Medicaid.
- Regarded as *Total Insurance's* **expert for impairment cases.**
- Stellar reputation for work in resolving **highly complex medical-legal** case issues.
- Uniquely qualified to interpret / summarize medical billings as **certified coder**.
- Medical knowledge acquired from more than 5 years of RN experience in Medical / Surgical, Neurosurgery, Critical Care / Trauma, Transplant, and Orthopedic Units.

AREAS OF EXCEPTIONAL REVIEW EXPERTISE

- Medical Treatment & Analysis Summaries
- Medical-Necessity Determination
- Negotiation Points / Deposition Questions
- Pharmaceutical (Medication)
- Length of Stay—Relative to Injury
- Experimental / Investigational Treatments
- Appeals Process

- Billing & Coding
- Medical Malpractice
- Injury / Illness Assessment
- Usual & Customary Charges
- Quality of Care—Relative to Injury
- Impairment Ratings
- Utilization Review / File Audits

Registered Nurse License, 1989
~ State of Wisconsin

Certified Professional Coder, 2006
~ American Academy of Professional Coders, Denver, CO

Medical Services Specialist   1/05–Present
TOTAL INSURANCE, Hartland, WI
Safeguard insurance payouts through comprehensive review of medical records for 300+ personal-injury claims annually. Develop case analyses and summaries. Advise adjusters regarding value of medical treatments. Prepare for complex, legal cases by interpreting claim and medical information for attorneys, providing negotiation points and deposition questions.

- Considered the **company authority for impairment cases** and one of a select few subject-matter experts in **medical billing and coding.**
- Recognized as top reviewer out of staff of 12—**exclusively assigned highest damage claim files** based on reputation for being thorough, accurate, and expedient.
- **Saved more than $3M** through uncovering unsubstantiated claims.
- Selected to **lead nationwide corporate training program** and chosen to advise committee developing software to detect fraudulent-billing practices.

Medical Records Review Consultant   1/05–12/05
HOMECARE SOLUTIONS LLC, Madison, WI
Reviewed and investigated 1,500+ home-healthcare records for potential Medicare fraud and errors (as independent contractor); uncovered irregularities in 60%+ of cases.

- Discovered circumstances that would have cost taxpayers **$40M+**; highest number of cases reviewed and largest savings out of staff of 10.

Page 1

68

Combination. *Linda Dobogai, New Berlin, Wisconsin*

The applicant wanted a resume for starting her own business in medical records instead of seeking employment with a firm. The writer used strong testimonials to help establish the applicant's

CAREER EXPERIENCE

"She consistently maintains the department standards for quality and compliancy, achieving 98% accuracy in quality reviews. Her knowledge has resulted in claims being adjudicated accurately by the department's guidelines and procedures." —**Roz. B, Claims Supervisor, Health Government Services, LLC**

EDUCATION

PROFESSIONAL DEVELOPMENT

Medical Review Specialist   6/99–12/04
HEALTH GOVERNMENT SERVICES, LLC, Milwaukee, WI
Regulated providers for Medicare and Medicaid through intermediary contractual arrangement with *Blue Cross Blue Shield United of Wisconsin*. Assigned up to 25,000 cases annually to review for medical necessity, guidelines compliance, and provider legitimacy. Advised attorneys and judges on medical appeals cases. Educated providers on proper claims procedures and Medicare policies.

- **Saved $34M+** through investigations that led to denial of 70% of claims.

Sabbatical   12/97–6/99
Focused on family development.

Registered Nurse—Marriott Managed Care   5/94–12/97
AETNA, Milwaukee, WI
Advised managed-care policy holders on treatment guidelines, collaborating closely with multidisciplinary medical teams across the nation. Educated medical personnel on preventative, preoperative, and discharge planning requirements for various medical conditions.

- Acknowledged for monitoring **highest number of caseloads** locally while concurrently and consistently **achieving 98% accuracy in quality reviews.**

Staff Nurse   5/89–5/94
WAUKESHA MEMORIAL HOSPITAL, Waukesha, WI
Provided high-quality care and education to patients in spinal cord injury, rehabilitation, neurosurgery / science, medical / surgical, orthopedic, transplant, and critical care / trauma units (28-bed unit average).

Bachelor of Science—Nursing, 1989
UNIVERSITY OF WISCONSIN, Madison, WI

Impairment Training Workshop—*AMA Guides to Evaluation of Permanent Impairment, 6th edition*, 2008
BRIGHAM & ASSOCIATES, Kailua, Hawaii

Medical Billing & Coding Seminars, yearly since 2004
AMERICAN ACADEMY OF PROFESSIONAL CODERS, Denver, CO

Various Medicare Seminars / Online Updates
Extensive number of trainings include such topics as Compliance Fraud, Outpatient Appeals, Ambulance Issues, and Outpatient Laboratory Values, among others.

credibility and identified how her work could benefit her targeted customer base (attorneys). The writer also used Microsoft Word text boxes, one for the section headings and one for the main text, to create the layout for this resume.

55 Southern Bend Way
Brentwood, New York 22222
(555) 555-0000 • labtech@health.com

LORI GREEN

LABORATORY TECHNICIAN

PROFESSIONAL **EXPERIENCE**	**Laboratory Technician** **Briarcliff Medical Center, The Islips, New York**	**1994–present** **Evening Shift**

▶ *Profile*

♦ 17+ years of comprehensive in-service training and experience managing multifaceted laboratory functions; A.A.S., Medical Laboratory Technology.

♦ Broadly cross-trained in areas that include, but are not limited to, hematology, phlebotomy and blood-bank procedures interfacing directly with professional staff and patients in ER, ICU, OR and Recovery.

♦ Perform and interpret laboratory tests, demonstrating a keen ability to identify and correct discrepancies; record and communicate test results.

♦ Recognized for ability to organize, prioritize, coordinate and perform tasks concurrently during periods of limited staffing and supervision.

♦ Ensure quality control of laboratory procedures, staff communication, equipment functionality, and OSHA/FDA compliance.

♦ Render in-house and off-site phlebotomy services utilizing exceptional organizational, time-management and interpersonal skills.

♦ Effectively train personnel in all areas of laboratory procedures; coordinate staff schedules; maintain timely and accurate computerized data entry.

▶ *Diagnostic Testing*

– Hematology	– Urinalysis
– Phlebotomy	– Coagulation
– Blood Bank	– Chemistry
– Bone Marrow Slides	– Serology

▶ *In-service Training*
15 years, ongoing

– CPR	– Infection Control
– Vital Signs	– Fire and Safety
– Venipuncture	– Information Systems
– Specimen Handling	– OSHA/FDA

▶ *Equipment*

– Beckman CX3, CX7	– Hemo-Cell-Dyne 1600
– TDX	– Coulter S+4
– IMX	– Coulter T-660

Secretary, Computer Department, Storage Warehouse **Space Savers, The Islips, New York**	**1986–1994**

♦ Provided secretarial support in areas of typing and customer service.

♦ Operated and maintained functionality of IBM and Hitachi mainframes to ensure accurate and timely processing of sensitive government information.

♦ Organized, labeled and supervised the release of tape inventory.

EDUCATION **Bachelor of Science, Medical Laboratory Technology, 1995**
Stony Brook University, Stony Brook, New York

69

Chronological. *Ann Baehr, East Islip, New York*

A Profile and three groups of skill areas embedded in the information about the current position in the Professional Experience section give this resume in effect a functional format.

CHRISTINA WOODS, RN

333 Sherman Street • Brentwood, New York 55555 • (555) 222-4444 • newnurse@health.com

EDUCATION

Bachelor of Science in Nursing, 2012; GPA 3.9
STONY BROOK UNIVERSITY, Stony Brook, New York

Certificate of Completion, Diabetic Nurse Education, 2011
LONG ISLAND UNIVERSITY *at* C.W. POST, Brentwood, New York

LICENSES & CERTIFICATIONS

New York State Registered Nurse License, 2012, # 555555
CPR; BLS Certification

CLINICAL TRAINING

Upheld high standards of nursing care for a diverse population of patients ranging from newborn to geriatric in a variety of settings including Medical Surgical, Pediatrics, ER, OR, PICU, and Ambulatory Surgery.

Assessment
- Performed total patient assessments including neurologic, cardiovascular, respiratory, gastrointestinal, genitourinary, IV site/line, PICC lines, CVP lines, surgical/trauma wound, nephrostomy tubes, trachiostomy, urinary catheters, NG tubes, G tubes, chest tubes, and ostomies.

Planning
- Educated patients and their families on disease processes, medical-surgical procedures, and broad aspects of therapeutic regimens, including medication and pain-management techniques.
- Attended in-service training on IV and PICC line management.
- As an observer, learned the legal role that chart-based medical records hold during court proceedings.

Implementation
- Followed aseptic procedures and provided care in accordance with universal precautions with an emphasis on surgical/traumatic wound care and debriding, intake and output, and ostomies.
- Administered oral and intramuscular and subcutaneous medications.
- Cared for perinatal and postpartum patients and their newborns, and evaluated fetal monitoring strips.

Evaluation
- Worked effectively with an interdisciplinary team and performed accurate charting procedures.
- Successfully recommended and implemented changes to the medical unit regarding assignment delegation and prioritization, resulting in a higher standard of patient care, and reassessed/revised plan of care as needed.

WORK HISTORY

Interim Office Manager, LONG ISLAND CARES, New Hyde Park, New York   10/07–present
Senior Fundraiser, UNICEF, Great Neck, New York   5/05–10/07

70

Chronological. *Ann Baehr, East Islip, New York*

This newly licensed RN had clinical training but no clinical experience. The writer placed office management experience at the end and made clinical training resemble clinical experience.

JULIE GREGORIO, R.N.
555 Elldin Street
Portland, ME 55555
(555) 555-4444 ♦ julieg@bmail.net

QUALIFICATIONS SUMMARY

Licensed Nursing Professional with 12 years of clinical experience in short-stay surgery/perioperative services and general medical-surgical units in major medical centers. Strengths include assessment, patient preparation, thorough documentation, providing quality care and patient education. Commended for outstanding clinical skills, teamwork, compassion, positive/supportive attitude and commitment to the nursing profession. Effective in establishing rapport and communicating with patients, family members, physicians and other healthcare professionals.

EXPERIENCE

PORTLAND HOSPITAL   Portland, ME
Registered Nurse—Perioperative Services   2002 to present

- Provide pre- and postoperative care for infant to geriatric patients in the Short-Stay Surgery and Recovery Unit of a 251-bed hospital. Responsibilities include on-call rotation for the Recovery Room.
- Prepare patients for all types of surgeries and one-day procedures, including arteriograms, CT guided biopsies, blood transfusions and IV infusions. This includes starting IVs, monitoring central IV lines, administering medications, giving enemas and so forth.
- Take patients' vital signs and complete medical history, medications, past surgeries and any prior problems with anesthesia.
- Educate patients and their families on preparation for surgical procedures and discharge instructions.
- Participate with clinical resources management in setting up home care by VNA as required.
- Maintain detailed patient documentation; document all required test results and medical clearance for surgery in patient charts.
- Train new nursing professionals on performing various procedures, including starting IVs.
- Apply strong planning, interpersonal and organizational skills in assuming responsibilities of Desk Nurse weekly. Ensure that all activities run smoothly and any issues are resolved.

- *Participated in redeveloping and improving the preadmission health system questionnaire.*
- *Invited to serve on the Policy and Procedure Review Committee.*
- *Commended twice by supervisor for demonstrating excellent knowledge and support during the JCAHO review process.*
- *Selected by management to assume Clinical Coordinator responsibilities as needed; commended for ensuring smoothly functioning unit activities.*
- *Presented an in-service training on day-stay surgery and recovery to OR nursing professionals.*
- *Selected as a Clinical Educator for nursing students.*
- *Chosen by the Marketing Department to represent the hospital in advertising activities.*

Recognized by supervisor for "consistent record of excellent pre- and postoperative assessments, plans and implementation with outcomes well documented. Delivers excellent patient care with compassion."

Staff Nurse—Medical-Surgical Unit   2000 to 2002

- Responsible for providing care to 16–32 adult and geriatric patients that included all types of general medical to surgical.
- Oversaw LPN and aides during shift and acted as charge nurse as needed on weekends.

continued ...

71

Combination. *Louise Garver, Broad Brook, Connecticut*

This nurse wanted a leadership role in her department, a role that required a broad-based background. To address this goal, the writer emphasized the nurse's projects/assignments in italicized,

Staff Nurse—Medical-Surgical Unit *continued* ...

- Administered medications, blood/blood products and IV fluids; checked vital signs; performed sterile procedures; monitored patients; prepared detailed documentation.
- Provided extensive patient education on procedures and home care.

PORTLAND MEDICAL CENTER　　　　　　　　　　　　　　　　Portland, ME
Student Nurse Intern　　　　　　　　　　　　　　　　　　1999 to 2000

- Acquired a variety of experience and nursing skills in 20-bed Telemetry/Cardiac Surgery Step-down Unit.

EDUCATION

Bachelor of Science in Nursing
PORTLAND COLLEGE, Portland, ME, 2000

Clinical Rotations

Geriatric Nursing, OB/GYN, Pediatrics, Psychiatric, Medical-Surgical, Social Services

Continuing Education

Women's Health

Epidural Analgesia

22nd Annual Anesthesia Symposium

Current Trends in Surgical Management of Patients with Radical Cystectomy

Listening to the Body

Pain Management in the Elderly

Pharmacology of Anesthetic Drugs: Applications in the PACU

Managing Legal Risks in PACU

Diseases within the Disease: Facing the Challenge of HIV Infection

Continuing Education Workshop for Clinical Educators

Acute Abdominal Pain

Same Day Surgery: State of the Art Nursing Care

Management of Patients with Peripheral Vascular Disease

Cholesterol Cardiovascular Disease

LICENSE / CERTIFICATIONS

State of Maine Nursing License

Basic Life Support Certification

Advanced Cardiac Life Support Certification

---

bulleted items and included a quote from a supervisor on page one. The writer added an extensive Continuing Education subsection on page two. With this resume, the nurse achieved her goal and was promoted to charge nurse.

JOHN R. DELROSARIO, RPA-C

701 Park Avenue • Setauket, New York 11771 • (631) 563-7209
johnrdelrosario@yahoo.com

PROFILE

Professional Forensic Investigator/Physician Assistant offering extensive forensic background and experience as a consultant for television/film. Successfully combine literary consultant experience and published crime-scene authoring. Natural ability to communicate professionally with individuals of all levels. Organized, detail-oriented, and efficient administrative abilities.

TRANSITIONAL SKILLS

➢ Investigated approximately 500 deaths a year, over a 25-year career, in role as Forensic Investigator, including homicides, suicides, accidental deaths, undetermined deaths, and deaths from natural causes.

➢ Supervised crime scene for Medical Examiner's Office; pronounced death, conducted physical examination of the deceased, investigated scenes, reconstructed accidents, and identified and preserved evidence.

➢ Advised detectives, crime-scene technicians, and morgue drivers.

➢ Obtained biological exemplars for evidentiary purpose at direction of police agencies, courts, or their authorized agents.

➢ Identified and established evidentiary value of items (i.e., samples for toxicological analysis), documented evidence, and directed removal while safeguarding quality and chain of evidence.

➢ Testified in court. Assisted in prosecutions in more than 1,000 DWI cases.

➢ Conducted formal lectures, educational programs, and conferences in forensic medicine for physicians, NYSSPA, and staffs.

➢ Provided regulatory reporting to OSHA, Long Island Police Departments, FBI, New York State Health Department, Centers for Disease Control, and Consumer Product Safety Commission.

➢ Participated in research of Huntington's Disease.

PROFESSIONAL EXPERIENCE

MEDICAL EXAMINER'S OFFICE • Riverhead, NY   **10/86 to 10/11**
Forensic Investigator
   Conducted independent and confidential investigations of deaths. Interviewed witnesses, recorded detailed observations of scenes, took photographs, collected evidence, and reviewed physician and hospital records. Obtained factual history and recorded events with emphasis on manner and circumstances of death. Prepared and submitted detailed reports.
   ➢ *Senior Forensic Investigator for Suffolk County Medical Examiner's Office investigating 1997 TWA Flight 800 disaster.*
   ➢ *Assisted in implementing new Medical Examiner's facility, 1996.*
   ➢ *Cofounder and creator of the "Forensic Investigator" role in 1986—replacing 20 P/T police surgeons and deputy medical examiner positions.*

STONY BROOK HOSPITAL • Stony Brook, NY   **10/99 to 7/01**
Hospice Nurse On-Call—P/T
   Provided comfort and patient care, and administered medications to 40–50 ill and dying patients. Interacted with family members and loved ones to educate them on patient status and care.

Prior to 1986, served as a Physician Assistant and EMT/ORT at several surgical and medical practice centers: Huntington Surgical Group, New York Group, Good Samaritan Memorial Hospital, and Massachusetts Memorial Hospital.

72

Combination. *Donna M. Farrise, Hauppauge, New York*

Strong page borders unite visually the two pages of this resume for a military veteran who was seeking to leave a long-term career as a forensic investigator to become a consultant for

JOHN R. DELROSARIO, RPA-C

(631) 563-7209 — Page Two — johnrdelrosario@yahoo.com

EDUCATION

Regents College, NY
Associate of Applied Science in Nursing, 1998

New York University, New York, NY
Bachelor of Science in Health Science Technology, 1982

State University of New York at Stony Brook School of Allied Health, Stony Brook, NY
Physician Associate, 1981

LITERARY CONSULTANT

Technical Adviser to Tom Philbin on *Precinct Siberia* crime novels for Fawcett Publishing: *Precinct Siberia / Undercover / A Matter of Degree / Cop Killer / Jamaica Kill / Death Sentence / Street Killer*
Antiquarian Book Dealer—Flitcraft Books

PUBLICATIONS

American Journal of Forensic Pathology:
"Open Revolver Cylinder at the Suicide Death Scene" (Pending)
Wrote Stories for *Physician Assistant Update Magazine*

CERTIFICATIONS / LICENSES

**Certification by The National Commission on Certification of Physician Assistants (NCCPA)—
#981744
New York State Licensed Registered Nurse—#426200
Registered Physician Associate—#000149**

MEMBERSHIPS / ASSOCIATIONS

Founding Member of New York State Society of Physician Assistants
Original Member of the American Academy of Physician Assistants
Pioneering Member of Physician Assistant Profession
Attended First Physician Assistant Program at the State University of New York at Stony Brook
Life Member of the First Marine Division Association

TASK FORCE SERVICE

Emergency Medical Service (EMS) Council of Suffolk County

MILITARY SERVICE

U.S. Navy, 1973–1979
2nd Battalion—1st Marines

television/film. Bold, centered, and underlined headings guide the reader's eyes downward through the two pages. Attractive 3-D, arrow-tip bullets point to the individual's transitioning skills and to his significant achievements as a forensic investigator.

Nancy Viggner, RN, BSN

555 Parston Road, Apt. 1, Wellington, WA 98888
(777) 777-1777 • nancyvig@tmail.net

Healthcare professional with more than 20 years of nursing experience demonstrates strengths in the following key areas:

- **Multi-Specialty Group Practice Management**
- **Medical and Clinical Services**
- **Clinical Process Improvement**
- **Total Quality Management**
- **Policy Development and Implementation**
- **Health Education and Training**
- **Provider, Staff, and Interdepartmental Facilitation**
- **Public Speaking / Event Management**

CAREER SUMMARY

CEDAR WOODS MEDICAL GROUP, Wellington, WA, 2006–present
Clinical Nursing Supervisor, 2007–present
Medical Records Supervisor, 2007
Referral Coordinator, 2006

- Supervise 100 clinical personnel and coordinate 20 specialty departments in compliance with group and regulatory standards.
- Recommend and implement departmental policies and procedures.
- Collaborate with colleges to set up extern programs, placements, and evaluations.
- Set up training classes and coordinate in-service education.
- Ensure accreditation processing / CPR recertification.
- Assess, adjust, and forecast staffing needs.
- Select, train, and evaluate all departmental personnel.
- Implement and develop OSHA and WISHA biohazard safety clinical training programs and specialized training.
- Set up, staff, and oversee MMG vaccine coordinators for public health department—vaccine implementation, benchmarking, etc.
- Collaborate with local hospitals, public agencies, insurance companies, and nursing homes to improve patient care delivery.

COMMUNITY COLLEGE, Wellington, WA, 2005
Adjunct Faculty Position

KAISER PERMANENTE MEDICAL CENTER
Rancho Cordova, CA, 2003–2004
Float RN—Internal Medicine, Pediatrics, and OB / GYN

CORVEL CORPORATION, Rancho Cordova, CA, 2002–2003
Supervisor / Medical Case Manager

KAISER PERMANENTE MEDICAL CENTER
Sacramento, CA, 1987–1998
Pediatric Advice Nurse, Relief Charge Nurse, Triage Nurse

UC DAVIS MEDICAL CENTER, Sacramento, CA, 1986–1987
Pediatric ICU Nurse, Relief Charge Nurse, ICU Float Nurse

" … great patient advocate… hardworking with a positive attitude… very supportive."

"…exceptional motivator." "…excellent leader."

" … straightforward and easy to work with… can analyze problems well and offer good solutions… willing to be flexible and try new ideas… learns very quickly."

"… flexible… personable, responsible… fellow employees respect her and find her fair."

"… exceeded our expectations in her teaching and management abilities… intelligent… self-reliant."

excerpts from performance evaluations

LICENSES / CERTIFICATIONS

Washington RN License, current

California RN License, current

HIV / AIDS Education Certificate, current

BCLS, current

Case Management Certificate, current

TQM Certificate, current

California Public Health Nurse, prior

Arterial Blood Puncture Certified, prior

ACLS / PALS, prior

NY Licensed Vocational Nurse, prior

PROFESSIONAL DEVELOPMENT

Member, Community College
  Advisory Board
Corvel Total Quality Management
Health Care Delivery Improvement
Workers' Compensation
  Claims Insurance
OSHA / WISHA Biomedical / Biohazard
  Waste
Clinical Safety Orientation
Patient Confidentiality
LastWord / Phamis

EDUCATION

Continuing Education Classes
  30+ hours annually
BS, Nursing, Adelphi University,
  Garden City, NY
Graduated with Honors cum Laude
Dean's List, 3 years

73

Combination. *Janice M. Shepherd, Bellingham, Washington*

This resume is distinctive because of the shape of the shaded area on page one and the dedication of page two to a Continuing Education Classes section. Bullets in the left column of page one

Nancy Viggner, RN, BSN

555 Parston Road, Apt. 1, Wellington, WA 98888
(777) 777-1777 • nancyvig@tmail.net

CONTINUING EDUCATION CLASSES

2012

May	Diabetes Update
April	Safety in the Workplace
	Referral Training
	Ambulatory Care Nursing Conference
March	Trainer, Biomedical / Biohazard Waste
February	Basic CPR—Recertification
January	Legal Documentation
	Minimizing Liability through the Medical Record

2011

December	Office Evaluation / Triage Nursing Review
November	Healthcare Delivery Improvement
October	Dealing Effectively with Unacceptable Employee Behavior
August	Surgical Emergencies
July	Stress Management / Biofeedback
	Conscious Sedation
May	Common Joint Pain / Problems
	Ambulatory Care Nursing Conference
April	Skin Cancer
March	Depression
February	Diabetes
	Basic CPR
January	Chest Pain

2010

November	Healthy Practices—Risk Reduction
	Strategies for Medical Office Staff
October	Hypertension
	Emotions
September	Rashes
	Immunization—Update 2010
July	Dizziness / Fainting
June	Headaches
April	Urinary Tract Infections
	Pediatric Palliative Case Project
	Telephone Triage
March	Cough
	Understanding Anger
February	Limb Pain
	Basic CPR
January	Upper Respiratory Infections

CONTINUING EDUCATION CLASSES EVERY YEAR PREVIOUS

point to key strengths and significant responsibilities in the candidate's role as Clinical Nursing Supervisor. In the right column, the excerpts from performance evaluations help overcome any doubts a reader may have about the candidate. Page two is a handy list of knowledge areas.

Susan D. Grant

0000 Any Street #4, Santa Cruz, CA 95062 • 555-444-4444

susan.grant@xxxx.com

Medical Support Professional...

with 3+ year history of bringing excellent skills to both front and back office, seeking a position to use positive attitude, strong work ethic and sensitivity to contribute to a high-quality, patient care team.

Described by Management As:

Skilled	Adaptive	Intelligent	Motivated
Thorough	Accurate	Caring	Valued
Hard Worker	Knowledgeable	Confident	Trusted

"In her position at Coast Medical, Susan worked a variety of positions and adapted to them all. She is a good Medical Assistant, and this proves to be a very good position for her. Susan is a good worker and would be an asset to whatever organization she joins."

Ashley Mendez, Back Office Medical Manager, *Coast Medical, Soquel, CA*

PROFESSIONAL EXPERIENCE

Family Caregiver/Case Manager   2008–2010

Provided full-time personal care support to terminally ill family member. Managed all medical appointments, medications, finances, insurance billing and transport.

COAST MEDICAL GROUP, Nuclear Medicine Department, Soquel, CA   2007–2008
Medical Assistant

Front Office: Guided each patient through registration, completion of insurance forms, and coverage determination. Answered approximately 70 phone calls daily. Updated and maintained medical records. Composed written and oral correspondence.
Back Office: Prepared appropriate instrument setup. Recorded medical history, determined and recorded vital signs, and prepared patient before doctor's entrance. Assisted physicians with patient exams and minor surgical procedures. Provided blood draws and cardiopulmonary resuscitation. Collected and prepared lab specimens while adhering to all OSHA and CLIA regulations. Facilitated EKG tests.

SCOTTS VALLEY ORTHOPEDIC, Scotts Valley, CA   2006–2007
Surgery Scheduler/Authorization Coordinator

Communicated with surgery centers, hospitals, insurance carriers and patients prior to and during scheduling to ensure billing concerns were met. Confirmed coordination of durable medical equipment and after-care arrangements.

SALINAS MEDICAL FOUNDATION, Salinas, CA   2004–2006
Lead Radiology Scheduler   2005–2006

Maintained smooth flow in highly understaffed office. Scheduled and prepared jackets for Nuclear Medicine, MRI, CT Scan, Ultra Sound, X-ray, Fluoroscopy and Mammography. Provided clear patient preparation instruction prior to procedures, both oral and written. Used MISYS and Epic software to ensure accurate handling of heavy phone traffic including STAT appointments and add-ons. Conducted effective communication with diverse medical staff; known for scheduling expertise. Trained new hires in scheduling. Performed well under high pressure while maintaining high level of organization.

page 1 of 2

74

Combination. *Kathy Kritikos, Aptos, California*

This applicant had special circumstances that seemed to her to be a possible hindrance to potential employers: she had left the workplace to care for a terminally ill family member for two years.

Susan D. Grant   susan.grant@xxxx.com   *page 2 of 2*

Desk Receptionist   2004–2005

Prepared patient files daily for techs and doctors in Radiology Department, a fast-paced environment. Processed an average of 50 calls per day, checked patients in, and confirmed with doctors that modalities performance had been reviewed by radiologist.

> *"Susan is intelligent and motivated, interested in learning and professional growth, handled multiple tasks and was very willing to assist wherever needed. Her work was thorough and accurate. Perhaps most important was her ability to provide personalized attention to patients. This was valuable as it aligned with our goal of quality service and high patient satisfaction."*
> **Linda M. Scottsley, MD, Medical Director, Dept. of Radiology, Salinas Medical Foundation**

EUGENE NEW TIMES, Eugene, OR   2002–2003

Classified Account Executive

Developed leads, sold ads, maintained/serviced current accounts, built new base.

HOLSIER REALTY COMPANY, EUGENE, OR   2000–2002

Senior Advertising Administrator

Conceptualized and designed marketing materials and Web site development. Implemented new billing system, acted as liaison between agents and vendors.

EDUCATION AND RELATED TRAINING

REGIONAL OCCUPATIONAL PROGRAM, Monterey, CA   2007–2008

Medical Assisting I

Completed 18-week course with emphasis on medical both front and back offices. Content included anatomy, medical terminology, ethics, patient exams, blood draw, lab tests, injections, patient care, insurance billing and coding, patient scheduling and communications.

Medical Assisting II

Completed 10 weeks of course; interrupted by family medical emergency.
◆ Maintained consistent high grades in upper 95% of class.

UNIVERSITY OF OREGON, Eugene, OR   1996

B.A. Business Studies, minor in Communications

◆ Earned 3.8 GPA

CERTIFICATIONS

AED/CPR for the Professional Rescuer, AMERICAN RED CROSS   Current

Medical Administrative Assistant, REGIONAL OCCUPATIONAL PROGRAM   2007

COMPUTER SKILLS

MS Office, Explorer, Outlook Express, Elysium, AMCIS, Soap Ware, Lytec, MISYS, Epic, Wise-Med

The writer presented this work as that of a Case Manager, which is exactly the job the applicant performed during this time, adding to her medical assistance experience. The testimonial on the first page helps to build reader confidence in the applicant's work.

Susan E. Day, CMPE

5555 Longmeadow Road
East Bay, NY 55555

555.555.5555
seday@email.com

Senior Healthcare Administrator/Manager/Consultant
*Dedicated toward making a positive change and promoting the highest standards
in the increasingly complex world of healthcare*

Success in overhauling and improving operations infrastructures; identifying inefficiencies in business and practice management systems; introducing automation; ensuring regulatory compliance; and implementing best practices to increase productivity, reduce error, and save time and money.

Named **Best Medical Practice Administrator** in the Northeast Region
by *New York Medical Journal*

Expertise in:

- Strategic Planning & Leadership
- Organizational Performance
- Business Development
- P&L Management
- Strategic Alliances/Relationship Development

- Technology Integration/Process Optimization
- Contract Negotiations
- Training & Education
- Executive-Level Presentations
- Thought Leadership

PROFESSIONAL EXPERIENCE & ACHIEVEMENTS

BROWN, LEWIS & JACOBS, M.D., P.A., New York, NY   1999—Present
Practice Administrator

Recruited to turn around well-established women's healthcare practice struggling with chaotic operations and management systems, and $600,000 in unbilled charges that threatened survival of the practice.

Built the roadmap and executed comprehensive change-management program that stabilized and positioned the practice for long-term growth and profitability in less than 1 year despite resistance to initiatives that challenged the status quo. Oversee all operations consisting of 2 facility locations, 3 physicians and nurse midwives, and 22 clinical/administrative staff.

Operations/Financial Performance
- Restructured all processes and service delivery protocols, garnering buy-in from physician-owners and staff. Identified revenue growth opportunities resulting in addition of new patient service offerings.
- Successfully negotiated fees and contracts with BlueCross BlueShield (BCBS) of New York, Aetna, Cigna, and United HealthCare that brought all contracts up-to-date and ensured appropriate reimbursement to meet current expenses and standards.
- Cut days accounts outstanding 31% and increased net collections ratio 95+%.
- Saved $150 in monthly processing fees by negotiating with LabGroup; recouped over $1,000 in IT expenses by negotiating a referral rebate from Eventure; secured additional $540 for 2 new referrals.

Business Development/Relationship Management
- Established strategic alliances with corporate and allied health providers/influencers at the local and national levels, and serve as Marketing Consultant to Thayer Pharmaceuticals and Inceptus. Credited with increasing practice visibility by securing recognition in national advertising campaign.
- Spearheaded professional development sessions and presented to a diversity of groups at high-profile meetings and special events.

Staff Training
- Authored employee manual, updated job descriptions, and delivered ongoing training programs that instilled autonomy and a sense of pride in staff, and maintained stable workforce.
- Developed and wrote HIPAA privacy manual.

Technology Leadership
- Led 2 practice management system conversions without any slowdown in revenue.
- Initiated and achieved transition from paper to electronic medical records.

continued...

75

Combination. *Alice Pendleton, Jacksonville, Florida*

The applicant wanted to explore additional consulting engagements, so the resume indicates the full scope of her abilities. The original resume had an Addendum with a complete list of

Susan E. Day, CMPE • seday@email.com   Page Two

Technology Leadership (continued)
- Work closely with BCBS of New York on the development of IT tools by serving as a Beta site.
- Updated provider and ancillary service information to enhance Web site and increase visibility in the healthcare marketplace.

Project Management
- Planned, redesigned, and negotiated prices for renovation of 5,100 sq. ft. satellite office.
- Designed a new 8,500 sq. ft. office building and coordinated relocation of staff and equipment with minimal downtime in productivity; recently renovated the building to accommodate 3 new exam rooms and generate additional revenue.

CITY UNIVERSITY PHYSICIANS, New York, NY   1998–1999
Office Manager—Oversaw daily operations for 3 physicians, 1 nurse practitioner, and staff of 15.

NEW YORK INSTITUTE, New York, NY   1997–1998
Instructor—Taught laboratory techniques including phlebotomy, blood pressure, and microscopic analysis to continuing education students in health administration program.

EAST BAY LABORATORY, East Bay, NY   1996–1997
Long-Term Care Coordinator—Assisted in establishing protocols and audited charts in long-term care facilities, labs, and physician offices to ensure laboratory work was accurately performed and coded for billing. Provided ongoing training to managers, physicians, and other healthcare professionals on coding updates. Increased reimbursable revenues 25% by coding to medical necessity. Helped ensure clean claims submissions to Medicare.

PRIOR EXPERIENCE—Phlebotomist and Team Leader at various labs in New York.

CERTIFICATION, EDUCATION & LICENSURE

Certified Medical Practice Executive, American College of Medical Practice Executives (ACMPE), 2004

Bachelor of Science in Health Administration, New York College, New York, NY, 1997
Graduated *cum laude,* member of honor societies

Licensed New York Nursing Home Administrator, 1997

AWARDS & HONORS

Received award for efforts in advancing the delivery of women's healthcare, Inceptus, 2009

Recognized for exceptional leadership in furthering the use of e-tools to serve consumers and enhance overall care, BCBS of New York, 2008

Best Medical Practice Administrator in the Northeast Region, *New York Medical Journal*, 2004

AFFILIATIONS

New York Medical Practice Management Association (NYMPMA) Immediate Past President, 2009; Member, Executive Committee, 2003–2009; President, 2008

Medical Practice Management Association (MPMA) Patient Advisory Committee, current

MPMA Obstetrics and Gynecology Organization (OBGO) 2005–2008; President, 2007

Northeast Medical Practice Management Association (NEMPMA) Secretary/Treasurer, 2002

TECHNOLOGY QUALIFICATIONS

Medical Manager, IDX, PrimeSuite; MS Word, Excel, and PowerPoint

*****

List of presentations & publications available upon request.

speaking engagements, presentations, and contributions to publications. Limited to a two-page resume, the writer put a line at the bottom of the second page to suggest that the applicant had done such things, which were important for consulting. The applicant got three job offers.

555 South Lime Street
Quarryville, PA 17566

Samantha C. Leeve

(717) 555-5555
scl3@xxxx.com

Healthcare: Operations & Quality Control Manager

Preserving Billions in Revenue Through Effective Operations and Relationship Management

Multitalented Healthcare Leader with more than 20 years of experience in all phases of emergency and primary care operations. Unique experience leading full medic operations in Iraq, building collaborative partnerships with multiple international entities to ensure excellent patient care. Known for no-nonsense, collaborative approach.

Turnaround Virtuoso with proven success in transforming chaos into order in fast-paced clinical environments. Well versed in global trends and international strategic partnerships with proven success in high-pressure situations. Deliver excellence by empowering teams and optimizing systems to raise the efficiency of care.

- Startup and Turnaround Operations
- Team Leadership and Motivation
- Supply Chain Management
- Procurement and Purchasing
- Quality Control
- Operations Management
- Process Improvement
- Contract Negotiations
- Strategic Alliances
- Risk Management
- Workforce Planning
- Training and Development

Professional Performance

MedGroup—Baghdad, Iraq   4/2009–4/2010
Startup provider of quality patient care in combat war zones. Known for clinical excellence and patient safety.

Key contributions: Recruited to streamline operations and build relationships with key government and commercial clients, mining growing demand for medical care during pullout of U.S. military and its clinical infrastructure. Played pivotal role in success of startup, overseeing operations as team more than doubled from 27 to 70+.

DIRECTOR OF MEDICAL OPERATIONS
Collaborative Partnerships | High-Stakes Negotiations | Supply Chain Management | Operational Leadership

Director of primary medical care emergency department and outpatient clinic on military base for Army Material Command. Led 70 staff members—physicians, nurses, lab techs, rad techs, support staff, and maintenance staff—tending to up to 60 patients per day. Staffed and developed medical teams, delivered physicals to U.S. military and client members according to Department of State standards. Repatriated deceased contract members to home countries, working with embassies across the world.

- **Delivered $5M in new revenue,** landing 4 major contracts for medical support in wake of military pullout.
- **Resolved "impossible" supply chain problem,** negotiating directly with U.S. embassy in Jordan to open delivery channels through military infrastructure.
- **Met regularly with Head Iraq Medical Surgeon as well as military's Infectious Disease Specialist** to discuss threat and contingency plans for H1N1 preparedness and other ongoing medical concerns for military and contract personnel.
- **Managed complex logistics of ~8 air evacuations a month** to countries throughout the world.
- **Enhanced ability to win military contracts** by reducing occupational injuries and recordable incidents.

Halliburton—Baghdad, Iraq   4/2006–4/2009
$11B, 57,000-employee provider of engineering, procurement, and construction services, operating in 45 countries.

Key contributions: Ensured high quality of care and preserved multibillion-dollar accounts under extremely difficult conditions. Provided excellent care to contractors and support staff. Established productive working relationships with colleagues, U.S. military, host national government, and subcontracting companies.

Continued...

76

Combination. *Kim Mohiuddin, San Diego, California*

The challenge for this candidate was that her competitors had degrees while she did not. She did, however, have a record of success in an extremely stressful environment: health clinics in

Samantha C. Leeve   scl3@xxxx.com   Page 2

Halliburton, continued

AREA MEDICAL SUPERVISOR (4/2007–4/2009)

Operational Excellence | Visionary Leadership | Process Improvement | Clinical Expertise | Collaborative Style

Led team of 11 paramedics for 10 outlying clinical operations, with occasional coverage of all 17 clinics. Treated up to 1,700 patients a month. Executed training of medics to increase collaborative relationships with Forwarding Operating Base (FOB) military medical staff. Demonstrated strong leadership skills to increase and maintain morale by communicating analysis of volume and success of clinic operations.

- **Spearheaded construction of long-needed, larger clinic**, writing the equivalent of a detailed business plan to gain permission from military and Halliburton. Solicited input from medics, worked hand-in-hand with architect, and oversaw construction, maintaining tight $100K budget.
- **Received 100% compliance audit**—almost unheard of—from Defense Contract Management Agency. Positive review came at a critical time, after another unit received a contract-threatening, level-3 warning.
- **Enhanced effectiveness of medics**, training them on how to build relationships with their military bases and performing root-cause analysis on frequent diagnosis and decision-making dilemmas.
- **Procured much-needed medical equipment** after predecessor had repeatedly tried and failed.
- **Achieved 100% mission completion** of up to 1,200 medical screenings per site, per month.

MEDIC (4/2006–4/2007)

Critical Thinking | Collaborative Alliances | Excellent Patient Care | Can-Do Attitude | Bravery Under Fire

Emergency and primary care to employees, subcontractors, and host nationals at 52 bases throughout Iraq.

- **Led successful closure of Abu Ghraib Halliburton medical facility**, taking initiative to assist U.S. military with critical inventory and infrastructure dismantling, meeting tight deadline in extremely hostile conditions.
- **Saved mission by retaining food services subcontractors** despite casualties in their ranks. Provided life-saving medical care for 8 workers and established twice-daily critical debriefing sessions with remaining staff. Received commendation from Inspector General for bravery in rendering care.
- **Established collaborative alliance with base, receiving FOB (Forward Operating Base) Coin**—an unheard-of honor for a civilian.

Lancaster Emergency Medical Services—Lancaster, PA   1999–2007

PARAMEDIC (1999–2007)

Process Redesign | Emergency Medicine | Conflict Resolution | Quick Thinking | Clinical Excellence

- **Honored for quality of care**, receiving 8 pre-hospital save commendations.
- **Improved colleagues' performance** as handpicked member of Performance Improvement team.
- **Collaborated to realize Lancaster General Hospital's new in-house paramedic division**, training new paramedics in delivery of best-in-class care.

Education and Training

Associate's degree in Para-Medicine—New York City Emergency Medical Service Division of Training
Certified Instructor of International Trauma Life Support (ITLS)—Lancaster Emergency Medical Services
Certified Instructor of Advanced Cardiac Life Support (ACLS)—American Heart Association
Adjunct Instructor, Course in Paramedics—Harrisburg Community College, 2000–2006

Iraq where she and her staff were frequently in the line of enemy fire. The writer used a hard-hitting tag line, keyword bars below each job entry, and a highlighted accomplishment overview with each company to emphasize the candidate's real-world effectiveness.

NICHOLAS D. ROBERTS
LNHA, ACSW, LCSW, M.Ed.

555.505.0505 • nd_roberts@xxxx.com

Nursing Home Administrator

Fiscally adept executive manager with an in-depth gerontology background, broad clinical expertise and a significant record of success in organizational leadership, operations, resource management, crisis management and service delivery. Innovative, detailed and decisive problem solver. Articulate and passionate . . . dynamic performer driven to impact quality of life for the elderly.

▶ **Key Strengths**

Budgeting	Multisite Management	Relationship Management
Capital Improvements	Networking	Risk Management
Compliance	Operational Turnaround	Safety
Communications	Policy/Procedures Development	Service Delivery
Conflict Resolution	Product Development	Staff Recruitment
Contract Negotiation	Productivity Improvement	Start-Up Operations
Efficiency Improvement	Program Management	Strategic Planning
Facility Design & Construction	Public Relations	Team Building
Marketing/Image Development	Quality Assessment/Improvement	Turnaround Management

LICENSES & CERTIFICATIONS

Florida Nursing Home Administrator	Certification, National Academy of Certified Social Workers
Georgia Health Facilities Administrator	Licensed Clinical Social Worker
(eligible for licensing in any state)	Certificated Level I Medication Aide

HEALTHCARE EXPERIENCE

Interim Executive Director　　2009–2010
BAYSIDE INDEPENDENT & ASSISTED LIVING, Tampa, FL

Aggressively recruited to fulfill a challenging 6-month turnaround assignment for 167-unit, for-profit facility with 12-acre campus and 6 off-site condominiums housing a total of 220 residents. Took immediate action to restore hands-on, responsive leadership to organization where predecessor had alienated both residents and staff and allowed a rancorous working environment to develop. Supervised a team of 60 healthcare professionals and support staff.

- Stemmed employee turnover by influencing positive organizational culture. Inspired cohesive team effort by establishing an "open-door" policy to address concerns, rectifying immediate issues, supporting staffers to show personal commitment, and implementing written policies and procedures that exemplified patient advocacy, respect and trust.
- Significantly raised organization morale and earned the respect of both residents and employees through personal leadership. Learned (and used) individuals' names, built relationships to show "someone cared," and delivered consistent high-quality patient care while focusing on attitude, fairness and consistency.

Administrator/Partner
HULA, INC., Tampa, FL　　2003–2009

Built, staffed and managed unique, 3-site, state-of-the-art model LTC (long-term care) facility for clients with various dementing ailments. Managed 36 employees: oversaw delivery of care for 25 residents.

- Rehabbed two existing homes in residential neighborhoods and constructed one new housing unit. Adapted living spaces to provide activities and programming to maximize clients' highest potential and daily quality of life.
- Built census from start-up to consistent waiting list.
- Recognized by former governor for pilot program reflecting best care for seniors with dementia.
- Served as model for Tampa Bay Hospital LTC facility; frequently hosted industry professionals desiring to see firsthand the highest quality care available in Tampa.
- Often conducted tours for students enrolled in University of Tampa graduate social work program.

Continued

77

Combination. *Ellie Vargo, St. Louis, Missouri*

This resume is substantial and well-crafted throughout. Although it has some information that may be considered negative, most long-term-care facilities (and many hospitals) deal with similar

NICHOLAS D. ROBERTS   555.505.0505 • nd_roberts@xxxx.com   Page 2

Administrator
JACKSON TERRACE, Jacksonville, FL   2002–2003

Managed turnaround assignment resulting from change in ownership and leadership: initiated corrective action to reverse decline of for-profit ICF (intermediate care facility). Implemented controls, established new policies and procedures, and tightened hiring practices in a challenging union environment. Oversaw 100 employees and delivery of care for 150 residents.

- Corrected numerous deficiencies identified in state survey before deadline.
- Converted vacant 7th floor into LTC for age-30 and younger clients. Provided age-appropriate activities, social interaction and outings. Marketed facility to the community; enrolled 25 residents.

Executive Director
ATLANTA MEDICAL CENTER, Atlanta, GA   1994–2002

Held full P&L and program-management accountability for a 317-bed Life Care Facility with more than $10 million in assets and an annual budget of over $2.5 million.

- Planned and executed $2 million building renovation.
- Established dementia program that surpassed client health expectations and revenues.
- Cut workers' comp claims and achieved lower insurance premiums by instituting formal safety education for employees. Saved over $100,000 annually.
- Established new foundation to generate revenue: raised more than $100,000 in the first year.

Early career includes management of hospital-based, nonprofit SNF (skilled nursing facility) struggling to overcome under-utilization and aggressive unionizing efforts, and a nonprofit residential treatment facility comprising 21 buildings on 32-acre campus, 3 off-site homes and daycare program serving over 50 clients.

ACADEMIC EXPERIENCE

Itinerant Professor/FLORIDA LEAGUE FOR NURSING, Tampa, FL   2006–2010
Adjunct Professor/UNIVERSITY OF TAMPA (Graduate School), Tampa, FL   2004–2006
Adjunct Professor/ATLANTA TECHNICAL COLLEGE (Allied Health Division)   1994–1999

Taught Gerontology, Quality Assurance, Marketing Long-Term-Care Facilities, How to Treat Dementia, How to Treat Combative Behavior, and Death and Dying to allied health professionals.

PROFESSIONAL LEADERSHIP & AFFILIATIONS

Vice President and Board of Directors: Florida Health and Human Services Society

Board of Directors and Administrator of the Year (nominated two consecutive years): Florida League of Nursing Home Administrators

Chair, Education Committee; Public Policy Committee: Tampa Alzheimer's Association

Chair, Board of Directors; Secretary: Tampa Committee on Aging

Board of Directors, Secretary: Hospital Missions Board of Florida

Respiratory Therapy Advisory Board: Atlanta Community College

Board of Directors: Florida Ambassadors

Board of Directors, Secretary/Treasurer: Hope's Faith

Board of Directors, Secretary/Treasurer: Health Care Family Society

Committee Member: Georgia League for Nursing

National Academy of Certified Social Workers

National Association of Social Workers

Buckland Community Betterment Federation

Georgia Association of Homes for the Aging

EDUCATION

30 postgraduate hours on Aging Issues, Treatment and Program Development
M.S.W., University of Tampa, FL
M.Ed. Georgia College and State University, Milledgeville, GA
B.A., University of Georgia, Athens, GA

situations. This older (60+) applicant secured a new position quickly because of his stellar performance record, superb qualifications, and well-articulated passion for affecting the quality of care for the elderly.

DEAN G. RAYBURN, SR.

dean5500@xxxx.com • 505.555.5005
500 Collins Avenue • Burghill, OH 55050

HEALTHCARE PROFESSIONAL
BUDGET CONTROLLER | PATHOLOGY ASSISTANT | EDUCATOR/TRAINER

Highly accomplished and visionary healthcare leader with extensive experience across clinical and laboratory settings, including lab start-ups, programs and projects management, sales, training, customer service, and hands-on expertise with medical equipment. Proficient in driving quality control and assurance by spearheading inspections, conducting continuing education courses, and implementing policies and procedures in accordance with accreditation agencies. Excellent problem solver and team leader who is capable of making high-risk decisions using facts and logic.

VALUE OFFERED

Diagnostic Testing & Interpretation	Training/Development	Cost Control	Quality Control
Performance Improvement	Quality Assurance	Staff Management	Inventory Control
Laboratory Operations	Research & Analysis	Customer Service	Outreach Programs
Drug Screening & Analysis	Strategic Planning	Inspections	Compliance

SYSTEMS / TECHNOLOGIES / EQUIPMENT

Lab Clinical System	Soft Lab Clinical System	Concur Business Expense Program	4Medica
Lab Information System	Glucose Monitoring Machine	Mass Spectrometer	MS Office

ACHIEVEMENT HIGHLIGHTS

✓ Streamlined workflow by inspecting 50+ sites to account for biomedical equipment and organization.

✓ Vital to developing 4Medica lab computer system, and updating and supporting systems for 40+ sites.

✓ Increased service accessibility and gained community appreciation by establishing lab outreach draw site.

✓ Promoted to laboratory shift supervisor by demonstrating leadership abilities and comprehensive knowledge of lab operations, mission, and scope.

✓ Launched lab at St. Joseph Urgent Care that passed first-year College of American Pathology Inspection (CAP).

✓ Instrumental in launching first-ever program to enable nurses to obtain lab specimens in the ER, which was adopted throughout the hospital floor.

✓ Key volunteer member of CAP inspection team that reviewed several healthcare system labs to ensure they met accreditation standards and to help achieve highest standards of excellence for patient care.

✓ Enhanced employee outlook and goals by volunteering to teach Continuous Quality Improvement (CQI).

✓ Improved lab services as Chairperson for laboratory and emergency room communication committee.

✓ Efficiently input productivity data that was used by upper management to ensure lab efficiency.

✓ Valued by director and management for exceptional job during first year as a Medical Technologist, and praised by doctors for prompt service and professionalism.

PROFESSIONAL EXPERIENCE / EDUCATION & CERTIFICATION—*next page*

78

Combination. *Jane Roqueplot, West Middlesex, Pennsylvania*

A large font size (11-point Cambria) ensures that the resume extends to full pages and exhibits adequate "white space." Key achievements appear in an Achievement Highlights section on the

*"Dean works hard at achieving his goals.
He has the ability of tackling tough problems and
following them through to a satisfactory conclusion.
He is logical and incisive. Dean is a good troubleshooter,
always seeking new ways to solve old problems."*

Results from recent Personal Style (DISC) Profile

PROFESSIONAL EXPERIENCE

ST. PAUL HEALTH PARTNERS, Yorkshire, OH   2000–Present
Laboratory Sales Representative
Recruited to initiate cold calls to physicians' offices, health clinics, and nursing homes and to head community outreach programs in order to grow business and provide employment opportunities. Manage four-county territory in Ohio, generating substantial sales. Lead continuing education courses for 20 phlebotomists to ensure they have current training and education. Manage scheduling for 14 offices and clinics weekly to ensure adequate staffing and service.

JOHN PAUL HEALTH CENTER, Wooster, OH   1987–2000
Medical Technologist/Shift Supervisor
Led and directed afternoon and midnight lab professionals as 2nd and 3rd shift supervisor. Performed and reported testing on patient specimens rapidly and with precision in support of urgent care functions. Provided excellent customer service and educated patients on testing procedures and requirements. Managed administrative operations of lab, quality control, and standards compliance for any and all accrediting agencies.

DILLON LABORATORIES, Barberton, OH   1985–1986
Medical Technologist
Performed emergency room drug screening and athletic drug screening to ensure accurate and timely toxicology screening and related clinical work.

EDUCATION & CERTIFICATION

M.B.A. in Marketing, Finance, Management, Quantitative Business Analysis and Accounting
YOUNGSTOWN STATE UNIVERSITY, Youngstown, OH

B.S. in Applied Science—Medical Technology/Chemistry
YOUNGSTOWN STATE UNIVERSITY, Youngstown, OH

Real Estate License
HONDROS COLLEGE, Westerville, OH

CONFIDENTIALITY RESPECTFULLY REQUESTED

first page to ensure that they will be seen by a hurried reader who looks at only the first page of resumes in a stack.

Sophie Habsburg, M.D.

5555 Lake Forest Road • Indianapolis, Indiana 55555
317.555.5555 • shabsburg@youremailaddress.com

Chief Healthcare Executive
~ Hospital & Healthcare System Leadership ~

Professional Services Champion ... Operations Builder & Leader ... Governing Board Advisor

Physician and MBA-educated healthcare executive with a notable career promoting high-quality hospital resources and programs that meet community needs. Savvy strategist and tenacious leader in identifying and executing short- and long-range plans that increase access, cut costs, mitigate risk, and deliver a profitable healthcare system. Confident, analytical, and enterprising change catalyst combining solid business acuity and financial acumen with a logical and diplomatic approach to overcoming complex industry challenges.

Key Strengths ...

☑ Strategic Planning & Tactical Execution	☑ Facility Structuring & Design
☑ Profit & Loss and Fiscal Control	☑ Management Service Organizations (MSO)
☑ Revenue Cycle Management	☑ Physician Practice Management
☑ Risk Assessment & Management	☑ Patient Safety & Delivery Outcomes
☑ Policy & Procedure Development	☑ Licensure, Auditing & Regulatory Compliance
☑ Process Reengineering & Improvement	☑ Multidiscipline Recruitment & Leadership
☑ Contract Negotiations & Oversight	☑ High Growth, Turnarounds & Start-ups

Career and Accomplishments

COMMUNITY HEALTHCARE—Indianapolis, IN • *1995 to Present*

Provide C-level leadership to an 112-bed community hospital with two outpatient and three family practice clinics boasting $350M in annual gross income and 1,200 employees.

Vice President of Professional Services

Drive hospital operations transcending multispecialty physician practices, service line management, regulatory compliance, risk management, quality, patient safety, and revenue cycle management. Play a pivotal role in leading strategic projects, overseeing the contractual process, and serving as a key liaison to legal counsel on all performance metrics and compliance issues. Direct the revenue cycle from service line development, charge description master and process development, and policy and procedure implementation through licensure, staff training, quality assurance and accreditation, and semiannual strategic review. Lead organizational development and change management directives across the entire healthcare system.

- Optimized community healthcare access 35%, decreased patient transfer rates 20%, and increased revenue 30% after developing multidisciplinary medical specialties, diagnostic, and hospital service lines.
- Cut claim denials and lost charges 28% by establishing a fee-for-service structure platform and increasing controls on financial transaction life cycle.
- Integrated five medical units into one newly constructed patient tower resulting in enhanced staffing, resources, and patient safety levels; led the entire project cycle from staging and relocation to finalization.
- Reduced policy premiums 15% and mitigated facility liability after instituting risk management strategies.
- Masterminded a unique corporate compliance model to integrate risk and quality management strategies while upholding compliance with CMS Conditions of Participation, as well as state and federal statutes.

... continued ...

79

Combination. *Susan Barens, Cleveland, Ohio*

Compare this resume with Resume 10, which was written by the same writer and has similar features. Noticing similarities and subtle differences can help you sharpen your focus in resume

- Spearheaded a Management Service Organization (MSO) to increase management oversight, provide services for employed physicians, and secure professional service contracts with hospital-based physicians.
- Achieved $1.2M in combined liability and workers' compensation savings after enhancing the system's loss / run and e-mod profile.
- Orchestrated a complete hospital evacuation initiative in response to a natural disaster; led the fiscal recovery process using insurance coverage for business interruption and FEMA funding.

Additional Career Highlights

<u>ST. JOHN HOSPITAL</u>—Cleveland, OH • *10+ years*

Leveraged formal medical training and hospital administrative expertise to enhance service lines of a not-for-profit hospital with two medical campuses.

Senior Director of Preventative Medicine and Occupational Health

Propelled service line expansion efforts impacting cardiology, preventative medicine, occupational health, and diagnostic services. Oversaw the entire project life cycle from initial primary and secondary services design through formal business modeling, implementation, and review. Directed clinical internship programs for the preventative medicine and clinical exercise physiology programs. Controlled outpatient facilities, monitored clinical outcomes / pathways, and served as an administrative liaison to the medical staff on quality assurance committees. *Additional details on St. John Hospital roles and career achievements presented during a personal interview.*

- Established all treatment protocols for multiple disease populations with results being published.
- Created and launched award-winning corporate wellness and industrial medicine programs.
- Recognized as a "Fellow to the Association" of the American Association for Cardiovascular and Pulmonary Rehabilitation after developing "Gold Standard" primary and secondary cardiac, pulmonary, and diabetic preventative medicine programs and services.

* Prior career as <u>Director of Cardiac Operations</u> with Hillcrest Hospital (5+ years) presented in person. *

Education and Credentials

THE OHIO STATE UNIVERSITY SCHOOL OF MEDICINE—Columbus, OH
MD—Metabolic and Cardiovascular Physiology

CASE WESTERN RESERVE UNIVERSITY—Cleveland, OH
Bachelor of Science in Chemistry (with honors)

American College of Healthcare Executives (ACHE) MBA-Level Curriculum Includes:

Healthcare Finance • Healthcare Management • Leadership • Healthcare Law • Physician Practice Management—AAMM

Professional Affiliations:

American College of Healthcare Executives (ACHE) • American Academy of Medical Management
Emergency Medical Treatment and Active Labor Act (EMTALA) Technical Advisory Group
Healthcare Compliance Association • Indiana Healthcare Association Leadership Fellow

~ Published Author and Accomplished Medical Researcher ~

analysis and apply a style to your own resume making. In this resume, an italicized description of each work-place "explains" it to a reader who may not know about each institution. The Education and Credentials section is more developed in this resume.

SHARON M. GREENE

55 Avery Street ▪ Boston, MA 00000 ▪ sharongreene@internet.com ▪ 555.555.5555

DIRECTOR OF HEALTHCARE OPERATIONS
Practice Management Services

EXPERTISE INCLUDES:

Best Practices in Healthcare Delivery ▪ Work Flow Optimization
Efficiency Initiatives & Process Reengineering ▪ Formulation & Implementation of Policies & Procedures
Team Leadership & Staff Training ▪ Budget Oversight
Committees & Task Forces: Continuous Quality Improvement & Physician Searches

---

PROFESSIONAL EXPERIENCE

MASSACHUSETTS HEALTH AND HOSPITALS CORPORATION, Boston, MA   2006–Present
Senior Director of Operations

LEAN Initiatives

- Improve medical service through analysis, restructuring, and training across the organization's 11 acute-care facilities.
- Meet with process owners (department heads) at each facility to identify issues in need of remediation. Define parameters of projects, including study metrics of time, cost, quality, and human development.
- Prepare training materials and personally conduct weeklong training in LEAN, educating employees to take an active role in reengineering operational processes for patient flow, quality of care, financial reimbursement, records management, purchasing, and scheduling.
- Bolstered reimbursements by improving clinical documentation and ensuring the accurate use of modifier coding.
- Updated contracts between hospitals to improve information sharing.
- Developed improved procedures to handle psychiatric emergencies at McLean Hospital.
- Reviewed task forces. Disbanded unneeded ones and merged the missions and efforts of others.
- Expedited administrative bottlenecks in the hiring process for physicians.
- Chair bimonthly conference calls with executive management.

Ambulatory Care Restructuring

- Delineated best practices in patient services as well as productivity benchmarks for physicians, which affected 45 primary-care clinics across the region.
- Convened MDs, RNs, and healthcare administrators to discuss issues related to patient flow and patient care.
- By senior management request, instituted an evaluation and subsequent set of initiatives to shore up efficiency and boost patient satisfaction. Outcomes, which were accomplished without an increase in staff, included:
  - An improvement in physician efficiency (3.2 patient visits-per-hour vs. 2 visits-per-hour).
  - An increase in patient satisfaction (65% to 75%).
  - An increase in employee satisfaction (73% to 80%).
  - A reduction in "no show" appointments by 23%.
- Implemented patient and staff surveys pre- and post-intervention.
- Organized all training and led a coaching staff of 15 plus two management consultants.
- Arranged and brought to fruition lectures led by nationally known experts in the field of patient-visit redesign to overcome resistance to new strategies.

BOSTON MEDICAL CENTER, Boston, MA   2005–2006
Director of Healthcare Operations, The Practice Clinics

- Oversaw operations at seven internal-medicine practice clinics.
- Managed a staff of 28, including physicians, nurses, medical assistants, heath educators, and administrative employees.

Continued…

80

Combination. *M J Feld, Huntington, New York*

This resume was for a senior-level healthcare administrator with much experience. The challenge was to cover everything but to keep the resume to two pages. For the first workplace, the writer

SHARON M. GREENE   sharongreene@internet.com   Page Two

Continued from page one…

Director of Healthcare Operations, BOSTON MEDICAL CENTER

- Accountable for a $2M budget. Reported to the finance committee regarding budget and cost-control issues.
- Revamped clinic hours and redeployed staff to higher-need departments.
- Increased clinic utilization by 27%—largely through community outreach efforts.
- Collaborated with Chief Compliance Officer and VP of Medical Affairs to discuss/resolve healthcare regulatory and compliance concerns.
- Served as a member of the Executive Management Team and as Chairperson for Clinic Review Council meetings.
- Oversaw special projects. Developed and maintained affiliation agreements.

HEALTH PLUS DEVELOPMENT CORPORATION (HPDC), Boston, MA   2002–2005
Consultant

- Provided consulting expertise to HPDC's clients, which included Massachusetts Health and Hospitals Corporation.
- Guided healthcare organizations by training teams to accomplish core program initiatives: patient-visit redesign, medical records integrity, patient-staff communication, and medical-error documentation and reporting.
- Conducted presentations to more than 70 multidisciplinary clinical teams on the principles and strategies of reengineering processes to increase efficiencies at ambulatory-care centers.
- Outcomes included structured visit scheduling, the standardization of medical charts, and fewer patient complaints related to appointment scheduling and physician access.

MASSACHUSETTS GENERAL HOSPITAL, Boston, MA   2000–2002
Internal Medicine Practice Administrator, *University Medical Practice Associates*

- Managed two multi-specialty practices employing a combined staff of 16.
- Increased patient visits by 21% through the implementation of walk-in and same-day appointment availability as well as the strategic utilization of physician assistants and nurse practitioners.
- Reduced hospital costs and improved patient access to care by championing the project of creating free-standing Faculty Practice Groups.
- Formulated the plans, designed the layout, and directed the consolidation of two departments to a new location, resulting in a cost savings of $120K in annual rent.
- Simplified the purchasing of supplies through the use of a group-purchasing organization. Negotiated vendor contracts, resulting in $65K in annual savings.

EARLY CAREER

Medical Practice Administrator, 1996–1999. NEW ENGLAND BAPTIST HOSPITAL, Boston, MA

Clinic Administrator, 1993–1996. STONY BROOK UNIVERSITY HOSPITAL, Stony Brook, NY

Administrator, Department of Medicine, 1990–1993. NORTH SHORE MEDICAL GROUP, Huntington, NY

EDUCATION

Master of Science in Health Care Policy and Management
State University of New York at Stony Brook, Stony Brook, NY

Bachelor of Arts, English (with minor in mathematics)
Hofstra University, Hempstead, NY

■ ■ ■

divided a long list of achievements into two groups with a subtitle for each group. For the Early Career section near the bottom of page two, the writer indicated only the dates, institution, and site for each position to ensure that the resume did not spill onto page three.

Tori Grace Ulrich

3 Woodland Court   (000) 000-0000
Knoxville, TN 00000   tori416@yahoo.com

Dietetic Technician/Clerk

EDUCATION   B.S., Home Economics, concentration in Nutrition—May 2012
Texas Christian University, Ft. Worth, TX
Maintained overall GPA of 3.45 while working part-time.

CAREER STRENGTHS

- ➢ Resourceful self-starter, effective in researching and analyzing data.
- ➢ Knowledge of marketing concepts and scientific principles related to food-product labeling and dietary information.
- ➢ Effective written and oral communications skills utilized in reporting evaluations on comparative products and educating adults on healthier lifestyle issues.
- ➢ Equally comfortable working independently as well as collaboratively in group efforts.

FIELD EXPERIENCE

- ➢ Observed and interviewed dietitians in the community to learn and evaluate their teaching techniques.
- ➢ Counseled two individual clients in weekly sessions on meal planning and exercise to achieve their weight-loss goals.
- ➢ Planned, organized, developed, and conducted lecture on nutrition to a group of recovering substance abusers.
- ➢ Teamed with another student to design a cycle menu for a nursing home, taking into account factors such as food specifications, portion costs, production schedules, and nutrient content.
- ➢ Practiced time-management, organizational, and assessment skills while involved in multiple ongoing projects that focused on planning, preparation, and attractive presentation of meals for specific dietary needs (i.e., diabetic or sodium-restricted populations).

EMPLOYMENT/COMMUNITY SERVICE

ELITE TEMPORARY AGENCY, Ft. Worth, TX   2010–2012

Various administrative assignments, including telemarketing. Gained experience in promoting an idea, basic computer proficiency (MS Word, Excel, and Access), paperwork organization, and dealing with customer problem-solving situations.

CHILI PEPPER'S GRILL, Ft. Worth, TX   2008–2010

Hired as hostess and later promoted to wait staff. Demonstrated superior abilities and was appointed as trainer for new employees.

PLEASANTVILLE NURSING HOME, Ft. Worth, TX   2008–2012

Volunteer, providing companionship to the elderly and assisting with meal service.

81

Combination. *Melanie Noonan, Woodland Park, New Jersey*

This graduating student wanted to portray education fieldwork as experience in her search for a position in the health/nutrition industry. The heading "Field Experience" accomplishes her aim.

Sara Applebaum, RN

55 Prince Avenue, Northport, New York 11768 • *residence* (555) 555-5555 • *cellular* (555) 555-5554

Career Interest: School Nursing

Offering a gentle disposition combined with strong diagnostic skills.
Physical Assessments—Safety & Public Health—Healthcare Documentation

NURSING EXPERIENCE

Registered Nurse, January 2010–Present. Syosset Community Hospital, Syosset, NY

- In a 40-bed medical-surgical unit, care for patients with a variety of medical conditions, including pre- and postoperative status.
- Conduct physical assessments, including evaluation of heart and lung functioning.
- Provide complete wound care and manage medicine administration through all modalities: oral, central line, intravenous, intramuscular, subcutaneous, and peg-tube routes.
- Attend to psychiatric patients temporarily placed on the unit. Assess cognitive/psychological states and implement detoxification protocols.
- Instruct family members on proper adjunctive support, including preventive care and medicine administration.
- Maintain accurate patient records in accordance with HIPAA regulations.
- Collaborate with physicians to assist in treatment plans.

Registered Nurse *(per diem),* April 2010–Present. Maria Regina Infirmary, Brentwood, NY

- Through physical and mental assessments, provide healthcare support to the residents of this convent.
- Evaluate environment for safety and comfort issues. Suggest and implement strategies for accident prevention.
- Handle medical crises with accountability for determining the proper course of action. Evaluate injuries and other medical issues and contact physicians or coordinate transfers to hospitals as warranted.
- Document all interventions and noteworthy events.

Nurse-in-Training Fieldwork, 2007–2009. St. John's Hospital, Huntington Hospital, Northport Veterans' Psychiatric Hospital, Syosset Community Hospital, and Nassau Community College Health Clinic.

- Participated in comprehensive clinical rotations, including the pediatrics unit at Syosset Community Hospital. Under supervision, evaluated children with the following conditions: asthma, dehydration, pre- and postop tonsillectomy, appendicitis, and hernia. Administered medicines PO and IM.

ADDITIONAL EXPERIENCE

Funeral Director, 1996–2006. Sunset Funeral Chapels, Deer Park, NY

- Coordinated all funeral plans for grieving families.
- Provided compassionate support, interacting with family members in an empathic, caring way.
- Conceptualized and completed several initiatives, including a reorganization of the office files and a child-friendly area within the chapel.

EDUCATION & TRAINING

Associate in Applied Science, Nursing (2009). Nassau County Community College, Garden City, NY

Associate in Applied Science (1995). SUNY Farmingdale, Farmingdale, NY

Certificate in Cardiopulmonary Resuscitation, *current*

82

Combination. *M J Feld, Huntington, New York*

This recently credentialed nurse had a 10-year career in funeral work and wanted a school nurse job. The writer minimized funeral experience and created a summary relevant to school nursing.

PAUL JEPSON

14 Westlake Drive
Framingham, MA 01702

paul@jepson.com

Cell: 508 875 1699
Residence: 508 789 0098

Senior Executive	**Healthcare / Medical**

Profile

Results-focused senior executive offering 20 years of experience positioning hospitals and healthcare facilities for growth, increased shareholder value, and refined business infrastructure. Acknowledged for capacity to build consensus and drive solutions that meet short-, medium-, and long-term goals. Communicative, energetic style coupled with strategic vision has transformed multimillion-dollar losses to strong profit performances in months, while projects under personal direction have won national awards for innovation. Expert in restoring profitability, assessing potential acquisitions, devising case-management programs, and managing sensitive cultural change integrations that challenge the status quo, yet win the unqualified support of key stakeholders and staff.

Areas of Expertise

- Organizational & Cultural Change
- Business Analysis & Management
- Executive Presentations & Negotiations
- Mergers & Acquisitions
- Healthcare Management & Operations
- Strategic Planning & Market Expansion
- Communications & Success Recognition
- Due Diligence Research & Recommendations

- Process Reengineering
- Business Development
- Not-for-Profit Organizations
- Clinical Process Revitalization
- Quality Healthcare Delivery
- Case Management Solutions
- Tendering Processes
- Hospital Business Administration
- Healthcare Industry Best Practices

Executive Performance

Change Management

Executed comprehensive change-management program for **Christian Church Community Care**—a not-for-profit organization that had experienced significant growth, yet remained stagnant in terms of processes and service delivery protocols. Incrementally introduced new philosophies and methods that automated routine tasks, cut inefficiencies, and slashed costs—winning the support of key stakeholders via step-by-step communication programs encouraging problem "ownership."

Cut administration errors by up to 15% and elevated direct nursing care by 200% through reduced reliance on administrative follow-up.

Program delivered return on $255K investment within 15 months, outstripping all board expectations.

• • •

Case Management

Spearheaded revitalized **case management practices** across New Zealand for the **Workplace Compensation Enterprise** as part of a $100M collaborative initiative to arrest escalating claims costs and introduce holistic infrastructure change. **Project managed $880K bid** against aggressive competition and presided over a team of 8 to design, develop, and commission an organizational-change project contributing **$37.5M per annum in savings.**

Against a backdrop of intense media and public scrutiny, **created transparent and accountable work practices** and regularly briefed the CEO to convey expected healthcare service improvements across New Zealand. Curtailed lead times, elevated customer service delivery, cut paperwork, employed dedicated caseworkers for each case, introduced recuperation plan negotiations, and reduced rehabilitation, compensation, and tail costs.

• • •

Due Diligence

Enhanced salability of business unit, conducting all due diligence work on behalf of **WorkComp.** Examined products, internal processes, liquidity, debt position, markets, demand and supply capabilities, competitors, management, and skill retention post-sale. Board fully embraced all product and service recommendations.

Continued

83

Combination. *Gayle Howard, Southbank, Victoria, Australia*

The applicant was "a consultant with vast experience in technology and project management to a number of diverse sectors, including healthcare." He believed that over many years as a

Paul Jepson paul@jepson.com page 2

Efficiency Improvements	Inadequate systems, procedures, and controls were the key challenges faced by **Hatchett Mitch Pathology.** Produced a complete suite of recommendations to refine workflows and internal controls and revamp business methods. Pruned costs and delivered 10% improvement in operational and customer service efficiencies.

• • •

Cost Savings & Revenue Growth	Revealed numerous cost-saving and revenue-growth opportunities to principals of **The Princeton Hospital.** Worked in partnership to deliver a long-term business/growth strategy, formalize information and clinical management, and optimize financial operations. Recommended methods to enforce compliance to debt collections, assume a stronger commercial stance, restructure divisions to prune budget expenditures, introduce technology enhancements, and review clinical management processes.
	Recommendations accepted and implemented across the board, resulting in **reduction in days' accounts outstanding from 90+ days to 9.** "Payment on Discharge" recommendation **tripled cash flows** and **slashed cost of debt by $200K per annum.**

• • •

Tender Evaluation	Countered public concerns over the integrity of **Burswood Health's** tender process in awarding the multimillion-dollar GADHH software project. Under "impossible" deadlines and a zero-tolerance error environment, meticulously re-evaluated assessment processes, tenders, and the veracity of solutions offered for effectively managing medical records/reports, admissions/transfers/discharges, surgery, theatre, pharmacy, billing, and more.
	Produced comprehensive report of findings to federal legal representatives citing minor "human error" breaches; tender was given "green light" and **system implemented with no political fallout.**

• • •

Hospital Metrics Analysis	Assessed financial health of the **South East Private Hospital** to leverage improved performances across all divisions at the lowest practicable cost. Analyzed all key hospital metrics that reflected desired outcomes and produced reports forecasting trends, winning management support.

Employment Chronology	**BUSINESS/TECHNOLOGY CONSULTANT**	7/2010–Present
	Devised a formal value creation model for management to analyze the validity of proposed infrastructure expenditures over multiple timeframes of up to 10 years.	
CAMDEN RAIL	Examined future business and technology infrastructures, and identified a need to realign perceptions and practices to reflect technology as a business "investment."	
	United existing processes with industry best practice to create a methodology that integrated seamlessly with evolving activity-based costing initiatives and strategic goals. **Model forecasted productivity savings of up to 30%,** together with improved focus on technology investments and business value.	

• • •

TRANTON INC.	**VICE PRESIDENT, BUSINESS DELIVERY**	6/2008–6/2010
Advanced business and technology solution provider servicing medical, healthcare, human resources, education, and executive management.	*Reported to Chairman & CEO (Monaco); Managing Director, Asia Pacific Projects: AUD $600K–$4 million*	
	Instrumental in transforming a fledgling business unit to the most prominent and successful unit in the group—despite the challenges of global downturns in technology.	
	As the pivotal operations-based driver, steered complete solution development phases—from creation to market launch and project implementation. Sustained momentum, scheduling, and delivery objectives, while simultaneously building client relationships through intense communication and scrutiny of individual business strategies, objectives, and infrastructure.	

Continued

consultant to the healthcare/medical sectors, he had gained enough knowledge to run a hospital. This resume targets the skills important for a hospital CEO and plays down the individual's technology background. Therefore, most of the resume is a functional resume for a CEO; the Employment Chronology section is about

Paul Jepson   paul@jepson.com

TRANTON INC., (CONTINUED)	Turned around employee reluctance for merging intellectual property development and client development areas by exposing key international staff to the advantages of linking these complementary operations; devised well-received training programs conveying future vision. Relocation saved $2 million per annum, and in service delivery areas **delivered 70% productivity improvement.**

Devised and developed corporate- and program-based activities spanning organizational management, corporate profile enhancement/creation, funding, capital raising, budgeting and planning, strategy and financial planning and execution, and business and market development.

• • •

UNISAVILLE AUSTRALIA LTD.

Business Solutions, Consulting, e-Business Divisions.

PROGRAM (EXECUTIVE) DIRECTOR, QUEENSLAND, AUSTRALIA   7/2002–6/2008

Reported to South Pacific Director, Sydney

Consulted to large corporates, healthcare/medical facilities, and government, and led team of 10 in project implementations, bids, and delivery of specialist healthcare engagements. Key catalyst in spearheading the innovative "Organizational Agility" practice that positioned the company for more responsive service delivery and allowed greater flexibility to meet market demand. Initiative prompted significant interest from the U.S.-based head office, inviting input on methods to drive cultural change.

Consultancies/Project Scope: Business strategy formulation, process reengineering, training and education, organizational and cultural change, operational analyses, executive guidance, productivity improvements, and cost-containment programs.

Project Highlights:

Winner, Gold National Government Productivity Award, for contributions in boosting employee productivity as part of a $15 million office management system for the Department of County Industries.

Reduced "tail" costs by $2 billion as part of a collaborative $100 million national business process reengineering initiative to contain spiraling litigation and accident insurance issues for the **Workplace Compensation Enterprise in New Zealand.**

Consolidated myriad disparate technology systems, designing a comprehensive knowledge base for the City of Bundaberg that connected all systems for consolidated access from all areas. **Cut annual running costs by 96%.**

• • •

CRAYDON & LINDSOM

SENIOR MANAGER   7/1997–7/2002

Direct Reports: 12 (managers, senior consultants, consultants, support staff)
Operational budget: $12 million

Profit-and-loss accountability in this senior management role overseeing daily operations while driving tactical market plans to capture new business within premium markets. With high fees and high-quality deliverables, expectations were strong and necessitated continuous monitoring. Steered client relationship-management strategies, delegated priorities, monitored project progress, identified trends, hired consultants, appraised staff performances, and positioned the business for continued prosperity.

Education

Master of Business Administration, University of Illinois, Urbana, Illinois

Bachelor of Science; *Majors: Management, Business Administration, Technology;* Monash University, Melbourne, Australia

Graduate Certificate in Quality, Worldwide Organization of Quality

---

technology. Note the use of boldface in the Executive Performance and Employment Chronology sections to call attention to the names of workplaces and significant achievements. The left column is used effectively to display performance subcategories, workplaces, and explanations in italic.

Hospitality

Resumes at a Glance

MARIANNE L. PERRAULT

900 East Shelter Road
Oldetown, Rhode Island 09999

Cell: (401) 555-6666
E-mail: marip@foxx.net
Home: (401) 333-8877

QUALIFICATIONS

➢ Proven ability to train, schedule, supervise, and effectively manage 60 employees preparing 1,000 airline passenger meals per day.
➢ Competent leader with extensive experience in prioritizing, delegating, and controlling work flow in municipal government and high-volume private-industry work environments.
➢ Proficient in effectively organizing, handling, and monitoring a wide variety of tasks.
➢ Comfortable with operating Microsoft XP/7, Corel, and Internet research on PC and Macintosh platforms.

EXPERIENCE

Food-Air Associates, Inc., Providence, RI
Vice President and Pricing Administrator for family-owned business, 2002–present
  o Manage accounts payable / receivable for very profitable, high-volume airline catering kitchen serving American, USAirways, United, Southwest, and Delta Air Lines.
  o Review and analyze monthly P&L statement generated by accounting firm.
  o Establish costs of goods and services; audit and reconcile inventory.
  o Negotiate contract terms with major airline clients.
  o Hire, train, schedule, and manage up to 60 employees.
  o Design and implement quality-assurance measures to maintain high standards and consistent business retention for clients serving a total of 1,000 passenger meals per day.

Oldetown Police, Oldetown, RI
Administrative Assistant to the Chief of Police (part-time), 2000–2002
  o Researched, prepared, and wrote grants for municipal benefit.
  o Assisted in assembling data for annual police budget submissions to town council.
  o Provided accurate, courteous responses to inquiries on police matters of a sensitive nature.

EDUCATION

John Phelps University, Newport, RI
  o Master of Science in Business Administration, 2002

Rhode Island University, Providence, RI
  o Bachelor of Science in Finance, 2000
  o Cecelia H. Belknap Scholar: GPA over 3.85 (four years)

VOLUNTEER

Providence Chamber of Commerce
Oldetown Animal League
Providence GRO-Business Associates
Air-Transportation League
R.I. Fraternal Order of Police

84

Combination. *Edward Turilli, Bonita Springs, Florida*

Two boxes make this resume different from most others. The hollow bullets also are not common. Boldfacing and italic make the name, headings, workplaces, jobs, and universities stand out.

CHERYL R. COOKMAN

1548 Northshore Blvd., #109   555-555-3697 (home)
Las Vegas, NV 05326   cherylcookman@ymail.com   555-555-5469 (cell)

FOOD SERVICE MANAGEMENT PROFESSIONAL
...Oklahoma Food Management Certification/Serve Safe Certified Instructor...
...Consistently promoted to higher levels of responsibility through exceptional work performance...

Well-qualified Food Service professional with strong management, decision making, supervision, and leadership skills. Proven ability to delegate, problem solve, prioritize projects, manage personnel, and meet deadlines without compromising quality. Create and implement menu plans, oversee food selection, contain cost, and maintain quality control. Computer literate: Word, Excel, and Internet. Bachelor of Arts. **Key skills:**

Culinary Arts:
- Superior culinary skills in food preparation, recipe experimentation/development, and full-service catering. Proven success in developing food budgets and negotiating contracts. Ensure cleanliness, quality, and food service standards and procedures. Significantly upgraded quality of food operations, profitability, and standards of service through innovative menu planning.

Staff Training & Motivation:
- Successful career record of motivating personnel to perform at high efficiency levels. Talent for recruiting, hiring, and developing support staff. Team player; always willing to share knowledge to attain corporate goals.

Leadership & Management:
- Exceptionally strong multitasking abilities. Planned and served catered affairs for 250+; developed menus, coordinated deliveries, and supervised personnel. Directed kitchen operations, purchasing budget, inventory planning, menu development and pricing, staff scheduling, vendor contracts, regulatory compliance, and food/labor cost and controls.

PROFESSIONAL BACKGROUND

BETTER LIVING, INC., Norman, OK   2002–Present
Publicly held, global food service management company. Divisions include Vending, Fine Dining, Schools, and Catered Dining.

Food Service Manager (2003–Present)
Oversee food service operations at 4 local high schools; provide lunch for student population of up to 950 at each location. Manage 17 staff, including food prep cooks, cashiers, cooks, and fryers. Recruit, train, schedule, and perform employee evaluations. Responsible for payroll, documenting man-hours, and tracking sick leave and vacation time. Accountable for volume sales on budget of $889K annually. Generate sales of $1,500–1,900 daily at each location; control $12K–15K inventory. Perform menu planning, inventory control, and purchasing. Design menus for special school events. Negotiate with outside vendors, conduct monthly staff meetings, perform end-of-day cash balances, handle bank deposits, submit vendor bills electronically, determine food pricing, provide sales/profit analysis, and conduct food reviews.

Performance Highlights:
- Reduced cost 11% through vendor negotiations.
- Increased profits 14% through in-house preparation of pizza.
- Recognized by senior-level management; consistently receive annual bonuses based on corporate budget expectations.
- Qualified to administer state-mandated Serve Safe test.
- Maintain 100% rating on county health inspections and corporate safety and health inspections.
- Boosted profits through maintaining food costs at 38–42%; exceed corporate budget of 47%.
- Facilitated smooth transition process during corporate merger.

Food Service Worker (2002–2003)
Fast-track promotion to management. Hands-on experience in all phases of food service operations.

Continued

85

Combination. *Cathy Fahrman, Tampa, Florida*

When a summary of qualifications indicates many skills, it is helpful to group the skills in some way to aid comprehension. Culinary Arts, Staff Training & Motivation, and Leadership & Management are three categories used as bold-italic subheadings to group this applicant's skills.

CHERYL R. COOKMAN

PROFESSIONAL BACKGROUND (continued)

THE AMERICAN DREAM, Norman, OK   2005–2010
Bed-and-breakfast hotel.

Caterer/Server/Bartender (part-time)
Provided catering services, including menu planning and food preparation, for special events; up to 180+ guests. Upscale dining with up to 5 main courses.

END OF THE DAY, Norman, OK   2007–2010
80-seat fine-dining restaurant serving lunch and dinner.

Caterer/Server/Bartender (part-time)
Provided catering services for special events and parties for up to 90+ guests.

WHOLESALE, INC., Norman, OK   1999–2002
Food and merchandise wholesaler.

Cake Decorator (2000–2002)
Decorated cakes for weddings and large parties.

Team Leader/Produce Department (1999–2000)
Oversaw produce staff, including scheduling and performance evaluations. Managed produce rotation, product ordering, and inventory levels.

Stock Person (1999)
Quickly promoted to Team Leader position (within 3 months).

EDUCATION

COLLEGE UNIVERSITY, Norman, OK
Bachelor of Arts, Fine Arts (2000)
Personally paid for all college expenses

CONTINUING EDUCATION

Diversity Training [2009; 2010]
Quality Assurance [2009; 2010]
Power of Many [2010]
Contribution Analysis and Pricing is Very Effective (C.A.P.T.I.V.E.) [2010]
Creating a dynamic, fun, and enjoyable working environment (FISH) [2010]
Profit Improvement Methods:
Interactive program focusing on learning and using the action planning process to improve profitability
[2009]
Beginner's Excel [2003]

CERTIFICATIONS

Serve Safe Certified [2009]
Oklahoma Food Manager Certified [2004]

In the Professional Background section, italic emphasizes a brief description of each workplace. Bullets draw attention to Performance Highlights for the current position. Many of these points are quantified with percentages.

Fred A. Simmons

555 Pilgrim Road ▪ Peekskill, NY 55555 ▪ (555) 555-5555 ▪ simmons@xxxx.com

Profile

Restaurant Manager with a proven track record of building and managing profitable restaurant operations through expertise in:

- **Business Management**—Broad-based experience encompasses P&L, budgeting, operations, human resources, purchasing, inventory, quality, customer service, sales and cost controls/reduction.

- **Training & Development**—Talent for recruiting, developing and motivating well-trained, productive management teams/staff focused on customer service excellence.

- **Project Management**—Exceptional organizational skills evident in the ability to plan and execute special projects, facility conversions/remodels and new business openings on time and within budget.

- **Sales & Marketing**—Demonstrated success in revitalizing failing businesses and achieving consistent sales/revenue growth.

Professional Experience

Ahern Corporation—New York, NY (2003 to Present)
RESTAURANT MANAGER

Recruited to manage $2.3 million restaurant operation that includes P&L accountability, sales, budgeting, staffing, training, customer relations, purchasing, inventory, quality and cost management. Supervise, motivate and develop management team of 4 plus 60–70 employees.

- Reorganized operations and staffing, building strong management team and crew through effective leadership and training.

- Delivered weekly sales growth of $2,500 and increased guest count by 4% over prior year while decreasing labor costs by 2%.

- Improved customer service by reorganizing systems and coaching staff in the consistent implementation of operational procedures.

- Instituted an effective train-the-trainer program to orient and develop new staff to achieve productivity goals quickly.

Darden Restaurants—Trenton, NJ (1990 to 2003)
RESTAURANT MANAGER

Took charge of 3 floundering restaurants as sole franchise operator chainwide, personally overseeing all aspects of operations, sales and marketing. Recruited and built solid management team, directing up to 50 employees.

- Turned around operations and achieved sales of $400,000 annually at each unit.

- Boosted sales growth by developing and implementing marketing programs and vendor stands in the community.

- Instituted training, sanitation and other programs to improve operations, food and labor costs.

- Created home delivery business catering to residential customers and businesses that contributed 10% increase in annual sales.

Continues

86

Combination. *Louise Garver, Broad Brook, Connecticut*

This restaurant manager wanted to become a hotel manager. The writer emphasized the applicant's skills and experiences that would be of interest to a potential employer in the hotel

Fred A. Simmons   simmons@xxxx.com   Page 2

Darden Restaurant—Baltimore, MD (1988 to 1990)
DISTRICT MANAGER

Recruited to direct $2.4 million district operations with 6 units employing 120 people. Accountable for all aspects of operations, including P&L, budgeting, staffing, training, scheduling and ordering. Managed catering program which generated 5% of total sales.

- Rebuilt crews throughout district and strengthened teams through strong leadership and training.

Reiter Corporation—Richmond, VA (1971 to 1988)
COORDINATOR—RESTAURANT DEVELOPMENT (1983 to 1988)

Promoted in recognition of performance to newly created corporate position in operations. Planned, scheduled and orchestrated all phases of restaurant modification/conversion projects throughout midwest and east coast regions. Conducted site surveys and teamed with operations, engineering and construction personnel on each project. Delivered numerous presentations to senior management on projects' status.

- Effectively managed remodel/conversion projects for 300–400 units over 5-year period, each one completed on time and within budget.

SUPERVISOR—RESTAURANT OPENING (1980 to 1983)

Selected to plan and spearhead new unit openings throughout midwest and northeast territories. Led team of 6 to assist manager in recruiting, staffing and training personnel for each new restaurant prior to grand opening. Chosen to manage numerous special projects in recognition of leadership, planning, organizational and operations expertise.

- Successfully opened 12 new stores on time, coordinating all grand-opening festivities.

Prior: Rapid advancement through progressively responsible positions in operations management at Reiter Corporation. Selected based on leadership, organizational and performance successes to manage new restaurant concept.

Education

Bachelor of Arts—Business Management
Evans College, Hamden, SC

Additional:

Management
Training and Development
Human Resources
Customer Service
Restaurant Operations

industry. The Profile section mentions four areas of expertise that are important to hotel operations. Similarly, for each workplace in the Professional Experience section, the writer lists with bullets his achievements of value to hotel-industry employers.

Matthew B. Taylor
CCM & CHE

5555 Lexis St., Unit 55
Austin, TX 55555
555.555.5555
taylormb@xxxx.com

GENERAL MANAGER

Operations & Financial Management | Long- & Short-Term Strategic Planning
Policy Development | Board & Committee Collaboration | Strength in Leadership

- Impeccable 22-year career ensuring the highest standards of dining & private club operations.
- Attract & retain talented employees to work together in delivering the vision of the board of directors according to new & established policies & bylaws.

PROFESSIONAL EXPERIENCE

AUSTIN COUNTRY CLUB, Austin, TX

Assistant General Manager   2009 to 2011

Visible leader committed to nurturing an exceptional staff while regularly interacting with the 900+ members of Texas's oldest country club.

- Oversaw clubhouse operations, including fine and casual dining, catering, banquets, housekeeping, maintenance, security, event sales and setup, and locker room upkeep, as well as F&B (food and beverage) and purchasing for the ice skating rink, swimming pool, and 18-hole golf course.

BAY VIEW CLUB, Horseshoe Bay, TX

General Manager   2006 to 2009

Created a compelling member/guest experience to differentiate this new, upscale residential community's private club from similar properties within the region.

- Led 5 department heads and administered operational and fiscal management of F&B, championship golf course, equestrian center, wellness center, off-site mountain club, lake house, on-site lodging, concierge, and award-winning cast-off cabin.
- Identified, prioritized, and directed all aspects of amenities to achieve the greatest ROI.
- Modified original clubhouse building plans to improve functionality and flexibility of use; drastically reduced costs without compromising quality.
- Analyzed industry trends and performed aggressive financial oversight to achieve the investors' objectives while exceeding member expectations; developed and periodically revised short- and long-term business plans to account for changing economic conditions.

UNIVERSITY OF KANSAS, UNIVERSITY CLUB / UNIVERSITY CATERING, Lawrence, KS

General Manager   2002 to 2006

Served as CEO for not-for profit, 1,800-member private club, including 2 dining rooms, a full-service catering operation, and 30,000 sq. ft. of event and meeting space spanning 3 buildings.

- Directed operations for on- and off-campus catering and oversaw F&B needs for a football stadium, 2 athletic arenas, an 18-hole golf course, and all major university events.
- Guided 7 department heads to maximize the productivity and profitability of 240 employees.
- Increased club dining traffic by 20% by cultivating a new dining concept; directed interior design, remodel, and renovation and led menu creation and marketing efforts.

Continued

87

Combination. *Melanie Lenci, Denver, Colorado*

The applicant's original resume had long paragraphs of information that would not be appealing to a potential employer. The writer broke up the paragraphs into shorter statements and listed

Matthew B. Taylor

555.555.5555
taylormb@xxxx.com

UNIVERSITY OF KANSAS, CLUB / CATERING, *General Manager* (continued)
- Successfully countered a $435K cut in budget by fostering a community outreach campaign and incentivizing sales staff to expand business within the community.
- Retired $1.2M in operating debt 2 years prior to goal.
- Managed priorities and developed strategic financial and operational direction and policies that served both the board of directors and the university administration.

CITY AND COUNTY OF DALLAS EVENT FACILITY, Dallas, TX
General Manager   1999 to 2002
Used a strategic partnership to secure a $5M contract to direct event facility operations.
- Decreased operating expenses by 12% and generated $500K in new business in initial year.
- Established a reputation for excellence while hosting 200 weddings per year.
- Expanded business through the addition of a full-service menu and a five-star chef.

THE LAWRENCE GROUP, Houston, TX
General Manager   1988 to 1999
Led conceptualization, launch, and management of ongoing operations for 5 unique Houston-area restaurants, including Titan's, Clear Water Brewing Company, Buffalo Ranch, Vincenzo's Italian Restaurant, and the Aztec Café.
- Established and oversaw development budgets, contributed to menu development, created and implemented operations standards, built and led strong staff teams, and acted as GM for each restaurant for 2+ years before transitioning to launch the next dining venture.
- Increased overall annual revenue to $13M and consistently surpassed yearly goals by 20%.

PERSONNEL MANAGEMENT

INTERNAL: Executive Chefs | Managers | Assistants | Servers | Accountants | Bookkeepers
Housekeeping | Concierge | Sales | Marketing | Construction | Maintenance
Golf Professionals | Golf Superintendents | Valet | Security | Human Resources

EXTERNAL: Auditors | IT | Marketing | Interior Design | Public Safety | Construction

CERTIFICATION

Certified Club Manager (CCM) ▪ CLUB MANAGERS ASSOCIATION OF AMERICA ▪ 2005
Certified Hospitality Educator (CHE) ▪ AMERICAN HOTEL & LODGING ASSOCIATION ▪ 2005
Corporate & International Protocol Consultant ▪ NEW YORK SCHOOL OF PROTOCOL ▪ 2004
Level One Sommelier ▪ THE COURT OF MASTER SOMMELIERS ▪ 2002

EDUCATION

MS in **Hotel & Restaurant Management** ▪ UNIVERSITY OF KANSAS, Lawrence, KS ▪ 2005
BS in **Business Administration** ▪ OHIO STATE UNIVERSITY, Columbus, OH ▪ 1984–1988
Leadership Studies ▪ UNITED STATES MILITARY ACADEMY, West Point, NY ▪ 1981–1984

these with bullets. In an interview with the applicant, the writer gathered additional figures and accomplishments and arranged all of this information plus keywords under bold headings. The result was a layout and presentation that presented the applicant as the professional he is.

| 5555 Waterwitch Cove Circle
Orlando, FL 55555 | **Kristine Juliet** | Cell: 555-555-5555
kjuliet@xxxx.com |

SENIOR EXECUTIVE

MULTIFAMILY PROPERTY MANAGEMENT | REDEVELOPMENT | ASSET MANAGEMENT

Growth-oriented real estate professional with more than 20 years of experience accelerating business goals by astute investment, lean operations, savvy supply-chain management, inventive marketing, and progressive tenant relations. Deep understanding of full multifamily investment life cycle, with the ability to manage HR, Finance, Business Development, and Marketing Departments, getting hands-on when needed.

Firsthand knowledge of materials sourcing in China combined with 10 years of focused hotel purchasing and management experience in the U.S., Caribbean, and Mexico, resulting in value-added redevelopment, high-occupancy management, and exceptional ROR on property investments.

Property Management
➤ Multifamily Operations
➤ Construction Management
➤ Redevelopment
➤ Real Estate Management
➤ Advertising / Marketing

Procurement
➤ Contract Management
➤ Project Management
➤ RFP Development
➤ International Business
➤ Export Programs

Hospitality Management
➤ Hotel / Restaurant Operations
➤ Strategic Planning
➤ Budgeting
➤ Human Resources

ACADEMIC CREDENTIALS

MBA, Executive Level, International Business Concentration
Crummer Graduate School of Business, Rollins College, Winter Park, FL

BSBA, Business Management Concentration—Elms College, Chicopee, MA

PROFESSIONAL EXPERIENCE

| KATHAY HOTELS, China
Consultant, Hospitality Business Development | 2011–Present |

Coordinated large-scale China hotel chain launch, currently on track to open on time and on budget. Recruited by former colleague for mission-critical 1-year assignment to develop new hotels and hotel operations for massive network, including limited-service and 5-star facilities. Manage all logistics and establish enterprise policies and procedures as well as organizational design.

➤ Set stage for successful September 2012 launch that will build from zero to 264 locations within 2 years.
➤ Resolved dearth of qualified staff by creating intensive training program with photo-rich materials and by building alliance with university, reaching out to English-speaking students with tourism industry experience.
➤ Fulfilled daunting procurement challenges, delivering world-class materials and construction used in underdeveloped areas to establish hotels as showpieces for broader government or business projects.
➤ Ensured quick ramp up to profitability, staffing at 50% capacity and 50% of standard employee-to-room ratio based on occupancy forecasts.

| ACE MANAGEMENT GROUP, LLC—Orlando, FL
COO / Vice President | 1995–Present |

Leverage broker relationships and lean remodeling processes to yield double- and triple-digit returns on major property investments. Hired to lead formation of new company through post-merger integration and manage Florida, Georgia, Virginia, Connecticut, and Ohio assets. Created business systems and processes from scratch, cultivating redevelopment and brokerage/due diligence services revenue. Direct full redevelopment life cycle—including acquisition, construction, management, and disposition—for $35M+ in acquisitions. Supervise Finance and Accounting team in asset modeling, financial reporting, budget creation, and fiscal planning. Also accountable for HR and Marketing departments. Manage up to 10K+ units and 58 properties at a time. $66M operating budget. 200 direct and indirect reports.

88

Combination. *Kim Mohiuddin, San Diego, California*

This applicant had a broad skill set that enabled her to manage effectively every aspect of major hospitality and real estate projects from renovations to launches. The writer put education near

Kristine Juliet	C: 555-555-5555 | kjuliet@xxxx.com	Page 2 of 2

ACE MANAGEMENT GROUP, LLC, continued

➢ Consistently exceed contractual ROR minimums (20%), yielding up to 100% profit by buying below market value, innovating materials sourcing for value-added construction, and creating dual exit strategy.

➢ Doubled redevelopment ROI, traveling to China and negotiating directly with suppliers to purchase high-value materials for the same price as mid- to low-tier materials from U.S. wholesalers. Avoided export fees by leveraging loophole commonly missed by U.S. importers.

➢ Enhanced business agility, creating additional option of easy condo conversion for potential buyers by executing top-notch redevelopment. Buyers just had to do legal work.

➢ Increased occupancy by codeveloping innovative quality guarantee that became industry best practice. Superior Service Program translates hotel management concepts for application to multifamily properties, assuring tenants of best-in-class maintenance and eliminating tenant-side risk by implementing penalties on property manager for poor performance.

➢ Exceed service level agreements and foster profitability by TQM (total quality management).

ITT SHERATON CORPORATION—Orlando, FL	1985–1995
Regional Director: Florida, Georgia, Caribbean, and Mexico	

Facilitated growth of Orlando office from startup to $50M business unit, helming Purchasing Resource and Unifood divisions. Established all operations, including supply-chain strategy, vendor selection and negotiation, export agreements, and purchasing division (for products and foods). Sat on ITT World Purchasing Board and prepared annual budgets and strategic plans. Supervised all regional hotel staff.

➢ Negotiated favorable pricing by pooling purchases of individual hotels.

➢ Kept offshore operating costs low, performing detailed supply-chain analysis weighing cost and logistics advantages of local, U.S., or alternative sourcing.

➢ Lowered materials costs by sourcing directly from China, gaining deep experience in Asian business practices.

➢ Played role in bringing new franchisees on board, championing their success by creating robust buying support network.

➢ Delivered $1.3M and $1.2M in YOY savings (1992 and 1993).

➢ Negotiated $30M annual supplies agreement for Southeast and Caribbean, chairing 25-member project team.

➢ Opened multiple new hotels throughout the territory.

HONORS, CREDENTIALS, AND TECHNICAL REPERTOIRE

➢ Honored with City of Orlando *Commissioners Award* for Crime Prevention Multifamily Redevelopment.

➢ Granted lifetime CPM (Certified Property Manager) by NAPM (National Association of Purchasing Management), 2004.

➢ Earned multiple awards and recognition.

Knowledge of:

MS Office \| Yardi Property Management \| AMSI \| BJM Property Management \| Rent Roll Property Management

Licensed Real Estate Broker, State of Florida

the top of the first page—even though the applicant was not a recent graduate—to balance the long, relevant list of keywords in the text box at the right margin. These are categorized to cluster related skills. For each position, a bold impact statement indicates her effectiveness.

CORY J. ERICKSON

5555 5ᵗʰ Avenue North ▪ Little River, MN 55555 ▪ 555-555-5555 ▪ cjerickson@email.com

SENIOR HOTEL MANAGEMENT

Accomplished Certified Hotel Administrator offering more than 19 years of progressive experience in the hospitality industry. Adept at analyzing, planning, and executing strategic solutions. Collaborative team leader with a proven talent for motivating staff to achieve organizational objectives.

Key Strengths

Budget Administration	Financial / Risk Management	Personnel Management
Project Management	Procurement	Training & Team Building
Forecasting / Strategic Planning	Sales, Marketing & Research	Process Improvement

PROFESSIONAL EXPERIENCE

SMITH MANAGEMENT GROUP, Little River, MN   June 2005–November 2010

Smith Management Group (SMP) provides hospitality development and management services for investment groups. Established in 1988, SMP has partnered to develop and operate more than 30 properties.

Director of Operations

Supervised four general managers and directed operations of four multiunit hotel properties, including 149-room property with annual revenues of $6.5 million. Collaborated with general managers, management team, and board of managers to oversee strategic planning, financial analysis, forecasting, and budgeting.

- Oversaw detailed logistics of preopening for two newly developed hotel properties (management recruitment, FFE procurement and placement, corporate and staff training, and site inspections).
- Conducted sales and marketing training, drawing on personal experience of successful results.
- Boosted bottom line by conducting post-opening financial analysis, administering changes, and reducing labor costs. Slashed electrical expenses by implementing "green" energy savings programs.
- Identified weaknesses and created an operations manual that outlined new procedures to enhance operations.

Key Accomplishments:

- Oversaw properties that earned corporate awards (top 5% in U.S.) for high employee satisfaction, superior guest satisfaction, and quality control.
- Spearheaded efforts to save time and increase productivity; overcame employee resistance and transformed accounting/payroll procedures into an up-to-date system.
- Implemented a new revenue management program to track and capture revenue opportunities; resulted in outperforming competitors in slow economic times (industry down 17%; SMP down only 5%).
- Succeeded in exceeding profits during sluggish economy by forging cost-containment initiatives (hiring/salary freezes, analyzing restaurant competitors, and modifying menu/prices).

SMITH HOTEL & SUITES, Little River, MN   April 1999–June 2005

Serving guests since 1965, Smith Hotel & Suites offers some of the finest lodging in the Little River area while consistently earning high ratings from guests.

General Manager

Managed a 68-room hotel property with annual revenues of approximately $1 million. Supervised 30 employees (recruiting, interviewing, hiring, training, performance evaluations, and terminations). Formulated and maintained a $700,000 budget; analyzed profit-and-loss statements to ensure a 30 to 35% occupancy rate.

- Succeeded in driving revenue growth from $0 to $1 million through networking, pinpointing business leads, marketing efforts, and thinking outside the box to capture and retain new customers.
- Awarded four consecutive corporate awards for outstanding service/cleanliness (2000–2003).

89

Combination. *Connie Hauer, Sartell, Minnesota*

Two double (thin-thin) horizontal lines enclose important information near the top of the first page. This is the place to snag a reader's attention. In the Professional Experience section, italicized

Cory J. Erickson	**cjerickson@email.com**	**Page 2**

Smith Hotel & Suites Continued . . .

- Accelerated profits in a highly competitive market by launching a "Stay, Shop & Play" package, targeting specific markets during seasonal events (accounted for 10% of annual revenues).
- Selected by corporate management to oversee opening procedures and facilitate training at new properties; handpicked to provide interim management for unexpected vacancies.
- Minimized turnover and achieved optimal staff performance by maintaining open lines of communication and leading by example (working side-by-side with staff); achieved 30% staff retention after four years.
- Ignited sales by conducting quarterly sales blitzes to corporations.

ANDERSON HOTELS, Little River, MN   December 1991–April 1999
Founded in 1980, Anderson Hotels is a family-owned facility that prides itself on delivering quality accommodations and personalized service.

Front Office Manager (May 1993–April 1999)

Promoted to manage front office duties for 103-room property, ensuring compliance with corporate standards, policies, and procedures. Supervised up to 20 employees including hiring, scheduling, and performance evaluations.

- Practiced yield management strategies to ensure optimal profits. Assessed cash flow shortfalls and instituted strategies to contain costs and drive profits:
  - ➢ Saved approximately $750/week by reducing selected expenses/purchases.
  - ➢ Minimized costs by negotiating new contracts with current vendors, as well as new vendors.
- Introduced a concept for improved service standards that was approved and adopted by owners.
- Managed all accounts receivables; generated and submitted financial reports to corporate office.

Food and Beverage Supervisor (December 1991–May 1993)

Oversaw the management and execution of banquets and catering events. Supervised 8 employees, including hiring, scheduling, performance reviews, and terminations.

- Developed and implemented a training program that motivated employees to optimum performance by tracking goals and establishing incentives to ignite sales.
- Analyzed weekly food and beverage budget and tracked profit and loss; assessed weekly forecasts of labor and revenue to evaluate staffing needs.
- Implemented a customized computer program to streamline procedures and improve tracking of sales.
- Recipient of two "Employee of the Month" awards for exhibiting excellent performance attitude.

EDUCATION & CREDENTIALS

LITTLE RIVER STATE UNIVERSITY, Little River, MN
Bachelor of Science; Major: **Management;** Minor: **Travel and Tourism**   1992

CERTIFICATIONS: **Certified Hotel Administrator**   2000

SEMINARS AND TRAINING

Building Business Features ~ Yield Management Training ~ Coaching and Team-Building Skills
Sexual Harassment Training ~ Diversity Seminar ~ Human Resources Training ~ General Manager Certificate

PROFESSIONAL AFFILIATIONS

American Hotel and Motel Association ~ State Innkeeper's Association ~ Little River Chamber of Commerce
Little River Convention and Visitor's Bureau Board of Directors; Chair of Travel and Tourism Committee

statements describe each workplace, and bullets point to significant achievements. Under the most recent workplace, a Key Accomplishments section calls special attention to the most important achievements.

Gerald F. Hewlitt

Hospitality Industry Specialist
Senior-level Operations Manager

Sales + Marketing + Owner Mentality + Technology + Daring Creativity = SUCCESS

Executive Profile

More than 20 years of experience in every facet of the hospitality industry in positions as general manager, consultant, or owner with a solid background in successful traditional and entrepreneurial venues. Use a real-world approach to problem solving and a deep well of experience to meet the challenges of this fast-paced, high-turnover industry.

- Have operated multiple restaurants accommodating 900+ patrons and managed events for up to 2,000 attendees while partnering with diverse management, overseeing a multitude of activities, and managing half-million-dollar budgets / P&Ls.

- Proven team-forming and motivational skills have delivered unmatched loyalty and a nearly unheard-of staff turnover rate of less than 25%, far below the 61% industry standard. Consistently develop cost-cutting and profit-building initiatives.

- Honed and demonstrated project-planning and management skills in supremely high-stress scenarios where failure was not an option and the wrong decision could end a career and / or deliver substantial personal loss.

- Skilled at simultaneously supervising several restaurants and projects. Directed management of two separate restaurants, 20 miles apart, for five years. Worked 18+ hours concurrently managing early-morning renovations and late-night operations.

- Use lifelong interest in computers / IT to enhance every business opportunity and activity from marketing to inventory control, menu preparation, and catering scheduling. Hold Certificate in Computer Science from Adelphi University (2009).

- Strategic business sense, uncompromising work ethic, and natural sincerity have helped create consistent profits and have won loyal support and motivation of customers, employees, partners, managers, community leaders, suppliers, and local officials.

Summary of Qualifications

- Multiunit operation management
- Multimillion-dollar P&L management
- Facility management
- Event management & promotion
- Troubleshooting & change management

- Project planning & systems development
- Advanced IT knowledge
- Risk management & inventory control
- Purchasing & negotiating skills
- Vendor sourcing & negotiating

- Sales / product / market analysis
- Food / labor / marketing cost controls
- Customer relations and satisfaction
- Human resources management
- Team-building & staff-retention programs

Career Development

PRESTIGE FOOD AND SPORTS ENTERPRISE, INC. (PFS), OYSTER BAY, NY
1996 to present

President and COO
Partner / Manager

PFS operated two consecutive successful theme restaurants on Long Island. Original concept, Charlie's Big City Grill, opened in 1997 as an 800-patron sports-bar restaurant much like the ESPN Zone restaurants.

- Charlie's grossed over $2 million in f / y 1998 and $2.4 million in f / y 2000 and 2001. Well-trained staff (only 25% turnover rate), value menu, and "almost as good as being at the game" mentality built a loyal customer base of young professionals, over-30 singles, families, and out-of-town guests.

- Restaurant was featured in numerous publications as a top sports bar/cafe, with Sunday NFL football afternoons attracting more than 1,500 guests.

In proactive response to increased competition from satellite dishes and sports-bar market saturation, renovated site and in 2003 transitioned Charlie's to the New Orleans Roadhouse, a Cajun menu "House of Blues"–style restaurant.

- Took only four months to plan and develop this restaurant / entertainment concept entirely new to Metro New York. Handled politicking / project planning necessary to get permits, plans, contractors, and equipment in place for summer renovation (slow season). Opened on Labor Day weekend 2003, two weeks ahead of schedule and below $750,000 budget.

- Negotiated with property-management company for an additional 10 years on lease and lower rent (both valuable assets for future sale). Fine-tuned, upgraded, and enhanced facility, including handicap access, risk management, and venue flexibility. Planned menu, hired kitchen staff, developed company's first employee manual, created marketing plans, and booked live entertainment.

- Now a top rhythm & blues showcase and popular Cajun / Creole dining destination, the Roadhouse was recently sold for a profit.

25 Bay Drive, Amityville, NY 11701
phone: 631-555-5555 ■ cell: 516-555-5555 ■ e-mail: GH.PFS@email.com

90

Combination. *Deb Dib, Medford, New York*

This resume has all the characteristics of many executive resumes that offer a greater amount of information: relatively smaller type; narrower margins for wider lines; adequate line spacing to

Gerald F. Hewlitt / page two of three

Career Development, continued

Key Leadership Initiatives at Prestige Food & Sports Enterprise

Developed Successful Theme Restaurant in Highly Competitive Area

Developed and operated a major theme restaurant in Nassau County, NY. Created concept and incorporated local venue elements into large-scale restaurant. Composed business plan and sought financing from U.S. Small Business Administration. Took possession of 10-year lease, construction, and physical development in less than four months. Driven by desire to succeed, took Charlie's Big City Grill from concept to creation in under a year.

Key Results:
- First year's gross sales exceeded $2 million, with sales growing by more than 20% in next four years.

Reduced Staff Turnover in High-Turnover Industry

Challenged with creating a strong team environment to reduce turnover of staff. Trained managers in "team management" principles, focusing on workplace pride. Compiled PC-based employee guidebook. Shared company's success with employees through annual bonuses, social gatherings, and benefit options.

Key Results:
- Delivered industry-low 25% turnover rate, even keeping 25% rate during renovation closure.
- Retaining competent and recognizable employees increased sales by building repeat-customer / staff bond.
- Increased service quality and customer loyalty through better, more-knowledgeable employees.

Managed Redevelopment and Construction of Successful Theme Restaurant

Challenged to co-develop and implement a new, next-generation theme-restaurant concept; to outperform, within five years, previous years' flat growth; to implement changes within a 90-day window; and to retain core customer base, as well as staff crucial to immediate success and profitability.

Identified key areas of planning and attention, set calendar, assigned management / partner responsibilities. Researched themes / concepts. Established $750,000 budget, developed project plan, and scheduled major construction for traditionally low-performing period. Renegotiated a lengthened lease, concessions for capital improvements, and lower rent. Established cooperative dialogue with town and county officials to expedite necessary permits and approvals.

Key Results:
- Completed construction of the New Orleans Roadhouse below budget and two weeks ahead of schedule.
- After renovation, year-one gross revenue rose to $2.6 million from $2.3 million.
- Reduced daily maintenance costs by 18% and energy consumption by 8%+ by updating infrastructure, HVAC, and layout.
- Achieved reduced insurance risk through facility changes that allowed full handicap accessibility.
- Retained market share, provided exposure to different market areas, and positioned firm for strong short-term growth.
- Booked live performances by top entertainers and expanded catering capacity.

Rebranded Local Restaurant to Attract New Customers

Challenged with marketing the New Orleans Roadhouse without conveying rural image. Recognized traditional radio spots did not take advantage of new theme, so explored and implemented 30- and 60-second local television spots with a major Metro NY cable television provider.

Key Results:
- Quarterly sales increased 21%. Ads generated qualified first-time customers and helped in rebranding.

Reduced Marketing Costs While Increasing Market Visibility to Targeted Customers

Challenged to develop effective, low-cost method of advertising to main customer base. Researched and implemented customer databases for direct-mail and target-marketing strategies, integrated direct-mail software for in-house mail sorting, and added POSTNET barcoding to meet USPS regulations. Appended 80,000-member database with phone numbers leading to telemarketing efforts. Eliminated manual removal of outdated customer information from database by using USPS National Change of Address files to automate process.

Key Results:
- Slashed direct-mail costs to 33%, from $63,000 to $42,000. Reduced marketing budget to 15%.
- Realized 3% to 7% annual postage and labor cost savings by updating database with USPS.

ensure white space between sections; and bullets, boldfacing, and italic to make important information more easily seen. To make the best use of the top third of the first page, the writer puts contact information at the bottom of each page. In the Career Development section, achievements are cast as five Key Leadership

Gerald F. Hewlitt / page three of three

Career Development, continued

THE LINDEN TREE CAFE, BABYLON, NY   **General Manager & Principal**
2007 to 2008 & 1990 to 2003

The Linden Tree Cafe is a well-established neighborhood cafe located in a historical building in one of Long Island's largest downtowns, Babylon, an urban / suburban town attempting revitalization from ongoing effects of "mall creep."

- In 1990 identified closed cafe as a good prospect—surrounding area's demographics were upscale, community revitalization efforts were strong, and circa-1880 building matched current trend for historic charm. Successfully negotiated 10-year lease with option to purchase building within five years at 1990 value, with half of paid rent credited towards purchase price.

- Working with Town of Babylon officials, the Babylon Historical Society, and the Chamber of Commerce, renovated building's façade to circa 1880, funding 70% of work through state and federal historic preservation funds. Purchased fixtures with no money down.

- Opened in November of 1990 and quickly established a local clientele. Then marketed to nonlocal population using regional magazine advertisements, popular radio stations, and supplier co-op ads.

- Cafe steadily grossed over $700,000 annually in early '90s. Although maintaining a historic building with apartments was an ongoing challenge, in 1994, purchased building at 1990 negotiated price of $110,000 rather than appraised price of $225,000.

- Restaurant's revenues began to falter in the late '90s as national recession reached Long Island, mall creep continued to deflect downtown business, town's road and sidewalk repairs limited access for months, and the large summer beach crowd started to gather at bayfront restaurants close to the ferries rather than in the downtown area.

- In 1998 planned complete building renovation including infrastructure, new kitchen, HVAC, handicap access, 100% fire sprinklers, increased dining area, and all-new outside dining area. To reduce effect on business, completed entire renovation in under four months. Kept core customer base informed of upcoming grand reopening with a 20,000+ newsletter mailing, and invited best customers and community leaders to menu tastings and mock service dining shortly before reopening.

- Renovation and new menu generated results above initial projection, but with unsteady growth. Decided to sell when a generous offer was received in 2002. Completed sale in 2003. Kept possession of building and separate real estate company; transitioned professional activities into new investment areas.

- New owners' establishment closed after only four years through owners' series of business-devastating decisions. Owners changed name and concept; invested heavily in fad, not trend; maintained business cash flow with questionable business practices; tarnished establishment's reputation; damaged property with brew-pub equipment; and drove away original clients.

- Determined to personally rebuild and reestablish business and then sell to a buyer or team who could maintain and enhance it. Repossessed property in winter of 2006, facing enormous challenges as landlord of a building in need of a tenant and as a member of a community that wanted to see / solicit a fine establishment in the area.

- Achieved this goal in less than 18 months with under $100,000 investment after reestablishing cordial community and business working relationships. Reopened in Spring 2007 with Chamber of Commerce celebrating the event with a party at the establishment in June 2007. In August 2008, business was sold for a profit and continues to develop.

Education and Certification

Bachelor of Science in Management, Adelphi University, Garden City, New York

Adelphi University, Garden City, New York
Certificate, 320 hours, Computer Science, 2009
Earned while running two businesses.

NY Continuing Education
MS Excel (2 days)
Advanced use of CorelDRAW software (2 days)

Hospitality Certifications
Food Service Manager's Certificate, No. 92122, County of Suffolk Department of Health Services
Food Service Manager's Certificate, Nassau County Department of Health

National Restaurant Association
Preventing Sexual Harassment in the Workplace
Restaurant Catering
Trends in Restaurant Design

New York Restaurant Association
Writing an Operation Manual (2 days)

25 Bay Drive, Amityville, NY 11701
phone: 631-555-5555 ■ cell: 516-555-5555 ■ e-mail: GH.PFS@email.com

Initiatives with bulleted Key Results specified for each initiative. Most of the results are quantified in dollar amounts and percentages. For the workplace mentioned on page three, the bulleted items tell in sequence the café's interesting history.

Human Resources

Resumes at a Glance

Joseph D. Morten

167 Helman Lane • Bridgewater, New Jersey 08807
908.555.5555 (H) • 908.444.4444 (Fax) • jMorten439@aol.com

HUMAN RESOURCES / CORPORATE TRAINING
Supervision ~ Business Management ~ Employee Relations ~ Coaching

Energetic, reliable and adaptable professional with a solid understanding of human resources, business operations and various corporate environments. Proven abilities in creatively identifying methods for improving staff productivity and organizational behavior. Recognized for ability to incorporate innovative management techniques into a multicultural workforce.

Results-oriented professional with excellent communication and interpersonal skills. Accurately perform challenging tasks with precision and attention to detail. Excel at organizing and setting up new procedures, troubleshooting and taking adverse situations and making them positive.

Competencies Include

- Human Resources Management
- Operations Management
- Teambuilding & Leadership
- Organizational & Project Management

- Training & Development
- Staffing Requirements
- Problem Resolution
- Employee Scheduling

Professional Experience

Waste Removal, *Plainfield, NJ (August 2005–September 2010)*
CFA Administrator
Waste Removal is the nation's largest full-service waste removal / disposal company
- Maintained and monitored multiple databases for the more than 120 pieces of equipment in the trucking company inventory.
- Generated accurate reports of budgets, repair costs, and personnel scheduling.
- Dramatically improved maintenance shop productivity through close budget monitoring.
- Served as a key link between management and mechanics, utilizing excellent interpersonal and communications skills. Acknowledged for improving the overall flow of information throughout the organization.
- Initiated, planned and managed the implementation of high-turn inventory-management systems and procedures. The new inventory system was credited with improving the performance of a high-volume parts operation.
- Assumed a leadership role in the company by completely reorganizing the physical inventory process to ensure greater accuracy and system integrity.
- Managed the successful integration of two new parts operations, turning a possible negative situation into a very positive one.

Easy Video Entertainment, *Colonia, NJ (March 2002–August 2005)*
Store Manager
Retail video rental and sales chain with more than 600 outlets and 5,000 employees worldwide
- Managed all daily store operations including a staff of 5 employees. Responsible for recruitment, hiring, firing, training, and scheduling of all staff members.
- Ability to train and motivate staff to maximize productivity and control costs with hands-on management and close monitoring of store budgets.
- Attained a 25% increase in sales over a 12-month period, leading all 45 stores in the district. The store ranked 40th in overall sales volume of the 600 stores in the company.
- Maintained a consistent Top 20 ranking for sales of high-profit coupon books.
- Used excellent leadership, team-building and communication skills to develop subordinates and encourage cooperation and responsibility. Ensured compliance with corporate HR programs.
- Developed and implemented creative and aggressive promotional techniques that resulted in the store consistently exceeding its sales goals.

Education

BA ~ Psychology, *FAIRLEIGH DICKINSON UNIVERSITY, Madison, NJ*

91

Combination. *Beverley and Mitchell I. Baskin, Marlboro, New Jersey*

The tilde (~), used to separate fields of activity in the profile, is echoed in the Education section at the bottom of the page. Each workplace in boldface is "explained" by a statement in italic.

Stephen Matthews

55 Roberts Road
Needham, MA 00000

555-555-5555
smatthews@email.com

HUMAN RESOURCES DIRECTOR

Expert in organizational effectiveness.

Recognized consensus-builder among diverse groups.

Innovative problem solver.

Strategic partner.

Effective executive coach.

Facilitator of management/staff collaboration to achieve business goals.

Watchdog against corporate legal liability and exposure.

VALUE PROPOSITION

Bringing **balance and simplicity** to Human Resources processes, **I create a competitive advantage** for the business that is reflected in the bottom line.

Proactive in anticipating problems and active in fixing things that break, **I attract and retain a highly skilled and motivated workforce** by implementing innovative and cost-saving programs.

LEADERSHIP

Employee Relations: Balance the company's best interests with the employees' needs to achieve business goals. Implement best management practices to maintain high morale in multinational and multisite businesses.

Staffing: Identify and define high-quality candidates in a tight job market and reduce cost per hire and turnaround time. Manage succession planning and employee development programs to build for the future and retain top talent.

Executive Coaching: Coach senior management to develop and communicate new strategy for continuous improvement and organizational effectiveness.

Organizational Development: Integrate cross-functional teams to change corporate culture and define common vision of success. Drive change targeted at strategic growth.

Benefits and Compensation: Develop and implement benefits and compensation programs that provide strong ROI.

Labor Law: Apply U.S. and international employment law to ensure compliance with regulations and minimize company's legal liability.

EXPERIENCE

JOHNSON MEDICAL SYSTEMS, Burlington, MA
Worldwide Director of Human Resources

2007–present

Provide the full spectrum of human resources support for worldwide imaging device division producing revenues approaching $1 billion. Manage all legal and compliance issues and perform executive-level consulting in organizational development, including coaching, results-oriented training, implementation, and strategic planning.

Key Accomplishments
- Improved employee satisfaction 20% by implementing division-wide 360-degree feedback process to identify and correct problem areas.
- Developed and instituted innovative staffing plan that reduced turnaround time (from time-to-post and time-to-fill) by 25%.
- Developed policies that addressed discrepancies between U.S. and German employment law.
- Simplified performance evaluation process to achieve buy-in throughout the division.
- Saved $500,000 by increasing employee retention and reducing associated cost of new hires; achieved competitive advantage by retaining top talent.

Continued

92

Combination. *Wendy Gelberg, Needham, Massachusetts*

This Human Resources Director wanted a distinctive resume to distinguish him from the competition. The Value Proposition points to the impact he has on his present company, and the phrases

Stephen Matthews—page 2   **555-555-5555**

EXPERIENCE (continued)

TECHNOCORP, Westborough, MA (headquartered in San Francisco)   2003–2007
Senior Human Resources Manager
Reorganized the management structure for a bicoastal Engineering Division, including internationally recognized experts in magnetic recording, electronics, and physics. Drove programs in continuous improvement and organizational effectiveness in a fast-paced and highly competitive environment, resulting in improved efficiencies and management excellence.

Key Accomplishments
- Built strong partnership with the executive staff to ensure that managers and employees worked collaboratively to achieve business goals across two sites. Implemented programs that drove high productivity and job satisfaction.
- Reduced staffing and compensation costs by $250,000 by developing hiring and pay programs based on individual development plans, succession plans, and workforce planning. Trained internal candidates to fill hard-to-staff positions.
- Provided executive coaching to Vice President of Engineering to identify leaders and structure the department to improve organizational effectiveness.
- Advised managers on fair hiring practices and employee performance issues to reduce corporate liability.

CONTINENTAL COMPUTER CORPORATION (acquired by XCom, 2003), Shrewsbury, MA   1988–2003
Senior Human Resources Manager, Worldwide Sales and Marketing Division Headquarters
Held positions of increasing scope and responsibility in various Continental departments, beginning as Management Development Consultant and finishing as Senior Human Resources Manager.

Key Accomplishments
- Oversaw the effective delivery of all human resources management, including compensation, recruitment, HR information systems, and university relations in a worldwide business with almost 4,000 employees and an annual operating budget in excess of $625 million. Managed a staff of 40 in a matrixed technical organization.
- Developed and implemented core programs in performance management and human resources planning that sharpened organizational effectiveness by providing managers with practical tools and critical information.
- Served as Human Resources Manager to five headquarters vice presidents.
- Introduced an innovative reward program that was essential to the retention of key employees and to the business's ongoing success.
- Implemented an Alternative Dispute Resolution (ADR) program with anticipated savings of millions of dollars in litigation costs.
- Provided leadership in XCom/Continental acquisition by identifying acquisition issues, determining and implementing best practices, and eliminating redundancies across both organizations.
- **Awarded:** Continental Achievement Award for Outstanding Contributions to Diversity Work (1999), Continental Achievement Award for Competitive Benchmarking (1998), Managerial Excellence Award (1991), and Educational Services Instructor Excellence Award (1991).

Prior experience includes Employee Relations Manager at Fidelity Investments, Training Manager at The Talbots, and Training Consultant at Polaroid Corporation.

EDUCATION

Certificate Mediation and Dispute Resolution, Metropolitan Mediation Services, Cambridge, MA
MBA   Executive Program, Babson College, Babson Park, MA
BA   Communications, Speech, and English, State University College of New York at Buffalo

in italic in the left column serve as a profile expressing further his value as an employee. Diamond bullets highlight extensive key accomplishments for each workplace. Note that a number of these accomplishments are quantified in percentages and dollar amounts.

AARON WALKER

5 Linden Avenue, Roslyn, NY 11576 ▪ aaronwalker00@aol.com
residence 555-555-5555 ▪ c*ellular* 555-555-4444

HUMAN RESOURCES PROFESSIONAL

PHR CERTIFICATE

Seeking a Generalist Role

Emphasis on:

Recruitment & Staffing • HRIS • Training & Development

Compensation • Salary Structures • Benefits Administration

Workforce Reengineering & Change Management • Job Task Analysis

Performance Appraisals • Employee Retention • Employee Communications

PROFESSIONAL EXPERIENCE

COMPUTER ASSOCIATES, Islandia, NY   2007–Present
Human Resources Specialist (2008–Present)
Human Resources Generalist* (2008)
Human Resources Associate (2007–2008)

   **Selected for rotational assignments as a leave replacement for other HR staff members.*

▪ ▪ ▪

HR Generalist Responsibilities and Achievements

Supported and provided HR-related guidance to general-management teams at two newly acquired facilities with a combined staff of approximately 130 employees.

- Contributed to a five-person team charged with establishing and implementing yearly **salary increases.**
- Managed a **job-reclassification project.** Conducted occupational research to determine if job titles were in sync with workplace norms.
- Assisted with **employee-performance** issues. Wrote disciplinary reports and developed a strategy for resolution.
- Reviewed **applicant résumés** and collaborated on **new-hire offers.**
- Tackled the **I-9 recertification** of approximately 2,800 employees at 12 locations. Through research, identified all employees whose paperwork was deficient. Trained support staff and line managers in proper documentation, which rectified oversights expediently and improved I-9 administration going forward.
- Articulated **corporate policies and procedures** to employees seeking clarification regarding payroll, disability, terminations, leaves of absence, and COBRA coverage issues.
- Authored a policies and procedures document to address the sometimes-confusing hiring categories of "rehires" and "reinstatements." Created and delivered **PowerPoint presentations** to the HR community, which, together with the written document, served as clarification on this issue.
- Regularly conducted the "benefits" portion of **new-hire orientations.** In one-hour sessions, provided information to 50+ employees.
- Participated in the **campus recruitment** program. Attended college fairs and **interviewed candidates** for internships and entry-level positions.
- Processed **employee data** for new hires and terminations.

Continued...

93

Combination. *M J Feld, Huntington, New York*

This person wanted a generalist role in human resources, which was not his most recent role. The writer grouped all the job titles at the top of the Professional Experience section and then listed

AARON WALKER

<u>**HRIS Responsibilities and Achievements**</u>

- Identified a significant administrative challenge regarding the inaccuracy of employee time-off accrual plans. Rectified the problem by creating an Access database linked to Lawson HRIS, which accurately provided the needed data.
- Designed, developed, and brought to fruition approximately 30 HRIS audits to ensure the accuracy of employee records. Defined audit parameters for compliance with federal, state, and company policies. Created numerous HRIS ad hoc reports as requested by the HR community and line managers.
- Improved the administration of employee sabbaticals by creating HRIS automation tools. In so doing, decreased processing time by approximately 50%.
- Represented HR Services during a company-wide Lawson system upgrade. As project manager, identified and advocated for the unique needs of the HR Services function. During implementation, served as trainer to the department's staff.

DEVELOPMENTAL DISABILITIES INSTITUTE, Brookville, NY   2004–2007
Residential Manager (2006–2007)
Assistant Residential Manager (2005–2006)
Direct Care Counselor (2004–2005)

- As residential manager, oversaw 20 direct-care counselors and one assistant supervisor.
- Hired approximately 15 direct-care counselors, all of whom became good employees. More than half were rated "exceptional."
- Developed and implemented a staff-training program that provided enhanced quality of care to residents and contributed to a reduction in employee attrition.
- Conducted in-depth analyses of residents' skills and abilities. Set appropriate skill goals based on present functional status. Instilled motivation to reach objectives.

EDUCATIONAL CREDENTIALS

Master of Business Administration, 2010. Hofstra University, Uniondale, NY

Bachelor of Arts, Psychology, 2004. Muhlenberg College, Allentown, PA

Professional in Human Resources (PHR) Certificate, 2008. Pace University, New York, NY
Workforce Planning & Employment, Performance Management, Compensation & Benefits,
Employee & Labor Relations, Occupational Health, Safety & Security,
Organizational Structure, Ethical & Legislative Issues

TECHNICAL SKILLS

Lawson HRIS System, Windows, Word, Excel, PowerPoint, Outlook, and Access

PROFESSIONAL AFFILIATION

Member, Society for Human Resource Management (SHRM)

■ ■ ■

the responsibilities and achievements the person had as an HR generalist. On page two, the writer similarly grouped positions for one institution to avoid repeating information that would be the same for each position. In resume-writing lingo, this process is called eliminating redundancy.

REBECCA J. EVANS

555.550.0055 • becky.evans@xxxx.com

BENEFITS ADMINISTRATION

**Health and Pharmacy Plans (PPO/CDHP) • Dental • Vision • Short- and Long-Term Disability
Medical/Dental Flexible Spending Accounts • Executive Medical Expense Reimbursement
Executive Deferred Compensation/Bonus Plans • Optional/Supplemental Life Insurance • AFLAC
EAP • 401(k) • FMLA • ADA • ERISA • COBRA • Compliance**

Critical thinker with comprehensive HR experience and proven results in strategic planning, resource management, policies/procedures development and team building. Confident rapport builder; effective in building productive working relationships based on approachability, professionalism and trust. Discerning communicator; effective at all levels from the front desk to the executive suite. Accomplished cost/benefits analyst and planner. Results-focused, systematic project manager. Skilled negotiator.

▼ ▼ ▼

Approachable, supportive and empowering team leader; skilled in using positive reinforcement to motivate performance and goal attainment. Innovative, resourceful and decisive problem solver. Extensively computer literate; proficient in HRIS (AS400/Infinium), RMIS (RiskMaster/STARS) and MS Office. Dynamic performer with a strong work ethic, a collaborative spirit and a passion for challenge.

EXPERIENCE

HEROD'S ENTERTAINMENT, INC., Joliet, IL   2000–present

Director, Benefits and Risk (2/07–present)
Have held progressively responsible roles impacting workers' compensation/insurance claims, risk management, benefits administration and staffing. Oversee Benefits & Risk Programs, including Short- and Long-Term Disability and Health, Dental, Vision, Prescription and Life Insurance benefits as well as 401(k) Plan and executive Deferred Compensation for up to 10,500 employees at the corporate office and 15 remote sites. Trained and supervise 26 on-site Risk & Benefits Managers.

Develop and manage ±$23 million annual budget. Compile monthly and quarterly reports to provide top management decision support. Manage Summary Plan Descriptions (SPDs) reflecting current plan provisions, property/casualty insurance renewal submissions, risk transfer tools (certificates of insurance, vendor contracts/agreements) and confidential employee records subject to strict compliance mandates.

Seek RFPs and conduct ongoing vendor evaluations to refine plan offerings and achieve cost-effective, competitive benefits packages to position Herod's Casino as "Employer of Choice" and attract/retain top talent. Develop and present the business case for program changes to senior leadership based on detailed cost/benefits analysis; participate in vendor selection.

Frequently collaborate with insurance adjusters, counsel and senior management on issues and litigation related to guest liability, workers' compensation and property/casualty insurance. Facilitate proactive complex issue resolution and attend court proceedings as necessary.

▸ Coordinated logistics for property/casualty self-insurance process facilitating $12 million in tax savings.

▸ Saved $.5 million in annual expense by recommending and establishing internal processing for insurance claims up to $5,000.

▸ Cut $30,000 in Third-Party Administration (TPA) expenses while also achieving verifiable records by implementing online, self-service benefits enrollment—a process tested through a pilot project and subsequently rolled out corporate-wide, 2008.

Continued

94

Combination. *Ellie Vargo, St. Louis, Missouri*

A pair of horizontal lines encloses areas of expertise with boldfacing to ensure that this important information will be seen. Then two paragraphs profile the applicant. Two themes are stressed:

REBECCA J. EVANS   becky.evans@xxxx.com   Page 2

HEROD'S ENTERTAINMENT, INC., Joliet, IL (continued)

▸ Implemented an internal audit process to ensure accurate benefits/risk databases and files as well as conformance to established processes and procedures across the organization.

▸ Set up Risk Management Information Systems (RiskMaster/STARS) at all locations.

Risk Manager and HR Generalist (5/05–2/07)
Collaborated in management transition and operational start-up after business acquisition. Refined job descriptions, integrated the workforce and restaffed positions as necessary to meet attitude and performance expectations.

▸ Authored comprehensive Risk Management Procedure Manual, standardizing policies and procedures enterprise-wide.

▸ Reconciled and monitored claims in excess of loss aggregate and/or deductible/SIR; filed for carrier reimbursements of more than $.5 million.

Risk and Benefits Manager (9/04–5/05)
Played an active role in staffing and opening new casino; conducted new-hire orientations for 700.

▸ Analyzed each casino position to accurately determine exempt/nonexempt job classifications and refined job descriptions.

▸ Introduced safety in the new property planning process, establishing model safety program adopted corporate-wide that delivered significantly reduced lost-time injuries and related costs.

Claims Risk Investigator (7/03–9/04)
Risk Manager (10/02–7/03)
Workers Compensation Administrator (9/00–10/02)

Additional early career experience in the insurance industry.

PROFESSIONAL AFFILIATIONS

Society of Human Resource Management (SHRM)
Risk Insurance Management Society (RIMS)

TRAINING & EDUCATION

"Leadership Gulf Coast," Mississippi Gulf Coast Chamber of Commerce
Problem Solving & Decision Making, Kepner Tregoe
Licensed Property & Casualty Agent
Numerous HR seminars and workshops

B.S., Business Administration, University of Chicago, IL

(1) the applicant's ability as a thinker, analyst, planner, and problem solver; and (2) her "people" skills as a leader, team builder, motivator, and negotiator. Under the first workplace, the writer indicates activities and successes in a series of short paragraphs.

Rachel McElroy, MBA, SPHR

5500 Grand View Drive • Kansas City, KS 50505

555.000.5050
rjmcelroy@gxxxx.com

Senior Executive in Human Resources with 10 Years of Experience

Driving the talent-management practices that mold human resources into an integral strategic partner in maximizing corporate productivity, improving employee satisfaction, and increasing profitability. Record of uncovering deficiencies in staffing procedures and policies and developing effective interventions that achieve measurable success and resonate with employees.

Full scope of HR expertise, including:

• Benefits and Compensation	• Employee and Labor Relations	• Workforce Planning
• Recruiting	• Learning and Development	• Policy Development
• Performance Management	• Succession Planning	• Rewards and Recognition

Professional Experience

Terrible's Casino and Resort, Kansas City, KS   *2008–Present*
Privately held, full-service hospitality operation offering casino gaming, hotel, banquet, and dining facilities. $45M annual adjusted gross revenue; 350 full-time equivalents (FTEs).

Human Resources Manager (Senior corporate HR position)
Drive full spectrum of HR initiatives to support business strategy, including recruiting, benefits, training, employee relations, engagement, incentive programs, performance management, and succession planning. Formulate and implement annual budget, including plan of action for benefit cost-containment. Write company-wide policies and procedures; collaborated with sister property, corporate, and outside counsel to draft company handbook.

Employee Engagement and Satisfaction
✓ Reduced turnover from **90.2%** in March 2008 to **35.5%** in July 2010 by developing and implementing a two-pronged approach:
  o Partnered with department managers to develop a "formula for success" by analyzing qualifications, experiences, and behaviors of top performers.
  o Implemented an employee-satisfaction survey in March of 2008, which delivered **2.3/5.0**; in June 2010, score increased to **4.2/5.0**.

Compensation and Benefits
✓ Transformed performance-management system from merit-based to skill-based by developing and executing a comprehensive training program to certify employees in multiple jobs with corresponding pay increases. As a result, regular FTEs dropped by **15%**, OT FTEs dropped from **3.61 to 1.10**, and payroll decreased by **$21K**.

✓ Aggressively pursued insurance plans that would deliver minimal premium increases year over year, leading to a nominal **5%** premium increase over a three-year period. Also introduced health-savings plan that achieved **21%** participation rate in first year.

✓ Analyzed, reworked, and wrote new job descriptions for all **96** salaried and hourly positions; created and implemented grade levels and salary structure.

Performance Management
✓ Instituted performance-management tool that rewarded desired guest-service behaviors, resulting in a documented increase in guest satisfaction.

✓ Increased efficiency and improved overall customer experience by combining two departments into one Guest Service Center. As a result, increased time on device by an average of 5 minutes, which generated **$98K+** in additional revenue while simultaneously reducing labor expenses by more than **$100K**.

Flexsteel, Lawrence, KS   *2006–2007*
Office-furniture manufacturer specializing in higher-end product line. Division of HNI, with revenues of $1.6B; 2,000 employees.

Member and Community Relations (MCR) Manager
Implemented all facets of HR function within manufacturing facility of 400+ employees, including training, employee relations, benefits administration, recruiting, and performance management. Promoted to corporate headquarters after only six months, driving strategic programs including semiannual 360-degree review process, EEO compliance, employee-satisfaction initiatives, staffing, and succession planning. Developed and delivered training programs on diversity, drug and alcohol awareness, harassment and respect, and performance management.

Page One

95

Combination. *Lesa E. Kerlin, Kirksville, Missouri*

A pair of horizontal lines encloses key information near the top of the first page: a profile in large type and areas of expertise formatted and bulleted in three columns. A statement in italic

Communications
- ✓ Bridged communication gap between factory managers and corporate team by building rapport and shifting perceptions so that MCR became a key strategic partner in major decisions.

Turnover Reduction
- ✓ Reduced turnover and improved quality standards by developing on-boarding program that stemmed from extensive focus groups' input as to the root causes of turnover.

Metrics
- ✓ Developed and implemented an HR metrics system that gave operational managers a complete statistical picture of MCR function in one location, including turnover rate, EEO compliance, employee-satisfaction scores, payroll, and OT. Reviewed data monthly with managers; used for goal setting, trending, and performance management.

Isle of Capri/Blues City Casino, Kansas City, MO   *2000–2006*
Publicly traded casino gaming company with 13 locations across U.S.

Director of Human Resources (Blues City)
Regional Training Manager (Isle of Capri & Blues City)
Recruiter (Isle of Capri)
Created a branded HR program that aligned with new Blues City brand and opened communication between two properties. Directed safety, benefits, employee relations, training, and recruiting functions; devised HR initiatives that aligned with company's strategic goals. Board member of corporate university; developed measurable training programs and succession plan for corporation.

Performance Management
- ✓ Enhanced work performance, reduced scheduling volatility, and significantly diminished work-related injuries by creating a team member recognition program that addressed deficiencies in the operation. **$20K** cost of program resulted in company savings of **$100K+**.

- ✓ Improved on-boarding practices by creating a company-wide training program that rolled out to all 13 properties after only one year. Program still in use today.

- ✓ Opened lines of communication between HR and operating managers by holding quarterly reviews with each manager, addressing their department's performance on turnover, employee-satisfaction scores, forecast vs. actual labor, time-to-hire ratios, and succession planning.

Strategic Management and Leadership
- ✓ Operated as key strategic partner during transition from Isle of Capri Casino to Blues City Casino; developed a balanced-scorecard approach to increasing revenues, decreasing labor percentages, improving turnover, and increasing profit. As a result, property transformed from **last to first** in one year.

- ✓ Demonstrated focused leadership as HR positions for the two properties combined; changed previous "us versus them" mentality to team-oriented "we" approach.

- ✓ Developed and facilitated monthly "best practices" meetings that brought together management teams from both properties to help create an atmosphere of collaboration instead of competition.

Education

University of Missouri–Kansas City
Master of Business Administration

Society for Human Resource Management
Senior Professional in Human Resources
Certificate of Specialization in Strategy

Truman State University, Kirksville, MO
Bachelor of Arts, Interdisciplinary Studies

Black Hawk College, Moline, IL
Certificate in Human Resource Management

Professional Affiliations

United Way of Kansas City Chapter
Cabinet Member

Medicount Management
Board Member

describes each workplace mentioned in the Professional Experience section. Significant achievements quantified with percentages and dollar amounts (in boldfacing) are clustered under separate subheadings to avoid one long list of accomplishments.

MARIA GONZALEZ

55 Matthews Drive ◆ Woodside, NY 55555
555-555-5555 Home ◆ 555-555-5554 Cell ◆ mgonzalez@xxxx.com

BENEFITS MANAGER
Strategic Benefits Analysis / Plan Design & Implementation
Plan Administration / Benefits Communications / Change Management

Strategic benefits manager and forward-thinking business partner who is effective in designing and implementing best-in-class benefit packages to foster positive corporate cultures and attract and retain top talent. Respected, influential leader; an effective communicator who is able to establish rapport with people at all levels in the organization while building a sense of confidence and trust.

Core Competencies

- Analyzing needs and designing well-conceived benefit plans, building best-fit solutions to meet business goals.
- Researching and justifying benefit programs, promoting new, innovative offerings to build competitive edge.
- Managing all aspects of benefits communications, developing and delivering messaging that demonstrates clear value to build acceptance of both popular and unpopular features.
- Flawlessly implementing programs and enhancements, overseeing all aspects to ensure smooth transition.
- Introducing improvements to facilitate program administration while maintaining the highest standards of customer service.

PROFESSIONAL EXPERIENCE

AXA EQUITABLE, New York, NY   2002 to present
Benefits Manager
Manage all benefit plans (medical, dental, life, disability, retirement, etc.) for 1,000 employees nationally and in 3 international locations for rapidly growing company, providing both strategic and administrative support for plans. Oversee annual renewal process, analyzing programs and benchmarking against others to maintain best-in-class status.

Promoted and launched new benefit plans…
…enhancing company's "employer-of-choice" reputation.

Strategic Benefits Management

- Provide strategic benefits management, conducting regular reviews of overall benefits package to ensure alignment with corporate goals. Benchmarked with competitors to maintain "best-in-class" standard, researching and justifying new programs to build competitive advantage. Among successes:
  - ✓ Advocated and won justification for first-ever EAP benefit, a well-received program that garnered extensive positive feedback from employees.
  - ✓ Recommended and launched hearing aid plan, a highly sought-after benefit.
  - ✓ Introduced adoption benefit plan that covered legal fees and travel expenses for adopters.
  - ✓ Revamped tuition reimbursement plan, eliminating waiting period while setting formal guidelines that made it more accessible to employees.
  - ✓ Successfully introduced mandatory mail-order prescription plan that saved $200,000/year, overcoming employee resistance by conducting on-site meetings at all locations that strategically addressed concerns by offering testimonials from employees who recognized advantages.
- Manage communications to educate employees on the value of benefits and the business needs that demand changes. Among successes, initiated creation of Total Compensation Statement, a communication tool used to demonstrate the intrinsic value of major benefit plans—and the company's contribution.
- Led effort to integrate separate retirement plans covering 2 different locations, offering solution that combined the best of both plans to deliver a best-in-class solution.

Continued

96

Combination. *Carol A. Altomare, Three Bridges, New Jersey*

For this benefits manager, the writer grouped accomplishments into strategic and tactical success-es, painting the manager as someone with a vision for building best-in-class benefits programs

Maria Gonzalez   mgonzalez@xxxx.com   Page 2

AXA EQUITABLE   Continued
Benefits Manager

Tactical Benefits Administration

- Introduced Paid Time Off program to replace archaic system. Easier to administer than other plans, program had added benefit of cultivating an empowering work environment that enhanced employee morale.
- Spearheaded development and launch of new benefits Web site, a one-stop resource that allowed employees to make elections online at their leisure. Solution minimized errors and reduced costs of what had been a labor-intensive process.
- Introduced system to automate premium payments, eliminating day-long manual process.
- Launched education series, bringing in external experts to provide guidance and advice on retirement plans.
- A sought-after benefits resource, earned reputation for knowledge and responsiveness, consistently providing quick and accurate answers to employee benefits inquiries,
- Leveraged excellent research skills to compile complete answers to tough employee questions, going "above and beyond" to provide assistance.

CHURCH & DWIGHT, New York, NY   2000 to 2002
Benefits Administrator
Administered all retirement, health, and welfare plans for 1,000 employees.
- Introduced first-ever HRIS database that automated HR processes, including benefits administration.
- Led special projects to automate administration of retirement and other benefit plans.

SMITH ARCHITECTURAL GROUP, New York, NY   1998 to 2000
Corporate Benefits Supervisor
Supervised 2 staff members in managing retirement, health, and welfare plans for more than 600 employees
- Managed open enrollment for health, welfare, and 401(k) plans.

ACE PROPERTY MANAGERS, New York, NY   1997 to 1998
Benefits Manager/Senior Benefits Administrator
Provided benefits support for 500 employees, administering all benefit plans.
- Designed HRIS benefits model to automate premium calculations and generate reports and statements.

PIEDMONT CAPITAL, New York, NY   1992 to 1996
Benefits Administrator
- Established new Benefits/HR function following separation from parent company.

EDUCATION/PROFESSIONAL DEVELOPMENT/AFFILIATION

B.A., English/Political Science, St. John's University, Queens, NY

Completed CEB's Course 1 and Course 3
Member, International Foundation of Employee Benefit Plans

TECHNICAL SKILLS

Databases: Ceridian Source 500, ADP HRPartner, Access, dBASE IV, EV4
Spreadsheet Applications: Excel, Lotus
Reporting Software: Crystal Reports, ReportSmith, Query Analyzer
Presentation Software: PowerPoint

and the know-how to implement them successfully. Notice the varied uses of horizontal lines in this resume and the mix of side and centered headings. Note also the thin underlining of certain centered headings and the names of the workplaces.

STACEY GAINES

5555 Barker Avenue | Freehold, NJ 07728 | 555-555-5555 | StaceyG@sample.com

HUMAN RESOURCES EXECUTIVE

Benefits and Compensation | Organizational Effectiveness | HR Initiatives

Seasoned Human Resources Executive with expertise in legal aspects of HR compliance, compensation, benefit plan design and taxation. Use respectful and skillful communication to enhance positive work cultures and inspire collaboration. An assertive manager with outstanding interpersonal, communications, negotiation, and people management skills. Demonstrate strategic thinking with innovative program ideas and the ability to execute same.

Core competencies include:

- **Benefits/Compensation Design and Administration**
- **Workforce Planning**
- **Process Improvement**
- **Strategic Planning**

- **Operational Streamlining**
- **Staff Management**
- **Team Leadership**
- **Training and Development**

EXECUTIVE PERFORMANCE

BENEFITS/COMPENSATION
Managed benefit administration processes and compensation plans while affirming alignment with business strategies. Ensured proper implementation and execution of said programs and initiatives.
- ✓ Achieved annual saving of $1.5 million for Access through successful renegotiations of vendor agreements with emphasis on executive benefits.
- ✓ Collaborated with Access's legal department to define executive benefit administration process, ensuring parity and nondiscriminatory practices in executive pay agreements.

Consultative Projects
- ✓ Redesigned annual incentive compensation plan for 5,000-personnel client, including base pay plan and full reorganization of job descriptions. Rewrote and reduced job descriptions from 5,000 to 1,000 in order to provide parity and company-wide consistency in function description, enhance cross-departmental job sharing and promotional opportunities, and properly align all with new compensation plan.
- ✓ Oversight for full compliance review for Fortune 50 client's qualified retirement plans. Reviewed 32 plan acquisitions over a five-year period, identified issues and suggested/implemented problem resolutions to ensure ongoing compliance. Developed and furnished plan administration procedures/protocols for corporate management to confirm effective plan management and execution.

ORGANIZATIONAL EFFECTIVENESS
Adept at assisting organizations to achieve goals with a proven ability for analyzing and improving corporate structure and procedures, staffing initiatives and employee development programs.
- ✓ Influenced corporate culture at Access through education and communication surrounding the benefits and need for diversifying the workforce. Established, implemented and conveyed policies and procedures for nondiscrimination hiring practices corporate-wide.

Consultative Projects
- ✓ Improved job analysis/workforce process ensuring adequate staffing plans, budget development and succession planning.
- ✓ Enhanced clients' hiring process through development of five-year workforce plan.

HUMAN CAPITAL
Skilled at enhancing revenue for new and existing clients.
- ✓ Furnished Deloitte & Touche's Fortune 50 clients with comprehensive 404 compliance reviews that resulted in client positive determinations by the IRS.
- ✓ Significantly increased revenue at multiple Deloitte & Touche offices within 12 months by $100,000+ by procuring, nurturing and maintaining income-producing relationships with Deloitte & Touche professionals.

Page 1

Combination. *Michelle Riklan, Morganville, New Jersey*

This resume makes good use of the important area between the contact information and the Executive Performance section, fashioning the core competencies as key phrases. The Executive

STACEY GAINES | 555-555-5555 | StaceyG@sample.com   **PAGE 2**

CAREER HISTORY

MAXIMUM HR, LLC, New York, NY   2005–Present
Maximum specializes in providing experienced Human Resources executives for just-in-time interim positions and special initiatives. Consultants are matched to clients based on client needs and consultants' areas of expertise.

Human Resource Consultant
Service clients by managing a variety of projects. Accomplishments include redesign of incentive plans, compliance reviews of acquired benefit plans through mergers and acquisitions, restructuring of company's salary plans for nonunion employees, redesigns of company's employee competency requirements and development of job family and function structure for nonbargaining employees.

DELOITTE & TOUCHE, New York, NY   2003–2005
Deloitte & Touche is a global leader in assurance, tax, transaction, advisory services and strategic growth markets.

Senior Manager, Human Capital
Recruited into Senior Management position to work with Tax and Audit clients in a consultative capacity in areas of Human Capital, specifically targeted Qualified and Non-qualified Retirement Plans, Health & Welfare plans, Stock Option Plans, Executive Incentive Plans and compliance (404[c]).

COOPER-EPSTEIN CONSULTING, INC., Cherry Hill, NJ   1994–2003
Cooper-Epstein Consulting, Inc., provides benefit design/implementation services to the health care industry.

Vice President, Client Services
Benefit Design Analyst
Rapidly promoted to position of increased scope and responsibility, managing staff of 20–30 design analysts, financial analysts and marketing representatives. Oversight for design team maintaining highest number of ongoing projects with a success rate surpassing 95%. Designed plan that was approved and purchased by clients and provided 50% new annual revenue for the organization.

ACCESS 2000, INC., Wyckoff, NJ   1990–1994
Fortune 100 company that manufactures and services elevators.

Manager of Benefits Administration
With three direct reports in compensation and benefits, responsible for complete benefit administration for Human Resource division including qualified retirement plans, Health & Welfare, EEOC and Risk Management. Administered all Executive-level incentive, compensation and non-qualified benefit plans.

EDUCATION, TRAINING AND CERTIFICATIONS

Bachelor of Arts, Psychology, **Adelphi University,** Garden City, NY

Membership: Society of Human Resource Management (SHRM)

Performance section clusters activities under three side headings with "Consultative Projects" as a side subheading for the first two headings. Check marks point to sentences and paragraphs rather than lines in a list. In the Career History on page two, workplace descriptions are in italic.

SCOTT T. FREEDMAN

505 Perryton Road   Des Peres, MO 00550
Home: **(555) 505-0055** Cell: **(555) 505-5500**
Stfree5@xxxx.com

HUMAN RESOURCES PROFESSIONAL

✓ Logical decision maker with a **Master of Science in Human Resources Management** and demonstrated work experience in recruitment, policy analysis, benefits compliance and development of systematic measurement tools to attain tangible results.

✓ **Certified Employee Benefit Specialist** with 20 years of proven success in employee group-benefit plan underwriting for small to mid-size organizations.

✓ **Diplomatic business acumen** with a strong will to coach, motivate and lead in a tactful manner, while being part of a team.

✓ **Analytical quality-focused professional** with compliant and objective awareness to organization factors that impact success.

PROFESSIONAL EXPERIENCE

Human Resources Generalist

♦ Successfully analyzed HR policies and coordinated reports of recommended revisions in alignment with organization objectives.

♦ Diligently researched and evaluated statistics and provision of time-off patterns to support the implementation of a PTO (Paid Time Off) program for an organization of 90+ employees.

♦ Compiled industry-specific Web sites to support workforce recruitment strategies, increase potential-talent pool and complement organization branding.

♦ Efficiently developed an organized applicant tracking system and a new-hire evaluation template that assessed the qualifications of candidates and supported hiring decisions.

♦ Improved team performance through quality-focused training techniques and coaching on adherence to client compliance specifications.

♦ Meticulously audited I-9 forms to reach full legal compliance for all employees and applied well-rounded generalist knowledge to all HR functions assigned.

Employee Benefits Administration

♦ Competently performed underwriting administration for fully insured, multistate groups and self-funded employer group-benefit plans.

♦ Thoroughly calculated group-benefit plan pricing for health, dental, life, disability and vision group-benefit plan products in accordance with client preferences.

♦ Administered employee group-benefit plan pricing within all government regulations to include HIPAA, COBRA, FMLA, ERISA and ADA federal mandates for group health insurance plans.

♦ Efficiently interacted with internal partners and clients to collaborate on benefit rates, revisions and policies for mutual understanding and consistent client pricing.

♦ Precisely audited account setup and billing structures to sustain quality and exceed client expectations.

♦ Contributed to company-wide projects to include the successful integration of HIPAA policies in the High Point Ohio market and compilation of data to predict profitability and maintain retention levels.

Continued on next page

98

Combination. *Jane Roqueplot, West Middlesex, Pennsylvania*

Slightly larger type and plenty of white space on page two make this two-page resume easy to read. A pair of horizontal lines (thin over thick) encloses each centered section heading, unifying

SCOTT T. FREEDMAN

505 Perryton Road   Des Peres, MO 00550
Home: **(555) 505-0055** Cell: **(555) 505-5500**
Stfree5@xxxx.com

PROFESSIONAL WORK HISTORY

TBU Telecom **HR Internship**	Pittsburgh, PA 2011–2012
Sun Health **Underwriting Consultant**	Pittsburgh, PA 2009–2011
American Blue Cross & Blue Shield **Senior Rating Analyst**	Pittsburgh, PA 2007–2009
High Point Blue Cross & Blue Shield **Senior Underwriter**	Cincinnati, OH 2002–2007
Castle Health Plan **Underwriting Manager**	St. Joseph, MO 2000–2002
Global Life Insurance Company **Group Underwriter**	St. Louis, MO 1996–2000
Bowman Health Care of Missouri **Group Underwriter**	St. Louis, MO 1992–1996

EDUCATION

La Roche College — Pittsburgh, PA
Master of Science, Human Resources Management
Major: Compliance and Administration
Graduated: May 2012

St. Louis University — St. Louis, MO
Master of Business Administration
Graduated: January 1994

University of Missouri — St. Louis, MO
Bachelor of Science, Business Administration
Graduated: May 1990

CERTIFICATIONS

Certified Employee Benefits Specialist (CEBS) — Fellowship
Certified Life Underwriter (CLU)
Certified Fraud Examiner (CFU)

MEMBERSHIPS & AFFILIATIONS

Association of Certified Fraud Examiners
2009–Present

International Society for CEBS
2002–Present

Toastmasters International
2002–Present

the resume visually. Like Resume 97, this resume summarizes experience in the lower part of the first page and provides a work history at the top of the second page. Notice how boldfacing calls attention to important information on both pages.

BILL CAVENDISH

555 Laurelwood Drive • Hopedale, MA 55555
555.555.5555 • bcavendish@example.com

Workforce Development Program Director

HUMAN RESOURCES • ORGANIZATIONAL DEVELOPMENT • PROJECT MANAGEMENT

Resourceful, well-respected, and influential senior-level training and development professional. Proactive business partner to senior management. Extensive experience in the design, delivery, evaluation, and enhancement of effective hands-on instructional programs that improve efficiency, increase productivity, enhance quality, and strengthen financial results. Professional career reflects 15+ years of progressive experience in administrative leadership, human resources management, resource utilization, and organizational development for blue chip corporations. Combine strong needs analysis, planning, organization, and consensus-building abilities in tandem with effective problem resolution, contract negotiation, and relationship-management skills. Highly articulate and engaging communicator; recognized as a creative leader with the aptitude to align training activities with overarching corporate goals. Proficient in the following areas:

Human Resources Management • Cross-Functional Project Management • Learning & Development Strategies
Vendor Management • Budget Control • Contract Negotiations • Instructional Design • Compliance
Change Management • Resource Planning • Networking • Team Building
Leadership Development • Program & Content Development • Multimedia & eLearning Strategies

CAREER HIGHLIGHTS

INK & PAPER, INC.—Framingham, MA   **1997–Present**
Office products company offering customers around the globe a wide range of office products including supplies, technology, furniture, and business services. With $20B in sales and 2,000 stores, the company serves businesses of all sizes and consumers in 25 countries.

MANAGER, Training & Development   **2006–Present**
North American Delivery Division (Sales & Customer Service)

Promoted to position of pivotal responsibility, coordinating with senior leadership to implement a highly effective training program for division managers across various business units; set and administer appropriate training action plans. Manage a $1.5M operating budget while advising and directing a team of 13 project managers, instructional designers, and trainers. Function as pivotal member of Service Improvement Management Team while partnering with key decision makers from all organizational business units spanning technology, customer satisfaction, knowledge management, and quality assurance personnel as well as IS, merchandising, and senior management in Retail and North American Delivery on crucial training initiatives.

- Piloted a **sales training program to harvest an 8% increase in average order sizes.**
- Coached and primed a 13-member project team to **foster over 30% in team promotions** for the past 2 years.
- Devised **first-ever company strategy for remote, instructor-led curriculum** for off-site/work-at-home associates.
- Pioneered management training certificate program for field managers; helped **garner promotions for 35% of program graduates** within a year of completion.
- Innovated, deployed, and manage an **online training tool ("Product Lab") used by 30,000+ associates across North America to drive revenue growth of 40% per year.**
- Established technology solutions for training and communication for contact center/customer service associates and management.
- **Instituted a 3-week-long training initiative incorporating instructor-led and eLearning tools for new customer service hires** to ensure peak performance levels equaling those of tenured agents within just 90 days; liaised with merchandising and marketing staff to deliver training to 2,000+ frontline customer service agents.
- Identify, secure, and manage vendor partnerships for short-term and long-term, multiyear relationships.

Continued

99

Combination. *Sandra Ingemansen, Matteson, Illinois*

This Training and Development Specialist had significant experience with implementing innovative eLearning initiatives for a major multinational office product corporation. With this resume

Bill Cavendish — page 2   bcavendish@example.com

MANAGER, Learning Technology   2001–2006
Corporate Human Resources Division (Ink & Paper University)

Appointed to high-profile role on Ink & Paper University management team with accountability to spearhead entire company-wide eLearning/distance learning technology program strategy, development, and implementation in compliance areas spanning harassment prevention, ethics training, safety, and quarterly corporate communication programs. Developed, instituted, and headed both content development and global training strategies for the company intranet and Web portal, InkandPaper@work. Total authority over eLearning budget development and administration as well as the budgeting, scheduling, instructional design, programming, and video/audio production of all learning technology projects.

- Aggressively negotiated contracts with vendors to **foster notable cost savings exceeding $1.2M per year.**
- Initiated a vendor collaboration to **institute a groundbreaking funding model** for pivotal training programs/tools, **capturing in excess of $1M in funding from product manufacturers** and counteracting any internal costs to the company.
- Led team to win the **Ned Nordham Group's 2006 Intranet Design Award.**
- **Created and delivered training programs to 50,000+** successful, thriving Ink & Paper associates.

DISTANCE LEARNING PROJECT MANAGER   2000–2001
Corporate Human Resources Division (Ink & Paper University)

Selected to project management role directing daily operations of the Ink & Paper Training Network (in-house interactive satellite television network that broadcasts training programs/communications to retail stores, remote offices, and distribution centers across North America). Guided, trained, and mentored a 3-member team of training specialists tasked with creating and facilitating delivery of all broadcast materials. Integrated the use of original training material including scripts and supporting resources to deliver dynamic training broadcasts for the network.

- Full ownership of contract management; continually **negotiated lowest possible costs for annual contracts with satellite provider.**

TRAINING & DEVELOPMENT SPECIALIST / INSTRUCTIONAL DESIGNER   1997–2000
North American Retail Division

Hired to key development position to study, devise, and implement an engaging training curriculum in support of store managers and associates of the North American Retail Division; performed in-depth needs assessment to identify training requirements, subsequently recommending viable long-term development solutions. Authored multimedia program content and organized outside vendors to deliver a high-tech program.

123 INVESTMENTS—Franklin / Boston / Andover, MA   1995–1997
Leading global money management firm with 70+ years of investment experience; $115B in assets under management.

TRAINER, Communication Services Division

Successfully created, established, and facilitated a 4-week training and orientation program to familiarize new staff members with division protocol; guided and mentored trainees throughout the training program.

- **Enlisted to deliver all training programs to support the opening of a new facility** in Andover, MA, because of previous success of newly established induction training program.

EDUCATION & CERTIFICATIONS

MASTER OF BUSINESS ADMINISTRATION, General Management (2010) *Executive MBA Program*
Alabama University—Auburn, AL

BACHELOR OF ARTS, Communications
East Coast College—Quincy, MA

Graduate Level Coursework in HR Management
University of Massachusetts, School of Business

HR Generalist Certificate Program
Society for Human Resource Management

he was recruited to a Director of Training position for a billion-dollar hospitality company seeking expertise in executive leadership development at its world headquarters.

Sarah Collins

PO Box 5555, Northland, KY 55555 • 555-555-0000 • scollins@gxxxx.com
http://www.xxxx.com/in/sarahcollins

Human Resources Senior Executive
HR Strategy • Organizational Development • Change Management

Dynamic "change engineer" who consistently drives business growth and profitability. More than 20 years of experience leading talent and organizational transformation, including 12 years with Brand Name Company. Deep expertise across all HR disciplines. Highly creative problem solver in the face of diverse challenges, including high-growth, global expansion, start-up, restructuring, acquisition, and merger integration.

Trusted and valued business partner to senior leaders. Highly effective people manager and team builder.

**Strategic Planning
Talent Acquisition, Development & Retention
Leadership Development, Succession Planning & Coaching
Organizational Design
Budget Management & Cost Containment
Consulting & Project Management
Team Leadership & Development**

Experience & Accomplishments

Sarah Collins Associates, Northland, KY   2008 – present
Independent consulting firm providing business leaders with creative, profitable, and proven solutions to lead employees through organizational transition.

CEO/Chief Change Engineer
Founded and now lead firm to offer expertise and results in high-change situations: acquisitions, integrations, downsizing, divestitures, and start-ups. Focus intensively on leadership, organization, and talent strategy and execution. Develop business, establishing and cultivating relationships with executives of diverse companies. Lead team of 5 associates.

- Delivered core strategy and specific action steps—accepted by executives and implemented in 45 days—for high-growth, privately held service company to decrease high employee turnover, improve morale and productivity, and transition organizational culture.
- Created and delivered career transition services to employees of 75-year-old business implementing first-ever layoffs; reduced company's legal risks and accelerated employability of laid-off employees.
- Crafted comprehensive toolkit adopted by leadership of Industry Alliance (300+ industry executives) to guide their transition of hundreds of employees through major industry downturn.

Lanston Global, Phoenix, AZ   2004 – 2007
Privately held global company created from consolidation of 3 businesses (one of which was Brand Name spin-off); $750 million in revenue, 4,000 employees, and 32 locations. Sold for 3.5 times earnings in 2007.

SVP, Human Resources
Tapped to lead HR and organizational strategy and development for newly formed company. Created and steered all talent strategy and practices as well as critical organization and culture change initiatives. Drove HR due diligence and integration for ongoing acquisitions. Led team of up to 30 professionals across multiple locations in U.S. and Canada. Managed multimillion-dollar budget.

- Led divestiture activities for Brand Name spin-off, ensuring seamless transition to new platforms and guiding new "start-up" experience for 1,000+ employees of 50-year legacy business.
- Spearheaded organizational and people integration of 3 independent businesses into single newly formed company; consolidated employee systems, processes, and tools while also enabling company's ongoing growth through acquisitions (400% in 3 years).

continued

100

Combination. *Cathy Alfandre, Easton, Connecticut*

The applicant's original resume was four pages and unfocused with no summary, no keywords, and no branding. She had great Human Resources experience, but it didn't come across clearly in

(continued...)

- Served on external and internal branding team; partnered with Marketing SVP to develop culture change tools and hands-on training, transitioning employees to new company vision, values, and customer service platforms within 1 year.
- Created and implemented diverse leadership development processes, including real-time, Web-based training for more than 500 leaders across more than 30 locations.
- Crafted critical new compensation strategy, including executive and sales compensation and other incentive plans for more than 4,000 employees, driving simplicity, market competitiveness, career development, and retention.
- Reduced company benefit costs by $500,000 in 1 year while maintaining high employee benefit satisfaction rates.

Brand Name Company, Atlanta, GA; Stamford, CT; Denver, CO; Phoenix, AZ   1992 – 2004
Global company with diverse holdings; ~$100 billion in revenue and 200,000+ employees.

VP, Human Resources
Promoted repeatedly through diverse businesses, eventually becoming HR leader for business of 1200+ employees in 8 locations. Also held short-term roles in marketing, business development, and operations. Led talent and organizational strategy and initiatives, including recruiting, development, and retention, leadership development and succession, OD and change management, and performance management. Managed staff of up to 6.

- Masterminded rightsizing and site consolidation activities for one business, resulting in 21% reduction in workforce with no legal, compliance, or employee-relations issues.
- Achieved 100% retention of identified Top 20% talent during downsizing in company and industry through performance, succession, and talent-retention processes.
- Crafted sales force compensation plan to improve recruitment and retention; drove first incentive payouts in 3 years and boosted satisfaction rates to 68% (up from 5%–10% with prior plans).
- Led HR team to exceed Six Sigma savings and process improvement targets by 34%.

Prior HR management experience at ABC Insurance and Consumer Brand Company.

Education

Master of Business Administration, Marketing
North University, School of Management, Everytown, IN

Bachelor of Arts, Mass Communications/Media
Hill University, Hill, GA

Professional Development Highlights

Brand Name Company:
- Exclusive 1–2 week executive leadership courses: Management Development, New Executive Leadership Symposium, Advanced HR Development
- Six Sigma Green Belt Certification
- Other courses: Change Acceleration Process, Strategy Skills, Facilitation Leadership, Diversity Leadership, Acquisition Integration, HR Due Diligence

Center for Creative Leadership: Certification, 360 Assessment Tools

College of Executive Coaching: Certification, Executive and Personal Coaching

her resume. The writer turned the original resume into this two-page resume to position the applicant for a senior HR role. Notice the use of lines, boldfacing, italic, bullets, tabbing, and line spacing to make the resume strong and easy to read.

GARRY CROSSLEY

66 Madrona Drive ~ Santa Monica, California 55555

555.555.5555 (A/H)   g_cross@hotmail.com

SENIOR HR EXECUTIVE

HR Infrastructure & Planning ~ Generalist Functions ~ Employment & Business Law

Multi-faceted, results-oriented Senior HR Executive with comprehensive experience demonstrating quantifiable achievements and expertise encompassing all facets of legal, management and human resource generalist functions. Combines unique blend of visionary leadership and executive business savvy with competencies to spearhead strategic planning and execution of core staffing, operational and administrative initiatives to drive overall HR, organizational and bottom-line financial performance.

- ♦ Multi-Site Operations Management ♦ Project/Financial Management ♦ Merger/Acquisition Integration
- ♦ Industrial/Employee Relations ♦ Benefits/Compensation Design ♦ Policy/Process/Systems Design
- ♦ Staff Performance Optimization ♦ Union/Non-Union Relations ♦ Business/Corporate Litigation

CAREER ACCOMPLISHMENTS

TimeField Corporation

- Revitalized morale of support services staff, improved client satisfaction and optimized overall organizational efficiencies through motivation/mentoring of underperformers and streamlining policies and procedures, including implementation of computerized work-order systems.
- Captured cost savings of $200,000 for contracted services within first year through elimination of previous reliance on expensive outside contractors.
- Transformed support services functions into high-producing team through execution of numerous turnaround strategies including corporate-wide conversion to Kronos computerized payroll system that secured improved attendance, payroll processing and performance-management functions.
- Consistently captured cost savings on premium renewals for employee benefit plans while obtaining improved benefit plans through facilitation of strategic negotiations.

PROFESSIONAL EXPERIENCE

TimeField Corporation, Los Angeles, CA   1995–Present
Human Services and Healthcare Provider to 25,000 clients locally, regionally and internationally with $60 million budget and 1,200 employees spanning 52 sites across four states.

General Counsel / Vice President of Support Services (1998–Present)

- Diverse role, accountable for $4 million budget and 13 staff, spearheading direction and execution of strategic initiatives to secure optimal performance across 10 functions encompassing legal, human resources, corporate and healthcare services procurement, risk management, training and development, information management, conference management and office services and telecommunications.
- Key member of executive team, providing ongoing tactical support, advice and presentations to President and Board of Directors in goal setting and achievement of corporate growth objectives.
- Distinguished track record for management and delivery of corporate-level functions and activities within HR, compensation/benefit administration, recruitment, training, performance management, diversity, EEO/AAP, HRIS, Safety, corporate-wide MIS, purchasing and risk management.
- Legal counsel handling a broad spectrum of corporate and program matters with sole responsibilities with investigation, negotiation, litigation and settlement across business law, employment law, commercial transactions, housing law, construction, real estate, elder-care law, corporate law, mergers and acquisitions, due diligence, bond financings, risk management and family law matters.

Continued

101

Combination. *Annemarie Cross, Hallam, Victoria, Australia*

As an executive, this individual had vast expertise. The writer put experience and achievements related to the applicant's goal toward the beginning of the document. She mentioned

PROFESSIONAL EXPERIENCE
(Continued)

Accomplishments
- Pioneered and directed five functions that improved organizational effectiveness, reduced costs and generated revenue including risk management, corporate purchasing, conference-management services, telecommunications and office services.
- Championed consistently high ratings from local, state and federal inspections, demonstrating leadership and direction expertise.
- Exceptional litigation record, winning 100% of 150 cases handled since 1998 within Administration, State and Federal court matters.
- Collected $700,000 in damages across broad spectrum of cases, and captured over $500,000 cost savings in legal fees by personally performing work previously assigned to external high-profile legal firms.
- Improved collection system and dispute-resolution system for three nursing homes, 550 hospital beds and 2,000 housing units through creation and execution of turnaround solutions.
- Designed, planned, executed and directed successful $400,000 telecommunications project.

Vice President of Support Services (1995–1998)

- Oversaw administration and operation departments with $6 million budget, including employee benefit programs and purchasing volume across 52 sites, with increasingly responsible duties proportionate to 300% budget increase during that time.
- Directed, supported and mentored 12–100 employees located at 50 sites across four states.
- Reviewed all employment disciplinary and employment law-related matters.

Accomplishments
- Re-engineered six core departments that facilitated 300% corporate growth.
- Achieved successful outcomes in all employment law matters, spearheading management of each case independently from beginning through completion.
- Captured significant improvement in staff morale and productivity through participative management style and introduction of innovative performance-optimizing strategies.
- Implemented strategic cost-reduction initiatives that secured consistent budget savings of 5%–10%.

Previous experience demonstrating expertise spearheading development and expedition of grievance-resolution and arbitration programs; litigation of unfair labor practices; and staff training and development across both public and private sectors, including Fortune 500 entity.

EDUCATION

UNIVERSITY OF CALIFORNIA, Los Angeles, CA
Juris Doctor

CAPITOL UNIVERSITY, Washington, DC
Master of Science—**Major: Industrial Relations**

STANFORD UNIVERSITY, Stanford, CA
Bachelor of Arts in Urban Studies

CERTIFICATIONS

Senior Professional in Human Resources—Society for Human Resource Management

less-related experience with a Fortune 500 company in a short italic paragraph at the end of the Professional Experience section. Achievements stand out in the Career Accomplishments section after the profile, and in the Professional Experience section under each left-aligned, italic Accomplishments subheading.

SUSAN J. ANDERSON

5960 Constantine Road
Orange, CA 92680

714.998.3012
Susan@aol.com

HUMAN RESOURCES INFORMATION SYSTEMS

**Implementation Consultant · Quality Customer Service & High-Level Retention
Account Executive · Corporate Start-Ups · Procedural Development
Corporate & Government Contracts · Skilled Negotiator · Strategic Planner
Sales Process/Full Life Cycle · Market/Competitor Research · Selling Models
Implementation Cycle · Product Solutions · Project Management · Payroll**

Solid career history in HRIS operations, including start-ups, reviewing and determining software solutions to payroll and HR issues, training, and project management. Keen eye for analyzing problems and determining viable solutions. Effectively manage the implementation cycle. Expertly control high-level client problem resolution. Develop and implement quality, "customer service first" environments, attaining significant levels of customer retention. Computer-savvy. Maintain extensive databases.

TECHNICAL PROFICIENCIES

Web-Based Recruiting Tools	HRIS	LANs/WANs	Excel	Word
Internet & Research	Web-Based HR/PR	Pivotal	Networks	Visio
Database Management	Tools	MS Office	PowerPoint	SQL Reporting
Client/Server Technology	Project Office			

PROFESSIONAL EXPERIENCE

Adrian Employer Services, Tustin, CA   1998–Present
Adrian is a payroll and HR solutions outsourcing company.

Project Manager (since August 2003)
- Implement and manage multiple projects integrated as a whole. Ensure consistent and integrated implementation of service initiatives across customer segments and business units. Deliver the total business solution on time and within budget.
- Collaborate with senior management, functional managers, and project managers to plan business and technology initiatives and budgets. Use formal and informal networks to accomplish program objectives. Identify and resolve project issues and manage project risk.
- Establish and manage cost, schedules, and performance of large, highly complex projects. Fully accountable for complex/diverse projects with a high degree of business risk.

Some Projects:
- Managed a multiproduct web-based implementation worth $300,000. Successfully moved a 2,000-employee global client from Windows-based PR/HR software to a web-based HR/Payroll package. Supervised a team of 10. Completed the project on time and under budget.
- Very carefully managed a sensitive issue and hostile client with an outstanding balance over $500,000. Directed a team of eight to troubleshoot complex issues, retain the business, and collect the balance due.
- Recently assigned to $300,000 employee self-serve assignment with a two-year scope.

System Consultant (3 years)
- Generated leads and secured new HRIS clients. Created and delivered proposals and demonstrations to key management personnel (user, technical user, buyer, and decision makers) meeting customer-specific requirements. Maintained a $6.1M quota annually. Proposed product solutions and applications working with IT directors for system requirements and functionality. Wrote RFPs for the sales team and clients.

Page 1

Combination. *Diane Hudson Burns, Boise, Idaho*

The person had a progressive employment history in a specialized field. She had been with the same company for several years, so the writer broke the employment section into bulleted

Susan J. Anderson, Page 2   Susan@aol.com

Professional Experience Continued...
- Effectively tailored responses and proposals using strategic and conceptual selling models to best position firm in the marketplace. Managed large and complex accounts (clients average 500 to 5,000 personnel).
- Created, tailored, and conducted product demonstrations, reinforcing solutions, and selling points, including Source Time and Attendance, Tax, Print Services, Travel and Expense software sales, software product demonstrations addressing feasibility of solutions, and implementation planning. Built technical credibility with prospects to turn sales to implementation cycle.
- Reviewed current technology trends and educated field staff in cutting-edge advances in Payroll & HR, Time & Attendance, recruiting, employee self-service, and benefit outsourcing during national product training for new hires as a product expert.

Account Executive/Project Management (9 months)
- Selected at the regional level to sit on a special project team to study customer retention with the intent to proactively manage and develop profitable, long-term customers.
- Met with clients to ensure complete customer satisfaction. Reviewed and recommended solutions to HRIS problems and suggested specific software. Managed conflict resolution.
- Developed an account strategy within each customer to establish trends and opportunities to capitalize on retaining and growing the customer base.
- Coordinated customer training. Conducted on-site customer visits. Negotiated long-term agreements.
- Managed the resolution of Accounts Receivable issues.

Implementation Consultant (1.5 years)
- Analyzed customers' payroll needs and provided recommendations for streamlining payroll processes and determining appropriate implementation strategy. Created and managed the overall detailed implementation project plan. Moved customers' payroll data to the company's Source 500 software. Negotiated contracts up to $2M.
- Trained customers on the Source 500 software. Provided quality ongoing customer support, ensuring the successful implementation of payroll, human resources, and tax filing accounts as measured by the customer start-up satisfaction results.

Mountain Top Health Services, Orange, CA   **1994–1998**
MT held the government contract for the joint services military HMO (TriCare) program, housing multiple large databases with hundreds of thousands of files and records.

Operations Supervisor
- Developed and implemented start-up plans/operations for the employing and operation of a call center with 500 employees. Implemented the database software and controlled large databases.
- Hired and trained 40 direct reports, set up a department, and staffed a call center with an additional 500 personnel. Determined all staffing requirements, providing timely hiring and training. Built provider networks, which booked appointments nationwide.
- Identified statistical data, providing accurate forecasting and trend identification. Conducted audits. Conformed to all government regulations. Tracked attendance, payroll, and performance ratings.

EDUCATION

Master of Arts in Organizational Management, University of California, Fullerton, 2004 (GPA: 3.98)

Bachelor of Arts in Interdisciplinary Studies with Concentration in Human Resources Management, University of Arizona, 1994
- Human Resources Intern, January 1993–June 1994 for Blue Cross & Blue Shield of Arizona

Project Management Institute, Tustin, CA, Member
■ ■ ■

paragraphs and included specific projects to attract the reader. A pair of thick-thin horizontal lines encloses a profile, a summary of responsibilities, and a multicolumn list of technical proficiencies. Brief descriptions of each workplace, plus a membership note at the end, appear in italic.

BRENDA HAMILTON

222 Lakeridge Place
Augusta, Alberta A1A 1A1
555.222.4444
bhamilton@email.com

HUMAN RESOURCES EXECUTIVE
Specialist in the Creation and Implementation of Leading-Edge Corporate HR Initiatives

DYNAMIC AND HIGHLY SKILLED STRATEGIC HR EXECUTIVE credited with building and leading award-winning and best-in-class Human Resources initiatives in the areas of cultural transformation, organizational change, e-Human Resources, and employee development. Career expertise designing, creating, launching, and leading innovative programs to enhance corporate culture, improve employee performance, and support change across the organization. Highly skilled in communications, mentoring, and integrating diverse teams around a common vision.

Key areas of speciality include

- Values-Based Initiatives
- Organizational Change
- Strategic Planning
- Merger & Acquisition Integration
- HR Policy, Process & Systems Design

- e-Human Resources
- Learning & Education
- Leadership & Mentoring
- Restructuring & Revitalization
- HRIS Technology Solutions

PROFESSIONAL EXPERIENCE

TELCO COMMUNICATIONS INC., Augusta, Alberta   2005–Present

Vice President—e-Human Resources (2010–Present)

Selected to lead the strategizing and implementation of a best-in-class online HR function integrating Recruitment, Performance, Recognition, and HR Administration for 30,000 employees nationally. Defined and spearheaded all strategic work to meet four key measurables: to build a self-service model, reduce HR costs, build a high-performance corporate culture, and enhance Data / IP skills across the organization. Concurrently responsible for Ombudsman, HR Website Design and Maintenance, Equity and Ethics, and Workplace Accommodation functions.

- Created in-house e-performance management system currently used by all managers across all lines of business enterprise-wide.
- Introduced a highly successful online data / IP learning curriculum and corresponding learning management system; success of program and efficacy of communications evidenced by 11,000 users within first 60 days.
- Sourced, purchased, and implemented RecruitSoft to enable and facilitate e-recruiting function.
- Championed and currently chairing e-Human Resources Steering Committee consisting of key cross-functional stakeholders.

Vice President—Learning Services / Chief Learning Officer (2008–2010)

Built, launched, and guided internal "corporate university" designed to provide training and performance enhancement across the areas of Technology, Management, Sales, and Marketing. Established Learning Services model, assembled the leadership team, and built the curricula to support and develop over 30,000 employees. Managed $22 million budget and 147-person staff.

- Recognized opportunity to sell technology, management, and sales training modules worldwide— concurrently managed this independent business entity that generated an additional $5 million in annual revenue.

Page 1 of 3

Combination. *Ross Macpherson, Whitby, Ontario, Canada*

This executive's many quality contributions justify the three-page format. Professional Accreditation & Education and Volunteer Leadership sections round out her outstanding qualifications. After a centered heading for the profile with centered key specialty areas in two columns, left-aligned

BRENDA HAMILTON
555.222.4444 • bhamilton@email.com

Vice President—Enterprise-Wide Change for People (2007–2008)

Seconded on 8-month project to spearhead and launch enterprise-wide cultural transformation to establish pillars of high performance across the organization. As leader of the "Energy Team," surveyed 1,000 employees, communicated and branded 4 core values, and launched supporting performance management system (Team Machine).

- Built communications strategy around hugely successful 4-hour "Igniter Sessions" that delivered new values, culture, and strategy to over 23,000 employees in person across 45 cities in less than 6 months.
- Following rollout, Pulse Check Analysis identified **78% increase** in how engaged employees were in TELCO values.
- Initiative recently won **International Verizon Leadership Award** for excellence in Leadership and Cultural Change (January 2012).
- Feature articles in *Telecom Edge* (May 2011) and *Business in Augusta* (December 2011).

Vice President—Human Resources (2005–2007)

Selected to lead all HR functions throughout TELCO Alberta—payroll, labour-relations, policy, compensation, and learning—and spearhead all critical HR process changes. Concurrently represented HR interests through 2 major corporate mergers.

- Led HR due diligence team for ABCTel merger—investigated HR practices, labour relations climate, contracts, and associated costs, and reported to Prime Due Diligence team.
- Created highly successful career transition structure and processes to support corporate restructuring—recognized as one of the top initiatives throughout North America for its creativity, support, efficacy, and feedback.
- Led successful cultural merger following purchase and integration of PEN-Tel.
- Spearheaded extensive values-based work to support ABCTel merger, effectively identifying, branding, and communicating the new organization's core values.

AGM LIMITED, Augusta, Alberta   1994–2005
(Alberta-based telecommunications company—merged into TELCO Alberta 2005)

Director—Employee Programs & Services (2002–2005)

Coordinated creation and maintenance of all HR policies and services prior to merger. Established and administered all policies concerning compensation, payroll, pension, administration, benefits, and labour relations.

- Beta-tested first SAP payroll in Canada—oversaw massive conversion process and led organization through smooth implementation.
- Successfully introduced a new flex benefit program accepted by both unionized and nonunionized workforce—effectively negotiated with all bargaining units and communicated program across entire corporation.
- Reduced costs through exhaustive cost analyses and updated policies annually to consistently meet proprietary and growth needs.

Director—Organization Development (2001–2002)

Selected to lead change-management priorities throughout AGM, with particular focus on restructuring initiatives in anticipation of PEN-Tel merger.

- Built highly successful career transition model to support restructuring—developed strategy, created and communicated process, and effectively supported restructuring of 2,800 employees representing 25% of the total AGM workforce.

section headings establish the layout for the rest of the resume. Boldfacing and underlining make evident the positions held at the different workplaces. Bullets point to the applicant's significant achievements. Many of these are quantified with numbers, dollar amounts, and percentages. Boldfacing highlights two exceptional

BRENDA HAMILTON
555.222.4444 • bhamilton@email.com

Director—Management & Quality Education (1998–2001)

Developed and launched in-house training and development division providing Total Quality training and Management development programs across the organization. Defined the strategy, developed the curricula, and coordinated the launch and management of all learning programs. Managed staff of 22 direct reports.

Previous AGM positions include
Finance Supervisor
Finance Training Supervisor
Total Quality Training

PROFESSIONAL ACCREDITATION & EDUCATION

Executive Management Program in Telecommunications	*University of Southern California*, 2010
Revitalizing the Workforce	*Center for Creative Leadership, Greensbow, NC*, 2005
Human Resource Executive Program	*University of Michigan*, 2004
PSOD (Organizational Development)	*National Training Labs, Alexandria, VA*, 1999
Personnel Administration (with Distinction)	*University of Augusta*, 1996
BA—Psychology / B.Ed.	*Pinehurst University*, 1987

VOLUNTEER LEADERSHIP

Advisory Board—*University of Augusta, Augusta, AB*	2010–Present
Advisory Board—*University of Augusta (TELCO Centre for Management Development)*	1997–2009
Board—*USC Center for Telecommunications Management (Marshall School of Business)*	2006–2008
President / Chair—*Skills Alberta, Augusta, AB*	1998–2006
Advisory Board—*Simon Pritchard University, Centennial, BC*	2006–2008
HR Management Committee—*Saint Royal College, Augusta, AB*	2006–2008
Chair—*Conference Board Education Forum*	1996–1999

achievements. Extra line spacing above each main section ensures adequate white space and avoids a crowded appearance. The overall impression is that the resume is long for good reasons.

Information Systems/Technology

Resumes at a Glance

RICHARD LEVINSON

0000 Preston Avenue ◆ Houston, TX 77000 ◆ (281) 000-0000 ◆ myname@aol.com

Software Programmer / Software Engineer

PROFILE

Talented software programmer with BBA degree, strong educational background in programming, and experience using cutting-edge development tools. Articulate and professional communication skills, including formal presentations and technical documentation. Productive in both team-based and self-managed projects; dedicated to maintaining up-to-date industry knowledge and IT skills.

Knowledge & Skill Areas:

- Software Development Lifecycle
- Object-Oriented Programming
- Problem Analysis & Resolution
- Web Site Design & Development

- Requirements Gathering & Analysis
- Technical & End User Documentation
- Software Testing & Troubleshooting
- Project Teamwork & Communications

TECHNICAL SUMMARY

Languages:	Java, C, C++, JSP, ASP.NET, Rational, HTML, SQL, Unified Process
Operating Systems:	Linux, Windows 7/Vista/XP
Object-Oriented Design:	UML, Design Patterns

EDUCATION

TEXAS UNIVERSITY, Houston, TX
Bachelor of Business Administration in Computer Science, 2010

- ◆ Earned place on President's List for 3 semesters (4.0 GPA)
- ◆ Member, Golden Key National Honor Society & Honors Fraternity
- ◆ Selected for listing in *Who's Who Among Students in American Universities and Colleges*

Relevant Coursework:

- Software Engineering
- Project Management
- Database Design

- Systems Engineering
- Differential Equations
- Classical / Modern Physics

- Calculus I, II, III
- Logic Circuits
- Systems Analysis

Project Highlights:

- ◆ **Software Engineering**—Served as Design Team Leader and member of Programming group for semester-long project involving development of software for actual implementation within Texas University Recreation Center. Determined requirements, created "look and feel" for user interface, and maintained explicit written documentation.

- ◆ **Systems Engineering**—Teamed with group of 4 in conceptualizing and designing client-server application to interconnect POS and inventory systems for retail outlet, delivering class presentation that highlighted specifications and projected $2 million in cost savings.

COMMUNITY COLLEGE, Houston, Texas
- ◆ 3.96 GPA / Concentration in Computer Science coursework

EXPERIENCE

DATAFRAME CONCEPTS, LLC, Houston, TX   2008–Present
Software Developer

- ◆ Worked with small team of developers to brainstorm and implement ideas for shipping/receiving software representing leading-edge concept within transportation industry.

- ◆ Planned and initiated redesign of existing standalone application, utilizing object-oriented design/programming and Java in creating thin-client GUI for new distributed system.

- ◆ Collaborated with marketing director in strategies to further business growth, including Web site enhancement that drove 65% increase in visitor interest for product offering.

104

Combination. *Daniel J. Dorotik Jr., Lubbock, Texas*

The applicant had limited work experience, so the writer emphasized skills and education and put the Experience section at the bottom of the resume.

FRANKLIN JOHNSON, MCITP

55555 55th Avenue ▪ Cell (555) 555-3925
Tigard, Oregon 97224 ▪ Home (555) 555-2953
www.careerfolio.com/mcitp ▪ fjohnson@careerfolio.com

NETWORK ADMINISTRATION / IS MANAGEMENT

Professional Profile

Service-driven IT professional with 13 years of experience in network administration, system maintenance, technical troubleshooting, team building, and infrastructure planning. Reputation for creative problem solving and effectiveness in resource management and cost control. Broad experience with diverse enterprise and network systems and remote administration.

- **Dedicated Team Leader:** Skilled in building motivated teams and supervising engineering and support staff in complex business and technical environments. Solid experience in coaching, staff training, goal setting, and performance evaluation.

- **Strategic Technology Planner:** Successful at developing long-range plans and managing application integration / data networking projects across multiple platforms. Current knowledge of technologies such as VPN, wireless, office automation, data communications, and SAN.

- **Seasoned Project Manager:** Organized and detail-oriented. Able to work under tight deadline pressure and consistently meet deadlines and quality goals. Accustomed to managing multiple projects and priorities in fast-paced, high-performance environments.

Certifications

MCITP—Server Administrator

MCITP—Enterprise Desktop Administrator 7

Experience

ABCO SYSTEMS—Salem, Oregon

Advanced Systems Administrator / Team Lead (7/10–Present)

- Coordinate the delivery of server engineering support and supervise the design of server solutions for multiple departments. Oversee and maintain 847 servers.
- Use Microsoft Virtual Server and VMware ESXi to design test environments and consolidate servers.
- Acquired extensive experience with SAN storage solutions, external storage arrays, data center operations, RAID configurations, firewall / security implementation projects, and small wireless LAN support.

Network Operations Supervisor (3/06–7/10)

- Managed and developed a team of 23 network engineers.
- Supervised the maintenance of 70+ Windows NT and Novell servers supporting a user base of 1,900 in Oregon, Washington, Alaska, Hawaii, California, Utah, Arizona, and Colorado.
- Maintained a SAN (80 servers) and related hardware. Installed and configured Novell NetWare and Windows 2008 servers and clients.
- Updated network systems.

—CONTINUED—

105

Combination. *Pat Kendall, Tigard, Oregon*

The design of this resume is easily grasped at a glance. Boldfacing is limited to occupational roles in the Professional Profile, company occupations in the Experience section, and the degree

FRANKLIN JOHNSON, MCITP

(5 5 5)   5 5 5 - 3 9 2 5   ▪   f j o h n s o n @ c a r e e r f o l i o . c o m

PAGE TWO

Experience *(continued)*

ADVO COMPUTER CORPORATION—Houston, Texas
Software Test Developer (Contract, 5/04–2/06)

- Developed test procedures for a line of laptop computers to ensure compatibility with multiple operating systems and hardware.
- Operating systems: Windows XP, Windows Server 2003, OS/2. Network operating systems: Novell 6.x, Microsoft Peer-to-Peer

AMERICAN DIGITAL SOLUTIONS—Irvine, California
Computer Technician / Technical Support Team (1/03–4/04)

- Provided technical support for end users (in-house, over the telephone, and online).
- Supported American Digital's line of hard disk drives; Windows, Windows NT, OS/2, Novell NetWare, and UNIX.

COMPUTER SOLUTIONS—Santa Ana, California
Computer Consultant (Contract, 12/00–1/03)

- Analyzed needs of small- to medium-sized firms to ensure optimum cost efficiency and productive use of applications and data processing, networking, and data communication systems.
- Developed custom configurations and installed IBM and Macintosh systems, standalone PCs, local-area networks, and Internet solutions.
- Provided onsite training and user support.

REQUIM CORPORATION—Irvine, California
Production Lead, Injection Molding (2/98–11/00)

- Oversaw department operations and capacity planning functions.
- Established production goals, prepared budget, and ensured that all quality, yield, and production standards were met.
- Supervised, scheduled, trained, and evaluated a 27-person injection molding crew.

Education

IRVINE COMMUNITY COLLEGE—Portland, Oregon
B.S. Mathematics (1998)

PROFESSIONAL DEVELOPMENT

- AC Nielsen Burke Institute: Tools and Techniques of Data Analysis
- AC Nielsen Burke Institute: Translating Data into Actionable Information
- Institute for International Research: Choice-Based Modeling Essentials
- Team Building: Improving Decision-Making Effectiveness
- Total Quality Management: Implementing, Leading, and Managing the Continuous Improvement Process
- Deming: Quality, Productivity, and Competitive Position
- Dale Carnegie: Effective Speaking and Human Relations
- Covey: Leadership Workshop / Seven Habits of Highly Effective People
- McNellis: Team Dynamics and Problem Solving

in the Education section. All-uppercase letters are used for the position-and-field banner at the top of the first page, company names in the Experience section, and the college name and Professional Development title in the Education section. Square bullets link the pages.

RAMJEET CHAPRA

5898 North Broome Street, Chesterfield, MN 22222
Home: 888-777-7777 ● Cell: 888-888-8888 ● RChapra@netzero.com

SENIOR TECHNOLOGY EXECUTIVE

Expert in Partnering IT with Enterprise Strategies, Operations & Goals

Ten+ years of IT management experience with world-class manufacturers and service providers. Known for exceptional technical proficiency and astute understanding of business operations / performance drivers across tech and management lines. Manage senior-level responsibilities far exceeding job titles.

Personal and business watchwords are EXCELLENCE—continuously strive for perfection; ECONOMY—seek simplicity and elegance in planning and execution; and ETHICS—demonstrate personal integrity in all endeavors.

Deliver exceptional rather than expected results through strategic thinking, innovative problem-solving, and managing teams / change for performance excellence. Self-directed, disciplined, flexible, confident, and ready for new responsibilities.

MANAGEMENT & TECHNICAL ABILITIES

Business & IT Vision, Strategy & Leadership ● Departmental Operations Management ● Organizational Restructure & Change
Project, Performance & Budget Analysis ● Project Planning & Management ● Systems Development & Implementation
Enterprise-Wide & Global Solutions ● Applications Analysis & Development ● Team Building ● Internal & External Customer Service

Operating Systems ● UNIX (several flavors), Windows (all versions), Linux, DOS
Languages ● C/C++, Perl, TCL, UNIX Shell Scripting, Visual Basic, VBA, Java, Javascript
Databases ● Oracle, DB2, Access, MySQL, Real-time databases
Software ● Business Objects Crystal Reports, MS Office, multiple other commercial packages
Comprehensive IT skills / project list available upon request.

EDUCATION

MS in Computer Integrated Manufacturing—4.00 GPA. Chatworth Institute of Technology, Chicago, IL, 2000
BE in Electronics & Communications—First Class Honors / 4.00 GPA. University of Bombay, India, 1994
Honors Diploma in Systems Management—Outstanding / Highest Grade. NIIT, Bombay, India, 1995

PERSONAL & BUSINESS DRIVERS

"Visionary, creative, out-of-box thinker; exhibits professionalism in the face of adversity; decisive when faced with chaos and uncertainty; [demonstrates] self-initiative." Director of IT ● *"Ramjeet has the ability to understand very complex technical issues and communicate them in an appropriate level of detail to whatever audience he is facing." Director IT Planning*

Business ● Get It Right the First Time
Invest appropriate time to fact-finding and planning. Dare to risk, act decisively with full-throttle effort into execution, and tenaciously move forward and achieve objectives, despite constraints and obstacles. *Example:* Independently authored and delivered technology presentations to staff and management to improve lagging knowledge of IT staff and allow CIO to forge ahead with new technology initiatives.

Technology ● Practice Pragmatic Application of Relevant Technology
Look to technology as first-line option / solution for enhancing operational performance, increasing productivity, improving efficiency, eliminating bottlenecks, reducing errors, and solving problems. *Example:* Improved performance of reporting from new general ledger (GL) system by identifying and addressing system bottlenecks.

Project Management ● Take a Big-Picture View
Create plan that fits scope; define and clearly articulate project goals and milestones (stretch, yet be realistic); assemble, coach, manage, and motivate team; intervene to resolve technical and business issues using problem-solving skills that are second to none. *Example:* Brought stalled project on track within two weeks by setting / communicating clear vision, goals, and milestones.

Leadership ● Interact, Motivate, and Lead by Example
Combine technical knowledge / proficiency with unique ability to identify / leverage individual strengths of team members; truthfully deliver good / bad news; avoid / mediate conflicts; encourage communication / cooperation; and inspire / lead professionally, functionally, and culturally diverse individuals / groups. *Example:* Negotiated with feuding teams to resolve issue hindering completion of PVCS systems implementation. Agreement enabled department to become more organized around change-management and change-audit efforts.

Page one of three

106

Combination. *Deb Dib, Medford, New York*

Why would a resume ever be four pages long? This dynamite resume illustrates why. It deserves close study. If you take the time to examine it, your effort will be rewarded with

PROFESSIONAL EXPERIENCE

UNIVERSAL LIFE INSURANCE COMPANY, Cranford, MN   **2007 to Present**

A division of AmerUs, an $18.3 billion holding company, ULICO develops, markets, and services a full line of life insurance and annuity products to consumer and business customers. Employs 1,200 in offices in Illinois, Missouri, Ohio, and New York.

IT SENIOR TECHNICAL / PROJECT MANAGER

Direct accountability for managing IT projects (conversions, installations, integrations, and upgrades) and providing systems / technical support to four operating locations and 1,200 users.

Provide technical / managerial oversight (design, development, implementation, and evaluation) to multiple intra- and intercompany projects and initiatives of strategic and tactical importance—business and financial reporting solutions; data warehouse and data marts; and Web-based applications for internal and external customers.

Distinctions

- *"Always the right man for the job."* CIO—Universal Life Insurance Company

- *"He would be a candidate to run any business unit or department ... [demonstrates] analytical and organizational skills, accountability, intelligence, customer focus, and leadership."* Current supervisor

- *"In the top 5% of the company. One of the most talented individuals I have had the pleasure to work with."* Former supervisor

- Recognized as the go-to for attacking and solving complex technology issues.

- Retained and given additional responsibility / authority in postmerger downsizing of staff in IT department from 65 to 30.

Business & Leadership Contributions

- Participate in enterprise-level IT strategy and department-level operations management. As internal IT consultant / advisor, interface routinely with top-tier corporate executives and senior department managers across all functional lines.

- Recommended and / or implemented high-impact initiatives for measuring, tracking, and improving productivity, business matrix, systems performance / data quality indicators, and product management / progress.

- Led training sessions on basics of Web servers and TCP / IP technology to members of IT department, enabling CIO to move forward with new technology initiatives.

- Credited with personal contributions to effecting enterprise-wide culture change, upgrading the technical competency of IT department personnel, opening channels of communication, and fostering cooperation among internal departments.

IT Projects & Results

- *Multiple-Phase Financial Reporting Project*—Succeeded in bringing lagging project back on track within four weeks. Restaffed project; worked with client to redefine requirements; renewed sense of urgency; and provided strong, decisive, technically astute leadership. (Project Manager and Team Lead)

- *Web-Based Project Tracking Solution*—Contributed technical expertise, innovation, and conceptualization of key business drivers to design, development, and implementation of IT solution providing instant / near real-time access to project information / status to internal and external customers. (Architect)

- *Enterprise Sales Reporting*—Managed recommendation, development, and implementation of data warehousing technologies for standardized and consolidated sales reporting. Provided one-stop-shop for information from multiple disparate systems as well as easy-to-use management dashboard. (Project Manager and Technical Lead)

- *Enterprise Reporting and Business Intelligence Solution*—Managed and coordinated enterprise-wide deployment of a standard corporate reporting and information-presentation solution. Coordinated activities of multiple team members and external consultants. Provided leadership and expertise for technical issues. (Project Manager and Lead Architect)

AUTO ELECTRONICS INC., Valley Stream, MO   **2000 to 2007**

Division of $26 billion company, Genius AutoSystems, originally formed by joining former major parts divisions. World's largest manufacturer and global distributor of automotive components, modules, fully integrated systems, and aftermarket replacement parts.

lessons in resume writing. In the profile, all the keywords are capitalized for emphasis. If you wonder why the Education section was put so near the beginning, check out the information. Someone whose under-graduate and graduate GPAs are 4.0, with an additional outstanding/highest grade in a related field, is

PROFESSIONAL EXPERIENCE, continued

SENIOR PROJECT ENGINEER, Factory Information Systems Group (FIS)—led team of three engineers
LEADER, Manufacturing Technology Team—led team of 12 global representatives

Technical lead for new department providing critical IT solutions / operational support for all manufacturing tracking and monitoring requirements. Reported directly to manager of FIS, indirectly to director of manufacturing engineering. Led teams in design, development, and implementation of IT solutions. Managed related functions and project cycles—staffing and training, resource planning and allocation, cost and progress analysis, on-floor testing and troubleshooting, and technical and business problem-solving.

Distinctions
- *"Give the task to accomplish [and] Ramjeet will quickly and efficiently assess the situation; make recommendations; marshal resources; and lead the effort by directing both business and technical resources."* Supervisor

- *"Ramjeet has more breadth of perspective than most engineers or managers."* Senior Engineer

- Earned numerous "Lightning Awards" for vision, innovation, and personal performance excellence.

- Chosen to lead global Manufacturing Technology Team (MTT). Traveled worldwide to conduct training and lead presentations on topics related to technology's role / value in high-performance manufacturing.

Business & Leadership Contributions
- Successfully lobbied for the formation of Factory Information Systems Group to replace outside systems vendor and expensive, ineffective applications. Played principal role in evolving department to become critical manufacturing partner.

- Led MTT meetings—cross-departmental, cross-functional, trans-global team of 12 involved in enterprise-wide IT strategies, projects, and solutions for the production floor.

- Served as internal IT consultant, advisor, and front-line point of contact to stakeholders—senior management, manufacturing managers, key department heads, and union representatives—in multiple global operational locations.

IT Projects & Results
- *Factory Information System*—Conceived and built proof of concept / prototype, and won consensus / approval for IT specifications and business matrix. Developed and positioned $200,000 project for 80-site global deployment and provided ongoing system support / improvement through MTT.

- *In-sourcing of FIS*—Facilitated $60 million to $80 million cost savings by recommending bringing project in-house, redefining IT strategy / specifications, and providing strong technical and managerial leadership throughout project cycle.

- *Web-Based Equipment & Manufacturing Management Solution*—Improved ability to monitor remote manufacturing equipment. Co-developed and built versatile Web-based front-ends, enabling management of manufacturing lines from any location, without need for specialized access software.

NPG GROUP, Bombay, India   **1999**

$149 million market leader in manufacture of industrial yarn and fabric and refrigerant gases—2,500 employees and operations in 14 locations throughout India, UAE, and U.S.

ASSISTANT MANAGER, Management Services Department

Assisted in management, systems operation, and supervision of 12 programming / technical support staff. Developed / implemented PERQS monitoring system within six weeks of hire. Designed, developed, and deployed methods-time ordering / product information. Reengineered and streamlined business / reporting processes.

SIDDIQUI MANUFACTURING COMPANY, Bombay, India   **1997 to 1999**

$790 million diversified enterprise—manufacturer, marketer, and distributor of wide range of durable consumer goods and industrial products in global markets.

SENIOR SERVICE OFFICER, CAD / CAM Division

Provided field support for CAD / CAM workstations, presale technical support, postsale hardware / software installation, and on-site and remote UNIX systems administration. Reduced time to connect machines to computers from 6–10 weeks to less than 2 hours. Assumed role of liaison to technology R&D teams. Provided client training.

someone to pay attention to. Take time to read the glowing testimonials in the Professional Experience section. The Critical Projects & Initiatives page provides proof of this candidate's abilities in a Challenge-Result-Strength format. This resume leaves no doubt that this candidate is worth interviewing.

RAMJEET CHAPRA

5898 North Broome Street, Chesterfield, MN 22222
Home: 888-777-7777 ● Cell: 888-888-8888 ● RChapra@netzero.com

CRITICAL PROJECTS & INITIATIVES

Expert in Partnering IT with Enterprise Strategies, Operations & Goals

Developed and delivered system that allowed company to manufacture new and profitable high-tech product.

As *Project Engineer, Auto Electronics Systems*, challenged to create new manufacturing data collection system and update / implement more functional companion systems. Researched, designed, and built proof-of-concept system. Worked with management to restore control of this initiative back internally (away from old system's outside vendor). Led team to write SOW (statement of work) and perform evaluation / bidding effort.

Result   State-of-the-art system is now in use in more than 80 global manufacturing sites, providing effective and standardized means to control, gather, and process data from the shop floor (product would have been extremely difficult, if not impossible, to build without functions of this system). System provided company with data gathering / archiving abilities as required by regulatory agencies.

Strength   *"I deliver cost-effective, functional systems and develop the team and business processes to enable the global deployment of these systems."*

Revitalized stalled mission-critical project.

As *Project Manager, Universal Life*, challenged to revitalize stalled project providing standardized way of supplying financial, accounting, and statutory reporting from company's new general ledger (GL) system. Reviewed client needs and team skill sets, and made staffing changes. Set up a formal project plan and assigned priorities. Provided technology assistance where required.

Result   The project was back on track and delivering high-quality reports to a happy client. Without this, the GL system would not have gone live, forcing enterprise to rely on previous-generation GL systems at much greater costs.

Strength   *"I understand and comprehend difficult situations, build and rally a team around a problem, and provide superior technical and project management to achieve tangible results."*

Standardized data gathering into a universal, cost-effective, and accurate reporting tool.

As *Project Manager, Universal Life*, challenged to implement new version of reporting tool while previous generation still ran live in production. In addition, solved multiple problems in data integrity. Brought together team of DBAs, data administrators, consultants, and end-users; developed project plan; and managed execution. Installed new version within five weeks with little user disturbance. Implemented Web-based tools to provide less complex user interface. Developed training plans to ensure success.

Result   Project has been adopted as the corporate reporting standard for the enterprise (postmerger). New version allows for easier reporting, simpler maintenance of the infrastructure, and saving licensing / maintenance costs.

Strength   *"I focus on business drivers and strive to provide the most effective and simple solution that can be standardized across the enterprise."*

Developed customer solution on personal initiative, directly leading to new contracts.

As *Senior Service Officer, Siddiqui Manufacturing*, took on personal challenge to resolve longstanding parametric software / training issue causing customer to work harder and longer to send designs out the door. Worked on program from home, on own time, to deliver solution, and implemented at customer's site during a regular service call.

Result   Customer was ecstatic that two-year problem was finally resolved and a parametric design now took 80% less time to execute. As a direct result, he renewed annual contract and within six months bought two more licenses.

Strength   *"I look to customer satisfaction as a business driver and strive to provide outstanding service and support to both internal and external customers."*

Built global consensus for crucial manufacturing enterprise system.

As *Leader, Manufacturing Technology Team, Auto Electronics Systems*, challenged to adopt a badly needed enterprise SOW for factory information systems (FIS) across all global sites. Organized virtual and on-site global team meetings (traveled to USA, Europe, and Mexico), leading team to consensus on final version.

Result   Standard FIS platform was adopted and evaluation / bid effort using this SOW was conducted. Company realized substantial savings in cost avoidance and implementation delays due to adoption of a common global standard.

Strength   *"Using initiative, team leadership, presentation, and persuasion skills, I build consensus and deliver cost-effective business benefits, keeping IT a value-add rather than a revenue drain."*

MARK K. MINADEO
773 Jefferson Street, Madison, WI 55715
(608) 663-5555 home ▪ markminadeo@gmail.com

Director, Software Development
Client-Server and Mainframe Applications Development Management

Business-savvy IT manager with track record of goal-surpassing performance delivering large-scale product development projects on time. Team builder and "big picture" thinker who maximizes productivity and team spirit. Pragmatic leader with M&A implementation and IPO experience. Hands-on software development experience with DBMS applications. Proven skills in:

☑ Product Life Cycle Management	☑ Vendor Partnerships	☑ Matrix Management
☑ Team Leadership / Motivation	☑ Software Engineering	☑ Technical Team Building
☑ Software Life Cycle Management	☑ Project Management	☑ Budget Forecasts / Savings

---

PROFESSIONAL EXPERIENCE

MADISON SOFTWARE SOLUTIONS, Madison, WI   2000–present
Market leader in enterprise database archiving and test data management software for information life cycle management. More than 2,100 customers (many Fortune 500) in 30 countries and 250 employees on 3 continents (North America, Europe, and Asia) with revenues in excess of $40 million.

Director of Development. Function as **VP of Development**; report to CEO (2007–present).
Matrix-manage client-server and mainframe development projects (full life cycle management), coordinating product life cycle (PLC) with Product Management, Documentation, and Quality Assurance (QA). Supervise 60 technical staff. Manage $6.6 million budget and budget forecasting.

ACCOMPLISHMENTS

- **Turnaround Management.** Turned around department struggling with failure to meet release-to-manufacture (RTM) dates and bug-laden products. Unified and rallied staffs from 4 departments around PLC timelines, meeting RTM dates 100% of time, on budget, and with no bugs.

- **Product Life Cycle Management.** Review enhancements for 15–20 products representing 80% of company's revenues. Oversee new product releases (3–4 client-server and 1 mainframe each year), which support 6 DBMSs and 4 platforms. Core product: DBMS Archive/Restore application that speeds DBMS response time while conserving system resources.

- **Vendor Management and Alliances.** Built 40 third-party vendor partnerships with companies such as IBM, EMC, and Oracle, integrating vendor apps for seamless customer experience. Diplomatically negotiated and resolved issues involving vendors, internal customers, and clients.

- **Human Resources and Talent Management.** Established and maintain 0% turnover in department (far below industry norms) through team building, vision "buy-in," improved cross-team communications, mentoring, and coaching. Oversee training and certification. Recruit, hire, and supervise 7–10 developers and staff annually for development of offshore operations in India.

- **Quality and Best Practices.** Implemented and monitor best-practice metrics and streamlined QA to increase efficiency and maximize resources. These initiatives, combined with a customer-first mentality, resulted in 100% client loyalty in competitive tech industry, as well as cost savings.

Continued

107

Combination. *Susan Guarneri, Three Lakes, Wisconsin*

Because this applicant wanted to stay in management at the director level, the writer started the resume with a hard-hitting summary of the applicant's management expertise, including

MARK K. MINADEO Page 2
(608) 663-5555 home ▪ markminadeo@gmail.com

Senior Developer (2000–2006)

- **Applications Development.** Created Windows-based DBMS Archive/Restore application, supporting top 7 most popular DBMSs, as team lead within 9 months. Became core product and established groundwork for additional software products.

- **Project Management.** Led team development of ancillary products that interface with third-party ERP/CRM applications, such as JD Edwards and PeopleSoft. Created new product allowing users to relationally edit, browse, and join DBMS tables across databases and database systems.

- **Productivity Improvements.** Created and programmed in-house automated source management system, standardizing source change process and product packaging for RTM. This utility increased productivity by removing duplication of work and eliminating potential errors.

- **Advanced Programming.** Designed and implemented high-volume, fast-performance DBMS load facility that could interface with top 7 DBMSs (PC platform). Created algorithms to improve processing of data terabytes (reduced 10-million-row run to 45 seconds).

Developer, COMPUTER RENAISSANCE, INC., New York, NY 1995–2000
Fortune 500 software development company (systems applications for mainframe).

- **Mainframe Development Project.** Teamed with 11 developers in partnered development effort with SBM to create and develop SBM CICS Plex Management system. Played key team role in designing main product features (message routing, monitoring, and workload management).

Developer, DATA PARTNERS, INC. (aka Applied Data Systems), New York, NY 1991–1995
Fortune 100 company—third-largest computer software company.

- **Advanced Development Programming.** Enhanced and maintained CA-ROSCOE (TSO-like facility permitting multiuser applications in single address space). Created and programmed ESTAE exits and Functional Recovery routines, facilitating synchronous task termination and coordination with main task. Wrote IPCS verb exits to analyze diagnostic materials obtained.

EDUCATION & TRAINING

Microsoft Project Training Seminar, New York, NY—September 2010
Best-Practices Conference, Philadelphia, PA—September 2010
SBM Share Conferences—2005 through 2010
UDB and Oracle DBMS Conferences—2005 through 2010
Associate's Degree, Computer Science, Suffolk County College, Suffolk, NY

TECHNOLOGY SUMMARY

Languages: C, C++, COM, VB, VBA, z/OS ASM, Java, z/OS JCL, HTML, JavaScript
DBMSs: Sybase, Oracle, UDB, DB2, Informix, SQL Server
Platforms: UNIX (Sun, HP, AIX), Windows (7, XP), z/OS, Linux
Software: Microsoft Office (Word, Excel, Access, PowerPoint), Project, Visio, Developer Studio, SourceSafe; CSI; PVCS; Subversion; XML; Middleware

a three-column list of proven management skills. The writer furthermore used boldfacing at the beginning of each bulleted accomplishment. She placed technical skills on the second page, including a Technology Summary at the end.

MICHELLE LEWIS, MBA   555.500.0055 • michelle_lewis@xxxx.com

BUSINESS ANALYST • PROGRAM/PROJECT MANAGER
Structured analysis and keen business insights to drive the business forward.

Dynamic performer with broad functional knowledge and leadership results in operations, marketing, technology utilization, process improvement, budget development and decision support. Articulate and persuasive communicator. Systematic planner. Approachable, supportive and unselfish team leader; skilled in building positive working relationships at all levels based on collegiality, accountability, discretion and trust. Inquisitive, value-added problem solver with a quick grasp of complex issues; expert in distilling random data into meaningful formats and seeing relationships that others miss. Visionary contributor with a collaborative spirit and a passion for challenge; prepared to exceed expectations.

♦ ♦ ♦

▶ **Key Competencies:** SAP ERP (FI, MM, PS, BWP, Business Objects), MS Office Suite, MS Project, SharePoint, Message Manager, Infrastructure Route, Business Requirements, Data Modeling, PCI Compliance

PROFESSIONAL EXPERIENCE

PROCTER & GAMBLE, Cincinnati, OH   1985–present

Held progressive cost analysis, budgeting, process reengineering and project/program management roles, aiding strategic planning and fostering sustained global business growth.

Senior Specialist/Business Manager, Information Technology (2000–present)
Fulfill a multifaceted expense analysis, gap analysis, strategic planning and budget development role within the Operations Network Services comprising Telecommunications, Data Networks, Messaging and LAN/WAN Support—functional areas with a total budget impact of nearly $50 million. Provide senior management with detailed decision support and recommendations regarding service costs, staffing, salary planning and capital budgets.

Using ITIL Foundations methodology in a project management framework, analyze and evaluate operational and volume metrics to effect bottom-up cost transparency and align Network Services with overall business goals. Observe processes and work flows; audit and measure deliverables against budget/project benchmarks and ROI goals; identify trends, threats and opportunities. Facilitate standard project planning and execution across all project/service teams.

▶ Allocate costs for a multitude of programs, program phases and projects, including full life-cycle software development and service delivery.
▶ Developed hourly workload management/staffing plan for 165 resources (employees and contractors) across 250 customer projects.
▶ Dramatically reduced invoice over-/underpayments by developing reliable metrics to determine vendors' actual cost of service and establishing SOPs to track contract expiration dates.
▶ Led multidisciplinary team effort that delivered transparency on an annual charge-back model of $17 million across 10 business units.
▶ Provided expert liaison to business units and Network Services, advancing communication flow, cross-functional understanding, mutual respect and morale.

Financial Risk Analyst/Corporate Human Resources, Safety and Risk Management (1995–1999)
Developed systems, processes and tools to ascertain risk/cost trends and budget impact of benefits, insurance, workers' compensation and claims management for a multinational organization and its strategic business partners. Collaborated with wholesalers, distributors and insurers to raise safety/cost awareness and obtain risk-history data. Developed and presented graphical analyses around cost, frequency and causes of accident and liability claims to aid development of strategic initiatives.

▶ Drove process reengineering effort that improved service delivery and resulted in a streamlined, agile and cost-effective HR operation. Participated in developing HR requirements and implementing SAP (HRBR) module.
▶ Created and managed online tools and resources providing a full range of HR services to employees via remote access.

Continued

108

Combination. *Ellie Vargo, St. Louis, Missouri*

The applicant has been working at the same company since 1985, so the Professional Experience section lists just one firm and the positions held at it. Start at the end of the section

MICHELLE LEWIS, MBA   555.500.0055 • michelle_lewis@xxxx.com   Page 2

▶ Advocated, implemented and managed data interchange by Information Systems Groups, strategic partners and certain vendors. Partnered with insurers to gain access to meaningful, accurate and timely information regarding risk, costs and ROI.

▶ Assisted in developing domestic and international performance benchmarks by risk area for two multinational corporations (Pepsi and 3M).

▶ Facilitated multiple interdepartmental committees to raise awareness of gaps in safety training, cost trends and risk reduction opportunities.

Supervisor POS Budgets & Analysis/Marketing, Brand Management (1992–1995)
Developed and managed annual budgets of $150 million+ for over 500 POS projects across 15 consumer brands. Performed ad-hoc analyses to forecast POS needs for product rollouts, brand extensions and/or new package introductions. Managed 4 support associates.

▶ Dramatically improved data and reporting quality by standardizing brand names across the enterprise.

▶ Revolutionized department operations (and earned promotion to supervisor) by leveraging opportunity arising from systems conversion (mainframe to client/server architecture) to implement database network. Administered 28-PC LAN on mixed VM/CICS, UNIX (RS-6000) and DOS/Windows platform.

▶ Designed PC applications to track and allocate costs based on POS distribution and develop cost analysis criteria by state, market coverage area or wholesaler test markets based on data extracted from Market Profile Report, Sales & Competitive Data and other sources.

▶ Analyzed and recommended annual budgeting scenarios based on historical trends, market coverage and/or sales projections. Developed statistics and graphics for "Fact Books" used by senior executives to support business decisions.

Field Request Coordinator/Marketing, Merchandising Systems (1989–1992)
Served as primary point of contact for POS promotional merchandise drop shipped to over 1,000 business partners and corporate personnel worldwide. Established priorities and ordered items from ±70 vendors nationwide. Issued "close-out" and "destroy" directives to vendors on national promotions.

▶ Updated, re-itemized and categorized 10,000-item merchandise catalog.

▶ Designed and managed application that reconciled merchandise requests against budgets and generated monthly activity/expense reports.

Statistical Analyst/Corporate Management Systems Group (1987–1989)
Tracked, analyzed and reported energy usage, residual sales and wastewater for 8 offshore production plants. Created charts, graphs, reports and presentations used across the enterprise for energy and environmental management purposes.

Communications Accounting Specialist/Corporate Management Systems Group (1985–1987)
Allocated $3 million monthly in telecommunications services provided to ±2,750 extensions in corporate departments. Worked at all levels within business units and service provider organizations to resolve billing issues. Simplified and automated the expense allocation process, exploding the use of these credit cards from 50 to 5,000+.

PROFESSIONAL TRAINING & EDUCATION

Certification, ITIL Service Methodology • Certification, CISA Candidate • Certification, PCI Compliance
Collaboration in Action • Strategic Service Management • Negotiating Skills for the IT Professional
Project Management Consulting

M.B.A., Emphasis: Finance, *honors graduate*
B.S., Business Management, Emphasis: Marketing, *honors graduate*
Chicago University, Chicago, IL

AFFILIATIONS

IT Financial Management Association (itFMA) • IT Service Management Forum (ITSMF)
Information Systems Audit and Control Association (ISACA)

and read upward to get a sense of the individual's progress with the company. Boldfacing makes it easy to spot these positions, and bullets point to significant achievements for each role. Key competencies are mentioned under the opening profile near the top of the first page.

THOMAS H. SULLIVAN, MA, MS

550 East Avenue • Atlanta, GA 55005 • 555.505.0050 • tom_sullivan@xxxx.net

INFORMATION MANAGEMENT ■ TECHNOLOGY IMPLEMENTATION
Accommodating dynamic growth through strategic application of tools and technologies.

Astute resource manager with broad functional knowledge and a proven record of results in strategic planning, program management, budget development, service delivery and relationship management. Strategic thinker with a big-picture focus and a firm grasp of detail. Comprehensive, collaborative planner.

■■■

Energetic project manager; expert in managing priorities, identifying critical issues and delivering positive results on time and on budget. Inspirational, supportive and unselfish team leader. Proactive complex problem solver. Dynamic performer with a passion for driving change that benefits all stakeholders.

■■■ PROFESSIONAL EXPERIENCE ■■■

Technology Manager
ATLANTA LIBRARY SYSTEM, Atlanta, GA   2007–present

Hold a dual leadership role for two entities: Atlanta Library System, a regional association of 134 member libraries within 11 counties surrounding Atlanta, GA; and PassLink, a consortium of 58 community and school libraries sharing association services. Oversee LAN/WAN network infrastructure and security; server backup; help desk support; telephony; online learning, videoconferencing and satellite television services; finance and accounting. Develop and administer $.6 million budget.

Administer Millennium ERP system (including Purchasing, Inventory Control, Data Warehouse, Circulation and Web-Based Catalog modules). Manage member relations; ascertain and meet common and unique technology needs. Provide directional leadership to 7 employees fulfilling technology implementation, training, help desk and network administration functions for member libraries.

- Hold an integral leadership role on the association's management team; participate in strategic planning and budget development.
- Oversee an infrastructure comprising 9 servers operating Windows NT, 2003 and 2000; Cisco firewall, router and switches; proxy server and spam firewall; Web hosting services; and 700 email accounts.
- Investigated and executed $95,000 in capital expenditures including state-of-the-art telephony system.
- Worked with outside consultant to update (and win majority approval for) consortium bylaws and Memorandum of Understanding, a year-long process that tightened controls and improved cash flow by clearly defining rights for services and payment terms.
- Centralized historically dysfunctional help desk effort by implementing off-the-shelf, dedicated software to facilitate transparent cross-functional problem solving, issue tracking, trend identification and accurate (state mandated) reporting.
- Facilitated formal change management process to standardize member library software configurations.
- Developed 2 revenue-generating service offerings: remote authentication of subscription databases (by proxy server) and downloading of multiple access book/journal records by member libraries.

Head, Systems & Access Services Department
GEORGIA STATE UNIVERSITY, Atlanta, GA   2001–2006

Reengineered services flowing from Circulation and Periodicals Service Desks, Interlibrary Loan functions and Information Systems. Directed technology implementation, systems/network administration and security, software development, asset tracking, safety and facilities maintenance for 300,000 s.f. building. Managed 49 employees and a $.3 million manpower budget.

- Served on management team; participated in strategic planning around space management, technology initiatives and security.
- Coordinated consortium of 3 academic institutions; served on 3 statewide consortium committees.
- Established Information Systems Office; recruited, hired and trained 5 team members.

Page 1

109

Combination. *Ellie Vargo, St. Louis, Missouri*

Every little touch can make a difference to distinguish one resume from a bunch on the reader's desk. The distinctive touches in this resume are the two horizontal lines enclosing the banner

THOMAS H. SULLIVAN, MA, MS   tom_sullivan@xxxx.net   Page 2

- Purchased 2 Dell Xeon servers and Windows 2003 OS; implemented LAN. Employed Active Director Policies and user profiles to control access and ensure backup of user data. Refined library's Web-hosting strategy and coordinated Web resources and services.

- Delivered $50,000 in annual savings as a direct result of work-flow efficiencies achieved through LAN.

- Achieved flawless (Millennium III ERP) system implementation within 6 months of hire. Conducted work-flow and requirements analyses; established system settings and configurations for online catalog system (WebPAC) and Acquisitions, Circulation, Cataloging and Serials Management modules. Deployed and delivered user training.

- Created and staffed help desk function; enabled user access to proxy server. Provided training resources and 2-tier hardware/software support to employees and library users.

- Planned and coordinated major renovation of Circulation Services, a project that required moving nearly .5 million books. Collaborated with ancillary departments to maintain service continuity throughout the construction process.

- Raised efficiency and improved morale by streamlining functions and assigning tasks based on talents/interests. Created software application to improve the payroll process for part-time employees.

- Tracked software licenses; managed furniture and capital equipment inventories.

- Played an active role on Information Technology and Student Admissions Committees.

Systems & Electronic Resources Librarian
WESLEYAN COLLEGE, Macon, GA   1997–2000

Revolutionized library services, communications and user access through automation. Delivered a variety of online and print information resources to library patrons; educated users on access and use. Managed one employee.

- Delivered $14,000 in labor savings through advanced technology.

- Implemented proxy server for remote access to subscription databases. Established help desk to provide training and support for patrons and employees.

- Evaluated and purchased diverse technology tools and subscription databases to accommodate the learning and research needs of students and faculty.

Circulation Supervisor/Web Page Manager/Archivist
ALBANY TECHNICAL COLLEGE, Albany, GA   1994–1997

Advised patrons on a variety of information tools and resources. Created and managed informational and educational exhibits for the library and college. Organized, indexed and managed artifact, archival and rare book collections. Created and managed Web site. Oversaw document delivery service for pharmacist conducting drug research for clients.

Two years of prior experience with South Georgia Technical College, Americus, GA. Managed Sumter County History Center records from the 1800s and early 1900s.

••• EDUCATION & TRAINING •••

M.S., Computer Information Systems, GPA: 4.0, Georgia State University, Atlanta, GA, 2005
- Named to Beta Gamma Sigma international business honor society and Alpha Sigma Lambda national honor society for nontraditional adult students.
- Inducted into Omicron Delta Kappa national leadership honor society.
- Recognized with College of Science & Mathematics "Honor Student Award."

M.A., Library & Informational Science, GPA: 4.0, University of Georgia, Athens, GA,1996

B.A., History, cum laude, GPA: 3.5; Bachelor of General Studies, Savannah State University, Savannah, GA, 1993
- Named to Phi Alpha Theta national history honor society.

containing a descriptive "slogan," the three square bullets enclosing each section heading, the placement of the position above the workplace in the Professional Experience section, the larger square bullets pointing to achievements, and the display of two master's degrees in the Education & Training section.

SAMUEL STEVENS

555 Beech Court, Cleveland, OH 55555 ▪ 555.555.4444 (cell) ▪ 555.555.5555 (home) ▪ stevens555@xxxx.com

INFORMATION TECHNOLOGY MANAGEMENT PROFESSIONAL

Team Leadership ▪ Strategic Analysis ▪ Process Improvement

PROFESSIONAL PROFILE

- **TALENTED MICROSOFT-FOCUSED IT MANAGEMENT PROFESSIONAL.** Technical expertise in business analysis, project management, architecture, and third-level support of network systems. Proven skills in project management utilizing wide range of technologies. Successful track record in broad range of projects, scopes, and fields, including public and private education, government agencies, automotive industry, healthcare, insurance companies, and financial institutions.

- **COMPREHENSIVE TECHNICAL UNDERSTANDING OF SERVER TECHNOLOGIES** in storage, Web, virtualization, IdM, and collaboration domains. Experience with server storage products, including Netapp and HP. Knowledgeable in directory services design, as well as migration and deployment. Expertise in systems analysis, investigation, problem resolution, data design, coordination, evaluation, road mapping, and modeling. Intricate understanding of process improvement, strategic analysis, and redesign.

- **SIX YEARS OF SUPERVISORY EXPERIENCE** directing and guiding team members. Reputation for exceptional leadership in managing projects, people, and processes. Ability to establish rapport and build collaboration at all levels. Experienced in recruiting candidates, mentoring professionals, and supporting ongoing career development. Successful record of team building and performance management.

- **EXPERTISE IN PROJECT MANAGEMENT AND ANALYSIS,** with extraordinary problem-solving skills. Proven ability to coordinate multiple projects in fast-paced environment, under high pressure, changing priorities, and tight deadlines. Demonstrated record of leading project teams to meet all customer specifications and expectations.

- **RECOGNIZED FOR EXCELLENCE IN COMMUNICATIONS AND RELATIONSHIP MANAGEMENT.** Adept at achieving performance objectives, with talent for influencing, motivating, and displaying organizational acumen within teams at all levels. Outstanding communication and technical writing skills, with experience creating highly effective proposals. History of preparing and conducting effective presentations and demonstrations to executives and decision makers.

PROFESSIONAL EXPERIENCE

"Sam carried a heavy load as the only Technical Team Lead for several months, and consistently went above and beyond to make himself available to help the team."
AAA SYSTEMS / PERFORMANCE EVALUATION

AAA SYSTEMS, CLEVELAND, OH   2004–PRESENT
Microsoft Technical Team Lead / Monitoring and Management Solutions Department

Provide technical leadership and project oversight as the Technical Team Lead. Mentor a highly utilized team of professionals, focused on delivering quality projects, ensuring customer satisfaction, and optimizing billable personal time utilized. Provide quality-assurance review and feedback on teamwork and deliverables, and coordinate team support for sales teams and technical specialists. Conduct weekly team meetings and regular one-to-one meetings with each team member. Work closely with team members to develop individual training plans, and provide support for continued professional development and growth. Screen and interview potential candidates for open positions.
Selected Achievements
- **System Center Configuration Manager and DDPS Engagements.** Successfully designed and implemented SCCM 2007 and SMS 2003 environments for more than 40 clients. Microsoft Technical Specialist in Windows 7 deployment design and pilot implementations.
- **Microsoft Projects.** Numerous projects involving entire realm of Microsoft infrastructure, while integrating additional technologies such as RSA and Cisco. Leader of Microsoft Security Center of Excellence Team.
- **Citrix Access Infrastructure Assessments.** Developed an assessment deliverable with potential solutions, best practices, recommendations, and scores, which enabled customer to quickly identify risks and rectify problems in the current implementation of Citrix. Worked closely with senior management, IT staff, and consulting engineers on configuration, procedures, processes, and recoverability.

PAGE ONE

110

Combination. *Vicki Brett-Gach, Ann Arbor, Michigan*

This IT Management Professional was about to be downsized, and the writer's task was to make evident the individual's worth to any prospective employer. The developed Professional

PROFESSIONAL EXPERIENCE, *CONTINUED*...

- **High Availability and Server Consolidation.** Designed and implemented a high-availability server consolidation solution for large life insurance company, with five data centers nationwide, and 8,000 employees. Enhanced business operations with cost-effective failover capabilities. Consolidated management, recovery, and storage costs. Developed migration methodology to provide a best practices approach to company staff. Allowed transfer of data from complex sources to single Windows cluster.
- **Technology Roadmap Planning.** Developed a Technology Roadmap with a Project Portfolio for large school district, and developed extensive plan to replace outdated processes.
- **Architecture Planning and Implementation.** Created a Systems Architecture Plan for large electrical products manufacturing company to upgrade aging systems with new hardware and software solutions. Reduced data center costs by three times, through faster technology, automated systems assurance, and replacement of equipment with smaller footprints.

ADDITIONAL PROFESSIONAL EXPERIENCE

BORDERS GROUP, CLEVELAND, OH   2002–2004
Senior IT Architect

KMART CORPORATION, CLEVELAND, OH   2000–2002
Technical Program Manager

KEYBANK, CLEVELAND, OH   1999–2000
Network Engineer

WATSON WORLDWIDE, CLEVELAND, OH   1997–1999
Systems Administrator

MILITARY EXPERIENCE

UNITED STATES ARMY   1989–1997
Sergeant

Military Honors
Decorated Desert Storm Veteran ▪ Army Commendation Medal ▪ Army Achievement Medal
Army Good Conduct Medal ▪ NCO of the Year Award

Military Training
United States Army Recruiting School ▪ NCO Academy Commandant's List Graduate
United States Army Primary Leadership Development Course

CERTIFICATIONS AND CREDENTIALS

Microsoft Certified Professional
Microsoft Technical Specialist II
Microsoft Systems Specialist II

TECHNICAL PROFICIENCIES

SELECTED SERVER STORAGE PRODUCTS: Netapp ▪ EMC ▪ HP

SELECTED SERVER AND CLIENT OPERATING SYSTEMS: Windows Servers (all versions)

SELECTED TECHNICAL INFRASTRUCTURE PRODUCTS: SCCM ▪ SMS ▪ SQL ▪ Exchange Server (all versions)

SELECTED VIRTUALIZATION PRODUCTS: VMWare ESX/GSX/Server ▪ MS Virtual Server ▪ SCVMM ▪ Hyper-V ▪ MED-V ▪ APP-V

SELECTED SECURITY PRODUCTS: Microsoft MIIS (idM) ▪ TMG ▪ UAG ▪ Rights Management Server (RMS) ▪ ISA
MS Forefront Endpoint Protection ▪ RSA Security SecurID ▪ Microsoft and Cisco implementation and integration

EDUCATION AND TRAINING

UNIVERSITY OF CLEVELAND
BACHELOR OF SCIENCE DEGREE (2008)
MAJOR: BUSINESS MANAGEMENT

Profile is a wall of solid information that signals to any reader that this candidate is a worker of substance. In case a reader may be overwhelmed by this information, the italic testimonial from a performance evaluation dispels that feeling.

INGRID IRVINGTON, M.S.

55 Mulberry Street ▪ East Brunswick, NJ 00000
(555) 555-5555 ▪ ingrid@xxxx.com

SENIOR IT MANAGEMENT PROFESSIONAL

**Process Reengineering...Organizational Redesign...Performance Improvement
Strategic Planning...Project Management...Operational Efficiency
Cost Savings...Team Leadership...Customer Satisfaction**

Innovative, performance-driven IT leader with a **15-year track record of success** developing world-class, technology solutions that exceed customer needs and promote satisfaction. Extensive background managing large, cross-functional teams within Fortune 500 and consumer products companies. Highly skilled in streamlining work flow and creating a team environment that increases productivity. Consistently identify and implement processes and procedures that save money and improve performance outcomes. As Manager of IT with Comcast, received prestigious **Director's Choice Award (2007) for developing most effective cost solutions and practices**. Recognized for stellar ability to effectively contribute to enterprise improvement efforts that have driven standardization and efficiency.

Technical Competencies

Hardware: Desktops, notebooks, handheld devices, Sun Solaris, UNIX & Windows Servers, CDMA Phones, CDPD devices, wireless modems, routers, hubs, and printers.

Software: MS Word, Access, Excel, Project, Outlook, Visio, and SQL; Adobe Acrobat, Photoshop, and Dreamweaver; Crystal Reports, Minitab, WinZip, and Drive Image.

Networking: TCP/IP, LAN/WAN, DSL, ISDN, and VPN.

Other: SharePoint 2007, relational databases, and Web site design.

CAREER HIGHLIGHTS

As Manager of IT at Comcast
- ✓ **Improved application performance by 85% and decreased average handle time by 1.4 seconds**, utilizing Six Sigma methodologies to measure application performance, track results, document case scenarios, and recommend process improvements. This resulted in **marked decrease in delays to customers and a yearly cost savings of $550K**.
- ✓ **Strategically planned and spearheaded launch of single common intranet**—SharePoint 2007—for all IT CSC Field Operation teams, allowing employees to log and track ongoing projects, out-of-office issues, accomplishments, hot topics, and round robins. Additionally, customized templates to meet specific needs of High Level Teams and individual IT locations.
- ✓ **Decreased average speed of answer time** by strategically placing monitors throughout Customer Service Center to enable supervisors, coaches, and managers to swiftly analyze queues and statistics.

As Manager of Wireless Data Support Centers at AT&T
- ✓ **Enabled 90% of calls to be answered within 30 seconds in 2005 (80% in 2004) and increased service levels** by providing real-time call volume statistics and reports.
- ✓ **Improved timeliness of new product and service rollouts and increased customer satisfaction** by collaborating with Marketing, Networking, and vendors on testing and configuration.
- ✓ **Motivated staff and helped to facilitate employee promotions** through individualized performance coaching and implementation of skill-building career development programs.

As Manager of Network Administration at AT&T
- ✓ **Consistently achieved a minimum of 95% customer satisfaction ratings** by anticipating customer needs and taking personal responsibility for exceeding customer expectations.
- ✓ **Received numerous recognition awards** for playing a critical role in several high-profile projects that have had a significant impact on the company's success.
- ✓ **Increased staff morale and reduced turnover** by consistently providing team members with understanding, support, and key contributions to team goals.
- ✓ **Wrote Security Policy article that was published in** *Windows NT Magazine* in 2003.

111

Combination. *Colleen Georges, Piscataway, New Jersey*

Areas of expertise are centered, boldfaced, and cast in the form of an inverted pyramid with ellipses. Boldfacing highlights key information in the paragraph that follows the pyramid, and

INGRID IRVINGTON, M.S. ▪ (555) 555-5555 ▪ ingrid@xxxx.com ▪ Page 2 of 2

PROFESSIONAL BACKGROUND

COMCAST, Sayreville, NJ
Manager of IT, 11/2006–Present
- Direct five cross-functional team members, overseeing system analysis, programming, telecommunications, and operations/support for 600 desktop clients and 30 servers.
- Enhanced customer satisfaction and saved unnecessary costs by converting IT Hotline to ACD system.

AT&T, Newark, NJ
Manager of Wireless Data Support Centers, 9/2003–11/2006
- Promoted into new position to provide tier-two advanced technical support and training to 3.5M data customers, nationwide internal customer support centers, network repair, telemarketing, sales teams, system engineers, and internal customers. Directed work of 40+ employees and managed $1.5M budget.
- Swiftly investigated and resolved users' wireless computer software and hardware communication problems and served as point person for escalations between tiers.

Manager of Network Administration, 6/1999–9/2003
- Managed a team of 10 to install/maintain hardware, software, and peripherals; design, configure, and support LAN/WAN networks; and support/provide troubleshooting for 3000+ nationwide customers.
- Reduced support time by installing nationwide System Management Server (SMS).

TECH SYSTEMS, Old Bridge, NJ
Project Manager, 6/1997–6/1999
- Implemented Six Sigma methodologies to reduce gaps in procedures and products. Redesigned database matrix and developed reporting process to measure opportunities and defects.
- Improved several help desk Service Level Agreements (SLA) and enhanced process flow between departments by developing and implemented Root Cause Analysis process flow using MS Visio.
- Improved existing PC image process, reduced field technician's setup process time, decreased customer downtime, and enhanced customer satisfaction by creating/updating image files for various models.

Z-TECH, South Amboy, NJ
Reporting Analyst, 11/1995–6/1997
- Promoted into position to develop and analyze agent/client reports, call metrics, and staffing forecasts.
- Saved thousands in service fees by designing Spike Data Report that enabled Strategic Accounts team to compare daily call volume trending to prior 8-week period, identifying which days impacted SLAs.
- Reduced daily manual editing time by 90 minutes per account by designing scripts (Excel macros) that collected raw data from CMS. Standardized reports across 20 accounts.

Help Desk Supervisor, 6/1994–11/1995
- Directed work of 20 Help Desk Technicians, overseeing scheduling, monitoring real-time calls, reviewing daily call logs, ensuring SLAs were met, analyzing ACD reports, determining call trend analysis, and acting as first-level management for all escalations.
- Facilitated weekly meetings to review trouble tickets, project plans, goals, and objectives and assessed agents' QA, providing remediation as necessary and ensuring agents met call efficiency targets.

EDUCATIONAL BACKGROUND

STEVENS INSTITUTE OF TECHNOLOGY, Hoboken, NJ
Master of Science in Computer Science

NEW JERSEY INSTITUTE OF TECHNOLOGY, Newark, NJ
Bachelor of Science in Computer Science

Professional Development:

Certificates of Achievement—Effective Business Writing, Civil Treatment for Managers, Coaching for Success, Visual Basic.NET, Java, Siebel Analytics, ITIL, and Six Sigma.

left-aligned labels cluster the technical competencies. Notice how the writer uses boldfacing to draw attention to achievements in the Career Highlights section, positions in the Professional Background section, and academic degrees and professional development in the Educational Background section.

STEVEN J. THOMAS — eLearning Technology Director

CAREER PROFILE

eBusiness/eLearning Management Professional experienced in the strategic planning, design, execution and leadership of enterprise-wide technology initiatives that support business systems, strengthen organizational capabilities and enhance productivity/efficiency. Proven record for delivering cost-effective projects on time and within budget. Expertise in technical training and development combines with equally strong qualifications in project management, operations/department management and systems integration. Recognized for building, mentoring and supervising teams responsive to meeting business demands for high-quality training products.

**Nominated for the 2004 Excellence Award for creating an electronic knowledge base
for all 300 training personnel across all business lines in company.
Recognized with the prestigious annual eLearning Best Practices Award in 2003.**

PROFESSIONAL EXPERIENCE

RYAN BECK FINANCIAL SERVICES, INC.   SAN DIEGO, CA
Director, eBusiness Technology Solutions Group   2002–Present
Assistant Manager, eBusiness Technology Solutions Group   2001–2002

Promoted to pioneer and direct group's development and maintenance of technology-based training initiatives and support functions, including Web-based Training, Online Help and Electronic Performance Support Systems (EPSS) for 2,000 internal and 20,000 external customers. Supervise team of 8 and provide eLearning expertise/support to technical trainers as well as managers company-wide. Manage vendor relationships and contract negotiations. **Selected Accomplishments:**

▶ **Selected to manage a major corporate initiative for the development and implementation of training in the release of a new higher-end technical product for preparing new teams to meet aggressive sales goals.**
  - Created the Project Management structure and standards for a complex project that included new product, operating model and technology components.
  - Led team of 11 in the development and implementation of training materials delivered on time and within budget.
  - Forged a collaborative partnership and team environment between 2 separate training departments that had never worked together.

▶ **Championed, persuaded senior management and introduced innovative eLearning technologies, processes and trends company-wide.**
  - Managed development and promoted to senior training and business leaders a Process-Based Assessment and Training method from idea generation to successful pilot implementation. Results led to enhanced work-flow processes: improved accuracy by 20% and time to perform tasks by 246%; 96% stated that training would increase their efficiency.
  - Led research on new simulation tool products reducing development costs by an estimated savings of $142K+ per year with a 174% EVA. Presented business case and won approval from senior leadership to implement.
  - Spearheaded creation of eLearning standards, processes and best practices, ensuring application of consistent methodology in program development among new and existing training personnel.

▶ **Led development of and delivered 4 Web-based training programs on time and within budget, effectively overcoming multiple obstacles.**
  - Took charge of the design and implementation of 2 concurrent Web-based training projects for 1,600 users that included eLearning, instructor-led training, distance learning and job aids for Loss Control System. Realized significant savings for the company over prior system rollout strategy.

continued…

5555 Sullivan Avenue • San Diego, CA 55555 • 555.555.5555 • sjthomas@xxxx.com

112

Combination. *Louise Garver, Broad Brook, Connecticut*

This applicant wanted to become a vice president at a larger organization and was successful in using this resume to advance his career. Below the applicant's name and position, a

STEVEN J. THOMAS
Page 2

<u>**Director, eBusiness Technology Solutions Group**</u> *continued…*

- Managed Web-based course design contributing to successful relaunch of Business Objects application for 1,400 users. Led training program development for business insurance analytical platform.
- Provided development direction, mentoring and consultation on a high-priority project for Web-based and Online Help training initiatives related to a business lines rating tool.

▶ **Initiated project, persuaded management and revamped 1,500-page online product manual providing key data on 48 states for 50,000 users. Streamlined and produced a searchable, more user-friendly Web format that is also easier and faster to maintain than prior version.**

ARRANSON TECHNOLOGY SYSTEMS, INC.	**SAN DIEGO, CA**
<u>**Training Consultant, Integrated Learning Solutions Group**</u>	**1999–2001**

Collaborated with clients and technical experts to develop Web-based Training, Computer-based Training and Instructor-led Training for proprietary ERP systems. Team leader for Web-based Training project, including interaction with internal and external clients, project planning, creation of design structure and standards, and instruction evaluation. Analyzed software design documents to determine system functionality. **Selected Accomplishments:**

- Coordinated multimedia training for 22,000 users of procurement systems, providing automated strategic, streamlined contract management support within a complete work-flow management solution.
- Designed multimedia program to train 8,000+ users of a financial system managing $36 billion annually.
- Developed a central record-keeping database, using Access and Active Server Pages.
- Created WBT using Microsoft Visual Interdev and performed HTML/VB Script edits.
- Authored user guides, job aids and train-the-trainer materials for an Ariba 7.0 eProcurement system.

ELECTRONIC INFORMATION TECHNOLOGIES, INC.	**NEW YORK, NY**
<u>**Technical Trainer**</u>	**1994–1999**

Provided end-user training on a proprietary ERP system to the finance and accounting organization of a government agency with16,000 employees. Led 12 other training instructors. **Selected Accomplishments:**

- Provided training on accounting systems for paying 5.7+ million people annually; trained personnel on vendor payments (total of $126 billion annually) and computerized accounts payable system.
- Contributed to development of instructional design standards for all financial management courses.
- Presented numerous courses on vendor pay; created and instructed a Microsoft Office training course.

EDUCATION

M.S., Management Information Systems
University of California, San Diego, CA, 2000

B.S., Workforce Education and Development
New York University, New York, NY, 1994

5555 Sullivan Avenue • San Diego, CA 55555 • 555.555.5555 • sjthomas@xxxx.com

truncated horizontal line with a shadow (which is replicated at the top of page two) is a different touch. Contact information appears at the bottom of each page. Boldfacing in the Career Profile and Professional Experience sections make winning information stand out. Academic degrees are clearly visible.

DONALD MONROE

0000 Wonder Avenue, San Diego, CA 99999 ■ 555-444-4444

donmon@sbcglobal.net

IT Management, Systems Administration
Operations / Technology / Engineering

Results-driven professional offering years of experience in planning, installation, and maintenance of computer systems including telecommunications ■ More than 20 years of experience in IT ■ Effective staff development, including training employees on IT policies, procedures, and software ■ Known for outstanding interpersonal and customer support skills ■ Technical Advisor for engineering projects and new technology development ■ Track record in cost-effective annual IT budgeting and forecasting ■ Established record in cost-saving contract negotiation ■ Ability to quickly assimilate new technologies in fast-paced, high-demand environment.

Selected Achievements

→ Achieved cost savings over $50,000 for Suntek in recurring costs through contract negotiations and updating technologies.

→ Reduced staffing costs by implementing fully automated phone system for sales and service-related calls, replacing need for receptionist.

→ Eliminated data loss for Jodex by configuring a standardized hardware/software solution for Web server data backups.

Core Technologies

Operating Systems	Software	Networking/Telecom
Windows Server 2000/2003	MS Office, MS Exchange	Cisco Routers, Switches, Hubs
XP Pro, Vista, Windows 7	Track-It, HelpDesk, Lotus Notes	Wifi, Firewalls and VPN clients
Windows 2000, 98, 95, NT	Veritas NetBackup, Backup Exec	PBX Maintenance, Voice Mail
UNIX, Linux, Novell NetWare	Visio, Antivirus, Spyware	Cabling: CAT5 Ethernet
DOS	Mozilla FireFox	Cabling: Phone patch-panel

PROFESSIONAL EXPERIENCE

SUNTEK CORPORATION   San Diego, CA   **2000–Present**
Network Engineer/Systems Administrator
- Successfully provide all PC/laptop and remote IT phone support for 50 employees as sole IT employee for Suntek.
- Manage finances, inventory, and day-to-day operations for IT department.
- Maintain the operation of all routers, switches, hubs, and servers including file storage, SQL, email, FTP, Novell, Web, and print.
- Administered all support for voice mail and PBX communications.
- Daily backup and restoration of server data, databases, and users.
- Active Directory and Exchange administration.

Page 1 of 2

113

Combination. *Kathy Kritikos, Aptos, California*

The distinctive, eye-catching feature is the Selected Achievements text box with right arrows for bullets. If you want to make certain that a reader sees important information about you,

DONALD MONROE   donmon@sbcglobal.net   Page 2 of 2

<u>PROFESSIONAL EXPERIENCE</u> ...continued

JODEX, INC   San Diego, CA   **2000**
Senior Internet Systems Administrator
- ◆ Managed and developed backup systems for fully managed, Web-hosted environments, including UNIX and NT/Win2000 platforms.
- ◆ Tested and deployed new technologies specific to backup software/hardware for disaster recovery of Web application and database servers.
- ◆ Primary Administrator for backup/restore requests, including customer relations relating to custom data backup solutions.

ALLIED FREIGHT SYSTEMS   San Diego, CA   **1997–2000**
Systems Administrator
- ◆ <u>NT Administration</u>: Implementation and support of PDC, BDC, file, mail, print, and applications servers.
- ◆ <u>UNIX Administration</u>: Setup of HP9000 D-class servers, including administration of users and applications.
- ◆ <u>BACKUP Administration</u>: Primary support for NT and UNIX platforms.
- ◆ <u>PC NETWORK Administration</u>: Supported more than 500 desktop and laptop users, both hardware and software, including Helpdesk by phone.

TECHNOLOGY FEDERAL CREDIT UNION   San Diego, CA   **1997**
Image Services Administrator
- ◆ Administrator for Novell 4.0 servers and CCMail and systems backup and primary desktop support for 75 staff members.

STARRA TECHNOLOGY CORP.   San Diego, CA   **1990–1997**
Engineer Technician/Equipment Support Lead/Network Administrator
- ◆ Managed PC setup and support for more than 100 office personnel.
- ◆ Directed and trained personnel in the maintenance, design, and calibration of disc drive test equipment.
- ◆ Implemented and maintained network systems, including Novell file and print servers, routers, hubs, repeaters, and cabling.
- ◆ Network administration for both Novell and UNIX platforms.

<u>EDUCATION</u>

SAN DIEGO COMMUNITY COLLEGE, San Diego, CA
A.S. in Electronic Technology

<u>CERTIFICATIONS</u>

Windows Server 2003 ■ Network Security I: Policy, Administration and Firewalls
Novell NetWare Administration ■ CheckPoint CCSA, CP2000
Lotus Notes Application Development I and II ■ UNIX Administration

consider putting it in a text box. The Core Technologies section groups technical skills in three columns with a heading for each column. Boldfacing makes the applicant's various positions and academic degree evident at a glance in the Professional Experience and Education sections.

LAURA RUSSELL

55 Prince Street | New York, New York 00000 | 555.555.5555 | laurarussell@xxxx.com

SENIOR NETWORK ENGINEER

Hands-on network engineer with more than 15 years of experience in the financial industry

Technologically sophisticated IT professional with solid history of leading all facets of project life cycles to align technology solutions with current and emerging business needs. Highly skilled in supporting trading applications and designing networks for low-latency electronic trading. Recognized by leadership team for dedication, reliability, and work ethic. Expertise in establishing global network connectivity to financial markets through network providers. ***Core competencies include:***

- Network Design & Implementation
- Project Management
- Helpdesk / Technical Support
- Troubleshooting & Problem Resolution
- Technology Evaluation & Deployment
- Network Administration
- Colocation Setup & Implementation
- Technical Documentation

> *"Laura is **one of the hardest working, most honest, and smartest people** I have ever worked with!"*
> —*Senior Network Engineer, Best Financial, LLC*

TECHNICAL PROFICIENCIES

Network Equipment:	Cisco Routers (800–7600 series) and Switches (2900–6500 series, including SUP 32 and 720), Cisco PIX/ASA Firewalls, Cisco Wireless AP, Cisco VPN 3000, Network General Sniffers, NetVcr, Mazzu, NetQos, Corvil, Infinistreams, Arista Switches Series 7124 and 7148SX (10 gig)
Network Protocols:	Multicast, TCP/IP, RIP, BGP, Eigrp, OSPF, IGMP, PIM, NAT, SNMP, VRRP, HSRP, IPSec, IKE, GRE, 802.11a/b/g/n, ISDN, PPP, PPPoE, Frame Relay, OC3, Metro-E, Dark Fiber

PROFESSIONAL EXPERIENCE

BEST FINANCIAL, LLC, New York, New York   2008 to Present
Senior Network Engineer

Architect solutions for equities, futures, foreign exchange, and other business units. Manage full life cycle of projects, to include requirements gathering, project planning, and network design, testing, and implementation. Lead implementation teams through network configurations and hardware installations. Coordinate efforts with exchanges, ECNs, vendors, business partners, and other stakeholders. Review, verify, and validate network documentation.

Notable achievements:

- Successfully interpreted business requirements to develop scalable and performance-oriented network solutions that support key business objectives.
- Gained hands-on experience building colocations to achieve greater latency decrease.
- Implemented firm's network security policy using Firewalls, Access-list, and Route Policy Filters.
- Improved knowledge sharing by facilitating post-implementation project reviews with engineering and operations groups to discuss technologies, connectivity, dependencies, and lessons learned.

> *"Laura was always motivated and accommodating. **She would stay late and do whatever was required**, always staying calm and positive."*
> —*IT Manager Equities, Best Financial, LLC*

...Continued...

114

Combination. *Michelle P. Swanson, Edwardsville, Illinois*

The applicant was very proud of her reputation among her peers, so the writer placed in gray text boxes without frames some of the individual's LinkedIn recommendations as testimonials.

ABC INVESTMENTS, INC., New York, New York   1997 to 2008
Network Engineer

Partnered with internal groups to analyze current and future business needs. Managed projects, such as migration of primary data center, working closely with vendors and trading partners. Designed and implemented secure dedicated server farms and DMZ to support vendor applications. Established connectivity for equities trading groups to all protected National Market venues as required by Regulation NMS. Multicast implementations for NYSE, ARCA, CME, NASDAQ, and X-Trader into firm's infrastructure. Built LAN-to-LAN VPN connectivity to business partners.

Notable achievements:

- Played key role in various initiatives to reduce costs and improve operational efficiency, which involved evaluating business needs and identifying opportunities.
- Enhanced network fault tolerance and simplified maintenance by deploying External Services Network architecture to global sites. Network had aggregation layer connecting to PIX Firewall and DMZ modules, and design employed EBGP, IBGP, and EIGRP to provide dynamic site-to-site failover, route aggregation, and simplified routing.
- Created multisite Global Order Routing network modules connecting into External Services Network aggregation layer. Migrated hundreds of critical connections from legacy DMZs and converted to dynamic routing to achieve external connection failures that required manual failover process to dynamically fail over below 10 seconds.
- Executed multiple high-profile data center migrations and consolidations with no business impact. Worked with development teams to identify/map connections, implemented network and firewall changes, and coordinated all testing efforts.

*"She can think outside the box and can **deliver highly effective solutions to meet firm objectives in high pressure environments.**"*
—*Market Data Manager, ABC Investments*

** *** **

CAREER NOTES: Prior success as Lead Technical Support Representative with Morgan Stanley & Co., Inc. Provided day-to-day support to equity and investment traders by resolving market data and network issues.

EDUCATION AND CREDENTIALS

Bachelor of Science in Mathematics and Statistics
NEW YORK UNIVERSITY, New York, New York
Magna cum Laude; Dean's List

Professional Development
Project Management PMI Course—Teachers College of Columbia University
Building Scalable Cisco Internetworks (BSCI) • Microsoft NT 4.0 Certification
Juniper Training-Firewall • Cisco Call Manager • Business Management

Affiliation
Member, Project Management Institute (PMI)

Note that the gray shading makes the three testimonials stand out. Clustering technical proficiencies under two side headings helps to break up a wall of imposing information. Centering information in the Education and Credentials section makes this information stand out.

JANE McDONALD, MTM

55 Orchard Road ◆ Ossining, NY ◆ (555) 555-5555 ◆ janemcd@xxxx.com

BUSINESS ANALYST—SYSTEM ANALYST

Leveraging analytical skills and keen attention to detail...
to develop and deliver top-quality business requirements and functional specifications.

Take-charge business analyst with proven expertise in driving the implementation of system projects, collaborating effectively with business stakeholders and developers to bring technology solutions into production. Meticulous professional known for ability to grasp business needs; translate them into clear, concise specifications; and develop detailed test plans to ensure virtual trouble-free applications. Respected business partner valued for solution-oriented style. High-energy project leader who can be relied on to get the job done.

EXPERTISE
- Requirement Gathering
- Specification Setting
- Product Testing
- User Documentation
- Release Management

CORE COMPETENCIES

- Driving technology projects, serving as link between business users and developers to ensure delivery of new solutions according to client requirements.
- Expertly mining for information to identify and understand client needs, recognizing and resolving potential disconnects before they become problems.
- Leveraging analytical nature, strong writing skills, and keen attention to detail to develop comprehensive requirements and test plans that facilitate successful project completion by minimizing miscommunication.
- Leading teams to drive process development and process improvement.

PROFESSIONAL EXPERIENCE

NEW YORK TECH GROUP, Yorktown, NY   2008 to present
Business/System Analyst

Drive Web site design/redesign projects for clients in the telecom field, serving as liaison between business owners and developers to collect, document, and communicate business and functional requirements.

- Working primarily on customer-facing and internal business applications for key client, earned reputation for service excellence, going "above and beyond" to ensure delivery of new solutions according to expectations.
- Handling complex customer-facing projects, developed requirements based on analysis of data from a variety of sources—customer call centers, online customer feedback, forum postings, interviews with stakeholders—making recommendations and offering solutions to meet unseen needs and address potential disconnects.
- Won praise from development team for thoroughness in documenting business requirements, providing meticulous detail to minimize costly, time-consuming miscommunications. Also acknowledged for providing detailed documentation of test results that facilitates troubleshooting.
- Established record of success in managing projects, instituting use of issues lists to keep open issues top of mind and ensure that appropriate progress toward addressing them is made.
- Gained praise from clients for performance excellence. Among successes, developed procedure for collecting Web site analytics from unauthenticated customer-facing application, quickly identifying and implementing solution for challenging, never-done-before process.

PRESTIGE BUSINESS SERVICES, White Plains, NY   2006 to 2008
Business/System Analyst

Joining Prestige as outsourced group from JP Morgan Chase, drove system projects while assisting manager in restructuring group and providing training and support to offshore systems analyst and development team.

- Successfully maintained work standards in challenging, ever-changing outsourced environment, developing meticulous business requirements and functional specifications in support of service assurance and domestic network access projects for key client.

115

Combination. *Carol A. Altomare, Three Bridges, New Jersey*

The challenge for this writer was to break away from a lot of technical jargon and the repetition of information for similar projects and to identify what this applicant would bring to a new

PRESTIGE BUSINESS SERVICES   Continued

- Provided comprehensive training and support to offshore teams, facilitating move of more and more work to offshore location.
- Participated in joint product improvement projects, gaining expertise in improvement methodologies, including collection of function points.
- Mastered and developed best practices for implementing WebSphere Business Modeler, a tool to document business processes. Trained business and IT teams in its use.

JPMORGAN CHASE, New York, NY   1990 to 2006
Business/System Analyst (2000 to 2006)
Production Support Manager (1998 to 2000)
Release Manager (1995 to 1998)
System Analyst/Software Developer (1990 to 1995)
Developed breadth of experience in various roles across JP Morgan Chase divisions.

- Hired as Software Developer, quickly earned reputation for speed and accuracy. Among successes, modularized list generation software, decreasing run time by 75%.
- Building expertise as developer/analyst, took on *de facto* leadership role after joining new group:
  - ▷ Tapped to join organization in disarray, helped bring structure and focus to analyst function. Thriving in new environment, quickly earned reputation as "go-to" resource for getting the job done, succeeding where other, longer-tenured staff did not.
  - ▷ Navigating in muddy water, identified key stakeholders and cultivated positive relationships built on confidence and respect. Gaining credibility, secured buy-in of stakeholders to propel projects forward.
  - ▷ Developed system specification templates and standardization guidelines to support rapid application development team.
- Promoted to Release Manager, developed and implemented practicable release schedule, moving organization from ad-hoc deployment mode to system of stable and predictable release. Managed production support trouble tickets, ensuring prompt response to production issues.
- As Business Analyst, successfully managed system enhancement projects for ordering, provisioning, and testing applications in support of domestic network access, strengthening reputation as project driver.
- Based on ability to get the job done, tapped to participate in projects to drive process improvement. Designed and developed "zero touch" reports to measure the effectiveness of automation in ordering, provisioning, and testing applications. Coordinated collection of Pareto reports.

Background also includes experience as media analyst/planner, supporting advertising campaigns for Fortune 500 companies.

EDUCATION

Master of Technology Management, Pace University, Pleasantville, NY
Bachelor of Arts, English/Journalism, Fordham University, Bronx, NY

TECHNOLOGY SKILLS

Languages:	COBOL, JCL, Assembler.
Applications:	Microsoft Office Suite (Word, Excel, PowerPoint, Access, Outlook), Microsoft Visio, Lotus Notes.
Tools:	SQL, Database Visualize, Squirrel, TOAD, Requisite Pro, WebSphere Business Modeler, Rational ClearCase, Rational ClearQuest, Use Case Methodology.
Standards:	Capability Maturity Model; Function Point collection.

job that other business or systems analysts might not. This resume displays at the right margin another kind of shaded text box that can capture a reader's attention immediately. Thin underlining draws attention to the Core Competencies heading and workplace names in the Professional Experience section.

JANE SMITH

5555 Hornet Drive • New York, NY 55555 • 555.555.5555 • jane.smith@xxxx.com

EXECUTIVE IT STRATEGIST & LEADER

C-level technology expert with 15-year track record of leading powerhouse design implementations and solutions, leveraging early career in finance and accounting.

"Listen, Document, Research, and Resolve" – Personal Driving Motto

Strategy & Planning	**Leadership**	**Technology**
Align IT initiatives to company goals and objectives with triangular business focus: customers, revenues, and future business. Collaborate with C-level and board-level decision makers to manage changing needs and devise overall strategic direction.	Known for building functional talent pools based on company operations and strategic needs. Impressive presentation skills, able to motivate and gain trust from audiences through personalized speaking style and subject matter expertise.	Generate competitive advantage through smart, strategic investment in cutting-edge and bleeding-edge ERP and related technologies. Leverage continuous research and 15+ years of experience to analyze technology potentials against business initiatives.

PROFESSIONAL EXPERIENCE

SWIFT CONSULTING, INC., 2007–PRESENT
IT consulting firm providing strategies and solutions to meet clients' information and business management needs.

Director, Project Management Services

Strategize enterprise and upper-middle market systems and consulting engagements valued up to $850K; design and implement mission-critical systems controlling finance, supply chain, job cost control, and operations. Collaborate with entire executive team to set IT direction of company and respond to dynamic / volatile economic market conditions. Direct team of 10 consultants, developers, and project managers. ***Key projects:***

⇒ **Designed and supervised development of single managerial control system for client that replaced a three-subsystem process for data management and reporting of accounting, purchasing, and manufacturing.**

⇒ **Formulated organization's project management methodology from ground up, affecting visibility of and communication on engagements; results included improved on-time deliverables, budget controls, and client satisfaction.**

⇒ **Introduced business intelligence solutions through company's main ERP publisher; initiative folded seamlessly into marketing budget and overall project implementation execution.**

STERNS & UPSON, INC., 2003–2007
Consulting and information solutions for ERP implementations and custom development engagements.

Manager, Consulting and Information Solutions

Leveraged expertise in accounting and finance to lead design, development, and implementation of ERP, managerial, and financial reporting systems serving midmarket clientele. Directed teams of up to 10 consultants and developers on projects ranging from small financial management engagements to major, enterprise-wide contracts. ***Solutions implemented:***

⇒ **Devised solution and led 15-person team that developed an integrated off-the-shelf system with a warehouse management structure for customized customer service system; system replaced a complex, time-wasting multiscreen application with a single-view program that resulted in client-side efficiencies and cost savings.**

⇒ **Mastered process logic to understand programmers' coding and created simple, effective chains of communication to stay on top of each project and relay information to clients.**

Page 1 of 2

116

Combination. *Kimberly Schneiderman, New York, New York*

The writer's goal was to present the applicant for a promotion to a CIO position (from a senior-level executive position). The resume brands the applicant as an "Executive IT Strategist &

JANE SMITH

555.555.5555 · jane.smith@email.com

TUPPER, INC., 1998–2003
Finance and distribution ERP systems implementations leveraging Microsoft Business and Sage Software Solutions.

Solution Consultant

Managed dual role in sales and consulting, handling everything from client-needs analysis to formulation and proposal of business solutions that supported enterprise and midmarket clients' objectives. *Products: Sage Software, Microsoft Business Solutions, and Crystal Reports.*

⇒ **Led frequent presentations for 50+ potential clients at company-sponsored marketing events; built reputation for handling open Q&A with expertise and insight that led to signed contracts.**

ARMSTRONG, LEVELOUR & KRUP LLP, 1997–1998
Accounting and business advisory firm providing Microsoft Business Solutions for small- to midsize clients.

Senior Consultant / Auditor

Implemented Microsoft Business Solutions of financial and distribution ERP systems for midsize clients in a variety of industries. Conducted financial audits, compilations, and tax return filings for enterprise and midsize clients. Controlled client's bookkeeping function as an outsource provider.

⇒ **Stepped into position cold and learned all aspects in the midst of high-pressure situations with clients; recognized by management for hitting the ground running.**
⇒ **Teamed with development staff to create custom payroll solution in Excel environment.**

FINANCE & ACCOUNTING BACKGROUND

JUNT TRAY.. **1996–1997**
Consulted with executive management on holdings and investments; created and analyzed real estate portfolio performance and risk assessment reports.

PILLY & WAGHTE LLP.. **1993–1996**
As Senior Accountant, conducted audits for enterprise and midsize clients; codeveloped investment pools for Resolution Trust Corp.; conducted property liquidation valuations; researched fraudulent accounting practices.

TIPPER REAP COMMUNICATIONS, INC.. **1990–1992**
Managed finance operations and financial reporting functions for this publisher of weekly advertising papers.

EDUCATION, AFFILIATIONS & TECHNICAL REPERTOIRE

FLORIDA UNIVERSITY, JASON PHILLY SCHOOL OF BUSINESS
Master of Business Administration (MBA): *Information Technology* · **Certificate in Accounting**

NYC COLLEGE, **Bachelor of Business Administration:** *Finance*

Certified Public Accountant (CPA) • American Institute of Certified Public Accountants (AICPA) • Beta Alpha Gamma, International Honor Society • Beta Gamma Omega, National Scholastic and Professional Fraternity

Application Expertise: Sage MAS 500, Office, Crystal Report Writer, FRx, Great Plains, Solomon Software, Transact-SQL, Visual Basic 6.

Industry & Process Expertise: Advertising, Construction, Manufacturing (Food, Specialty Retail, Medical Supplies), Securities Trading & Back Office Operations, Professional Services, Real Estate, Printing, Supply Chain Management.

Leader" having several areas of corporate expertise, cast in three columns. This resume displays the applicant's leadership qualities rather than hands-on work, a personal driving motto that reflects her work style, and as many achievements as possible to show management experiences.

JOHN P. LOOMIS

5555 S Michigan Blvd #555, Dayton, OH 55555
550-555-5555 • jploomis@xxxx.com

SUCCESSES

Gained CNET "Best All Around Hosting Service" for company.

Key in gaining major commercial and celebrity clients, including Jason Buller, KVC Digital and Tony Swan.

Personally closed major media Web site accounts.

Personally recruited to work for Linux Systems, Inc.

Selected for prestigious SourceForge Project.

Specifically chosen by clients, including TransWorldHosting, to manage their projects.

Personal accounts became employer's largest accounts out of 5,000 total.

Successfully helped clients through infamous 2007 migration disaster.

Quickly became company's resident Linux expert.

Chosen for post-Level III escalations for special clients.

ADVANCED LINUX SYSTEMS ADMINISTRATOR

"Where escalations stop"

Talented Senior Systems Administrator with 20 years of continually advancing experience in all aspects of IT program/project design and management and systems design and management with particular expertise in Linux systems. Expert in Web servers, email management, VPS, database management and LAMP. Accomplished at debugging, scripting, e-commerce and routing, security and anti-spam applications. **Combine expert knowledge of particular applications with big-picture overview of systems functions; able to effectively analyze systems to identify trouble spots.**

Effective Level III troubleshooter, combining technical skills with strong and strategic outlook. Proven program/project management abilities. Member of SourceForge project team developing open source alternatives to proprietary software. Excellent communications and people-management skills.

PROFESSIONAL EXPERIENCE

LOOMISWEB HOSTING SERVICES, Dayton, OH   **2002–Present**

Web server management/consulting firm offering Web server administration and Web site management services with as many as 30,000 domains under management, including commercial, not-for-profit and academic Web sites.

Owner/Consultant
Lead team of 12 technicians to direct management of up to 30,000 domains including manufacturing, ecommerce, advocacy and private sites to ensure client problem solving, expansion and 24/7 uptime.

Final point for all escalations after levels I, II and III have passed them on. Provide 24/7 monitoring/response for both hardware and software needs, including system monitoring, problem diagnosis, backups, account, permission maintenance, mailflow, traffic analysis, team response and escalation management.

Direct all configuration, process automation for patches, file changes, software installation/removal and other routine processes. Lead project manager for new product development; evaluate client needs, expand accounts by upselling with newly developed applications.

- Developed innovative, new Tritico mail-handling system for effective spam removal, archiving and redundancy that successfully handles 7M emails per month.

- Key in attracting and keeping major media Web site clients, including *Politics Today* magazine and Choices radio network, and maintaining system integrity during dramatic traffic spikes.

- Gained major commercial and celebrity clients, including founders of Bob & Co. and PetDen, Jason Buller, KVC Digital and Tony Swan.

Continued

117

Combination. *Patrick Moore, Rio Rancho, New Mexico*

The writer's challenge was to provide a competitive resume for an IT manager who was in his 40s, entirely self-taught, largely self-employed, and without official credentials. The large,

COMPETENCIES

Systems Administration
Systems Analysis
Project/Program Management
Web Servers
Information Systems
Network Administration
VPS
LAMP
Testing
QA/QC
Business Analysis
Needs Analysis
IT Strategy
IT Security
Mail Archiving
Database Management
Technical Support
Technical Writing
Policy Development
Deployment/Migrations
Client Relations
Negotiations
Customer Service
Ecommerce
Programming

TECHNICAL SKILLS

FTP • MYSQL • POP • SMTP
HTTPD • Cloud-Based Systems
SpamAssassin • Cpanel Mail
WHM • OsCommerce
Miva Merchant • OpenWebmail
NewMail • SourceForge
Tritico • Perl • AWK • SED
Bash Windows • Mac • Linux

VINCENZA/ LINUX SYSTEMS, Dayton, OH   **1999–2002**

Pioneer of Web-hosting automation software offering Web-hosting solutions and infrastructure services to Web-hosting client companies. Staff of 400. Sold to Linux Systems in 2000, now owned by Prestige.

System II Administrator

Specifically recruited by Vincenza management. Administered over 1,000 Web servers serving clients including hosting companies and small businesses. Provided support to clients. Member of team maintaining KnowledgeBase for clients and technical support staff. Quickly mastered Linux to become staff DNS and Sendmail expert. One of just three administrators selected for large-client Client Relations Group tasked with resolving escalated or special client needs. Own clients became Vincenza's largest and fastest-growing clients.

- Key in gaining CNET "Best All Around Hosting Service" award for company.

- Chosen for analytic and client service abilities as one of few employees retained by company when it was sold to Linux Systems.

- Chosen to represent company on SourceForge project to evaluate, accept or refuse SourceForge project applications.

WEBSYSTEMS, Allentown, PA   **1997–1999**

IT staffing and services company, part of the international staffing and workforce services giant Systems Group. WebSystems provides IT support and staffing for applications, network infrastructure, end-user support and communications technology needs.

Desktop and Network Support Specialist

Consulting member of in-house team providing IT support to ARG Bank's Y2K preparation involving replacement and configuration of over 5,000 workstations and related hardware at both ARG Towers and the Steel Tower in Pittsburgh. Transferred to Lowell Insurance team providing Y2K remediation involving replacement and configuration of almost all of client's IT equipment.

INNOVATIONS DATA SYSTEMS, Oxnard, CA   **1993–1997**

Start-up subsidiary of Innovations Group providing real estate tax data to real estate industry, with 300 employees.

Research Analyst, Assistant Network Administrator

Researched county records, plat maps and other sources to create county-specific real estate information databases. Responsible for maintaining office network during evening shift, including troubleshooting and repair.

EDUCATION AND PRESENTATIONS

Bachelor's degree, Liberal Arts (Seminar-type Great Books program),
Hillmount College, Oxnard, CA

Provided core staff training on Sendmail, Apache and DNS.

shaded text boxes in the left column of each page display important successes (page one) and list competencies and technical skills (page two). This resume now resembles those of other workers who have been company employees rather than self-employed.

Tom Henderson

555 Bingham Circle ❑ Omaha, NE 55555 ❑ Phone: (555) 555-5555 ❑ Email: tom@xxxxx.com

INFORMATION TECHNOLOGY MANAGEMENT

SERVICE CONTINUITY MANAGEMENT | DISASTER RECOVERY | RISK MANAGEMENT

A highly skilled ITSCM professional with nearly 10 years of enterprise-level experience in planning, development, continuous improvement, strategic implementation, integration, and execution of Risk Management, Business Continuity, and Crisis Management. A motivational leader who can easily work in and navigate a dynamic and sometimes ambiguous environment. Committed to personal development and with the ability to learn quickly and adapt to business needs/priorities as needed.

AREAS OF EXPERTISE

- Strategic / Tactical Planning
- Risk Assessment and Contingency Planning
- ITIL / ITSCM / SDLC

- Project Management
- Crisis Management
- Information Assurance
- Contract Negotiations

- Data Loss Prevention (DLP)
- Service Continuity Strategy
- Program Governance and Execution

CERTIFICATIONS

Certified Business Continuity Professional (CBCP)
Certified Information Systems Auditor (CISA)
Certified Information Systems Security Professional (CISSP)
Information Technology Infrastructure Library (ITIL) V2 Foundation Certification
Organizational Change Management (OCM)

PROFESSIONAL EXPERIENCE

IBM CORPORATION
ITSCM PROGRAM MANAGER, Canton, OH   (2009 – PRESENT)

Provide practical guidance on the design and implementation of integrated end-to-end processes based on proven industry best-practice guidelines for a $15.6 billion-per-year provider of power management products/services with 80,000 employees worldwide. Manage all components of business recovery, business resumption, contingency planning, and crisis management—including Disaster Recovery plans and attestation—to ensure that critical business systems are available in accordance to agreed time frames and standards.

ACHIEVEMENTS

- Standardized the approach for Disaster Recovery Planning/Response/Restoration using continuous improvement methodology across 440 global locations incuding primary internal data centers.
- Avoided an estimated $7 million loss due to penalties, lost business, etc., through effective planning and coordination of Disaster Recovery measures required after a critical power outage interrupted service delivery from the primary data centers.
- Reduced site SOX audit visits from external 3rd party partner 50% by leading effort to create perpetual inventory feeds of separated workforce members, making those feeds available to systems automatically and available to administrators of systems across the enterprise.
- Instrumental in creating a process by which Application Service Providers (any partner hosting or processing IBM data that would otherwise reside within IBM data centers or sites) apply so that the risk presented to IBM was identified and assessed (50+ partners applications processed, reviewed, assessed, and use-or-not-use determination rendered).

CONTINUED ...

118

Combination. *Angela Jones, Lincoln, Nebraska*

Boldfacing highlights key information in the profile paragraph near the top of the first page. Horizontal lines both separate and direct attention to the Areas of Expertise and Certifications

PROFESSIONAL EXPERIENCE - CONTINUED

EASTMAN-KODAK CORPORATION
IT MANAGER, London, England   (2008 – 2008)
Ensured the execution of specific strategic functions and implemented high-end, business-wide, critical strategy resulting in translating the IT strategy into action. Provided guidance, planning, and direction for business unit(s); maintained budgets; and proactively allocated resources and time for the business units or functions they supported.

- Provided direction for local Computer Room operations, incident and problem management, service-level management, and critical business process planning and execution.
- Promoted teaming skills to ensure cross-training within team; motivated staff for successful project results.

ACHIEVEMENTS

- Effectively managed an annual budget of 1.75 million British Pounds with signing authority of up to $15 thousand for justifiable expenses with approval of the Plant Manager.
- Led a Disaster Recovery response/recovery/restoration effort at the site after power substation maintenance caused high-voltage backfeed that destabilized network, ERP, communications, and storage.
- Created and implemented the first-ever IT disaster recovery plan for the site.

ACCENTURE
E-BUSINESS / E-COMMERCE MANAGER, Columbus, OH   (2007 – 2008)
Worked cross-functionally with a team of technology and business professionals to develop and implement from inception to completion Web-based projects that support key business strategies.

- Managed a $1.25 million budget with an additional $500 thousand contingency available if necessary.
- Integrated Web technology into business processes where it had not been present before throughout the Order to Cash Cycle.

ACHIEVEMENTS

- Successfully negotiated internal supplier costs that resulted in a 3-year cost avoidance of $235 thousand.
- Managed activities, efforts, and products for development and moved Web-based solutions to production—all within a 3% variance to forecast and budget.

AON CORPORATION
SENIOR INFRASTRUCTURE ANALYST, Northbrook, IL   (2004 – 2007)
Provided day-to-day support that included problem analysis and resolution of hardware and software issues, program and configuration modifications for projects, quality assurance testing, and coordination of technology installations.

ACHIEVEMENTS

- Mentored the infrastructure team in project management, Windows back-office server technologies, and troubleshooting. 100% pass rate by team members on Windows NT and Windows Server 2003 tests.

DYNATECH INFORMATION SYSTEMS
SYSTEMS ENGINEER / HELP DESK ANALYST   (2002 – 2004)

EDUCATION

MASTER OF BUSINESS ADMINISTRATION
University of Phoenix—Los Angeles, CA
BACHELOR OF SCIENCE — SYSTEMS ANALYSIS
University of California—San Diego, CA

sections. Note that important certifications appear in the first half of the first page instead of after university degrees at the end of the second page. A subheading for achievements directs attention to them for each workplace except the last one mentioned.

CHRISTOPHER M. LANTZ ———————————————————————

555 First Avenue • New York, New York 55555
Residence (000) 000-0000 • Cellular (000) 000-0000 • cmlantz@email.usa

TECHNOLOGY MANAGEMENT PROFESSIONAL

Innovative and performance-driven management professional with 20+ years of hands-on information technology experience and comprehensive knowledge of creating and implementing strategic plans to ensure quality product and service delivery. Proven success in developing, managing and integrating advanced technology to support operational strategies and proven ability to merge technology platforms to structure a highly functional performance-oriented IT organization.

Information & Technology Solutions • IT Infrastructure • Process Improvements
Operational & Strategic Planning • Project Management • Profit & Loss • Contract Negotiations

VALUE OFFERED ———————————————————————

- Effectively lead and manage complex projects involving reengineering processes, network operations, IT coordination and change management to improve overall performance and operational efficiencies and achieve optimal results.

- Expert in developing tactical plans, IT strategies and management systems and executing business-specific telecommunication solutions to meet corporate and client demands while remaining under budget.

- Proficient in negotiating vendor contracts and service maintenance agreements that identify cost-savings opportunities and conducting diverse cost/benefits analysis.

- Well-developed listening and communication skills. Establish and build sound business relationships with clients, executive personnel, process team managers, peers and employees to instill teamwork and create productive teams.

CAREER EXPERIENCE ———————————————————————

HEALTH CENTER, INC., New York, New York, **5/2009–Present**
(Global Healthcare Products Manufacturer)

MANAGER—TELECOMMUNICATIONS

Direct and manage voice and data communication infrastructure. Oversee operations of telecommunication systems and product testing/service delivery and manage contract negotiations for this corporation with annual revenues of $5.5M. Evaluate and determine implementation of hardware/software applications and interface with key vendors to ensure quality service delivery to 1,500+ internal customers.

Establish project goals, develop and carry out strategic plans and recommend service standards, procedures and policies to support company objectives. Administer and lead regional professional staff, project managers and technical analysts. Manage corporate budget of $3M and report to the Director of Information Technology.

NOTABLE CONTRIBUTIONS

- *Incorporated measurable methods within Service Level Agreements (SLA) to ensure quality data network operations and service delivery of global data transmissions:* Consulted with company suppliers and renegotiated contract deliverables to provide minimal data service interruptions and monthly SLA reporting and attached clause to reimburse Health Center, Inc., for non-SLA compliance. Prioritized system traffic to ensure successful access to key business systems for end users. Conducted monthly supplier meetings to review network monitoring reports, SLA compliance, service interruptions, order activity and invoicing.

Page 1 of 3

119

Combination. *Maria E. Hebda, Trenton, Michigan*

This individual wanted a new position to better use his technical and leadership talents in information technology and project management. The writer demonstrated the individual's

HEALTH CENTER, INC., New York, New York, **5/2009–Present** (continued)

NOTABLE CONTRIBUTIONS (continued)

- *Decreased annual telecom expenditures $120K without communication service downgrades or elimination of services:* Analyzed telecom marketplace, networked with industry experts to understand "best in class rates" and determined factors to ensure that suppliers provided lowest rates for identical service delivery. Evaluated contract proposals, selected service providers and negotiated contract terms.

IT PROJECT CONSULTANT, New York, New York, **6/2007–5/2009**

INDIVIDUAL CONSULTANT

Provided diverse global companies with assertive tactical plans to simplify business operations and processes, integrated sophisticated data systems and services, created maintenance programs and incorporated high-tech internal data security systems. Industry client base included financial services, pharmaceutical sales, global chemicals and consumer products.

NOTABLE CONTRIBUTIONS

- *Reduced employee travel costs $300K for client company within 30 days of contract assignment:* Introduced availability of e-commerce business tools that provided state-of-the-art communication resources to frequently traveling employees. Wrote brochure content that was distributed to employees and provided employee training sessions in utilizing e-commerce tools—web, audio- and videoconferencing. Change of business operations positioned client company to decrease employee travel and increase productivity due to physical accessibility of "on hand" personnel.

- *Enhanced security level of global internal data and voice over Internet protocol (VoIP) systems for client company, which protected 500+ vendor communication systems from hackers:* Teamed with Cisco and Avaya to gain knowledge of security issues with pertinent equipment. Established project objectives with key stakeholders and conveyed technical approach to assure parties that systems from suppliers were secure. Incorporated 24/7 monitoring element that applies latest security patches and program updates upon system notification.

ABC PHARMACEUTICALS, Albany, New York, **3/1991–6/2007**
(Pharmaceutical Company)

SENIOR MANAGER—GLOBAL VOICE/VIDEO/REMOTE-ACCESS TECHNOLOGIES, *1/2004–6/2007*

Led global functions that managed voice and data contract negotiations, including telecom contract initiatives corresponding with SLA, and oversaw $40M annual budget. Directed global strategies for remote access and voice and video communication products and established corresponding product security standards accordingly. Managed video hardware, networks, bridging and technical services scheduling. Led and supported 12 local and remote management personnel, analysts and consultants.

TEAM LEADER—VOICE/MULTIMEDIA TECHNOLOGIES, *2/2003–1/2004*

Led and supported multiple sites, which consisted of 1,100 global research and executive personnel. Led voice/video strategic planning activities as well as operations activities. Managed $2M technology budget and supervised an eight-member team consisting of exempt and contractor personnel.

PROJECT MANAGER—VOICE/VIDEO, *1/2002–2/2003*

Developed and managed product and sales strategies for voice/video products. Coordinated system design, vendor negotiations and implementation activities for Avaya, Northern Telecom, Siemens and Octel. Appointed Feature Development Team Chairman for the ABC customer advisory council.

strengths and areas of expertise through career achievements presented as Notable Contributions. Each one of these begins with an underlined statement in italic. This kind of consistent formatting enables the reader to glance at all three pages and spot each contribution quickly. A partial line after the person's name serves

CHRISTOPHER M. LANTZ ————————————————————

ABC PHARMACEUTICALS, Albany, New York, **3/1991–6/2007** (continued)

NOTABLE CONTRIBUTIONS

- *Cut telecom expenses $5M within 24 months after company reorganization and assumed overall responsibility for regional and global communication budgets:* Partnered with business leaders to fully understand global vs. country budget priorities. Held semiannual meetings to clarify systems technology and its ability to meet current and future business requirements. Implemented telecommunication solutions, which amplified global remote access and established ATM-based data network backbone that included full network redundancy and rendered wide-range individual/group video services.

- *Merged Rhone-Polenc and Hoechst Marion Roussel telecom units to form the Telecommunications Business Unit, which was recognized for exceptional performance on key initiatives:* Developed job titles and associated position descriptions to meet business requirements, assigned individual/team objectives and recruited management team leaders. Conducted monthly meetings, facilitated team building exercises and provided direction and support to create cohesive productive teams.

- *Increased manpower efficiency and decreased employee traveling costs:* Persuaded corporate executives to install videoconferencing hardware in prime locations to conduct global divisional and technical meetings to reduce travel expenses while maintaining global business interactions. Researched, purchased and installed video hardware and facilitated training workshops on use and features. Installed video scheduler that managed room reservations globally and based on various time zones. Videoconferencing increased workforce efficiency while promoting global interaction among coworkers.

ENTRY-LEVEL POSITION

TELECOMMUNICATIONS ANALYST, *3/1991–12/2001*

CAREER DEVELOPMENT

IN-HOUSE TRAINER/FACILITATOR:
Sales Force Remote Access & Voice Mail User Training Seminars, Data Remote-Access Workshops, Videoconferencing Training, 2004–2008

PROFESSIONAL DEVELOPMENT:
Cisco Networker Conference and VoIP Seminar, 2004–2008
Project Management Seminar, 2006–2007

PROFESSIONAL AFFILIATION:
XYZ Management Institute, Member, 2005–Present

EDUCATION

BOSTON UNIVERSITY, Boston, Massachusetts
Bachelor of Science, Communications

as a header on each page. A partial line after the Value Offered and Career Experience headings makes it easy to see the beginning of these two key sections. Small caps are a welcome change from upper- and lowercase formatting.

Law

Resumes at a Glance

MARIANNE TANTILLO

555 Kelly Drive North, Morristown, NJ 00000
555-555-5555 • mtantillo@email.com

QUALIFICATIONS PROFILE

Highly organized, experienced, and multilingual **legal assistant** with solid background assisting attorneys in all phases of legal groundwork including client intake and trial preparation.

➢ In-depth experience conducting extensive research and gathering data relevant to high-profile cases and proceedings.

➢ Fluent in English and Italian to interact easily and effortlessly with international clients, accumulating and inputting data while remaining composed under pressure.

➢ Recognized for being highly efficient, punctual, organized, and detail-oriented.

➢ Diverse experience includes assistance in all facets of family law and personal injury law practice.

➢ In-depth knowledge and experience with all legal documentation and trial preparation procedures, as well as outstanding administrative support skills.

PROFESSIONAL EXPERIENCE

BACHMAN, STONE, MYERS, LLP, Attorneys at Law, New York, NY   2007–Present
Legal Assistant

Provide legal assistance for this leading national personal injury law firm with more than 50 years of experience and a high verdict record. Prepare legal documents, including written reports, pleadings, affidavits, and briefs, and file pleadings with court. Contact clients and arrange intake meetings. Conduct research and gather facts relevant to cases, entering information into company database. Identify, organize, and input information pertaining to individual claims, including types and amounts of damages requested. Research and determine appropriate laws, judicial decisions, and legal articles relevant to assigned cases.

• Contacted and corresponded with more than 1,000 clients worldwide, gathering and inputting information relevant to such high-profile drug litigation cases as Fen-Phen, Celebrex, Avandia, and Vioxx, including the drugs' adverse reactions and deleterious effects.

• Interacted with more than 500 "Ground Zero" clients, gathering and organizing data relevant to claims, including symptoms and damages requested.

ALEXA P. SOTO, Attorney at Law, New York, NY   2004–2007
Legal Assistant / Secretary

Coordinated office activity and maintained financial records. Prepared affidavits and other legal documents, handled client correspondence, organized and maintained files, and filed pleadings with court clerk. Served as witness to will signings and arranged client intakes and interviews.

• Recognized by supervisors for being highly efficient and exceptionally detail-oriented.

EDUCATION AND ASSOCIATIONS

Bachelor of Arts degree in Political Science *(anticipated graduation May 2012)*
MONMOUTH UNIVERSITY– West Long Branch, NJ

Member, Global Learning Opportunities and Business Experiences (G.L.O.B.E.) Program

Member, National Association of Legal Assistants

120

Combination. *Karen Bartell, Massapequa Park, New York*

This applicant was seeking another position in her field. The writer stressed the candidate's experience, abilities, bilingual skills, worker traits, and knowledge.

MARTHA SAYLES

555 Morrow Lane
Carson, Ohio 55555
(555) 555-5555

SUMMARY

Paralegal professional with 9 years of experience. Strengths include

- Extensive paralegal and administrative support experience in private law practices.
- Outstanding planning and organizational skills with keen attention to detail.
- Effective interpersonal communications with management, judges, court clerks, attorneys, and clients.
- Knowledge of bookkeeping and probate accounting.

EDUCATION

Certificate in **Paralegal Studies**
Bay Path College, Carson, Ohio, 2006

EXPERIENCE

PETERSON, MEYERS AND GALLIHAN   Carson, Ohio
Paralegal   2006 to present

Perform various paralegal and administrative support functions for several criminal and personal injury attorneys. Ensure smooth office operations and foster positive client relations in busy practice.

◊ Prepare computerized court documents including summonses, complaints, agreements, evictions, and other materials.
◊ Participate in meetings with clients and attorneys in the preparation of legal materials and court appearances.
◊ Interface and serve as liaison with court clerks, judges, arbitrators, clients, and opposing attorneys.

BARLOW AND WILSON   Carson, Ohio
Paralegal   2003 to 2006

Performed various paralegal functions and concurrently managed all administrative aspects of general law practice. Hired, trained, and supervised support staff. Organized and maintained efficient work flow, earning recognition for productivity.

◊ Managed estates valued up to $500,000 for incapable clients; functions included processing income, paying bills, and hiring personal care attendants.
◊ Prepared all probate court accounting for estate administrators.
◊ Researched information and prepared Last Wills and Testaments for clients.
◊ Prepared selected court documents including summonses, complaints, and wage executions.
◊ Utilized investigative and research skills to obtain information for serving court papers.

121

Combination. *Louise Garver, Broad Brook, Connecticut*

The individual was seeking a position in a larger firm where she could use her office management and paralegal skills to handle more responsibilities. This resume helped her to reach her goal.

Ann Wharton

555 Oak Lane • Milwaukee, Wisconsin 00000 • (555) 555-5555 • annwharton@email.com

Judicial Assistant

Talented and dependable legal support professional with 10+ years of experience

Ethical, personable **Legal Secretary** offering exceptional work ethic and "can-do" attitude. Repeatedly recognized for balancing accuracy and speed to produce quality work. Proficient with Microsoft Office, WordPerfect, and Windows operating systems. Type 80 wpm.

Legal Document Drafting/Review ♦ File Tracking and Maintenance ♦ Calendar Management
Proofreading and Editing ♦ Correspondence Preparation ♦ Organization and Planning
Receptionist Duties ♦ Client Communications/Service ♦ Litigation Support ♦ Transcription and 10-Key

Experience Highlights

- Served as temporary **Judicial Assistant to Magistrate Judge Julian Bergmann**, providing comprehensive legal secretarial support. Processed mail, reviewed and edited decisions, typed correspondence, and received and distributed pleadings.
- Updated contracts database for Office of the U.S. District Court, Eastern District of Wisconsin.
- Received, screened, and routed telephone calls, serving as first point-of-contact for judges, attorneys, and employees of the Clerk's Office and Department of Justice.

Career Chronology

LEWIS PETERSON KRAWIEC, S.C., Milwaukee, Wisconsin • 2005 to 2012
Legal Secretary
Supported three attorneys in tax, healthcare, and environmental law matters. Drafted and revised heavy volume of pleadings and correspondence. Communicated regularly with judicial staff, clients, opposing counsel, sheriff's offices, and government agencies. Coordinated with other departments on workload and key tasks. Reviewed and assembled documents used as exhibits. Maintained calendar, contact list, and status list of open files. Responded to inquiries from process servers and court reporters.
- Played key role in setting up e-room for healthcare department, which provides access to PDF copies of executed agreements, minutes, and other corporate documents.
- Coached new associates on policies, procedures, and performance expectations. Created reference materials with document samples and step-by-step instructions.
- Selected for two-year assignment to support the only attorney handling commercial foreclosures.

LEGAL PLACEMENT SERVICES, Milwaukee, Wisconsin • 2004 to 2005
Legal Secretary
Delivered full range of legal secretarial services through full-time, temporary assignments. Clients included U.S. Court of Appeals for the Seventh Circuit; XYZ Global, Inc.; and Lewis Peterson Krawiec, S.C.
- Completed temporary Judicial Assistant assignment with U.S. District Court, Eastern District of Wisconsin.

HASSAKIS LAW OFFICE, Milwaukee, Wisconsin • 2001 to 2004
Legal Assistant
Provided administrative support to one attorney and one paralegal specializing in personal injury, products liability, workers' compensation, legal malpractice, and medical malpractice. Drafted and revised large volume of legal documents and correspondence. Opened, organized, and updated files.
- Tasked with multiple additional duties associated with working in a small law office.
- Communicated directly with clients on case status/updates, court procedures, and depositions.

Education

SANDERS COLLEGE, St. Clair, Wisconsin
Associate of Arts in Legal Secretarial Studies

122

Combination. *Michelle P. Swanson, Edwardsville, Illinois*

The applicant wanted a highly competitive Judicial Assistant position. She had been a temporary worker in such a position about seven years earlier, as shown in the Experience Highlights section.

CHLOE CHANDLER

cchandler1@gmail.com   555 Swan Avenue, Miami, Florida 55505   555.555.5050

CORPORATE ATTORNEY

➤ Versatile, skilled Attorney with more than 15 years of experience and expertise in these areas:

- Legal Research & Consultation
- Mediation & Negotiation
- Document Drafting & Editing
- Risk Analysis
- ERISA Knowledge
- Legislation Review & Analysis

➤ Strong background advising in-house fiduciaries of cash balance and 401(k) plans with combined assets of more than $6B and 35,000 participants, as well as service providers regarding 401(k) plans (including automatic enrollment and qualified default investment alternatives), the establishment of public school retirement plans, and ERISA 403(b) plans under final 403(b) regulations.

➤ Analytical, thorough researcher and problem solver; able to communicate complex subject matter in simple terms.

➤ Excellent collaborator with a proven ability to provide effective legal advice; learns quickly and adjusts easily to rapid changes.

PROFESSIONAL EXPERIENCE

PLEDGE INSURANCE, Miami, Florida   2005–Present
Consistently promoted throughout career for outstanding performance; received greater responsibilities with each position while continuing to manage previous assigned roles.

ASSISTANT GENERAL COUNSEL–PRIVATE-SECTOR RETIREMENT (2011–Present)

- Provide legal advice and risk analysis to private-sector retirement plan business that provides the financial products for small-business retirement plans through third-party administrators offering 401(k), 403(b) and governmental 401(a) plans.
- Draft legal documents and provide legal opinions regarding automatic enrollment and qualified default investment alternatives, resulting in the company gaining a competitive edge in marketplace.
- Advise the company on legal issues regarding ERISA 403(b) plans and public school 403(b) plans, enabling them to attract and retain millions of dollars in plan assets.
- Review and respond to legal pleadings, subpoenas, documents, and correspondence from the Department of Labor (DOL) and outside counsel.
- Draft, review, and negotiate contracts and agreements with third-party administrators, plan sponsors, and brokers.

ASSISTANT GENERAL COUNSEL–RETIREMENT PLANS (2010–2011)

- Served as the primary ERISA counsel for $6.2B defined benefit plan converted to a cash balance plan.
- Successfully maintained the cash balance plan's tax-qualified status by providing daily legal advice to the company.
- Advised administrative committee regarding their fiduciary duties for cash balance and 401(k) plans and provided legal advice regarding discretionary decisions, thereby preventing potential lawsuits.
- Worked with office of investments regarding representations made involving ERISA assets to protect Pledge from costly prohibited transactions.
- Drafted cash balance plan incorporating provisions of merged plan and negotiated provisions resulting from the merger and acquisition of a major life insurance company.
- Provided current analysis of new cases, legislation, and regulations in order to maintain plan compliance with current laws.

Continued

123

Combination. *April Walters, Columbus, Ohio*

The writer used bullets in a profile to emphasize areas of strength. A large gray text box, containing the applicant's name, contact information, and position, creates a commanding look

SENIOR COUNSEL (2008–2010)
- Successfully negotiated conflicts regarding plan benefits with outside counsel and customers, significantly reducing Pledge's liabilities.
- Collaborated with the Florida Legislative Service Commission to successfully draft and refine durable power of attorney statutes that became laws published in the Florida Revised Code in 2011.

COUNSEL (2005–2008)
- Reviewed all domestic relations orders and powers of attorney for Pledge 401(k) and cash balance plans to confirm they met compliance with ERISA and internal policies.
- Provided research and analysis of DOL and IRS promulgations and current case law to ensure compliance.
- Drafted amendments to Pledge 401(k) and cash balance plans to maintain the tax-qualified status.
- Provided legal advice regarding self-correction of issues identified during a third-party audit to maintain the tax-qualified status.

GENEVA BANK, Indianapolis, Indiana   1996–2004
TRUST, ESTATE, AND TAX OFFICER (1998–2004)
- Administered estates of up to $3B from opening to closing of estate.
- Completed, filed, and negotiated with IRS attorneys in regard to estate, split-interest trust, grantor-retained annuity trusts, income, exempt organization, charitable remainder interest trusts, and private foundation tax returns.

COLLATERAL LOAN REVIEW OFFICER (1996–1998)
- Analyzed collateral loan documents for large commercial loans to ensure compliance with state laws and bank policies.
- Proposed, initiated, documented, and drafted a loan-review training manual to develop consistent procedures used to train new loan officers.

EDUCATION

Juris Doctorate, NOTRE DAME LAW SCHOOL, Notre Dame, Indiana

Bachelor of Arts, Journalism, PURDUE UNIVERSITY, West Lafayette, Indiana

LICENSES & PROFESSIONAL AFFILIATIONS

Licensed to practice law in Florida and Indiana

2005–Present, Member, Central Florida Association of Corporate Counsel (CF-ACC)

2010–Present, Member and Certified Toastmaster (Speaker), Pledge Toastmasters, Miami, Florida

that is sustained by the shaded text boxes for the section headings and the replication of the candidate's name at the top of page two. Note the italic statement with the current workplace that highlights the applicant's record of consistent promotions and greater responsibilities.

R o b e r t a   J e n n i n g s

555 E. Alabama Avenue • Aurora, CO 00000 • 555.555.5555 • rjesq@atti.net

Corporate Counsel

Accomplished corporate counsel with more than ten years of experience devising and implementing practical solutions to complex problems. Skilled in dispute resolution and client management. Articulate communicator and clear, concise writer with polished presentation and interpersonal skills. Impeccable ethics and integrity.

Areas of Expertise

Real Estate • Transportation • Commercial Transactions

Professional Credentials

Admitted to Colorado Bar, 2002
Juris Doctor, University of Denver, College of Law (Top 20% of Class)

Legal Expertise

- Property Acquisition/Sales/Transfer
- Property Leases/Deeds
- Trespass Claims/Relocation Issues
- Easements/Right of Way
- Tower Site Agreements
- Evictions
- Default Letters/Releases
- Condemnation Actions

Professional Experience

The Broe Companies, Inc., Denver, CO   **2006–Present**

Associate General Counsel since 2009. In-house counsel for privately held company with holdings and operations in commercial real estate, senior living communities, railroad and related transportation services and healthcare technology. Served as Director of Legal Affairs, 2006–2009. Legal expertise includes

Contracts	Manage contracts process, including negotiations, dispute resolution and collections for equipment sales and leases; commercial property acquisitions and leases; vendor agreements; confidentiality agreements; service agreements for start-up operations.

✓ Process high volumes of contracts in short timeframes. Meticulously review each contract. Prudently select points to argue, winning them in negotiations.
✓ Successfully negotiated corporate accounting and telecommunications software usage contracts.

Litigation Management	Direct and determine litigation and resolution strategy for commercial, property and personal injury disputes; prepare reports advising CEO, CFO and Managing Director of status of company legal matters. Serve as the liaison between corporate and outside counsel and facilitate exchange of information.

✓ Select and retain outside counsel as needed. Weigh the merits/costs of the case against the efforts necessary to establish relationship with outside counsel, and make go/no-go decisions.
✓ Strive for speedy resolution through mediation and arbitration to reduce costs.
✓ Encourage clients/departments to budget for litigation to meet budget objectives.

Page I

124

Combination. *Roberta F. Gamza, Louisville, Colorado*

This lawyer wanted to test the waters and see how marketable she was. The writer demonstrated the lawyer's value and growth within her profession. A distinctive feature is the use of two

R o b e r t a   J e n n i n g s

555.555.5555 • rjesq@atti.net • Page 2

Intellectual Property	Manage company's intellectual property portfolio and provide advice on trademark-related issues.
	✓ Creatively resolved several naming disputes, avoiding costly litigation.
Human Resources	Handle resolution of wrongful termination, discrimination, sexual harassment and ADA claims; provide counsel on immigration matters, use of independent contractors and development of personnel policies and procedures.
	✓ Resolved more than 80% of discrimination and wrongful-termination claims without incurring incremental costs and avoiding lengthy litigation.
Risk Management	Served as primary liaison between subsidiaries and insurance carriers; evaluated, monitored and settled claims; ensured compliance with policy reporting requirements. Provided legal assistance in company's efforts to establish captive insurance company.
	✓ Established timely notifications and accurate record keeping of all incidents and claims.
	✓ Interpreted insurance coverage/policies for all concerned parties.
Corporate Formation Records Maintenance	Supervised formation and records maintenance for company subsidiaries structured as corporations, limited liability companies and partnerships.
	✓ Formed companies in 20 different states, Canada and the Caribbean.
	✓ Developed database and maintained accurate corporate records in compliance with IRS regulations for 200 companies.

Law Office of Bertrand F. Marsh, P.C., Denver, CO   **2004–2005**
Associate Attorney. Firm's primary undertaking was defense of a Fortune 500 company in multimillion-dollar litigation involving sale of product technology. Supervised paralegal team in responding to discovery requests; responsible for privilege review of documents responsive to discovery requests.

Project Attorney, Denver, CO   **2002–2003**
Clients included Colorado Attorney General, Colorado Department of Natural Resources and PRC Environmental Consulting, Inc., a U.S. Environmental Protection Agency contractor. Researched and wrote regarding federal and state hazardous substances, water and air-quality regulations in support of state's position in clean-up negotiations. Investigation, verification of evidence and compilation of reports for use by EPA in identifying and bringing actions against potentially responsible parties in environmental clean-up actions.

Affiliations
Member, American Corporate Counsel Association
Member, Colorado Bar Association

Education
J.D.   University of Denver, College of Law, Denver, CO, 2001
B.A.   International Studies, Rutgers University, New Brunswick, NJ, 1996

columns to indicate—by categories in the left column and details in the right column—the lawyer's areas of expertise at the most recent workplace. Check-mark bullets draw attention to achievements listed for each of the categories. The two columns add to the impression of adequate white space.

DENNIS E. RIGGS

1234 Carrolton Drive • Bloomington, IL 61704 • 309.555.5555 • deRiggs@aol.com

CORPORATE COUNSEL
Litigation Management ~ Attorney Management

Dynamic, proactive Corporate Counsel with **multiple responsibilities and the ability to direct a large staff. Outstanding leadership and teambuilding strengths** that generate optimum productivity and performance from legal staff. Excellent communication and presentation skills. Proven capabilities in litigation, mediation, and arbitration. Supervise the selection process for retaining outside attorneys.

Possess the vision necessary to develop and implement successful action plans. Demonstrated proficiency directing multiple ongoing cases in a productive and cost-effective manner.

Areas of Expertise

- Litigation Management
- Attorney Management
- Arbitration/Mediation
- Legal Review
- Risk Management/Remedial Measures

- Institutional Litigation
- Organizational Compliance
- Mentoring/Teambuilding
- Claim Audits
- Project Management

Professional Experience

LIBERTY MUTUAL INSURANCE, *Bloomington, IL*
Counsel — 2010–Present
Assistant Counsel — 2006–2010
Attorney — 2005–2006

Promoted twice over a five-year period after demonstrating exceptional legal and managerial expertise. Acknowledged for superior interpersonal skills and the ability to interface with individuals of all levels.

Leadership:
Senior Management Bonus Committee member; *Legal Resource Management Committee member*; *Section Interview Team*; *Corporate Summer Intern Mentor*; *About Our Business Table Leader*—Selected to conduct multiple six-hour corporate business presentations to all staff, from administrative to executive level personnel.

Litigation:
Manage complex institutional bad-faith litigation for the state of West Virginia (trial and appellate).

- Select and hire attorneys, assign cases, and oversee all aspects of the litigation (state and federal).
- Review suits, evaluate corporate institutional exposure, and formulate strategies. Conduct interviews of company employees to determine exposure of cases.
- Determine whether to proceed to trial or negotiate settlements.
- Provide updates to executive management concerning multimillion-dollar exposure cases. Advise on strategy, progress, and resolution.
- Direct trial/deposition preparation of all levels of institutional personnel (administrative to executive).
- Additional duties include the management, review, and assignment of cases in other states on an as-needed basis.
- Assist in drafting public relations message points concerning high-profile cases.
- Television interview preparation of retained counsel concerning insurance industry issues.

Managerial Responsibilities:
Manage all phases of the litigation budget and supervision of 10 to 15 outside attorneys and staff.

- Interview, select, and negotiate the contracts of outside attorneys.
- Assist in the formulation of corporate legislative strategies for West Virginia.
- Create remedial measures/risk-management strategies concerning institutional litigation.
- Interview prospective in-house attorneys for the corporate law department and provide hiring recommendations.
- Conduct corporate executive and regional management presentations as needed concerning status of institutional litigation. Report on compliance issues.
- Interview corporate summer interns and provide hiring recommendations.
- Conduct statewide claim file audits.
- Accountable for the approval of all litigation fees and expenses with check-signing duties.
- Assist in the administration of support-staff evaluation.

Continued

Combination. *Beverley and Mitchell I. Baskin, Marlboro, New Jersey*

Boldfacing makes key information stand out in the profile. Large diamond bullets direct attention to each area of expertise. Four categories—Leadership, Litigation, Managerial

Professional Experience *(Continued)*

Corporate Achievements:
- Supervised more bad-faith jury trials than any other member of the department.
- Authored corporate law department's *Guidelines for Employee Deposition Preparation.*
- Managerial responsibility for two of Liberty Mutual's top five institutional bad-faith states (volume and financial exposure): Pennsylvania, '05 to '06 and West Virginia, '06 to present.

LIBERTY MUTUAL INSURANCE, Baltimore, MD
Claim Litigation Counsel   2000–2005

Trial counsel for lawsuits ranging from auto bodily-injury claims to premises liability injuries. Composed opinion letters related to potential exposures. Prepared all motions and other materials needed for trial. Conducted EUO (fraud investigations) proceedings of insureds and provided advice on the merits of claims (accept or deny). Assisted in the interviewing and hiring recommendations of prospective in-house trial attorneys.
- Tried more jury trials than any other member of the 300+-member department.
- Selected to provide presentations to claim management on trial strategy.
- First-chaired approximately 100 jury trials, which required excellent time-management and organizational skills.
- First-chaired approximately 40 bench trials; conducted approximately 200 to 250 depositions.
- First-chaired approximately 30 arbitration/mediations.
- Demonstrated ability to communicate thoughts and ideas to advance the causes of individual insureds, as well as the corporation.
- Supervised and trained younger attorneys and summer interns.

KESSLER, HARDY AND FARRELL, Landover, MD
Associate   1999–2000
Law Clerk   1997–1999

Practices included insurance and medical malpractice defense. Drafted motions, legal memoranda, opinion letters, and briefs concerning a variety of insurance and medical issues. Drafted all forms of discovery and conducted depositions. Second-chaired medical malpractice trial.

LIBERTY MUTUAL INSURANCE, Fairmont, WV, and Frederick, MD
Claims Representative   1994–1996

Responsible for all phases of the investigation, evaluation, and negotiation of automobile claims presented by insureds and claimants for bodily injuries and property damage.

Personal Lines Underwriter (Intern)   1993

Assisted in the evaluation and determination of the acceptance of insurance risks involving personal property.

Education

UNIVERSITY OF MARYLAND SCHOOL OF LAW, Baltimore, MD ~ Juris Doctor   1998
FAIRMONT STATE COLLEGE, Fairmont, WV ~ BS (Cum Laude), Business Management   1993
All-American—Football

Bar Admissions and Affiliations

Maryland   1998
District of Columbia   2000
U.S. Court of Appeals, District of Columbia   2000
U.S. District Court, Maryland   2000
U.S. Court of Appeals, Fourth Circuit   2000
U.S. District Court, District of Columbia   2000

CPCU—Insurance Institute of America, ongoing
Multiple national institutional litigation seminars
Powell/Tate Media Communications Training (print & television)
National Institute of Trial Advocacy School—Diploma   2002
Licensed Maryland Real Estate Agent
Automobile Insurance Claim School
Basic Insurance Claim Course
Basic Insurance Course
Personal Lines Underwriting Course
Toastmasters International

Responsibilities, and Corporate Achievements—are used to indicate aspects of the applicant's professional experience at the Bloomington, Illinois, site of his employer. Smaller type enables the reporting of more information in the allotted space. Dates of promotions are easily seen.

PATRICIA JUHASZ

555 Riddle Avenue • Smithtown, NY 55555 • (888) 999-0000 • Pjuhasz@telcomm.net

Legal Assistant/Paralegal Assistant

Experienced Legal Assistant with excellent office management and client-attorney relation skills seeking an entry-level Paralegal Assistant position where a working knowledge of legal terminology, general law, and legal proceedings, and continuing education in Paralegal Studies, will be utilized and expanded. Bring experience working within a Legal Department/Collection Agency environment in the following select areas:

Civil Litigation…Collections…Settlements…Affidavits…Skip Tracing…Attorney Sourcing & Selection
Bankruptcies…Judgments…Liens…Summonses & Complaints…Estate Searches…Statute of Limitations

PROFESSIONAL EXPERIENCE

Legal Assistant, Legal Recoveries, Inc., Lake Grove, NY   2008–present

Joined this Collection Agency's legal department at a time of unit-wide staffing changes. Responsible for managing a high volume of civil litigation case files for major accounts that partially included Century Detection, Credit Union of New York, AB Bank National Association, and St. Mary's Hospital.

- Collaborate extensively with internal departments including collections, medical billing, finance, production, special projects, and clerical to obtain, verify, and process documentation pertaining to the status of more than 50 weekly referred collections cases forwarded to the legal department.
- Carefully source and select nationally based bonded attorneys utilizing the *American Lawyers Quarterly, Commercial Bar Directory, National Directory List,* and *Columbia Directory List;* determine the appropriate choice upon obtainment and review of résumés, copies of insurance policies, and court filing fees.
- Perform estate searches and integrate traditional investigative methods and the DAKCS database system to gather account histories and case-sensitive documentation for attorneys including debtors and guarantors, credit bureau reports, court affidavits, judgments, skip-tracing records, bankruptcy notices, banking statements, proof of statute of limitations, proof of assets, and trial letters.
- Maintain communications with attorneys and clients from point of referral/discovery to trial phase to facilitate and expedite case settlements that historically award clients a minimum of 80% in recovered funds.

EDUCATION

Bachelor of Science in Paralegal Studies, 2008
ST. JOSEPH'S COLLEGE, Brentwood, NY

COMPUTER SKILLS

Windows XP/7; WordPerfect and Microsoft Word; DAKCS

EARLIER WORK HISTORY

Administrative Assistant, State Insurance, Patchogue, NY   2007–2008
Office Support Assistant, Financial Association of America, Inc., Islip, NY   2005–2007
Appointment Coordinator, Phlebotomy Services, Huntington, NY   2001–2006
Senior Office Support Assistant, AB National Bank, Hicksville, NY   1996–2001

126

Combination. *Ann Baehr, East Islip, New York*

The focus in this resume is on the most relevant experience. Earlier experience is put near the bottom. Keywords are used to indicate areas of expertise at the end of the profile. The page border is shadowed.

Law Enforcement

Resumes at a Glance

JENNIFER GONZALES

334–30 Kissena Blvd., Flushing, NY 55555 • (555) 222-7777 • JGonzales@lawandorder.net

Seeking a position in the field of

Law Enforcement

CITY——STATE——FEDERAL——PRIVATE

➢ Highly motivated, energetic law enforcement student with strong work ethic and professional goals.
➢ Bring five years of experience in office support and retail sales positions while attending college full time.
➢ Bilingual with an articulate fluency in English and Spanish; personable, easygoing communication style.
➢ Meet challenges head on; work well in stressful situations and in a fast-paced setting.
➢ Analytical with a lot of common sense, intuitive instincts, and ability to think outside of the box.
➢ Maintain excellent research, organization, time-management, and problem-assessment/resolution skills.

Education

Bachelor of Arts, Forensic Psychology—expected August 2012
John Jay College of Criminal Justice, New York, NY
Honors Candidate: Psi Chi Chapter National Honor Society in Psychology

Academically trained in criminalistics and psychology:

Select Courses: Analysis of Criminal Behavior, Concepts of Forensic Science, Abnormal Psychology, Physical Fitness in Law Enforcement, Criminal Law, Group Dynamics
Select Projects: Crime Scene Observation, Forensic Study of Microscopic Fibers, Fingerprint Analysis

Work Experience

Receptionist, Volvoville, Massapequa, NY	4/06–Present
Payroll Clerk, People's Alliance Federal Credit Union, Hauppauge, NY	4/08–7/08
Sales Associate, Annie Sez, East Northport, NY	2/06–6/06
Senior Sales Associate, Rainbow Shops, Commack/Bay Shore, NY	9/05–2/06

• Provide front-desk representation, clerical support, and customer service for Volvo and subsidiary, Land Rover, directing customer traffic with a proven ability to maintain open lines of communication.

• Managed more than 50 business payroll accounts utilizing cross-trained experience in teller and payroll services.

• Prepared and uploaded weekly exempt/non-exempt payroll data into network system for clients to download.

• Completed mandatory training that included a film study on a mock robbery to learn observation techniques.

• Held increasingly responsible sales positions, achieving recognition for over-quota floor sales and cashier management skills, and manager-requests to return during school breaks based on performance and reliability.

• Provided excellence in customer service while assisting in all areas of inventory and display merchandising.

Computer Skills

Windows XP/7; Microsoft Word, LexisNexis, PsychInfo, Criminal Justice Abstracts, InfoTrak Health, Sociological Abstracts, Internet research

127

Combination. *Ann Baehr, East Islip, New York*

Including four areas of interest directly below the Law Enforcement heading broadens this resume for use at job fairs and networking events. When this new graduate is applying for a specific job, however, she should change the heading to match the type of hiring organization.

BRUCE S. ALEXANDER

1010-L Park South Drive ▪ Charlotte, NC 28888
Home: (704) 555-5555   Cell: (704) 666-1111
shadowman@earthlink.net

CAREER PROFILE

Results-oriented professional with more than 15 years of security management and **law enforcement** experience in both the military and private sector, including drug surveillance, anti-terrorism activities, nuclear security and operations leadership. Highly developed situational problem-solving and analytical skills. Advanced knowledge of military (grounds) weapons, special experience identification (SEI) training and drug-testing procedures. Expert Marksman and Security Craftsman (7-Skill Level). Consistently commended for professionalism and outstanding performance—played key role in several major operations and investigations. Qualified by:

▪ Investigative Techniques	▪ Emergency Response	▪ Cross-Cultural Relations
▪ Conflict Resolution	▪ Search & Seizure	▪ Physical Security & Theft Prevention
▪ Supervision & Training	▪ Technical Surveillance	▪ Community Partnerships

---

AWARDS & RECOGNITION

- Air Force Achievement Medal (First Oak Leaf Cluster) for Outstanding Achievement, 2001
- Air Force Achievement Medal for Outstanding Achievement, 1995
- Air Force Commendation Medal, 1995
- Armed Forces Expeditionary Medal, 1999
- National Defense Service Medal, 2009–2012

PROFESSIONAL EXPERIENCE

U.S. AIR FORCE—Charleston, SC   2009–2012
Patrol Supervisor
Second-in-command of day-to-day operations. Led and trained staff of 15–20 personnel, including supervisory staff of 5. Conducted general law enforcement protection activities. Apprehended, controlled and detained suspects. Conducted interviews with witnesses and suspects. Provided first-responder action. Developed, planned and implemented security force programs.

- As member of 13-person team, provided surveillance and security for sites in Spain, Italy, Saudi Arabia, Afghanistan, Pakistan, Turkmenistan and Uzbekistan. Conducted interrogations of two Saudi intelligence officers.

- Participated in apprehension of 44 illegal aliens, serving as preliminary investigator. Performed discovery and analysis; interviewed suspects, gathered evidence and filed report.

- Played key role in defusing many internal incidents involving military personnel (e.g., smuggling and illegal possession of firearms, criminal domestic violence and violent assault altercations).

MONTGOMERY COUNTY SPECIAL POLICE & SAFETY SERVICE, INC.—Raleigh, NC   2004–2009
Special Police Officer (2007–2009)
Security Officer (2004–2007)

128

Combination. *Doug Morrison, Charlotte, North Carolina*

The individual was seeking a new position in law enforcement with either a federal or state agency. He possessed a strong security, surveillance, and covert operations background in

-2-

MONTGOMERY COUNTY SPECIAL POLICE & SAFETY SERVICE, INC. (CONTINUED)
Provided security service to 12 Bank of America facilities. Investigated suspicious activities, complaints and reports of violence. Worked with other law enforcement officers throughout the Raleigh area.

- Improved charge/arrest rate through better surveillance while providing onsite security.

- Arrested 15 suspects for acts of domestic violence, breaking and entering, traffic felonies and possession of illegal drugs.

U.S. AIR FORCE—Southeast Region, U.S.   March–July 2000
Shift Leader, Night Crew
Supervised 13-member team as leader during a major drug operation in southwestern U.S. Collaborated directly with U.S. Border Patrol, U.S. Customs Service and local police officials.

- Directed designated activities during 3½-month covert investigation of a major drug enterprise leading to the seizure of 250 lbs. of marijuana, 6 kilos of uncut cocaine, 1 lb. of crystal methamphetamine ("ice") and 1 lb. of heroin, and the indictment of numerous individuals.

- Awarded the Air Force Achievement Medal for outstanding service achievement, March 2001:

> Recognized by senior officials for "outstanding achievement while performing as team member of Joint Task Force Six Mission . . ." Cited by commander for "playing vital role in this unique narcotics smuggling activity," including surveillance, analysis of intelligence reports, mapping of reconnaissance areas and instruction and supervision of personnel.

U.S. AIR FORCE   1993–1999
Fire Team Leader/Squad Leader (Staff Sergeant, E-5)—Charleston AFB, Charleston, SC (1998–1999)
Assigned to 315th Security Force Squadron (SFS)/437th SFS
Participated in air base security activities to protect federal government resources and property in Cairo, Egypt vicinity, as well as Joint Task Force in Southwest Asia. Worked closely with Egyptian military police and Special Forces, among others.

- Received Armed Forces Expeditionary Medal for contributions in training of U.S. Armed Forces personnel in intelligence gathering and security operations.

Security Specialist (Sergeant, E-4)—Kirtland AFB, Albuquerque, NM (1993–1997)
Led 2-person team. Planned, coordinated and supervised field threat protection (Level 1) operations.

- Distinguished with the Air Force Achievement Medal (contributions during July 28–September 2, 1995 mission) and the Air Force Commendation Medal (identification of sniper location and use of cross-cultural diplomacy, among other mission activities in Europe).

EDUCATION

B.S., Human Sciences, Gardner-Webb University, Boiling Springs, NC, 2004
A.A.S., Law Enforcement Technology, Central Piedmont Community College, Charlotte, NC, 2002
U.S. Air Force: N.C.O. Preparatory Course, *Distinguished Graduate* (2nd among 52), 1996; N.C.O. Academy, 2004; Security Forces Training (7-Skill Level), 2007.
Civilian: Introduction to Community Policing, January 2008; BLET, State of NC, 2008

the military—in both domestic and international operations. The writer created a three-column box in the Career Profile section to draw attention to important qualifications. Another box on the second page makes conspicuous the person's Air Force Achievement Medal for outstanding service.

CHARLES WILSON

2158 Hampton Lane, Cincinnati, OH 45219
513.426.9568
cwilson@ci.cincinnati.oh.us

CAREER PROFILE

A results-oriented, high-energy LAW ENFORCEMENT LIEUTENANT with 20+ years of progressively responsible experience in the Public Service area. Highly developed administrative and analytical skills as evidenced by the ability to continuously improve division operations. Qualified by:

Investigative Techniques	DEA Certification	Evidence Collection
Police Media Relations	Supervision & Training	Emergency Response
Conflict Resolution	Search & Seizure	Technical Surveillance
Protection Programs	Defense Management	Professional Development

PROFESSIONAL EXPERIENCE

CINCINNATI POLICE DEPARTMENT, Cincinnati, OH   1994–Present

Lieutenant of Detective Division, 2007–Present
Lieutenant of Patrol Division, 2006–2007
Sergeant of Patrol Division, 2004–2006
Detective Division—Forensics, 2002–2004
Field Training Officer, 1999–2002
Patrol Officer, 1994–1999

Prior police experience in various security positions, 1991–1994

KEY ACCOMPLISHMENTS

- Supervise seven investigators assigned 330+ cases per year who gather and analyze sufficient evidence in major crime cases, resulting in an average solvability rate of 40%.

- Supervised three-year investigation of a major drug enterprise leading to the seizure of 200 kilos of cocaine and the indictment of 40+ individuals on state and federal charges.

- Increased charge rate 10% due to advanced investigative techniques and technology training.

- Redesigned police department schedules to allow for 100 hours per year of in-service training for all officers in the department.

- Modernized Detective Division's infrastructure by purchasing new computers and reconfiguring office space to allow for increased communications.

- Equipped cruisers with laptop computers and CAD-RMS (Computer-Aided Dispatch—Records Management System) software, increasing report-writing efficiency and reducing paperwork 80% for Patrol Division officers.

- Led Patrol Division with 50 drunk-driving arrests, accounting for 10% of total arrests.

- Updated forensic lab equipment and coordinated training for all officers, leading to increased evidence-collection capabilities for the police department.

- "Police Officer of the Month" presented by the Cincinnati Police Department—October 2003.

-Continued-

129

Combination. *Sharon Pierce-Williams, Findlay, Ohio*

During 20 years of working for the police department, this detective never needed a resume. He was completing a BA degree; thinking of retiring from the force; considering future career

CHARLES WILSON

2158 Hampton Lane, Cincinnati, OH 45219
513.426.9568
cwilson@ci.cincinnati.oh.us

Page 2

EDUCATION

UNIVERSITY of CINCINNATI, Cincinnati, OH
Bachelor of Arts Degree
Major: Criminal Justice
GPA: 4.0 Anticipated Graduation: 2014

TERRA COMMUNITY COLLEGE, Fremont, OH
Associate in Law Enforcement Degree
GPA: 3.84 *Magna Cum Laude*
Distinguished Alumni Award, 2011

NORTHWESTERN UNIVERSITY TRAFFIC INSTITUTE, Evanston, IL
School of Police Staff and Command (19 semester hours)

FEDERAL BUREAU of INVESTIGATION NATIONAL ACADEMY, Quantico, VA
Criminal Justice Education (17 semester hours)

OHIO PEACE OFFICER TRAINING COUNCIL (386 hours), Fremont, OH—**Top Honors**

PROFESSIONAL DEVELOPMENT

FBI U.S. Department of Justice, Media Relations for the Law Enforcement Executive,
    Quantico, VA—2011
Crime Stoppers Annual Training Conference, Pueblo, CO—2011
Combating Violent Crimes in the 21st Century Information Sharing Conference, MAGLOCLEN,
    Cleveland, OH—2010
FBI Hostile School Environment: Causes and Solutions Conference, Cleveland, OH—2009
Exploring Economic, Electronic and Financial Crimes in Our Society Information Sharing
    Conference, MAGLOCLEN, Atlantic City, NY—2009
Crime Stoppers International Conference, Gillette, WY—2008
Crime Trends in America, MAGLOCLEN, Pittsburgh, PA—2008

AFFILIATIONS & LEADERSHIP

Board of Crime Stoppers of Cincinnati, **Law Enforcement Coordinator/Liaison,** 2007–Present
Benevolent Protective Order of the Elks #75, **Chairman of Youth Activities,** 2011–Present
Free and Accepted Masons of Ohio—32nd Degree, 2012
Fraternal Order of Police Lodge #20 Member, **President,** 1999–2000

CONTINUING EDUCATION

Ohio Department of Health, Alcohol Testing, Approval & Permit Program, Senior Operator Permit
Search and Seizure Update, Cincinnati Academy (16 hours)
The Dispatch Institute: Liability and Public Image Concerns in Public Safety Telecommunications
Laws of Arrest, Search & Seizure, Firearms Training (50 hours)
Ohio Peace Officer Training Council, Evidence Technician (40 hours)
Lucas County Coroner Forensic Medical Sciences, Evidence Related to Blood (8 hours)
Front-Line Effective Police Supervision Skills (14 hours)
Defensive Tactics Training (16 hours)
Public Safety Training, Saving Our Own Lives (16 hours)
FBI U.S. Department of Justice DEA, Basic Narcotics and Dangerous Drug Law Enforcement (80 hours)

options; and realizing that it was time to put his credentials, experience, and accomplishments on paper.
This resume is a past winner of the "Best Law Enforcement/Security Industry Resume," as determined by the
Professional Association of Resume Writers.

Tom Collier

000 15th Street ▪ Oakland, CA 00000 ▪ name@aol.com
Home: (000) 000-1111 ▪ Cell: (000) 000-0000

LAW ENFORCEMENT OFFICIAL

*With Track Record of Strengthening Safety/Security Programs and Success in Providing
Community of Oakland with 20+ Years of Excellent Public Service*

Dedicated law enforcement officer with more than 20 years of experience in planning and managing investigations, security, public service, and police force activities. Strong qualifications in budgeting, personnel affairs, training, resource management, public safety, and emergency response. Excellent research and problem-solving skills; maintain strict confidentiality on sensitive information. Confident public speaker with experience in media and civic leadership relations. Reputation for strong work ethic and uncompromising devotion to service.

SPECIFIC SKILL AREAS

- Public Safety Programs
- Emergency Response
- Internal Investigations
- Crisis Communications
- Team Building & Leadership

- Community Event Coordination
- Policy & Procedure Development
- Budget Planning & Management
- Staffing, Training & Retention
- Time & Resource Allocation

- City Council Presentations
- Community Outreach
- External Communications
- Regulatory Compliance
- Media & Public Relations

AWARDS & RECOGNITIONS

Service Above Self Award, "Outstanding Community Service" — by Oakland Rotary Club (2006)
Two-Time Recipient, County Outstanding Peace Officer Award — by Oakland College (1992 & 1993)
Representative, Advisory Committee in Washington, DC — selected by CA Police Chiefs Association (2009)

PROFESSIONAL EXPERIENCE

CITY OF OAKLAND POLICE DEPARTMENT — Oakland, CA   1989–Present
Assistant Chief of Police (1995–Present)
Shift Supervisor (1990–1995)
Police Officer (1989–1990)

Distinguished 20-plus-year career ensuring public safety for city of Oakland with culturally diverse population. Progressed rapidly through strict promotion requirements to handle increasingly responsible positions, culminating in supervisory duty for staff of 25 employees. Hold key accountability and co-responsibility for budget management, staff training, lead work on investigations, program/policy development, and public safety programs, along with regulatory documentation and filing requirements. Maintained consistent performance in core law enforcement disciplines. **Selected Accomplishments:**

TEAM BUILDING & LEADERSHIP

- Use tact and professionalism in responding to citizen complaints against officers and allegations of misconduct, applying corrective strategies on minor infractions and stricter measures on serious offenses.
- Co-developed Employee Evaluation program that enhanced targeting of strengths/weaknesses and resulted in measurable, sustainable performance improvements.
- Earned high level of loyalty from staff and maintained excellent retention rate through fair, consistent evaluations and modeling effective on-the-job performance in both criminal and administrative matters.

PROGRAM & DEPARTMENT DEVELOPMENT

- Recognized for contributions to organizational development through supervision of following departments:
  - *Patrol Division*
  - *K-9/Animal Control*

  - *Investigation Division*
  - *School Resource Office*

  - *Communications Division*
  - *Community Policing Division*

...Continued...

130

Combination. *Daniel J. Dorotik Jr., Lubbock, Texas*

Usually, personal information is not included in a resume—often to avoid breaking sensitive regulations about hiring. The personal information at the bottom of page two was judged

Tom Collier

Professional Experience, Continued

(PROGRAM & DEPARTMENT DEVELOPMENT)

- Modified key departmental policies to reflect changes in the law following high-profile court cases that involved such issues as high-speed pursuit, search and seizure, and domestic violence.
- Implemented new technologies and applications that resulted in increased efficiency and accuracy for file and records management functions.

CRISIS MANAGEMENT & RESPONSE

- Repeatedly recognized by citizens, community groups, and supervisors for quick-thinking, calm, and correct response to multitude of crisis and emergency situations, both in the field and as shift supervisor.
- Developed strong relationships with members of Fire Department and local/regional emergency medical services that led to improved, expedited emergency responses.

COMMUNITY & CITY COUNCIL RELATIONS

- Built good will between citizens and police department over 20-year period, with emphasis on youth crime prevention and community service initiatives.
- Deliver well-received, comprehensive presentations to City Council of Oakland detailing department's year-to-date statistics and activities from written report.

EDUCATION & TRAINING

Associate Degree in Law Enforcement
COLLEGE, Oakland, CA (1989)

Selected Professional Development Coursework:
Asset Forfeiture & Racial Profiling ▪ Leadership Principles ▪ Supervising Problem Solving ▪ Cultural Diversity
Leadership Survival Skills ▪ Manpower Allocation & Deployment ▪ Chief's Administrative Conference
Law Enforcement Liability ▪ Command Staff Leadership Series ▪ Principles of Management

* 576 hours total in professional development. A comprehensive course list will gladly be provided upon request.

Certifications & Licenses:

- Master Peace Officer, 2010
- Intermediate Peace Officer, 1998
- Peace Officer License, 1991
- Advanced Peace Officer, 1998
- Instructor Proficiency, 1994
- Basic Peace Officer, 1990

AFFILIATIONS & CIVIC INVOLVEMENT

Member—City of Oakland Police Association (1998–Present)

Advisory Board Member—County Family Center (2002–2006)
Advisory Board Member—County Children's Welfare Board (2005–2011)

President—Girls Softball (2003–Present)
President—Youth Soccer League (2003–2005)
President—Girls Little Dribblers Association (2006–2007)

PERSONAL

Married, 23 years, to Sandra Collier, Nursing Supervisor at Oakland Clinic
Three children: Amy (22), Josh (19), and Alyssa (16)

appropriate for this candidate because background checks on personal information are standard in the field of law enforcement, and he was being hired to represent the community. Information about his affiliations and civic involvement paints him as a model citizen.

Joe Johnson

55 Sunset Shores
Costa Mesa, CA 55555

Cell: (555) 555-5555
joe.johnson@xxxx.net

Objective: LIEUTENANT

A results-oriented, high-energy Patrol Sergeant with 20+ years of progressively responsible experience in the Public Service area. Highly developed leadership and analytical skills as evidenced by the ability to continuously improve division operations. Areas of expertise and qualifications include:

Conflict Resolution	Flexible & Adaptable	Policies & Procedures
Decisive Problem Solver	Front Line Supervisor	Professional Development
Effective Communicator	Investigative Techniques	Search & Seizure
Emergency Response	Organized/Time Management	Staff Reports
Evidence Collection	Performance Evaluations	Supervision & Training

PROFESSIONAL EXPERIENCE

CITY OF ORANGE POLICE DEPARTMENT, Orange, CA   1992 – Present

Patrol Sergeant (5/11–present)
- Oversee law enforcement field activities and office operations.
- Assist officers with investigations and reports.
- Supervise and perform investigative, patrol, traffic and administrative duties.
- Jail Supervisor: Maintain and manage jail records, personnel, policies and procedures.
- Field Training Sergeant: Coordinate training, mentor and evaluate new employees.
- Serve as Acting Watch Commander, as needed, and Department Communicable Disease Coordinator.

Patrol Corporal / Field Training Officer (11/06–5/11)
- Supervised and managed field operations personnel, including preparation of supervisory reports.
- Trained, mentored, coached and supervised new officers; mentored and taught experienced officers.
- Provided supervisory assistance during major incidents.
- Promoted and trained employees on the COPPS philosophy.
- Conducted in-service training and promoted team building.
- Recruited the most qualified police candidates with complete background investigations.

Financial Crimes Detective (9/03–11/06)
- Supervised and directed personnel during numerous criminal investigations.
- Directed multiagency investigations dealing with financial crime violations.
- Obtained and served approximately 10 financial crime search warrants for suspects and supporting documents involving monetary losses in the hundreds of thousands of dollars.
- Networked with numerous outside agencies for more complete and efficient investigations.
- Facilitated off-site seminar to improve division effectiveness and enhance employee relations.
- Trained and supported patrol officers in Financial Crime Investigations.
- Improved communication between divisions with implementation of "Briefing Bulletin."

Narcotic Detective / Tactical Team Member (6/99–8/03)
- Conducted narcotic, Vice and A.B.C. investigations in Brea and Yorba Linda.
- Operated in an undercover detective capacity to further narcotic investigations.
- Maintained TEAM concept with fellow employees to enhance investigations.
- Trained patrol and detective division members in high-risk entry and tactical deployments.
- Participated in over 75 narcotic-related search warrants.
- Networked and collaborated with Probation, Parole and A.B.C. supervisors and investigators.
- Supervised and evaluated personnel throughout numerous investigations.
- Worked with fellow detectives investigating sex crimes, financial crimes and crimes against persons.

Regional Narcotics Suppression Program (10/96–6/99)
- Participated in approximately 30 narcotic search warrants, seizing in excess of three million dollars and hundreds of pounds of illegal narcotics.
- Successfully worked with employees from several outside agencies in the investigation and prosecution of large-level narcotic violators.
- Conducted law enforcement surveillances with state, county and federal agencies.
- Aggressively sought "Case Agent" status on several high-profile investigations.

131

Combination. *Pearl White, Irvine, California*

A bold horizontal bar separates the contact information from the important opening section, which contains an objective, a profile, and (in three columns) areas of expertise and

Joe Johnson   **(555) 555-5555**   **Resume – Page 2**

School Resource Officer (8/94–10/96)
- Maintained demanding Brea schools D.A.R.E. program schedule.
- Supervised children in teaching arena.
- Worked in a TEAM environment with fellow D.A.R.E. officers.
- Spoke and answered questions at Brea City Council meetings.

Field Training Officer (9/93–8/94)
- Provided training and supervision to new officers.
- Continued to pursue personal education goals and expectations.
- Conducted community education seminars.

Patrol Officer (5/92–9/93)
- Provided criminal investigations that led to the arrest and conviction of hundreds of suspects.
- Worked with other officers in TEAM approach.
- Provided court testimony in numerous felony/misdemeanor/infraction cases.

EDUCATION and TRAINING

Supervisor School: Temporary Holding Facility, Anderson & Associates, Anaheim, CA, 2011

Sexual Harassment Update, Orange, CA, 2011

Bachelor of Arts: Organizational Management, July 2003
Vanguard University, Orange, CA

Administration of Justice/Liberal Arts, 1983–1986, 1989, 1992
Goldenwest College, Huntington Beach, CA

D.A.R.E. Training Program

AWARDS and CERTIFICATIONS

- Two commendations for field arrests and investigations
- Reserve Police Officer of the Year Award, 1990
- Advanced Post Certificate
- Certified Background Investigator

PROFESSIONAL AFFILIATIONS

- California Narcotic Officers' Association
- California D.A.R.E. Officers' Association
- Orange Police Department Special Response Team (Tac-Team)
- Police Officers Research Association of California
- Orange County Financial Crime Investigators Association
- International Association of Financial Crime Investigators
- State of California Background Investigators Association
- Treasurer, Orange Police Officers Association

SPECIAL ASSIGNMENTS

- City of Orange B.E.S.T. Committee Member
- Police Budgeting Seminar Attendee
- Orange Senior Center Liaison
- Detective Bureau Offsite Facilitator
- Orange L.E.A.D.S. Liaison (Law Enforcement Automated Data System)
- Orange Police Department Parole and Probation Liaison Officer

COMMUNITY VOLUNTEER ACTIVITIES

- Locate resources for shelter and medical needs as a liaison among the homeless, the City of Orange and Social Services.
- Orange Police Department liaison with City of Orange senior citizens.

qualifications. This is the important location in which a reader's attention can be won or lost. Shaded text boxes for the section headings unify the resume's two pages visually. The Professional Experience section displays the applicant's impressive record of promotion within one police department.

JASON E. HOLMES

5500 Pine Avenue
Yorkshire, Ohio 55505

jholmes5@xxxx.com

Cell: 550-505-5005
Home: 550-550-0505

LAW ENFORCEMENT MANAGEMENT

▶ Dedicated law enforcement officer with 20+ years of management experience and high standards of law enforcement ethics and professionalism. Foster a sense of mutual respect among department members. Notable oral and written communication skills facilitate conveying objectives and delegating tasks. Readily share opinions on solving work-related problems.

▶ Thrive as leader in a team environment. Possess talent to motivate and work with people at all professional levels across a complex organization. Promote a commitment to high standards of excellence in serving the community. Excellent troubleshooter; exercise good judgment under stress.

▶ Prioritize and manage heavy work flow. Driven to achieve goals employing principles and practices of supervision, training and record keeping. Logical and incisive in problem-solving activities. Make objective decisions.

▶ Communicate effectively with individuals at all levels of the department through established credibility, trust and respect. Cultivate established rapport/trust to achieve mutual agreement.

▶ Spearhead personnel strategies and new programs to enhance overall department performance. Control overtime to manage salary budget. Motivate and inspire personnel to promote programs and mission of the police department.

▶ Knowledgeable in use of proprietary computer programs for law enforcement organizations and also MS Word, Excel, PowerPoint and Outlook.

PROFESSIONAL EMPLOYMENT

City of Yorkshire Police Department — Yorkshire, Ohio   *1977–Present*
   CAPTAIN (highest rank in department), **Shift Commander** *(1997–Present)*
   ACTING CHIEF OF POLICE *(2003)*
   LIEUTENANT, Officer in Charge of Juvenile Division *(1987–1997)*
   DETECTIVE, Criminal Investigation *(1981–1987)*
   PATROLMAN *(1977–1981)*

- Oversee operations of C-Patrol Division since 2003 and served as previous commander of B-Patrol Division. Supervise 40+ personnel (lieutenants, sergeants, patrolmen and civilians). Manage scheduling, training, implementing departmental policies, rules, regulations and general orders. Direct crime prevention and apprehension of criminals.

- Developed positive relationship with the public. Established and maintain positive working environment for all employees. Reduce crime by promoting proactive patrolling and zero tolerance.

- Capably respond to emergencies and make decisions. Ensure personnel are fully trained and follow established policies and procedures. Secure adequate staffing levels and compliance with guidelines. Monitor performance. Keep accurate records.

- Asked to serve as Acting Chief of Police in 2003. Demonstrated exceptional ability for proactive management: readily identified what needed to be done and formulated and implemented steps to achieve objectives.

- Key member of committee that rewrote operational regulations (General Orders Manual) of the police department. Competently address media to brief the public regarding criminal activities.

- As Commander of Juvenile and Domestic Violence Division from 2002–2003, supervised approximately 14 police officers, supervisors, investigators and clerks.

- Served as Officer in Charge of Juvenile Division from 1987–1997, managing approximately 9 officers, detectives and clerks.

Continued on next page

132

Combination. *Jane Roqueplot, West Middlesex, Pennsylvania*

To avoid repetition in stating similar duties for related jobs, the writer lists the applicant's various positions like a work history and then presents highlights of the entire range of experience

PROFESSIONAL DEVELOPMENT

Federal Bureau of Investigation: National Academy Session #217, 2004
Department of Justice: Dignitary Security Protection, Commander (Vice, Narcotics & Intelligence), Narcotic Investigations, Narcotic Enforcement for Police Officers, Gang Investigations/Enforcement
San Francisco Police Department: Tactical Operations & Intelligence
Los Angeles Sheriff's Office: SWAT Academy Training
San Francisco State: Homicide Investigation, Internal Affairs Investigation, Police Management

PROFESSIONAL SUMMARY

Affiliations

- San Bruno Police Officers Association
- Federal Bureau of Investigation National Academy Association

Awards & Commendations

- Certificate of Appreciation, Parker Heights Neighborhood Association, 2010
- Captain Andrew Lewis Memorial Award for Community Service, Ridgeview Neighborhood Association, 2010
- Letter of Commendation from Federal Bureau of Investigation: Joint Task Force Operation, 2002
- Letters of Commendation from Mayor's Office: Sting Operation, 1992; Project Breakdown, 2000; Joint Sting Operation—Silicon West CHP with FBI, 2002
- Community Award for Outstanding Police Dedication, San Bruno Department of Parks, Recreation, and Neighborhood Services, 2002
- Medal of Valor, San Bruno Police Department, 1991

Community Involvement

- **Latino Youth Forum:** Public Safety Task Force Committee
- **San Bruno Parks, Recreation, and Neighborhood Services:** Project Breakdown
- **SNI Richmond/Forbes—Community project dealing with neighborhood gang suppression and rebuilding:** Partnered with multiple city departments to develop and implement new police techniques to combat gang and narcotic activity. Techniques were cited in project report as desirable for use in future projects.

Military Service

U.S. Army (6 years), Honorable Discharge

---

so this special information is put conspicuously at the bottom of the first page and not buried at the end of the second page, which is sometimes a resume's boneyard. Note the use of boldfacing for emphasis on both the first and second pages.

ROBERT DAVIS CAMPBELL

555 East Lakeshore Road ▪ Whitmore Lake, MI 55555 ▪ 555.555.5555 ▪ rdcampbell@xxxx.com

POLICE CHIEF
ANN ARBOR POLICE DEPARTMENT

PROFESSIONAL PROFILE

- **Over 20-year track record as Law Enforcement Professional,** with extensive Senior Management experience, most recently as Detective Sergeant. Recognized for outstanding leadership skills with people, processes, and projects. Unwavering commitment to excellence during entire career.

- **Michigan Certified Public Manager.** Comprehensive testing followed 324 hours of training and study, including coursework in Strategic Planning, Quality Improvement, Ethics, Media Relations, Internal Investigations, Budget Management, and Problem Analysis.

- **Certified Unified Tactics Instructor.** Certified Emergency Readiness Instructor. SWAT Team member.

- **Background in policy development and implementation** for the Department, as well as in Budget Management. Working knowledge of National Incident Management System.

- **Firsthand experience in wide range of law enforcement positions,** including Patrol Sergeant, Police Detective, and Patrolman. Experience serving as Deputy Sheriff for the Dexter County Sheriff's Department.

- **Ability to guide teams and build collaboration at all levels.** President of the Michigan Sergeants Association. Coordinator of New Police Recruit Physical Ability Testing.

- **Organized and analytical,** with exemplary problem-solving skills. Sound judgment and reliability; calm and effective under high pressure and in crisis mode. Decisive, detail-oriented, and results-driven.

PROFESSIONAL EXPERIENCE

ANN ARBOR POLICE DEPARTMENT, ANN ARBOR, MI   1993–PRESENT

Detective Sergeant (2008–present)
Direct all criminal investigations, respond to each critical incident, and oversee any required internal investigations. Review reports and arrests generated by Patrol Officers. Supervise three Detectives and all related investigative processes. Conduct ongoing evaluation of staff and complete required evaluation forms.

Unified Tactics Instructor (2004–2008)
Developed, coordinated, and delivered the "Use of Force" Training used by the entire Police Department. Managed the effective organization of the information, implementation of the instruction, and proper documentation of training completed by each Officer.

Patrol Sergeant (2000–2004)
Managed all shift and patrol duties, including Dispatch Control. Oversaw all reports and arrests, and supervised adequate levels of staffing, scheduling of personnel, and allocation of resources. Directed the field training process for all new Officers.

Police Detective (1997–2000)
Conducted criminal and background investigations, and oversaw all search warrants, subpoenas, and electronic recordings.

Continued

134

Combination. *Vicki Brett-Gach, Ann Arbor, Michigan*

This Detective Sergeant was applying for the position of Police Chief in the department for which he had worked for 19 years. Boldfacing in the Professional Profile emphasizes the

PROFESSIONAL EXPERIENCE, *CONTINUED*...

Patrolman (1993–1997)
Served as Senior Field Training Officer, Shift Commander, and SWAT Team member. Performed accident investigations, and served as Crime Scene and Evidence Technician. Certified as Intoximeter Operator.

DEXTER COUNTY SHERIFF'S DEPARTMENT, DEXTER, MI   1991–1993

Deputy Sheriff
Served as SWAT Team member. Managed operations of jail facilities. Provided security and investigation assistance as the Dexter High School Officer.

EDUCATION

EASTERN MICHIGAN UNIVERSITY, YPSILANTI, MI
MASTER OF ARTS IN CRIMINAL JUSTICE (2008)

WAYNE STATE UNIVERSITY, DETROIT, MI
BACHELOR OF ARTS IN POLICE SCIENCE (1991)

CREDENTIALS

MICHIGAN CERTIFIED PUBLIC MANAGER (2012)
UNIVERSITY OF MICHIGAN

CERTIFIED UNIFIED TACTICS INSTRUCTOR (1998)
STATE OF MICHIGAN DEPARTMENT OF JUSTICE

CERTIFIED EMERGENCY READINESS INSTRUCTOR (1998)
STATE OF MICHIGAN DEPARTMENT OF JUSTICE

ADDITIONAL ADVANCED LEADERSHIP TRAINING

University of Michigan, Ann Arbor, MI
Leadership in Police Organizations (2008)

University of Michigan, Ann Arbor, MI
First-Line Supervisory Training (2008)

PROFESSIONAL AFFILIATIONS

Michigan Sergeants Association
President (current) ▪ *Vice President (former)* ▪ *Treasurer (former)*

Michigan Law Enforcement Training Officers Association
American Academy of Certified Public Managers
Michigan Society of Certified Public Managers
Force Science Training Institute
Concerns of Police Survivors

information that would be of greatest interest to those reviewing applications for the vacant position. If you start with his first departmental position of Patrolman and read "up" the resume, you can gain a better sense of the individual's promotions within the department.

CASEY JONES, CFE

23 West Point Place · Jones, MD 43533 · 555.555.5555 · cjones@xxxx.com

SENIOR-LEVEL INVESTIGATOR & SECURITY PROGRAM EXPERT

15+ years with *major computer manufacturers* and other entities leading investigations and security-prevention initiatives in Asia, Europe, South America, North America, and Australia.

Specialist in Investigating and Managing

Global Security Programs & Strategic Planning · Law Enforcement & Agency Relationships · SOX & Reporting Compliance Issues · Supply-chain Thefts · Protection of Personnel, Property & Products · Gray Market & Counterfeit Rings · Government Payoffs & Corrupt Practices · Data Collection, Analysis, Interviews & Online Research · Technology-driven Prevention & Investigation Tactics · Online Fraud Controls · Team Training Programs · Available for Travel

Career Highlights

⇒ **Recognized for recovering up to $20M in equipment through investigations of counterfeit and gray-market activities, with subsequent involvement in criminal prosecution as an expert witness.**

⇒ **Spoiled a corrupt government pay-off practice within 3 months while helping guilty parties save face—a valuable cultural business practice in the local area.**

⇒ **Foiled $1M internal expense fraud and bribery ring led by corrupt manager and two staffers.**

⇒ **Created and operated numerous fictitious broker businesses to lure corrupt product dealers and thwart counterfeit and gray-market sales.**

⇒ **Maintain key relationships with law enforcement professionals in FBI, other federal agencies, major crimes units, and police in major cities across North America.**

⇒ **Leverage technology know-how to develop online fraud controls, create globally-relevant information databases, and identify unscrupulous business practices affecting company.**

PROFESSIONAL EXPERIENCE

COPEN BROS, 2007–PRESENT
Leader in corporate investigations, training, and consulting.
U.S. · Australia · Hong Kong · India · Malaysia · Singapore · Thailand

Investigations Manager

Lead investigations and advise clients on corporate security measures that result in additional revenues, loss prevention, loss recovery, and brand protection. Currently on assignment with major technology company with damaging product security issues.

Corporate Investigations

⇒ **Fortune 500 Computer Manufacturer:** Leading comprehensive due diligence investigations of potential suppliers in Hong Kong, Singapore, Australia, Malaysia, Thailand, and India to determine civil and corporate integrity of companies and their principals; set up and manage fictitious international broker company to investigate and run undercover buys of suspected counterfeit computer peripheral products.

⇒ **Medical Records / Storage Company:** Facilitated company's 15% growth (3 new major accounts) by providing key consultative services affecting employee background checks, records protection, technology, access control measures, and alarms.

⇒ **Oil & Gas Contractor:** Ended nearly $10K theft of specialty diesel fuel with quick and direct investigation encompassing interviews with contractor's customer and staff.

⇒ **Tele-technology Company:** Recovered $100K in computer equipment and enabled criminal prosecution of individuals by probing questionable online sales and arranging buys of stolen products; took investigation from launch to conclusion within 6 weeks.

135

Combination. *Kimberly Schneiderman, New York, New York*

The writer gleaned information from the earlier part of the applicant's career—mostly what is reflected on page two—to display impressive accomplishments in the Career Highlights on page

CASEY JONES, CFE

555.555.5555 • cjones@xxxx.com

HOOPER COMPUTER CORPORATION, 2001–2007
Global supplier of computer technology.
North America • Latin America • Europe • Asia

Global Investigations Manager

Managed global internal investigations of white-collar fraud, anticounterfeit and brand protection issues, and supply-chain theft. Overhauled global investigative structure, bringing uniformity and clarity to procedures worldwide. Communicated directly with CEO, CFO, CLO, and business-unit presidents throughout tenure.

Global Investigations	⇒ Managed investigations of multimillion-dollar gray market and counterfeit rings in South China and Latin America; directed undercover product buys and served on-site during warehouse raids.
	⇒ Recovered $20M in product by ending global supply-chain theft ring encompassing cargo hijacking, armed robberies, and contractor scams; implemented ensuing loss-prevention tactics.
Program Management	⇒ Teamed with vendor to develop global integrated security reporting database and information depository to thwart criminal activity through immediate identification of questionable people and activities.
	⇒ Transformed investigation department's internal reputation from one of "rogue cop" to a strategic, prevention-focused group that worked collaboratively across business units worldwide; built strong cross-functional relationships and developed comprehensive investigation guidelines and situational decision / escalation trees.
	⇒ Initiated local community "give-back" initiative with sponsorship of the Kids Club—a charity to support education of children of fallen law enforcement officers in Houston.

YEVTEL NETWORKS, 1995–2001
Global supplier of networking and communication technology.
North America: California • Florida • Georgia • Nevada • New York • Ohio • Washington

---

Senior Advisor, Corporate Security • Advisor, Corporate Security • Security Specialist

Brought on to manage security, access controls, and investigations at 7 U.S. regional sales offices and eventually at 50+ sites across North America; aggressively promoted through ranks as direct result of strategic investigation approaches and methodologies. Worked extensively with law enforcement authorities including U.S. Attorney, FBI, Secret Service, U.S. Postal Inspection Service, and local major crimes divisions.

Investigations	⇒ Thwarted $10M+ nationwide equipment-theft ring resulting in $2M in product recoveries and 5+ convictions; led 18-month / 5-state task force; brought findings to FBI and major crimes units in New York, LA, and Seattle; and testified as expert in 2 criminal trials.
	⇒ Orchestrated investigation of internal $1M expense-claim fraud and bribery ring involving 3 staff and managers; worked closely with Dallas FBI and U.S. District Attorney for prosecution.
Program Development	⇒ Launched external professional services program to implement antitheft programs at subcontracted telephone carrier sites around U.S. with potential revenues of $300K.
	⇒ Coordinated executive protection and technical surveillance countermeasures for 4 major corporate functions annually.

EDUCATION & CERTIFICATIONS

BACHELOR OF SCIENCE, CRIMINAL JUSTICE, WEST VIRGINIA STATE UNIVERSITY

CERTIFIED FRAUD EXAMINER • NETWORK MANAGEMENT SECURITY CERTIFICATION

LICENSED PRIVATE INVESTIGATOR • REID INTERVIEW AND INTERROGATIONS—LEVEL I AND II

---

one. This resume is rich in design features, with its horizontal and vertical lines, shaded text boxes (some with frames), distinctive arrow bullets, and tables. Which of these features could you use to advantage in your resume?

LOUISA KAY ACETO

555 Water Place | Alexandria, VA | 55555 | (555) 555-5555 | LouisaKay@xxxx.com

---

STAFF ANALYST, CASE MANAGEMENT

DISPLAY COMMITMENT TO CLIENT SERVICE THROUGH DEGREE OF COMPETENCE AND STRENGTH OF CHARACTER

Expertise securing and coordinating services for clients, analyzing criminal histories, documenting research for trends and patterns, and helping the organization achieve its mission

---

Analytical, research-driven, law enforcement professional with 9 years of experience working within the criminal justice system as a peace officer and recreation therapist. Passionately engage the client in treatment process, assess client's needs, develop a service plan, link the client with appropriate services, monitor client progress, intervene with sanctions and advocate for the client when necessary. Uncover and apply best strategies to bring about faster solutions. Perform at an exceptionally high level in fast-paced environments and those reliant on structured processes and protocols. Regarded as "pinch-hitter," willing to assume on-call and backup duties for the better good of the agency.

CAREER TRACK & CONTRIBUTIONS

AXEL GOVERNMENT SOLUTIONS (currently TRINET Government Solutions)—Alexandria, VA   2012
Headquartered in Loveland, Colorado, Axel Government Solutions is a leading provider of investigative and security services to the federal government and a select group of private sector clients. Investigators: 2,000
Background Investigator. Conducted background investigations to determine employment suitability of persons who require access to sensitive and classified U.S. Government information…conducted face-to-face interviews with subject and his/her neighbors, employers, friends and family.
- Performed record searches at police agencies, courthouses, educational institutions, financial institutions and medical health facilities, and produced top-notch, clear and concise reports and summaries.

MICHIGAN HIGHWAY PATROL—Detroit, MI   9/2007–9/2011
Peace Officer. Successfully completed the Michigan Highway Patrol (MHP) Cadet Academy Training…served as a sworn peace officer…enforced Michigan state laws, vehicle regulations and penal code…investigated misdemeanor and felony violations and wrote arrest reports.
- Automated a haphazard overtime distribution process system, transforming it from chaos to order, improving efficiency and reducing time spent on allocation.
- Fairly and equitably allocated overtime to—and tracked overtime requests for—120 officers.
- Developed outstanding rapport and relationships with agents at County Jail, dramatically reducing booking times.
- Received unprecedented zero complaints in four years from convicted persons.
- Managed ad-hoc administrative receptionist duties, always portraying a professional image by phone or face-to-face.

MICHIGAN DEPARTMENT OF CORRECTIONS AND REHABILITATION—Detroit, MI   11/2002–11/2007
MICHIGAN DEPARTMENT OF MENTAL HEALTH—Detroit, MI   2/2002–11/2002
Recreation Therapist. Delivered holistic therapy to acute psychiatric inmates during one-on-one and group recreation sessions…wrote daily progress reports on all inmates in treatment center…acted as first therapist on staff at substance abuse treatment facility as part of a treatment team that included a psychiatrist, psychologist, licensed clinical social worker and registered nurse…developed and implemented treatment plans for recipients.
- Wrote and implemented policies and protocol manual for recreation therapy services to be administered at facility, and educated team on necessity of procedure, still in place today.

FORMAL EDUCATION

2 years of graduate coursework completed in Public Health (2004) – Michigan State University, East Lansing, MI

B.S. in Recreation Administration, Therapeutic Recreation option (2001)
Michigan State University, East Lansing, MI

136

Combination. *Laura Labovich, Bethesda, Maryland*

The prominent shaded text box makes this resume immediately different from most other resumes. Boldfacing helps to make the applicant's various positions stand out.

Management

Resumes at a Glance

*C*ollins Mackey

5th Street • Centereach, NY 55555 • (555) 444-2222

OFFICE MANAGER

Bringing 25+ Years of Office Administration and Full-charge Bookkeeping Experience as Follows:

◆ Accounts Payable / Receivable	◆ Expense Control	◆ Human Resources Management
◆ Weekly Payroll	◆ Account Management	◆ Staff Training and Supervision
◆ Credit and Collections	◆ Account Reconciliation	◆ Customer Service / Client Relations
◆ Statement Billings	◆ Month-end Closings	◆ Computerized Processes

PROFESSIONAL EXPERIENCE—*Overview*

Recognized throughout longstanding career for ability to develop, implement, and manage full-charge, computerized bookkeeping functions while overseeing multifaceted office administration procedures.

- As Office Manager for August Publications, fully manage company-wide accounting and reporting functions for five subsidiaries, as well as weekly payroll processes for 45 salaried employees.

- Liaison between senior management, employees, and clients to ensure proper lines of communication critical in addressing myriad problems and issues requiring immediate attention and resolution.

- Manage Accounts Payable/Receivable and expense-control procedures, including bank and account reconciliation, cash receipts, disbursements, finance charges, billings, invoicing, purchase order and inventory verification, chargebacks, rebates, and preparation of daily bank deposits.

- Negotiate and enforce collections to recover funds and expedite the clearance on delinquent accounts.

- Collaborate extensively with external auditors, providing in-depth assistance with periodic corporate audits.

- Perform thorough credit analyses, research financial histories, and review account status as a prerequisite to qualifying new accounts, authorizing purchases, and extending/increasing lines of credit of up to $200,000.

- Establish and maintain Human Resources–related employee files reflecting salary increases, deductions, garnishments, benefits, payroll exceptions, and W-2 withholdings, exercising a high level of confidentiality.

- Skilled at interviewing, hiring, training, and evaluating employees in areas of accounting procedures.

- Research account transactions, demonstrating a keen ability to recognize and resolve discrepancies.

- Follow through on timely and accurate month-end closings and financial reporting activities.

WORK CHRONOLOGY

Office Manager	August Publications, Hauppauge, NY	2004–present
Office Manager	Quality Insurance, Huntington, NY	1994–2004
Office Manager	DSG Management Corp., Melville, NY	1991–1993
Controller's Assistant	Georgia Interiors, Farmingdale, NY	1987–1991
Credit/Collections Supervisor	EastTel Sales Corp., New York, NY	1986–1987
Accounts Payable/Receivable Clerk	Syobel Corp., New York, NY	1981–1986

COMPUTER PROFICIENCIES

Windows XP/7; MS Word and Excel; WordPerfect; Lotus; Peachtree Accounting

EDUCATION

Bachelor of Arts, Business Management/Accounting, Banes College, 1990

137

Combination. *Ann Baehr, East Islip, New York*

The writer condenses extensive experience onto one page, using keywords, an Overview section representing many similar positions to avoid repetition, and a compact Work Chronology section.

LAURA D. WENN

899 Lancona Road
Dallas, TX 00000

(555) 555-5555
ldw56@yahoo.com

RETAIL MANAGEMENT PROFESSIONAL

Nine years of retail management experience demonstrating a consistent track record of outstanding sales, merchandising and customer service results. Equally strong qualifications in all areas of fine jewelry department operations: P&L, budgeting, inventory control, training, security and other functions. Effective communicator, leader and problem solver who builds teamwork and possesses the initiative to exceed goals.

EXPERIENCE

LAWRENCE FINE JEWELRY CORPORATION, Seattle, WA (2003–present)
Progressed rapidly from part-time position to manager at several stores, including the following:

Manager—G. Fox, Randolph Mall, Dallas, TX (2009–present)
Manager—G. Fox, Valley Mall, Phoenix, AZ (2005–2009)
Manager—G. Fox, Turner Mall, Tucson, AZ (2004–2005)
Assistant Manager—G. Fox, Forest Mall, San Antonio, TX (2003–2004)

Summary of Responsibilities

Operations Management—Hold profit and loss accountability; manage all aspects of day-to-day department performance of stores ranging from $500,000 to $2M in annual sales. Direct sales, inventory control, visual merchandising, housekeeping, security, administration and compliance to company policies/procedures. Managed 2 stores concurrently over 4-month period with highly successful sales results during busy Christmas season.

Staff Supervision & Training—Supervise teams of up to 13 fine-jewelry specialists. Experienced in recruiting, selecting, training, developing, scheduling and supervising associates. Motivate staff to achieve performance goals and ensure productive department operations.

Customer Relations & Service—Develop and manage customer relations to maximize service satisfaction, promote goodwill and generate repeat/referral business that contributes to sales growth. Monitor and resolve any service issues.

Selected Achievements

- Increased Randolph store sales from $1.1M to $1.4M (27%) in 2010 and maintained .02% shrink—well below company average of 2.1%.
- Increased percent-to-store sales at Valley Mall from 2.8% to 5.2%, surpassing company average of 2.5%. Grew annual sales at Valley Mall from $.8M in 2005 to $1.1M (37%) in 2006, $1.4M (27%) in 2007, $1.7M (21%) in 2008 and $2M (18%) in 2009.
- Selected by Regional Manager to serve as Training Store Manager for the region; recognized for the ability to recruit quality candidates who have successfully advanced with the company.

Awards

- Earned **Branch Manager of the Year** and **Branch of the Year** awards in 2010 in the Southwest Region.
- Twice named **Manager of the Year** out of 50 stores in 2008 and 2006 in the Southwest Region.
- Winner of 3 sales performance awards in 2010: **Goal Achievers, Best Increase in % to Store** and **Best Event Business. Christmas Contest** winner in 2009, exceeding sales goal by 15%.
- Selected runner up for 3 awards in 2010: **Best in Operations, Best Visual Department** and **Best Buyer Communication.** Ranked #3 in **Christmas Contest** in 2010, exceeding sales goal by 21%.

EDUCATION / PROFESSIONAL DEVELOPMENT

B.A., Retail Management, Valhalla College, Dallas, TX

Completed various company-sponsored training courses in management, personnel recruiting, staff training and development, sales, customer service and related topics.

138

Combination. *Louise Garver, Broad Brook, Connecticut*

This retail manager was applying for a position with a competitor in Arizona. She had held positions with the same responsibilities at several stores. To eliminate repetition, the writer summarized key duties.

marlene weist

Administrative / Accounting Support

PROFESSIONAL PROFILE

Conscientious and detail-oriented with solid training in accounting and practical knowledge of business operations, administrative support, office procedures, and problem solving. Bilingual (English and Spanish).

* Proven ability to manage multiple projects simultaneously and continuously streamline processes and procedures.
* Exceptionally well organized with well-developed verbal and written communication skills.
* Computer literate (PCs and Macs). Thoroughly familiar with database management systems, flowcharting, and entity-relationship diagramming. Advanced proficiency with Microsoft Word, Excel, PowerPoint, and Access; QuickBooks; and Quicken.

EXPERIENCE

WASCO & COMPANY, LTD.—Seattle, Washington
Office Manager / Executive Assistant (2007–Present)
Provide administrative and accounting support to owners of closely held corporation and numerous affiliated companies (i.e., three investment companies, two property-management companies, and a small-business investment corporation).

* Handle accounts-payable functions for seven companies.
* Prepare reports and reconcile checking and money-market accounts.
* Work closely with office manager and in-house CPA to streamline accounts payable and accounts receivable.
* Initiated the complete reorganization of a complex, out-of-date filing system.

DAYMON ASSOCIATES, INC.—Tualatin, Oregon
Administrative Assistant (2005–2006)
Coordinated office staff of 16, maintained files, managed records, and oversaw employee scheduling.

* Worked with buyers to place orders.
* Interfaced with vendors, coordinated product shipping, and resolved vendor and customer problems.
* Functioned as liaison between Tualatin office and the Idaho-based warehousing facility.

EDUCATION

WASHINGTON STATE UNIVERSITY—Seattle, Washington
Post-Baccalaureate Accounting Certificate (2006)
Course work: Accounting Information Systems, Intermediate / Advanced Financial Accounting, Introductory / Advanced Taxation, Auditing Concepts and Practices, Management Accounting, Business Law

ADDITIONAL PROFESSIONAL DEVELOPMENT
Introduction to Investments, Portland Community College (Fall 2004)
Practical Bookkeeping, Elliott Bookkeeping School (Summer 2005)

PERSONAL

Climbed all three mountains in the South Sister Wilderness Area.
Willing to relocate.

CONTACT ME

m-weist@careerfolio.com

139

Combination. *Pat Kendall, Tigard, Oregon*

This e-resume, taken from the Web, has adequate white space as blank lines between main sections and their parts, giving an uncluttered look and making each part easy to see and read. The hyperlink in the Contact Me section is easy for a potential employer to click and use to set up an interview.

Victoria Chamberlain

5441 Sycamore Lane
St. Louis, MO 00000

(000) 000-0000
vchamberlain@aol.com

CAREER PROFILE

15+ Years of Diversified Experience and Documented Contributions in Office Management, Human Resources, and Insurance Disciplines

Dedicated, quality-focused professional offering strong qualifications in office administration, service delivery, personnel affairs, and insurance-related activities, including claims adjustment and customer service. Precise, detail-oriented worker with proven skill in managing large volumes of information and facilitating multiple tasks in deadline-driven environment. Sound judgment and decision-making skills. Recognized at every step of career path for positive attitude and work effort; maintain highest professional ethics and standards.

Core Competencies:

Workflow Planning and Prioritization

▪ ▪ ▪

Time and Resource Optimization

▪ ▪ ▪

Regulatory Compliance Filing and Recordkeeping

▪ ▪ ▪

Team Member Training and Mentoring

▪ ▪ ▪

Service Quality Improvement

▪ ▪ ▪

Customer Needs Assessment

▪ ▪ ▪

Quality Control Standards

▪ ▪ ▪

Loan Administration

▪ ▪ ▪

Budget Management

▪ ▪ ▪

Creative Problem Solving

▪ ▪ ▪

Interviewing, Hiring, and Retention

▪ ▪ ▪

Public Presentations

RELEVANT EXPERIENCE

COUNTY EXECUTIVE DIRECTOR, 1999–2011
**X County FSA Office ▪ Y County FSA Office
Z County FSA Office ▪ A County FSA Office (trainee)**

Amassed track record of results spanning more than 10 years of management in a government-funded agency supporting local farmers and producers. Scope of responsibility included program management, staffing and training, community and Board of Director meetings, loan administration, quality assurance, and regulatory compliance in deadline-driven environment.

Continually monitored member and staff activities, identifying and analyzing key financial data and performance indicators, applying cost-benefit analysis to decisions, and demonstrating strong understanding of organizational missions and capabilities.

Drove achievement of organizational goals
❑ Projected confidence and took decisive steps to achieve objectives.
❑ Kept efficiency levels high and produced consistently top results, earning recognitions for exemplary performance:
  - **Finished regularly in top 10 among 100+ counties statewide in timely, on-target payment submissions.**
  - **Earned consistent recognition from State of Missouri for efforts in establishing and maintaining excellent operations.**

Provided excellent service to program recipients
❑ Wrote newsletters, press releases, and other informational materials to keep farmers/producers abreast of new developments.
❑ Implemented emergency procedures to aid program members during disaster/crisis events. Authorized loan extensions in special situations.

Motivated and contributed to enhanced team performance
❑ Trained and mentored staff through series of changes from manual to automated systems, engaging in one-on-one training to ease transition.
❑ Selected to train State of Missouri employees based on crop insurance and appraisal knowledge.

Continued

140

Combination. *Daniel J. Dorotik Jr., Lubbock, Texas*

The shaded box displaying core competencies is eye-catching and draws attention to important keywords. The Career Profile and Relevant Experience sections offset the Other Experience section, which is silent about the dates of the person's earlier jobs. Bulleted accomplishments for

Victoria Chamberlain   vchamberlain@aol.com   **Page Two**

OTHER EXPERIENCE

Federal Crop Insurance Corporation ■ *St. Louis, MO*

CONTRACT CLAIMS ADJUSTER/FIELD SUPERVISOR

Hired as field representative in charge of appraising crops and determining cause of loss on per-situation basis, earning promotion within two years to oversee all job assignments, recruit and train new employees, review insurance claims, and make final determinations on courses of action. Managed adjusting activities over multicounty territory and assigned losses to field staff. Addressed and resolved customer issues, including management of complex claims resolutions. Worked in tandem with Underwriting Department.

<u>Accomplishments:</u>

- Earned appointment as District Reviewer covering entire district area, with responsibility for employee reviews, random loss claims, and assistance with unusual/controversial claims.
- Built strong, sustainable relationships with farmers and producers by providing excellent service while protecting company interests and bottom line.
- Developed advanced abilities in analyzing and tracking claims results, pinpointing and correcting deficiencies, and delivering presentations to management regarding evaluations.
- Built loyal, top-performing staff through prudent hiring decisions and ongoing training initiatives.

ABC Insurance Company ■ *St. Louis, MO*

PROGRAM ASSISTANT

- Assessed program compliance and worked directly with customers to answer questions and solve small- and large-scale problems.
- Fulfilled various objectives in filing, mail/courier services, and general office duties.

PROFESSIONAL DEVELOPMENT

Professional Development Coursework:

- ❑ Executive Director Management Training, Parts I and II
- ❑ Time Management/Stress Management
- ❑ EEO/Civil Rights Training
- ❑ Farm Loan Training
- ❑ Federal Crop Insurance
- ❑ Certified Appraiser—All Crops
- ❑ Instructor & Sales Training

Computer Skills:

MS Word and Windows, WordPerfect, proprietary applications, PC and mainframe computer systems

these experiences, however, are signs of management potential. Note in the Relevant Experience section the underlined statements about achievement, service, and teamwork. Because this person lacked a college degree, the resume writer chose to use a Professional Development section instead of a more-standard Education section to end the resume.

MELINDA FORMAN

7765 Hazel Lane
(555) 555-5555 Portland, OR 00000 mforman@hotmail.com

NONPROFIT MANAGEMENT PROFESSIONAL

Operations/Project Management: Proven record in conceiving and transmitting vision into reality, mission into action and philosophy into practice. Strategic planning expertise combines with dynamic leadership, resulting in the efficient operation of organizational programs. Focused problem solver who identifies organizational needs and delivers effective solutions on time and under budget in both nonprofit and business environments.

Human Resources/Training: Recruiting, mentoring and supervising staff in the delivery of quality programs. Creation and facilitation of staff development, leadership training and other workshops. Adept at fostering cooperation and building successful cross-functional team relationships at all levels in multicultural environments.

Fiscal & Grant Management: Planning and administration of all financial and budgeting activities related to program operations, including preparation of audits and financial reports as well as securing grant funding.

Program Development/Community Relations: Experienced in designing and managing innovative programs that achieve organizational goals. Effective in developing community partnerships and building awareness for organizational activities/events through public relations, fundraising and outreach efforts.

CONSULTING EXPERIENCE

FORMAN GROUP, Portland, OR
Independent Contractor/Consultant (2005–present)

Consult with companies to provide expertise in the areas of strategic planning, training and development, operations, information technology, sales and customer service. **Major Engagements:**

♦ **Lane-Brown Consulting Group:** Designed content and facilitated various sales training programs for management-level personnel of client companies in diverse industries. Created templates and developed processes for core consulting projects; designed and implemented e-business website to market organizational development products. Contributed to development and design of human resources policy and procedural manuals.

♦ **McKenzie Worldwide:** As consultant/liaison with 500+ staff members of the Business Consulting Practice, provided strategic planning for technology projects, including ongoing technical support coordination, research, resolution of high-end customer issues and continuous improvement. Contributed to development of an effective implementation process to assess resource requirements, communications and accountability procedures.

♦ **First Bank:** Provided leadership support for an online banking project and trained 12 project managers on desktop tools; maintained and authored key project database; maintained and audited $250,000 in asset inventory. Assisted in defining project scope, scheduling of resources and cost controlling.

♦ **Morris Corporation:** Contributed technical support and project management capabilities to ITS Group Field Engineering, Professional Services and Sales. Effectively defined project scope, scheduled resources and controlled costs. Produced key documents: critical path analysis, project implementation plans and fault escalation procedures.

NONPROFIT MANAGEMENT EXPERIENCE

TJ CHILDREN'S ASSOCIATION, Portland, OR
Program Director (2004–2005)

Provided strategic planning and leadership in the administration of youth programs for boys and girls ages 5–18 of diverse multicultural backgrounds. Scope of responsibilities included operations, human resources, financial/grant management, program development, fundraising, facilities, marketing, public relations and community outreach. Recruited, trained and supervised staff of 10. Managed $300,000 annual budget. **Key accomplishments:**

♦ Initiated and implemented innovative programs such as anger management, diversity awareness, book club, boys' programs, coed programs and girls' program incorporating health/fitness, self-esteem and related themes.
♦ Led successful efforts in preparation for American Camping Association Accreditation; managed programs that surpassed all governmental standards.
♦ Redesigned, revitalized and expanded a floundering day-camp program, increasing attendance to 400 participants.
♦ Built a cohesive team environment through training, staff/leadership development and diversity initiatives.
♦ Wrote grants and secured funding from a variety of private and governmental resources for new programming.

♦ Continued ♦

141

Combination. *Louise Garver, Broad Brook, Connecticut*

This person had started a consulting business so that she could control her hours while raising children. Now that they were in school, she wanted to return to nonprofit management. Her original four-page resume listed every short-term consulting assignment and buried nonprofit

CAMP ROSEN, Portland, OR
Program Director (2002–2004)

Initially managed the 8-week residential camp program and subsequently selected for the Program Director position to increase minority participation and staffing as well as design and manage day-camp program. Directed all aspects of approximately 50 youth programs annually serving 1,100 girls of all economic and social backgrounds. Accountable for program design, development and delivery, staff recruitment and training, and day-to-day management of facilities and operations. Program specialty areas included HIV/AIDS training for adults and youths and life skills planning. Community outreach efforts included public relations and presentations to various groups. Managed $250,000 annual budget. Ensured continuing accreditation with local, state and camping associations. **Key accomplishments:**

- Designed and implemented leadership training program for teenage girls; program included mentoring and job skills training.
- Expanded the introduction of innovative programs in health and safety, HIV/AIDS awareness, environmental education, conflict resolution, recreational and others.
- Succeeded in building minority staffing by 50% and minority campers by 75% through active recruitment efforts. Designed and delivered training to national and international teams. Infused troops with new program options.
- Produced public relations and recruiting materials; researched and authored articles on current issues affecting girls, which were published in area newspapers.
- Member of fund-raising council, planning and coordinating annual event generating $200,000.

PORTLAND YOUTH CENTER, Portland, OR
Program Director (2000–2002)
Assistant Program Director (1999–2000)
Village Director (1995–1997)

Joined organization while attending college and promoted through series of progressively responsible management positions to direct summer camp for 200 urban youth. Recruited, mentored and trained team of 60 multicultural staff members in all aspects of program operations. Responsible for fiscal management, marketing, community outreach, program development and other functions. Supervised, tracked and monitored program activities. Developed and coordinated administrative policies, procedures and controls. Administered $500,000 annual budget.
Key accomplishments:

- Initiated and facilitated organization's first leadership training and several other programs for boys and girls, including opening programs for physically challenged individuals.
- Increased year-round programming and boosted participation in leadership training and camping programs.
- Worked closely with the Board of Directors on strategic planning, program direction and funding. Partnered with community groups and social service agencies in services administration throughout the year.
- Recruited numerous volunteers as member of Board of Directors to serve on special committees of the American Camping Association.

EDUCATION

B.S. in Sociology, University of Oregon, Portland, OR, 1997
Participated in study-abroad programs in South America, France and Italy.

Additional:

Completed Camp Training courses
Previously certified to teach CPR/First Aid courses

COMPUTER & OTHER SKILLS

Microsoft Office suite (Word, Excel, PowerPoint), Microsoft Project
Foreign-language skills: Conversational Spanish and French

experience at the end. She looked like a job hopper and was getting no interviews. The writer created a two-page resume that put nonprofit experience first. The person received multiple job offers within two months.

9727 Sunrise Avenue, Philadelphia, PA 00000

Home: (000) 000-0001
Cell: (000) 000-0002

Barbara Lindsey

E-mail: lindseyb@taskforce21.org

Executive Profile

Offering more than 20 years of broad-based management advisory experience, combining administrative, sales, and marketing skills in challenging multitasking environments. Successful in utilizing a consultative approach to access key decision makers or benefactors, network effectively, and create synergistic relationships. Excel in focusing the efforts of diverse groups to work toward common goals. Strong ability to plan and organize high-level business affairs while maintaining efficient control of financial and human resources. Areas of expertise include

- Program design, development, and implementation
- Project management
- Staff training and team leadership
- Special event planning and management
- Scheduling, logistics, and detail coordination
- Negotiations and contracting
- Public relations

- Budget development, allocation, and monitoring
- Community outreach
- Proposal and grant writing
- Fundraising and promotional campaigns
- Policy and procedure implementation
- Public speaking and presentation delivery
- Computer literacy

Professional Experience

PHILADELPHIA IN THE 21ST CENTURY TASK FORCE at Rutgers Camden Law School   2007–Present
A public and privately funded task force of civic leaders drawn from the professional, philanthropic, cultural, and social sectors of the metropolitan region, established to evaluate Philadelphia's strengths, assess its role in the regional economy, and articulate a vision of the city in the decades ahead.

Director of Community Development

- Joined the Task Force in its early stages as an Assistant to the Executive Director. Assigned to special project to coordinate a dinner meeting for 26 prominent attendees from the fields of healthcare, education, foundations, and community development, which culminated in the establishment of a Board of Directors.

- Successfully accomplished this initial effort and demonstrated further abilities to manage the day-to-day affairs of the Task Force, freeing executive's time to focus on organization development strategies. After 3 months, was promoted to Administrative Director.

- Took charge of all planning and details for subsequent monthly Task Force meetings as well as workshops, seminars, dinners, and related activities, all within very tight lead times.

- Carried out primary mission of the Task Force in directing compilation of an inventory of City of Philadelphia assets, designed to attract future investors in the city's economic development. Managed student interns who assisted in completing this large-scale project within a $250,000 budget and 18-month timeline.

- Produced the *Directory of City Assets* book, which the Task Force made available and distributed as a public service to libraries, educational institutions, businesses, and cultural organizations throughout the City of Philadelphia.

- As representative of the Task Force, conveyed a professional image and played a critical role in fulfillment of its goals by chairing or participating in several advisory committees within the community. These included the Regional Plan Association, Philadelphia Arts Council, United Way of Greater Philadelphia, and Rutgers Camden Law School.

- Sat on the Advisory Board of the Northeast Regional Economic Development Conference to plan for its being hosted in Philadelphia in 2011.

(Continued)

Combination. *Melanie Noonan, Woodland Park, New Jersey*

A "different" font (Lucida Handwriting) for the individual's name and for centered headings sets the tone for this resume. Comments about the current workplace are in italic and draw

Barbara Lindsey   lindseyb@taskforce21.org   Page 2

WEBBER AGENCY, Camden, NJ   2003–2007

Employee Benefits Consultant

- Consulted and acted on behalf of the client companies to analyze health benefits, perform cost comparisons, and recommend solutions to lower employer costs. Maintained a book of business that included nonprofit agencies, state-funded Community Action programs/day care centers, and municipalities.

- Represented University Health Plans, the HMO of the University of Medicine and Dentistry of New Jersey (UMDNJ) in its initiative to expand from Medicare only to a commercial managed-care company. Implemented strategy that facilitated introduction of the plan to a large corporation, a large financial institution, and county government.

- Served as codirector for the State Health Benefits open enrollment, coordinated special events, and developed marketing strategies for on-site campaigns and health fairs in conjunction with local hospitals.

COMED HMO, Philadelphia, PA   1997–2003

Marketing Manager/Senior Account Executive, New Jersey and Eastern Pennsylvania

- Increased new business and expanded existing customer base throughout the state of New Jersey and was promoted to Philadelphia corporate office after 3 months. Managed a staff of 22 in the sale of group health insurance to commercial accounts as well as the sales efforts of account executives, service representatives, and telemarketing staff to increase market share and obtain sales goals.

- Increased existing business by 150% through restructuring former market strategies and improving customer service.

- Successfully led the marketing department to attain sales quota and meet budget for the first time in 6 years.

- In conjunction with the Director of Marketing: Developed and implemented marketing policies and procedures; designed and delivered sales training modules that became procedure for all new hires; conducted presentation skills training for all field sales representatives.

CUSTOM INFORMATION SOFTWARE, Haverford, PA   1995–1997

Sales Supervisor/Field Sales Training Coordinator

- Hired as sales representative and promoted within 9 months after increasing territory 50% through new business with accounts such as QVM, Parsons Corp., and Columbia National.

- Supervised a staff of 5 in marketing IBM mainframe software education seminars to data processing personnel. Trained and acted as consultant to 20 sales representatives on sales techniques.

- Conducted internal sales training, which consisted of formal instruction sessions and interactive workshops, including team building, assertiveness training, and listening skills.

GLK CONSULTANTS, Princeton, NJ   1992–1995

Account Representative

- As consultant to the data processing industry, marketed systems/applications to programmers and support personnel.

Education

UNIVERSITY OF ROCHESTER, Rochester, NY   B.A. Psychology, 1992

---

attention. Bullets point to important information: first, the areas of expertise in the Executive Profile, and then the achievements in the Professional Experience section. Achievements are presented for each of the workplaces. Small caps highlight workplace names and the university's name.

KATHERINE RANDALL

5555 S.W. 55th Circle	www.careerfolio.com/krandall	Cell 555-555-5555
San Diego, California 97334		krandall@careerfolio.com

AWARD-WINNING PRODUCER, WRITER, DIRECTOR
video • television • radio

PROFILE

Nine years of combined experience in studio / location shooting, broadcast programming, production troubleshooting, marketing, promotional planning, and contract negotiation. Solid network of film industry contacts and up-to-date knowledge of industry trends, events, and key film festivals.

Core Skills:

- **Production Management:**
  Business-savvy project manager with proven ability to supervise large film crews, coordinate complex production schedules, and manage budgets up to $100,000. Successful at managing simultaneous media / video projects and troubleshooting pre- and postproduction problems.

- **Public Relations:**
  Enthusiastic spokesperson. Accustomed to functioning as production liaison to community leaders, city bureaus, government agencies, neighborhood associations, and local businesses.

- **Filmmaking / Video Editing:**
  Expertise in studio and location lighting and layered audio design. Skilled at creating studio sets and directing the use of camera dollies, butterflies, lighting cookies, camera cranes, studio lighting grids, and other high-end video production equipment.

- **Advanced Computer Skills:**
  AVID Media Composer, Photoshop, Dreamweaver, Flash, AfterEffects, InDesign, Word, Excel, and PowerPoint.

EXPERIENCE

GRANTREE PRODUCTIONS—San Diego, California

Senior Media Production Manager (2007–Present)
Produce and package public relations and marketing messages for mass media production company. Coordinate concurrent mass media and video production projects.

- Supervise professional production crews and on-camera talent.
- Coordinate subcontractors in the television studio and during location shoots.
- Serve as senior consultant to government, nonprofit, and commercial accounts.
- Develop and execute media plans for TV, radio, and print campaigns.
- Function as chief scriptwriter, producer, and director for all major news, documentary, public relations, and marketing communication projects (video, radio, Internet / Web).
- Create and manage line-item media production budgets.
- Prepare and present bids and budgets for government contract work.

(Continued)

143

Combination. *Pat Kendall, Tigard, Oregon*

A pair of lines encloses the contact information, making it easy to reference this information at a glance. Large, left-aligned headings mark the resume's main sections, making evident its

EXPERIENCE *(Continued)*

FREELANCE FILM PRODUCTION—Phoenix, Arizona
Art Director / Project Manager (2003–2007)
Representative Projects:

- Managed $75,000 Art Department budget on location in Phoenix.

- Supervised crew of 28. Negotiated salaries, coordinated scheduling, and resolved complex production problems.

- Functioned as a liaison to community representatives and local law enforcement to ensure trouble-free shooting and compliance with contract and permit requirements.

- Provided technical and creative support for several high-profile movie projects in conjunction with the Arizona Film / Television Advisory Council.

- Served as a point of contact for 22 people working under a 5-month television filming deadline.

- Oversaw wardrobe, property department, and set decorating.

- Maintained full-scale offices to support three departments.

AWARDS

FIRST-PLACE WINNER—San Diego Regional Video Competition
Professional Video / Short Drama Category: *Fear of Flying*

AUDIENCE CHOICE AWARD—Chicago Film Festival
Most Powerful Film of the Festival: *Renaissance Women*

EDUCATION

PORTLAND STATE UNIVERSITY—Portland, Oregon
Master of Arts, Mass Communication (2009)

ALBANY COLLEGE—Albany, New York
Bachelor of Arts, Communication (2007)
Emphasis: Film and Television Production

MONTANA STATE UNIVERSITY—Bozeman, Montana
Film and Video Production (2002–2004)

COLUMBIA COLLEGE—Chicago, Illinois
Art History / Theatre Design (2002)

AFFILIATIONS

AMPA—Arizona Media Production Association

overall design. Boldfacing helps the applicant's core skills, positions, and academic degrees stand out. Square bullets on both pages unify the resume visually, and plenty of white space makes the resume uncluttered throughout. Some small caps give the resume class.

JACKSON BRAUN

3000 Peak Vista Drive • Dallas, TX 55555 • Home: (000) 000-0000 • Cell: (000) 000-0001
jbraun@bmail.com

EXECUTIVE PROFILE

Successful executive with 22 years of proven success in revitalizing failing business units. Proven career record of producing multimillion-dollar profits through pinpointing operational inefficiencies and encouraging the revitalization of employee morale and corporate culture change. Possess solid understanding of food distribution industry in diverse markets and cultures, including profit and loss, market analysis, operations analysis, and logistics. Demonstrated ability to communicate business principles to distribution center personnel on all levels in order to facilitate change and initiate turnaround. Expertise in

◈ Cost Reductions   ◈ Profit Generation   ◈ Strategic Planning

◈ Distribution Management   ◈ Process Redesign   ◈ Multisite Operations

◈ Operations Start-Up   ◈ Multilevel Communications   ◈ Sales/Market Growth

CAREER EXPERIENCE

CST CORPORATION   2008–PRESENT
DIVISIONAL DIRECTOR OF OPERATIONS, Houston, TX
Recruited for abilities to successfully revitalize failing business units. Currently responsible for more than $1 billion in annual sales from Fort Worth, Oklahoma City, and San Diego facilities. Accountable for all P&L, equipment, utilities, personnel, and operating procedures. Directed overhaul from the ground up of San Diego distribution center, including bringing warehouse, offices, refrigeration, and transportation facilities up to code and fully staffing the center. Mobilized correction of gross inefficiencies in Oklahoma City and Fort Worth facilities, resulting in quick turnarounds. Facilities currently maintain monthly profits.

◈ Launched San Diego distribution center and built into a profit-producing facility within 3 months.

◈ Reduced substantial losses at Oklahoma City distribution center of $6 million per year to generating a profit within 3 months. Cost per case drastically fell 85–90 cents per case—excluding marketing monies—resulting in $8+ million turnaround (running rate).

◈ Directed operational changes in Fort Worth center, resulting in cost per case drastically falling from $2.35 per case to $1.80 per case, with $5+ million gain in profits realized in 4 months (running rate).

GALLEY'S FOOD SERVICE, INC.   2004–2008
GENERAL MANAGER, Lincoln, NE
Recruited to modernize operations in return for potential significant equity position. Restructured business financially and reorganized personnel. Monitored P&L and administered daily supervision of staff. Developed strong relationships with key accounts. Boosted bottom-line profitability in order to strengthen personal purchasing position.

◈ Achieved notable increase in profits, including a 60% increase in 2005, a 26% increase in 2006, and an 11% increase in 2007. (All profits are EBIT.)

(continued)

144

Combination. *Michele Angello, Aurora, Colorado*

Unique dot-in-a-diamond bullets point to areas of expertise in the Executive Profile and to accomplishments in the Career Experience section. Horizontal lines enclosing section

jbraun@bmail.com   **JACKSON BRAUN** (Page 2)   **Cell: (000) 000-0001**

CAREER EXPERIENCE (continued)

NAUTILUS FOOD SERVICE, INC.   2000–2004
DIVISION PRESIDENT, Sioux City, IA
- ◈ Initiated operational changes within one year that revitalized Sioux City center from 7-year record of losses to $350,000 EBIT in fiscal 2002.

BEST FOODSERVICE, INC.   1991–2000
DIVISION PRESIDENT, Boca Raton, FL
EXECUTIVE VICE PRESIDENT, Baltimore, MD
Accountable for all P&L and administration of all personnel, including sales, procurement, marketing, operations, customer service, finance, transportation, and warehouse staff. Directed $450 million distribution center with 1,350 employees, overseeing sales, procurement, and marketing.
- ◈ In 1994/95, transformed Schmidt acquisition with 9 straight years of losses to a turnaround of $250,000 EBIT, an overall gain of $1 million.
- ◈ Negotiated additional $1.2 million in additional EBIT through fourth-quarter vendor buy-in conference.

EDUCATION

University of Notre Dame, Notre Dame, IN
Executive M.B.A. Program. Accepted into exclusive program; completed 8-week course prior to acceptance of Best promotion and transfer.

University of Houston, Houston, TX
Best Management School, 1991

Ivy League University, East Coast, PA
Bachelor of Arts, Business Administration
  Honors—Received full scholarship for music and sports. Varsity baseball, Captain; Theta Delta Chi, President and Treasurer; All-Conference Outfielder, State of Pennsylvania; Recruiter and Mixed Quartet member.

HONORS & AWARDS

CST Corporation, Distribution Company of the Year—2011
Best Foodservice, Branch of the Year—1999
Nautilus Food Service, Highest Margin and Highest Sales Gross—Attained awards 11 out of 12 months
Galley's Food Service, National Sales Award
Numerous Sales Awards

headings make the overall layout easy to see. The writer uses a larger font size (12 points) for the text in the Executive Profile to make that information stand out from the resume's other information (at 11 points). Note that all the achievements are quantified in some way.

MICHAEL MANN

5499 Greenland Place • Columbus, Ohio 43227
Home: 614-374-9786 • Cellular: 614-554-1321 • E-mail: mikemann@copper.net

PLANT OPERATIONS • PRODUCTION MANAGEMENT

AREAS OF STRENGTH & EXPERTISE

• OSHA Compliance	• Productivity Improvement	• Startup/Turnaround
• P&L Responsibility	• Staff/Union Oversight & Development	• Recruiting/Staffing
• Project Management	• Toyota Production Systems	• Inventory Management
• 5S Philosophy	• Manpower/Production Forecasting	• Plant Reorganization
• Kanban	• Government/Military Compliance	• Lean Manufacturing
• Kaizen Events	• OSHA Regulations/EPA Regulations	• ISO 9000 and QS 9000
• Union Negotiations	• Budgeting & Expense Reports	• Production Engineering
• Employee Relations	• Union-Free Management	• Expense Control
• Contract Negotiations	• Strategic Planning & Initiatives	• C/N/C and N/C Machines
• Quality Control	• Policy/Procedure Development	• Performance Evaluations
• Time Management	• Contract Review/Recommendation	• Vendor Negotiations

CAREER HIGHLIGHTS

- **Appointed by VP of North American Operations as point person to spearhead launch of assembly plants with new product lines supplying Big 3 automotive manufacturers.** Seamlessly started new assembly facility in Oberlin, Ohio, and received accolades from customer, Ford Motor Co. **Operations Manager ... Jackson Industries**

- **As 5th leader in 7 years, took plant from break-even to $7.5 million on $57 million in gross sales.** Increased profitability from $4.5 million to $6.7 million in 12 months and improved profitability from 6.5% ROI in 2000 to 11.1% ROI in 2001 and 10% in 2002. **Production Manager ... Dominic Company**

- **Increased operating profits to more than $4 million in 2006 and set operating income records eclipsing 20% after assuming plant with operating loss in 2003.** Brought plant to profitability via knowledge of Lean Toyota Production System, 5S, and Kaizen continuous improvement programs, along with extremely close watch on waste affected by scrap, rework, poor productivity, and poor quality. **Plant Manager ... Princess Productions**

PROFESSIONAL EXPERIENCE

JACKSON INDUSTRIES ... Grove City, Ohio   August 2007 to Present
Second-largest bedding manufacturer in U.S.; privately held company employs more than 2,500 people and operates 18 plants in U.S. and Puerto Rico. Operation is 1 of 18 plants nationwide and second-highest in sales.

Operations Manager
Administer entire scope of operations and profit/loss outcomes throughout $60 million, 180,000-square-foot facility supported by approximately 240 union employees (facility serves 6 Midwest states). Brought in to turn around performance and improve operating culture throughout production floor. Develop and administer capital and operating budgets.

Direct reports include supervisors and management throughout production, quality, shipping and receiving, purchasing, customer service, and HR. Circulate floor to oversee and ensure productivity expectations, expense controls, quality output, equipment/facilities maintenance, safety/sanitation/security, shipping/delivery, and inventory.

- **During tenure, plant set operating income records with percentages at 21% for several months.** Brought accountability, quality, safety, communications, and supervision, elevating plant to second-place ranking out of 18 plants.

145

Combination. *Janice Worthington, Columbus, Ohio*

Three columns of bulleted keywords under Areas of Strength & Expertise eliminate the need for an opening summary. A reader who looks favorably at the keywords may be more likely to read

MICHAEL MANN

- **Improved on-time delivery to 97% from 60% by developing scanning procedures.** Customer delivery improvements ultimately resulted in elevated customer satisfaction.

- **Reduced 2007 incident rate more than 36% over 2008.** Facilitated reduction after working with Bureau of Workers' Compensation on testing/survey of safety perception and received **$50,000** grant from BWC to improve ergonomic opportunities throughout operation.

- **Facilitated progression of operations with implementation of 5S philosophy (Sort, Set in Order, Shine, Standardize, and Sustain—essential in lean manufacturing structure).** Also implemented one-piece flow versus batch system.

PRINCESS PRODUCTIONS ... Ada, Ohio   November 2003 to July 2007

Sheet metal fabrication facility specializing in welding, painting, and assembly of product, supplying Big 3 automotive manufacturers as well as telecommunications industry.

Plant Manager

Oversaw operations and administered $50 million profit/loss performance in 225,000-square-foot tier-one lean manufacturing facility supported by 325 unionized hourly and 25 administrative associates. Hired and mentored staff and directed management throughout manufacturing, quality assurance, research and development/tool and die, materials, maintenance, and paint line systems departments. Supervised production; quality; research and development; ISO 9000, QS 9000, and NQA audits; supply procurement; shipping; and facilities maintenance. Also performed plant reengineering and vendor sourcing. Contributed to JD Edwards conversion.

- **Amidst business growth and increased production demands, hired and trained 75 associates (bringing total to 325) in 6 months.** Also established standards for new hires.

- **Successfully guided plant through QS & ISO 9000 compliance subsequent to departure by quality manager.** At time of hire, plant was going through QS 9000 audit and immediately drafted procedures and policies vital to certification. **Pivotal in 3 successful ISO 9000, QS 9000, and NQA audits.**

- **Appointed by president to attend Ashland University, recognized in top echelon nationwide for lean manufacturing colleges.** Education facilitated implementation of lean/cellular manufacturing, one-piece flow systems, and several innovations to aid production.

DOMINIC COMPANY ... Rochester, New York   June 1998 to June 2003

Global market leader in automotive systems and facility management and control.

Production Manager

Assigned to new facility to ensure operations performance throughout 150,000-square-foot tier-one JIT manufacturing and assembly facility grossing approximately $1.5 million monthly. Operating in extremely fast-paced and mistake-free environment, supplied seating for Ford Econoline Van, with product installed within 4 hours of production. Responsible for performance and development of 2 superintendents, 6 supervisors, and more than 200 nonunion employees; directed quality control, shipping, and receiving, as well as equipment and facilities maintenance and safety. **Promoted from Product Line Manager and Shift Superintendent.**

- **Instrumental in seamless setup and layout of 3 new JIT manufacturing facilities with nearly 1 million square feet of production and warehousing space.** Contributed to equipment purchase and ergonomics; hired and trained employees; and established standard process controls for assembly operation, including fixturing, robotic welding, and fabricating.

- **Worked in concert with Ford engineers, addressing continuous-improvement processes, industrial engineering, and resolution of quality-control issues.** Frequently visited Ford plant, established/maintained relations with all organizational levels, and maintained knowledge of Ford Q1 inspection process and ISO 9000.

EDUCATION

ASHLAND UNIVERSITY ... Ashland, Ohio
Candidate: Master of Business Administration, 2012

MOREHEAD STATE UNIVERSITY ... Morehead, Kentucky
Bachelor of Science in Industrial Technology, 1992 (GPA 3.2)

and absorb the details in the Career Highlights and Professional Experience sections. The strategy of beginning with an extensive list of keywords is worth considering for someone with many years of work experience. Lines help define the resume's main sections.

AVAILABLE FOR RELOCATION

John Savage
maintenance reliability engineer

1000 State Drive
Memphis, Tennessee 38100
901.555.5555—js1@tide.net

"Your contribution over the past 10 years has been a key factor to our success."
— Site General Manager

"Finding a better way to do something is what helps us become the best in the business."
— Production Manager and Maintenance Manager

WHAT I CAN OFFER TopLine

❏ Moving maintenance from a cost center to a **productivity center** as well ❏ Getting the right information to the right people in time to **save money and boost production** ❏ **Building and motivating teams** who think of my suggestions as their own good ideas ❏ Solving the right problems—the first time ❏ **Forging "success partnerships" with vendors**

RECENT WORK HISTORY WITH EXAMPLES OF PROBLEMS SOLVED

❏ **Chemical Operator** *promoted over 250 tough competitors to be* **Industrial Maintenance Mechanic;** *promoted over 70 others (some more senior) to be* **Industrial Maintenance Leader;** *promoted before 75 others to be* **Maintenance Coordination Leader,** GE, Centerville, Tennessee   94–Present

Our plant operates 24/7 from its 300 acres of production space. Our 425 employees produce polycarbonate resins and engineered plastics as raw materials for products that range from automotive instrument panels to CDs and DVDs.

Serve as direct reporting official for 12 maintenance mechanics.

Gave management the production maintenance reports they needed to run the business after others tried—and failed—using our mainframe. Led 20 team members from across three states to build our new reporting system. *Payoffs:* **Saved $240K in direct labor.** Now every team member has immediate, on-site ability to track more than 48K stock items and assets. Project **on time and on budget**. **Our system now the GE standard.**

Got control of our high nonfill rate by overhauling our MRO (maintenance, repair, and operations). Did my homework to marry best practices to just the right metrics applied to just the right data points. Replaced our expensive, twice-yearly inventory with a rolling system. *Payoffs:* The new approach easily handles 10,900 stock issue requests. **Nonfill rate dropped to zero and stayed there for 16 months.**

Helped management rethink how we could comply with tough EPA standards for our transformers. Proposed, and got complete support for, an approach that let us get maximum ROI from existing equipment. *Payoffs:* My fix complete in just a few days for only $30K—**$720K less than the cost of the original plan.**

Worked closely with the production team to solve a chronic problem that caused too many costly production-line shutdowns. When I reevaluated vendor's equipment against EPA standards, I saw a new engineering solution that promised a long-term solution. *Payoffs:* We **met Federal regulations better than ever** and we **saved $140K** in raw materials.

Championed the idea of predictive maintenance as a complement to preventative maintenance. Sold senior management on the idea and my approach to implementing it. *Payoffs:* **Reduced production budget by $900K** *and* **increased production 12.5 percent.**

More indicators of performance **TopLine** *can use …*

146

Combination. *Don Orlando, Montgomery, Alabama*

This resume (and others by this writer) stands out from resumes by others in many ways. Note the creative use of font enhancements (boldfacing, italic, bold italic, and small caps) and font

Built a mutually beneficial relationship with vendors that served us, them, and our customers better. Tapped into their expertise to redesign a critical component that didn't fail gracefully. *Payoffs:* **Lowered replacement part cost by 35 percent. Saved $110K more** by tripling the MTBF.

❑ **Industrial Maintenance Mechanic,** Delta Chemical Company, Longview, Louisiana

83–93

EDUCATION AND PROFESSIONAL DEVELOPMENT

❑ Pursing BS, Education, with special emphasis on Adult Education in Industrial Operations
Center State University, Centerville, Tennessee   Degree expected in 12
❑ *Earning this degree at night and on the weekends while working 50 hours a week.*

❑ Associate Degree (Applied Technology)
Union State Technical College, Memphis, Tennessee   03
❑ *Completed this degree while holding down a 50-hour-a-week job.*

❑ Reliability-Centered Maintenance Training, Manufacturing Technologies, Inc.   11
❑ *Volunteered for this 88-hour course. One of 20 selected from a field of 200 eligibles.*

❑ Electrical and Instrumentation Craft Training, National Center for Construction Education
and Research   Jul 07

❑ Planning and Scheduling Maintenance Management Resources, Hartford Steam Boiler
Company   06
❑ *Selected and funded by my employer for this week-long workshop.*

❑ Millwright Craft Training, National Center for Construction Education and Research Dec 02

COMPUTER SKILLS

❑ Expert in EMPAC, a purchasing, asset, work-management, and maintenance software suite.
❑ Proficient in Primavera, a project planning and management software package; MS Word,
Excel, PowerPoint, Outlook, and Money; and Internet search protocols.

PROFESSIONAL ACCREDITATIONS

❑ **Certified Systems Administrator for Enterprise Maintenance Planning and Control** by
Corker International   09
❑ Certified Instructor in millwright craft training from the National Center for Construction
Education and Research   07

PROFESSIONAL AFFILIATIONS

❑ Member, Program Advisory Committee for Electrical and Instrumentation Programs, Union
State Technical College, Memphis, Tennessee   Since Mar 07
*Selected by the president to help guide how the college matches its curriculum with industry best
practices.*

styles (sans serif and serif). The word *Payoffs* presents quantified information about achievements in a novel way. Headers (at the top of pages) and footers (at the bottom of pages) impress on the reader the need for confidentiality.

Victor Valencia, Ph.D.

5555 N. Richmond
Chicago, IL 60616

valenciaphd@comcast.net

Residence: 555.337.4322
Cellular: 555.665.8799

SENIOR SCIENCE AND TECHNOLOGY MANAGER

CTO / PROJECT MANAGER / INTELLECTUAL PROPERTY / BUSINESS DEVELOPMENT

Spearheading Innovative Technology Solutions That Drive Change in a Career Spanning 14 Years

Technically sophisticated and business-savvy management professional with solid experience managing technology start-ups, state-of-the-art operations, cross-functional teams, IP assets, and organizational expansion projects to achieve competitive market advantages. Adept at spearheading technological innovations, new-product delivery, and commercialization. Successful at delivering simultaneous large-scale, mission-critical projects on time and under budget. Recognized industry pioneer with 2 patents, 11 patent applications, 36 invention disclosures, and 27 periodical articles / conference papers. Bilingual: English / Spanish.

Representative industries served:

- Medical Devices
- Printing and Imaging
- Surface Mount Technology (SMT)
- Displays
- Packaging
- Nanotechnology
- Radio Frequency Identification (RFID)
- Coating
- Fuel Cells and Batteries

TECHNOLOGY / MANAGEMENT EXPERTISE

- Groundbreaking Research Programs
- R&D Lab Management
- Full Life-Cycle Project Management
- SBIR Management
- Strategic / Operational Planning
- New-Product Development
- Quality / Reliability / Performance
- Competitive Benchmarking
- Technical Staffing

CAREER PROGRESSION

SUPER CAPACITOR TECHNOLOGY, INC.—Chicago, IL, and Guadalajara, Mexico   2010–Present
Designer and manufacturer of the world's leading supercapacitors
Chief Technical Officer / Business Development Manager / Regional Sales Manager

Recruited as key member of start-up management team that orchestrated commercialization of supercapacitor technology transfer from CSIRO. Upon building successful technology operations in Mexico, transferred to U.S. to launch the North American business enterprise. Contracted with global customers and vendors. Supervised 12 direct reports (scientists, research engineers, and technicians).

HIGHLIGHTS OF ACCOMPLISHMENTS:

- **Captured the company's first multimillion-dollar sale** with the global leader in class 12 GPRS PC modems. Research team formulated an electrolyte that exceeded the design specifications by 15%. SCT won 100% of the business. No competitors could meet specifications, driving them from this market.

- **Piloted SCT's full life-cycle, solution-focused business model in the U.S.** As technology liaison, initiated business contact, generated design win, and oversaw contract manufacturing to ensure quality product delivery.

- **Chaired IP Asset Management Team that leveraged one of the industry's most viable portfolios.** Led team that included senior managers, key scientists, and an IP Attorney.

- **Captured 60%+ market share** for supercapacitors used in GPRS modems worldwide. Secured additional clientele, including the world's most recognized CPU and leading digital still camera manufacturers.

- **Reduced prototype failure rates from 85% to 1%** via innovative performance testing and packaging technologies. **Dramatically improved product yields.** Patent pending.

- **Achieved 80% cost reduction** by designing and equipping 2 state-of-the-art research and coating laboratories. **Invented thin film coating** formulations, techniques, and testing processes.

Continued

147

Combination. *Murray Mann, Chicago, Illinois*

Vertical alignment looks good in resumes, and this well-designed resume displays careful vertical alignment. See, for example, the two three-column lists in the first two sections of the

Victor Valencia, Ph.D.

valenciaphd@comcast.net

CAREER PROGRESSION, CONTINUED

ADVANCED RESEARCH INSTITUTE—Los Alamos, NM
Principal Research Investigator / Senior Scientist (Ultracapacitors)
Project Manager (Advanced Battery)

2003–2010

HIGHLIGHTS OF ACCOMPLISHMENTS:

◆ **Managed** SBIR project.
◆ **Led research team** that developed advanced battery technologies for the USAF.
◆ **Achieved greater control** of process and 100% increase in throughput by inventing novel method of depositing capacitive material onto a substrate.

VANGUARD TECHNOLOGIES—Houston, TX
Senior Research Scientist (Lithium Ion Batteries)

1999–2003

HIGHLIGHTS OF ACCOMPLISHMENTS:

◆ **Developed formulations** for thin polymer electrolytes with emphasis on conductivity, coatability, and UV or E-Beam cross-linking, resulting in greater uniformity of coatings and longer battery life.
◆ **Performed full IP analysis** of competitive products and manufacturing technologies. Evaluated carbon materials and methods of particle size reduction.

PATENTS AND PUBLICATIONS

Patent	9,876,543	Cathode-active material blends of Li.sub.x Mn.sub.2 O.sub.4. **Cited in 36 other patents.**
Patent	9,123,456	System and method for impregnating a moving porous substrate with active materials to produce battery electrodes.
Patents Pending	11	Supercapacitor performance and manufacturing technology.
Invention Disclosures	36	Various materials and process improvements focused on Li Polymer batteries. Some disclosures incorporated as trade secrets in preference to patenting.
Periodical Articles / Papers, Posters	27	Authored / coauthored articles published in peer-reviewed journals. Delivered papers, seminars, and 15 poster presentations at professional conferences.

PROFESSIONAL PROFILE

EDUCATION

PhD Physical Science
MASSACHUSETTS INSTITUTE OF TECHNOLOGY
Cambridge, MA (2003)

Thesis: EXAFS for Polymer Batteries. Structure conductivity in doped thin-film polymer membranes. Funded by USDOE and Energy, Inc.

BSc (Honors) Applied Chemistry
INSTITUTO DE TECNOLOGÍCO
Monterrey, Mexico (2000)

BTech HD Physical Sciences
INSTITUTO TECNOLOGÍCO
Monterrey, Mexico (1996–1999)

AFFILIATIONS

Diversity Committee
American Association for the Advancement of Science (AAAS)

Regional Chair
The Society of Mexican-American Engineers and Scientists, Inc. (MAES)

Member
Society of Hispanic Professional Engineers (SHPE)

Member
Latino Alumni of MIT (LAMIT)

TECHNOLOGY SKILLS

Manufacturing Science, Materials Engineering, Electrical Engineering, Quality Control, Electrochemistry, Competitive Analysis, Reverse Engineering, Advanced Polymers, Device Testing, Packaging Processes, Selection and Design, Anticipatory Failure Determination

COMPUTER SKILLS

Operating Systems: Windows, Macintosh, UNIX

Programming Languages: BASIC, Visual Basic, C/C++

resume. The bullets in the lower list are carefully aligned vertically below the bullets of the upper list. This kind of precision usually does not appear in a resume that is thrown together. Another distinctive feature is the five-row, three-column table on page two, which also displays good alignment.

SHARON C. CLEMENTS

2721 Abernathy Drive, Columbia, MD 21044
(410) 997-7521 Home ▪ (703) 771-8113 Mobile ▪ sharonclem@newmedia.com

Operations & Management Executive
Area Director / Regional Director ▪ General Manager ▪ Operations Manager

General/Operations Management professional with proven expertise in expanding product/program lines, increasing revenue streams, and capturing market share in highly competitive Health and Fitness industry. Doubled membership income and gross revenues within one year (2010–2011). Leadership role in health and fitness clubs expansion (15 greenfields and 10 acquisitions).

Hands-on P&L role in strategic planning and initiative management, multisite operations, recruitment and training (60 management and 1,000 line staff), team building, and project management. Met or exceeded revenue/development expectations for 20+ years. Experienced in:

- ☑ Revenue & Market Expansion
- ☑ Staff & Management Development
- ☑ Budget & Financial Performance
- ☑ Change Management
- ☑ Sales & Marketing
- ☑ HR Management
- ☑ Start-ups & Acquisitions
- ☑ Business Development
- ☑ Branding & Technology

PROFESSIONAL EXPERIENCE

FITNESS CLUBS INTERNATIONAL, Washington, DC (corporate headquarters)   1990–2012
Leader in Health & Fitness Industry, ranked 2nd in U.S. and 7th worldwide (based on revenues) with 365,000 members at 132 clubs and 7,200 employees.

General Manager—Columbia Fitness Club (CFC), Columbia, MD (2009–2012)
Full P&L responsibility for sports club ranked 1st in suburban DC market. Managed 20,000 SF club with 2,000 members and supervised 40 management and line staff. Key player in strategic planning, business development, operations, sales and marketing, brand building, PR and community relations, customer service/retention, human resources, administration, and technology performance.

ACCOMPLISHMENTS

Challenged in company restructure and brand-building initiative to deliver smooth-running, profitable operations and sales in high-profile fitness club facility. By 2011 Voted "Best Health Club" in DC-Metro area. Key contributor to market dominance on East Coast. Introduced new product and service lines, negotiated cost reductions (from 10% to cost of item), collaborated in succession planning and team building, and led revenue and profitability increases (demonstrated by financial metrics below):

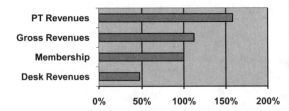

2011 v. 2010
PT Revenues: $509,136 v. $197,225
Gross Revenues: $1,863,790 v. $881,506
Membership: $1,544,748 v. $768,564
Desk Revenues: $27,541 v. $18,774

Continued

Combination. *Susan Guarneri, Three Lakes, Wisconsin*

The writer's challenge was to condense a 22-year career with one company into two pages. The writer dedicated the first page to a Management Summary, keyword list, and most recent

Area Manager—CFC, Columbia, MD (2005–2009)
Oversaw operations and explosive growth of suburban DC clubs. Full P&L responsibility for Sales and Marketing, Systems, Finance, SOP, Customer Service, Multiunit Management, HR, Initiative Management, Succession Planning, Recruiting, Training, and Management Development.

- **Start-up and Acquisition Leader.** Delivered strong revenues and development results in soft market: Spearheaded growth from 1 club with 500 members (starting revenues of $1.4M) to 6 clubs with 13,200 members and annual revenues of $14.5M (2009). Clubs ranged in size from 20,000 SF to 200,000 SF on 23 acres. Managed and motivated team that grew to 550 employees. Chosen as member of Washington, DC, Mayor's Health & Fitness Council Committee in 2009.

- **Technology Improvements.** Played key team role in 2008–2009 rollout of Club Networks, an integrated enterprise software solution for sales reporting with online point-of-sale/real-time sales, tracking, financial, and reporting capability. In 2006 successfully launched automated Fitness Database, as well as online direct payroll processing IT system (Kronos).

General Manager—Washington, DC, Fitness Club (DCFC), Washington, DC (1996–2005)
Directed operations of largest sports club in DC market (8 locations), with full P&L responsibility. Supervised 30–60 management and line staff, including recruitment, training, and staff development.

- **Acquisitions and Revitalization.** Designated Lead Management Trainer for New Manager Orientation, including Senior Management. Initiated Employee Cross-Training Programs; New Employee and Customer Service seminars; monthly performance incentives; and SOPs for training, operations, maintenance, tracking, and production. Negotiated cost-saving contracts with outside vendors. Oversaw multimillion-dollar club renovations.

- **New Technology and Products.** In 1997 transitioned club from manual to computerized system for sales tracking (Sales, Leads, and Management System software), increasing accuracy and turnaround time for sales reporting. First to introduce electronic funds transfer.

Previous FCI Career History:
Progressive promotions from Sales Consultant through Sales Supervisor to Area Membership Supervisor (supervised 36) as company grew from 3 to 9 locations. Set year-over-year (YOY) sales records, presold and assisted in opening 7 clubs, and initiated performance-improvement processes.

EDUCATION & AWARDS

Bachelor's Degree Program, University of Maryland, College Park, MD
Certificate, Managing Performance, American Management Association (AMA), 2005
Certificate, The Manager's Role in Professional Management, AMA, 2004
International Racquet Sports Association (IRSA) Conventions & Seminars, 1992–2004

Fitness Clubs International (FCI) Management & Sales Awards
Service Recognition Award for Outstanding Achievement in Sales & Marketing, 2005
Certificate of Achievement "Employee Primer" Award, 2003
Certificate of Achievement for "greatest drop in cancellation percentage," 2002

accomplishments, including a sales chart and beside it quantified figures. The second page plays up management jobs. In the Education & Awards section, the phrase "Bachelor's Degree Program" indicates that the person attended a university but did not earn a degree.

LISA DAVIDSON

5555 West King Street, Honolulu, Hawaii 00000 • (808) 555-5555 • ldavidson@coconut.org

*Seeking **Management** position in a*
NONPROFIT ORGANIZATION

QUALIFIED TO PERFORM

- *Mission Planning and Implementation*
- *Organizational Development*
- *Leadership Training*
- *Marketing Communications*
- *Media Relations*
- *Public Relations*
- *Corporate Relations*
- *Fund-Raising*
- *Grassroots Campaigns*
- *Community Outreach*
- *Educational Programming*
- *Member Development and Retention*
- *Member Communications*
- *Volunteer Recruitment*
- *Volunteer Training*
- *Special Events Management*

EDUCATION

Columbia College, Columbia University—
New York, NY
B.S., English Literature
(Journalism/Ancient Religions concentration)
- Editor of campus weekly magazine
- Awarded Cornell Woolrich Fellowship

PROFILE

18+ years of experience in dynamic organizational settings, including past 8 years in positions of bottom-line accountability. Background includes history of creating and building various small businesses. Effective communicator highly skilled in multiple environments—public speaking, groups, and one-on-one. *Core skills include*

Organizational Leadership	Project Management
Persuasive Communications	Problem Resolution
Staff Management	Training and Development
Presentations	Workshops
Customer Service	Cross-Cultural Awareness
Research	Written Communications

PROFESSIONAL HISTORY

Career and Life Coach   **2005–Present**
Honolulu, HI; Seattle, WA; Florence, Italy; London, England

Consult with and advise—in person and by telephone—clients of a variety of personal backgrounds and professional levels. Select clients include lawyers, child services professionals, nonprofit board members, nonprofit fund-raisers, artists, and cultural diversity trainers. Work closely with one assistant on scheduling matters.
- Successfully partner with clients, assisting them through major life transitions.
- Conceptualize, plan, and write all marketing materials for life- and career-development workshops.
- Communicate with media regarding workshop promotional plans. Consistently attract 5 to 20 participants.
- Mentor other professional teachers and workshop presenters on planning, implementation, and problem resolution.
- Publish quarterly client newsletter with circulation of 150.
- Have designed and led weekly workshops on subjects ranging from stress management to decision making.

Certified Yoga Instructor   **2000–Present**
Honolulu, HI; London, England

Currently perform private therapeutic sessions. Have taught daily classes of up to 40 students, including new-student orientations. Handle all administrative functions.
- Employ various levels of persuasive communication according to individual students' levels, expectations, and goals.
- Have assisted hundreds of people in recovering from injuries, addiction, and stress, helping them develop positive mind and body attitudes.

PROFESSIONAL HISTORY Continued on Page 2 →

149

Combination. *Peter Hill, Honolulu, Hawaii*

The applicant had a successful business/entrepreneurial background and wanted a nonprofit management position. The writer plays up the variety of the applicant's core skills, job positions

(808) 555-5555   **LISA DAVIDSON**   LDAVIDSON@COCONUT.ORG
Page 2 of 2

Founder/Manager/Sales Representative   **2007–2009**
Handworks, Inc.—Seattle, WA

Accountable for bottom-line success of this on-site chair-massage service at natural food supermarket franchises. Contracted out and supervised 11 massage therapists. Acted as liaison between customers, employees, and corporate management.
- Spearheaded comprehensive public relations campaign to educate public about services.
- Successfully planned and built business from scratch. Sold it after only two years.

Jin Shin Jyutsu Practitioner   **2004–2009**
Private Practice—Seattle, WA

Built thriving private practice providing Japanese *Jin Shin Jyutsu* style of bodywork.

Founder/Manager/Sales Representative   **2004–2005**
Davidson Delicacies—Seattle, WA

Managed all aspects—production, sales, distribution—of this wholesale natural food venture, including materials procurement, kitchen operations, order fulfillment, and account maintenance. Negotiated terms for 20+ accounts throughout Seattle area.
- Launched and grew profitable business, starting with no knowledge of business world or industry.
- Positioned company for success by implementing unique marketing message. Attracted attention of national buyers (including a national food distributor).
- Created *Climbing Cookie* and other unique-concept products. Customers still ask for them at area stores.

Administrative Assistant   **2002–2003**
The Family Schools—Seattle, WA

Oversaw all front- and back-office operations for experimental alternative school program of the Seattle public school system. Program focused on community development of elementary school programs.

Program Assistant   **2000–2002**
Neighborhood Initiative Programs—Seattle, WA

Accountable for program and event planning for this government-funded leadership training and education for low-income and minority communities. Wrote grant proposals, press releases, business communications, and marketing materials. Assisted in design of Community Leadership Training Program.

Communications Assistant   **1999–2000**
Williams & Stevenson—Baltimore, MD

Collaborated to compose marketing proposals and newsletter pieces. Managed administrative functions in communications department of this international law firm.

Communications Assistant   **1994–1998**
Pratt, Gregg & Nakamoto—Baltimore, MD

Charged with authority to assess prospective client case potential. Generated press releases and marketing materials for this entertainment law firm. Researched and wrote one partner's weekly column for New York newspaper.

held, qualifications, and work experiences to make her appealing to a wide range of organizations. The two-column look of the first page helps convey a sense of diversity. The reader can see at a glance something of the individual's qualifications, education, and experience.

Candace L. Kugle

520 E. Ogden Avenue   000-983-8882
Naperville, Illinois 06060   ckugle@internetservice.com

PROFESSIONAL QUALIFICATIONS AND KEY STRENGTHS

Professional manager with a broad-based background in business development, human resources, personnel management and store operations. Strong leadership and motivational skills; proven ability to quickly build rapport, establish trust, and train and motivate people of all levels. Recognized for professionalism, positive mental attitude, commitment to excellence and demonstrated ability to communicate and interact effectively with senior management, associates and customers. Big-picture focus on company goals has produced increased efficiencies in production and sales.

*Human Resources Management • Interviewing/Training/Developing Personnel • Benefits-Wage Administration
Project Management • Expense and Inventory Control • Policies, Programs and Procedures*

CAREER HIGHLIGHTS

Human Resources

- Established training priorities for 110 stores throughout Illinois, Wisconsin, Minnesota, Iowa and Michigan.
- Recruited personnel at college campuses.
- Evaluated human resources programs and directives.
- Ensured proper execution of federal and state laws and customer service initiatives.
- Evaluated hiring decisions and identified high potential field management personnel.
- Presented benefits and corporate policies overview to new hires.

Management

- Improved expense control; identified efficiencies for controllables and salary expenditures.
- Enhanced management/staff team productivity through motivational training and mentoring.
- Responsible for overall store operations.
- Developed and sustained new and existing business.
- Contributed to store-management team effort to maintain efficient operating conditions and ensure in-stock position.

EMPLOYMENT HISTORY

General Manager, WESTRIDGE APPAREL, Schaumburg, Illinois, 08/07 to Present
- Supervised all aspects of the opening of the Weekend Only Warehouse concept store.
- Recruit, hire and train sales staff.
- Schedule sales and support staff.

General Manager, VENTURE CORPORATION, Chicago, Illinois, 09/06 to 08/07
- Executed merchandising and operations for hardlines /softlines.
- Controlled office/freight receiving procedures; salary budgets.
- Supervised management staff, emphasizing sales performance and high standards of store operations.
- Directed complete remodeling of assigned fashion areas.
- Trained management personnel in operations and supervision.
- Managed job assistance efforts for multiple stores during business close-down.

Previous roles:

Regional HR Trainer, Ft. Wayne, IN—09/03 to 09/06	**Fashion Manager,** Quincy, IL—04/92 to 11/98
District Manager, Ft. Wayne, IN—11/99 to 09/03	**Apparel Manager,** Green Bay, WI—04/89 to 04/92
Softline Manager, Garden City, MI—11/98 to 11/99	**Assistant Manager/Trainee,** Kenosha, WI—07/88 to 04/89

EDUCATION

University of Michigan, Ann Arbor, Michigan
Bachelor of Science in Clothing, Textiles and Design (cum Laude), 1988

150

Combination. *Pat Chapman, Naperville, Illinois*

This individual had retail management experience and wanted to move into human resources management. The writer plays up human resources both in the profile and in the Career Highlights.

Manufacturing

Resumes at a Glance

BAXTER A. LEEDS

45 Kaiwan Street   Taipei, Taiwan   555-05050505   bestoys@xix5.net

PROFESSIONAL GOAL

Opportunity in the toy manufacturing industry where experience in creative product development, team leadership, and mass production will contribute to business growth and success in the USA and Asia.

PROFESSIONAL PROFILE

- Successful background in the toy industry with a leading manufacturer in both the USA and Asia.
- Highly creative in design, construction, and production of seasonal, novelty, and licensed products.
- Broad understanding of living and working in Asia; knowledge of customs, beliefs, and culture.
- Dedicated commitment to quality products, expense control, and customer satisfaction.
- Valued by colleagues for work ethic, team leadership, creativity, and open-mindedness.

EXPERIENCE

BESTOYS, INC.—Taipei, Taiwan   **2000–Present**
Creative Director
USA-based toy company with manufacturing operations in Taiwan.

Creative Product Development
- Manage product aesthetic and function during product engineering and development process.
- Conceptualize in 3D with mechanical ability to develop pattern, starting with minimal item definition.
- Strong knowledge of model-building techniques and experience with all relevant materials.
- Collaborate with company's CEO and Asian Division President on product development initiatives.

Management/Team Leadership
- Direct 100-member Taiwan prototype staff in all phases of the prototyping/manufacturing process.
- Independently supervise work, coping with fluctuating work loads while maintaining accuracy to product design without missing deadlines.
- Effective interpersonal skills and a respect for people of all backgrounds and nationalities.
- Communicate via e-mail with USA product management on daily item needs and changes.

Manufacturing for Mass Production/Licensed Products
- Skilled in meeting mass production costs, scheduling, and engineering specifications.
- Work directly with BesToys' Asian engineering staff and production vendor engineering on item construction to meet aesthetic, function, schedule, and item cost.
- Manufacture a vast number of products including boys', girls', spring, seasonal, novelty, and licensed products for vastly successful brand names.
- Effectively complete a large volume of licensed goods for sale/distribution in various world markets.

Key Contributions

- Opened a new prototype facility in Taiwan to meet increased corporate demands, maximize output of sales samples, and reduce prototyping costs.
- Utilize a management style of empowerment, support, and assertiveness in meeting deadlines.
- Monitor and control USA designs built in Taiwan to ensure highest quality standards.

EDUCATION

BFA with Honors
Marketing and Advertising Design—Santa Rosa Fine Arts Academy, Santa Rosa, California, 2000

■■■■■■■■

151

Combination. *Billie Sucher, Urbandale, Iowa*

The applicant brought the writer "vast pages of information about his background." The writer organized and categorized this information into keyword/skills areas to showcase his experience.

FRANKLIN S. CLARK

555-555-5555   55 W Main Street – Decatur, Indiana 55555   ClarkDirects@xxxx.com

CORE BUSINESS & OPERATIONAL DEVELOPMENT DIRECTOR

MANUFACTURING • NOT-FOR-PROFIT • MULTISITE MANAGEMENT
Successful at Building High-Performance Teams and Establishing Operational Excellence

High-performance, results-driven Director of Manufacturing with a career focused on visionary leadership, productivity, cost-reduction improvements, and functional management of multisite manufacturing operations. Combine tactical execution of strategic initiatives with effective management and motivation of staff/team members to enhance quality, customer service, and bottom-line financial performance.

Lean Manufacturing	Strategic Planning & Execution
Process Analysis & Reengineering	Productivity Optimization
Performance Improvement	Quality Control
Analysis & Problem Resolution	Mergers, Acquisitions & Strategic Partnerships
Cost Reductions	Profit Growth

EXPERIENCE NARRATIVE

Pulp Paper Goods, Berne, IN   2003–Present
#1 Paper Goods Manufacturer established in 1903 and focused on serving churches throughout the U.S.

Director of Manufacturing   **2007–Present**
Executive management confidante involved in strategic planning and tactical implementation of continuous improvement and Lean Manufacturing initiatives. Support aggressive initiatives and drive lasting cultural changes within multiplant divisional operations; successfully led transformation to lean enterprise.

- Contributed to unprecedented growth from $10M to $30M in revenues.
- Achieved major financial performance improvements; built rapport with all levels of management and skilled workers and skillfully implemented Lean concepts and improved net income from 12% to +30% over three-year period.
- Defined goals and developed/implemented Value Stream organizations; realized significant improvement and greater focus on customer service.
- Improved on-time delivery; used SMED methodology and led initiatives to reduce inventory by 70%.

Plant Manager   **2003–2007**
Recruited to manage manufacturing operations for a three-shift, union shop located within a 200,000 sq. ft. facility. Held direct accountability for P&L performance, scheduling, and strategic planning; adeptly created flow of material and information within a traditional manufacturing environment.

- Combined tactical execution of strategic initiatives with strong leadership of cross-functional staff and development of key alliances to capture and enhance overall quality, productivity, and bottom-line financial performance; proficiently improved work flow and reduced labor expenses by 20%.
- Served as catalyst for change to optimize productivity; analyzed operations and identified/implemented a capital investment to permanently eliminate the number-one customer quality concern.
- Positioned company for continued growth and profitability through the development of strong plant leadership staff; transformed plant into customer-focused/continuous-improvement operation.

Continued

152

Combination. *Tammy Shoup, Decatur, Indiana*

The writer's challenge was to showcase the depth of the applicant's manufacturing experience, which far outweighed his academic training. His objective was to move forward with his

555-555-5555 **Franklin S. Clark** ClarkDirects@xxxx.com

Experience Narrative, Continued

TrueValveManufacturing, New Haven, IN 1991–2003
Global leader in motion and control technologies, engineering innovative products and systems to increase their customers' productivity and continued success.

Production Manager *1998–2003*
Coordinated production priorities with team leadership while ensuring cost efficiencies and fostering continuous improvement through Toyota Production System Methodology.

- Drove a series of successful productivity, quality, and operating improvement programs; realized substantial increase to production outputs.
- Facilitated team meetings, Quality Operation System (QOS) meetings, and problem-solving teams.
- Motivated production employees to achieve team goals.

Plant Scheduler *1996–1998*
Analyzed capacity requirements planning (CRP) and communicated with sales, manufacturing, and supplier to prioritize schedules and meet customer demands for shorter lead-times.

- Introduced and implemented Lean Manufacturing Principles including one-piece flow cells, Kanban, and Heijunka Scheduling; expertly reduced work-in-process inventories by 60%.

ADDITIONAL EXPERIENCE
Garnered experience analyzing work flow and developing procedures to standardize work, streamline processes, communicate work directives, provide strong and decisive leadership, and increase efficiencies.

Process Technician
Challenged to analyze operations and assist with the development and launch of new products.

Team Leader
Facilitated communications to ensure smooth flow of daily production, attain set goals, and maintain high level of quality for all parts built.

EDUCATION & PROFESSIONAL DEVELOPMENT

Seek out and participate in seminars and classes to bolster knowledge and stay abreast of cutting-edge methodologies.

Excellence in Manufacturing I & II • Lean Accounting • Strategic Decision Making • Creating Continuous Flow Workshop • Facilitation and Coaching • Customer Value Management • Shingo Prize Cell Redesign • Collective Bargaining • Workplace Organization • Union Strike Avoidance • Physical Inventory Control • HR Legal Processes • Value Stream Mapping • University of Michigan Lean Manufacturing

ASSOCIATE OF SCIENCE, BUSINESS MANAGEMENT
Institute of Learning, Goshen, IN

manufacturing career by learning through focused sources instead of further academic training. The table on page one makes areas of expertise easy to read. The Education & Professional Development section indicates the candidate's alternative nonacademic educational experiences.

ADAM BRADFORD

555 Foxwood Lane, Granby, GA 55555
H (555) 555-0000 ▪ C (555) 555-0001
a.bradford@xxxx.com

MANUFACTURING LEADER
PLANT MANAGEMENT ▪ SUPPLY CHAIN ▪ OPERATIONS

Unwavering customer focus, deep experience, and intense commitment to manufacturing excellence.

Exceptional record of top- and bottom-line results—revenue growth, cost reduction, and improvements in efficiency, productivity, customer service, and quality.

Valuable combination of strategic business insight gained from diverse experience *and* pragmatic ability to execute and deliver.

Production
Logistics & Distribution
Materials Management
Technology
Financial Management
People Leadership
Change Management

EXPERIENCE

Porter Power Systems USA   **2000 – Present**
Global manufacturer of power equipment (both commodity and highly engineered products); €5.1 billion in annual revenues, 53 plants worldwide, and ~13,000 employees.

DIRECTOR OF PLANT OPERATIONS, Artsville, GA (2005 – Present)
Lead facility of 250 employees working 7 days per week / 24 hours per day in continuous manufacturing process. Oversee operations, process engineering, and maintenance (9 direct reports), plus HR, Quality, Production Planning, and Logistics (5 indirect reports). Direct recruiting, training, and compensation processes. Assume full accountability for plant P&L (~$300 million in annual sales, variable budget of $10.8 million, and fixed budget of $4.3 million).

- Increased overall plant output by 15% (~$30 million in additional sales) by guiding lean production (SMED) initiatives, production scheduling changes, and raw material reformulations.
- Strategized and drove $3.5 million capital expansion in addition to $1 million annual capital budget.
- Realized annual labor efficiency gains of up to $100,000 each year, net of benefits increases.
- Improved on-time shop order delivery from 85% to 97% and overall quality index by 23%.
- Transferred 3 new product lines and 5 new product families into plant within 8 months.
- Introduced daily Right First Time (RFT) measurement system, improving results from 90% to 95% on critical plant equipment within 6 months.

DIRECTOR OF LOGISTICS, Lenox, GA (2001 – 2005)
Promoted to take on production planning and scheduling, raw materials procurement, and finished goods warehousing, distribution, shipping, and receiving for all North American facilities (3 plants) in California, Quebec, and Georgia. Managed 8 direct reports—2 managers in each plant and 2 in division office.

- Spearheaded new cost control measures—such as increasing use of recycled reels from 5% to 30% and consolidating freight loads—saving $500,000+ within first year.
- Saved 10% in freight tariffs through negotiation and contracting with third-party logistics group.
- Drove implementation of new, ERP-integrated systems to semiautomate demand planning, production scheduling, and lead-time management.

DIRECTOR—RAW MATERIALS AND PRODUCTION PLANNING, Coleman, GA (2001)
RAW MATERIALS MANAGER, Coleman, GA (2000 – 2001)
Managed production planning and procurement of raw materials (~$175 million) for all 3 North American facilities. Oversaw inventory levels of raw materials and finished goods. Directed timing and flow of materials to support production. Managed 1 materials buyer/planner in each plant.

- Implemented statistics-based, easy-to-use, production planning and inventory control tools that reduced finished goods inventory while improving speed and service to customer.
- Reduced division-wide raw material inventories to less than 5 days on-hand—~20% reduction—while accomplishing Purchase Price Variance goals.

Page 1

153

Combination. *Cathy Alfandre, Easton, Connecticut*

The applicant's career had been in manufacturing, but his original resume did not present his record of results in a compelling manner. The writer positioned him for Plant Manager roles by

Capital Tools—A Division of Capital Industries   **1994 – 2000**
Manufacturer of power tools; $765 million division of Capital Industries.

MATERIALS MANAGER, Summit, GA (2000)
MANAGER OF MATERIALS AND ENGINEERING, Summit, GA (1999)
Directed master scheduling, purchasing, shipping, receiving, and packaging, as well as engineering, new product development, capital management, and database management. Continued to serve as SAP lead for plant. Managed 11 direct reports and capital and raw materials budgets.

- Crafted centralized purchasing and master scheduling processes, elevating plant's buying power and saving more than $550,000 in purchasing costs in 5 months.
- Converted inventory management from manual, weeklong process to automated 1-day process.
- Reduced inventory by 10.2% in 5 months.
- Supported engineering consolidation of another facility into Summit plant.

ENTERPRISE BUSINESS SYSTEM (SAP) IMPLEMENTATION TEAM MEMBER, Acme, TN (1997 – 1999)
Tapped for Manufacturing Management / Production Planning (MMPP) SAP implementation team. Led Production Planning, Inventory Management, and Procurement configurations.

- Redesigned and automated numerous business processes during implementation; realized immediate cost savings and improvements to planning, product flow, and inventory tracking.
- Trained users at all levels in large groups (60+ people), small groups, and one-on-one.
- Implemented system in 9 plants and 2 distribution centers, on budget and 2 months early (on 24-month schedule).

FOCUSED FACTORY MANAGER, Summit, GA (1996 – 1997)
FOCUSED FACTORY MANAGER, Stanton, GA (1994 – 1996)
Led manufacturing, engineering, capital management, quality, production planning, and purchasing for 55-person (Stanton) and 180-person (Summit) focused factories. Managed 10 self-directed work teams.

- Achieved 60% productivity increase at Stanton and 25% labor efficiency improvement at Summit—highest levels ever at this plant—through implementation of empowered work teams and synchronous manufacturing methods.
- Spearheaded significant customer service improvements and introduction of new products, driving sales at Stanton from $13 to $18 million in 2 years.
- Implemented combined machining/assembly cell and reduced cycle time from 6 weeks to 2 weeks.

Capital Industries   **1992 – 1994**
Global power tools manufacturer; annual revenues of $6.5 billion (2012).

MANUFACTURING TRAINING PROGRAM

- Recruited for rigorous 2-year management training program with four 6-month assignments: Manufacturing Engineer, Materials Management, Design Engineering, and Manufacturing Supervisor.
- Completed series of 1-week training courses: Manufacturing Concepts Workshop, Advanced Technology for Manufacturing, and Finance for Non-Financial Managers.

SPECIAL SKILLS & KNOWLEDGE

- SAP—Purchasing, Inventory Management, Physical Inventory, Production Master Data, Planning, Repetitive Manufacturing, Discrete Manufacturing, and Kanban.
- Kaizen, 5S, TPM, TQM, SMED, Design of Experiments, and Six Sigma projects.
- Deep technical expertise with diverse analytical, database, presentation, and drafting software.

EDUCATION

Southern American University, Coleman, GA
MASTER OF SCIENCE IN MANAGEMENT

State University, Ramsey, SC
BACHELOR OF SCIENCE IN MECHANICAL ENGINEERING (Minor in Spanish)

making his expertise, leadership abilities, and bottom-line impact "jump off the page." She achieved this effect with the quantified and bulleted achievement statements for each of the candidate's workplaces, plus the italicized descriptions of three of the workplaces.

Orville Smith

o.smith@xxxx.ca

55–55 5th St., Vancouver, BC V1A 1A1   Cell: (555) 550-5555

Operations Manager

Extraordinarily resourceful leader with 15 years of experience delivering business and profit growth in start-up and mid-size companies.

Key Competencies

Organizational Leadership • Customer & Labour Relations
Lean Production • Industrial Engineering & Optimization • Project Management
Quality Management (ISO 9001) • Strategic Sourcing & Procurement

Career Highlights

- Grew manufacturer from start-up to 95% supplier to local car manufacturers. (Soucar)
- Achieved all annual budget and revenue targets while operating in extraordinarily difficult political and economic environment. (Soucar, Vinage)
- Implemented statistical process control techniques to control manufacturing. Drove product reject rate from around 14% to less than 0.3% , achieving A+ supplier rating and authorization to deliver directly to customer assembly line. (Soucar)
- Managed design and construction of 75,000 sq. ft. warehouse and installation of new U.S. $400 thousand polyurethane soft cushion production line. Brought both projects in on time and on budget and enabled 40% sales increase. (Soucar)
- Regularly negotiated supply contracts that enabled company to achieve double-digit margin goals. (Soucar, Vinage)

Relevant Professional Experience

Immigration / Educational Sabbatical, 2010–Present
Pursued several certifications to update business knowledge to "cutting edge" North American standards.

Soucar, Caracas, Venezuela
General Manager, 1996–2009
Car seat manufacturer with over U.S. $20 million in annual sales.
Directed and carried full P&L responsibility for start-up car-seat manufacturer. Prepared and presented annual production and capacity plans based on customer demand forecast. Met production deadlines, quality standards and customer requirements. Set pricing; developed expense control and systems / technology integration. Implemented and supervised compliance with safety regulations (similar to OSHA and WHMIS).

- Grew business from initial start-up to lead supplier to local subsidiary of Asian auto manufacturer.
- Minimized inventory from five days to three hours, and elevated customer service ratio to 100% by implementing JIT delivery system including double Kanban system to pull finished products from warehouse.
- Developed ISO 9000 quality management system to monitor and control manufacturing operations and administrative functions.
- Hired and trained key workers. Grew workforce to 150 while maintaining 90% retention rate.
- Negotiated all management objectives in return for acceptable concessions in union agreements.
- Achieved long-term supplier contracts yielding double-digit gross profit margins.

Page 1 of 2

154

Combination. *Tim Cunningham, Vancouver, British Columbia, Canada*

This applicant had trained in the United States but had built his entire career in South America in an antibusiness political environment. After emigrating to Canada, he needed a resume that

Vinage, Caracas, Venezuela
Procurement & Development Manager, 1993–1996
Venezuelan manufacturer / subsidiary of Asian automobiles.
Oversaw contract management process from initial planning and preparation of requests for proposal (RFPs) through source selection and negotiations, contract administration and closeout. Directed supplier certification program: evaluating suppliers on production capacities, quality management systems, and continuous improvement programs. Supervised all stages of supplier manufacturing operations. Led team of 6 design engineers, 3 purchasing agents and an assistant.

- Negotiated long-term open contracts with key local and international suppliers valued at over $100 million. Implemented "release system" to communicate short- and long-term requirements.
- Successfully managed Local Content program which integrated the fabrication of locally made automobile components. Increased use of locally manufactured products by 15% in two years.
- Coordinated design and fabrication of over 100 auto parts valued at more than $5.2 million. Met quality, scope, budget and time constraints, enabling 40 successful new vehicle launches.

Education

Bachelor of Science, Industrial Management, University of Alabama, Birmingham, AL, USA

Professional Development

Completed:
Certificate in Project Management, University of British Columbia, Vancouver, BC
Project Management Professional, Project Management Institute (PMI)
Certified Supply Chain Professional, The Association for Operations Management
ISO 9001:2008 QMS Internal Auditor, RABQSA *(International Certification Service)*
WHMIS for Managers and Supervisors, Canadian Centre for Occupational Health & Safety (CCOHS)
Health & Safety for Managers and Supervisors, CCOHS
Competent Communicator, Toastmasters International

In progress:
Villanova University, Villanova, USA
Master Certificate in Contract Management (completion, 08/12)

The Association for Operations Management, APICS
Certified in Production and Inventory Management (anticipated completion, 12/12)

American Society for Quality
Certified Quality Engineer (anticipated completion: 12/12)

American Society for Quality
Lean Six Sigma Black Belt (anticipated completion: Spring 2013)

Computer & Language Skills

Intermediate to advanced user of MS Office, MS Project, Share Point and Dynamics RMS
Fluently bilingual in English and Spanish

Professional Affiliations

Project Management Institute
The Association for Operations Management, APICS
American Society for Quality
Purchasing Management Association of Canada
Toastmasters International

would highlight his transferable skills in such a way that employers would discount his lack of familiarity with Canadian business culture. This resume brought him four job interviews within one month and helped him win two job offers.

JAMES MATTESON

5555 Buckskin Circle, Yorba Linda, CA 55555   555.555.5555 • j.matteson@xxxx.com

Global Plant Management, Operations and Supply Chain Excellence

Award-winning, hands-on operations and multisite manufacturing leader with broad-based experience managing high-tech, global organizations and complex programs across diverse industries and geographies. Highly organized, self-sufficient innovator **comfortable with any size organization from the boardroom to the factory floor**. Able to draw from and leverage extensive team building and process improvement experience as well as **Project Management Professional (PMP) and Six Sigma Black Belt Certifications. Results-oriented trendsetter with an impressive track record of achieving immediate and significant improvements** in cost and cycle-time reduction, quality and safety improvement and overall profitability. Recognized as an organizational coalition-builder and growth catalyst with the **ability to instill a fresh perspective and infusion of positive and productive energy.** Top Secret/SCI Security Clearance. Winner of *IndustryWeek* magazine's America's Best Plants Award. Expertise includes:

Multisite Plant Operations • Full P&L • Global Supply Chain (Asia & Mexico) • Turnarounds • EBITDA Improvement
Current Good Manufacturing Practices • Cash and Asset Management • Low-Cost Region Sourcing
Acquisition Due Diligence and Integration • CA & FDA Food & Drug Manufacturing • Key Results Areas and Metrics
ASQ Lean Manufacturing / Six Sigma Certified • Logistics Management • ISO 9001, 13485 & 14001

CAREER HIGHLIGHTS

Amin Corporation
Gardena, CA • 2011–2012

Privately owned, 105-employee and 40,000-sq.-ft. single-plant business specializing in made-to-order extruded, radio frequency welded plastic liquid packaging and filling services with ~$5M in annual revenue. Markets served include pharmaceutical, consumer goods, cosmetic and industrial.

GENERAL MANAGER
Recruited to transform distressed business operations as fully autonomous company leader. Deployed full-scale infrastructure revitalization strategy impacting staff, facility, technology systems, inventory management, new product development, manufacturing equipment and processes. Elevated company image as platform for new private-label product launch with pioneering marketing strategy introducing new company logo, tagline, Web site, trade show promotion plan, branding initiatives and fresh product development to target new markets and rejuvenate existing customer groups.

- Recruited and built a new leadership team to boost Amin's operating cash flow by 88%, doubling EBITDA and increasing sales by 21%. Improved margins by 11%; reduced receivables by 34% and inventory by 17%.
- Captured more new business in first 6 months of 2012 than in the preceding 2 years combined, focusing on new product development initiatives and untapped markets.
- Designed balanced scorecard to measure performance against key metrics and establish new roles, responsibilities and primary areas of focus for management staff; served as catalyst for performance improvement.
- Compressed lead times from 8 to 3 weeks and drove strict compliance to FDA cGMP's and a factory 5S program resulting in efficiency gains of 50%+ and dramatic improvement in customer satisfaction.

Wellesley Corporation (Spectra-Physics)
Irvine, CA • 2008–2011

Leading worldwide manufacturer and distributor of precision components and systems used for development and application of laser products; $400M annual revenue across 13 global manufacturing sites and 5,000 employees. Markets served include photonics and high-technology instrumentation.

VICE PRESIDENT, Operations & OptoElectronics Technologies (China)
Appointed to lead launch of low-cost electronics manufacturing, assembly and distribution plant in Wuxi, China, as well as establish and develop local optics and electrical- and mechanical-component supply base. Accountable for all facets of project including a full-scale global country and market assessment, facility design and construction, process and systems design as well as product transfer from plants in the U.S. and Europe. Established standard financial, manufacturing, logistics, warehousing and distribution strategies—incorporating best practices and elements of Wellesley global manufacturing plant strategies. Headed up staff recruitment activity, leading 12 direct and 22 dotted-line reports. Served as lead strategist and hands-on manager across every function in the supply chain, consistently delivering below a $25M operating budget.

- Partnered with Wellesley global plant management to analyze direct material product portfolio and determine technologies best suited for transfer to China, enabling revenue growth of $8.3M and $15.4M in 2010 and 2011 respectively.

Continued

155

Combination. *Sandra Ingemansen, Matteson, Illinois*

The applicant had been in manufacturing from the ground up across many sectors, including government, commerce, life and health sciences, aerospace, and emerging technologies.

- Achieved a 43% improvement in corporate Cost of Poor Quality ($8.1M), 3.9% standard direct material costs ($4.2M) and reduction in inventory of $14.2M from 2009 through 2010 utilizing Toyota Production System (TPS).
- Restructured information management and measurement of direct material expenditures to provide plant management with significantly improved visibility and install a cost-reduction priorities and opportunities model for application across company-wide disciplines.
- Collaborated across 13 manufacturing sites to establish standardized metrics, Key Results Areas (KRAs) and accompanying action plans—providing a platform from which all company improvement activities were managed.
- Set records for least number of lost-time accidents and lowest severity rate through effective management teamwork.
- Drove backlog/overdue down at every facility and improved overall on-time delivery from 88% to 96% in less than a year.

Northern Grammus Ltd.
El Segundo, CA • 2000–2008

With 120,000 global employees and $33B in annual revenue, company is a leading designer, systems integrator and manufacturer of military aircraft, defense electronics, precision weapons, and commercial and military aero structures.

DIRECTOR, Enterprise/Operational Excellence & Continuous Improvement *(2005–2008)*
Appointed to manage 14 direct reports and standardize the project execution portfolio by integrating Lean, TPS, System, Six Sigma and Kaizen Event methodologies.

- Drove savings of $3.5M+, fostering consistent 97% project implementation rate and 93% on-time completion rate.
- Integral in new business development; took the helm during proposal activity to win a $100M NASA Global Precipitation Measurement Program contract.

PROGRAM MANAGER, SBIRS High GEO Payload and GMI Programs *(2003–2005)*
Accountable for leading 20 direct reports and 400 staff. Delivered 2 geosynchronous Space Based Infrared Sensor (SBIRS) USAF payloads while managing all facets of this $460M program. Instrumental in scoring .99 on SPI and CPI for 2004–2005 for $104M in budgeted Cost of Work Scheduled.

PLANT MANAGER, GeoCorp–Aerojet *(2000–2003)*
Led and mentored 20 direct management reports with oversight of 1,150 staff in multiplant operations. Controlled annual budget of $78M and reduced overhead expenses by 7%+ annually. Recognized for breaking lowest lost-time injuries/accident severity records, subsequently winning America's Best Plants Award by *IndustryWeek* magazine.

United Waverley Tech Corporation
Hartford, CT • 1987–2000

BUSINESS UNIT DIRECTOR, Hamill Sands *(1996–2000)*
Strong record of advancement during 13-year tenure for this diverse, $55B multinational corporation with more than 200,000 employees. Promoted into directorship role for reducing customer overdue rate by 73%, inventory by 28% and operating expenses by 19% in just under a year while overseeing 315 personnel and all operations for United's $95M Propulsion and Engine Control division. Managed processes including composite structures, blades, machined parts and propeller final assembly & test.

OPERATIONS CENTER MANAGER, Hamill Sands *(1991–1996)*
CORPORATE SUPPLY CHAIN MANAGER, Corporate Office *(1989–1991)*
SENIOR BUYER & MIDWEST REGION MANAGER, Sivorsky Aircraft *(1987–1989)*

EDUCATION & PROFESSIONAL DEVELOPMENT

MBA, International Business, *University of New Haven, CT*
BS, Economics/Finance and Accounting, *Bents University–Waltham, MA*
Advanced Program Management Certification, *University of Defense Acquisition–Fort Belvoir, VA*
Project Management Professional (PMP) Certification, *Project Management Institute (PMI)*
Six Sigma Black Belt Certification, *American Society for Quality (ASQ)*
Dale Carnegie Public Speaking Certification
Karrass Effective Negotiating Certification

He didn't mind working in the trenches but wanted a more strategic-level position as a VP or Director of Operations within any of these sectors. The writer refocused the applicant's resume for these roles, and he soon secured two interviews.

LEE WARNER

355 Thomas Drive
Trenton, NJ 55555

Home: (555) 555-5555
leewarner@xxxx.com

PLANT / OPERATIONS / GENERAL MANAGEMENT EXECUTIVE

Multisite manufacturing plant/general management career building and leading high-growth, transition and start-up operations in domestic and international environments with annual revenues of up to $680 million.

Expertise: Organizational Development • Productivity & Cost Reduction Improvements • Supply Chain Management • Acquisitions & Divestitures • IPOs • Plant Rationalizations • Safety Performance • Customer Relations • Change Agent

---

CORE COMPETENCIES

Manufacturing Leadership—Strong P&L track record with functional management experience in all disciplines of manufacturing operations • Developing and managing operating budgets • Spearheading restructuring and rationalization of plants and contracted distribution facilities • Initiating lean manufacturing processes, using SMED principles • Establishing performance metrics and supply-chain management teams.

Continuous Improvement & Training—Designing and instituting leadership enhancement training program for all key plant management • Instituting Total Quality System (TQS) process in domestic plants to promote the business culture of continuous improvement and leading ISO 9001 certification process.

New Product Development—Initiating plant-based "New Product Development Think Tank" that developed 130 new products for marketing review, resulting in the successful launch of 5 new products in 2000.

Engineering Management—Oversight of corporate machine design and development teams • Developing 3-year operating plan • Directing the design, fabrication and installation of several proprietary machines • Creating project cost tracking systems and introducing ROI accountability.

PROFESSIONAL EXPERIENCE

BEACON INDUSTRIES, INC., Maspeth, NY (1994–Present)
Record of continuous promotions to executive-level position in manufacturing and operations management despite periods of transition/acquisition at a $680 million Fortune 500 international manufacturing company.

Vice President of Manufacturing (1997–Present)

Senior Operating Executive responsible for the performance of 7 manufacturing/distribution facilities for company that experienced rapid growth from 4 plants generating $350 million in annual revenues to 14 manufacturing facilities with revenues of $680 million. Charged with driving the organization to becoming a low-cost producer. Established performance indicators, operating goals, realignment initiatives, productivity improvements and cost-reduction programs that consistently improved product output, product quality and customer satisfaction.

Achievements

- Selected to lead corporate team in developing and driving forward cost reduction initiatives that will result in $21 million saved over the next 3 years through capital infusion, process automation and additional rationalizations.

- Saved $13 million annually by reducing fixed spending 11% and variable overhead spending 18% through effective utilization of operating resources and cost-improvement initiatives.

- Cut workers' compensation costs 40% ($750,000 annually) by implementing effective health and safety plans, employee training, management accountability and equipment safeguarding. Led company to achieve recognition as "Best in Industry" regarding OSHA frequency and Loss Workday Incident rates.

- Reduced waste generation 31%, saving $1 million in material usage by optimizing manufacturing processes as well as instituting controls and accountability.

- Enhanced customer service satisfaction 3% annually during past year (measured by order fill and on-time delivery percentage) through supply-chain management initiatives, inventory control and flexible manufacturing practices.

- Trimmed manufacturing and shipping-related credits to customers from 1.04% to .5% of total sales in 1999, representing annual $1.8 million reduction.

- Decreased total inventories 43% from 1997 base through combination of supply-chain management, purchasing, master scheduling and global-utilization initiatives.

- Rationalized 3 manufacturing plants and 6 distribution facilities, saving $6 million over 3 years.

156

Combination. *Louise Garver, Broad Brook, Connecticut*

This applicant's company was being downsized because its industry was declining steadily. He used this resume to make an industry change and was successful. Core competencies

General Manager, Northeast (1994–1997)

Assumed full P&L responsibility of 2 manufacturing facilities and a $20 million annual operating budget. Directly supervised facility managers and indirectly 250 employees in a multiline, multicultural manufacturing environment. Planned and realigned organizational structure and operations to position company for high growth as a result of acquiring a major account, 2 new product lines and 800 additional SKUs.

Achievements

- Reduced operating costs by $4.5 million through consolidation of 2 distribution locations without adverse impact on customer service.

- Accomplished the start-up of 2 new manufacturing operations, which encompassed a plant closing and the integration of acquired equipment into existing production lines for 2 new product lines without interruption to customer service; achieved 2 months ahead of target and $400,000 below budget.

- Increased operating performance by 15% while reducing labor costs by $540,000.

- Reduced frequency and severity of accidents by 50% in 3 years, contributing to a workers' compensation and cost avoidance reduction of $1 million.

- Decreased operating waste by 2% for an annual cost savings of $800,000 in 2 manufacturing facilities.

- Negotiated turnkey contracts for 2 distribution warehouses to meet expanded volume requirements.

- Maintained general management and administrative cost (GMA) at a flat rate as sales grew by 25% annually over 3 years.

ROMELARD CORPORATION, Detroit, MI (1980–1994)
Division Manufacturing Director (1989–1994)

Fast-track advancement in engineering, manufacturing and operations management to division-level position. Retained by new corporate owners and promoted in 1994 based on consistent contributions to revenue growth, profit improvements and cost reductions. Scope of responsibility encompassed P&L for 3 manufacturing facilities and a distribution center with 500 employees in production, quality, distribution, inventory control and maintenance.

Achievements

- Delivered strong and sustainable operating gains: increased customer fill rate by 18%; improved operating performance by 20%; reduced operating waste by 15% and reduced inventory by $6 million.

- Justified, sourced and directed the installation of $10 million of automated plant equipment.

- Implemented and managed a centralized master schedule for all manufacturing facilities.

- Reduced annual workers' compensation costs by $600,000.

- Created Customer Satisfaction Initiative program to identify areas of concern and implemented recommendations, significantly improving customer satisfaction.

Prior Positions

Manufacturing Manager (1987–1989)
Plant Manager (1986–1987)
Engineering Manager (1984–1986)
Plant Industrial Engineer (1980–1984)

EDUCATION & PROFESSIONAL DEVELOPMENT

Bachelor of Science in Manufacturing Engineering
New York University, New York, NY

Continuing professional development programs in
Executive Management, Leadership and Finance

are grouped under four topics to avoid a long list of statements. In the Professional Experience section an Achievements subheading for each workplace calls attention to accomplishments quantified by dollar amounts and percentages. Prior positions are referred to briefly near the end.

Alex C. Parker, Jr.

5555 Valley Drive • Canton, OH 55555
(555) 555-5555 • AlexParker@xxxx.com

Plant Engineering Manager

High-achieving Engineering Management professional with an impressive record of optimizing processes and systems, identifying and implementing cost savings and improving efficiency, quality and profitability in a high-speed manufacturing environment. Easily assimilate to new environments and technologies to quickly identify capital improvement project opportunities, develop project plans and implement efficient installation solutions. Results-driven leader adept at cultivating collaborative environments and leading engineering and maintenance teams when utilizing processes that minimize costs while maximizing output speed and product quality.

Systems Implementation • Capital Projects Conception & Execution • Project Management
Budgets & Cost Controls • P&L • Product Flow & Quality Improvement • Process Reengineering
ISO 9001 / 14001 • Lean Manufacturing • Employee Development • Preventative Maintenance

PROFESSIONAL EXPERIENCE

SIEMENS DEMATIC, Akron, OH • 09/2006–06/2010
Engineering & Maintenance Manager
Oversaw $4M in engineering and capital projects annually. Directed maintenance operations using a maintenance budget of $8.5M to drive process improvements for the wire and rope mills and 2 physical plants.

- Supervised 27 technicians, a maintenance manager, a mechanical supervisor and an electrical supervisor.
- Implemented lean manufacturing practices in both manufacturing and maintenance areas and began Six Sigma Green Belt Certification; prompted maintenance team to earn ISO 14001 and 9001 Certification.
- Collected and analyzed equipment breakdown data and enforced practices to reduce breakdowns by 15%.
- Decreased maintenance upkeep spending by $165K; negotiated better pricing with vendors, set up inventory system to alleviate overstocks, performed analysis to determine target areas to effectively reduce spending, etc.
- Led $250K lead pan replacement project; observed similar process in the UK before developing and implementing a plan to use in-house maintenance staff to complete the majority of the work; completed ahead of schedule and $20K under budget.
- Directed $475K strander installation project; finished on time and $60K under budget.
- Established preventative maintenance (PM) programs for machines in the rope mill based on value stream analysis results; incorporated environmental PM program in the wire mill.
- Earned ISO 9001:2008 Internal Auditor Certification.
- Implemented and trained others on maintenance management software system, Manager Pro Plus.

NELSON PUBLISHING, New Albany, OH • 12/2002–09/2006
Maintenance Supervisor
Administered a $6M annual budget while managing all maintenance and engineering projects and activities for 3 physical plants and the grounds.

- Decreased breakdowns by over 30% and lowered total maintenance department spending by over 10%.
- Established spare parts inventory based on repair data history; reduced equipment downtime and costly overnight shipping fees by having pertinent replacement parts on hand.
- Provided leadership and direction to 11 maintenance technicians and 13 temporary employees.
- Launched a window replacement initiative that actualized $15K in annual energy savings.

page 1

157

Combination. *Melanie Lenci, Denver, Colorado*

The applicant was anxious about being laid off in a weak economy. The writer filled this resume with many facts, figures, and bulleted accomplishments. The applicant was shocked to get

OHIO STEEL PLANT, Canton, OH • 09/1985–06/2002
Engineering & Maintenance Manager, 01/01–06/02
Managed a budget of $8.8M to drive all maintenance and engineering initiatives.

- Analyzed parts usage and reset inventory min/max limits to decrease inventory by 20% ($131K); negotiated the return of unneeded parts back to their vendors and sold other unneeded parts to companies still using them.
- Adjusted for volume and reduced the variable repair cost by $75K.
- Improved scheduling, enforced overtime restrictions and implemented PM system to lower total maintenance department spending by over 12%.
- Created and implemented a repair request system; earned a 95%+ completion rate in just 5 days.
- Supervised 9 maintenance journeymen, 2 porters and 2 engineers.

Engineering Manager, 01/99–12/00
Directed Engineering Department projects and activities within a budget of $4.2M per year.

- Led improvement projects, including the $1.5M tube mill rearrangement project and the $5M pilger mill installation project, which was completed on time and $70K below budget.
- Managed 3 engineers and 1 maintenance supervisor; developed maintenance and engineering training plans.
- Saved over $16K per year after evaluating furnace belt performance and implementing recommendations.

General Foreman, 09/90–12/98
Provided hands-on plant management for a $20M+ specialty seamless stainless steel tube and pipe manufacturing facility.

- Supervised 3 shift foremen, a training coordinator and 75 hourly production employees in a 24/7 operation; generated team buy-in and established training plans for all foremen and hourly personnel.
- Increased output by 29% to transform a mill that had never produced more than 5.5M ft. to one producing 7.2M ft. per year.
- Determined and scheduled regular weekly PM efforts, contributing to an increase in on-time delivery from 60% to 92% and a reduction in breakdowns by 30%.
- Launched internal study that led to a change in acid concentration usage, increasing bath life from 3 to 5 weeks and decreasing acid usage by over 37%.
- Lowered internal rejection rate from 2.5% to 1%.
- Developed and led the safety initiative; established a record of no-lost-time accidents for 15 months by establishing and documenting rules promoting safety and consistently enforcing violations.
- Led production, planning, warehouse and maintenance teams to achieve ISO 9002 Certification.
- Established regular shift meetings; meetings initially created a forum for employees to vent and share frustrations, but regular meetings eventually turned into a productive time for employees to share concerns and ideas and contribute to effective solutions.

Supervisor of Industrial Engineering, 11/89–08/90
Senior Industrial Engineer, 09/85–10/89

TECHNICAL SKILLS

Proficient with Microsoft Excel, Access, Word, Outlook, PowerPoint and Project, as well as dBASE III, AS400 SQL Querying, BPCS, Minitab, Elke and Manager Pro Plus (maintenance management systems), etc.

EDUCATION

BS, **Mechanical and Industrial Engineering,** Ohio State University, Columbus, OH
AS, **Engineering Science,** Shawnee State University, Portsmouth, OH

many calls for interviews and was told that this resume made him stand out ahead of the pack. His only complaint was that the resume made such a good impression that he was called in for the first interview and would have preferred to be last. He accepted a position he has thrived in since.

DAVID L. KENNERLY, MS, BS

555.505.0505 • davidkennerly@xxxx.net

MANUFACTURING ENGINEER

Top performer with uncommon versatility and a leadership record of results in process improvement, cost reduction and team building/training. Knowledgeable in manufacturing methods, production/maintenance processes, work flow planning, robotics, conveyor systems, pneumatic and hydraulic equipment, PLC, preventive maintenance testing procedures and multiple skilled trades. Expert in extending machine life.

■ ■ ■

Inspirational team leader with high expectations and a relaxed mentoring/coaching approach. Intuitive learner with a quick grasp of productivity tools and technologies. Fluent in MS Project, MS Office Suite, Lotus Notes and Factory Information Systems. Value-added, resourceful problem solver with a "can-do" attitude, a passion for aggressive goal attainment and a reputation for delivering on the bottom line.

■ EXPERIENCE

NISSAN NORTH AMERICA, Nashville, TN   1998–present

Total Productive Maintenance/Total Maintenance System Facilitator (3/07–present)
Administer Computerized Maintenance System (CMS) throughout Nashville Assembly Plant, ensuring compliance to recommended priorities, schedules and best practices across all jobs performed by millwrights, pipe fitters, electricians, carpenters, toolmakers and painters in 12-acre automotive production facility. Ensure compliance to timelines, benchmarks and performance expectations. Hire, train, schedule and evaluate 8 employees. Supervise HVAC and facilities personnel as necessary.

Hold weekly review meetings to discuss progress on maintenance issues with plant leadership and area managers. Complete 85–90% of maintenance tickets within 60 days—fulfilling corporate standard.

- Implemented plantwide Total Productive Maintenance (TPM) initiative in cooperation with multiple unions representing skilled trades and production workers.
- Achieved first TPM checkpoint on schedule, earning "Bench Mark Facility" recognition for establishing the corporate-wide performance standard. Cut downtime 30%, elevating throughput in pilot area.
- Reduced unexpected equipment failure by introducing Predictive Maintenance Program incorporating oil analysis, thermography, ultrasonic detection, chain stress and chain wear testing procedures.
- Delivered 20% annualized savings on maintenance labor (±5,500 hours) by streamlining procedures.
- Improved conveyor uptime 30% by addressing conveyor issues through biweekly lubrication meetings.

Maintenance Facilitator (4/03–2/07)
Directed maintenance and repair of body shop manufacturing equipment, including robotic and automated sealer systems and power and free Sys-T-Mation and Bliechert conveyor systems. Motivated and managed 17 employees.

- Slashed Framing downtime 50% by creating and installing inverted carrier stabilizer wheel detection system to detect missing parts on carriers.
- Delivered 30% increase in pipe fitter productivity by eliminating redundant procedures and standardizing maintenance procedures across all 3 shifts.
- Achieved unique 100% manpower versatility on second shift by cross training on all machinery.

Lead Maintenance Supervisor (4/00–3/03)
Maintenance Supervisor (5/98–3/00)
Oversaw, documented and reported preventive maintenance and repair of conveyor programmable logic controls, pneumatic and hydraulic equipment, mechanical systems and HVAC systems. Purchased and controlled replacement part inventory. Managed 49 maintenance supervisors and employees.

- Established centralized parts storage area and standardized parts on breakdown carts to facilitate quick repairs for 85% of common breakdowns.

Continued

158

Combination. *Ellie Vargo, St. Louis, Missouri*

Square bullets are used variously to separate paragraphs in the opening profile, to make evident the location of each section heading, and to point to significant achievements for

DAVID L. KENNERLY   555.505.0505 • davidkennerly@xxxx.net   Page 2

- Implemented weekend schedule for routine preventive maintenance.
- Reduced the cost of new door conveyor 40% by salvaging and reusing legacy conveyor drives.
- Cut installation costs by standardizing and optimizing equipment; reduced mean time between repairs by staging parts and repair equipment; and improved mean time between failures by installing part detection systems.

SCOTT AIRCRAFT COMPANY, Wichita, KS   1984–1998

Foreman Assembly Production (12/96–5/98)
Supervised wire bundle installation and final assembly of aircraft models. Monitored schedules, cycle times and realization. Motivated and managed up to 15 employees.

Specialist Manufacturing Methods Engineering (5/92–11/96)
Developed and implemented standard manufacturing methods, work flow plans and time standards for the Skyhawk and Skylane aircraft programs. Trained and managed up to 12 employees.

- Served as Variability Reduction/Process-Based Management Coordinator; analyzed production lags and implemented corrective action.
- Delivered 15% labor savings by developing Shop Planning Book containing detailed assembly instructions and precedence diagram(s) illustrating assembly sequence and required manpower.
- Achieved significant reduction in paint cycle prep time by establishing team to correct aircraft mold-line nonconformances.
- Automated troubleshooting of electronic and mechanical issues by laptop computers.

Senior Engineer Production Technology (3/88–4/92)
Justified and wrote specifications for equipment and systems needed to support manufacturing processes (e.g., electrical/electronic testing equipment; mechanical, environmental control and communications systems).

- Earned Integrated Product Division's "Step Above Award" for delivering $2 million in savings through alternative cooling method for avionics used in several aircraft models.
- Recognized with Scott Aircraft "President's Award" for results achieved in radioactive tracking assignment covering all production facilities nationwide.
- Achieved $30,000 in annualized savings (and "Bonus Award") by revising damaged fastener removal procedure.
- Initiated "Hand Tool Control" program to reduce tool loss.

Engineer Production Technology (1986–1988)
Associate Engineer Production Technology (1985–1986)
Mechanic/Electrician/Radioman Production (1984–1985)

■ AFFILIATIONS

Society of Manufacturing Engineers (SME)

■ EDUCATION & TRAINING

M.S., Organizational Management, University of Tennessee, Knoxville, TN
B.S., Aircraft Maintenance Engineering, Texas A & M University, College Station, TX
FAA Airframe & Powerplant Mechanic's License

each workplace in the Experience section. The use of square bullets throughout is a device that unifies the resume's two pages visually. Achievements in each set of accomplishments are quantified with percentages, numbers, or dollar amounts. The last two sections are center-justified.

Darren McConnell

(555) 555-5555
mcconnell@comcast.net

5555 Roland Road
Atlanta, GA 55555

MANUFACTURING OPERATIONS EXECUTIVE

Customer- and quality-focused business executive who provides the strategic vision and leadership that drive operational process, productivity, efficiency and bottom-line improvements at multisite manufacturing organizations.

Expert in combining financial and business planning with tactical execution to optimize long-term gains in performance, revenues and profitability. Breadth of experience in quality and manufacturing operations, including lean concepts, Six Sigma, root cause and Corrective Action Preventive Action (CAPA) analysis, team concepts total preventive maintenance, setup reduction and standard work. Leadership philosophy promotes employee participation in creative problem solving to contribute to organizational success.

Career Highlights:

Change Agent: Transformed a struggling business unit by using Kaizen principles that slashed hourly costs from $120 to $59, boosted on-time delivery from 48% to 97%, increased productivity metrics from 43% to 98% and reduced scrap from $1.65 million to only $325,000—all within 2 years.

Quality and Customer Champion: Instituted a CAPA and Quality Control Process Control (QCPC) that cut escapes to customers by 45% in 6 months and reduced Material Review Board (MRB) scrap by $3.4 million.

Team Builder and Coach: Boosted productivity 30% in a union operation by listening to root issues, forming teams to troubleshoot problems and fostering strong relationships among salaried and hourly staff.

PROFESSIONAL EXPERIENCE

BROWNSTONE CORPORATION, Atlanta, GA   2009–Present
VICE PRESIDENT OF OPERATIONS

Direct all manufacturing and assembly functions of 15 instruments produced by Brownstone and Worldwide Service. Manage team of 130 plus supplier and buyer relationships. Accountable for $25 million in OEM sales and $35 million in service warranties. Implement quality metrics to track business needs and lead diverse projects. Collaborate with R&D on products in development.

➢ **Rescued an OEM manufacturing operation struggling with declining employee motivation, poor process flow and escalating rework inventory at 34% of work in process.** Initiated multiple process improvements for work instructions, tooling and testing—creating a visual factory. **Results:**

- 53% reduction in work in progress (WIP), beating operating costs for 2 quarters.
- Cost-per-unit decrease of $100 below goal, with instruments now priced at $434 less than 2009.
- Excellent finished-goods inventory with no backorders for 2 consecutive quarters.
- Improved employee knowledge of business operations and streamlined product flow.

➢ **Tapped to lead development of Worldwide Service Strategy and rolled out the new initiative in the Netherlands in February 2011.** Established standard quality metrics such as value stream mapping (VSM), employee training and technical protocols for service upgrades and bulletins that improved communication and instrument repair services worldwide. **Results:**

- Clipped turnaround time from 38 to 22 days in 6 months, with a target goal of 2 days by year's end.
- Decreased turnbacks in process by 48% and reduced integration issues by 63%.

Page 1

159

Combination. *Louise Garver, Broad Brook, Connecticut*

The individual wanted to move to the next level in his career path but couldn't do so at his company. The writer created a strong profile that mentions three leadership strengths with

➢ **Initiated physical inventory of MRB Material, which included $5.3 million of unused inventory and potential scrap.** Implemented controls for inventory management, created teams to rework inventory and worked with suppliers to resolve issues. **Results:**

- Cut MRB to $1.9 million in 6 months with only $200,000 of scrap; reduced new orders on materials by 40%.
- Established compliant controls on inventory supporting Sarbanes-Oxley. Created more of a can-do attitude among employees.

➢ **Executed daily tracking procedures for Cost of Poor Quality, daily production output and financial tracking for instrument costs. Results:**

- Consistent daily production output; below-budget average product cost, optimizing the bottom line; 62% reduction in run rate.

ARRON CORPORATION, Atlanta, GA   1991–2009
Fast-track progression to senior-level operations management positions of multimillion-dollar divisions and business units with multiple product lines.
GENERAL MANAGER (2006–2009)

Challenged to turn around a nonperforming operation and effected a successful culture change throughout the division that focused all personnel on product quality and delivery plan execution. Supervised a team of 300 in repair operations and held full P&L accountability for budgeting, sales and asset management. Tasked with new product implementation and growing the existing line. **Results:**

➢ **Built sales from $32 million to $73 million in 2009. ROS spiked from 11% to 28% of the business fixed at 15% ROS opportunity with military contracts. Results:**

- Cut average turnaround time (TAT) from 76 days to 18 with on-time delivery percentage ending at 98% through rollout of lean concepts and standardized repair processes.
- Customer satisfaction ranked 6.3 out of 7.

➢ **Devised plan that addressed monumental issues with aged material and uncontrolled inventory. Worked closely with other businesses to launch the unit's inventory management system and SAP, as one of the first units to implement system company-wide. Results:**

- Led unit to win recognition as the flagship of all aftermarket businesses in inventory control, as well as achieve the best Sarbanes-Oxley audit in the company in 2008.
- Wrote off $5 million in inventory by building cribs and putting controls in place to better manage materials, allowing unit to become compliant with Price Waterhouse audit criteria.

➢ **Spearheaded strategies that improved processes and delivery performance and reversed losses of $1,000 per unit delivered, saving a $17 million military contract that was in jeopardy.** Teamed with the Contracts department to amend a military contract, recouping more money for products serviced.

BUSINESS UNIT MANAGER (2000–2006)

Brought on board to reduce costs, improve delivery performance and correct major quality issues. Directed a team of 146 and managed $14 million budget. Cut hourly production costs by $27 and improved delivery from 53% to 98% by creating a visual factory and established cells in machining areas.

Prior: Quality Unit Leader/Senior Supervisor (1996–2000); Quality Supervisor (1991–1996)

EDUCATION

Executive MBA — UNIVERSITY OF GEORGIA, Atlanta, GA, 2008
BS in Business — UNIVERSITY OF NORTH CAROLINA, Raleigh, NC, 2006

achievements to support those strengths. The Professional Experience section tells the applicant's success stories and shows the range of his abilities. He sent his first resume to a major industry player in his community, and he landed a new position at the level he was seeking.

Roseanne Sullivan

"the glue of the company"

PO Box 555, Charlestown, NH 55555-5555

Rhsnh05@xxxx.com • Cell: 555-555-5555

http://www.linkedin.com/pub/roseanne-sullivan

OPERATIONS MANAGEMENT

PROFESSIONAL QUALIFICATIONS

Extensive background managing all aspects of plant operations for technology and manufacturing companies. Track record of saving money and delivering the highest possible ROI. Will go above and beyond to help the company succeed and exceed expectations of customers and colleagues. Areas of expertise include:

Strategic Planning & Execution	Staff Development/Turnover Reduction
Budget Planning, Development & Control	Client Value-Focused Business
Cost Reduction with Quality Improvement	Exceptional Customer Service
Operational & Financial Risk Management	Production & Inventory Control
Purchasing & Supply Chain Management	Continuous Process Improvement

Computer Skills: Proficient with MS Office (Word, Excel, PowerPoint, Access), Sage Peachtree software, and Intuit QuickBooks, and savvy at learning new programs.

PROFESSIONAL EXPERIENCE

Operations Manager, Frontier Design Group LLC, Lebanon, NH   3/06–Present

Manage a set of contract manufacturing services, internal testing processes, and external fulfillment operations that support the company's growth in the area of digital audio hardware. Evaluate and deliver analysis of finances: AP, AR, Payroll, Cash Flows, Income, and Balance statements. Guide and support the research & development group in the area of parts sourcing, price negotiations, database management, and price/cost analysis. Plan and attend 3 trade shows annually (1 international) to develop new business for our digital audio product line.

- Built our network of 50 domestic retailers and 30 international distributors for our digital audio product line by cultivating relationships and implementing outstanding customer service protocols.

- Led the team to bring our test process in-house, which decreased our failure rate by 25% and reduced the product cost by 15%.

Continued

160

Combination. *Mary Ellen Brew, Merrimack, New Hampshire*

The shaded text box is the feature that catches the eye first. A large font size and adequate white space help to spread out the resume over two full pages. Boldfacing appears in strategic

Roseanne Sullivan   Rhsnh05@xxxx.com   Page Two

Operations Manager, The Sperry Group, Springfield, VT   8/04–2/06

- Directed a short-term manufacturing operation for the production of (200) foam-in-place packaging systems. Developed budgets, fitted up a suitable space, hired and trained manufacturing employees, purchased material, and documented the manufacturing process.

- Collaborated with the customer to transfer the manufacturing technology to a contract manufacturer for increased volume production.

Purchasing Manager, Fostex Research & Development, Hanover, NH   6/02–4/04

- Identified and implemented a plan to reduce the cost of the bills of material for the Foundation 2000 audio production system by 25%, thus allowing the product to be manufactured in the United States instead of in Asia.

- Initiated a project to reduce the vendor base from 50+ vendors to 15 key vendors, creating a dedicated core of suppliers whose performance was easier to measure and monitor.

- Designed and implemented new specific sourcing support to the R&D group by improving vendor management and analysis.

Purchasing Manager, New England Digital Corp., Lebanon, NH   3/92–6/00

- Demonstrated synergistic teamwork that propelled the company's growth from $5M to $23M over an 8-year period with skillful commodity management of integrated circuits, disk drives, and electromechanical material used in the production of the state-of-the-art Synclavier music production system.

- Directed the purchasing operation's adoption and implementation of Just In Time and Lean Manufacturing practices.

- Established in-house stores for long lead time and high-cost material that increased inventory turns by 30%, enabling vendors to invoice for weekly use.

EDUCATION

Bachelor of Arts, Political Science, Elmira College, Elmira, NY, 1982
Certificate, Advanced Graduate Studies, Foundations of Management, University of MA, Amherst, MA, 2003

places: the applicant's name, her career field, the section headings, and the work positions held. Note the descriptive phrase for the applicant that appears under her name. A simple, five-word phrase can catch a reader's attention and build respect for the applicant.

Bernard T. Bailey

123 Main Street
Park Point, IL 00000

555-555-5555
xxxx@aol.com

HIGHLIGHTS OF VALUE TO A POTENTIAL EMPLOYER

- In-depth knowledge of **manufacturing and distribution operations and logistics**, with a particular strength in improving efficiency with effective **supply-chain analysis, production planning and scheduling.**
- Hands-on experience in **materials forecasting, purchasing and inventory management.**
- Versatile problem-solver, especially in the application of technology to the planning process, as well as day-to-day operations.
- Computer and related equipment skills: Microsoft Office suite, Crystal Reports, Novell NetWare, PCs, HP printers.

PROFESSIONAL EXPERIENCE

Northern Industries, Inc., Portland, OR, 2000 to Present
Local Systems Administrator / Corrugator Scheduler for the Pleasant Park, IL, plant of this major manufacturer of corrugated containers and point-of-purchase products. Firm recently merged into the XYZ Company.

- Maintain plant LAN systems; provide training and first-line user support for systems issues.
- Install and repair computer equipment.
- Plan and direct production schedules for two-shift machine operation.
- Forecast, purchase and manage raw materials inventory within sales budget.
- Manage finished-for-release inventories for key accounts.
- Provide expertise for sales and production departments to establish new product requirements.

Tech Systems, Park Point, IL, 1998–2000

- Established and operated a company selling and servicing computer products for small businesses.

ABC Housewares Manufacturing, Inc., Western Park, IL, 1993–1998
Assistant Warehouse Manager

- Developed significant improvements in layout and operational procedures to increase productivity.
- Installed warehouse management computer system; provided liaison to data processing staff and system vendor.
- Trained operations staff and led the transition to new procedures.

Additional experience gained with the following:

- **Distribution Systems Analyst** with **DDD Corporation,** Chicago, IL, 1986–1993. Completed projects to develop and maintain layouts of multi-warehouse distribution center, analyze material-handling requirements and branch store inventory sharing, and research computer support requirements.
- Intelligence Analyst with the U.S. Army, 1975–1982, and the Central Intelligence Agency, 1982–1983.

EDUCATION

Big State University, Big State, IL
Bachelor of Science in Administrative Science, 1986

161

Combination. *Christine L. Dennison, Lincolnshire, Illinois*

Companies assume that mature applicants want a high position or high salary, but this applicant wanted only a "decent" amount of responsibility. The writer presents him as low-key and reliable.

Media

Resumes at a Glance

LAURA A. PAUL

lapaul@xxxx.com . . . . 555.555.5555 . . . . Mukwonago, Wisconsin

MULTIMEDIA SPECIALIST

Television Production . . . Web Design . . . Online Multimedia . . . Photography

Featuring 8+ Years of Providing High-Quality Technical Direction and Production Services
Excellent Record in Meeting Deadlines—Solid Commitment to Professional Development

TECHNICAL SKILLS SUMMARY

- **TELEVISION / VIDEO PRODUCTION:** Editing, camera operation (robotic and manual), floor direction, technical direction, switching, lighting and set design, teleprompter, graphics, utility, SD & HD systems transmission, and digital media.
- **WEB DESIGN / ONLINE MULTIMEDIA / PHOTOGRAPHY:** HTML, CSS, ASP, Flash, Web audio / video; digital cameras; and fully designed 3 Web sites.
- **COMPUTER:** Adobe Photoshop, Illustrator; Visual Basic; Macromedia Dreamer; Director; MS Word, Excel, PowerPoint, Outlook; After Effects; various types of editing software (including AVID and Adobe Premier); DEKO Graphic Systems; INews and Control Air Operations; Louth Master Control System; and Sat Truck.

RELEVANT EXPERIENCE

CW MILWAUKEE—Milwaukee, Wisconsin   2008–Present
Engineering Technician
As sole third-shift technician, execute Master Control of all overnight programming, ensuring schedule compliance, managing discrepancies, and recording show feeds. Operate 6 robotic studio cameras for daily early morning newscasts. Track transmitter reading during the night and maintain FCC compliance for the Emergency Alert System (EAS).
- Improved efficiency and ease of overnight operations by designing and implementing computerized-contact tracking system for dealing with unexpected circumstances.

JOHNSON BROADCAST GROUP—Milwaukee, Wisconsin   2006–2008
Technical Director
Hired into lead role to provide technical direction for Channel 5 *News at 9* daily program. Operated teleprompter and edited headline segments. Directed various small live pieces; edited and ran audio. Additional responsibilities included switching, operating, and shading robotic cameras, and controlling digital-video effects (DVE) and still-store devices.
- Selected to train several peers in technical direction and editing technique.

Freelance Production   2004–2009
Successfully completed numerous projects that included:
- TIME WARNER CABLE—Acted as technical director and audio operator for televised high school sporting events; operated cameras in filming 4th of July parades for local cable programming. Other functions included switching, audio, and utility.
- MUKWONAGO SCHOOL DISTRICT—Provided technical direction and operated camera for broadcast of school board meetings on the school's cable channel.
- MILWAUKEE AREA TECHNICAL COLLEGE—Operated camera for 3-day coverage of educational symposium.

MILWAUKEE PUBLIC TELEVISION CHANNELS 10 & 36—Milwaukee, Wisconsin   2004–2006
Production Staff Member
Played various roles: camera operation, floor direction, lighting and set design, editing, audio production, teleprompting, and switching.

EDUCATION

MILWAUKEE AREA TECHNICAL COLLEGE
- **Associate's degree, Television Production**, 2005—Named *Second Year Production Student of the Year* in 2005
- **Associate's degree, Visual Communications**—Anticipated graduation in 2013

162

Combination. *Linda Dobogai, New Berlin, Wisconsin*

The applicant was open to several different multimedia fields, so the writer used a clip-art image representing multifaceted interests, plus a Technical Skills Summary showing a range of abilities.

Marilyn Forester

900 Limrock Avenue
Windsor, CT 00000
(555) 555-5555
mforester@yahoo.com

Career Profile

Results-oriented Sales, Marketing and Account Management Professional with a solid history of verifiable accomplishments in the competitive broadcast arena. *Key Strengths:*

- Proven ability to identify and acquire new accounts, retain existing clients, design creative promotions and generate revenues and profitability.
- Effective negotiator with expertise in the sales process; adept at selling conceptually by using qualitative information.
- Committed to building long-term relationships and finding solutions to address customer needs, resulting in mutual growth.
- Sales leadership skills to train and mentor new recruits to achieve results.
- Computer proficient in Tapscan, Qualitap, Media Master, Target One and other software programs.
- Bilingual in English and Spanish.

Professional Experience

<u>WPTX-AM & WPTX-FM</u>, Hartford, CT   2002–present
Part of Channel Communications One, a global organization that owns and operates numerous radio stations, television stations and billboard companies, as well as holds equity interests in other media companies.

Account Executive (2004–present)
Promoted to build new and expand existing account base in the greater Springfield metropolitan and northern Connecticut territory. Experienced and successful in selling advertising on both stations (adult contemporary and news/talk formats). Build strong partnerships with local direct clients and advertising agencies in the local, regional and national marketplace. Accountable for sales and marketing strategies, copywriting, proposal writing and promotional planning.

- *Grew annual revenues from zero base to more than $380,000, developing and managing 75 accounts.*
- *Won 2011, 2010, 2009 President's Club Award; consistently recognized as one of the top performers.*
- *Chosen out of 15 account executives from 3 different radio stations to win 2011 Team Spirit Award for leadership and outstanding sales performance.*
- *Designed several creative promotional tie-ins that generated profits for both the radio station and clients.*
- *Cultivate and maintain strong, ongoing relationships with clients while working collaboratively to meet their advertising needs. Commended for excellent service and follow-up.*
- *Selected by management to train and mentor new account executives, providing effective coaching in sales techniques, marketing strategies, proposal writing and related topics.*

Business Manager (2002–2004)
Coordinated accounts payable, accounts receivable and payroll for 70 employees at both stations. Posted entries to the general ledger, invoiced customers and performed credit checks as well as collections. Prepared month-end and year-end closings and financial reports for corporate management.

- *Implemented system that cut days outstanding by 50% (down to 30–60 days), significantly reducing backlog of past-due accounts and bringing accounts receivable under control.*
- *Instituted credit approval system where none previously existed, which included performing extensive account research and reconciliation.*
- *Initiated recordkeeping system for accounts payable that improved accuracy and ensured on-time payments.*

Education

Bachelor of Arts in Communications, UNIVERSITY OF CALIFORNIA, Riverside, CA, 2001

163

Combination. *Louise Garver, Broad Brook, Connecticut*

The individual was planning to relocate and was seeking a similar position. The writer emphasized the depth of the applicant's skills, experience, and achievements. The person got a new job quickly.

JASON PETERS

928 Arthur Road • Port Reading, New Jersey 22222 • (333) 333-3333 • jpeters@aol.com

Media manager whose accomplishments reflect effective leadership, an innovative mindset, strong sales and client management skills, and expertise in identifying effective means of corporate communications

SUMMARY OF QUALIFICATIONS

Forward-thinking professional with 15 years of experience in the audio-visual services field. Demonstrated expertise in both the development of promotional materials and the production and orchestration of media events. Innovative and resourceful with strong grasp of how to best reach target audiences. Proven record in delivering communications solutions that hit the mark. Respected business partner with extensive array of industry contacts. Able to successfully identify client needs and create cost-effective programs that are consistent with company image and style. Valued for vision in finding new and better ways to do business. Effective leader who embraces the ideals of customer satisfaction and encourages creativity and risk-taking to make it happen. Top-notch communications skills. Effective in adapting messages to regional, national, and international audiences. Progressive in outlook and quick to adopt new technologies.

PROFESSIONAL EXPERIENCE

MEDIAMASTERS, Franklin Park, New Jersey   Apr 1997 to present
Business Development Manager – New Jersey (Mar 2002 to present)
Manage department of six, overseeing all aspects of client engagement and client projects. Develop promotional materials to generate new business. Communicate with prospects to identify needs, developing and presenting client proposals and implementing project plans. Hired as technician, earned promotion to assistant manager after only one year. Earned second promotion to current position in 2002.

- Successfully manage company advertising to bring in new prospects. Designed brochure sent out in mass mailing and developed multimedia advertising plan that integrated print ads, radio spots, and website to promote services.

- Designing creative and cost-effective proposals, successfully built client base and customer confidence while ensuring frequent repeat business. Grew client base by 60% since becoming manager, successfully bringing on several major well-known international companies.

- Developed innovative presentation proposal for major client that saved thousands of dollars by converting a company warehouse into a temporary theatre, eliminating the need for offsite facilities. Plan was later adapted and successfully used to orchestrate cost-effective presentations for many other clients.

- Positioned company to compete more effectively for staging contracts by successfully streamlining labor and eliminating waste to significantly reduce program costs.

- Developed webcast for well-known car manufacturer that allowed CEO to address employees from overseas location, saving both time and money.

EDUCATION & CONTINUING DEVELOPMENT

WESTERN UNIVERSITY, Sunnyvale, California
Bachelor of Science in Radio, Television and Film (Emphasis: Media Management)
➢ Worked at Panavision, scheduling, operating and maintaining film and video equipment.

Seminars and Workshops:
Writing, Producing and Directing Workshop, American Film Institute
Media Management Program, ICIA
Extensive product training on Sony and Panasonic products

TECHNOLOGY SKILLS

PowerPoint ◆ Word ◆ Excel ◆ Internet ◆ Script Writing ◆ Video Editing ◆ Video Shooting ◆ Video Teleconferencing

164

Combination. *Carol A. Altomare, Three Bridges, New Jersey*

This media manager wanted to show that he could "do it all" in developing and coordinating media events and in communicating effectively. The writer uncovered and displayed his innovativeness.

JOHN A. DAVIS

555 Morgan Hill Road ▪▪ Atlanta, GA 55555 ▪▪ 555.555.5555 ▪▪ jad@cox.net

Media Professional
Marketing ▪▪ Operations ▪▪ Production ▪▪ Programming

Award-winning management professional with 13 years of television operations experience, including marketing, promotions, sales and strategic partner development. Significant contributor to revenue growth through innovative programming, promotional events and other sales-related opportunities.

Proven Competencies

- Strategic Marketing Planning
- Promotions
- Production
- Program Development
- Media Buying
- Operations
- Partner Development
- Team Building & Leadership
- Negotiations
- Vendor Relations
- Sales/Presentations
- Project Management
- Writing/Editing
- Audio Engineering
- Videography
- Marketron Research Tools

Awards

Georgia Association of Broadcasters
- Television Promo of the Year:
  1st Place, 2010 and 2009
- PSA of the Year:
  2nd Place, 2010

Georgia Vision Awards
- Best of Show (1), 2006
- Gold (1), 2008
- Silver (2), 2009
- Bronze (2), 2010

Telly Awards
- Media Promotion, 2010
- Videography, 2002

Atlanta Ad Club Award

Southeast Regional Emmy Award, 2011

Career Achievements

WAXT-TV, Atlanta, GA
<u>Creative Services Director</u> (2007 to Present)

Designed and executed innovative marketing strategies, which significantly improved station's ratings, recognition and revenues. Spearhead creative direction for all promotional campaigns and on-air strategies, including setting superior quality standards to maximize on-air impact. Built and lead team of 4 in all promotions and production activities.

Monitor commercial projects to help develop highly effective mass-media messages for clients. Write and produce majority of station's award-winning custom promos. Personally handle/oversee daily promo placement, execute media buys and manage budget.

Act as station's spokesperson and key contact on network/programming and station events. Participate with senior management in strategic program-planning initiatives that impact acquisitions and on-air broadcast schedule.

<u>Marketing/Branding</u>: **Overhauled station's branding and developed its professional on-air image.** Orchestrated more effective promotional events and contests; improved promo placement.

- **Optimized limited off-air promotional budget by cultivating strong cross-media relationships** that generate free publicity and support programming. **Negotiate lowest rates for spot buys.**
- **Launched a subbrand,** creating open, close and bumpers that **maximize audience identification** with WAXT.
- **Drove creation, planning and production of successful ongoing revenue-generating programs.**

Bottom Line …

Helped propel ratings to record levels within station's 14-year history.

- Average ratings in Adults 18–49 Monday–Friday jumped 34.7% for 5p–6p, 100.7% for 6p–8p and 40.4% for 8p–10p time periods.
- As of 2/12, station placed 2nd in both traditional and common prime time ratings in all key demographics.
- Station achieved 3rd-place status sign-on to sign-off for the first time.

Generated more than $200,000 through nontraditional revenue streams with creative program development such as WAXT Kids News, Weatherline and LegalLine.

Page 1

165

Combination. *Louise Garver, Broad Brook, Connecticut*

This individual wanted to relocate and apply his management skills in a position in programming, marketing, production, or creative services at a TV station. The writer used underlined

WAXT-TV *continued*…

- **Sales Promotions & Production**: Interface with Sales and clients to review and facilitate all sales-driven promotions to ensure successful completion and maximum impact tied to station's goals. Oversee and handle writing and production of all spots. Create and manage all phases of contesting, from developing official rules to tracking all winner-related activity.

  - Lead every station in the market in implementing the FCC's mandated station identifications as show promotion opportunities, thereby reinforcing station branding.
  - Eliminated inaccuracy of on-air promos by developing an intuitive promotional numbering system.

- **Affiliate Marketing / Off-Air Event Sponsorships**: Heightened station awareness to become the preferred media partner for nonprofit groups, driving cause-marketing efforts while strengthening community ties. Established, nurture and manage ongoing relationships with local chapters of the American Heart Association, American Cancer Society and Juvenile Diabetes Research Foundation, among others.

  - Expanded station recognition and audience awareness by initiating, negotiating and overseeing event sponsorships with several local organizations.
  - Led American Cancer Society's PSA creation publicizing various initiatives. Spearhead and represent station at the Atlanta Mayor's Cancer Awareness Day—an annual multiorganization coalition.
  - Invited to join the Champlain Valley Crime Stoppers' Board of Directors and chaired the Executive Director Search subcommittee.

- **Media Buying**: Cost-effectively manage and execute all media buys ($90,000 annually) of off-air media (radio, print and cable) based on CPPs and GRPs, including final production and trafficking.

  - Developed traffic system and sophisticated Excel spreadsheet to facilitate placement of media buys while reconciling co-op advertising with WAXT, WB and syndicators.

- **Technology**: Concurrent responsibility as computer network administrator for 25 on-site and remote users. Previously, as master control supervisor, managed 7 people and wrote procedures for creating the best-quality video on the air with the fewest errors possible.

  - Replaced antiquated system on Windows Server 2008 with separate Zix anti-spam email server solution, providing capacity to handle future IT demands.

- **Elected and serve on Promotional Advisory Council. Elected as Secretary in 2010.**

Master Control Operator (1999 to 2006)

Operated and maintained audio, video and satellite equipment. Filled in as news audio engineer as needed and periodically directed taped news segments and live weather updates. Managed switching from programming to commercials and ensured feeds were of top broadcasting quality. Rotated through news, promotions and film departments, expanding industry knowledge.

- **Tapped to fill role of audio engineer** by demonstrating self-taught expertise of audio equipment.

Education

Bachelor of Arts in Communication with **Emphasis on Mass Media,** 1999
Georgia State University, Atlanta, GA

Computer & Technical Skills

Proficient in Microsoft Word, Excel and PowerPoint

subheadings in the Career Achievements section and created a separate column to showcase the person's diverse range of competencies and accomplishments in his industry. He wanted to work at a particular station, and he was chosen from several hundred applicants.

ALEXANDRA M. DUPONTE

555 Center Court, Hollywood, CA 00000
555.555.5555 Email: a.duponte@xxxx.com

MEDIA & PUBLIC RELATIONS PROFESSIONAL

Award-winning and dynamic professional with broad scope of experience combining broadcasting, media production, public relations/speaking and community outreach, with sales, marketing, business and operational expertise. Leader and overachiever with unsurpassed dedication to organizational success. Offer expertise in human resource and customer relationship management, employee training and development, and product and business expansion. Strong capacity to promote workforce harmony and efficiency through strong sensitivity and multicultural literacy. *Areas of expertise include:*

COMMUNICATIONS

- Entertainment & Media Production
- Educational / Informative Broadcasts
- Public Relations / Community Outreach
- Event Leadership & Sponsorship

SALES & MARKETING

- Business & Marketing Plans
- Customer Focus / Relationships
- News & Press Releases
- Presentations & Demonstrations

MANAGEMENT

- Recruitment & Training
- Operations Oversight
- Budgeting / Allocation
- Technological Control

PROFESSIONAL EXPERIENCE

TELEVISION HOST
Plasco Television—Daytime, Burbank, California, 2004–Present

Interview guests for daily live television lifestyle and entertainment show. Assist with program scheduling. Recruit and train employees and volunteers in all aspects of broadcast production. Represent company at public and private events. Educate and inform the public on issues of interest and concern including healthcare, family life, community safety and inspirational events.

Selected Accomplishments

- Serve as Master of Ceremonies at public and private events, representing Plasco Television to establish goodwill and presence in the community.
- Serve as assistant producer to book 90% of show's featured appearances.
- Demonstrate dedication to organizational success by providing help and assistance in all production areas, maintaining composure in high-profile, stressful settings while promoting ease and confidence in others.

SALES & MARKETING MANAGER
Centrex Homes, San Jose, CA, 1999–2004

Managed sales office, recruiting, training and scheduling local and remote sales staff. Developed business and marketing plans. Created and implemented employee sales incentives. Submitted weekly/monthly progress and status reports to senior-level management. Directed and participated in public relations and trade show events.

Selected Accomplishments

- Won five high-value newspaper and magazine feature articles because of exceptional public relations and negotiation skills, increasing sales and company recognition.
- Consistently rated as top sales person; won numerous monthly and annual sales awards.
- Authored and implemented sales staff training manual.

EDUCATION & CREDENTIALS

BACHELOR OF ARTS IN MEDIA AND COMMUNICATIONS (2000)
University of California, Los Angeles (UCLA), Los Angeles, CA

Publications:

Duponte, Alexandra. 2002. "Media in the Twenty-first Century." *The New Media*. Sacramento, CA: Blum Publishing, Inc.
Duponte, Alexandra. 2002. "A New Dawn." *The New Media*. Sacramento, CA: Blum Publishing, Inc.

166

Combination. *Karen Bartell, Massapequa Park, New York*

The applicant hosted a daytime television show and wanted new challenges. The writer highlighted areas of expertise in the top third of the resume and emphasized award-winning achievements.

ELIZA BOWDEN

555 Junction Drive | St. Louis, Missouri 00000 | elizabowden@xxxx.com | 555.555.5555

MEDIA EXECUTIVE
Distinguished career leading development, programming, and production efforts in local and national markets

Award-winning, innovative strategist with repeated success developing original, cutting-edge programming content to maximize revenue and visibility. Expertise in identifying top-performing programs and maximizing effectiveness and placement to meet organizational needs. Skilled communicator able to translate strategic goals into actionable solutions. Expert presenter with background in serving as host, spokesperson, and on-air talent. ***Core competencies****:*

Strategic and Long-range Planning	Broadcast / Cable Operations Leadership	Branding / Image Development
Content Strategy & Development	Best Practices / Policies & Procedures	Trend Identification & Analysis
Budget Planning / Administration	Online / Offline Marketing Campaigns	Team Building & Leadership
Public & Community Relations	New Revenue Stream Development	Fund-raising & Development

PROFESSIONAL EXPERIENCE

KXYZ—MISSOURI PUBLIC TELEVISION (PBS), St. Louis, Missouri   1997–Present
Executive Producer & Membership Director
Drive revenue generation by leading multimedia fund-raising and marketing programs, to include programming, production, product placement, direct mail campaigns, Web promotions, and social media initiatives. Maximize member retention and acquisition by directing strategic planning and creative/editorial efforts. Supervise up to 30 employees and volunteers. Maintain strong relationships with television and entertainment industry contacts, staff, and vendors. Oversee messaging and brand placement across all platforms. Produce original concepts for on-air and Web promotions.

- **Attained more than 40% of gross on-air revenue** by acquiring independent programming and original content to distinguish KXYZ brand.
- **Generated $18M+ with 5% annual revenue growth** by identifying outreach strategies and diverse program niches.
- **Defined new revenue streams** by leveraging partnerships and implementing turnkey and original concepts.
- **Streamlined operations and improved outreach** by strengthening cross-departmental and vendor communications.
- **Identified and maximized placement of top-performing pledge programs**.

SHIMMING MEDIA, LLC, St. Louis, Missouri   1999–Present
Executive Producer / Marketing Consultant
Hold full P&L responsibility for production and marketing organization. Manage and consult on business development, proposal creation, contract negotiation, product development, and employee training functions. Oversee budgeting and report generation. Write scripts and direct and guide projects from concept to delivery phases.

- Released "Your Health" program, DVD, and companion workbook, **securing more than 100 airings in 20+ PBS markets nationwide**.
- **Produced 86 episodes of "Televideos"** for broadcast and cable distribution.
- **Served as spokesperson** for Anderson Regional Hospital's "Your Health" TV and PBS national pledge events.
- **Streamlined production and postproduction efforts** by introducing improved methodologies.

EDUCATION

WASHINGTON UNIVERSITY, St. Louis, Missouri
Bachelor of Arts in Communication, Emphasis in Television & Film Production

167

Combination. *Michelle P. Swanson, Edwardsville, Illinois*

Note the alignment of the core competencies: left alignment of the left column, center alignment of the center column, and right alignment of the right column, making a pleasing arrangement.

KRISTIN L. ANDREWS

555.505.5500 • kandrews@xxxx.net

MEDIA/COMMUNICATIONS DIRECTOR
Strategic thinker with keen awareness of what constitutes a "big" story.

Poised spokesperson and prolific published writer with significant achievement in communicating mission, organizing events, generating positive PR and inspiring others to action. Energetic project manager with demonstrated success in designing and executing both grassroots and sophisticated media campaigns.

■ ■ ■

Dynamic speaker and presenter. Engaging rapport builder; effective in building productive partnerships and alliances based on veracity, follow-through and trust. Investigative problem solver; expert in finding creative ways to present perennial stories. Top performer with a collaborative spirit, an expansive network of media relationships, and a passion for inspiring others to action with a compelling message.

■ EXPERIENCE ■

KENTUCKY DIVISION OF CONSERVATION   2007–present

Energized media efforts to enhance awareness of the Division's mission and clarify its purpose in helping Kentucky residents connect with wildlife and the outdoors. Leveraged publicity opportunities to deliver measurable increases in nature-center traffic, volunteerism and special-interest class attendance.

Metro Media Specialist
Develop and execute strategic initiatives around the Division's mission: managing and preserving forest, fish and wildlife resources through education and outreach. Identify and develop long-term funding sources; foster strategic partnerships and alliances among regional and national agencies, nonprofit organizations and corporations. Plan and coordinate special events in cooperation with strategic partners.

Manage all aspects of print and broadcast media communications within the geographic area surrounding Lexington. Write and distribute press releases, articles and leave-behind materials. Provide reporters and producers related tools and resources to make their jobs easier—and gain leverage in negotiating story/ad placement. Coordinate and produce biweekly interviews and story packages for television, radio and cable outlets in the Lexington market. Provide information to school districts and chambers of commerce to aid in educational and tourism efforts. Solicit public-speaking engagements.

- Achieved publication of special-interest articles in 144 print media outlets including *Lexington Herald-Leader* and *Kentucky Conservationist*. Wrote, contributed to or promoted numerous articles and events annually: 160 in 2007, 364 in 2008 and 300+ in 2009.

- Produced and hosted "Conservation Currents" for WLEX-TV Channel 18.

- Promoted subject-matter experts to the media and won coverage for annual events including Eagle Days, Mobile Aquarium, Kids' Fishing Day, Maple Sugar Days, hiking opportunities and Lexington Conservation Area programs airing on WDFB, WRLF, WFLE, WBUL, WMXL and WKED radio.

- Achieved feature articles, mentions and calendar notes in prominent publications including *Nature Conservancy Magazine* and *Kentucky Living*. Mentioned in *Nature Conservancy Magazine* as "best place in the country to watch eagles" and "4th best place in the country to watch birds" (for Lexington Conservation Area), 2008. Contributed to Mammoth Cave feature published in *Kentucky Living*, 2009.

- Organized public forums on potentially volatile subjects including bow hunting as a solution to deer overpopulation in West Fayette County. Provided informational materials, assembled speaker panels, set up audiovisual equipment and engaged media participation. This effort resulted in successful bow hunts in two suburban communities that had previously rejected deer kills of any type.

- Organized and managed publicity for national conference attended by 1,200 guests. Produced registration materials and signage; orchestrated speaker logistics.

- Developed monthly newsletter with timely articles that reaches more than 13,000 households, schools and nongovernmental agencies.

Page 1

168

Combination. *Ellie Vargo, St. Louis, Missouri*

The opening section between horizontal lines is a profile to capture the reader's attention. Centered headings guide the eye down through the resume. The Experience section spans two

KRISTIN L. ANDREWS   555.505.5500 • kandrews@xxxx.net   Page 2

- Created 28-page *Conservation Resource Guide* featuring answers to common questions regarding hunting and fishing in Kentucky.

- Manage relationships with local media outlets and partnerships/alliances with agencies and organizations including Army Corps of Engineers and Brigadoon State Nature Preserve.

- Develop written responses ("fact sheets") to defuse crises and minimize negative impact of sensitive and/or potentially damaging information.

- Organize convention exhibits, select appropriate literature and coordinate staffing schedules for All Equipment Expo, Boat & Sport Show, Working Women Survival Show and Forest Products Conference.

- Promote the agency, its mission and its dedicated employees through frequent media appearances and speaking engagements with civic and community groups.

ETHICAL SOCIETY OF CINCINNATI   2004–2007

Outreach and Events Manager
Increased nonprofit's visibility in the community through an assertive public relations approach. Wrote frequent news releases to publicize visiting speakers, solicited corporate underwriters for radio programming, organized special events, and leased building space to community groups to raise interest in the organization's mission among Lexington media outlets.

- Organized (and negotiated sponsorships for) National American Ethical Society convention attended by 650 attendees.

- Developed Web site content and graphic links.

MARKETING ON CALL OF CINCINNATI OHIO   2002–2004

Administrator
Interviewed and screened applicants for marketing and graphics positions. Produced and managed an extensive database of corporate clients and freelance employees.

CONNECT ONE   2001–2002

Account Supervisor
Supervised, coached and tracked the performance of 40 associates executing special projects for AT&T. Edited and coordinated telemarketing scripts.

CINCINNATI COUNTY PARKS   1999–2001

Coordinator, Volunteer Services/Eggleston Park
Planned and executed media campaigns to publicize annual festivals, art installations and volunteer opportunities. Established volunteer training programs; conducted meetings and appreciation events. Oversaw staffing schedules in gallery gift shop.

■ **PROFESSIONAL AFFILIATIONS** ■

Lexington Regional Commerce and Growth Association
Public Relations Society of America
Community Service Public Relations Council

■ **EDUCATION** ■

B.S., Communications/Sociology, GPA: 3.7, Ohio University–Athens, 1999

- *Who's Who Among Students in American Universities and Colleges*
- Dean's List; Leadership Program

pages. Boldfacing highlights the applicant's positions, and square bullets point to significant achievements for the current and most recent position. The Professional Affiliations section is centered for a sense of variation.

ELLIOT WAGNER

5 Henry Hudson Avenue · Hoboken, NJ 55555 · 555.555.5555 · ewagner@xxxx.com

EXECUTIVE MEDIA OPERATIONS & BUSINESS EXPERT

C-level streaming media expert with 20-year track record of
leading digital media initiatives, business development, and operations.

"Bringing traditional broadcast values and disciplines to a new digital generation."
Personal Driving Motto

Streaming Media Expertise	**Leadership**	**Technical Expertise**
Led foray into "new media" during its infancy—serving as key driver of technology, productions, and online initiatives that delivered results, captured audience attention, and translated to revenues.	Known for collaborative working style and ability to form productive and loyal relationships with clients, executive teams, and subordinates. Sought out by previous clients and staff to provide expertise on projects and initiatives.	Recognized for building state-of-the-art, budget-restricted production facilities; handling projects from drawing schematics to managing vendor deliverables, including planning and execution of a 20K sq. ft., 24x7 broadcasting facility.

Media Production · Operations Management · Leadership

VICE PRESIDENT, MEDIA SERVICES
GREAT MEDIA CORPORATION, 2000–PRESENT

Oversee streaming division's P&L of $1.5M–$3M annually, with 13 staff and managers. Previous positions include General Manager, Director of Streaming Operations, Director of Systems Operations, and Regional Manager. Originally brought in as consultant to help ramp up services and deliverables following Great Media's unsuccessful contract proposal during tenure with VGR. **Clients:** YRCTV, POTUS, Jet Mobile, BooksRUs, Wave Radio, Sports Now, Workhouse, REW, New Reach Media, *Florida Times,* Bell Pharma, and Ducky Music.

Business Development	⇒ Designed and built first-ever dedicated, origination-based 750 sq. ft., $1.2M encoding facility that brought in $1.5M annually since 2001 and provides encoding of live and on-demand video; entire build and move completed with 100% up time and zero customer loss.
	⇒ Built the facility from which Sports Now launched and became one of first companies to provide streaming of live content to cell phones; assisted third-party client (Workhouse) in landing contract and executing broadcast for 2004 and 2006 sports association play-offs.
Operations & Leadership	⇒ Took on and transformed ineffective systems operations group following Hopper Media's bankruptcy and acquisition by Great Media with resulting 60% staff layoff and consolidation of services; reduced response time issues of Tier 1, 2, and 3 problems to just 10 minutes—a 30% reduction—and dropped total tickets in cue to just 70 from 500+; maintained 100% of clients ($20M annual revenues) during bankruptcy while increasing customer satisfaction results.
	⇒ Established much-needed policies and procedures that enabled sales department to work cohesively with video and technology groups; created client questionnaires and standardized specs lists; developed procedures to bid jobs, capture expenses, identify costs, and forecast profits; instituted formality of assignments within group and appointed a group manager to oversee projects.
	⇒ Recruited, shaped, and currently lead longest-tenured operations staff across corporation; recognized with President's Club award—only of a handful of non-sales professional recipients in company history—for impact on revenues and business development in streaming video division.

Page 1 of 2

169

Combination. *Kimberly Schneiderman, New York, New York*

The applicant wanted to be prepared for a job change because he was getting calls from recruiters. The three-column table categorizes his different responsibilities. Note that the

ELLIOT WAGNER

555.555.5555 • ewagner@xxxx.com

VICE PRESIDENT, OPERATIONS / PRODUCTION
TIPPER INTERACTIVE, 1997–2000

Created streaming video—then a new delivery mechanism—that encompassed 20+ production projects on three channels simultaneously and included live shows from comedy clubs from across the U.S. Directed $1.5M P&L with 15+ production and freelance crews for what was one of the first Internet-only video channels.

Operations & Technology

⇒ Built 20K sq. ft. production facility that launched three Internet channels—comedy, crime, and romance—handling initial planning, technology selection, schematics, and vendor management.

⇒ Configured Web technology and engineering resources that led to broadcast of 40 hours of content and five weekly live comedy shows streamed from New York, Toronto, Denver, and Chicago.

⇒ Saved company $10K monthly by negotiating new deal with streaming service provider; negotiated carriage contract with Media Height for cable distribution (company folded prior to project launch).

Early Career Highlights

Good Images, Owner ———————————————————————————

➢ Grew company from a solo operation to a five-man crew and 15+ freelancers—managing operations that served ENG/EFP, equipment, and production needs of ABC, BCD, CDE, and DEF—during a time of dynamic change and unconventional approaches in broadcasting.

➢ Key projects include shooting of *Top Raps Show, Heavy Metal Magic, Events Galore,* and *The Gifford Armstrong Show,* among others in NYC, LA, and Europe.

➢ Produced and shot Robert Brown's first full-length concert video featuring the Jive Band.

Night Entertainment Television, Director/Engineer ———————————————

➢ Designed and engineered high-tech audio and video system that sparked a 10-year run of *The Jason Strum Radio Show* featuring four robotic cameras and three isolated cameras operated remotely without interference to live radio show; promoted to show director within two weeks of completion.

Digital Vision, Director of Digital Networks ———————————————————

➢ Increased quantity of channels offered by transforming analog cable head-end into digital platform; gained significant territory expansion without use of high-cost, low-return cellular transmitters by using dark fiber network to link three major sites that delivered wireless signals; upgrade resulted in 10K new customers across NYC boroughs.

Big Apple Pay-per-view, Chief Engineer ———————————————————————

➢ Researched, planned, and directed building of one of the first multichannel, all-server-based playback facilities in a landmarked NYC building; facility ultimately played 10 unique channels simultaneously and saved company $1.32M annually by bringing technology in-house.

Additional career experience includes senior-level engineering and operations positions with highly regarded media companies and production houses in New York City.

Education

Bachelor of Arts, Communications
University of Oklahoma

Early Career Highlights are without dates so that they could be reordered to mention the most impressive highlights first. The bullets are different in this section to keep it visually different from the chronological arrangement of the current and most recent workplaces.

MICHAEL FRAMEWORK

555 Beach Street ▪ Miami, FL 55555
mframework@xxxx.com ▪ 555.555.0000

SENIOR BROADCAST EXECUTIVE

Industry Knowledge ▪ Relationship Management ▪ Revenue Growth

Veteran sales driver with 25+ years of experience maintaining long-standing, collaborative relationships with key industry leaders in the South, Midwest and Northeast, capturing $350 million in total revenue. Persuasive presenter and consensus builder with the ability to negotiate favorable agreements in competitive and volatile markets. Knowledge of technological innovations in HD digital and Internet broadcasting.

Keen business acumen in implementing strategic sales and marketing plans, analyzing revenues, controlling expenses, forecasting profits and maximizing market share. Inspirational and authentic leader with the ability to earn trust, clarify purpose, align organizational systems and unleash individual talents.

EXPERTISE

- New Business Development
- Account Management
- Strategic Planning
- Contract Negotiations
- Business Forecasting
- Media Relations
- Customer Service
- Financial Analysis
- Change Management
- Team Leadership & Mentoring
- Brand Creation & Management

PROFESSIONAL EXPERIENCE

ABC RADIO, INC.
Fourth largest radio broadcasting company in the United States, owning, operating and/or servicing 86 stations in 19 markets with 2,100+ employees.

Vice President / General Manager, WMMM-FM / WNNN-FM, Miami–Fort Lauderdale, FL   2001–2012
Managed all aspects of successful broadcast operation: sales, programming, business, advertising, engineering and technology advances. Supervised multiple sales managers producing local, national, Internet and event marketing revenues. Created dynamic marketing plans, increasing audience share, ratings and revenue. Facilitated transition to HD Radio and Web site launch.

- **Recruited, hired and retained top talent at all levels.** *"His unbridled energy, enthusiasm and knowledge of the product will ensure our success!"* Press Release, 4/7/2005.
- **Collaborated with General Manager of WEDR-FM and WHQT-FM** in Miami, creating cluster synergy of 4 stations for sales and operations.

XYZ RADIO, INC.   1996–2001
One of largest major market operators in the United States operating 130 radio stations. Participated in formation of Chicago's #1 revenue-producing marketing group composed of 7 formerly independent stations.

Vice President / General Manager, WWWW-FM / WYYY-FM, Chicago, IL

- **Spearheaded successful format change** from classic rock to talk by successfully recruiting top on-air talents Howard Stern, Jonathon Brandmeier and Steve Dahl.
- **Propelled station to #1** in male demographic ages 25–54 and to top 5 among adults ages 25–54.
- **Increased revenue from $12 million to more than $25 million in 5 years**, growing sales staff from 12 to 25 representatives.
- **Assisted with sale of WYYY to Spanish Broadcasting, Inc.,** as deregulation began in 1996.

Continued...

170

Combination. *Ginger Korljan, Phoenix, Arizona*

The shaded text box at the right margin is an eye magnet that attracts a reader's vision immediately to the applicant's areas of expertise. The two paragraphs to the left are a summary profile

MICHAEL FRAMEWORK   mframework@xxxx.com • 555.555.0000   Page Two

---

MNO RADIO, INC.   1984–1996

Vice President / General Manager, WBBB-FM / WCCC-FM, Chicago, IL (1992–1996)
Recruited to manage classic rock station WBBB with revenue of more than $11 million. Hired new sales, programming and marketing managers, successfully integrating new management into the fabric of MNO RADIO/WBBB.

- **Instrumental in start-up and purchase of Beasley Broadcasting station WCCC**; changed format to all 1970s music on C-107.9.

Vice President / General Manager, WXXX-AM / WZZZ-FM, Miami, FL (1988–1992)
Modified sleepy, old-line talk format into dynamic talk/sports market leader, #1 in ratings and revenue.

- **Recruited on-air personalities** Neil Rogers and Rick & Suds, resulting in ratings increases in the key adult 25–54 and men 25–54 demographics, consistently ranking top 1–3 in the market.
- **Propelled WXXX to #1 billing station in Miami market** by handpicking and mentoring top sales managers.
- **Successfully renegotiated NFL/Miami Dolphins and NCAA/University of Miami Hurricanes contracts** resulting in significant savings and reducing Dolphins deal by $750,000 in first year.
- **Changed format of WAAA from rock to successful adult contemporary music**, renamed WZZZ in 1991. Format today remains market leader in ratings and revenue, known as 97.3 The Coast.

General Sales Manager, WLLL-FM, Chicago, IL (1984–1988)
Directed all aspects of sales, including local and national revenues.

- **Participated in transformation of failed contemporary hit radio format to successful rock format within 3 months.**
- **Bolstered revenue from $2 million to more than $8 million** in 4 years by restructuring sales teams and implementing new revenue programs.

POSITIONS PRIOR TO 1984

Early career characterized by top performance in sales and management positions for national radio representative companies in Atlanta and New York, covering Philadelphia, Washington and Baltimore.

EDUCATION AND TRAINING

BA in History, WAKE FOREST UNIVERSITY, Winston-Salem, NC

Continuing Education

- Talent-Focused Management, Customer-Focused Selling Systems—Center for Strategic Sales
- Wharton School of Business Training Seminar
- Mentor-Cox Enterprises, Inc., Mentor-Mentee Program
- Creative Problem-Solving Workshop—Gerry Tabio

Professional Affiliations

- Member, Florida Association of Broadcasters
- Former Member, Arbitron Radio Advisory Council
- Executive Board of Directors, Special Olympics Miami–Dade County
- Former Board of Directors, Starlight Foundation
- Knights of Columbus

of the applicant and his experience. Note how the writer uses italic effectively to describe chief workplaces, declare the applicant's chief responsibilities for each specified position, and highlight a glowing testimonial for the current position.

Sloane T. Hillier

<u>*Permanent Address*</u>	814-436-3709	<u>*School Address*</u>
1 Roberts Court	sth178@psu.edu	289 East Grant Avenue
Morganville, NJ 07751		State College, PA 16801

Assistant Media Planner

Experience	**BBCS WORLDWIDE INCORPORATED,** New York, NY
	Intern Summer 2011
	◆ Responsible for proper execution of media plans on the HBO account.
	◆ Worked with the HBO planning team to evaluate media opportunities for this major account.
	◆ Helped evaluate all print executions before final approval by HBO.
	EASTERN OPINION INCORPORATED, Middletown, NJ
	Administrative Assistant Summer 2010
	◆ Responsible for medical data accumulation and categorization for this medical malpractice firm. Participated in case review sessions.
	◆ Helped organize materials for attorneys to aid in their case presentations. Practiced accurate data management and quality-control procedures.
	RIVERVIEW MEDICAL CENTER, Red Bank, NJ
	Intern/Speech Pathology Assistant Summer 2009
	◆ Assisted the Director of the Speech Pathology Department with patient testing, medical charting, record keeping, and patient nutrition.
	◆ Worked with physical therapists, occupational therapists, and speech pathologists to administer patient care in the Brain Trauma Unit.
	HAPPY TIME DAY CAMP, Millstone Township, NJ
	Day Camp Group Leader Summer 2008
	◆ Supervised junior counselors and communicated with parents and camp director. Responsible for campers ages 11 through 13.
Education	**PENNSYLVANIA STATE UNIVERSITY,** University Park, PA
	BS, Communication Disorders, 2012 (expected). Overall GPA 3.46—Dean's List.
	LORENZO DE MEDICI INSTITUTE, Florence, Italy Spring 2011
Honors	Golden Key National Honor Society, Dean's List, Health and Human Development Honor Society, Order of Omega National Greek Honor Society
Activities	**National Student Speech, Language, and Hearing Association** 2009–2011
	Attended and participated in monthly colloquia led by professional speech pathologists, audiologists, and professors.
	Sigma Delta Tau Sorority 2008–Present
	Torch **Magazine Representative:** Wrote for the national sorority magazine. Informed other chapters across the country of our sorority's accomplishments and activities.
Computer Skills	Microsoft Excel, Microsoft PowerPoint, Windows 7, Ad Spender

171

Combination. *Beverley and Mitchell I. Baskin, Marlboro, New Jersey*

To make a resume in this format, simply create columns with tabs, putting headings in the left column and data in the right. Note that unlike most resumes for new graduates, this resume lists Experience before Education, which draws attention to a relevant internship.

Sales and Marketing

Resumes at a Glance

JOSEPH NEVINS
joe505@xxxx.com

SALES PROFESSIONAL

Outgoing and determined sales professional with experience driving sales; exceeding quotas; and leading training initiatives, new business development, and product launches across industries. Recognized as top-ranking sales performer with keen ability to competitively launch and position products within large territories to new and existing accounts. Successfully coach, mentor, and develop high-performance sales representatives to aggressively market and promote products.

PROFESSIONAL EMPLOYMENT HISTORY

Sales Representative — 2007 to Present
DUNCAN RESOURCES, Shippenville, PA
Drive sales in transportation industry, with focus on prospecting consumers needing to transport steel and other heavy, dense freight. Execute territory-specific sales strategies to expand business and revenue in two states.

✓ Promoted from outside sales, a 1099 postion, to inside sales postion with benefits due to sales success.

✓ 400% boost in outside sales generated between January 2008 and January 2009 by attaining new business through extensive research, thorough presentations, and excellent closing skills.

✓ $4 million in revenue growth achieved by effectively managing territory spanning western Pennsylvania, from Erie to Pittsburgh, and eastern Ohio, from Cleveland to Columbus.

✓ Maintained profit percentage despite economic decline, gaining $400,000+ in a 12-month period between 2009 and 2010.

✓ Negotiate $500,000 annual account with D.L.M., a world-class provider of precision machined components.

Account Manager — 2007
THE BOTTLING GROUP, Franklin, OH
Oversaw 12 accounts, with responsibility for following sales through and strengthening relationships. Managed eight merchandisers by delegating tasks/handling scheduling while staying within budget.

✓ Launched Pepsi Max into all 12 accounts, including Walmart and Giant Eagle.

✓ Increased revenue by negotiating with managers and persuading them with the advantages of placing Pepsi Max in high-traffic areas.

✓ Obtained 5% sales increase and competitive advantage over Coca-Cola by adding new displays.

Sales Representative — 2006 to 2007
UNIVERSE CORPORATION, Franklin, PA
Provided sales leadership to new employees, training them on features and benefits of all facility service products. Leveraged skill in aggressive cold calling with excellent phone skills to schedule appointments. Consistently met sales targets by presenting to customers based on needs, gaining commitment from prospects, negotiating multi-year agreements, and closing new business.

✓ Achieved fast-track promotion within six months of start date because of tenacity and exceeding quota.

✓ Respected as top selling representative in region in terms of volume and number of accounts sold.

✓ Maintained weekly sales average that was 25% over quota, as well as 130+ dials, 30 cold calls, and 7 new appointments per week.

Manager — 2004 to 2005
HOMER'S PIZZA, Shippenville, PA
Supervised and trained up to seven employees in a fast-paced setting. Ensured safety in store, including food preparation and equipment. Controlled financial aspects, including preparing daily bank deposits, product cost controls, waste control, damages, and theft. Assisted owner with purchasing, inventory, and sales forecast.

✓ Improved employee productivity by instructing them in equipment use and safety, customer relations, sales, and product knowledge.

✓ Increased sales 10% by contributing up-to-date managerial perspective to forecasting.

EDUCATION | TRAINING

Bachelor of Arts in Accounting & Business Administration
3.34 GPA | Dean's List for five semesters | Chi Eta Sigma Honors Society
MERCER COLLEGE, Greenville, OH *Relevant Coursework:* Accounting | Marketing | Human Resources | Finance

Basic Sales School, UNIVERSE CORPORATION, Franklin, PA

VALUE OFFERED

✓ Sales Growth
✓ Territory Development
✓ Competitive Analysis
✓ New Business Development
✓ Presentations
✓ Management
✓ Product Launch
✓ Team Leadership
✓ Customer Relations
✓ Needs Assessment
✓ Strategic Planning
✓ Sales Training
✓ Account Management
✓ Negotiation
✓ Prospecting
✓ Closing

DETAILS FROM DISC PROFILE OF SALES CHARACTERISTICS

"Joseph is always **driven towards completion of his sales goals,** and he wants to be in a position that allows him to meet these goals.

He is **comfortable in a sales environment** that contains variety and/or high-pressure situations.

He **loves the challenge presented by sales.** He sees closing the sale as a great opportunity to **compete with himself and others.**

Joseph frequently **closes soon and often,** plus he will **secure many sales** that the competition has sold but failed to close."

CONTACT INFORMATION
505 Spangle Road
Shippenville, PA 00550
555.505.5005
joe505@xxxx.com

172

Combination. *Jane Roqueplot, West Middlesex, Pennsylvania*

The distinctive feature in this resume is the shaded text box in the right column, containing values in keywords and key phrases, plus an extended testimonial from a DISC profile of sales characteristics.

Joseph Rockford

55 Briarfield Drive ♦ Great Neck, NY 55555
555-555-5555 (h) ♦ 555-555-0000 (c) ♦ jrockford@email.com

Summary	Marketing Executive with international experience and proven ability to increase customer retention, expand market share, and drive revenue. Background includes partnering with executive team to set strategic direction. Excellent track record of developing relationships with Fortune 500 clientele.
Work History	**Supercomp/Megatech,** New York, NY, 2006–present **Director, North American Marketing** Oversaw a $4 billion North American electronic storage device business, managing 48 direct reports and a specialized sales force, through a major acquisition of Supercomp by Megatech.
Achieved a 95% success rate in customer retention during a corporate merger.	• Developed a customer incentive program that resulted in 95% customer retention of Supercomp key accounts, worth $400 million. • Increased market share and penetration 10% by providing training to Gold Star customers prior to acquisition. • Coordinated an award-winning trade show for 6,500 sales reps from North and South America to introduce new product lines. • Retained as one of only two Supercomp employees following acquisition due to extensive knowledge of Megatech's product line.
	Supercomp, New York, NY, 2002–2006 **Worldwide Product Marketing Manager** Developed the overall strategy for international marketing programs throughout North America, Europe, and Asia-Pacific.
Captured $100M in new revenue.	• Drove a marketing strategy that produced $100M in new-product sales through multiple product launches, including new products, software, and services. • Designed training programs that resulted in a 15% increase in the North American market share. • Spearheaded Supercomp's rise to the #3 vendor in the business by developing an overall global marketing strategy that expanded product placement in Europe and Asia-Pacific.
	Software Specialties, Dover, DE, 2000–2002 **Product Marketing Manager** Managed all aspects of marketing the company's product line of customized business management software and database applications.
Led 18% growth in Fortune 500 accounts.	• Developed a sales strategy that resulted in an 18% increase in sales and revenues of $45M, marketing to clients that included McDonald's, Sears, Stop & Shop, Walgreen's, Barnes & Noble, and General Electric.

Continued

173

Chronological. *Wendy Gelberg, Needham, Massachusetts*

This individual hoped to take the next step up the corporate ladder. The chronological format showcases his career's upward progression. The writer used a sidebar format in the left column

Joseph Rockford

Page 2

555-555-5555 (h) ◆ 555-555-0000 (c) ◆ jrockford@email.com

Work History (continued)	**Supercomp,** New York, NY, 1994–2000 **Product Marketing Manager** Managed product launches for numerous product lines, leading cross-functional teams to meet deadlines for deliverables.
Penetrated new markets worth over $15M in revenue.	• Coordinated and implemented corporate marketing programs for new storage system technology. Secured large, strategic orders, including Chase Manhattan Bank (worth $10M over a four-year period), John Hancock (worth $4.5M), and Liberty Mutual (worth $2M). • Drove sales by overseeing design improvements that ensured that engineering teams addressed customer needs.
Viewed as "Market Expert."	**Area Marketing Consultant,** New York, NY, 1990–1994 Provided marketing support for several product launches. • Wrote and managed marketing plans, product positioning, and collateral content creation. • Conducted focus groups and usability testing to gather customer feedback. • Furnished sales support with product and application knowledge. Provided understanding of market, competition, and sales process. Recognized by management as "market expert."
	Capital Camera Corporation, Cambridge, MA, 1992–1994 **Marketing Coordinator** Performed inside sales, customer service, consulting, and campaign management for camera and film products.
Education	**MBA,** Harvard Business School, Boston, MA **BS, Marketing,** Bentley College, Waltham, MA Ongoing professional development includes • Managing in the Global Business Environment • International Management in the High-Tech Industry

to highlight the person's strong accomplishments and to draw the reader's eye to statements that demonstrate the impact the individual had on the organizations he had worked for. Sidebar statements paraphrase information in nearby bulleted statements.

Charles W. Broadway

4200 Centre Street   Montgomery, Alabama 36100   cbroad555@aol.com   ☏ 334.555.5555

WHAT I CAN OFFER **TOPLINE** AS YOUR NEWEST **SALES PROFESSIONAL**

○ Penetrating and holding **new markets,**

○ Gathering and leveraging **sales intelligence** faster than our competition,

○ Mastering our customers' business so well we **anticipate** their **needs,**

○ Putting together "win-win" sales deals that yield **enduring profits,**

○ Communicating so powerfully that **sales** are **closed**—at every level from shop floor to boardroom, and

○ **Managing risk** prudently.

RECENT WORK HISTORY WITH EXAMPLES OF PROBLEMS SOLVED

○ *Hired away by the CEO to be* **Sales Development Manager** *and then promoted over four more experienced eligibles to be* **Sales Director,** Arista Corporation, Montgomery, Alabama   Oct 09 to Present
Arista is the world's largest auto transmission manufacturer.

Supervise three regional sales managers directly. Lead a territory that covers all of America east of the Mississippi River and portions of Canada. Build and defend a travel budget of $400K. My district generates $45M in annual sales.

Chosen by the President to **guide us into a new market** dominated by four tough competitors. Found, and really listened to, all potential customers. Identified our market niche. Then made the calls that led to **20 presentations nationwide,** many at presidential levels. *Payoffs:* **From $0 sales to $3.5M** in sales in just 16 months.

Moved faster than our competition to discover an RFP before it hit the street. When none of our products met this customer's needs, **put together a win-win deal** that shared both risks and profits. *Payoffs:* When I showed our customer's CEO how I could **save him $2M** over the life of the contract, I **won a $4M contract for us.**

Used polite persistence to **"steal" a customer from a competitor** who had served them for a decade. Soon uncovered our competitor's weakness. **Carefully timed and executed "cold calls"** on the right people. *Payoffs:* By appealing right to their specific needs, brought in **$8M** in the last two years alone.

Saw opportunity a potential customer missed—even after he awarded his contract to another company. Tracked our competitor's performance right up until contract renewal. *Payoffs:* My presentation, made on the same day as other firms, carried the **sale: $4M** over several years—even though we weren't the lowest bidder.

174

Combination. *Don Orlando, Montgomery, Alabama*

A resume that's different from all the others gets attention. Hiring officials want to know what a new employee can do for the company. This resume is distinctive in indicating immediately

Charles Broadway	**Sales Professional**	334.555.5555

Uncovered an unmet need in a major market. Worked with the customer and a manufacturer to design a new product. Persuaded our leadership to invest $200K in the prototype I knew we would need for the competition. *Payoffs:* **Won a $14M sale** and **took away our competitor's dominance** in this market.

Picked up the signs that a competitor's customer wasn't happy, and then found out why. Got a 100-percent response to our needs-analysis survey to define the best new product for the market. *Payoffs:* **Profit margin up** four percent—**double the industry average.** My methods became the **corporate standard** for customer analysis.

○ Plant Manager, Plantar Corporation, Montgomery, Alabama   May 03 to Sep 09

○ **Sales Manager for Business Products,** Mylar Corporation, Montgomery, Alabama
Mar 01 to May 03

EDUCATION & PROFESSIONAL DEVELOPMENT

○ MPA, Auburn University—Montgomery, Montgomery, Alabama   05

○ BS, Troy State University, Troy, Alabama   01
Earned this degree while working 10 hours a week.

○ Instructed classes in Value Analysis for Product Improvement and Cost of Sales
01 to 03

Selected from five more-experienced professionals to teach these six-week courses, preparing 100 sales professionals to represent up to ten different products.

IT SKILLS

○ Expert in proprietary **sales, billing, and customer contact software** suite; proficient in Outlook, Word, Excel, PowerPoint, and Internet search methods

what the sales applicant can bring to "TopLine." Uncommon bullets point to six boldfaced sales results of top importance to executives responsible for sales: getting and keeping new markets, beating competitors, anticipating customer needs, staying profitable, closing sales, and controlling risk.

BURT A. THOMPSON

5555 Main Street • Trenton, Michigan 55555 • bthompson@email.usa

(000) 000-0000 • Fax (000) 000-0000 • Cellular (000) 000-0000

**PRODUCT SALES & MARKETING • ACCOUNT MANAGEMENT • NEGOTIATIONS • INFLUENTIAL SELLING
PRESENTATION & COMMUNICATIONS • PUBLIC RELATIONS • CUSTOMER SERVICE**

Dynamic and results-driven sales professional with nearly nine years of comprehensive sales and marketing experience. Proven sales talent to cultivate strategic relationships, increase customer base, and maximize account sales. Persistence in achieving goals that leads to professional success while building corporate value. Business- and computer systems–literate and willing to relocate. Qualification highlights include

- Highly skilled in communicating effectively with company buyers, marketers, peers, and management

- Proven ability to meet targeted goals, build professional relationships with a diverse customer base, maximize sales opportunities, and present a professional sales image

- Excellent business-to-business sales skills and talents, with comprehensive knowledge in brand imaging and product presentations, pricing, and promotions

- Strong leadership, organizational, time management, and mentoring skills

- BS degree—Business Management

PROFESSIONAL EMPLOYMENT

ABC MEDICAL (Medical Device Company)
Headquarters—Seattle, Washington, **6/2008–Present**

Sales Representative

Manage and direct sales of diverse ultrasound medical products for the entire Michigan region, including the Upper Peninsula. Introduce new products, attain and expand new and existing business, educate medical staff on clinical applications, and perform monthly/quarterly sales forecasting. Consult with key decision makers, conduct in-services, routinely follow up with clients, and provide customer support.

<u>NOTABLE ACHIEVEMENTS</u>

Achieved product sales exceeding $1M within 16 months of hire: Conducted due-diligence research of marketplace, determined needs of target audience, provided nurse managers and nursing staff with in-service training (equipment use and results reporting), and presented overall product value and benefits.

Landed first-ever sales to the XYZ Medical Center's Children's Hospital, Local University Hospital, and Local Women's Hospital: Developed sound and trusting business relationships with urologists and OB-GYN staff closely connected with the Medical Value Analysis team, became part of their professional network, and gained support from affiliated physicians to introduce and present product line to decision makers.

Increased product hospital sales more than $200K within 12 months, representing increase of hospital usage by 37%: Developed strategic promotional campaigns, offered trade-in incentives, strengthened business relationships with nurses and physicians, and closed sales with 5 non-user hospitals.

Increased on-hand scanners at Local University Medical Center, ABC Hospital, Smith-Boyd Hospital, USA Health, Jenkins Hospital, and XYZ Healthcare Hospital: Identified need for additional scanners to sufficiently accommodate facilities, consulted with head nurses, and provided nursing staff with trial runs to demonstrate advantages of additional on-hand scanners, which decreased number of patient catheterizations and increased nursing staff's utilization and efficiency.

AWARDS / SPECIAL RECOGNITION
- Million Dollar Club Award, 2010
- Top Sales Performer—Northern Region, 2009
- Company-Wide **#1** Sales Representative, 11/2008; 7/2009
- Company-Wide **#2** Sales Representative, 3/2009
- Exceptional Sales Performance—110% of Quota, 2009
- Ranked #6 of 35 Sales Representatives Company-Wide, 2009
- Rookie (#2) of the Year Award—111% of Quota, 2008
- Exceptional Sales Performance—111% of Quota, 2008

175

Combination. *Maria E. Hebda, Trenton, Michigan*

The first page packs a wallop in being almost entirely a strong profile, a list of notable achievements, and a bulleted list of awards and special recognition. The reader may expect the next

BURT A. THOMPSON   (000) 000-0000 • Cellular (000) 000-0000 • bthompson@email.usa • **Page 2**

WAGEPAY (Payroll Processing Corporation)
Wyandotte, Michigan, **6/2005–5/2008**

Sales Representative *(12/2005–5/2008)*
Associate Sales Representative *(6/2005–11/2005)*
Presented product line to end users and developed referral network to build client base. Provided client consultations, conducted payroll audits, and managed territory for more than 100 CPA firms, 11 financial institutions, and more than 450 clients. Served as sales training leader and mentor; evaluated and "job shadowed" new-hire sales associates. Built company payroll client base through cold calling and interfacing with potential customers.

NOTABLE ACHIEVEMENTS

Influenced 19 CPA firms to refer newfound clients to WagePay within 36 months, which accounted for 45% of business and generated more than 100 new client accounts; created sales strategy delivering values and benefits of partnering with WagePay, positioning customer to focus on more "profitable" business aspects.

Ranked #3 of 700 sales representatives identifying major market referral sales (clients having more than 75 employees and/or requiring special reporting needs) for fiscal 2007.

AWARDS / CAREER DEVELOPMENT
- Level 1 Diamond Club Member—Closed 300+ Product Sales, Fiscal Year 2007 / 2008
- Top Sales Performer Award—148% Revenue, 2007
- Overachieving Award—138% of Quota, 2007
- MVP Award—132% of Quota, 2007
- District Rookie Award—102% of Quota, 2007
- Exceptional Sales Performance Award—100% of Quota, 2006
- Exceptional Sales Performance Award—130% of Quota, 2006
- "Competitive Edge Selling"—Tom Hopkins Seminar, 2007

SEARS (Department Store)
Southfield, Michigan, **6/2001–6/2005**

Merchandise Manager, Children's Department (Ann Arbor / Southfield, Michigan) *6/2003–6/2005*
Determined quarterly merchandise buys for department to maximize sales, profit, and merchandise investment, which generated over $5M in company sales. Managed merchandise inventory, performed data analysis, and instituted strategic sales tactics. Oversaw 25 direct sales associates supervising 225 employees.

Merchandise Management Trainee, Men's Department (Taylor, Michigan)
Employee Internship, *1/2003–6/2003*
Successfully completed comprehensive 6-month management training program and promoted to Merchandising Manager due to excellent performance.

NOTABLE ACHIEVEMENTS

Increased school uniform sales 100%: Analyzed previous-year business practices and determined need for school uniforms in the Detroit area and marketed to targeted buyers.

Achieved highest department sales gain: Boys, Girls, and Infants among 11 store chains, averaging 9% above other sales managers in Boys and Girls and 3% in Infants.

Saved company nearly $7K: Increased productivity and reduced "paid-not-work" hourly wages.

Decreased employee absenteeism 50%: Effectively communicated with sales associates, promoted teamwork, and conveyed their vital role in the company's success.

EDUCATION
MICHIGAN STATE UNIVERSITY
BS—Business Management
Dean's List

page to be weak by comparison, but it has more lists of notable achievements and more awards. Almost all the achievements are quantified in some way with dollar amounts, figures, and percentages. The awards also are quantified heavily with percentages.

DAVID R. PERLMAN

405 Weatherspoon Drive
Ehldridge, NC 56974

(555) 555-1834
daveperl@yahoo.com

SALES / ACCOUNT MANAGEMENT EXECUTIVE
...Consistently exceed corporate goals & increase key account base...

Well-qualified executive with proven expertise in global/national sales, strategic marketing, team building, and contract negotiations. Re-acquired major corporate account and increased sales 220%; committed to a high level of customer service to build trust and enhance sales. Highly motivated to outperform the competition; consistently set and achieve personal goals above corporate expectations. Exceptional "deal closing" expertise; keen understanding of corporate dynamics. PC literate; B.S., Business Administration.

CORE STRENGTHS

...National Accounts / Building & Maintaining Long-term, Loyal Business Relationships...
...Consultative Selling / International Expertise / Team Building / New Business Development...
...Creative & Strategic Planning / New Product Introduction / Sales Process Planning & Implementation...

CAREER BACKGROUND

THE WIRELESS NETWORK, Walson, NC   1998–Present
2nd largest global provider of cellular, voice, and data applications.

International Corporate Account Manager (2010–Present)
Fast-track promotion to oversee corporate, city, county, and federal clients. Manage 10 national contracts and 20+ remote accounts in the NC market. Market voice and data to multimillion-dollar accounts. Negotiate contracts; team with business care personnel and account managers to increase data sales. Train clients on features of Extranet (Web-based site for customer service and new products). Function as remote account manager for national accounts not based locally.

Executive Account Sales Manager (2010)
Tasked to drive government account sponsorships in 8 counties serving 13 retail locations. Focused on city, county, and federal clients. Managed advertising and marketing initiatives for national accounts.
Highlights:
- Increased sales by 31% (1st year).
- Acquired major government account (Marion County elections), resulting in $3M annual revenues.

Senior International Account Manager (2005–2009)
Accountable for attaining corporate sales quotas, increasing revenues, acquiring 80+ new high-profile national accounts per month ($7M+ in annual revenues), and maintaining existing accounts. Managed 1 sales associate and 75 accounts. Teamed with other professionals to create high-impact PowerPoint presentations for new clients. Extensive interaction with clients and business sales departments to facilitate resolution of customer service and billing issues.
Highlights:
- Decreased client churn 7.5% below industry standards.
- Successfully initiated and closed federal government contracts through attention to detail and response time, resulting in 12% increase in annual revenues.
- Re-acquired and grew Buy It Here Online Network account 220% through aggressive leadership and advertising strategies.
- Consistently exceeded sales goals; maintained 122% average status of corporate expectations.
- Coordinated quarterly on-site benefit expos for large nationally contracted companies, which increased gross activations by 7%.
- Recruited new accounts, including United Shipping, Pepsi, and Warethon.
- Achieved 197% sales quota (2010); ranked 3rd in the state and 36th nationwide.
- Elite *10 Top Producers* (2009); 151% quota (4th Quarter); 116% quota (2nd Quarter); 104% quota (1st Quarter).
- *Presidents Club Winner* (2005, 2006, 2009, 2010).
- Awarded *Top Federal Account Executive* (2nd Quarter 2008).
- *Gold Club Winner* (2007).
- Ranked among the *Top Producers* in NC (2005–2009).

Continued

176

Combination. *Carol Heider, Tampa, Florida*

Center justification is evident in part of the profile, in the Core Strengths section, and in the small sections on the second page. An advantage of center justification in sections with short

CAREER BACKGROUND (continued)

THE WIRELESS NETWORK, Walson, NC (continued)

Corporate Account Executive (2000–2005)
Promoted to senior-level management following merger acquisition of One Cellular. Managed major account acquisition and maintenance for large corporate clients ($500K+ annual revenues) through target research and cold-call sales. Territory included central North Carolina and 9 surrounding counties. Served as mentor for sales associates. Managed 2 sales executives and 120+ accounts. Conducted weekly sales meetings.
Performance Results:
- Increased account base by 25 accounts.
- Personally recruited University of New Bedford and ABC accounts.
- *100% Club Achiever* (1998–2000; 2002–2004).
- *Top Producer of Voice Mail Sales* (2003).
- *North Carolina Rookie of the Year Award*—Corporate Accounts Division (2000).
- *Circle of Excellence Award* (1999); determined through employee balloting for integrity, team player, displaying good judgment, pursuit of excellence, and customer satisfaction skills.

EDUCATION

UNIVERSITY OF NORTHERN CALIFORNIA, Bakersfield, CA
Bachelor of Science, Business Administration (1992)
Activities: Dean's List

CONTINUING EDUCATION / TRAINING

The Best Sales Training
Getting There Sales Training
Magic Sales Training
Know Your Client Sales Training
SPIN Training
Microsoft Word & Outlook training classes

ACTIVITIES

Board of Directors, Wireless International
Board of Directors, Lend a Hand
Captain, Neighborhood Watch
Volunteer, "Adopt A Family"

CERTIFICATIONS

Account Management & Maintenance (AMM) certified

COMPUTER EXPERTISE

Microsoft Excel, PowerPoint, Word, and Outlook; Internet

phrases is that the reader's eyes can travel quickly down the center of the page. Bold italic draws attention to positions held, to Highlights and Performance Results sections, and to the candidate's academic degree. The Highlights and Performance Results sections present quantified achievements and notable awards.

Roland C. Cameron

150 Elm Street
St. Louis, MO 55555

(555) 555-5555
rcameron531@msn.com

Senior Account Executive

★**Technology Sales**
★**Hardware / Software / Services**
★**Consultative Sales / Large Account Wins**
★**B2B / B2C / Channel Sales**

Differentiated by...

TOP PRESENTATION, CLOSING & STRATEGIC ACCOUNT MANAGEMENT SKILLS

Resulting in...

MULTIMILLION-DOLLAR ANNUAL SALES / CONSISTENT QUOTA OVERACHIEVEMENT

TOP-PRODUCING SENIOR ACCOUNT EXECUTIVE. Ranked #1 in sales in both Fortune 500 technology companies and IT start-ups. Expert at turning around territories with histories of declining sales and turning them into revenue leaders. Combine technical proficiency with consultative sales skills to close top-dollar sales. **Engineering Bachelor's degree plus MBA.** Power user of PowerPoint. Hands-on technical grasp of software and hardware. Experienced sales manager / leader.

IT SALES HIGHLIGHTS

SALES REPRESENTATIVE
PhoneWeb Communications—*VoIP (Voice over Internet Protocol) start-up,* St. Louis, MO (2010 to Present)

- **Forged key technology evaluation agreements with 2 Fortune 50 firms.**
- Hired and trained a sales team of 5.

SALES REPRESENTATIVE
Hartwell Networks—*Early-stage networking company,* St. Louis, MO (2008 to 2010)

- **Finished the final quarter with #1 ranking (out of sales team of 10), closing $2.9 million in sales (143% of quota).**
- **In a tough market, closed important deals:** RE Lighting, Southwestern Univ., Medco Laboratories, and BankWest.

SALES REPRESENTATIVE
River Networks/Truro—*A merger of Truro (routers) with Solidoptics (hubs, switches),* St. Louis, MO (2003 to 2008)

- **At Truro, ranked #1 for 3 years running in new accounts closed (out of 10 reps).** Ranked in top 2% nationally (3rd-highest sales numbers out of 125 sales reps).
- **Closed multimillion-dollar deals** with Topflight Airlines and GermanBank.
- **Finished FY 2007 at 125% of quota.**
- **Turned around a problem account with a global banking firm.** Innovated a successful strategy to package services with hardware that in turn resulted in successful cross-selling of Solidoptics products into the account.
- **Established customer service as a competitive advantage** in a strong field of competitors, including Cisco Systems. Won customer trust and loyalty by assigning a dedicated support person to global accounts.
- **Sold a $3.5 million services agreement** for hardware and software maintenance to a large account. Path-breaking approach became a best-practices model that was adopted company-wide.

Page One

177

Combination. *Jean Cummings, Concord, Massachusetts*

The writer faced a number of challenges. The individual was facing age issues. That meant not going back too far and using a different format for earlier experience. Typical of many IT

Roland C. Cameron, Page Two

(555) 555-5555
rcameron531@msn.com

SALES MANAGER—EASTERN REGION
Boston LAN Systems—*A $35M hub and router vendor,* Boston, MA (1999 to 2003)

Recruited to turn around the Eastern Region. Territory had a history of declining sales volume and low revenue-per-rep metrics. Charged with selling complex integration deals. Used management skills, coaching, and sales expertise to lead sales team to peak performance. Hired, fired, mentored, and trained representatives.

- **Catapulted the worst-performing region out of 6 into the top position within 13 months,** winning Regional Manager-of-the-Year award for 2000, despite a corporate environment of generally declining sales.
- **Transformed the sales team, bringing a minimally productive sales team of 10 to a top-performing, lean group of 7 reps who sold $9.9 million total in 2000,** averaging $1,610,000 per salesperson. (In 1999, the larger, inherited team averaged only $667,000 per rep.)
- Closed the largest sale ($3.1M) in the company's 10-year history.

EARLIER SALES & SALES MANAGEMENT ACHIEVEMENTS

★ As VP of Eastern Region Sales for a communications technology startup:
- Opened a huge sales territory, built a sales force of 6, and led them to $12 million in sales revenues in 2 years.
- Leading by example, **finished #1 in sales in 1989, 1990, and 1991 out of 12 reps in all.**
- **Closed a $6 million aerospace company deal** at a time when that sale accounted for 33% of total corporate revenues.

★ For a telecom giant, excelled as an individual sales contributor while managing a branch office of 67:
- **Led sales team of 10 to achieve 237% of quota.**
- Instrumental in closing 2 major accounts, including the **largest deal among all 9 local branches** (to supply data modems to a hospital supply company's 2,200 locations).

★ As Regional Sales Manager for Global Data Corporation:
- **Turned around the weakest of 16 regions and led 25 reps to finish in #1 position nationally at 191% of quota.**
- Using diplomatic and negotiation skills, avoided threatened litigation, **saving the company $550,000.**
- **Rescued $1.3M** in revenues by turning around a troubled account.

★ At IBS, as Marketing Representative for the Data Processing Division:
- **Attained 7 consecutive 100% Clubs and 2 Golden Circles, averaging 200% of quota.**

EDUCATION & SALES SKILLS

Master of Business Administration
Washington University, St. Louis, MO

Bachelor of Science in Electrical Engineering
University of Missouri, Rolla, MO

Sales Skills: prospecting, qualifying leads, making presentations, sales closing, solution sales, consultative sales, channel sales, direct sales, customer needs assessment, field sales management, key account management, negotiation, sales cycle management, sales training, team building / leadership

salespersons, this individual had worked recently for many start-ups and early-stage companies. His biggest wins were earlier in his career. The writer's approach was to catch the reader's attention, qualify him for his target, indicate his value in a profile, and show his worth in the rest of the resume.

STEVEN YOUNG

| 00 Highland Way | Ramsey, NJ 07436 | syoung@optonline.net | cell: 000-000-1111 | 000-000-0000 |

SUMMARY

Creative Wordsmith and Marketer with finely honed ability to communicate compelling value and benefit propositions while simultaneously improving profitability and quality and reducing expense. Exceptional Copywriter and Researcher with more than 15 years of diversified expertise in writing and producing catalogs, fax broadcasts, direct-mail brochures, press releases, magazine print ads and Internet promotions in deadline-driven environments.

PROFESSIONAL EXPERIENCE

GIFTS AND MORE, New York, NY ....2003–2011 & 1994–2000

COPY MANAGER (2003–2011)

Managed all aspects of copy production for the largest catalog brand of this $180 million cataloger and e-retailer. Wrote, edited, proofread, typeset, conducted extensive product research and assisted with layout design. Created web site promotions. Oversaw in-house and freelance writers and proofreaders.

- Partnered with Copy Director to generate a dramatic jump in sales of personalized products by writing highly effective, targeted product copy and messaging.
- Wrote compelling copy that grew revenues of opening spreads to record highs.
- Reduced annual expense $20,000 by utilizing proofreader to write basic copy and creating a greatest hits headline library.
- Shortened work cycle by 5 weeks to allow buyers more time and flexibility in decision-making.
- Implemented a new catalog database that streamlined workflow to keep production on schedule during the busy holiday season.
- Participated in the launch of the expanded web site, which tripled sales in first year.
- Significantly increased visual appeal and product density by writing more-concise copy.
- Developed easier-to-read type treatment that better highlighted selling points.

SENIOR COPYWRITER (1998–2000) / COPYWRITER (1994–1998)

Wrote product and direct-mail copy, edited and proofread. Assisted with layout revisions and interacted with print house to address copy-related issues.

- Authored copy for many of the company's all-time best sellers: *Weather Wreath* pulled in $1 million in its first season.
- Saved thousands of dollars in print corrections by on-site visit to printing facility.
- Key contributor to company's exceeding return rate goal by creating copy that clearly communicated value and benefit proposition and appropriate details.
- Recognized by *Catalog Age Magazine* for effective copywriting techniques—1999.
- Awarded *Employee of the Month* for superior performance—1997.

RESEARCH DATA, New York, NY...2001–2003

COPYWRITER / CREATIVE SERVICES MANAGER

Directed staff of 5 freelance copywriters. Oversaw all aspects of writing and design of print advertising, direct-mail and special promotions for this research, consulting and business intelligence firm with $32 million in annual sales. Conceptualized, wrote and designed print ads and direct-mail pieces for books, reports and company services.

page one

178

Combination. *Fran Kelley, Waldwick, New Jersey*

This person's unique value was that he was a creative writer who also could keep an eye on a firm's expenses and profitability. The writer highlighted these aspects in the opening summary.

STEVEN YOUNG • syoung@optonline.net • cell: 000-000-1111 • 000-000-0000   **page two**

PROFESSIONAL EXPERIENCE, continued

RESEARCH DATA, New York, NY, continued

- Dramatically improved profitability of brochures and increased sales by enhancing visual appeal, writing hard-hitting copy and reducing print costs.
- Slashed advertising costs by 25% annually.
- Produced more than 100 brochures and 15 fax broadcasts each year under extremely tight deadlines.
- Designed and implemented web marketing strategies.
- Elevated press coverage by initiating and developing relationships with the *Wall Street Journal*, the *New York Times, USA Today, Newsweek, Fortune* and CNN.
- Designed a special offer for top report buyers that generated more than $30,000 in additional annual revenue.

BEST BUSINESS SUPPLIES, Ridgewood, NJ...2000–2001

COPYWRITER / EDITOR

Oversaw all copywriting and copyediting for this $100 million business-to-business firm that sold specialty papers and presentation products. Participated in catalog design and selection of featured cover products.

- Major contributor behind the launch of a new presentation catalog.
- Revitalized copy in instructional books on brochures and newsletters.
- Selected to judge customer catalog contest.

MARKETS INTERNATIONAL, New York, NY...2000

COPY CHIEF

Directed all writing and corporate communications: in-house, client and contract assignments for this national marketing firm with $5 million in annual revenues.

- Crafted surveys—mail and telephone—to identify prospects.
- Designed and wrote focused, clear and powerful marketing proposals, presentations and member benefits brochure to present firm's lead-generation and direct-mail programs.

CONSUMER REFERENCE, New York, NY...1991–1994

COPYWRITER / EDITOR / SENIOR MERCHANDISING ANALYST

Composed product, direct-mail and narrative copy for catalog and product reference guides for this multimillion-dollar consumer service company.

SMYTH, SMYTH & JONES, Washington, DC...1989–1991

LEGAL ASSISTANT / PROOFREADER

Wrote executive summaries of public programs for this large communications law firm that represented radio and TV broadcasters. Edited and proofed legal documents. Managed a library of pleadings.

EDUCATION

MA—International Development	AMERICAN UNIVERSITY—Washington, DC
BA—Political Science	MARIETTA UNIVERSITY—Marietta, OH
Semester abroad	UNIVERSITY OF BRUSSELS—School of International Business—Brussels, Belgium

TECHNICAL SKILLS
Mac & PC experience

Advanced: QuarkXPress	Proficient: Microsoft Word and Excel, and FileMaker Pro

A chief concern for the writer was to create a format that, like the applicant's copy, was easy to read and engaging. Note in the Professional Experience section the use of "dot leaders," the strings of periods that direct the reader's eye across the page to dates at the right margin.

Mokena, IL 55555

Carole Ross

708-555-5555
Carole.Ross@xxxx.com

SENIOR MARKETING & STRATEGY EXECUTIVE

Meaningful Marketing. Bottom-Line Results.

High-impact leader with 20 years of experience executing successful, integrated marketing programs and product launches that translate into value for established and growing brands. Rally cross-functional resources to cultivate diversified channels, enter new markets, and direct complex promotional and advertising campaigns. Rare ability to combine solid analytics with innovative strategy and impeccable execution. Deep experience in online and offline customer acquisition as well as traditional and social media.

➢ Sales and Marketing Integration	➢ Strategic Planning	➢ Cross-Functional Team Leadership
➢ New Product Development/Launch	➢ Agency Relations	➢ B2B & B2C Customer Acquisition
➢ Market Research/Insights	➢ Live Events & Webinars	➢ Brand Positioning/Management
➢ Concept Development/Execution	➢ Trade Shows	➢ Multimedia Promotions/Advertising

PROFESSIONAL EXPERIENCE

MARTIN & MARTIN, LLP – Chicago, IL   2004–Present
$450M professional services firm with 2,400 professionals and 23 offices nationally. Provides audit, tax, and consulting services to mid- and large-size companies globally. Top-10 firm nationally based on number of audit engagements (2009).

ASSOCIATE DIRECTOR

Doubled Marketing-generated pipeline—and supported $70M in total revenue—by transforming Marketing from support organization to proactive business partner. Executive accountability for marketing and marketing innovation firmwide. Lead cross-functional team in advertising/messaging, international marketing, new product development, lead generation/nurturing, marketing research/insights, and market/business analysis. Responsible for $1M operating budget and building business cases for new investments.

Made top- and bottom-line improvements...

➢ **Spurred $3.5M t0 $7.5M in sustainable annual sales through multitouch, integrated marketing programs,** generating 100–150 new clients per year with a $350K marketing budget.

➢ **Boosted qualified leads 50% and inside sales capacity 20%** by designing comprehensive lead generation, qualification, scoring, and nurturing system. Sourced and implemented marketing automation tool; developed demand creation segmentation model, and executed lead nurturing, lead scoring, and Sales training components.

➢ **Catalyzed Marketing organization's effectiveness by unifying its role across 5 business units and 11 horizontals.** Spearheaded strategic marketing planning process. Integrated business objectives and marketing plan, establishing relevant metrics and common vocabulary.

Cemented brand value with internal stakeholders, industry analysts, and clients...

➢ **Heightened brand awareness internally, improving recall 15%.** Conceived firmwide print ad campaign that leveraged brand differentiators and featured Martin & Martin partners, highlighting relationship-centered culture.

➢ **Raised firm visibility and credibility within primary market** by developing original research and related brand positioning to demonstrate understanding of CFO needs. Coordinated internal and external subject matter experts and translated results into PR/external byline opportunities, white papers, webinars, and marketing campaigns.

➢ **Established firm's first social networking program,** leading evaluation of the medium and creating a business case and full-scale strategy. Established Social Network Advisory Council to remediate issues and serve as strategic think tank.

Page 1 of 2

179

Combination. *Kim Mohiuddin, San Diego, California*

The writer had two challenges. The first was that this candidate had many accomplishments. To avoid a "sea of bullets," the writer categorized the accomplishments under value-added

Carole Ross 708-555-5555 | Carole.Ross@xxxx.com

PROFESSIONAL EXPERIENCE, continued

DELOITTE – Chicago, IL	2001–2004
Big 4 accounting and consulting firm. $20B+ annual sales.	

MARKETING DIRECTOR

Transitioned Midwest Marketing organization from passive order taker to growth driver. Sales and profitability responsibility for 13-office Midwest area as member of leadership team in Marketing and Tax departments. Led up to 15 direct reports in marketing, communications, event marketing, and database management activities. $2M budget.

➢ **Built strong relationship with Midwest leadership team,** initiating expansion strategies and increasing Marketing input 800% (measured by increase of floor time in leadership strategy meetings from 30 minutes to 4 hours).

➢ **Improved close ratio 25%** by improving ad-hoc proposal tracking system to capitalize on market opportunity. System was responsible for 20 additional clients in first quarter and hundreds of clients overall.

➢ **Strengthened middle-market practice,** initiating national go-to-market strategy that included structure, process, marketing, tracking, and reporting plan components. Implemented across $2B national line of business.

➢ **Reduced cycle time for core functions and improved data integrity** by improving technology and processes.

CHIEF OUTSIDERS – Chicago, IL	2000–2001
Full-service interactive/Web agency based in Dallas, TX. Clients included P&G, General Mills, and Eli Lilly.	

VICE PRESIDENT, CLIENT SERVICE

Catalyzed expansion into lucrative Chicago market by developing business plan that resolved critical capability gaps and organizational obstacles. Hired 22 people. Led client service and business development.

➢ **Spurred game-changing business with General Mills, Comdisco, and Abbott Labs** by developing interactive and integrated marketing strategies.

➢ **Added $2.2M in revenue** by leading business development personnel in targeting and closing key sale.

EARLY CAREER HIGHLIGHTS

Focused on **NEW PRODUCT DEVELOPMENT** for NESTLÉ and CITIBANK, managing project budgets up to $10M. Also gained experience in a variety of industries as a senior leader in a direct marketing agency and as an independent consultant.

CITIBANK: Created new $10M revenue stream with minimal investment. Recognized value of shelved line-of-credit product. Created business plan, sold project to CEO, updated technology, and launched within 90 days.

NESTLÉ: Transformed cost-savings idea into profitable new product concept. Leveraged failed plan to cut costs by reducing beef in corn beef hash (uncovered by self-managed work team in manufacturing facility) into new product idea, flavored corn beef hash. Managed successful national launch, orchestrating product development, packaging, naming, merchandising, financial projections, and associated marketing.

EDUCATION

MBA, Marketing, University of Chicago Booth School of Business, Chicago, IL

BA, English Literature, Ripon College, Ripon, WI

---

headings. The second was that the applicant had valuable experience at big companies in her early career, but indicating her duties would have aged her. The writer used a brief Early Career Highlights section to indicate their benefit without revealing her years.

DANIEL MURPHY

55 S. Gilmore Street ▪▪ New York, NY 55555
Home: (555) 555-5555 ▪▪ Mobile: (555) 555-4444 ▪▪ danmurphy@xxxx.com

REGIONAL SALES MANAGEMENT

Seven years of consistent achievements as a top-ranked key account manager with sporting goods retailers.

Both manufacturer and retailer experience include extensive regional sales and key account management roles selling sports products and apparel through "big box" and specialty retail environments. Excel in establishing consultative-style working relationships and extraordinary trust level with accounts and management to grow sales volume and profitability through sales of premium-priced products that produce dramatically higher sell-through than competitors.

Customers' and Supervisors' Comments

"Dan is the best sales rep in the building." Vice President

"Besides being great at establishing trusting relationships, Dan is a take-charge person who is able to present creative ideas and communicate the benefits." Account Supervisor

"Dan is the hardest working and most dedicated rep we have." Corporate Buyers at Key Accounts

PROFESSIONAL EXPERIENCE

Retail Brand, Inc.   **New York, NY**
ACCOUNT MANAGER (2003 to 2009)

Hired based on sales results and strong account relationships to take over major retail account with 160 stores in 23 states generating $2.5 million per year for the leading performance sports apparel company. Scope of responsibility more than doubled to 468 stores in 48 states and $10 million in sales following merger. Managed company's second-largest account in the country with a large product line consisting of premium-priced men's, women's and youth retail products with 2 major launches annually, including 40–50 new items each year. Negotiated sales agreements of up to $22 million.

Results delivered include:

✓ **Dramatically increased shipped revenues each year** from $10 million to $55 million (represents 71% of total business at a key account).

✓ **Exceeded plan each year** (2003–2007) and increased sales in 2008 despite recession. On track to achieve 2009 sales plan.

✓ **Maintained a 50+% gross margin rate on a major account** without using credits or discounts.

✓ **Ranked in top 2 each year out of 20 sales reps.**

✓ **Awarded as Salesperson of the Year (2005) out of 15 reps.**

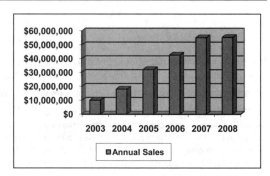

✓ **Facilitated rapid revenue growth of both accounts** by accelerating order frequency and setting up weekly scheduled shipments of automatic replenishment items. **Results: Cut lead time by two-thirds, which increased sales by more than 20–30%.**

EDUCATION

Bachelor of Arts, Business Management | Cornell University, New York, NY

180

Combination. *Louise Garver, Broad Brook, Connecticut*

This applicant was downsized. The quotations and chart helped to communicate his value for highly competitive positions. With this resume he found a new position in a related industry.

LYDIA HOWE

SALES MANAGEMENT | GENERAL MANAGEMENT | OPERATIONS

MANAGEMENT PROFESSIONAL

Results-oriented management professional with extensive experience heading sales and operations, new business development, and product launches—generating significant sales growth and optimizing operational performance. Successful coaching, mentoring, and building high-performance teams to achieve sales and business objectives. Well versed in conceptualizing and implementing best-in-class sales and customer training programs and strategies to identify and capture new market channels and revenue opportunities. Highly effective at establishing and maintaining solid customer relationships to deliver profitable sales. Core competencies include:

Sales Turnarounds	Organization	Sales Growth	Daily Operations
Customer Service	Scheduling	Product Knowledge	Sales Training
Target Marketing	Turnarounds	Team Leadership	Competitive Analysis

DELIVERED RESULTS

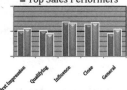

Sales Strategy Index™ Results
Most Effective Sales Strategies

- Recognized as Café of the Year in 2009 for outstanding operations.
- Saved company $15,000 to $18,000 per month, resulting in #1 rank for café.
- Spearheaded 12-week effort to transition and assimilate 16 new management teams in new market.
- Selected by executive management to open new stores and/or turn around poorly performing locations to achieve sales and volume targets.
- Instrumental in current location's sales volume increase of 8% within two months.
- Consistently succeeded in challenge to create efficient operation, achieve sales and profit goals, boost customer satisfaction, and improve employee retention.
- Satisfactorily implement marketing programs with results of annual audits showing no deficiencies.
- Ensure adequate staffing to serve 60% of daily clientele within four-hour window.

EMPLOYMENT HISTORY

POWER'S BAKERY / DAVISON VENTURES   1998–Present

FRANCHISE AUDITOR, Multiple locations (2009–Present)
GENERAL MANAGER, East Mercer, OH (2005–2009) $250,000 per month sales
GENERAL MANAGER, McDaye, OH (2002–2005) $160,000 per month sales
GENERAL MANAGER, Clover, OH (2001–2002) $130,000 per month sales
ASSISTANT MANAGER, Woodrow, PA (1998–2001)

Responsible for assessing operating practices, financials, training, security, and cleanliness for 145 cafés. Derive "best practices" to help maximize profits and support General Managers to ensure standards are met. Report directly to CFO and Regional Director of Operations. Provided leadership and direction in daily operation, including customer service, food and labor costs, safety, sanitation, product preparation, bank deposits, vendor relations, and recruitment. Accountable for training and supervising 40 to 45 staff members and 7 managers in serving 1,000 to 1,200 guests per day.

McDUGALS / DAVISON VENTURES   1995–1998

Fast-track promotion from **CREW MEMBER** to **SHIFT MANAGER** to **ASSISTANT MANAGER**

Assisted manager in store operations, with responsibility for using pre-shift and shift planning tools to meet volume demands. Supported marketing and promotions to maximize sales. Trained staff in all aspects of restaurant service, including personnel policies, security, and safety procedures. Contributed to hiring, performance appraisals, and employee retention.

EDUCATION / TRAINING / CERTIFICATIONS

Pre-MBA Program in Marketing, Accounting, Finance, LLOYD THOMPSON UNIVERSITY, Lloyd, OH

Bachelor of Science in Political Science/Sociology, OLDTOWN COLLEGE, Oldtown, OH

Safe Serve Certification, LAWRENCE TOWNSHIP, OH, HEALTH DEPARTMENT

Fluent in American Sign Language

5055 Blackberry Lane ◆ Youngstown, OH 55055 ◆ 555-550-5505 ◆ lhowe5555@xxx.com

181

Combination. *Jane Roqueplot, West Middlesex, Pennsylvania*

The graph in the Delivered Results section is the distinctive feature that makes this resume stand out.

LUCAS M. SPELLMAN

5500 BINGHAM ROAD · PITTSBURGH, PA 55555 · 555.000.5555 · lucaspellman@xxxx.com

ACCOUNT EXECUTIVE—NEW BUSINESS DEVELOPMENT
SALES MANAGEMENT—TEAM LEADERSHIP

AREAS OF EXPERTISE

TERRITORY DEVELOPMENT	MEDICAL DEVICE SALES	NEGOTIATIONS/CLOSING SKILLS
STRATEGIC PLANNING	CONSULTATIVE SALES	KEY PROJECT MANAGEMENT
PRESENTATIONS	TEAM LEADERSHIP	ACCOUNT RETENTION

MEDICAL SALES EXPERIENCE

Watson Therapy Products
Manufacturer and leading provider of compression therapy systems

Senior Account Manager April 2010–Present

Full account responsibilities promoting and selling compression therapy solutions to Vascular Surgeons, Podiatrists, Surgical Oncologists, Therapy Clinicians, and VA Health Systems throughout PA, WV, MD, DE, and DC.

- Assist in educating Surgeons, PA-Cs, CRNPs, and PTs/OTs on identifying various candidate types for optimum treatment results from products.
- Create individual account solutions through development of strategic marketing plans based on consultations and patient population.

East Coast Medical Products, Inc.
Provider of negative pressure wound therapy, bariatrics, and wound care solutions

Regional Sales Manager November 2007–April 2010

Directed team of three Sales Reps and two Clinicians to market and sell negative pressure wound therapy, bariatric products, and wound care solutions to Directors of Nursing, Wound Care teams, Surgeons, and Purchasing Department heads throughout PA, OH, and WV.

- Recognized for successfully converting more than 50 Skilled Nursing Facility and Wound Center accounts in a highly competitive region.
- Delivered 121% of quota, Q1 2010.
- Consistently achieved 101% of regional quota and 117% of territory quota during tenure.
- Authored protocols and procedures manual to conduct and evaluate product trials, which was adopted for company-wide use.
- Established territory budgets and sales goals and trained, coached, and mentored sales team to achieve expectations.

Barnes Healthcare
America's leading provider of integrated home healthcare products and services

Account Executive July 2005–November 2007

Specialized in promoting respiratory disease products and treatment protocols with sales energies focused on Cardiologists, Pulmonologists, and Internal Medicine Physicians in the hospital setting.

- Delivered 107% of goal expectation during tenure.
- Billable revenue of territory increased to $2.7M from $2.1M.
- Consistently billed 31% more per month over previous years' recorded revenues.

MILITARY EXPERIENCE

United States Navy, 2000–2003

❑ E5/Second Class Petty officer	❑ National Defense Ribbon
❑ Distinguished Military Graduate	❑ Good Conduct Medal Winner

EDUCATION

Bachelor of Science, Health Administration. Minor: Business
University of Illinois at Champaign, 2005, Dean's List

182

Combination. *Sari Neudorf, St. Louis, Missouri*

The Areas of Expertise section, placed within a table without side and bottom lines, catches immediate attention for this Senior Account Manager. Note the effective use of boldfacing.

3
P·A·R·T

Best Cover Letter Tips

Best Cover Letter Tips at a Glance

Best Cover Letter Writing Tips

In an active job search, your cover letter and resume should complement one another. Both are tailored to a particular reader you have contacted or to a specific job target. To help you create the best cover letters for your resumes, this part of the book mentions and debunks some common myths about cover letters and presents tips for polishing the letters you write.

Seven Myths About Cover Letters

The following bold statements are common myths about cover letters. Keep reading to discover the truth about these key job search documents:

1. **Resumes and cover letters are two separate documents that have little relation to each other.** The resume and cover letter work together in presenting you effectively to a prospective employer. The cover letter should mention the resume and call attention to some important aspect of it.

2. **The main purpose of the cover letter is to establish a rapport with the reader.** A resume shows that you *can* do the work required. The main purpose of a cover letter is to express that you *want* to do the work required. But it doesn't hurt to display enthusiasm in your resume and refer to your abilities in your cover letter.

3. **You can use the same cover letter for each reader of your resume.** Modify your cover letter for each reader so that it sounds fresh rather than canned. Chances are that in an active job search, you have already talked with the person who will interview you. Your cover letter should reflect that conversation and build on it.

4. **In a cover letter, you should mention any negative things about your education, work experience, life experience, or health to prepare the reader before an interview.** The purpose of the cover letter is to get an interview, not get screened out of one. You might bring up these topics in the first or second interview, but only after the interviewer has shown interest in you or offered you a job. Even then, if you feel that you must mention something negative about your past, present it in a positive way, perhaps by saying how that experience has strengthened your will to work hard at any new job.

5. **Removing errors from a resume is more important than removing them from a cover letter, because the resume is more important than the cover letter.** Both your resume and cover letter should be free of errors. The cover letter is usually the first document a prospective employer reads, and the first impression is often the most important one. If your cover letter has an error in it, chances are good that the reader may not bother to read your resume or may read it with less interest.

6. **To make certain that your cover letter has no errors, all you need to do is proofread it or ask a friend to do so.** Trying to proofread your own cover letter is risky, even if you are good at grammar and writing. Once a document is printed, it has an aura about it that may make it seem better-written than it is. For this reason, you are likely to miss typos or other kinds of errors.

   Relying on someone else is risky, too. If your friend is not good at grammar and writing, that person may not see any mistakes either. Try to find a proofreader, an editor, an English teacher, a writer, or an experienced secretary who can point out any errors you may have missed.

7. **After someone has proofread your letter, you can make a few changes to it and not have someone look at it again.** More errors creep into a document this way than you would think possible. The reason is that such changes are often done hastily, and haste can waste an error-free document. If you make *any* change to a document, ask someone to proofread it a final time just to make sure you didn't introduce an error during the last stage of composition. If you can't find someone to help you, the next section gives you advice on how to eliminate common mistakes in cover letters.

Tips for Polishing Cover Letters

You might spend several days working on your resume, getting it just right and free of errors. But if you send it with a cover letter that is written quickly and that contains even one conspicuous error, all your good effort may be wasted. That error could be just the kind of mistake the reader is looking for to screen you out.

You can prevent this kind of tragedy by polishing your cover letter so that it is free of errors. The following tips can help you avoid or eliminate common errors in cover letters (and in your resume as well). If you become aware of these kinds of errors and know how to fix them, you can be more confident about the cover letters you send with your resumes.

Using Good Strategies for Letters

For the most part, cover letters follow a standard business letter format. The following tips concern some details you might overlook:

- **Use the postal abbreviation for the state in your mailing address.** See the first tip in the "Contact Information" section in Part 1.

- **Make certain that the letter is addressed to a specific person and that you use this person's name in the salutation.** Avoid using such general salutations as Dear Sir or Madam, To Whom It May Concern, Dear Administrator, Dear Prospective Employer, and Dear Committee. In an active job search, you should do everything possible to send your cover letter and resume to a particular individual, preferably someone you've already talked with in person or by phone or e-mail and with whom you have arranged an interview. If you have not been able to make a personal contact, at least do everything possible to find out the name of the person who will read your letter and resume. Then address the letter to that person.

- **Adjust the margins for a short letter.** If your cover letter is 300 words or longer, use left, right, top, and bottom margins of 1 inch. If the letter is shorter, you should increase the margins' width. How much to increase them is a matter of personal taste. One way to take care of the width of the top and bottom margins is to center a shorter letter vertically on the page. A maximum width for a short cover letter of 100 words or fewer might be 2-inch left and right margins. As the number of words increases by 50 words, you might decrease the width of the left and right margins by two-tenths of an inch.

- **Use left justification to ensure that the lines of text are readable and have fixed spacing between words.** The letter will have a "ragged" look along the right margin, but the words will be evenly spaced. Don't use justification (having each line begin and end even with the page margins) in an attempt to give your letter a printed look. Unless you do other typesetting procedures, such as kerning and hyphenating words at the end of some lines, full justification can make your letter look worse by giving it some extra-wide and extra-narrow spaces between words.

Using Pronouns Correctly

Pronouns are a common source of cover letter problems. The following tips provide advice on how to handle such issues:

- **Use *I* and *My* sparingly.** When most of the sentences in a cover letter begin with *I* or *My*, you might appear self-absorbed, self-centered, or egotistical. If the reader is turned off by this kind of impression (even if it is a false one), you could be screened out without ever having an interview. Of course, you need to use these first-person pronouns sometimes, because most of the information you put in your cover letter is personal. But try to avoid using *I* and *My* at the beginnings of sentences and paragraphs.

- **Refer to a business, company, corporation, or organization as *it* rather than *they*.** Members of the Board may be referred to as *they*, but a company is a singular subject that requires a singular verb and pronoun. Note this example:

  > New Products, Inc., was established in 2010. It grossed more than $1 million in sales during its first year.

- **If you start a sentence with *This*, be sure that what *This* refers to is clear.** If the reference is not clear, insert a word or phrase to clarify what *This* means. Compare the following:

  > I will e-mail my revised application for the new position to you by noon on Friday. *This* should be acceptable to you.

  > I will e-mail my revised application for the new position to you by noon on Friday. This *method of sending the application* should be acceptable to you.

  A reader of the first example wouldn't know what *This* refers to. Friday? By noon on Friday? The revised application for the new position? The insertion after *This* in the second example, however, tells the reader that *This* refers to the use of e-mail.

- **Use *as follows* after a singular subject.** Literally, *as follows* means *as it follows,* so the phrase is illogical after a plural subject. Compare the following:

Incorrect:	My plans for the day of the interview are as follows:
Fixed:	My plans for the day of the interview are these:
Correct:	My plan for the day of the interview is as follows:
Better:	Here is my plan for the day of the interview:

In the second set of examples, the improved version avoids a hidden reference problem—the possible association of the silent "it" with *interview.* Whenever you want to use *as follows,* check to see whether the subject that precedes *as follows* is plural. If it is, don't use this phrase.

Using Verb Forms Correctly

The following tips relate to verb usage:

■ **Make certain that subjects and verbs agree in number.** Plural subjects require plural forms of verbs. Singular subjects require singular verb forms. Most writers know these things, but problems arise when subject-verb agreement gets tricky. Compare the following:

Incorrect:	My education and experience has prepared me...
Correct:	My education and experience have prepared me...
Incorrect:	Making plans plus scheduling conferences were...
Correct:	Making plans plus scheduling conferences was...

In the first set, *education* and *experience* are two separate things (you can have one without the other) and therefore require a plural verb. A hasty writer might lump them together and use a singular verb. When you reread what you have written, look out for this kind of improper agreement between a plural subject and a singular verb.

In the second set, *making plans* is the subject. It is singular, so the verb must be singular. The misleading part of this sentence is the phrase *plus scheduling conferences.* It might seem to make the subject plural, but it doesn't. In English, phrases that begin with such words as *plus, together with, in addition to, along with,* and *as well as* usually don't make a singular subject plural.

■ **Whenever possible, use active forms of verbs rather than passive forms.** Compare the following:

Passive:	My report will be sent by my assistant tomorrow.
Active:	My assistant will send my report tomorrow.
Passive:	Your interest is appreciated.
Active:	I appreciate your interest.
Passive:	Your letter was received yesterday.
Active:	I received your letter yesterday.

Sentences with passive verbs are usually longer and clumsier than sentences with active verbs. Passive sentences often leave out the crucial information of who is performing the verb's action. Spot passive verbs by looking for some form of the verb *to be* (such as *be, will be, have been, is, was,* and *were*) used with another verb.

In solving the passive-language problem, you might create another, such as using the pronouns *I* and *My* too frequently (see the first tip in the "Pronouns" section). The task then becomes one of finding some other way to start a sentence while keeping your language active.

■ **Be sure that present and past participles are grammatically parallel in a list.** What is true about parallel forms in resumes is true also in cover letters. See "Parallel Structure and Consistency" in Part 1. Present participles are action words that end in *-ing,* such as *creating, testing,* and *implementing.* Past participles are action words that usually end in *-ed,* such as *created, tested,* and *implemented.* These types of words are called *verbals* because they are derived from verbs but are not strong enough to function as verbs in a sentence. When you use a string of verbals, control them by keeping them parallel.

■ **Use split infinitives only when *not* splitting them is misleading or awkward.** An *infinitive* is a verb preceded by the preposition *to,* as in *to create, to test,* and *to implement.* You split an infinitive when you insert an adverb between the preposition and the verb, as in *to quickly create, to repeatedly test,* and *to slowly implement.* About 50 years ago, split infinitives were considered grammatical errors; these days, however, opinion about them has changed. Many grammar handbooks now recommend that you split infinitives to avoid awkward or misleading sentences. Compare the following:

Split infinitive:	I plan to periodically send updated reports on my progress in school.
Misleading:	I plan periodically to send updated reports on my progress in school.
Misleading:	I plan to send periodically updated reports on my progress in school.

The first example is clear enough, but the second and third examples may be misleading. If you are uncomfortable with split infinitives, one solution is to move *periodically* further into the sentence: "I plan to send updated reports periodically on my progress in school."

Most handbooks that allow split infinitives also recommend that they not be split by more than one word, as in *to quickly and easily write.* A gold medal for splitting an infinitive should go to Lowell Schmalz, an Archie Bunker prototype in "The Man Who Knew Coolidge" by Sinclair Lewis. Schmalz, who thought that Coolidge was one of America's greatest presidents, split an infinitive this way: "*to instantly and without the least loss of time or effort find...*"[1]

Using Punctuation Correctly

Refer to the following tips when you need a quick refresher on correct punctuation:

■ **Punctuate a compound sentence with a comma.** A compound sentence is one that contains two main clauses (a group of words containing a subject and a verb) joined by one of seven conjunctions (*and, but, or, nor, for, yet,* and *so*). In English, a comma is customarily put before the conjunction if the sentence isn't unusually short. Here is an example of a compound sentence punctuated correctly:

> I plan to arrive at O'Hare at 9:35 a.m. on Thursday, and my trip by cab to your office should take no longer than 40 minutes.

The comma is important because it signals that a new grammatical subject (*trip,* the subject of the second main clause) is about to be expressed. If you use this kind of comma consistently, the reader will rely on your punctuation and will be on the lookout for the next subject in a compound sentence.

---

[1]Sinclair Lewis, "The Man Who Knew Coolidge," *The Man Who Knew Coolidge* (New York: Books for Libraries Press, 1956), p. 29.

■ **Be certain not to put a comma between compound verbs.** When a sentence has two verbs joined by the conjunction *and,* these verbs are called *compound verbs.* Usually, they should not be separated by a comma before the conjunction. Note the following examples:

> I *started* the letter last night *and finished* it this morning.

> I *am sending* my resume separately *and would like* you to keep the information confidential.

Both examples are simple sentences containing compound verbs. Therefore, no comma appears before *and.* In either case, a comma would send a wrong signal that a new subject in another main clause is coming, but no such subject exists.

Note: In a sentence with a series of three or more verbs, use commas between the verbs. The comma before the last verb is called the *serial comma.* For more information on using the serial comma, see the first tip in the "Punctuation" section in Part 1.

■ **Avoid using *as well as* for *and* in a series.** Compare the following:

Incorrect:	Your company is impressive because it has offices in Canada, Mexico, as well as the United States.
Correct:	Your company is impressive because it has offices in Canada and Mexico, as well as in the United States.

Usually, what is considered exceptional precedes *as well as,* and what is considered customary follows it. Note this example:

> Your company is impressive because its products are innovative as well as affordable.

■ **Put a comma after the year when it appears after the month.** Similarly, put a comma after the state when it appears after the city. Compare the following pairs of examples:

Incorrect:	On January 10, 2011 I was promoted to senior analyst.
Correct:	On January 10, 2011, I was promoted to senior analyst.

Incorrect:	I worked in Springfield, Illinois before moving to Dallas.
Correct:	I worked in Springfield, Illinois, before moving to Dallas.

■ **Put a comma after an opening dependent clause.** A dependent clause is linked and related to the main clause by words such as *who, that, when,* and *if.* Compare the following:

Incorrect:	If you have any questions you may contact me by phone or e-mail.
Correct:	If you have any questions, you may contact me by phone or e-mail.

Actually, many writers of fiction and nonfiction don't use this kind of comma. The comma is useful, though, because it signals where the main clause begins. If you glance at the example with the comma, you can tell where the main clause is without even reading the opening clause. For a step up in clarity and readability, use this comma. It can give the reader a feel for a sentence even before he or she begins reading the words.

- **Use semicolons when they are needed.** See the second tip in the "Punctuation" section in Part 1 for the use of semicolons between items in a series. Semicolons also are used to separate two main clauses when the second clause starts with a *conjunctive adverb* such as *however, moreover,* or *therefore.* Compare the following:

Incorrect:	Your position in sales looks interesting, however, I would like more information about it.
Correct:	Your position in sales looks interesting; however, I would like more information about it.

The first example is incorrect because the comma before *however* is a *comma splice,* which is a comma that joins two sentences. It's like putting a comma instead of a period at the end of the first sentence and then starting the second sentence. A comma may be a small punctuation mark, but a comma splice is a huge grammatical mistake. What are your chances of getting hired if your cover letter tells your reader that you don't recognize where a sentence ends, especially if a requirement for the job is good communication skills? Yes, you could be screened out because of one little comma!

- **Avoid putting a colon after a verb or preposition to introduce information.** The reason is that the colon interrupts a continuing clause. Compare the following:

Incorrect:	My interests in your company *are:* its reputation, the review of salary after six months, and your personal desire to hire people with disabilities.
Correct:	My interests in your company *are these:* its reputation, the review of salary after six months, and your personal desire to hire people with disabilities.
Correct:	My interests in your company are its reputation, the review of salary after six months, and your personal desire to hire people with disabilities.
Incorrect:	In my interview with you, I would like *to:* learn how your company was started, get your reaction to my updated portfolio, and discuss your department's plans to move to a new building.
Correct:	In my interview with you, I would like to discuss *these issues:* how your company was started, what you think of my updated portfolio, and when your department may move to a new building.
Correct:	In my interview with you, I would like to learn how your company was started, what you think of my updated portfolio, and when your department may move to a new building.

Although some people may say that it is acceptable to put a colon after a verb such as *include* if the list of information is long, it is better to be consistent and avoid colons after verbs altogether.

■ **Understand the use of colons.** People often associate colons with semicolons because their names sound alike, but colons and semicolons have nothing to do with each other. Colons are the opposite of dashes. Dashes look backward, whereas colons usually look forward to information about to be delivered. One common use of the colon does look backward, however. Here are two examples:

> My experience with computers is limited: I have had only one course in programming, and I don't own a computer.

> I must make a decision by Monday: That is the deadline for renewing the lease on my apartment.

In each example, what follows the colon explains what was said before the colon. Using a colon this way in a cover letter can impress a knowledgeable reader who is looking for evidence of writing skills.

■ **Use slashes correctly.** Information about slashes is sometimes hard to find because *slash* often is listed in grammar reference books under a different name, such as *virgule* or *solidus.* If you are unfamiliar with these terms, your hunt for advice on slashes may lead to nothing.

At least know that one important meaning of a slash is *or.* For this reason, you often see a slash in an expression such as ON/OFF. This usage means that a condition or state, such as that of electricity activated by a switch, is either ON *or* OFF but never ON *and* OFF at the same time. This condition may be one in which a change means going from the current state to the opposite (or alternate) state. If the current state is ON and a change occurs, the next state is OFF, and vice versa. With this understanding, you can recognize the logic behind the following examples:

Incorrect:	ON-OFF switch (on and off at the same time!)
Correct:	ON/OFF switch (on or off at any time)
Correct:	his-her clothes (unisex clothes, worn by both sexes)
Correct:	his/her clothes (each sex had different clothes)

Note: Both his-her and his/her are clumsy. Try to find a way to avoid them. One route is to rephrase the sentence so that you use the plural possessive pronoun *their* or the second-person possessive pronoun *your.* (Campers should make their beds before breakfast. Please make your beds before breakfast.) Another way is to rephrase the sentence without possessive pronouns. (Everyone should get dressed before going to breakfast.)

■ **Think twice about using *and/or*.** This stilted expression is commonly misunderstood to mean *two* alternatives, but it literally means *three.* Consider the following example:

> If you don't hear from me by Friday, please call and/or e-mail me on Monday.

What is the person at the other end to do? The sentence really states three alternatives: just call, just e-mail, or call *and* e-mail on Monday. For better clarity, use the connectives *and* or *or* whenever possible.

■ **Use punctuation correctly with quotation marks.** A common misconception is that commas and periods should be placed outside closing quotation marks, but the opposite is true. Compare the following:

Incorrect:	Your company certainly has the "leading edge", which means that its razor blades are the best on the market.
Correct:	Your company certainly has the "leading edge," which means that its razor blades are the best on the market.

Incorrect:	In the engineering department, my classmates referred to me as "the girl guru". I was the youngest expert in programming languages on campus.
Correct:	In the engineering department, my classmates referred to me as "the girl guru." I was the youngest expert in programming languages on campus.

Note this exception: Unlike commas and periods, colons and semicolons go *outside* double quotation marks.

Using Words Correctly

Poor word choice in a cover letter can keep you from getting called in for an interview. These tips can help you choose your words wisely:

■ **Avoid using lofty language in your cover letter.** A real turn-off in a cover letter is the use of elevated diction (high-sounding words and phrases) as an attempt to seem important. Note the following examples, along with their straight-talk translations:

Elevated:	My background has afforded me experience in...
Better:	In my previous jobs, I...

Elevated:	Prior to that term of employment...
Better:	Before I worked at...

Elevated:	I am someone with a results-driven profit orientation.
Better:	I want to make your company more profitable.

Elevated:	I hope to utilize my qualifications...
Better:	I want to use my skills...

In letter writing, the shortest distance between the writer and the reader is the most direct idea.

■ **Check your sentences for excessive use of compounds joined by *and*.** A cheap way to make your letters longer is to join words with *and* and to do this repeatedly. Note the following wordy sentence:

Because of my background and preparation for work and advancement with your company and new enterprise, I have a concern and commitment to implement and put into effect my skills and abilities for new solutions and achievements above and beyond your dreams and expectations. (44 words)

Just one inflated sentence like that would drive a reader to say, "No way!" The writer of the inflated sentence has said only this:

> Because of my background and skills, I want to contribute to your new venture. (14 words)

If you eliminate the wordiness caused by this common writing weakness, an employer is more likely to read your letter completely.

■ **Avoid using abstract nouns excessively.** Look again at the inflated sentence in the preceding tip, but this time with the abstract nouns in italic:

> Because of my *background* and *preparation* for *work* and *advancement* with your *company* and new *enterprise,* I have a *concern* and *commitment* to implement and put into *effect* my skills and *abilities* for new *solutions* and *achievements* above and beyond your *dreams* and *expectations.*

Try picturing in your mind any of the words in italic. You can't because they are *abstract nouns,* which means that they are ideas and not images of things you can see, taste, hear, smell, or touch. One certain way to turn off the reader is to load your cover letter with abstract nouns. The following sentence, containing some images, has a better chance of capturing the reader's attention:

> Having created seven multimedia tutorials with my digital camcorder and HP Pavilion Media Center PC, I now want to create some breakthrough adult-learning packages so that your company, New Century Instructional Technologies, Inc., will exceed $50,000,000 in contracts by 2012.

Compare this sentence with the one loaded with abstract nouns. The one with images is obviously the better attention-grabber.

■ **Avoid wordy expressions in your cover letters.** Note the following examples in the first column and their shorter alternatives in the second column:

at the location of	at
for the reason that	because
in a short time	soon
in a timely manner	on time
in spite of everything to the contrary	nevertheless
in the event of	if
in proximity to	near
now and then	occasionally
on a daily basis	daily
on a regular basis	regularly
on account of	because
one day from now	tomorrow
would you be so kind as to	please

Trim the fat wherever you can, and your reader will appreciate the leanness of your cover letter.

■ **At the end of your cover letter, don't make a statement that the reader can use to reject you.** For example, suppose that you close your letter with this statement:

> If you wish to discuss this matter further, please call me at (555) 555-5555.

This statement gives the reader a chance to think, "No, I don't wish to." Here is another example:

> If you know of the right opportunity for me, please call me at (555) 555-5555.

The reader may think, "I don't know of any such opportunity. How would I know what's right for you?" Avoid questions that prompt yes-or-no answers, such as "Do you want to discuss this matter further?" If you ask this kind of question, you give the reader a chance to say no. Instead, make a closing statement that indicates your optimism about receiving a positive response from the reader. Such a statement might begin with one of the following clauses:

> I am confident that...

> I look forward to...

In this way, you invite the reader to say yes to further considering your candidacy for the job.

Exhibit of Cover Letters

The following Exhibit contains sample cover letters that were prepared by professional resume writers. The names, addresses, and facts have been changed to ensure the confidentiality of the original senders and recipients. Each letter, however, retains the essential substance of the original.

Use the Exhibit of cover letters as a reference whenever you need to write a cover letter for your resume. If you have trouble starting and ending letters, look at the beginnings and ends of these letters. If you need help with writing about your work experience, describing your abilities and skills, or mentioning some of your best achievements, look at the middle paragraph(s). Search for features that will give you ideas for making your own cover letters more effective.

As you examine the Exhibit, consider the following questions:

1. **Does the writer show a genuine interest in the reader?** One way to tell is to count how many times the pronouns *you* and *your* appear in the letter. Then count how many times the pronouns *I, me,* and *my* occur. Although this method is simplistic, it nevertheless helps you see where the writer's interests lie. When you write a cover letter, make your first paragraph *you*-centered rather than *I*-centered. Review the first tip under "Using Pronouns Correctly," earlier in Part 3.

2. **Where does the cover letter mention the resume specifically?** The purpose of a cover letter is to call attention to the resume. If the letter fails to mention the resume, the letter has not fulfilled its purpose. In addition to mentioning the resume, the cover letter might direct the reader's attention to one or more parts of the resume, increasing the chances that the reader will see the most important part(s). It is not a good idea, however, to put a lot of resume facts in the cover letter. Let each document do its own job. The cover letter's job is to point to the resume, not repeat it verbatim.

3. **Where and how does the letter express interest in an interview?** The cover letter's immediate purpose is to call attention to the resume, but the *ultimate* purpose of both the cover letter and the resume is to help you get an interview with the person who can hire you. If the letter doesn't convey your interest in getting an interview, it has not fulfilled its ultimate purpose.

4. **How decisive is the writer's language?** This question is closely related to the preceding one. Does the writer express interest in an interview directly or indirectly? Does the person specifically request an interview on a date when the writer will be in the reader's vicinity, or does the person only hint at a desire to meet the reader someday? When you write your own cover letters, be sure to be direct and convincing in expressing your interest in an interview. Avoid being timid or wishy-washy.

5. **How does the person display self-confidence?** As you look through the Exhibit, notice the cover letters in which the phrase "I am confident that..." (or a similar expression) appears. Self-confidence is a sign of management ability but also of essential job-worthiness. Many of the letters display self-confidence or self-assertiveness in various ways.

6. **How does the letter indicate that the person is a team player?** From an employer's point of view, an employee who is self-assertive but not a team player can spell T-R-O-U-B-L-E. As you look at the cover letters in the Exhibit, notice the letters in which the word *team* appears.

7. **How does the letter make the person stand out?** As you read the letters in the Exhibit, do some letters present the person more vividly than others? If so, what does the trick—the middle paragraphs or the opening and closing paragraphs? Use what you learn here to help you write distinctive cover letters.

8. **How familiar is the person with the reader?** In a passive job search, the reader will most likely be a total stranger. In an active job search, chances are good that the writer will have had at least one conversation with the reader by phone or in person. As you look through the cover letters in the Exhibit, see whether you can spot any letter that indicates that the writer has already talked with the reader.

After you have examined the cover letters in the Exhibit, you will be better able to write an attention-getting letter—one that leads the reader to review your resume and to schedule an interview with you.

THOMAS DORAN   555-123-4567

April 29, 2012

Mr. Alex J. Madrid
Advertising Director
Creative Spanish Advertising, Inc.
5555 Ignacio Road
Concordo, Mexico YZ555-55

Dear Mr. Madrid:

A **bachelor of arts in advertising, a minor in marketing** from Academia University, and experience building several competitive advertising campaigns add credibility to my candidacy for an advertising position with Creative Spanish Advertising, Inc. Your *Today's Journal* classified ad for an advertising assistant sparked my interest. The enclosed resume reflects an **energetic, highly competitive, and committed** individual with **relevant experience.** The following **achievements and personal characteristics** are additional reasons to take a closer look at my qualifications.

CONTRIBUTING IDEAS THAT WORK...

- Provided advertising skills as **integral team player** on several campaigns. Fully involved in creating a plan book and **creative brief** to promote awareness of how the state lottery uses funds to better the state public school system. Contributed to **all aspects of project.**
- Earned a place on the Advertising Coalition Student Competition Team of 2012 due to **abstract concepts** and **creative impact.** Incorporated **appeal techniques** in the creation of a four-year integrated marketing communications plan book for auto dealership. Chosen for **creative team.**

EXPERIENCE THAT BRINGS INSIGHT...

- Used initiative to gain opportunity and funding for **foreign study programs** in Mexico and Holland. Studies covered **Spanish, international marketing, management, and law.** Submersion into these cultures and observation of foreign **advertising techniques, nontraditional media,** and **economic structures** greatly enhanced **insight** into international business.
- Gained a stronger **acceptance of differences,** expanded **cultural awareness,** and became more **self-reliant and confident** through **travel experiences** and **interaction with people of diversity.**

PROFICIENCIES THAT REFLECT DISTINCTION ...

- Creative idea generation and problem solving for unique presentations.
- Brainstorming and openness to new ideas for increasing productivity.
- Group facilitation and organization for effective teamwork.
- Effective decisions based on overall picture for positive outcomes.
- Interpersonal skills such as mediation and negotiation for maintaining strong business relationships.
- Effective writing talent for creative copy.
- Mac and IBM computer literacy with experience in QuarkXPress, Adobe Illustrator and Photoshop, and Microsoft Works and Word for optimum layouts.
- Conversational Spanish for interfacing with peers and clients.

I will contact you within the week to confirm receipt of my resume and set up a **personal interview** at your convenience. In the meantime, thank you for your time and consideration.

Sincerely,

Thomas Doran

Enclosure: Resume

5555 55ᵗʰ Street ▪ Camary, Texas 55555 ▪ tdoran@yahoo.com

Edith A. Rische, Lubbock, Texas

The letter has only two paragraphs. Sandwiched between them are three sections with bulleted achievements, areas of development, and personal qualifications. See Resume 7.

Lara Carson　　　　　　　　　　　555 South Hill Road • Los Angeles, CA 55555
Home: 555.555.5555 • Mobile: 555.555.4444　　　　E-mail: laracarson@hotmail.com

Date

Name
Title
Employer
Address

Dear _____:

As a native speaker and Spanish teacher, I believe my skills and talents can make a long-term contribution to your school. My qualifications include teaching Spanish to nonnative speakers at a language-based institute that promotes intercultural understanding through learning communicative-language skills and cross-cultural awareness. In addition, I privately instruct children in learning Spanish.

You will find that I am skilled at developing and presenting stimulating lesson plans for students of differing learning abilities and that I possess a communicative teaching style. You will also notice that I am collaborative and team-oriented in my approach, building strong rapport with students, professionals, parents and staff members. In addition, I continually receive outstanding evaluations from my students, who reinforce my teaching strengths and the skills I have helped them develop.

The accompanying resume details the experience I will offer your organization. If you need a dedicated teaching professional whose passion for teaching is clearly evident in the classroom and who would enjoy making a difference in your school, then I would welcome a personal interview.

Please know that I am planning on relocating to your community in Florida and will make myself available for interviewing. I will contact you in two weeks to explore the possibility of an in-person meeting.

Sincerely,

Lara Carson

2

Louise Garver, Broad Brook, Connecticut

The first two paragraphs show that this candidate is more than just another Spanish teacher. The third paragraph indicates that she is truly interested in the position. See Resume 38.

WALTER D. SAKS

98 Ben Franklin Drive
P.O. Box 219
Cherry Hill, New Jersey 07896   wdsaks@aol.com

Home: (609) 888–1111
Cell: (609) 888–5555
Home Fax: (609) 888–7777

<Date>

<Title, Name of Hiring Manager>
<Name of Company>
<Address>
<City, State ZIP>

Dear <Courtesy><Last Name>,

Throughout my 40-year career in real estate development and construction, I have built and led numerous successful development, construction, and property management companies. For each organization, I have provided the strategic, marketing, financial, and operating expertise to deliver strong earnings and sustained revenue streams. Please consider the following in addition to my resume:

- 15+ years of management experience in a general contracting company, including construction management, owner/client negotiations, subcontract scope designs and negotiations, project cost accounting/reporting, design-build, estimating, purchasing, design/expense analysis, and bidding.
- 15 years of experience in real estate development and management, including site selection, building conception designs, establishing and maintaining owner associations, acting as representative on condominium boards, and establishing budgetary goals and life expectancies of building and site features.
- Recognized as a credible professional within the real estate community of New Jersey; proven track record of closing early sales/leases and meeting client delivery requirements.
- Leadership of more than $190 million in construction projects, with complete development and management responsibility for more than 470 projects ranging from commercial renovations to major new construction projects.
- Astute business manager with an outstanding ability to build dynamic teams and generate strong results; successfully assembled teams to solve engineering, architectural, and mechanical problems associated with all phases of construction and development.

As a successful entrepreneur, I possess a wealth of positive, proven methods and solutions to diverse obstacles. Most significant is my ability to drive projects through complex political, community, and governmental channels. By providing a strong community vision and decisive action plan, I have won the support of community, political, business, and financial leaders—support critical to project funding, development, and profitable sales/leasing. In addition, my enthusiasm for the entire process, from product conception and planning to delivery and sales/leasing, is undaunted by any negativity or economic difficulty. There is always a consumer for a product selected and executed with pride and grace.

I would welcome the opportunity to discuss how my credentials and expertise can benefit your organization, and will therefore contact your office next week to arrange a mutually convenient time for us to meet. In the interim, I thank you for reviewing this letter and the accompanying material.

Sincerely,

Walter Saks
Enclosure

Jennifer Rushton, Sydney, New South Wales, Australia

The writer expanded this three-paragraph letter after the first paragraph by adding five bulleted items about experience, esteem, scope of accomplishments, and outstanding managerial abilities. See Resume 63.

555 ● 555 ● 5555

B. Rae French

5555 Toton Avenue ● Skyview, Texas 79000
brfrench@nts-online.net

May 27, 2012

Sally Monarch
Human Resources Director
CORPORATE AMERICA
5555 Broadview Lane
Macro City, Texas 99999

...an ordinary person who is motivated, enthusiastic, who has dreams, and who works hard; who has the ability to laugh, to think, to cry; and who can give the gift of belief to other people can accomplish anything.

Unknown

RE: CORPORATE TRAINER

Dear Ms. Monarch:

After a successful eight-year teaching career in academia, I am seeking change. To be more specific, as a **corporate trainer,** I hope to realize more latitude for **creativity** and **original training techniques** in a company where upward mobility is an option. **Communication, interpersonal relations, coordination, and organization** are among my most highly developed skills—all practical resources for managing a corporate training program. The enclosed resume reflects a **multitalented, energetic achiever** who enjoys making **positive contributions.**

The following **additional skills** further exhibit a **strong candidacy** for a corporate trainer position:

Interpersonal / Communication Skills
- **Personable, cheerful demeanor** and a **relaxed style** cultivate an **effective learning environment.**
- **A sense of humor makes training enjoyable.**
- **Perceptiveness** and **attentiveness** allow appropriate **responses to student needs.**
- Ability to develop **rapport and trust** with a **diverse population** strengthens **trainer / trainee relationships.**
- **Articulation** and **good grammar** ensure **clear, credible delivery** of **instructions** and **training materials.**

Leadership Qualities
- Readiness to **assume responsibility** and **accountability** alleviates stress on upper management.
- **Integrity, diligence,** and **commitment** model **leadership** and **reflect distinction.**
- **A positive attitude** and **willingness to adapt to change** suggest **cooperation** and **easy transitions.**
- **Discernment, prioritization,** and **delegation** encourage **teamwork** and **productivity.**
- **Analytical thinking** and **common sense** foster **effective problem solving.**
- **Proven training techniques** fortify **information retention.**

Administrative Abilities
- **Restructuring curriculum** and **writing directives** supplement **program development.**
- Capacity to **coordinate activities, focus on details,** and **follow up** promotes **smooth-running events.**
- **Organization** and **forward planning** imply **efficiency** and **successful outcomes.**
- **Time management, multitasking,** and **follow through** facilitate **consistently met deadlines.**

I am **confident** that my abilities can benefit your company's training department, and consider a **personal interview to be mutually beneficial.** Relocation is an option for the opportune job offer. I will contact your office within the week to confirm receipt of my resume and set up an appointment at your convenience. Thank you for your consideration.

Sincerely,

B. Rae French

Enclosure: Resume

4

Edith A. Rische, Lubbock, Texas

The novel page border sets this letter apart from most cover letters. The letter appears to set the applicant apart from other applicants through the bulleted lists of skills. See Resume 47.

Bill Raymond, CFA

555 Lowell Street
Lawrence, MA 01746

billraymond@alumni.mit.edu
978-555-1210

May 22, 2012

Mr. Tom Marston, Director of Fixed Income
International Financial Investments, Inc.
200 Federal Street, 26th Floor
Boston, MA 02110

Dear Mr. Marston:

In response to your search for the **Money Market Analyst/Portfolio Manager** position your firm placed on Bloomberg, I bring more than 15 years of experience in the market.

My years of experience at Boston Investors, Inc., including more than a dozen years managing money market portfolios, indicate that I could step right into this position and add value immediately. It combines my passion for analysis with my knowledge of money markets.

Your Needs	**My Qualifications**
CFA, MBA degree or equivalent	◆ CFA since 1996
	◆ B.A. in Economics from M.I.T.
Several years of experience in Money Markets, fund analysis and trading	◆ More than a dozen years of experience managing taxable 2a-7 funds
Creating credit files	◆ Created institutional 2a-7 from scratch, including credit files

My enclosed resume provides further details of my accomplishments. I look forward to discussing a career opportunity with you. I will call you in the next few days to discuss your company's needs in greater detail.

Sincerely,

Bill Raymond
Senior Vice President
Boston Investors, Inc.

Enclosure

Gail Frank, Tampa, Florida

The "Your Needs...My Qualifications" two-column table is distinctive. Diamond bullets and the additional line about the MIT degree suggest that the person's qualifications surpass the reader's needs.

BRENDA B. STEVENS

5555 55th Street ■ Ft. Cloud, Mississippi 55555 ■ *(555) 555-5555*

May 12, 2012

TROY PHARMACEUTICALS
5555 Magnum Street
Ft. Cloud, Mississippi 55555

Re: Pharmaceutical Sales Specialist, Code SPMDT

Dear Human Resources Coordinator:

I am committed to improved patient care, a quality that characterizes value to medical professionals. As an *established pharmaceutical sales representative* covering the whole of Mississippi, I offer *beneficial industry knowledge* from *six years of experience.* It would be an honor to represent TROY, a highly regarded pharmaceutical company whose mission to enhance and preserve quality of life coincides so closely with mine.

The enclosed resume reflects a *match between my credentials and your requirements for the pharmaceutical sales specialist position.* A qualification summary follows:

JOB REQUIREMENTS	PERSONAL QUALIFICATIONS
Five years of sales experience, preferably pharmaceutical	▪ *Six years of proven success* in the pharmaceutical / medical sales industry. ▪ *Established rapport with 200+ Mississippi physicians* specializing in a spectrum of healthcare disciplines.
Bachelor's degree	▪ *Bachelor of Science* in political science with minor in public relations.
Project and account management experience	▪ Exclusively *acquired six-figure surgical center account,* orchestrated *total equipment installation,* and *troubleshot logistical problems.* ▪ Employ *continuous customer contact, needs assessment, and strategic planning* to manage and grow 180+ accounts.
Sales / persuasion skills	▪ Consistently rank in *top 10% of regional sales* representatives for exceeding 100% of annual sales goals. ▪ Use *scientific / consultative sales approach* to gain customer acceptance of products and services.
Communication and presentation skills	▪ Relate to physicians through *lighthearted, yet authoritative, communication style* to create enjoyable sales environment. ▪ Incorporate analogies, illustrations, sales / detail aids, and humor into presentations and training seminars to *engage audiences, retain interest, and improve comprehension.*

Given a *pre-established client network, technical knowledge, and personal values,* I am confident I would well serve TROY PHARMACEUTICALS' goals and objectives. I hope to *share business development ideas* during a personal interview, and look forward to scheduling an appointment at your convenience. In the meantime, thank you for your consideration.

Sincerely,

Brenda B. Stevens

Enclosure: Resume

6

Edith A. Rische, Lubbock, Texas

This similar "Job Requirements...Personal Qualifications" two-column table shows that you can easily expand the Qualifications column to suggest that your qualifications outweigh the job's requirements.

SUSAN ENGLE

70 West Nordham ■ Wyckoff, NJ 07465

email: sengle@msn.com   cellular: 000-000-1111   000-000-0000

Date

Name
Title
Company Name
Company Street Address
Town, State, ZIP

Dear Mr. / Ms. _____:

As a Senior Financial Analyst with more than 10 years of progressively responsible finance / accounting experience in public, private and nonprofit environments and with expertise in U.S. / U.K. GAAP, I am an excellent candidate for the position of _____. My career includes both supervisory and individual contributor positions, and I have been successful in both roles. The following are some of my career highlights:

- Able to rapidly and flawlessly execute financial consolidations and reportables, including budgets, forecasts and strategic plans with both domestic and international reporting.
- Within 5 days, completed North American Industry Classification System (NAICS) codes for a $152 million acquisition.
- Unveiled a $2.5 million dividend through thorough analysis of joint venture financial data.
- Certified in Hyperion and Hyperion Enterprise.
- Highly proficient in Essbase and Excel.

Attached is my résumé for your review. I am confident that my demonstrated expertise would add value to your firm and contribute to your continuing success.

I will contact you in the near future to set up a time to discuss your needs and my qualifications further.

Very truly yours,

Susan Engle

Attachment: résumé

Fran Kelley, Waldwick, New Jersey

After an opening paragraph that refers to the applicant's excellence and successfulness, bullets point to abilities, quantified achievements, certifications, and software proficiencies.

ELANA M. AVILES   555 Lakeview Drive • Wyandotte, Michigan 55555
                                                              (555) 555-5555 • eaviles@email.usa

January 4, 20XX

Ms. Janet Richardson, Board of Education
Local School District
555 Timber Lane
Wyandotte, Michigan 55555

Dear Ms. Richardson,

As an Eastern Michigan University graduate with a Bachelor of Science in Elementary Education, I look forward to applying my academic training and teaching experience to continue helping students establish and achieve their personal goals. I take a sincere interest in seeing that students under my direction take advantage of the vast resources available to them and presenting these learning tools in a way to promote effective learning.

Instilling students with self-confidence, encouragement, and moral support helps children believe in themselves while being rewarded for their efforts. Establishing a sound student/teacher relationship is a large contributing factor in motivating students to take an active role in developing their education in various subject areas. This is my personal belief and how I view my position as a teaching role model to my students.

I am certified in the State of Michigan to educate K–5 as well as certified to educate 6th–8th grade students with emphasis in the Science subject areas. I am also a member of the Michigan Education Association (MEA), as well as the Michigan Science Teachers Association (MSTA). My goal is to acquire a teaching position with the Local School District, which will allow me to provide your students with the support and tools necessary to achieve and succeed.

I appreciate your time and consideration in reviewing my resume and I would welcome a personal interview to discuss my qualifications further. I will follow up with you next week and look forward to speaking with you soon.

Regards,

Elana Aviles

Enclosure

8

Maria E. Hebda, Trenton, Michigan

This applicant for a K–8 teaching position expresses her interest, personal beliefs about education, certifications, and desire for an interview.

Elizabeth Swanson

3461 N. Drake Ave. #324
Chicago, IL 60624

773-555-2166
eswanson4@ymail.com

Dear Superintendent:

In many cases a child's first experience in school sets the stage for the rest of his or her educational career. Is school hard and intimidating? Or is it fun and welcoming? I believe school should be the latter, and for more than 18 years I have worked hard as a prekindergarten teacher to make sure that every student gets the best start possible in my classroom. I am forwarding my resume to you in consideration for an appropriate position as a member of your district's early childhood teaching staff.

One of my strengths is preparing and presenting a developmentally appropriate curriculum to meet the cognitive, social, emotional and physical needs of students and to thoroughly prepare them for the leap to kindergarten. Because I have worked with children from diverse backgrounds and skill levels, I am adept at modifying the lessons to meet my students' individual needs. Another strength is my ability to elicit the cooperation and involvement of parents within the classroom as well as schoolwide. This is another aspect of the strong foundation I am trying to lay for children as they begin their education.

Outside the classroom I work hard to be a leader and role model. I have participated in many extracurricular leadership capacities, including being elected as a faculty representative to my school's Board of Education. I am aware of the issues and problems facing youth and their families, and I continually advocate for young children.

I am confident you will agree my maturity and experience can be an asset to your district's early childhood program. Therefore, I will contact you to arrange an opportunity to discuss my strengths and potential contributions. Thank you for your time and consideration.

Sincerely,

Elizabeth Swanson

Enclosure

Janet L. Beckstrom, Flint, Michigan

This person wanted a job with a public school district after many years in a parochial school setting. The writer presents the applicant as experienced. See Resume 35.

Darrin Wilson

1124 Liberty Street, 3rd Floor • Chester, PA 18940 • 267.757.5462 • dWilson53@excite.com

MARKET RESEARCH ANALYST

Dear Sir/Madam:

As a research professional, I understand that success depends on a strong commitment to *customer satisfaction.* Executing the basics and using logic and reasoning to identify the strengths and weaknesses of alternative solutions, conclusions or approaches to problems are key to increasing performance and market share. I believe that my background and education reflect a commitment and ability to find solutions to these challenges. I developed excellent skills in **project coordination and the design and development of research projects** that increased the effectiveness of my organization.

I am considered an energetic, aggressive and innovative leader who is extremely client-oriented.

My position encompasses multiple tasks and responsibilities that include the following:

♦ Examining and analyzing statistical data to forecast future trends and to identify potential markets.

♦ Designing and implementing new formats for logging and transferring information while working as part of a team researching data and statistics.

Thank you for your consideration. I approach my work with a strong sense of urgency, working well under pressure and change. I look forward to meeting with you personally so that we may discuss how I may make a positive contribution to your organization.

Sincerely yours,

Darrin Wilson

Enclosure

10

Beverly and Mitchell I. Baskin, Marlboro, New Jersey

This four-paragraph letter displays bulleted responsibilities introduced by the third paragraph. Boldfacing of phrases in the first paragraph calls attention to concerns that are of interest to the reader.

Robert V. Carlino

6 Phillips Drive • Princeton Junction, NJ 08550 • (609) 209-8349 • rCarlino17@aol.com

CHIEF FINANCIAL OFFICER

June 12, 2012

Mr. John Promo
President
American Construction
PO Box 1844
Bridgewater, NJ 08807-0884

Dear Mr. Promo:

As a Certified Public Accountant with solid experience as a **Chief Financial Officer** and a **Vice President of Finance,** I understand that success depends on the bottom line, with special attention to financial and managerial teamwork. I believe that my background and accomplishments have proven to be a productive combination.

Throughout my career, I have been assigned increasing responsibilities and significantly contributed to corporate growth. I believe I have mastered the art of contact management, corporate networking, and personal relationship building. In doing so, I developed a working knowledge of several service-oriented industries, including Architectural, Engineering, and Construction.

Following are some accomplishments of which I am proud:

- Increased shareholder distribution from zero in 2003 to $1.3 million and $1.5 million in 2006 and 2007, respectively, in spite of a 20% revenue shrinkage over the same time period.
- Improved cash flow more than $3 million in 6 months.
- Grew profit margin from 3% to 10% for 3 consecutive years, *the best in company history*.
- Reduced overhead from 170% to 120% in direct labor.
- Trimmed DOS 21% from 85 to 67 days.

Thank you for your consideration. I am a forward thinker and a team player who has a strong commitment to my people and the organizations I work for. I look forward to speaking with you to discuss how I may make a positive contribution to your operation.

Sincerely yours,

Robert V. Carlino

Enclosure

Beverly and Mitchell I. Baskin, Marlboro, New Jersey

The design is like that of the preceding letter, but it is flexible. The differences are in the expansion of the second paragraph and the greater number of bullets after the third paragraph.

MEG ANISTON

555 Overlake Street, Oakland, CA 94601
510-555-4242

maniston@earthlink.com
Fax 510-555-4243

May 22, 2012

VISIONEER FINANCIAL PRODUCTS
ATTN: Position #5490
56 Hillside Drive, Suite 285
Oakland, CA 94601

Dear Hiring Professional:

In response to your search for a quality sales professional, I bring more than 15 years of experience in financial sales and consultation.

I am an extremely high-energy and innovative salesperson who leads by example. I consistently produce strong results with a high degree of integrity, dedication and organized communication skills.

Many of my achievements are due to my ability to create and maintain rapport with clients. This quality, coupled with a drive to think strategically and capitalize on opportunities, has given me a track record of success. Some highlights include

- Consistently exceed sales quotas and bring in new accounts
- Closing rate over 80%
- Client retention of 92%
- Increased revenue by 146% within first 6 months of current position
- Annually generated $14–20 million in revenue
- Hired, trained and developed team of 85 people
- Created and delivered hundreds of impactful presentations and meetings

My resume and a summary page provide further details of my accomplishments. You will note that I have worked for some major companies and have progressed in responsibility levels. I look forward to discussing yet another career opportunity with you. I shall contact you next week to arrange a meeting so we may discuss your company's needs in greater detail.

Sincerely,

Meg Aniston

Enclosure

12

Gail Frank, Tampa, Florida

This letter is for someone who doesn't have a degree but who has a strong work ethic and a results-oriented attitude. Diamond bullets call attention to the person's qualifications.

MARIA M. LEAL

(555) 555-5555 (H)   555 Quad Street, Prairie Stream, Texas 55555   **(555) 555-0000 (C)**
mariamleal@mindspring.net

April 29, 2012

Mr. Francis Rolly
Assistant Superintendent for Personnel Services
Prairie Stream Independent School District
5555 Main Street
Prairie Stream, Texas 55555

Re: GENERIC ADMINISTRATOR APPLICATIONS   *All our children deserve teachers who believe their students can learn and who will not be satisfied until they do.* —Joe Nathan

Dear Mr. Rolly:

Please accept this letter of application and resume as representation of sincere interest in an **administrator position** within the Prairie Stream Independent School District. Not only have I been a PSISD Title I educator for the past 13 years, but I am proud to be a product of PSISD, wherein I was raised. Additionally, a **master of education in educational leadership, with a mid-management/principal certification, and a master of education in elementary education, with a specialty in math,** add to my qualifications for this esteemed position. However, though I offer an impressive educational background, nothing can replace the hands-on teaching and administrative experiences afforded me by tenure at Heartgood Elementary. My record at Heartgood of **strong interpersonal, communication, and problem-solving skills** speaks for itself.

Over the years, I have contributed to the implementation of several money-saving and learning-centered enhancements. I have

- Consistently returned from training seminars to **empower the staff** and teachers with newly gained knowledge, an endeavor for staff development that has saved substantial funding.
- Initiated inventory awareness, **cutting costs** on ordering manipulatives and supplies that could be acquired or shared by teachers from existing inventory.
- Helped **transition** first-graders to second-grade spiral math curricula by restructuring their program to coincide with Sharon Wells' math curriculum.
- **Increased TAAS/TAKS scores** through tutor programs. I am highly involved in implementing other excellence programs and directing academic team competitions.

The following communication and interpersonal practices also reinforce credibility for an administrator position. I

- Regard **personal contact** as the first and optimum vehicle for relating needs and information.
- Use **assertive communication,** calm demeanor, active listening, compromise, and negotiation to create win-win situations.
- **Overcome resistance** by communicating both perspectives of an issue, as well as the cause, need, and expected outcome. Then offer positive choices.
- **Acknowledge everyone**—teachers, staff, students, parents, and visitors—for overall success in education.
- **Know every student by name,** especially the challenging ones, and interact with them at every opportunity. Relate to each of them in the manner that works with that particular child.
- **Support teachers** in every way feasible: with resources, encouragement, help, positive feedback, and coaching/mentoring. Instill pride with positive comments.
- **Make parents partners** in their children's educations. Draw on their strengths and treat them with respect. Invite them to participate wherever possible.
- Set **high expectations** to increase performance.

You will find me an exceptional candidate for an **instructional specialist or principal position.** Outstanding references are at your disposal upon request. Since the opportunity to further discuss your needs and my qualifications will be mutually beneficial, I look forward to an upcoming **personal interview.** In the meantime, thank you for your consideration.

Sincerely,

Maria M. Leal

Enclosure: Resume

13

Edith A. Rische, Lubbock, Texas

This letter has only four paragraphs, but a developed first paragraph and many substantial bulleted items after the second and third paragraphs fill a page—even with small print.

GEORGE POWELL

SENIOR EXECUTIVE ● STRATEGY ● MARKETING ● LEADERSHIP

2859 Albany Avenue, Littletown, PA 22222
Home: 444-444-4444 ● Cell: 555-555-5555
E-mail: GeorgePow@yahoo.com
Website: www.GPowell.info

October 31, 2012

«First_Name» «Last_Name»
«Title»
«Company»
«Postal_Address»

To become healthy, consumer electronics companies will need to find new sources of revenue while developing sustainable areas of differentiation that are in tune with customer needs and wants.

Dear «Courtesy_Title» «Last_Name»:

These are tough times in the consumer electronics industry.

As a seasoned senior-level marketing professional with a Fortune 100 background, start-up experience, and cross-industry expertise, I can help. Coupled with experience in communications and IT, my background provides a thorough foundation to position «Company» for the coming convergence of PCs and consumer electronics.

With a profound understanding of computing and Internet trends, as well as the wants, needs, and buying behaviors of potential customers, I can anticipate and evaluate the issues associated with this new market direction. By taking a holistic approach to planning, I can leverage the strengths of your organization through targeted strategic and marketing efforts. I know how to drive vigorous strategy development and implementation, construct solid organizational and product line plans, optimize the use of funds, and, most importantly, get it right the first time!

Critical marketing and revenue-generating strengths and contributions include the following:

Identifying opportunities to reposition uncompetitive / limited market products.
To protect a $42 million revenue stream and slow margin erosion, I repositioned a networking product line to meet an emerging need in enterprise networking (Intel). Faced with a slow developing market, I created a pre-market product concept that produced 50% of the firm's revenue in its first 18 months and opened doors with Apple, IBM, and several telcos (GPC).

Constructing powerful positioning, differentiation, and value propositions.
As a consultant, I developed a market identification methodology that became a key differentiator, driving sales of lucrative planning exercises (PAL Associates and Graves).

Understanding channels of distribution and the use of hybrid channels.
During my career I received hands-on education about resellers and their targets (Intel)...worked with communications resellers and top PC distributors (Teleos and DEBCOM)...established a channels-consulting practice (Graves)...and conducted a global study of networking-product distribution channels (IBM).

Using in-depth experience in the marketing / planning process for successful product launch.
Working as a consultant, I have assisted several Fortune 100 firms—including IBM, Telcordia, Lucent, and HP—with strategic and go-to-market planning. As a senior manager, I have been directly involved in product launches, including servers at Intel, the award-winning LAWN at DEBCOM, and ISDN products.

«First_Name», having enjoyed the experience of operating a successful consulting firm for six years, I find I miss the challenges associated with developing markets. That is why I am contacting you—to discuss bringing my strategic and revenue-generating expertise to «Company». Let's schedule an informal exploratory meeting to review your needs and my ideas. I will call you next week and look forward to speaking with you soon.

Sincerely,

George Powell

Enclosure

14

Deb Dib, Medford, New York

Another way to develop a letter so that it fills a page is to add a paragraph for each item in a series of items introduced by a colon. In this letter, the colon is after the third paragraph.

555 Reynolds Road
Berlin, Maryland 21811

410-555-8080
czenith@hotmail.com

CHARLENE ZENITH
PHARMACEUTICAL SALES REP

To: Schering Plough, Pharmaceutical Division
Re: Online Posting #2651

In response to your search for a **quality pharmaceutical sales professional,** I bring more than 8 years of experience in sales. I am a quick learner with a strong track record of recognizable increases of sales in my product. People describe me as an extremely high-energy and innovative salesperson who leads by example. I consistently produce strong results with a high degree of integrity, dedication and organized communication skills.

Many of my achievements are due to my ability to create and maintain rapport with clients. This quality, coupled with a drive to think strategically and capitalize on opportunities, has given me an extremely high client retention rate. My work managing the egos and needs of corporate clients and celebrities will transfer well to a pharmaceutical sales environment. I thrive on setting aggressive goals and then meeting them.

I meet and exceed all the qualifications detailed in your online job posting:

Your Needs	My Qualifications
B.A. degree or equivalent.	◆ B.A. in Communication Studies with a Concentration in Public Relations from Virginia Polytechnic Institute.
Previous outside business-to-business sales experience.	◆ More than 3 years of experience as Marriott Event & Sales Manager, selling to top corporate clients.
Demonstrated sales and communication abilities.	◆ Results include 90–95% retention of clients, $1.3 million direct contribution to profit, and highest area market share. ◆ Developed all promotional materials, collateral and sales kits for the property.
Excellent interpersonal, organizational and time-management skills.	◆ Outgoing, dynamic personality. ◆ Have run hundreds of events and tournaments that require outstanding time-management and service skills. ◆ History of thriving on networking, prospecting and working odd hours to meet diverse client needs.
Computer office suite literacy at an intermediate level.	◆ Sourced and installed network for entire office, plus developed database systems to facilitate administrative work and increase available selling and service time.
Valid driver's license and safe driving record.	◆ Licensed in the state of Virginia; safe record.

My resume provides further details of my accomplishments. If you will add me to the interview roster for this open position, I'll be ready...anytime or anywhere!

Thank you,

Charlene Zenith

15

Gail Frank, Tampa, Florida

Still another way to expand a letter is to create a "Your Needs...My Qualifications" two-column table. This one is keyed to the items in an online job posting.

AMY VESTAL

Target:

Events Planning

Ideas are the root of creation.

—Ernest Dimnet

5555 55th Street
Flower, Texas 79400

avestal@aol.com

(555) 555-1234

May 12, 2012

Rita Coleman
Vice President of Marketing
CAPITAL IDEAS AND EVENTS
5555 Main Street
Crestview, Texas 79000

RE: Events Planner / Marketing Position

Dear Ms. Coleman:

Generating creative ideas spanning from decorating to effective problem solving energizes me! Other talents include **planning and coordinating the logistics of complex projects or exciting events, revitalizing a failing business, and increasing profits through innovative marketing strategies.** Additionally, a **bachelor's degree** adds credibility to my candidacy for the above-named position.

Upon reviewing the enclosed resume, you will discover a background rich in **sound leadership, skillful negotiation, effective networking, and active public relations experience,** all of which have enhanced the promotion of several personal businesses. As an entrepreneur, I have an understanding of the factors needed to run a winning business—insight that can enhance relationships with the business community.

The following character traits would reward any employer:

Personal Trait	Company Benefit
Ownership of responsibility—	*Sound leadership.*
Perceptiveness and understanding—	*Effective interaction with team.*
Attentive listening—	*Accurate response to customer needs.*
Loyalty, honesty, and diligence—	*Company distinction.*
Competitiveness and optimism—	*Increased profits.*
Self-motivation and resourcefulness—	*Stimulated productivity.*
Passion—	*Dedicated service.*
Energetic action—	*Met deadlines.*

A personal interview at your convenience would be mutually advantageous. I will contact your office within the week to set up a meeting. In the meantime, **thank you for your valued time and consideration.**

Sincerely,

Amy Vestal

Enclosure: Resume

16

Edith A. Rische, Lubbock, Texas

In this two-column cover letter, the left column is shaded slightly to define the column visually. Content within the column is centered and spread down the column for a balanced look.

BRIAN LANGE

2400 Daphne Way
Walnut Creek, CA 94000

925-555-0000
BrianLange@pacbell.net

April 12, 2012

Mr. Henry Newton
Vice President, Administration & Operations
Alliance Technical, Inc.
111 Pontiac Drive
Santa Cruz, CA 95060

Reference: Employment Opportunity—Director of Customer Service & Support

Dear Mr. Newton:

Could you use a senior manager with a track record of building and managing teams that ensure strong customer satisfaction by providing high-quality solutions to customer issues? If so, I believe you will find the enclosed resume worth a close look.

Throughout the past several years, I have enjoyed leading my own teams and working with cross-functional groups to analyze and resolve a variety of customer concerns. In addition to establishing and mentoring customer-focused teams, I also gain great satisfaction from improving the way things are done and the results that are achieved, either by streamlining existing methods or by creating and implementing new processes and procedures. Continuous improvement is more than a buzzword to me!

At both Prentiss and Acquire, I spearheaded development of the entire infrastructure, policies and procedures, while simultaneously carrying out all the standard management responsibilities—including staff recruitment, hiring and training. I also participated in major budget development, planning and management activities. At Acquire, the initiatives I led enabled the company to turn around relationships with several key customers, which prevented loss of that business.

My combination of management and technical strengths has repeatedly proven valuable to employers. I utilize it to plan and manage complex technical projects while also accomplishing management objectives related to those projects. For example, I drove the establishment of an international Critical Customer Escalation department that substantially reduced escalation time and, as a result, greatly improved the customer support experience.

In the current challenging business environment, I believe my strong experience can benefit employers who need to produce exceptional results. Specifically, I am confident I can add substantial value to Alliance Technical as the Director of Customer Service and Support, and I would like to arrange a personal interview to discuss your needs. I will call you within the next few days to follow up and, if appropriate, schedule an interview. I look forward to speaking with you.

Sincerely,

Brian Lange

Encl.

17

Georgia Adamson, Campbell, California

This applicant wanted to move up in customer-relations management in either a technical or nontechnical company. The letter refers to both management and technical strengths.

CHAD BERRY

2614 Belleshire Drive	chadberry@aol.com	Residence: (317) 555-3009
Indianapolis, IN 46201		Office: (317) 555-7794

Michael Moore, Director
Department of Public Safety
50 W. First Street, 2nd Floor
Indianapolis, Indiana 46201

February 7, 2012

Dear Director Moore:

Submitting a letter explaining my "vision of a safe and secure Indianapolis" would be hollow rhetoric if it were not supported by 25 years of accomplishments and leadership. Whether leading a crew into a blazing four-story building or leading our community of firefighters into a dangerous future where new enemies are behind local catastrophes, I believe three questions are fundamental to the leadership of our next Chief of the Indianapolis Division of Fire:

Will this Fire Chief know where he is going?
I have lived in Indianapolis throughout my entire life. My loyalty to Indianapolis is unsurpassed in comparison to others who may be less familiar with our city's governmental system and various communities. As I have steadily progressed through the leadership ranks within the Department, I have maintained a focused view on the wider administrative, political, and public relations concerns that must be proactively addressed. From **Captain** to **Battalion Chief** and from **Deputy Chief** to **Assistant Chief,** I have always been motivated by a clear picture in which community safety and security are prioritized and realized. As Fire Chief, I want to go where Indianapolis has long wanted to go.

Will this Fire Chief know how to get there?
As you know, a candidate's past performance is the best indicator of future results. At all levels of my experience with the Indianapolis Division of Fire, I have enjoyed a thread of achievements that reflects my qualifications in creating and executing effective citywide safety/security strategies while serving as Assistant Fire Chief. Do I know "how to get there"? If you review my résumé, my achievements speak for themselves. I am only the second African-American to attain the rank of Assistant Chief in the history of the Indianapolis Division of Fire. I received a commendation from the Indiana Senate for exemplary services to the Division of Fire, and I have been honored with the Achievement of Excellence Award from the Indianapolis African-American Firefighters' Association.

Will this Fire Chief inspire others to follow?
Throughout my career, my greatest resource has never been my qualifications or the rank I held over my subordinates. It is my ability to inspire others from a passion for my neighbors' well-being. There is a stark contrast between delegated authority and personal responsibility. With delegated authority, subordinates follow a leader because the superior holds a higher rank. With personal responsibility, individuals willingly follow their leader, inspired by his unyielding commitment to shared ideals, his professional success, and his personal sense of well-being.

A great leader motivates subordinates to grow into better individuals because they serve a purpose greater than themselves. Such a team I have built on numerous occasions, and I look forward to repeating my success on a greater scale as the next Chief of the Indianapolis Division of Fire. I will contact you next week to set up a time for an interview.

Sincerely,

Chad Berry

Jason Worthington, Columbus, Ohio

This applicant, wanting to be the new fire chief, considers three questions of importance. They provide a novel structure for the letter, capturing and holding the reader's attention.

BILL STEADMAN, CPP

CORPORATE EXECUTIVE ● CHIEF SECURITY OFFICER

"Security is always too much...until it's not enough."
— Daniel Webster

«Date»

«First_Name» «Last_Name»
«Title»
«Company»
«Postal_Address»

Dear «Courtesy_Title» «Last_Name»:

Within minutes, the disastrous events of September 11, 2001, transformed our conceptualization of corporate security—changed its significance, scope, and strategy—from an optional "diligence" to an absolute requirement. Undoubtedly, the 15,000+ companies that were directly affected that day have since created, expanded, and / or upgraded corporate security.

In these perilous times, today's socially and financially conscientious enterprise is obligated to take a serious, urgent, and comprehensive approach to protecting infrastructure, property, and people from internal and external threats. Globally, companies are reprioritizing corporate security in their plans and actions, despite the soft economy.

Today's conundrum? Do more with less—again! This is where I come in! Through 20+ years of experience in the planning, deployment, and management of full-scale corporate security programs, I can provide <Name of Company> with the capacity to efficiently and cost-effectively avoid / mitigate risk and loss. In addition, I bring the added value of senior-level executive achievement, advanced academics, and an understanding of technology.

The following are highlights of my successes:

- Served as Head of Security for all of Your Cable's corporate entities and assets and managed related strategies, projects, and inventories for corporate headquarters and two operating divisions. Controlled $7 million capital and expense budget.

- Assisted SVP of Security (solid line to CEO) with enterprise-wide budget and team oversight ($24+ million / 800+ employees).

- Contributed to $1+ million in annual cost savings related to corporate security.

- Formed and managed an internal organization—Intelligence Services Group—as a solution to employee and vendor security issues.

- Planned and managed technology-based security—personnel, proprietary, and intellectual property protection—systems projects representing investments, some in excess of $1 million.

- Contributed to post-9/11 strategic plans and actions for high-profile venues and events (e.g., West Side Arena, Lyman Recital House, and Senior GMA Tournament). Consulted on Metropolis Plaza security issues after the '93 bombing.

<Name of Contact>, if you see value in the breadth of my experience, scope of my knowledge, and caliber of my management qualifications, please get in touch so we can set up a meeting. I look forward to discussing your needs and my solutions. I can guarantee you a substantial ROI.

Sincerely,

Bill Steadman

Enclosure

vulnerability assessment ● access security ● event security ● workplace / employee security
executive protection ● electronic surveillance / countermeasures ● competitive intelligence / countermeasures
emergency preparedness ● crisis response ● intellectual / proprietary property protection

25 Bristol Road, Smallville, New Jersey 33333 ● Home: 444-444-4444 ● Cell: 777-777-7777 ● E-mail: bstead@verizon.net

19

Deb Dib, Medford, New York

The writer put bulleted successes, keywords, and contact information in a footer (a designated area) at the bottom of the page in order to sell the need for security at the top with the Webster quotation.

Edward Field
16 Land Street
Streator, IL 55104
Cell: 312.555.0514

edfield@hope.com

(Customize/personalize name and address here, or write:)

Dear Hiring Executive:

I believe that you will find my experience as Director of Finance very intriguing. I specialize in financial analysis, budgeting, planning, acquisitions and mergers. In addition, my background includes detailed product pricing analysis to ensure success in highly competitive markets.

Currently, I am Director of Finance and Business Development at Hi-Technologies, a software development company. My duties include establishing pricing strategies and authoring business plans, which have raised $5 million in capital over the last year.

At my previous position, I was Director of Finance for Automart, Inc., a startup procurement automation firm. I negotiated the sale of the company for $20.5 million and performed all due diligence and contract review.

Prior to that position, I was the Financial Manager at a $250 million healthcare services company. I reported directly to the President and directed the corporate strategic planning process, leading the annual budget process for four business units with revenues of $150 million.

With my strong financial expertise and operational experience, including advising the decision makers, I strongly believe that my skills in the following areas can bring you continued success:

→   Financial planning and analysis
→   Budgeting and planning
→   A strong knowledge of acquisitions and mergers

I would like to discuss mutual business interests and will contact you in a few days to set a convenient time for us to meet. Thank you for your time and consideration.

Sincerely,

Edward Field

20

Steven Provenzano, Streamwood, Illinois

Because the six paragraphs are short, the tempo in reading them is quick. This means that the reader is more likely to read the entire letter. Bullets point to skill areas.

List of Contributors

The following professional resume writers contributed the resumes and cover letters in this book. I have included contact information about these writers to make it easy for you to contact them if you want a particular writer to develop your own resume and cover letter. Resume and cover letter numbers after a writer's contact information are the numbers of the writer's resumes and cover letters included in the Gallery, not page numbers.

Australia

New South Wales

Sydney

Jennifer Rushton
Keraijen
Level 14, 309 Kent St.
Sydney, NSW 2000, Australia
Phone: +61 2 9994 8050
E-mail: info@keraijen.com.au
Website: www.keraijen.com.au
Member: CDI, CMA, AORCP
Certifications: CERW, CARW, CEIC, CWPP
Resume: 63
Cover letter: 3

Victoria

Hallum

Annemarie Cross
Advanced Employment Concepts
PO Box 91
Hallam, Victoria 3803, Australia
Phone: +61 3 9708 6930
Fax: +61 3 9796 4479
E-mail: success@aresumewriter.net
Website: www.aresumewriter.net
Member: CMI, PARW/CC, CDI
Certifications: CEIP, CARW, CPRW, CRW,
  CCM, CECC, CERW, CWPP
Resume: 101

Southbank

Gayle M. Howard
Top Margin
8 Kavanagh St., Suite 1402
Southbank, Victoria 3006, Australia
Phone: +61 3 9020 5601
Toll-free: 1300 726 669
E-mail: getinterviews@topmargin.com
Website: www.topmargin.com
Member: CDI, CMA, AORCP
Certifications: MRW, CERW, CRPBS, JLRC,
  CARW, MCD, CCM, MRWLAA, MCPLAA,
  CRS-IT, CWPP
Resume: 83

Canada

British Colombia

Vancouver

Tim Cunningham
Fast & Focused Resume Service
401–1330 Hornby St.
Vancouver, BC V6Z 1W5, Canada
Phone: (604) 418-7094
Toll-free: (800) 514-6208
Fax: (604) 681-4182
E-mail: tim@ffresume.com
Website: www.ffresume.com
Member: PARW/CC
Certification: CPRW
Resume: 154

Ontario

Whitby

Ross Macpherson, MA
Career Quest
131 Kirby Crescent
Whitby, Ontario L1N 7C7, Canada
Phone: (905) 438-8548
Toll-free: (877) 426-8548
Fax: (905) 438-4096
E-mail: ross@yourcareerquest.com
Website: www.yourcareerquest.com
Member: CMA, PARW/CC
Certifications: CPRW, CEIP, CJST, Personal
  Branding Strategist
Resumes: 43, 103

China

Shanghai

Peter Hill
P.H.I. Consulting
Phone: + 86 137.7448.0436
(For full listing, see Honolulu, Hawaii, United States)

United Kingdom

England

Leeds, West Yorkshire

Sandra Ingemansen
President, Résumé Strategies
(See permanent address: Matteson, Illinois, United States)
29 Cromwell Court
10 Bowman Lane
Leeds, West Yorkshire
LS10 1HN, United Kingdom
Phone: (312) 212-3761 (USA)
E-mail: sandra@resume-strategies.com
Website: www.resume-strategies.com
Member: CDI, NRWA, PARW/CC
Certification: CPRW
Resumes: 3, 59, 64, 99, 155

United States

Alabama

Montgomery

Don Orlando, MBA
The McLean Group
3001 Zelda Road, Suite 400
Montgomery, AL 36106
Phone: (334) 264-2020
E-mail: dorlando@yourexecutivecareercoach.com
Member: CDI, CMA, PARW/CC
Certifications: CPRW, JCTC, CCM, CCMC, CJSS
Resumes: 41, 146, 174

Arizona

Phoenix

Ginger Korljan, MEd
Take Charge Coaching
2202 N 38th St.
Phoenix, AZ 85008
Phone: (602) 577-9306
Fax: (602) 943-1171
E-mail: ginger@takechargecoaching.com
Website: www.takechargecoaching.com

Member: CDI, NRWA
Certifications: NCRW, CCMC
Resumes: 25, 170

California

Aptos

Kathy Kritikos
Best Impression Resumes & CareerPower Workshops
2788 Wimbledon Dr.
Aptos, CA 95003
Toll-free: (800) 428-8065
E-mail: bestimpression05@yahoo.com
Website: www.mybestimpressionresumes.com
Member: NRWA
Certification: CCMC
Resumes: 74, 113

Campbell

Georgia Adamson
A Successful Career
180 W. Rincon Ave.
Campbell, CA 95008-2824
Phone: (408) 866-6859
Fax: (408) 866-8915
E-mail: success@ablueribbonresume.com
Websites: www.ablueribbonresume.com and
    www.asuccessfulcareer.com
Member: CMI, NRWA, PARW
Certifications: CCM, CEIP, CPRW, JCTC, CCMC
Resumes: 55, 133
Cover letter: 17

Irvine

Pearl White
A 1st Impression Resume & Career Coaching Services
41 Tangerine
Irvine, CA 92618
Phone: (949) 651-1068
Fax: (949) 651-9415
E-mail: pearlwhite1@cox.net
Website: www.a1stimpression.com
Member: NRWA, PARW/CC
Certifications: CPRW, JCTC, CEIP
Resume: 131

Los Angeles

Vivian VanLier
Advantage Resume & Career Services
6701 Murietta Ave.
Los Angeles (Valley Glen), CA 91405
Phone: (818) 994-6655
Fax: (818) 994-6620
E-mail: vivianvanlier@aol.com
Website: www.careercoach4u.com
Member: CMA
Certifications: CPRW, JCTC, CEIP, CCMC, CPRC, CPBS
Resume: 15

Orange

Nita Busby
Resumes, Etc.
438 E. Katella, Suite G
Orange, CA 92867
Phone: (714) 633-2783
E-mail: resumes100@aol.com
Website: www.resumesetc.net
Member: PARW/CC
Certifications: CPRW, CAC, JCTC
Resume: 48

San Diego

Kim Mohiuddin
Movin' On Up Resumes
San Diego, CA
Phone: (619) 550-2901
E-mail: info@movinonuresumes.com
Website: www.movinonupresumes.com
Member: CDI, NRWA
Certification: NCRW
Resumes: 18, 76, 88, 179

Valencia

Myriam-Rose Kohn, MA
JEDA Enterprises
27201 Tourney Rd., Suite 201
Valencia, CA 91355-1857
Phone: (661) 253-0801
Toll-free: (800) 600-JEDA
Fax: (661) 253-0744
E-mail: myriam-rose@jedaenterprises.com
Website: www.jedaenterprises.com
Member: CDI, CMA, NRWA, PARW/CC
Certifications: CPRW, CEIP, JCTC, CCM, CCMC, CPBS, CJSS
Resume: 32

Colorado

Aurora

Michele Angello
Corbel Communications
19866 E. Dickenson Pl.
Aurora, CO 80013
Phone: (303) 537-3592
Toll-free: (866) 5CORBEL
E-mail: corbelcomm1@aol.com
Website: www.corbelonline.com
Certification: CPRW
Resume: 144

Denver

Melanie Lenci, MAS
Résumé Relief
Denver, CO
Phone: (720) 379-6878
Mobile phone: (303) 241-6103
Fax: (303) 496-0357

E-mail: ml@resumereliefonline.com
Website: www.resumereliefonline.com
Member: CDI, NRWA, PARW/CC
Certifications: CPRW, CEIP
Resumes: 29, 87, 157

Fort Collins

Ruth Pankratz, MBA
Gabby Communications, LLC
Fort Collins, CO
Phone: (970) 310-4153
E-mail: Ruth@GabbyCommunications.com
Website: www.gabbycommunications.com
Member: NRWA, NCHRA (Northern Colorado Human Resources Association)
Resume: 26

Louisville

Roberta F. Gamza
Career Ink
Louisville, CO 80027
Phone: (303) 955-3065
Fax: (303) 955-3065
E-mail: roberta@careerink.com
Website: www.careerink.com
Member: CMA, NRWA
Certifications: JCTC, CEIP, JST
Resume: 124

Connecticut

Broad Brook

Louise Garver, MA
Career Directions, LLC
Broad Brook, CT
Phone: (860) 623-9476
Fax: (860) 623-9473
E-mail: Louise@careerdirectionsllc.com
Website: www.careerdirectionsllc.com
Member: CDI, CMA, NRWA, PARW/CC
Certifications: CPRW, JCTC, CEIP, CPBS, CJSS, CCMC, MCDP, COIS, Certified Career Coach
Resumes: 9, 19, 38, 71, 86, 112, 121, 138, 141, 156, 159, 163, 165, 180
Cover letter: 2

Durham

Jan Melnik, MA
Absolute Advantage
PO Box 718
440 Higganum Rd.
Durham, CT 06422
Phone: (860) 349-0256
Fax: (860) 349-1343
E-mail: CompSPJan@aol.com
Website: www.janmelnik.com
Member: CMA, NRWA, PARW/CC
Certifications: MRW, CCM, CPRW
Resume: 61

Easton

Cathy Alfandre
Catherine A. Alfandre, LLC
PO Box 453
Easton, CT 06612
Phone: (203) 445-7906
E-mail: calfandre@earthlink.net
Website: www.cathyalfandre.com
Member: CMA
Certification: MRW
Resumes: 100, 153

Florida

Bonita Springs

Edward Turilli, MA
AccuWriter Resume Service
Phone: (239) 298-9514 (FL)
Phone: (401) 268-3020 (RI)
E-mail: accuwriter@comcast.net
Website: www.resumes4-u.com
Member: PARW/CC, CRW.com
Certifications: CPRW, CRW
Resume: 84

Clearwater

Edward McGoldrick
Resume Professors
2775 Hyde Park Place
Clearwater, FL 33761
Phone: (727) 692-9010
Toll-free: (866) 990-8821
Toll-free fax: (866) 990-8821
E-mail: emcgoldrick@resumeprofessors.com
Website: www.resumeprofessors.com
Member: PARW/CC
Certification: CPRW
Resume: 2

Jacksonville

Alice Pendleton
Your Résumé Strategy
Jacksonville, FL 32259
Phone: (904) 891-2040
Fax: (904) 230-4247
E-mail: alice@yourresumestrategy.com
Website: www.yourresumestrategy.com
Member: PARW/CC
Certification: CPRW
Resume: 75

Tampa

Cathy Fahrman
Resumes by Professionals
10220 Woodford Bridge St.
Tampa, FL 33626
Phone: (813) 282-0105
Fax: (813) 926-0170

E-mail: cathy@resumesbyprofessionals.com
Website: www.resumesbyprofessionals.com
Member: CMA, PARW/CC
Certification: CPRW
Resume: 85

Gail Frank, MA
Frankly Speaking: Resumes That Work!
10409 Greendale Dr.
Tampa, FL 33626
Phone: (813) 926-1353
Fax: (813) 926-1092
E-mail: gfrank01@tampabay.rr.com
Website: www.callfranklyspeaking.com
Member: CMA, NRWA
Certifications: NCRW, CPRW, JCTC, CEIP
Resume: 46
Cover letters: 5, 12, 15

Carol Heider
Resumes by Professionals
10220 Woodford Bridge St.
Tampa, FL 33626
Phone: (813) 282-0105
Fax: (813) 926-0170
E-mail: carol@resumesbyprofessionals.com
Website: www.resumesbyprofessionals.com
Member: CMA, PARW/CC
Certification: CPRW
Resume: 176

Valrico

Cindy Kraft
Executive Essentials
2209 Whitney Place
Valrico, FL 33595
Phone: (813) 655-0658
Fax: (813) 354-3483
E-mail: Cindy@CFO-Coach.com
Website: www.cfo-coach.com
Member: CMA, CDI
Certifications: CPBS, COIS, CCM, CCMC, CPRW, JCTC
Resume: 56

Hawaii

Honolulu

Peter Hill
Distinctive Resumes
Honolulu, HI
(Also Shanghai, China)
Phone: (808) 384-9461
Phone: +86 137.7448.0436 (Shanghai, China)
E-mail: pjhill@phi-yourcareer.com
Website: www.phi-yourcareer.com
Member: CDI, PARW/CC, Five O'Clock Club Guild of
  Career Coaches

Certifications: CPRW, CERW, Certified Five O'Clock
  Club Career Coach
Resumes: 45, 149

Idaho

Boise

Diane Hudson Burns
Career Marketing Techniques
3079 N. Columbine Ave.
Boise, ID 83713
Phone: (208) 323-9636
E-mail: diane@polishedresumes.com
Website: www.polishedresumes.com
Member: CMA, PARW/CC
Certifications: CPRW, CPCC, JCTC, CEIP, FJSTC, CCM,
  CLTMC, CCMC
Resume: 102

Illinois

Chicago

Murray A. Mann
Global Diversity Solutions Group, LLC
5651 N. Mozart St., Suite B
Chicago, IL 60659
Phone: (312) 404-3108
Toll-free: (877) 825-6566
E-mail: murray@globaldiversitysolutions.com
Website: www.globaldiversitysolutions.com
Member: CDI, CMA, NRWA
Certifications: CCM, CPBS, COIS
Resume: 147

Edwardsville

Michelle P. Swanson
Resume Results
218 Hickory St.
Edwardsville, IL 62025
Phone: (618) 307-5589
Fax: (618) 307-5599
E-mail: michelle@ResumeResultsOnline.com
Website: www.resumeresultsonline.com
Member: NRWA, PARW/CC
Certification: CPRW
Resumes: 30, 114, 122, 167

Lincolnshire

Christine L. Dennison
Dennison Career Services
16 Cambridge Lane
Lincolnshire, IL 60069
Phone: (847) 405-9775
E-mail: chris@thejobsearchcoach.com
Website: www.thejobsearchcoach.com
Member: PARW/CC, Greater Lincolnshire Chamber of
  Commerce
Certification: CPC
Resume: 161

Matteson

Sandra Ingemansen
President, Résumé Strategies
(See temporary address: United Kingdom; England;
Leeds, West Yorkshire)
PO Box 43
Matteson, IL 60443
Phone: (312) 212-3761
E-mail: sandra@resume-strategies.com
Website: www.resume-strategies.com
Member: CDI, NRWA, PARW/CC
Certification: CPRW
Resumes: 3, 59, 64, 99, 155

Naperville

Patricia Chapman
CareerPro-Naperville, Inc.
520 E. Ogden Ave., Ste. 3
Naperville, IL 60563
Phone: (630) 983-8882
Fax: (630) 983-9021
E-mail: pat@career2day.com
Website: www.career2day.com
Member: CMI, CDI, NAFE
Certification: CRW
Resume: 150

Streamwood

Steven Provenzano
President, ECS: Executive Career Services & DTP, Inc.
Streamwood, IL 60107
Phone: (630) 289-6222
E-mail: Careers@Execareers.com
Website: www.Execareers.com
Member: PARW/CC, BBB
Certifications: CPRW, CEIP
Cover letter: 20

Indiana

Decatur

Tammy Shoup
Breakthrough Résumés
Decatur, IN 46733
Phone: (260) 223-1821
E-mail: awordpro@aol.com
Website: www.breakthroughresumes.com
Member: CDI, PARW/CC
Certification: CPRW
Resume: 152

Iowa

Urbandale

Billie Sucher, MS
Billie Sucher Career Transition Services
7177 Hickman Rd., Suite 10
Urbandale, IA 50322

Phone: (515) 276-0061
E-mail: billie@billiesucher.com
Website: www.billiesucher.com
Member: CDI, CMA, SHRM
Certifications: CCM, CTMS, CTSB, IJCTC
Resume: 151

Maryland

Bethesda

Laura M. Labovich, MLRHR
Aspire! Empower! Career Strategy Group
8910 Seneca Lane
Bethesda, MD 20817
Phone: (703) 942-9390
E-mail: lauramichelle@gmail.com
Website: www.aspire-empower.com
Member: CDI, CMA
Certifications: Guild Certified Five O'Clock Club Career
  Coach, CARW, CCM, JCTC
Resume: 136

Massachusetts

Concord

Jean Cummings, MAT
A Resume For Today
Concord, MA
Phone: (978) 254-5492
E-mail: jc@YesResumes.com
Website: www.aresumefortoday.com
Member: CDI, NRWA, PARW/CC
Certifications: CPRW, CPBS, CEIP
Resume: 177

Franklin

Rosemarie Ginsberg
Career Planning Solutions
Franklin, MA 02038
Toll-free: (888) 271-2999
Member: CMA
Certifications: CPRW, CEIP, CFRW, CWPP, CECC;
Certificate of Subject Mastery in Comprehensive
  Proofreading
Resume: 34

Needham

Wendy Gelberg, MEd, CAS
Gentle Job Search/Advantage Resumes
21 Hawthorn Ave.
Needham, MA 02492
Phone: (781) 444-0778
Fax: (781) 455-0778
E-mail: wendy@gentlejobsearch.com
Website: www.gentlejobsearch.com
Member: CMI, NRWA, PARW/CC
Certifications: JCTC, CEIP
Resumes: 92, 173

Tyngsboro

Jeanne Knight
Jeanne Knight, Career and Job Search Coach
PO Box 286
Tyngsboro, MA 01879
Phone: (617) 968-7747
E-mail: jeanne@careerdesigns.biz
Website: www.careerdesigns.biz
Member: CDI, CMA, NRWA
Certifications: JCTC, CCMC
Resume: 53

Worcester

Joellyn Wittenstein Schwerdlin
The Career Success Coach
Phone: (508) 459-2854
Fax: (508) 459-2856
E-mail: joellyn@career-success-coach.com
Website: www.career-success-coach.com
Member: CDI
Certifications: CPRW, CCMC, JCTC
Resume: 51

Michigan

Ann Arbor

Vicki Brett-Gach, BFA, MA
BEST RESUME, LLC
2132 Stephen Terrace
Ann Arbor, MI 48103
Phone: (734) 327-0400
Fax: (734) 913-0633
E-mail: bestresume12345@aol.com
Website: www.bestresume12345.com
Member: PARW/CC
Certification: CPRW
Resumes: 110, 134

Flint

Janet L. Beckstrom
Word Crafter
1717 Montclair Ave.
Flint, MI 48503
Phone: (810) 232-9257
Toll-free: (800) 351-9818
Fax: (810) 232-9257
Toll-free fax: (800) 351-9818
E-mail: janet@wordcrafter.com
Website: www.wordcrafter.com
Member: CMA, PARW/CC
Certifications: ACRW, CPRW
Resume: 35
Cover letter: 9

Trenton

Maria E. Hebda
Career Solutions, LLC
Trenton, MI 48183
Phone: (734) 676-9170

E-mail: maria@writingresumes.com
Websites: www.WritingResumes.com
www.certifiedresumewriters.com (Resource Guide)
Member: CDI, NRWA, PARW/CC, ICF
Certifications: CPRW, CCMC
Resumes: 119, 175
Cover letter: 8

Minnesota

Sartell

Connie Hauer
CareerPro Services
PO Box 76
Sartell, MN 56377
Phone: (320) 260-6569
Fax: (320) 253-5245
Website: www.mncareerpro.com
Member: PARW/CC
Certification: CEIP
Resume: 89

Missouri

Kirksville

Lesa E. Kerlin, MPA
LEK Consultants
1703 Meadow View Drive
Kirksville, MO 63501
Phone: (660) 626-4748
E-mail: lesa@lekconsultants.com
Website: www.lekconsultants.com
Certification: CPRW
Resume: 95

St. Louis

Sally McIntosh
Advantage Resumes in St. Louis
11921 H Villa Dorado Dr.
St. Louis, MO 63146
Phone: (314) 993-5400
Toll-free: (888) 919-9909
Toll-free fax: (866) 728-9323
E-mail: sally@reswriter.com
Website: www.reswriter.com
Member: CDI, NRWA
Certifications: NCRW, JCTC
Resume: 58

Sari Neudorf
SDN Consulting
428 Hickory Glen
St. Louis, MO 63141
Phone: (314) 283-6976
E-mail: Sari@sdnconsulting.biz
Member: CDI, NRWA, PARW/CC
Certifications: CPRW, CPBA, CEIC
Resume: 182

Ellie Vargo
Noteworthy Resume & Career Services, LLC
2190 S. Mason Rd., Suite 303
St. Louis, MO 63131
Phone: (314) 965-9362
Toll-free: (866) 965-9362
Fax: (314) 965-6222
E-mail: ev@noteworthyresume.com
Website: www.noteworthyresume.com
Member: CDI, CMA, PARW/CC
Certifications: MRW, CPRW, CCMC, CFRWC, CEQS
Resumes: 77, 94, 108, 109, 158, 168

Nebraska

Lincoln

Angela Jones
Haute Resume & Career Services, LLC
3201 S. 33rd St., Suite G
Lincoln, NE
Phone: (402) 484-6819
Toll-free: (866) 695-9318
Toll-free fax: (866) 596-0153
E-mail: Angie@ANewResume.com
Website: www.anewresume.com
Member: CDI, CMA, NRWA, PARW/CC
Certifications: CPRW, CEIC
Resume: 118

New Hampshire

Merrimack

Mary Ellen Brew, MBA
"Anything is Possible!"
Certified Résumé Writing & Career Coaching
23 Mason Road
Merrimack, NH 03054
Phone: (603) 490-9901
E-mail: coachbrew@live.com
Member: PARW/CC
Certifications: CPRW, CPCC
Resume: 160

New Jersey

Flemington Area

Carol A. Altomare
World Class Résumés
PO Box 483
Three Bridges, NJ 08887-0483
Phone: (908) 237-1883
Fax: (908) 237-1883
E-mail: caa@worldclassresumes.com
Website: www.worldclassresumes.com
Member: CDI, CMA, PARW/CC
Certifications: ACRW, MRW, CPRW, CCMC, CJSS
Resumes: 4, 5, 12, 16, 22, 23, 31, 96, 115, 164

Freehold

See Marlboro.

Iselin

See Marlboro.

Marlboro

Beverly Baskin and Mitchell I. Baskin
BBCS Counseling Services
6 Alberta Dr.
Marlboro, NJ 07746
Also at Iselin, NJ; Princeton, NJ; and Freehold, NJ
Toll-free: (800) 300-4079
Fax: (732) 972-8846
E-mail: bev@bbcscounseling.com
Websites: www.baskincareer.com and
 www.resumewriternj.com
Member: NRWA, NCDA, NECA, MACCA, AMHCA,
 NJCA
Certifications: EdS, MA, MS, LPC, MCC, CPRW,
 CCHMC, NCCC, PE
Resumes: 8, 28, 50, 52, 91, 125, 171
Cover letters: 10, 11

Morganville

Michelle A. Riklan
Riklan Resources, LLC
Street 200 Campus Drive, Suite 2D
Morganville, NJ 07751
Phone: (732) 761-9940
Toll-free: (800) 540-3609
E-mail: Michelle@riklanresources.com
Website: www.riklanresources.com
Member: CDI, CMA, NRWA, PARW/CC, CTL
Certifications: CPRW, CEIC
Resumes: 65, 97

Piscataway

Colleen Georges, EdD
Colleen's Career Creations
614 Putnam Ave.
Piscataway, NJ 08854
Phone: (732) 910-5714
Fax: (732) 903-1064
E-mail: dr.colleen@gmail.com
Website: www.colleenscareercreations.com
Member: CDI, PARW/CC
Certifications: CPRW, CPCC, CCC, CPLC, CNLP, LPC
Resumes: 66, 111

Princeton

See Marlboro.

Waldwick

Fran Kelley, MA
The Résumé Works
PO Box 262
Waldwick, NJ 07463
Phone: (201) 670-9643

E-mail: FranKelley@optimum.net
Website: www.careermuse.com
Member: CMA, NRWA, PARW/CC, SHRM
Certifications: CPRW, SPHR, JCTC
Resume: 178
Cover Letter: 7

Woodland Park

Melanie Noonan
Peripheral Pro, LLC
560 Lackawanna Ave.
Woodland Park, NJ 07424
Phone: (973) 785-3011
Fax: (973) 256-6285
E-mail: PeriPro1@aol.com
Member: NRWA, PARW/CC
Resumes: 81, 142

New Mexico

Rio Rancho

Patrick Moore
Résumé Specialties
Rio Rancho, NM
E-mail: resumespecialties@gmail.com
Certification: ACRW
Resume: 117

New York

East Islip

Ann Baehr
Best Resumes of New York
East Islip, NY 11730
Phone: (631) 224-9300
E-mail: resumesbest@earthlink.net
Website: www.e-bestresumes.com
Member: CDI, CMA, NRWA
Certification: CPRW
Resumes: 1, 33, 69, 70, 126, 127, 137

Hauppauge

Donna M. Farrise
Dynamic Resumes of Long Island, Inc.
150 Motor Pkwy., Ste. 401
Hauppauge, NY 11788
Phone: (631) 951-4120
Fax: (631) 952-1817
E-mail: donna@dynamicresumes.com
Website: www.dynamicresumes.com
Member: CMA
Certification: JCTC
Resume: 72

Huntington

M J Feld, MS
CAREERS by CHOICE, Inc.
205 East Main St., Suite 2–4

Huntington, NY 11743
Phone: (631) 673-5432
Fax: (631) 673-5824
E-mail: mj@careersbychoice.com
Website: www.careersbychoice.com
Member: NRWA, PARW/CC
Certification: CPRW
Resumes: 80, 82, 93

Long Island

Linda Matias
CareerStrides
Long Island, NY 11717
Phone: (631) 456-5051
E-mail: linda@careerstrides.com
Website: www.careerstrides.com
Member: NRWA
Certifications: NCRW, CIC, JCTC
Resume: 54

Massapequa Park

Karen Bartell
Best-in-Class Résumés
4940 Merrick Rd., Suite 160
Massapequa Park, NY
Phone: (631) 704-3220
Toll-free: (800) 234-3569
Fax: (516) 799-6300
E-mail: support@bestclassresumes.com
Website: www.bestclassresumes.com
Member: CDI, CMA, PARW/CC
Certification: CPRW
Resumes: 11, 120, 166

Medford

Deb Dib
Executive Power Brand
Medford, NY
Phone: (631) 475-8513
E-mail: DebDib@ExecutivePowerBrand.com
Website: www.executivepowerbrand.com
Member: CDI, CMA, NRWA
Certifications: CG3C, CPBS, CCMC, NCRW, CPRW,
  CEIP, JCTC, COIS
Resumes: 90, 106
Cover letters: 14, 19

New York

Kimberly Schneiderman
City Career Services
New York, NY 10034
Phone: (917) 584-3022
Fax: (214) 580-5328
E-mail: kimberly@citycareerservices.com
Website: www.citycareerservices.com
Member: CDI, NRWA
Certifications: NCRW, CLTMC, CEIC
Resumes: 21, 116, 135, 169

Poughkeepsie

Kristin M. Coleman
Coleman Career Services
Poughkeepsie, NY 12603
Phone: (845) 452-8274
E-mail: kristin@colemancareerservices.com
Member: CMA
Resume: 39

North Carolina

Asheville

Dayna Feist
Gatehouse Business Services
265 Charlotte St.
Asheville, NC 28801
Phone: (828) 254-7893
Fax: (828) 254-7893
E-mail: Gatehous@aol.com
Website: www.bestjobever.com
Member: CDI, CMA, NRWA, PARW/CC
Certifications: CPRW, JCTC, CEIP
Resume: 42

Charlotte

Doug Morrison
Career Power
5200 Park Road, Suite 227
Charlotte, NC 28207
Phone: (704) 527-5556
Toll-free: (800) 711-0773
E-mail: dmpwresume@aol.com
Website: www.CareerPowerResume.com
Member: CDI
Certification: CPRW
Resume: 128

Julian

Laurie Mortenson, MEd
LegWork Résumés and Career Services
4446 Old Julian Road
Julian, NC 27283
Phone: (336) 233-1338
E-mail: connect@legworkresumes.com
Website: www.legworkresumes.com
Member: CDI, NRWA
Certification: CCMC
Resume: 20

Ohio

Athens

Melissa L. Kasler
Resume Impressions
306 W. Union St.
Athens, OH 45701
Phone: (740) 592-3993
Toll-free: (800) 516-0334

Fax: (740) 592-1352
E-mail: resume@frognet.net
Website: www.resumeimpressions.com
Member: PARW/CC
Certification: CPRW
Resumes: 37, 44

Cleveland

Susan Barens
Career Dynamics
Cleveland, OH 44138
Phone: (440) 610-4361
E-mail: susan@yourbestmarketingtool.com
Website: www.yourbestmarketingtool.com
Member: CDI, PARW/CC
Certifications: CPRW, IJCTC
Resumes: 10, 79

Columbus

April Walters
Jewish Family Services
1070 College Avenue
Columbus, OH 43209
Phone: (614) 559-0205
Fax: (614) 231-4978
E-mail: awalters@jfscolumbus.org
Website: www.jfscolumbus.org
Member: CMA, NRWA, PARW/CC
Certifications: CPRW, PHR
Resume: 123

Janice Worthington
Worthington Career Services
6636 Belleshire St.
Columbus, OH 43229-1510
Phone: (614) 890-1645
Toll-free: (877) 9Resume (973-7863)
Fax: (614) 523-3400
E-mail: Janice@WorthingtonCareers.com
Website: www.worthingtoncareers.com
Member: CDI, CMA, NRWA, PARW/CC
Certifications: CPRW, JCTC, CEIP
Resume: 145

Jason Worthington
Worthington Career Services
6636 Belleshire St.
Columbus, OH 43229-1510
Phone: (614) 890-1645
Toll-free: (877) 9Resume (973-7863)
Fax: (614) 523-3400
E-mail: JasonWorth@NetZero.com
Website: www.worthingtoncareers.com
Member: CDI
Certification: CEIP
Cover letter: 18

Jeremy Worthington
Buckeye Resumes
2092 Atterbury
Columbus, OH 43229-1510
Phone: (614) 861-6606
Fax: (614) 737-6166
E-mail: Jeremy@BuckeyeResumes.com
Website: www.buckeyeresumes.com
Member: CDI
Certifications: CARW, CCTC
Resume: 67

Findlay

Sharon Pierce-Williams, MEd
The Resume.Doc
609 Lincolnshire Ln.
Findlay, OH 45840
Phone: (419) 422-0228
Fax: (419) 425-1185
E-mail: Sharon@TheResumeDoc.com
Website: www.theresumedoc.com
Member: Findlay–Hancock County Chamber of
  Commerce
Certification: CPRW
Resumes: 62, 129

Oregon

Tigard

Pat Kendall
Advanced Resume Concepts
14928 SW 109th Avenue
Tigard, OR 97224
Phone: (503) 639-6098
Fax: (503) 213-6022
E-mail: pat@reslady.com
Websites: www.reslady.com and
  www.careerfolios.com
Member: NRWA
Certifications: NCRW, JCTC
Resumes: 105, 139, 143

Pennsylvania

Blue Bell

Christopher J. Bilotta, MBA
Resource Development Company, Inc.
925 Harvest Drive, Suite 190
Blue Bell, PA 19422
Phone: (215) 628-2293
Toll-free: (888) 628-2293
E-mail: chrisb@rdcinc.com
Websites: www.rdcinc.com,
  www.jobmetrx.com, and
  www.christopherbilotta.com
Member: PARW/CC
Certifications: CPRW, CPA
Resume: 60

Reading

Darlene Dassy
Dynamic Résumé Solutions
14 Crestview Drive
Reading, PA 19608
Phone: (610) 678-0147
E-mail: darlene@dynamicresumesolutions.com
Website: www.dynamicresumesolutions.com
Member: CDI
Certifications: CERW CIJSE
Resume: 36

West Middlesex

Jane Roqueplot
JaneCo's Sensible Solutions
3493 Sharon Rd.
West Middlesex, PA 16159
Phone: (724) 528-1000
Toll-free: (888) JANECOS (526-3267)
Fax: (724) 528-1703
E-mail: janeir@janecos.com
Website: www.janecos.com
Member: CDI, NRWA, PARW/CC
Certifications: CPBA, CECC, CWDP
Resumes: 13, 27, 78, 98, 132, 172, 181

Rhode Island

Edward Turilli, MA
Phone: (401) 268-3020
(For full listing, see Bonita Springs, FL)

Tennessee

Smyrna

Teauna Upshaw
Workforce Initiatives
PO Box 1134
Smyrna, TN 37167
Phone: (615) 848-4799
E-mail: Teauna@workforceinitiatives.org
Website: www.workforceinitiatives.org
Member: NRWA
Resume: 24

Texas

Lubbock

Daniel J. Dorotik Jr.
100PercentResumes
5401 68th St.
Lubbock, TX 79424
Phone: (806) 783-9900
Fax: (806) 993-3757
E-mail: dan@100percentresumes.com
Website: www.100percentresumes.com
Member: NRWA
Certification: NCRW
Resumes: 6, 40, 49, 104, 130, 140

Edith A. Rische
(No longer accepting work)
Lubbock, TX
Member: NRWA
Certifications: NCRW, JCTC, ACCC, CPBS
Resumes: 7, 14, 47
Cover letters: 1, 4, 6, 13, 16

Washington

Bellingham

Janice M. Shepherd
Write On Career Keys
Bellingham, WA
Phone: (360) 738-7958
Fax: (360) 306-8225
E-mail: janice@writeoncareerkeys.com
Website: www.writeoncareerkeys.com
Member: CMA
Certifications: CPRW, JCTC, CEIP
Resume: 73

Wisconsin

New Berlin

Linda Dobogai, MS
Aberlene Resume & Career Services, LLC
13585 West Maple Ridge Rd.
New Berlin, WI 53151
Phone: (414) 425-6375
Toll-free fax: (866) 569-4103
E-mail: Linda@aberleneresume.com
Website: www.aberleneresume.com
Member: CMA, PARW/CC, NCDA (National Career
   Development Association)
Certifications: CPRW, MCDP (Master Career
   Development Professional through NCDA)
Resumes: 68, 162

Three Lakes

Susan Guarneri, MS
Guarneri Associates
6670 Crystal Lake Rd.
Three Lakes, WI 54562
Phone: (715) 546-4449
Toll-free: (866) 881-4055
E-mail: susan@AssessmentGoddess.com
Website: www.assessmentgoddess.com
Member: CDI, CMI, PARW/CC, CTL
Certifications: MRW, CERW, CPRW, JCTC, CEIP, COIS,
   CMBS, NCC, NCCC, MCC, DCC, CG3C, CCMC
Resumes: 17, 57, 107, 148

Professional Organizations

If you would like to contact the resume writers' organizations for more recommendations of resume writers in your area, see the following information.

Career Directors International (CDI)
(Formerly Professional Résumé Writing and
Research Association)
Phone: (321) 752-0442
Toll-free: (888) 867-7972
E-mail: info@careerdirectors.com
Website: www.careerdirectors.com

Career Management Alliance (CMA)
(Formerly Career Masters Institute)
A Division of Kennedy Information
1 Phoenix Mill Lane, Fl. 3
Peterborough, NH 03458
Phone: (603) 924-0900, Ext. 640
Fax: (603) 924-4034
Website: www.careermanagementalliance.com

The National Résumé Writers' Association
(NRWA)
Toll-free: (877) THE-NRWA or (877) 843-6792
Website: www.thenrwa.com (or www.nrwa.com)

Professional Association of Résumé Writers &
Career Coaches (PARW/CC)
1388 Brightwaters Blvd., N.E.
St. Petersburg, FL 33704
Phone: (727) 821-2274
Toll-free: (800) 822-7279
Fax: (727) 894-1277
E-mail: PARWhq@aol.com
Website: www.parw.com

Occupation Index

Resumes are indexed according to current or last positions indicated. Job goals do not appear in this index. **Numbers are resume numbers in the Gallery, not page numbers.**

Features Index

The following commonly appearing sections are not included in this index of resume features: Work Experience, Work History, Professional Experience, Related Experience, Other Experience, Employment, Education (by itself), Student Teaching, and Additional Information. Variations of these sections, however, are included if they are distinctive in some way or have combined headings.

As you look for features that interest you, be sure to browse through *all* of the resumes. Some important information, such as Accomplishments, may not be listed here if it is presented as a subsection of another section. **Numbers are resume numbers in the Gallery, not page numbers.**